Through a Fiery Trial

Building Washington
1790–1800

Bob Arnebeck

MADISON BOOKS
Lanham • New York • London

Published by Madison Books
4720 Boston Way
Lanham, Maryland 20706

3 Henrietta Street
London WC2E 8LU England

Distributed by National Book Network

The paper used in this publication meets the minimum
requirements of American National Standard for
Information Sciences—Permanence of Paper for
Printed Library Materials, ANSI Z39.48–1984. ∞™
Manufactured in the United States of America.

Library of Congress Cataloging-in-Publication Data

Arnebeck, Bob.
Through a fiery trial : building Washington,
1790-1800 / Bob Arnebeck.
p.   cm.
Includes bibliographical references and index.
1. Washington (D.C.)—History.   2. City planning—
Washington (D.C.)—History—18th century.   I. Title.
F197.A76   1990
975.3'01—dc20   90–42343 CIP

ISBN 0–8191–7832–2 (cloth : alk. paper)
ISBN 1–56833–027–8 (pbk. : alk. paper)

To my father who died,
and my son who grew

Contents

1793

1794

1795

Sixteen pages of illustrations follow page 374.

Preface

In the beginning was the swamp. At least that is what I had imbibed since my youth. Yet I had never run across any tales of any particular frogs, snakes, or close encounters with quicksand. Having for years lived a very humble existence off of peddling amusing vignettes on Washington history, I waded into the affair. When I discovered that there was no swamp, and published the fact to the world, the "members of the District of Columbia Historical Records Advisory Board" took me to task. They should know, but I had my doubts. As I dug deeper into the history of early Washington, not only did I continue to find it essentially dry, I found it rife with good stories that had never been told. The swamp was the least of it.

I confess I still began to write the story as a piece of vindication, but in Washington today one can still walk in the eighteenth century. Nowhere in the streets to be sure, not even in Georgetown. There are stretches of Rock Creek Park—tangles of Rock Creek Park, would be a better way of putting it—where one can say 'twas ever thus. After frequent walks there I realized that history is not for our delectation. It was. When I began writing I resolved to put Pierre L'Enfant in his place. When I said goodbye to L'Enfant I couldn't help but cry. Not that I succumbed to breathing heavily in my narrative. My rule was to let the men and women there do the emoting—and they were not shy about it either. I let them draw the inferences. Yet, ironically, by clothing them in all their rhetoric which others have been content to snip-snap, I found at the end of it all that I felt a little naked. It is fashionable to emblazon what it all means on one's chest so it might seem more cowardice than modesty to duck the scholarly question: Washington 1790–1800 = . . . , and do no more than invite the reader to a 700-page walk in the tangles. But why not? You need the exercise.

Acknowledgments

After years of trying not to be drowned by the chitchat of journalism, I found being all alone in front of a microfilm reader exhilarating. Not a few times, say, while changing reels, I found myself thanking old editors and colleagues for encouraging me to write about the past. Among them are Shelby Coffey, the late Marion Clark, Steve Petranek, Bill MacKaye, and Bill Hamilton at the *Washington Post*; Danny Zwerdling and John Ydstie at National Public Radio. At times I needed help making sense of what I was seeing on the microfilm. Ken Bowling served as a source of information, commented on the manuscript, and most importantly inspired me in the belief that history is alive. James C. Riley gave me guidance on Dutch loans. The staffs of libraries and archives were invariably helpful, especially at manuscript reading rooms of the Library of Congress and the Historical Society of Pennsylvania. Special thanks to Linda Stanley who let me scratch the dusty shelves that bore the North American Land Company papers. The hospitality of Barbara and Leo Kuter made it possible for me to stay near enough to the HSP so I could use it. Bobby Hunter, G. T. Hunt, and Bill Curtis read portions of the manuscript and offered encouragement. My wife, Leslie Kuter, read the whole thing and then some, and cheered at the right passages. My agent Rafael Sagalyn picked me up out of the swamp and his assistant Lisa DiMona believed in my revisions and sold the book. The folks at Madison Books left nothing to be desired, especially Jed Lyons, Chuck Lean, and Lynn Gemmell. Copy editor Kenneth Hale's efforts are greatly appreciated. Stephen Kuter displayed inexhaustible patience and skill in perfecting maps of Washington. I hope these maps will set a new standard for historical maps. Land elevations were such a crucial factor in eighteenth-century life that no map should be without them. And three little guys helped in big ways. Beachey-bird and Perley Poore danced over my word processor, and Ottoleo pushed the right buttons and kept me in the tot lots digging the dirt of Washington.

1. A Fiery Trial

George Washington should have eagerly anticipated the turn of the century. In 1800 Congress was due to fulfill the commitment it had made in 1790 to move from Philadelphia to the permanent capital on the Potomac. Blessing the capital city that bore his name as it opened for business would have been the apogee of a glorious career. But it was not to be. Rather than inspire the sixty-seven-year-old demigod to cling to life, the dismal state of the embryonic capital so dampened Washington's spirits that a case can be made that the city killed him.

A man with such an iron constitution and even stronger will should have at least tried to fight the swollen throat that robbed him of breath that December night in 1799. Many accused Washington's doctors of excessively bleeding him, but at the patient's command an assistant overseer drained an amount of blood that startled on-lookers. Washington recognized and accepted his impending death well before the doctors tried to save him. Biographers cite all that as the crowning example of Washington's nice sense of duty. In Roman times it might have been called suicide.[1]

The upbeat view of Washington's death is bolstered by the penchant his biographers have for not taking the city of Washington seriously. Yet worries about the city crowded out the pleasures of retirement. A week before he died, Washington vented his spleen at the whole nine years of missed opportunities. One commissioner of the city who Washington had appointed, sounded an alarm at the opinion of the attorney general that the commissioners had no legal authority to accept the loan they desperately needed to get the public buildings ready in time. Washington insisted the power was there but was not surprised at yet another roadblock to developing the city.

"By the obstructions continually thrown in its way, by *friends* or

1

enemies, this city has had to pass through a fiery trial. Yet, I trust will, ultimately, escape the ordeal with éclat. Instead of a *fiery trial* it would have been more appropriate to have said, it has passed, or is on its passage through, the ordeal of local interest, destructive jealousies, and inveterate prejudices; as difficult, and as dangerous I conceive, as any of the other ordeals."

In an earlier letter he had intimated, in an uncanny premonition, that day of éclat would likely come in one hundred years.[2] He had only himself to blame. As president he had chosen the site of the city in March 1791. Six months later, the commissioners he appointed named the city Washington. In 1792 he approved plans for the city and the president's house, and in 1793 for the Capitol. He also picked the men to build the city. In 1797, at his retirement, it was widely held that Congress would move to the Potomac in 1800 only if George Washington were still alive. In his retirement, Washington continued to promote the city, and in 1798, to relieve fears that there would not be enough houses to accommodate congressmen, he decided to build two large town houses on the northwest slope of Capitol Hill. Today a hard-to-find stone in the park between Union Station and the Capitol marks the spot.

The nightmare began. The builder would not attend to the work and, once he did, promptly inflated costs to well over what Washington expected to pay. Such extravagance forced Washington to try to get a bank loan. He had a visceral dislike of banks. When he was elected president in 1789 he was a little short of the funds he knew he would need to establish himself in New York City in the style befitting his new office. The Bank of Alexandria refused him a loan. In 1799 the bank promised a loan, which did not prevent him from protesting "the ruinous interest." That was only the half of it: when Washington went to get the money he was appalled to learn that he had come begging on the wrong day.

"Not being well enough acquainted with the rules of the bank," he informed his agent in a letter he wrote in late November 1799, "I suffered what are called discount days, to pass over before I applied; for which reason the business there must remain over until after Tuesday of next week."[3]

Death bequeathed those vexations to his heirs. The pain to the city's founder was all the greater because his expectations had been so high.

*   *   *

The logic that assured the greatness of the city was so persuasive that even on his deathbed Washington could not have renounced it. The Potomac extended farthest to the west of all the American rivers that flowed into the Atlantic. And the portages between the upper tributaries of the Potomac and the rivers that flowed to the Ohio were so short as to invite the assertion that the true end of the Potomac was Lake Superior. Even without the capital on it, the Potomac would be one of the great rivers of the world. But with the capital, the combined attractions of politics and commerce assured that the city would soon become the metropolis of the new nation.

As Washington lay dying, Tobias Lear, his secretary who hovered over his bed, was the living example of the failure of the commercial capital on the Potomac. Lear was the first presidential assistant to try to trade in on the contacts made while in public service. After serving Washington from 1786 to 1793, he toured Europe soliciting business for T. Lear and Company, which he hoped would become the mercantile house to reckon with in the City of Washington. Lear managed all the outer trappings of a going business, including a wharf and warehouse along the Potomac just east of its confluence with Rock Creek, but by 1799 he was virtually bankrupt, eking out a living as Washington's secretary once again.

What went wrong?

Eventually it became expedient to blame the slow development on swamps. But what historians have faulted Washington for won the applause of contemporaries. The city was not built on a swamp. The salient feature of the terrain that impressed almost all visitors in the 1790s was the forest-covered hills. That long tongue of land that seems to lap into the Potomac for relief, always in vain on summer days, did not exist in Washington's day. Engineers brought Hains Point out of the river in the 1880s. And the land west of the Washington Monument where Lincoln sits today was all river in the 1790s. The city of Washington had a long shoreline, lined with bluffs since leveled, overlooked by a succession of plateaus affording picturesque vistas.

Cities on hills are not unusual today, and the hills of Washington pale in comparison. In the 1790s most cities were seaports built largely on flat land. Philadelphia at the time was a slab of land about two miles wide and three miles long between the Delaware and Schuylkill, just north of 7,000 acres of marshland. And New York hadn't grown to SoHo, which at that time was so low that some called it swamp. So in 1790 Washington was an eyeful. It stretched five miles over hill and dale from the Navy Yard on the Eastern Branch (what is now called the Anacostia), to Rock Creek, 5,000 acres all told, about the size of London.

In 1790 it was undoubtedly a most picturesque site for a city. But despite the expectations of speculators, in 1799, with only about a few thousand people, it was the most vacant city in the world. With plan in hand, one could understand that much of the emptiness was to become public gardens, but in 1799 the two public buildings were still work sites surrounded with brick kilns, clay pits, and a generous sea of mud whenever it rained. The Mall was pastureland with a generous stand of trees.

Newcomers might trust that in the near future the wastes would be civilized, but Washington knew the might-have-beens and could no longer feed on hope. As Washington lay dying, Pierre Charles L'Enfant was being kept by a Swedish admiral in Philadelphia. Washington had not seen him since January 1792. The president had begged the young French architect to expedite the completion of the engraving of his plan of the city so that a waiting world could see the opportunity in the offing. But L'Enfant had another agenda: complete control of the construction of the city. His plan was his trump card, and L'Enfant held it too long. Delay led to recriminations, which led in turn to insults. Washington insisted that L'Enfant serve at the pleasure of the three city commissioners. L'Enfant refused, leaving the president with an unfinished plan and the one man in the world who he thought could effect it refusing to serve.

Rather than rally around the president, the handful of men who owned most of the land in the city rallied around L'Enfant, virtually declaring the city aborted unless the visionary Frenchman returned to the job. He had been careful to cut large avenues into every section of the city, opening up every proprietor's neck of the woods and giving even modest landholders the conviction that their holdings were worth a quarter million dollars.

As the proud L'Enfant fell from grace, an ingratiating Bostonian named Samuel Blodget took his place and more. He packaged a loan, had the plan of the city engraved, submitted a design for the Capitol, sold the commissioners' lots, the proprietors' lots, and his own city lots, drew up plans for the national university Washington often talked about creating, and stayed long enough in the city to be appointed superintendent before heading north again to oversee the half dozen schemes he had afoot in Philadelphia and Boston. By a process that frankly defied Washington's understanding, all Blodget's plans degenerated into a seven-year ordeal to salvage a $350,000 lottery he organized in an effort to finance construction of a $50,000 hotel in the city which would be the grandest in the nation. As Washington lay dying, his unfinished houses looked down upon Blodget's unfinished hotel, unoccupied and ripe for lawsuits.

Washington finally decided that Blodget was nothing more than a scheming speculator, which did not prevent him from welcoming an avowed speculator, James Greenleaf, with open arms. With his charm and bankroll, this young Bostonian made Blodget seem like a peddler. Whether he learned the arts of salesmanship and promotion in Holland where he amassed his fortune or was simply born smooth is not certain, but he touched all the right chords. He had an unfailing way to win friends in high places. He offered to buy their western lands. His generosity was fueled by sure knowledge of a million-dollar line of credit in Holland. When it was not forthcoming, he saw to it that lawsuits tied up the more than 6,000 lots Washington encouraged the commissioners to sell to him cheaply. As Washington lay dying the suits filled the dockets of every level of courts in Maryland. The lives Greenleaf ruined were many. In 1797 Noah Webster, his brother-in-law, cursed him for cheating good people only to feed a train of "rogues and whores."

No one cursed Robert Morris. He was the only man in the country whose fame, buttressed by great wealth, was nearly on a par with Washington's. When Morris bought out Greenleaf to save the day in the federal city, Washington was grateful to his old friend. That only increased the embarrassment when Morris was unable to pay the public for the lots on which Greenleaf had also failed to complete payment. Morris was an avowed monopolist and along with his partner John Nicholson attempted to take complete control of Washington real estate, not to mention 6 million acres of land from New York to Georgia. Nicholson once calculated that their Washington holdings were worth $10 million. He made that calculation while barricading himself in a Washington hotel room in fear of the sheriff serving a writ for nonpayment of debts. Morris and Nicholson had a corporate structure still admired by historians of business organization. They lacked cash. In 1798 Washington visited Morris as he did his penance in Philadelphia's Prune Street debtors' prison.

While he welcomed them initially, Washington did not appoint Greenleaf, Morris, and Nicholson. However, the men he appointed as commissioners of the city charged with building the president's house and Capitol were so self-serving as to demoralize the most ardent supporters of the city. Washington forgave his commissioners much, and while the rest of the world despised or ridiculed them, he always supported them. He had one complaint. Not one would build a house and live near the Capitol slowly rising on the hill. If only one would do so, he told them over and over again, the work would go on better and jealousy among the proprietors would subside. But the last thing those lawyers, doctors, and gentlemen commissioners wanted to do was be near the slaves and Irish laborers who evinced little respect for their betters, not to mention the skilled workers who knew infinitely more about the business than the commissioners.

So the proprietors, each who had so much to gain, never worked together. In 1790 Washington tried to end the feuding between land owners in the eastern and western ends of the city. As he retired in 1797 three proprietors alerted him to a plot by the western proprietors to make Congress sit in the president's house so they would be nearer to Georgetown. A week before he died Washington learned that a proprietor was telling people in Philadelphia that no houses had been built next to the Capitol and that those coming to the city for the opening of Congress would have to live in Georgetown. At that very moment Washington was draining his bank account to build two houses next to the Capitol.

*   *   *

Just as the Constitution was to be "the machine that would go of itself," so Washington was to be the city would grow of itself, another example of the Enlightenment ideal of self-regulation. Other than some money Maryland and Virginia contributed, the taxpayers need not spend a dime on the city. Magnificent public buildings would be financed by the sale of city lots; as the buildings rose, the value of lots would increase, financing more improvements. Skilled craftsmen and artists from around the world would be attracted by the incipient grandeur and make it even grander.

"After the law had established that there should be a city, Genl. Washington seems to have thought that enough had been done towards *making* it," Benjamin Latrobe wrote in 1806. Latrobe knew as much about the city as any who had not lived there before 1800 because as superintendent of public buildings he was trying to undo much of the damage that had been done. In his letter to a European correspondent, he continued his critique of the general: "He himself built two indifferent houses in it. Every thing else was badly planned and conducted. L'Enfant's plan has in its contrivance every thing that could prevent the growth of the city. . . . Genl. Washington knew how to give liberty to his country, but was wholly ignorant of art." Latrobe despaired of redeeming the public buildings he was hired to finish—". . . these buildings were badly designed, [and] they are still more indifferently executed."

Kinder critics would characterize the city as one of "magnificent distances" or "magnificent intentions." Latrobe marveled at "this *Gigantic Abortion.*"[4]

Three early biographies of Washington, by Parson Weems, John Marshall, and Washington Irving, do not even allude to Washington's close connection to it. It was a far cry from the days when men gloried at their chance to embody the greatness of the man in the city.

That contemporaries were embarrassed by the city's slow development is telling, because standards were not that high. If Williamsburg ever was picture-postcard perfect, by the end of the eighteenth century most of its buildings were in ruins.[5] Most American towns and farms were ramshackle affairs dedicated to the proposition that when things got too bad it was time to move on. Finished in 1800, the Capitol began falling apart in 1803.

The founding of Washington became a topic on which less said was better. Pedagogues delight in associating an achievement in engineering with each period of American history. And there is a succession of genuine achievements to remember: the Erie Canal, the rail link to the West, the Panama Canal, the atomic bomb, the conquest of outer space. Each of these focused the political, commercial, and scientific talents of the age. The founding of Washington was the moon shot, the Panama Canal of the 1790s. How ineptly the politicians, financiers, lawyers, and engineers managed the affair has been forgotten and the tardy development attributed to a swamp.

But just because it goes so against the American grain is no reason not to tell the story.

1783–1790

2. Congromania

In June 1783 eighty unpaid soldiers marched from Lancaster to Philadelphia to redress their grievances. By the time they surrounded the statehouse in Philadelphia on Saturday, June 21, their mutiny had grown. Over 400 men fixed bayonets in an effort to attract the attention of the Pennsylvania Council. Since they were soldiers of the Pennsylvania Line, they wanted the council to give them permission to elect new officers who could present their case to Congress, which met in the chamber below the council. Congress was not scheduled to meet that Saturday, but members gathered anyway, resolved to deal with the mutiny.

The leaders of Congress asked the president of Pennsylvania, who was at the council meeting above, to summon the Philadelphia militia for the protection of Congress. Knowing that the citizens of Philadelphia were not unsympathetic to the plight of the unpaid soldiers, the president demurred. Congress promptly decided to adjourn and reconvene in Princeton, New Jersey. As the congressmen filed out of the statehouse, no harm was offered to them by the mob. In return, months later, before death sentences were carried out against the leaders of the mutiny, Congress pardoned them.

The citizens of Philadelphia immediately suspected something fishy. The knowing said that Congress had hit on the only way possible to engineer its removal from the city. Wits named a new species of insanity—"congromania"—for where else would anyone want to meet than in the leading city in the country? "We shall laugh at it hereafter over a glass of wine," Thomas Willing, a prominent Philadelphia merchant, wrote to his son-in-law. "They must finally sit down *here* and here *only*."

During the Revolution Congress hightailed it out of Philadelphia a number of times, going to Lancaster and York in Pennsylvania and Baltimore to avoid being captured by the British, but they always came back. And it soon became obvious that the tiny village of Princeton was to be but a way station. The president of Congress that year was Elias Boudinot of New Jersey, and around his dinner table he began talking up Elizabeth Town, New Jersey, as just the spot for the capital. In fact, he owned a large house there, and he would gladly make arrangements for its use. Charles Thomson, secretary of the Congress, was only amused.

"It is true," Thomson wrote to his wife, "the place is inflicted with mosquitoes in summer and lying low and near marshes may be liable to intermittents in the spring and fall, but these are trifling when it is considered that by fixing the residence of congress there the value of his estate will be increased and he will have an opportunity of letting his house at a good rent."

Such was the scramble to house Congress that the only way the body could muster a majority to agree on a new home was to split its sessions between Trenton in the north and Georgetown in the south. And until Georgetown could be made ready, Annapolis would do as a meeting place. What puzzled one wit was what would then become of the equestrian statue that Congress had resolved to build in honor of George Washington. Would it be put on wheels and dragged to and fro between the two capitals?

The two-capital solution began to come asunder as soon as Congress tried to meet in Annapolis. For an embarrassingly long time they could not get a quorum. Sessions in Trenton were not much happier either, especially after friends of the city asked for $100,000 to make it a suitable capital. Congress simply did not have the money because it relied on the voluntary contributions of the states and most did not want to see money wasted on Trenton or Georgetown. In 1785 Congress finally answered the siren song of Manhattan, which had room to spare.[1]

The Constitutional Convention met in Philadelphia in 1787, and clearly memories of 1783 were fresh in delegates' minds, because the Constitution empowered Congress to establish a federal enclave not larger than one hundred square miles where it would meet and have exclusive jurisdiction. But still, having the old gang back gave Philadelphians the illusion that all was forgiven. Then it came time for the old Congress still meeting in New York to decide where the new Congress should convene. Agreement was impossible. No city,

New York, Trenton, Philadelphia, Wilmington, or Baltimore, could muster a majority. Finally, rather than see the union come asunder on such an issue—to the laughter of all the world—Virginia voted to keep Congress in New York. James Madison, a Virginia congressman, explained the decision to George Washington, who was keen on having the capital on the Potomac, this way: New York was too far north ever to be the permanent capital of the union. Better put it there provisionally than in Pennsylvania, where it might stay forever.[2]

*   *   *

The New York Common Council raised $65,000 to change the old city hall at Wall and Nassau Streets into an ornate Federal Hall to house Congress. Pierre L'Enfant, a French military engineer who had risen to the rank of major in the American army, designed the renovated building. His last public project had been to organize a festival in support of the Constitution. Its pièce de résistance had been a float honoring Alexander Hamilton, carried down the street by a band of stalwarts, and the influential Hamilton never forgot L'Enfant. George Washington thought so highly of L'Enfant's building that he saw to it that the architect gave Martha a personal tour.[3]

No one expected to stay in New York long. Pennsylvanians began engineering for removal to their state immediately. Madison was content to keep the question of the capital off the very full agenda. As time passed, the West would become more populous. The greater the importance of the West, the more likely it was that the capital would come to the banks of the Potomac.

Busy as Congress was in establishing courts and executive departments, levying taxes, and passing the Bill of Rights, many members could not resist trying to make deals for the capital. New Yorkers were mindful of the general sentiment that their city would not do as the permanent capital of an empire spreading west. But such was their zeal to keep Congress in the city that when the death toll from an August fever epidemic increased, the Common Council ordered churches to stop tolling their bells at funerals lest congressmen fear the bells might soon toll for them. New York congressmen decided to defeat any immediate removal to Philadelphia by making a deal to put the permanent capital on the Susquehanna, and while that site was prepared Congress would stay in New York.

When Madison got wind of that package, he tried to effect a deal of his own. But he was too late. So he did the next best thing. When the bill came to the floor, he expressed amazement that so momentous a decision could be made by members outside the chamber in a secret conclave, rendering the arguments in favor of any other site futile. Madison fumed that if the delegates to the Virginia ratifying convention could have known of the trick played on Virginia that day, they would have never joined the union. This taunt did not strike fear in the hearts of the opposition. Indeed, they took it out of context and began claiming that Madison was such a sore loser that he preferred disunion to having the capital anywhere else but on the Potomac.

Another Virginia congressman, Richard Bland Lee, presented the basic case for placing the capital on the Potomac. It was in a more central position than the Susquehanna and had better communications with the West. And since it was the most southern spot mentioned as a possible site, it must have the most salubrious climate. Theodore Sedgwick, a representative from Northampton, Massachusetts, was ready for that. "It is the opinion of all the eastern states," he said, referring to what we call New England, "that the climate of the Patowmack is not only unhealthy, but destructive to northern constitutions. It is of importance to attend to this, for whether it be true or false, such is the public prepossession. Vast numbers of eastern adventurers have gone to the Southern states, and all have found their graves there. They have met destruction as soon as they arrived."

In his rebuttal, Madison managed the issue of health by describing the Potomac as a western river, not a southern one. The Potomac capital would be near Hancock, Maryland, 250 miles from the Atlantic. So compared with the site proposed on the Susquehanna, roughly near Harrisburg, the Potomac site "is considerably farther from tide-water. . . . and generally speaking, as we retire towards the western and upper country, we are generally removed from the causes of those diseases to which southern situations are exposed."

The bill to place the capital on the Susquehanna passed 31 to 17 in the sixty-four-member House. Back along the Potomac, many were dumbfounded at Congress's action. David Stuart, who had married Martha Washington's widowed daughter-in-law and who handled personal matters for the Washington family, wrote that Alexandrians wanted the president to veto the bill. A word from Washington, much less a veto, would have prompted the Senate to kill the bill, but no word was forthcoming.

However, the men who concocted the deal made one crucial error. They did not get interested senators to sign on, especially the powerful Robert Morris of Pennsylvania. After George Washington, Morris was the great man in New York that year. The days of unassailable reputation of Hamilton, Jefferson, and Madison were yet to come. Morris came to town with a sobriquet that has never failed to impress Americans: he was the richest man in the country. Critics who scoffed that he accumulated his wealth by self-dealing while he was the financier of the revolutionary government made such a small dent in the man's renown that Morris himself asked the new Congress to appoint a committee to investigate his accounts.

Morris did not want the capital on the Susquehanna for the very good reason that he owned land opposite Trenton at the falls of the Delaware. He had no trouble breaking up the coalition in favor of the Susquehanna. The House voted in favor of the Susquehanna only on condition that the Susquehanna be opened to navigation, thus threatening that the new capital in central Pennsylvania would supplant Philadelphia as a commercial center. Soon Morris had a number of Philadelphia congressmen disavowing their vote in the House. The other senator from Pennsylvania lived and owned land along the Susquehanna, and so of course supported the bill. William Maclay was no match for Morris whose whirlwind of intrigue so disgusted Maclay that he raged in his diary, "This day marked the Perfidy of Mr. Morris in the most glaring colors." Maclay had heard him say time and again that he would vote for the Susquehanna. Instead during the debate, while Maclay sang the praises of Pennsylvania's central river, Morris was "running backwards and forwards like a boy, taking out one senator after another. . . ." He was taking them to a knot of nothern senators who stayed off the floor, evidently cutting deals. New York would keep the capital, Morris assured all, at least for three years. Vice President Adams, Maclay thought, slowed down the business of the day to help Morris in his designs.

Then Morris and his friends came back into the chamber ready to amend the bill to put the capital in Germantown, then a suburb of Philadelphia. Charles Carroll of Maryland made the usual plaint of the Potomac's friends when it looked like they were going to lose. If the capital was in Philadelphia, the union was certain to separate. Not fretting at that, Morris turned the heads of his colleagues with money. The House bill had authorized a $100,000 loan from the Treasury to defray some of the cost of the public buildings in the capital. Morris rose and said that was unnecessary. If the capital was in Germantown the state of Pennsylvania would donate $100,000 to the enterprise. Maclay got up in protest. The state had made no such offer, and he asked Morris the authority on which he made his claim. In his diary Maclay described Morris's reaction: "He now came forward the Great Man & the Mercht. and pledged himself that if the state would not, He would find the money." His allies from New England came forward promptly with a suggestion that the state getting the capital pledge $100,000 toward building the city.

Friends of the Potomac tried to amend the bill to put the capital on the northern bank of the Potomac. Just as Richard Bland Lee had extolled the Potomac, so Richard Henry Lee spoke of its good climate, fertility and reach into the West. Only seven senators voted for the Potomac. Morris came forward with his amendment, the capital in Germantown on condition that Pennsylvania give $100,000. The vote on Germantown was a tie, 9 for and 9 against. Vice President Adams said that if he had his druthers Congress would meet in New York and Philadelphia, alternating every four years. But "as Pennsylvania had offered the money," he voted for Germantown. Maclay lost all heart. The next day a colleague mentioned that "a trifling amendment" would be added to the bill in the House, sending the bill back to the Senate so it could be killed. Maclay didn't care. The friends of the Potomac were more stouthearted.

The Senate acted in late September and everyone was shooting for an October 1 adjournment. Weary House members seemed to be inclined to accept the Senate bill, an indication of how shallow support for the Susquehanna was. A Maryland member wrote that "there is such jobbing and bargaining on this subject, that it is impossible to say what will be the vote. . . ." Madison then discovered a flaw in the bill. Once the government moved to the new capital, Congress, as required by the Constitution, would have exclusive jurisdiction over the federal enclave, but what law would prevail until Congress took over? Madison alerted his colleagues that the bill should provide for the laws of Pennsylvania to apply. In the waning days of the session, the House passed the Senate bill with Madison's amendment. The Senate ran out of time and postponed the bill to the next session.[4]

3. Revulsions of Stomach

If the Potomac can be said to have a poet, George Washington is that poet. He went up and down it as a surveyor, army officer, speculator, and landlord, and as president of the Potomac Company, he sought the shortest route to the Ohio valley. Washington quizzed every knowledgeable man he met about the web of creeks and rivers that tumbled out of the mountains. Here was a landbound search for a northwest passage, and for an old surveyor and retired general nothing seemed more exciting. Rarely does a reader of Washington's diaries sense that he is listening in on Washington's conversations with himself. But upriver, the diary sings.

"From Spurgeon's to one Lemons," ran a 1784 entry, "which is a little to the right of McCullochs path, is reckoned 9 miles, and the way not bad; but from Lemons to the entrance of the Yohiogany glades which is estimated 9 miles more thro' a deep rich soil in some places and a very rocky one in others, with steep hills and what is called briery Mountains to cross is intolerable but these might be eased and a much better way found if a little pains was taken to slant them."

Upon stepping down as commanding general in 1783, Washington wanted nothing more than to farm. Only one public project, he said, would interest him: opening the navigation of the Potomac from Georgetown to Cumberland. By 1785 he was president of the Potomac Company. James Madison remarked on his enthusiasm: "The earnestness with which he espouses the undertaking is hardly to be described." With the commerce of the West coming down it, Washington thought land values along the river would double, and he had 20,000 acres. Although putting the capital on the Potomac was not necessary to assure the greatness of the river, Washington thought that the river could assure the greatness of the capital. Indeed, sales of lots continually increasing in value, not federal appropriations, could finance magnificent public buildings. George Walker, a Georgetown merchant who styled himself "A Citizen of the World," boasted in a Maryland newspaper that a capital six miles square just across Rock Creek from Georgetown would rise to such commercial importance that land bought for £15 an acre could be sold for £400 an acre, thus raising over £4 million, over $10 million, to be applied to making magnificent public buildings. [An American pound was worth $2.66. An English pound sterling was $4.65 and a guinea about $5.][1]

Washington's enthusiasm was infectious, so although he did not express an opinion, friends of the Potomac were not idle. The major result of Morris's grand gesture to guarantee $100,000 for a capital in Germantown was a general agreement among politicians that the state winning the capital should provide the seed money to build the public buildings in it. The federal government should never have to pay a cent. The Virginia Assembly appropriated $120,000 for a city on the Potomac and challenged less populous Maryland to appropriate a proportionate amount, $72,000. Merchants of Georgetown and Alexandria wrote a memorial to Congress in favor of the gateway to the West, which challenged insinuations about the health of the Potomac valley.

"Perhaps no part of America can boast of being more healthy than the Potomack in general; and we have been more astonished at the objections which have been made to fixing the seat of government on it, from a supposed deficiency in this respect than any other; the country is almost entirely high and dry, with plentiful streams of pure water throughout the whole extent of it: and are not these the principal circumstances which conduce to health in every climate?''

The memorial also explained why the river was not yet a great highway of commerce. Two years of high water had prevented the clearing of rocks and building of canals to open the river. The delay was opportune for New England merchants, because as yet, ''upon the Potomack are but few merchants of large capital, and but very little shipping.'' A capital in Pennsylvania would play into the hands of the already dominant merchants of Philadelphia.

Adam Stephen, an upriver ironmonger and promoter, wrote his own broadside defending the river: ''In order to remove some groundless prejudices which Mr. S—dg—k and others entertain . . . , I beg leave to mention a few facts that are incontrovertible. . . . A certain DANIEL THOMPSON, born in a cave on the banks of the Delaware, before there was a house built in Philadelphia, died lately on Opeckon,'' which flowed into the Potomac. Stephen also listed men in the valley who lived to the ages of 109, 107, and 102, and three who were still alive at 97, 92, and 90.

Another anonymous effusion defended not the river as a whole but Georgetown, Alexandria, and vicinity. The author, John O'Connor, was an Irishman who came to America in 1788 and immediately began trying to drum up backers for a book he wanted to write describing the United States. He saw in the debate over the government's residence an opportunity to display his descriptive abilities: ''From every ascent, and in every dale, Georgetown will affect the imagination in presenting new beauties,'' from Georgetown College to the riverside warehouses, ''brick, four story high, large and capacious.'' He thought Georgetown should be the capital so that what is now called Theodore Roosevelt Island could be fortified to ''shelter the Archives of the United States from the invasions and cannons of the universe.''

Then O'Connor let his enthusiasm glide downstream to the Eastern Branch. ''This branch is wide, and deep enough to receive all the ships in the river Thames, and with signal advantage over the latter; for it runs through very high lands, forming such a diversity of coves, and vast basons, under the protection of elevated hills, almost perpendicularly impending, as if, formed by nature, for the express purpose of sheltering ships and commerce from the rage of the North-west wind. . . . Gentlemen's country seats, or the mansions of Ambassadors, could not appear more happily from any situation, in the world, than these variegated hills. The residence of Notley Young, Esquire, on the [Potomac] river, . . . not inferior to the palaces of some European princes, is the first object to attract the traveler's attention.''

Not mentioned were the huts of Notley Young's 265 slaves scattered in the low areas surrounding the great house.[2]

*   *   *

When Congress convened in January, Treasury Secretary Alexander Hamilton presented a report on funding the debts incurred during the Revolution, which put the residence debate, and not a few other matters, on the back burner. Hamilton asked Congress to refund at face value with new bonds every piece of paper money printed to pay soldiers and suppliers during the war. That seemed just, but it was notorious that most soldiers and many suppliers exchanged their notes for specie or services at less, often far less, than face value. So the holder of the most worthless state notes, heretofore being bought by speculators for pennies on the dollar, could come to the Treasury and get a bond equal to the face value of the money that would pay six percent interest for twenty years to boot. In addition, Hamilton tried to make the debt as large as possible, arguing that a large debt, far from depressing the economy, would cause it to boom because the interest-bearing notes would be themselves as good as gold. There would be more sound money in circulation, hence more prosperity, such were the "blessings," as Hamilton put it, of a large public debt.

Congressmen soon realized that such a public blessing could become a particular blessing for some. Hamilton's assistant secretary, William Duer, leaked details of the report to his associates in the financial community of New York. That the federal government would fund at par the money printed by Congress had already been anticipated, and the value of those notes had risen steadily. A tip that it would fund the state debts at par opened a fertile field for speculators. Backed by a Dutch loan, Duer and his friends dispatched agents to begin buying up state notes at vastly depreciated prices before Hamilton's plan became public. The most fertile area for buying up notes was North Carolina, where they were available from the unknowing for a quarter on the dollar. Among Duer's associates in the surefire scam were some congressmen from New England and New York. Hamilton himself seemed to be above the dealing. Congressman James Jackson of Georgia fumed at the ships "freighted with money" to buy up state notes from unsuspecting holders. He wished that the Congress was sitting on the banks of the Susquehanna or Potomac, away from the speculators of New York.

The sticking point in Hamilton's proposal was federal assumption of state debts, and for less emotional reasons. Two states, Massachusetts and South Carolina, had the lion's share of the debt, and other states, such as Virginia and Pennsylvania, had paid off some of the debt or were in the process of doing so by accepting state notes for the purchase of back lands. The argument that a blow struck against the British in Massachusetts or South Carolina was a blow struck for all wore a little thin when it became apparent that most of the money would be given to speculators. Virginians opposed it because Virginia's debt was relatively small. But being the most populous state, Virginia would bear the heaviest burden in paying the taxes to fund the debt.

The provision to assume state debts was defeated in the House. Hamilton's friends in Congress did not give up. They made it clear that it was all or nothing. If state debts were not assumed, all debts would go unpaid, including the loans from Holland and France so instrumental in winning the war. In that case, the union might as well dissolve or revert back to the Articles of Confederation.

With all this going on, Congress postponed deciding its future home. In April the House decided headway could be made on the issue if the question of the permanent residence was separated from the temporary residence. Satisfying the get-out-of-New-York lobby, it passed a bill to convene for its next session in Baltimore. The friends of New York in the Senate refused to separate the issues, thus allowing them to play the friends of the Potomac off against the friends of Pennsylvania, all in an effort to keep Congress in New York, next to Wall Street. But with the stalemate over assumption of state debts there was something dearer to New York speculators than the proximity of congressmen. Duer and his associates stood to lose a bundle if state debts were not assumed.

Pennsylvania had enough congressmen against assumption that Morris offered to deliver votes for assumption if Hamilton delivered votes for a Pennsylvania capital. In early June they thought they had a deal, but Hamilton discovered that if Congress left New York, Senator Rufus King of that state would switch his vote on assumption. Hamilton and Morris looked to Virginia for help. Morris gambled that making Philadelphia the temporary capital for ten years would be good enough because no city would ever be built on the Potomac that could lure Congress away. Hamilton approached Jefferson, who two years later wrote an account of the transaction. He recalled how Hamilton, looking uncharacteristically disheveled and ill at ease, confronted him outside the president's lodging and claimed that the union was about to come asunder over assumption. Professing ignorance of the issue—Jefferson had just got off the boat bringing him home from Paris, where he had been the U.S. minister—the secretary of state arranged a dinner with Hamilton and Madison. Hearing Hamilton's plea, Madison agreed that although he could not himself vote for assumption, he would stop organizing the opposition to it provided Hamilton would offer some help on that other knotty issue, the capital.

"It was observed, I forget by which one of them," Jefferson recalled, "that as the pill would be a bitter one to Southern States, something should be done to soothe them, that the removal of the seat of Government to the Patowmac was a just measure, & would probably be a popular one with them and would be a proper one to follow assumption."

To uphold their end of the bargain Madison and Jefferson agreed to get the two Virginia congressmen whose districts bordered the Potomac, Alexander White and Richard Lee, to vote for assumption. And Charles Carroll in the Senate and Daniel Carroll in the House, both from Maryland, became supporters of assumption.

Lee readily agreed to the deal after being assured by Madison that if Georgetown was given the capital, Alexandria would be included in the federal district. White, "with considerable revulsions of stomach," according to Jefferson, also finally agreed.

Hamilton never gave his version of the deal, but a pamphlet published two years later by a political ally accused Jefferson of forcing the crisis. Virginians had seemed content with assumption until Jefferson arrived from Paris. Then, directed by the secretary of state, they raised objections to assumption while making it clear that the price for their support was the capital on the Potomac.

One contemporary observer thought the most intriguing part of the deal was not what Virginia, Maryland, and Pennsylvania gave and got, but what the friends of New York got for giving up the capital. Apparently, for some, assumption was not enough. Theophile Cazenove, the agent for several European banking houses, hinted in a June 23 letter to his clients that the partisans of New York would resist, but "several secret interests" would take care of them, such was "the labyrinth of intrigue."

As for the actual mechanics of the deal, the Senate passed the residence bill by two votes. The genius of Hamilton as a wirepuller was economy. The bill then went to the House, where Madison had to beat back an attempt to amend the bill to make Baltimore the permanent capital. He assured members that the Senate would not vote for Baltimore, and indeed, that body had defeated that city before. Most of the New Englanders kept quiet. They obviously knew a deal was on. But Elbridge Gerry of Massachusetts raised the issue of health once again. In reply a Virginia member pulled out a report Gerry had written for the Confederation Congress in 1784, after he had led a committee to Georgetown to see if it would be a suitable site for the capital. Back then Gerry thought the area northwest of the city too rough and the plain behind the city suitable, and "about a mile and a half on the river below Georgetown, there is also a District which commands fine prospects. Some part of it is low, but the residue is high and pleasant."

Gerry apparently had an explanation for his change of heart, but unfortunately the reporters of the debate did not record it. What made headlines, so to speak, was Gerry's taunt that the bill was a sham because everybody knew that once Congress returned to the comforts of Philadelphia it would never give them up for the rigors of the wilderness. Fisher Ames privately characterized it as a fight between the grog shops of Philadelphia and New York as to which one should get the congressional tippling trade. Editors around the country picked up on Gerry's gibe and credited Morris with bamboozling the Virginians.

The votes on assumption of state debts came three weeks later. The Senate passed the measure again. Over in the House, Madison spoke against assumption and Alexander White publicly said he had not made up his mind. But when the vote came, White upheld the bargain. Assumption passed by six votes.[3]

4. On Peter's Slashes Plantation

Congress did not select the site of the federal district. It authorized Washington to place it anywhere along 110 miles of the river between the Eastern Branch and the mouth of the Conogocheague. The public buildings, which were to be built under the supervision of three commissioners appointed by the president, had to be on the Maryland side of the river. In letters back to Virginia before the residence bill was passed, Jefferson and others had referred to Georgetown as the future capital, but Washington was not about to rush his decision. On August 29, he conferred with Jefferson and Madison about how to implement the law. He thought Jefferson, as secretary of state, should be the executive officer in charge, and they both valued Madison's advice.

With a taste for architecture and a collection of the plans of European cities, Jefferson was eager to get down ideas for the capital city itself, that portion in the federal district where the public buildings would be. Assuming the city would have streets in a grid pattern like Philadelphia, he wanted to avoid crowding and promote health and beauty by devoting nine squares to a large public park. The president's house and garden should have two whole squares, and the public market a whole square. And to further prevent crowding, streets should be at least a hundred feet wide. Jefferson even had building regulations in mind, explaining in his memo to Washington, "In Paris it is forbidden to build a house beyond a given height, and it is admitted to be a good restriction. It keeps down the price of ground, keeps the houses low and convenient, and the streets light and airy. Fires are much more manageable where houses are low."

Madison was more familiar with the thinking of the president and knew that he liked to take care of first things first. He suggested that "the President inform himself of the several rival positions; leaving among them inducements to bid against each other in offers of land or money."[1]

*   *   *

Jefferson and Madison turned tourists on their trip home to Virginia that September. Rather than take the beeline through Baltimore, they went to Chestertown, Maryland, and took a boat across Chesapeake Bay to Annapolis. After a night at the village of Queen Anne they had breakfast at a Bladensburg inn run by an old black woman named Margaret Adams, who told them how white competitors were harassing her because George Washington chose to stay with her.

They reached Georgetown in time for dinner and met with the prominent gentlemen of the town, who proposed a grand tour of the area in the morning. The outing began by crossing the area between Rock Creek and Tiber or Goose Creek, which flowed along what became Constitution Avenue. They had breakfast at Notley Young's mansion south of the Tiber overlooking the Potomac, then returned to Colonel Uriah Forrest's house in Georgetown for dinner, and ended the day with a boat tour up to the Little Falls. Landowners kept joining the group, which numbered thirteen when the tour ended.

At the president's direction Jefferson met with three men in particular: Benjamin Stoddert and William Deakins, prominent Georgetown merchants, and Daniel Carroll of Duddington, the nephew of the congressman who switched his vote on assumption. The nephew owned most of the land along the Eastern Branch. Jefferson impressed upon them that there had to be enough land and enough money to build a city, and that the money to build the public buildings had to come from the sale of the land. Apart from the initial contributions of Maryland and Virginia, totaling $192,000, state governments could not be relied on. And no federal contribution to the city should be expected. Jefferson suggested that the 1,500 acres necessary for a city be sold to the government for twice the market value of the land before the designation of the site as the capital. Jefferson reported to the president that the three showed "great zeal" for the project, and "they seemed to approve the proposition for the 1,500 acres."

Jefferson also discussed the boundaries of the federal territory with the three landholders. He reported to Washington that they agreed that Alexandria, Virginia, should be included. And so that Alexandria would not hang naked at the southern tip of the district, Jefferson opined that congress should be asked to extend the permissible eastern boundary of the capital to include the eastern bank of the Eastern Branch, which he thought should be the commercial center of the city.

"In locating the town," Jefferson continued, "will it not be best to give it double the extent on the eastern branch of what it has on the river? The former will be for persons in commerce, the latter for those connected with the government."[2]

*   *   *

The president kept his own counsel. On October 13 nine Georgetown landowners offered their lands in that city and vicinity for the federal capital, "on such terms as" General Washington "shall determine to be reasonable and Just." Three days later Washington inspected the lands around Georgetown, "with," the newspaper reported, "the principal Gentlemen of this town." He asked them to have a map of the area prepared, and the next day he rode off toward the Conogocheague.

Samuel Davidson, a Georgetown merchant and land speculator, wrote to a London merchant, "There does not a doubt remain but that the Federal City will ere long rear its head in the vicinity of this town—The President has viewed and appeared much pleased with the situation between Rock Creek and the Eastern Branch. . . ." All of which did not yet inspire Davidson to buy land in the area.

But Washington also encouraged landowners upriver. Both Hagerstown and Williamsport, at the confluence of the Conogocheague and Potomac, gave him a grand reception. At Williamsport he looked over the lay of the land. And his guide, Colonel Elie Williams, thought he seemed well pleased with the site. He also toured the Sharpsburg area, some ten miles downriver from Williamsport, and finally the area where the Monocacy joins the Potomac, thirty miles north of Great Falls. Senator Charles Carroll of Maryland owned 10,000 acres in the area.

From each of the rival sites Washington asked for a map and an offer of land. On the map he wanted the boundaries marking landownership, plus all the springs pinpointed, and the high and low lands characterized. He wanted to know which areas were subject to floods. Unfortunately, the map of the Georgetown area is not extant, but it seems evident that Washington had his eye out for unhealthy swamps.

Francis Deakins, the brother of William Deakins who was arranging for a survey to be made of Georgetown, handled the negotiations in the Monocacy area. On November 12 he sent "a draught of the lands you viewed about this place, with the offers the proprietors has made." Deakins was not enthusiastic.

"You'll have to consider our neighbours as retired industrious planters having no income but the produce of their farms, not more than adequate support for their families, as a Reason why they have not been more liberal." Deakins had "faint expectations" of the Monocacy area "possessing superior advantages to any other place."

Yet John Darnall, a kinsman of Carroll's from the same neck of the woods, got excited by the prospects and sent Deakins a description of the surrounding areas, where slate and limestone for buildings were readily available. Deakins sent Darnall's letter on to Washington. And a John Chisholm made his own map of the area, waxing enthusiastic about the majestic Sugarloaf Mountain, which overlooked the site.

The survey that the landholders around Sharpsburg sent was "laid down as directed by your Excellency." The town was four miles off the river, and the lands designated for donation flanked the road to the ferry to Shepardstown, in what is now West Virginia. The price was £3 an acre, but there was a gap of "600 acres of land here in dispute between the heirs of Michael Myers and the widow of the Col. Spriggerty."

The Williams family controlled much of the land around Williamsport, a city they had just ambitiously laid out. Today the streets of Williamsport are probably the widest of any small town in America. Otho Williams, a general to his brother the colonel, grandly offered any land Washington wanted, only saving his family burial plot. He assured the president that if fairly compensated, those who bought lots in Williamsport would gladly give up their land. But in case there was trouble, Williams offered to get the Maryland legislature to give the federal government power to take lands held by people with small holdings who might get in the way of the grand design. In addition, although he did not think that the provision of the law that allowed the government to accept monetary donations toward the project was dignified, Williams proceeded to get a subscription started in Washington County, Maryland, where both Williamsport and Sharpsburg were, and Berkeley County, Virginia (now West Virginia).[3]

*   *   *

On returning home, Washington received a more particular offer from the proprietors of the land between Rock Creek and the Tiber. They signed an agreement offering their land on the following terms: £15, or $40, an acre with every third lot reconveyed to the proprietors, plus they reserved the "exclusive privilege of taking off the woods from their respective lands." The tracts they agreed to sell were marked on a map, which is now lost.

Exactly when Washington received the offer and his reaction to it are not known. The Georgetown rumor mill smiled on that area's chances. A mid-November letter from Samuel Davidson to a London merchant claimed that the future abode of Congress was to be built "on Peter's slashes plantation" across Rock Creek, the cleared land owned by Robert Peter roughly where Washington Circle, or 23rd Street and Pennsylvania Avenue, is today.

To judge from what remains in his papers, Washington was indeed concentrating on the Georgetown offer. What worried him were the owners of the lots of a nonexistent town called Hamburg or Funkstown. In 1765 Jacob Funk, a German immigrant, bought 130 acres surrounding an inlet, now near 22nd and C Streets Northwest. In 1771 he divided it up into 287 lots and sold them mainly to his fellow immigrants, mostly in Hagerstown, a center of German settlement in Maryland. The lots had originally cost £5, and the 150 Germans who owned them thought they were worth little more.

Benjamin Stoddert and Deakins used Washington's worry to try to get him to play his hand. They wrote to Washington that they "were determined to commence a purchase of [the lots], meaning to accommodate the Public without any private advantage, but we were deterred from carrying this into effect by the consideration that if they should not be wanted by the public, they would remain a considerable loss on our hands." That did not prompt Washington to show his cards.

By mid-December the Maryland legislature passed a law (at the prodding of both the Georgetowners and General Williams) giving the commissioners of the federal city the power to condemn lots needed for the city. With that in his arsenal, it would seem Washington had no more reason to be coy. But he kept his counsel, not even mentioning the federal city in the annual message he gave to Congress on December 8, 1790.[4]

1791

5. Heavy Rain and Thick Mist

It is not as if Washington was in unfamiliar territory. The process of organizing a new city was very familiar to Americans in the eighteenth century: land was bought or donated, plats were made, and lots were sold, usually all under the watchful eye of trustees often sanctioned, if not appointed, by the state legislature. Washington never explained the reason for the delay. General Williams finally decided it was a ruse, that Washington was keeping up the hopes of upriver sites while trying to get the Georgetowners to lower their price. More likely he probably decided that to be strictly legal he had to name the commissioners, who were the parties to whom land was to be given, before designating the site. On January 22 he named the three commissioners and on January 24 he informed Congress that he had designated the area between and including Georgetown and the Eastern Branch as the federal district and asked Congress to amend the law so that the eastern bank of the Eastern Branch and the town of Alexandria could be included which meant it would include 1,200 acres of woodland that Washington owned.

*   *   *

By asking Congress to extend the boundaries of the federal district, Washington made the capital a political football once again. "This seems like unsettling the whole affair," Maclay wrote in his journal. "I am really surprised at the conduct of the President. To bring it back at any rate before congress is certainly the most imprudent of all acts."

Madison in the House and Charles Carroll in the Senate were at least careful about when they brought the measure to the floor. The

33

great debate that January was over Hamilton's national bank. Virginians led by Madison opposed the bank in toto as unconstitutional. The proponents of the bank countered that the Virginians feared that Philadelphia with the bank would get such a grip on Congress that it would never leave for the Potomac. So Carroll introduced the legislation after the passage of the bank bill was certain.

The Senate still postponed a vote. Alexander White explained to worried Alexandrians, "the President must within that period approve or disapprove the bill for establishing a bank." Maclay opposed it because he thought the commissioners, not the President should pick the site. His obstinacy, Maclay thought, was the occasion for a visit from Jefferson, who, with "more than Parisian politeness, . . . talked politics, mostly the French difference and the whale-fishery; but he touched the Potomac, too, as much as to say, 'There, oh, there.'" The President signed the bank bill and Congress extended the federal district to include Alexandria and the east bank of the Eastern Branch.

Despite his love affair with the Potomac, George Washington did not marry himself to the site southeast of Georgetown like some blushing groom. He had spent a lifetime dickering with land titles in surveys, sales, and legal disputes. The passionate believer in the future glory of the river easily turned into the stickler for indisputable title to the land. The agreement the landowners signed pledging their lands to the project was not a deed. And not all of the landowners signed. Not for nothing did Washington appoint a prominent lawyer to the three-person commission that was to build the new capital.

Thomas Johnson was a lawyer, politician, and land speculator, and, when Washington stepped down, he became president of the Potomac Company. He fought to open the river with Washington before the war and during the war proposed to his fellow members of the Continental Congress that Washington lead the American army. Then he served as governor of Maryland when, with British troops eager to discipline rebellious officials, it took courage to be a governor. He was small in stature, blunt in language, and, at fifty-nine, Washington's age, not about to be bamboozled. His one regret was that, despite ample plantation, an ironworks, and thirty-eight slaves, he was not as wealthy as he wished to be.

The other Marylander Washington appointed to the commission, Daniel Carroll, lived near the federal city, at the source of Rock Creek in Montgomery County. He was a cousin of the more famous Charles Carroll of Carrollton but was no slouch when it came to wealth and sway in Maryland. He owned fifty-two slaves and his aged mother, who lived close by, owned another thirty-nine. He signed the Constitution and represented Maryland in the first Congress, where he switched his vote on assumption of state debts to help get the capital on the Potomac and lost his reelection bid because of it. He owned thousands of acres along the Potomac, and he actively engaged in land sales. Surprisingly, he did not own many acres in the federal enclave, but his relatives controlled that stretch of the Potomac. He owned only two lots in Carrollsburg, a small town that was planned but never built at the confluence of the Eastern Branch and the Potomac. At sixty-one he was Washington's and Johnson's peer in age, but unlike those stalwarts he was prone to lose his nerve. He regularly traded political gossip with Washington's protégé, James Madison. And he spent his waning days as a congressman in Philadelphia trying to forward Thomas Johnson's efforts to get a loan for the Potomac Company through Theophile Cazenove from Dutch banks.[1]

The third commissioner, David Stuart, was not the usual Virginia planter-politician. He was a planter-doctor living in Abingdon, Virginia, not far from Mount Vernon. Married to Martha Washington's widowed daughter-in-law, he was treated as a family member by Washington. He had served in the Virginia legislature and was active in the Potomac Company. Most important, he wrote frank letters to Washington. All three commissioners were men Washington was comfortable working with, and as far as is known their appointment elicited no adverse reactions. The Residence Act did not require Senate confirmation.

*   *   *

Washington did not wait for the commissioners to familiarize themselves with the task at hand. He had his secretary of state take charge of the initial phase of the project. In early February Jefferson sent Andrew Ellicott, the geographer general of the United States, to lay the boundary lines of the ten-mile square. Then the president wrote to Stoddert and Deakins asking them to act as the government's agents "in the most perfect secrecy," and buy the land needed for the city. The presidential proclamation only set the boundary of the ten-mile-square district. The next steps were to choose the area in that district on which the capital city would be built and to buy the lands needed for the public buildings and grounds. Stoddert was a merchant who, along with his partner, Uriah Forrest, was synonymous with Georgetown's prosperity. He owned a thousand acres north of Georgetown and could be expected to buy more.

Washington described his quandary to them as he viewed the competing virtues of the land along the Eastern Branch and the lands adjacent to Georgetown. He could not decide between the natural advantages of the former and the convenience of the latter. "These advantages have been so poised in my mind as to give it different tendencies at different times. There are lands which stand yet in the way of the latter location and which, if they could be obtained for the purposes of the town, would remove a considerable obstacle to it, and go near indeed to decide what has been so long on the balance with me."

With most of their property in and around Georgetown, Deakins and Stoddert became zealous in an effort to clear obstacles to buying a parcel of land adjacent to Georgetown. Meanwhile, Washington had Commissioner Carroll try to soften up his kin holding land on the Eastern Branch.

Stoddert had to persuade only a handful of men to sell their land, but within a week he alerted the president to a snag. Robert Peter, whose land, rumor had it, would be the site of the building housing Congress, wanted more than the £15 an acre agreed to back in November. The president pondered that and in a February 17 letter told Stoddert to go as high as £25. The president also had an idea to get around other stingy proprietors. The law passed by Maryland allowed for the confiscation of a limited amount of land roughly the extent of Hamburg or Carrollsburg. However, if Stoddert went ahead and bought the Hamburg lots, "we shall be free to take, on the terms of the act, so much of any other lands in our way, and consequently those whose proprietors refuse all arrangements." So he authorized Stoddert to buy Hamburg lands at not more than £25 an acre. Stoddert and his friends had already been doing just that. By February 21 he and five other area landowners had signed an agreement to sell the lots in Hamburg that they had been buying up.

Upping the price to £25 placated Peter but not David Burnes, who owned most of the land bordering Tiber Creek. All of the proprietors understood that the government would divide the land it took into lots and then return a sizable portion for the proprietor to market for his own profit. But Burnes wanted to keep a farm and reserved 100 acres of his 350-acre tract. Burnes had long been a thorn in the side of his neighbors. In 1784 he had forcibly ejected Dick Goose-quill, a tenant of Carroll of Duddington, off the eastern end of his tract at the foot of what would become Capitol Hill. The resulting case was still in court. In 1786 he had raised enough fuss about encroachments on his northwestern line that the matter went to three arbitrators. Yet for all the atavism, he was wont to bad-mouth the tobacco plantation that his father had bought in 1764.

It had a 20-by-26-foot house (at what would become 17th and D Streets Northwest) built of plank save for the large stone chimney, one corn house 24 by 12 feet, and one tobacco house 40 by 24 feet and "almost blown down." As for his land, six acres were in "timothy meadow very much grown up with sedge." The rest was "chiefly cut down, and worn out, very much grubbed and washed. One hundred acres or more which lays on the road leading from the Eastern Branch ferry to Georgetown on the right hand will not bring one barrel of corn per acre. . . ."

The president did what he could to help persuade Burnes to cooperate. He had Jefferson send Pierre L'Enfant to the city with instructions to begin mapping the lands along the Eastern Branch. Washington told Deakins and Stoddert not to be alarmed because, with L'Enfant along the Eastern Branch, Washington hoped "that the proprietors nearer Georgetown who have hitherto refused to accommodate, will let themselves down to reasonable terms."[2]

*   *   *

L'Enfant had not been unmindful of the plans to build a new capital, and in 1789 he wrote to Washington expressing his interest in planning a city worthy of a great empire. As far as is known, only one other man, Joseph Clark, who had designed public buildings in Annapolis, offered his services. Having seen samples of L'Enfant's military drawings and portraits, his design for the medal to be worn by the brotherhood of officers in the Society of the Cincinnati, his work on Federal Hall, and perhaps some of the altars and houses he had done in New York, Washington was impressed with L'Enfant's taste and ability. He also liked the young man and could think of no other man in the world as qualified to plan the city and the public buildings, who was also available.

The first task Washington wanted L'Enfant to perform, as Jefferson explained to him in a March 7 letter, was to make "drawings of the particular grounds most likely to be approved for the site of the Federal town and buildings." The important point was to begin on the Eastern Branch to scare Burnes.

The 36 year old Frenchman arrived in Georgetown late on the evening of March "after having traveled part of the way on foot and part on horseback leaving the broken stage behind." On the next day he presented himself, as instructed, to the mayor of Georgetown who "appeared to be much surprised." But after thinking upon the matter for a day, the mayor gave L'Enfant what he needed: three men to help him make the survey. Meanwhile L'Enfant damned the "heavy rain and thick mist" and rode across Rock Creek, past a tottering log house and Peter's tobacco house, through forests between the Pearce and Burnes farms, up through the forests on Jenkins Hill, then down through the Carroll farms to the Eastern Branch. Ignatius Fenwick, who farmed the land for Carroll, had a house at the point; Notley Young's mansion was up on the Potomac; his brother William had a house up on the branch. All three houses were surrounded at a convenient distance with shacks for slaves. There were fishing huts at strategic points on shore and a ferry landing below some log houses. In his letters L'Enfant did not mention what man had wrought. He was enthralled with the lay of the land, the springs, and what could be done.

"As far as I was able to judge through a thick fog," he wrote to Jefferson, "I passed on many spots which appeared to me really beautiful and which seem to dispute with each other who command in the most extensive prospect on the water. The gradual rising of the ground from Carrollsborough towards the ferry road, the level and extensive ground from thence to the bank of the Potowmack as far as Goose Creek present a situation most advantageous to run streets and prolong them on grand and far distant point of view. The water running from springs at some distance into the creeks appeared also to me possible to be conducted without much labor, so as to form ponds for watering every part of that spot."[3]

In Georgetown L'Enfant stayed at Suter's Fountain Inn, where Ellicott also bedded when he did not camp out in the field. Georgetowners were gratified to see Ellicott, but surveying the faraway district lines was tame work. The only thing interesting about Ellicott was his black assistant, Benjamin Banneker, who was held up as living proof that Jefferson was wrong in his *Notes on Virginia*. Blacks were not "void of mental endowments." Banneker, then sixty years old, did not do much of the laborious field work. He helped Ellicott with astronomical calculations and left the job some time in late April.

L'Enfant was a decidedly more intriguing arrival, and he was not shy about explaining what he was doing. The *Georgetown Weekly Ledger* reported that he was "employed by the President of the United States to survey the lands contiguous to Georgetown, where the Federal City is to be built. His skill in matters of this kind is justly extolled by all disposed to give merit its proper tribute of praise. He is earnest in the business and hopes to be able to lay a plan of that parcel of land before the President on his arrival in this town."

L'Enfant's claim that he was laying out the city startled proprietors who trusted that the president himself would decide where the public buildings were to go. Worse still, L'Enfant's traipsing around the Eastern Branch did not budge Burnes. And L'Enfant ruined any effect his merely looking at the area would have, by getting excited about it. Indeed, L'Enfant did not care for the land west of Tiber (or Goose) Creek. "It seems to be less commendable for the establishment of a city, not only because the level surface it presents is but small, but because the heights from beyond Georgetown absolutely command the whole."

Stoddert complained to the president, which threw Washington into a momentary panic. He asked Jefferson, "What steps had I best take to bring matters to a close with Burn's, and by declaring at *once* the site of the public buildings, prevent some inconvenience which I see may arise from the opinions promulgated by Mr. L'Enfant?"

Jefferson promptly drafted a proclamation placing the capital city north and west of the Tiber, next to Georgetown; drew a map of such a city (Jefferson placed the president's house around today's 24th and G Streets Northwest and the Capitol at about 15th and G Streets Northwest); and wrote to L'Enfant telling him to stop surveying near the Eastern Branch and move over toward Georgetown. "There are certainly considerable advantages on the Eastern branch," he wrote, "but there are very strong reasons also in favor of the position between Rock Creek and Tyber, independent of the face of the ground. It is desired that the proper amount should be in equilibrio between the two places till the President arrives, and we shall be obliged to you to endeavor to poise their expectations."

Meanwhile, Stoddert was not idle. In a February 26 letter to the president, Burnes made it clear that it was not money or cussedness that caused his obstinacy. He just did not like the way Stoddert was going about things. "I presume to address you with great deference," Burnes wrote, "on a subject in which I think my own character, reputation and interest involve. Reports have been circulated here that some designing speculative men have been making you offers for the property which I among others gave up to you on certain conditions stipulated in a paper which we all signed giving you the power to make any advantage therefrom towards erecting the Federal city, & I am the more inclined to believe that speculation is in view from an offer which I have lately had for a further part of my property on the specious pretext that it will be necessary to give it up to complete your design. . . ."

But although he did not trust Stoddert, to prove he had no ill will toward the president, he offered seventy-nine more acres at £15 an acre. The president informed Stoddert, who then tried to allay Burnes's suspicions. "The truth is," Stoddert wrote, "I have no object, but a public one. I think it of the utmost importance to Georgetown that the President should fix on the situation offered him from this neighborhood for the federal city—and I think the only chance of his so doing will be by making the offers as unexceptionable as possible.''

To end his holdout, Stoddert offered to give Burnes £1,000 if he agreed to give up all of his land. If the president took the land, Burnes would still get the £25 an acre for selling it. "Fixing the federal city on the Eastern Branch, would destroy Georgetown in which I have a good deal of property that would thereby be rendered of little or no value," he explained to Burnes, "and I think that unless the offer from this side of Goose Creek should be much better than those from the Eastern Branch, that Carrollsburg will carry it.''

Burnes made the deal. Stoddert gave him £100 up front, promised 200 more in a year, and assumed the debts Burnes had with Deakins and James Lingan, another Georgetown merchant who also stood to profit by Burnes's cooperation. But although able to buy off Burnes, Stoddert could not cool L'Enfant's enthusiasm for the Eastern Branch.[4]

*   *   *

As he trekked from the Eastern Branch to the ridge called Jenkins Hill, near a beautiful spring halfway up the hill, L'Enfant saw the stone foundation of a house 56 by 48 feet with a considerable pile of bricks nearby. This was where Daniel Carroll of Duddington, the commissioner's nephew, hoped to build his future home. (Duddington was the name of the 500 acres he owned.) L'Enfant suggested that he not finish his house until the decisions about the capital were made. Carroll decided to delay building but did not soften the hard stand he took about giving up land to the government. His uncle had to report to the president that offers from Carrollsburg were "backward.''

L'Enfant's plans for Carrollsburg were going forward. In the evenings, back in Georgetown, Jenkins Hill was about all that L'Enfant was writing to Philadelphia about. Despite the continued bad weather—including "a fall of snow and stormy wind which succeeded for these three days past''—he managed to survey the area between the Eastern Branch and Jenkins Hill. He had trouble completing the survey south of the hill, "leaving for a better time swampy parts which were rendered absolutely impassable by the heavy rain which overflowing all the low ground determined me to confine myself on the high land."

The inconvenience of the "swampy parts" did not sour him on the area. He wrote to the president describing a city entirely oriented around the hill. Commerce would center on the Eastern Branch, with the public buildings on the ridge that ran from Jenkins Hill east to the branch: "From these hights every grand building would rear with a majestic aspect over the country all around and might be advantageously seen from twenty miles off." The southern boundary stone at Hunting Creek near Alexandria would be in view, making that point a great spot for "a majestic column or a grand pyramid."

L'Enfant projected a grand avenue to run from a bridge over the Eastern Branch roughly at C Street Southeast to a bridge to be built over the Potomac at the Three Sisters rocks (a few hundred yards west of today's Key Bridge). The commercial centers at the eastern and western extremities of the avenue would compete to connect with the governmental center. The city would grow like a tree. He wanted the city's growth to "be foreseen in the first delineation in a grand plan." This could not be the usual grid, which "could only do on a level plain and where no surrounding object being interesting it becomes indifferent which way the opening of streets may be directed." A grid was "tiresome and insipid and it never could be in its origin but a mean continuance of some cool imagination wanting a sense of the real grand and truly beautiful."[5]

6. Diabolical, Frenzical Disorder

L'Enfant confessed that he was "engaged in the most fatiguing work which I ever had to perform" and was at it "constantly," but he still had not produced a map that Washington could use when he arrived in Georgetown on March 28. Undoubtedly, L'Enfant told the president about the rain and snow. However, Andrew Ellicott and his men suffered through the same weather and managed to continue surveying the forty-mile boundary of the ten-mile square. The thirty-seven-year-old surveyor even persevered despite a painful bout with the flu. Of course Ellicott was an old hand at roughing it. He had just completed the survey of the border between Pennsylvania and New York near Lake Erie.[1]

Washington immediately saw L'Enfant's point. When he arrived, intent on designating the sites for the Capitol and the president's house, the drizzle would not stop. He tried to tour the area with the commissioners, but thanks to "a thick mist" he "derived no great satisfaction from the review." He also remained unsatisfied with the offers from the proprietors. His effort to get the Georgetown and Carrollsburg factions to keep a low price and enlarge their offers of land had backfired, unleashing "their fears and jealousies . . . counteracting the public purposes." L'Enfant suggested enlarging the city to include both factions. Washington had been thinking along the same lines, and Commissioner Carroll, who had been riding around the other side of the Eastern Branch "exceedingly pleas'd at the numerous & various beautiful prospects," liked the idea too. The president called a six o'clock meeting of the proprietors, eighteen men and one woman, at Suter's tavern.

The president was not wont to meet with citizens, preferring contact buffered by ceremony, but he held the floor and talked at length. He summarized his speech in his diary: "I represented that the contention in which they seemed engaged, did not in my opinion comport either with the public interest or that of their own; that while each party was aiming to obtain the public buildings, they might by placing the matter on a contracted scale, defeat the measure altogether; not only by procrastination but for want of the means necessary to effect the work;—That neither the offer from Georgetown or Carrollsburgh, separately, was adequate to the end of insuring the object. That both together did not comprehend more ground nor would afford greater means than was required for the federal City; and that, instead of contending which of the two should have it they had better, by combining more offers make a common cause of it, and thereby secure it to the district, other arguments were used to show the danger which might result from delay and the good effects that might proceed from a Union.''

Which is to say that Washington threatened to make no decision on where the city should be rather than choose between the competing interests. The proprietors had two problems. With commissioners and surveyors on the scene, they worried about who would decide where the public buildings would go. The president assured them that he would make those decisions and that since there would be a house for Congress and another for the president, each side of the city could share in the benefits arising from proximity to those buildings. He promised a plan of the city that would be engraved for wide distribution as soon as possible, and he declared that work on the buildings would begin the following summer. The other problem was that the size of the city, upward of 5,000 acres, diminished the value of each lot. Washington observed "that Philadelphia stood upon an area three by two miles, and that if the metropolis of *one State* occupied so much ground, what ought that of the United States to occupy?"

As a final palliative for landholders worried about the bottom line, Washington told the commissioners to prepare for an October sale of city lots, to be held early enough for Northern members of Congress to come down and buy, and late enough for Southern members on their way to Philadelphia.

That night Washington broke bread with the commissioners and select proprietors at Colonel Forrest's house in Georgetown. Washington never forgot the young officer who lost his leg at the battle at Brandywine. On the next day, March 30, an agreement was prepared in which the proprietors agreed to give all their land to two trustees with the understanding that the president would pay £25 for each acre used for public buildings and parks. The commissioners would divide the remaining land, exclusive of what was needed for streets, and direct the trustees to convey half of the lots back to the proprietors. The remaining half would be marketed by the commissioners to raise money to pay the proprietors for their land and finance the construction of the public buildings. The proprietors would not be paid for the land taken by streets but would be paid for trees the commissioners wanted preserved. They could also buy the land their houses stood on from the commissioners for £12½ an acre if the land was not needed for public purposes.

The proprietors at the meeting signed the agreement. Burnes had not attended, but Stoddert explained that getting his signature was a mere formality. Jonathan Slater, who worked a plantation along Jenkins Hill, had just sold his 500 acres for £20 an acre to an Englishman lately setting up as a merchant in Baltimore. That was too central and too large a tract to be left out. Washington had an express rider summon the new owner, William Prout, who was overjoyed since he had not really counted on his land being in the city itself. He gushed to his brother back in England that "the President treated me with the greatest politeness." Prout gladly signed.

Washington left it to Thomas Johnson to draw up the individual deeds each proprietor would sign over to the trustees, and to do what was needed to get the far-flung lotholders of Hamburg and Carrollsburg to exchange their old lots for new. He gave L'Enfant and Ellicott "some directions . . . with respect to the mode of laying out the district—Surveying the grounds for the City and forming them into lots." He left for Mount Vernon, well satisfied.[2]

* * *

The *Maryland Journal* hailed the agreement in a notice obviously written by a proprietor. The new city's site was described as "surpassed by no spot on earth, of equal extent, for commercial advantage and elegance of situation." L'Enfant agreed; in a letter to Hamilton he expressed confidence that lots would sell quickly and for high prices, then confessed that he felt "a sort of embarrassment" in lauding a situation he was so involved in, but he assured

Hamilton "that no position in all america can be more suceptible of grand improvement, more capable of promoting the rapide increases of a city nor better situated to secure an infinity of advantages to gouvernement. . . ."

After he opened the next day's mail the president crowed that the agreement came in the nick of time. Jefferson alerted him that the Pennsylvania legislature had appropriated money to build a hall for Congress and a house for the president in Philadelphia. The president used the news to rally the commissioners: "This (although I do not want any sentiment of mine promulgated with respect to it) marks unequivocally, in my mind, the designs of that State, and the necessity of exertion to carry the Residence Law into effect."

No matter what Philadelphia did, Washington was not about to back off. On April 4, before leaving on his two-month tour of the Southern states, he prodded L'Enfant to grab as much land as he could. "Although it may not be *immediately* wanting, it will nevertheless encrease the Revenue—and of course be beneficial, not only to the public but to the individuals also hereafter in as much as the plan will be enlarged, and thereby freed from those blotches which otherwise might result from not comprehending *all* the lands that appear well adapted to the general design. . . ."

Jefferson wrote to L'Enfant with the same advice. Twenty-five pounds an acre was such a good price L'Enfant should include all the land he could. Jefferson congratulated L'Enfant on his being dubbed by the president to propose a plan for the city and readily agreed to L'Enfant's request for plans of European cities. Jefferson sent down his private collection. Then the secretary of state hurried on to what he supposed would be L'Enfant's next assignment, designing the public buildings. For Congress he advised copying "some one of the models of antiquity which have had the approbation of thousands of years." For the president's house he preferred something modern, "which have already received the approbation of all good judges." He listed three examples, including the Galerie du Louvre.

Jefferson had his eye on the private buildings too. On the same day that he wrote to L'Enfant, he wrote to Washington offering to have copies made of the drawings he had of the fronts of various

European mansions and distribute them "gratis" in Georgetown so they "might decide the taste of the new town."[3]

*   *   *

No one was happier about the deal than George Walker, "A Citizen of the World," whose scheme outlined in January 1789 was being fulfilled. Some proprietors mindful of Walker's contribution promised to give him lots to show their gratitude, but he wanted to be a major player. Knowing of L'Enfant's enthusiasm for the crest of Jenkins Hill, he reasoned that the area between there and the Eastern Branch, the center of commerce he had prophesied would fuel the engine to make a grand capital, would be extremely valuable. So he paid £10,140 ($27,000) for 358 acres extending from the Eastern Branch in a rectangle that would be five blocks wide all the way up to 5th and G Streets Northeast.

Yet, as happy as Walker was, Prout matched it. His purchase of Slater's land, he claimed to his brother in England, "is the only thing talked of in this country from Boston to Georgia. There never was a purchase made that ever made such a stir. . . . Since it is known that the city will be in my land it is allowed to be the greatest purchase ever made in this country and I have been offered twenty thousand pounds for my bargain as soon as it is paid for but I would not take double that sum." Completing payment was the trick, and Prout asked his brother for a loan; no wonder he was bragging.

Not all of the proprietors were that excited. Edward Pearce, who had the farm north of Burnes, decided to cash in as soon as possible. After all, it would take time for the city to be planned and divided, and until that was done no one would get £25 an acre. To survive, he could continue to farm his land, but Pearce decided to sell. A week after he signed the March 30 agreement, he sold 150 acres in the tract known as Port Royal, just northeast of where the White House would be, to the Georgetown merchant Samuel Davidson, who paid $6,000 and traded a 500-acre farm on the Gun Powder River north of Baltimore. Plus the merchant gave Mrs. Pearce a chintz pattern.

Admittedly, it took Davidson, who had assured correspondents for two years that the capital would be next to Georgetown, a long time to put his money where his mouth was, but he entered into the deal with the true spirit of the day: "Yesterday I was violently seized with that diabolical, frenzical disorder, which have raged with such fury and pity for some time over the Federal City," he wrote to George Walker, "and to which, poor Prout and yourself fell victims. . . . You will sympathize, with others, over this my inevitable ruin, and believe me insane." In a more serious vein he urged a Virginia friend to hurry "to Georgetown where the ague and fever was never known. . . . We are all here in very high spirits in consequence of the Grand Federal City being fixed in the vicinity of this town. The commissioners and surveyors are now actively engaged in the business."

As if to cap off the deal, on April 15 the commissioners organized one of those ceremonies that remind us that marking boundaries and laying stone was the true religion of the day. The southernmost boundary stone of the district was laid with all of the proper Masonic rituals. However, the crowd was sparse. Someone forgot to tell the citizens of nearby Alexandria.[4]

*   *   *

On the eve of the ceremony five proprietors led by Stoddert protested that L'Enfant was expanding the city beyond even the grand size the president wanted; "taking Land we never had it in contemplation would be required," they argued, "would only tend to lessen the value of the rest, without any real benefit to the public, as the price of the lots would diminish, in proportion as the number for sale increased."

Walker and Davidson quickly got off a letter of their own urging the commissioners not to back off. "And we confide that you will not accede to any system that may mutilate, disfigure or render inconvenience, the great Metropolis of America. Whatever might drop from the President, in course of conversation concerning the Lands to be occupied by the City, we do not consider conclusive; as it would not be expected he could, with precision determine, what might be proper to include within its limits, the great object in view being the founding (of) an elegant, convenient and agreeable Capitol for the Union.''

The commissioners sent the letters to the president, then on his way to South Carolina, and asked what to do. They assured him that L'Enfant and Ellicott would continue to work ''according to their idea of your Instructions as if the conveyances had been made in the utmost extent.'' And then the commissioners returned to what appears to have been their major task that spring; notifying the 200 or so people who had bought lots in the never built towns of Hamburg and Carrollsburg that they could exchange those lots for a new lot in the capital.

The bundle of complaining letters caught up to Washington when he was in Charleston. They caused him much pain. He had been lauding the patriotism and good sense of the landholders all during his Southern trip. He hoped the complainers would realize that when he talked to them he had no map, and he recollected qualifying all his remarks with the word ''about.'' And then he reiterated one of the arguments he used at the March 29 meeting: ''if the Metropolis of *one State* occupied so much ground, what ought that of the United States to occupy?''[5]

7. Major L'Enfant Proceeds

On April 22, Congressman William Loughton Smith, on his way from Philadelphia to his home in Charleston, South Carolina, came to Georgetown. Smith had been one of the leaders of the faction opposed to placing the capital on the Potomac. There was reason to believe that a critic had just come to the would-be town, but Smith was charmed by the tour L'Enfant gave him.

"The Major pointed out to me all the eminences, plains, commanding spots, projects of canals by means of rock creek, eastern branch, & a fine creek, called Goose Creek, which intersects the plan of the City; the place intended for the Presidents palace, States House for Congress, public buildings, mercantile part of the City along the Eastern Branch, Quays, bridges, etc. magnificent public walks & various other projects. . . . The ground pleased me much; the Major is enraptured with it; nothing he says, can be more admirably calculated for the purpose; Nature has done much for the place, & with the aid of art it will become the wonder of the World. I propose calling this new Seat of Empire Washingtonople."

Back at the tavern he heard the important talk: "Land in the neighborhood which sold before for five or seven pounds an acre has been sold for thirty or forty pounds."[1]

Save for the president down in Charleston, no one seemed concerned about the complaints of Stoddert and his friends, including those gentlemen themselves. The wisdom passed around Georgetown was that soon there would be a million dollars available for building the capital city. Commissioner Carroll assured James Madison that "the sales of lotts will produce at least 300,000 pounds for public use. This with the grants from Virga & Marylnd will amt to near a Million of dollars. The produce from the sale of the public property will certainly be very productive, some of opinion, considerably more so than what has been mentioned." The city was taking "a deep root. The hopes of the adversaries to it must diminish, as confidence among ourselves encreases." Carroll summarized his optimism in one striking phrase: "Majr L'Enfant proceeds."[2]

With such projections a momentary snag in finding $2,000 to pay current expenses caused not a riple of concern. President Washington, on his way through Richmond, tried to get a small advance on the $120,000 the state of Virginia had promised, but at the moment the state treasury was bare.

*   *   *

Before leaving, Washington had pointed out the spot toward Georgetown where he wanted the president's house to be. So

L'Enfant redirected his attention from the Eastern Branch to the Tiber, which bisected the slowly rising plane that stretched two and a half miles from the western rim of Jenkins Hill to Georgetown. That point on the hill was, L'Enfant thought, "a pedestal waiting for a monument." But what was the plain below? He could have put the Mall between the two buildings, letting the western half of the city be a governmental park, while the east would grow into a commercial center. But he rejected that idea and decided to make the midpoint between the buildings the "foundation" of the city. ". . . The nature of the local[e] is such as will made everything concur to render a settlement there prosperous—" L'Enfant explained in his usual poor English. "There it will benefit of the natural jalousie which most stimulate establishments on each of its opposed limits it will become necessarily a point of reunion of both and soon become populouz."

Not a mall but a bustling commercial avenue would connect the two buildings and help prove L'Enfant's essential argument that diagonal avenues up to 160 feet wide—a colossal width in those days—"will make the long distances of the city seem shorter and promote the growth of the city." To accentuate the angle of the avenue, he nudged the president's house "somewhat more in the wood and off the creek." The flaw in the arrangement was the shallow Tiber. In an April 10 letter to L'Enfant, Jefferson premised his organization of the city on the shallowness of that creek. He thought the governmental core of the city should be "about the Tyber" because "it will be of no injury to the commerce of the place, which will undoubtedly establish itself on the deep waters towards the Eastern branch and mouth of Rock creek; the water about the mouth of the Tyber not being of any depth."

L'Enfant saw that the Tiber could be easily turned into a canal. It would not be a backwater but a lifeline for the bustling "foundation" L'Enfant saw to the north of it. As he later explained to the president, a canal, easily opened from the Eastern Branch to the mouth of the Tiber, "will undoubtedly facilitate a conveyance most advantageous to trading Interest it will insure the storing of marketts which, as lay down on the map, being erected all along the canal and over grounds proper to shelter any number of boats will serve of Mart Houses from w[h]ere when the city is grown to its fullest extent most distant markets will be supplied at command.''

The earth needed to fill the Tiber to form the canal would come from the hills south of the Tiber, allowing the area to be formed into a mall, affording a perfect pedestal for the equestrian statue of George Washington that would be directly south of the president's house. To add grandeur to the eastern end of the Mall, L'Enfant added a crowning touch that would make the canal the mainspring of the whole: a grand cascade, "issuing from under the base of the Congress building may there form a cascade of forty feet heigh or more than one hundred waide which would produce the most happy effect in rolling down to fill up the canall and discharge itself in the Potowmack of which it would then appear as the main spring when seen through the grand and majestic avenue intersecting with the prospect from the palace at a point which being seen from both I have designated as the proper for to erect a grand Equestrian figure.''

In filling out the plan, L'Enfant used the same logic that he used to form the core of the city. Two strategic points along the river would serve as forts. As a measure of defense, diagonal avenues had to be cut from them to the principal buildings. Not that every government building had to be seen from the two principal buildings. To denote the freedom of the judiciary from political influence, the avenues from Judiciary Square would not run to them. Squares designated for markets had to be served by diagonal avenues to facilitate access. With such an extensive city, the diagonal avenues proliferated. Each area of the city had to feed off the vitality of other areas.[3]

*   *   *

The president returned to Mount Vernon in early June. He did not rush to Georgetown to straighten out the proprietors who balked at signing the deed. L'Enfant did hand-deliver his plan on the 22nd, but the president did not elaborate on it in his diary. He finally went to Georgetown as previously planned, when it was convenient for his return to Philadelphia.

This time he did not conduct his business at Suter's inn. Commissioner Carroll had found doing business in a tavern inconvenient and expensive, so he rented a nearby house for "a month or two," hoping that "the President may likewise find it convenient for what business he may have during his stay in George Town." On the 27th he met with the commissioners at nine o'clock and then with all the proprietors. He cleared up the misunderstanding about the size of the city without signing away his or the commissioners' rights. He took Ellicott aside and redirected some boundary lines so a spring Stoddert owned would not be included in the city, thereby diminishing the size of the city.

On June 28 the commissioners drew up the final deeds and Washington went with L'Enfant and Ellicott to see if he liked where L'Enfant had put the president's house. He did not. On the 29th a large crowd gathered at Suter's tavern, and the president explained the plan "in a speech of some length." He explained that the diagonal avenues "would not be so numerous." The president's house would be more to the west "for the advantage of higher ground." L'Enfant had not put the executive offices on the plan, so Washington explained that they would flank the president's house. His cabinet had complained of being so bothered by visiting congressmen that they feared the confidentiality of their papers and sometimes had to go home to get work done. George Walker worried that there were fewer public buildings in the eastern end of the city. Washington agreed that the exchange could be put over there. Washington noted in his diary that the plan was viewed "with much pleasure that a general approbation of the measure seemed to pervade the whole." L'Enfant fielded particular inquiries from proprietors, answering those who asked about public improvements enthusiastically and being coy with Carroll of Duddington, who asked if he could finally get to work on his house. L'Enfant did assure Notley Young that his house was not in jeopardy. The proprietors deeded their lands to the trustees.

Before leaving for Philadelphia a little after four the next morning, the President set two priorities for the commissioners: preparations for an October 17 auction of lots and beginning work on the canal. The *Georgetown Weekly Ledger* summarized his performance this way: "The moment he appeared, all difficulties vanished."

On June 30 the commissioners asked newspapers around the country to publicize the date of the sale. In consultation with Washington, they determined the terms buyers had to meet: eight percent down and the rest in three equal yearly payments. The commissioners also solicited proposals, due by July 20, for "perfecting a Canal" through the Tiber and connecting to James Creek, which emptied into the Eastern Branch near its confluence with the Potomac. L'Enfant's task, with Ellicott's aid, was to complete his plan and lay out the city in lots so that there would be a map to see and something to sell at the October auction. He told Washington that he expected to be in Philadelphia in late August with the final plan in hand.[4]

*   *   *

L'Enfant and Ellicott worked well together, although they were rather different characters. They were both getting all their expenses paid. L'Enfant's bill at Suter's tavern was twice that of Ellicott's. Ellicott was often surveying the district line, where he and his men lived in a camp, while L'Enfant was holding court at the tavern. Both men supervised a handful of men. No one complained of Ellicott's treatment, but L'Enfant had a special touch. He saw that his men got two ounces of chocolate butter in their daily ration. And although L'Enfant was the complete enthusiast, Ellicott was not that impressed with the environs. He was especially amused as he cut the line in Virginia, where Washington owned 1,200 acres. He wrote to his wife on June 26th: "for near seven miles on it there is not one House that has any floor except the earth. . . . We find but little Fruit, except Huckel berries, and live in our camp, as retired as we used to do on Lake Erie. . . . As the President is so much attached to this country, I would not be willing that he should know my real sentiments about it. But . . . this country intended for the Permanent Residence of Congress, bears no more proportion to the country about Philadelphia, and Germantown, for either wealth or fertility, than a Crane does to a stall-fed Ox!"

But the major difference between Ellicott and L'Enfant was that the surveyor had no greater interest than doing his job. L'Enfant wanted to build a city like no other. Their happiest collaboration was when Ellicott lined the site of the building for Congress so that a longitudinal meridian that could be designated zero degrees, thus replacing Greenwich, England, ran through the center of it. L'Enfant marked that meridian, giving full credit to Ellicott, on his plan.

Ellicott was only one of the men L'Enfant prodded into doing something special. He persuaded Robert Peter, who owned the land in the capital just across from Georgetown, to offer to share the cost of building wharves where Rock Creek met the Potomac. Peter sent a proposal to Washington, who forwarded it to the commissioners with clear indications that he approved. L'Enfant also formed close friendships with the merchant proprietors who were fellow bachelors. Davidson also boarded at Suter's tavern and gladly loaned L'Enfant a few pounds when he needed it. George Walker was so confident in L'Enfant's energy that he announced the closing of his Georgetown store, asked his debtors to pay up, and offered to sell "one of the best pews in the Presbyterian Church." He was setting out to move four miles east to his land in the city near the Eastern Branch.[5]

*   *   *

The three commissioners worked without pay, which they did not mind. No one envisioned them as working full time in the city. But they did need money to pay expenses, which already amounted to $6,000, principally for surveying. Accounts could be settled at the end of the year with L'Enfant, Ellicott, and their men, as well as with Dr. Worthington, who agreed to bleed and administer doses of the bark to them when they fell sick, but bakers and grocers could extend credit for only so long. The commissioners tapped William Deakins to be their treasurer, offering a commission on any money he handled, which did not prove especially remunerative because the first money the commissioners spent was advanced by Deakins. The commissioners asked Virginia and Maryland for the money, granted to the city, but none was forthcoming. The state of Virginia still couldn't advance any because the treasury remained bare. The state of Maryland had money, but the treasurer of the state decided that it would be illegal to give any money to the commissioners before January 1, 1792. At the same time a Georgetown builder, George French, offered to dig the canal for £22,000.

By July 24 Carroll was getting worried: "The objects of the Commission conferred on me I find intricate & complex'd, much more extensive & important than was expected," he explained to Madison. Worse still, the position involved him in a conflict of interest because of an unnecessary spat between L'Enfant and his nephew. After seeing the plan at the June 28 meeting with Washington, Carroll of Duddington asked L'Enfant if his house was outside of what would become public land. L'Enfant promised to look over the situation but did not. Carroll told his uncle that he planned to tell his workmen to begin putting the house on the foundation on July 29. Commissioner Carroll immediately set off with his nephew to find L'Enfant but could not find him in the surveyors' camp or Georgetown.

On August 2, Carroll and his colleagues told the president that with an empty treasury little could be done. After sending another letter to the governor of Virginia begging for money, they decided not to contract for the construction of the canal or for the wharves Peter wanted to build, for which they were to pay two thirds of the cost. If Virginia did not come through, the only hope for funds was the October sale, but L'Enfant was not progressing fast enough: "The survey and plan of the City is not in the forwardness we wish; we have hopes still given us that they will be in such a state tho' not complete as to begin the sales the 17th of October. . . . Major L'Enfant proposes to visit with you soon with his drafts for your confirmation."

Metaphorically, as he wrought his plan L'Enfant was bringing order to chaos, but in reality, confusion seemed to follow in L'Enfant's wake. In mid-August Ellicott and his men ran the line of New Jersey Avenue southeast of the Capitol site, and the eastern side cut off seven feet of the just completed wall of Daniel Carroll's house. Ellicott was not perturbed, explaining to Carroll that L'Enfant had said the width of the street could be reduced from 110 to 100 feet to save the building. Ellicott's explanation was at once reassuring and disconcerting. He said the plan was "mere fancy work, and would be very different when completed," so "it was idle to be alarmed at what was then doing."[6]

A letter L'Enfant wrote to the president on the progress he was making did not mention Carroll's house, but L'Enfant confessed that he was confused. Axe-men, mostly slaves, felled trees on Jenkins Hill and along the avenues leading from it. The trees belonged to Carroll, and L'Enfant expected him to remove them. Carroll let them lie, which L'Enfant blamed for slowing down his surveyors. He dreaded the prospect of the city developing piece-meal. To work, it needed simultaneous development at several key spots, few of which would be surveyed into lots by October 17. His original vision, as expressed in the April 8 letter to Hamilton, that city lots would sell briskly had become clouded. On August 19 he wrote to Washington urging him to postpone the October sale.

"This business had proved more tedious than at first considered," he explained. Only two areas were adequately cleared, the crest of Capitol Hill and the future site of the White House. For those spots were "exhibiting the most sumpetous aspect and claiming already the sufferage of a crowd of daily visitors both natives and foreigner. . . ." The unremoved timber clogged the area northwest of the future site of the Capitol, precisely the area that L'Enfant viewed as the foundation of the city, where, he explained to the president, "The grand avenu connecting both the palace and the Federal House, . . . and also the several squares or area such as are intended for the Judiciary Court—the national bank—the grand church—the play house—market and exchange—all through will offer a variety of situation unparalleled in point of beauties—suitable to command the height price in a sale."

Another area that had to be settled first was between the canal and Pennsylvania Avenue, where there will be a proper stand for shops and houses that "in a short time will increase to a number sufficient to afford a convenience in the intercourse of business and to procure proper accommodation to Congress member and every officer and other people attached to the executive."

Not only were those areas confused by fallen timber. It was impossible to lay them out in lots by October 17 because the proprietors who were supposed to give L'Enfant surveys of their property had not. L'Enfant warned that unless all was in readiness a sale of lots would interest only speculators. Not enough people knew about the sale, and the down payment required—eight percent—was so small that it would attract only a "few Individuals speculating [and] wanting means or inclination to improve" the lots they bought. L'Enfant even hinted darkly at a conspiracy to defeat the plan of the city being hatched between certain proprietors and bands of speculators in other cities.

The sale "will favor the plotting of a number of designing men whom in Georgetown in particular are more active than ever and use of every means to set themselves in a situation to cross the operation of the plan adopted, and whom in concert with society forming in Baltimore and in other places unfriendly promise to engross the most of the sale and master the whole business."

The best way to increase the value of the land was to improve it, not to sell lots to speculators. Improvements should be financed with loans secured by unsold lots, plus each of the sixteen states could control a square and compete in improving them. L'Enfant repeated an idea Walker had published in 1789: "Every particular religious society" could develop a free donation of land. Amid the proprietors anxious to know exactly how much their lands were worth and writing to a president convinced that the nation's capital could be built without the expenditure of any federal money, L'Enfant pleaded that it was "essential to pursue with dignity the operation of an undertaking of a magnitude so worthy of the concern of a grand empire. . . ."

L'Enfant's way of making a case was as baroque as his plan for a city. But underneath the numerous diagonals of his entreaties was an unmistakable stubbornness. If the nation wanted a great city, L'Enfant concluded his long letter, they had to do it his way: "It is in this manner and in this manner only I conceive the business may be conducted to a certainty of the attainment of that success."[7]

8. Grandeur, Magnificence, and Novelty

In 1791 no one took L'Enfant's complaints about felled trees seriously. Americans since the early seventeenth century had been seeing the future through a mess of fallen trees. And although the president heeded the other issues L'Enfant raised, he thought they should be resolved by the commissioners. Not that there was any acrimony when the two men met. Although he could write a mean letter, L'Enfant was too charming a man to bring up difficulties face to face. When difficulties had to be addressed, L'Enfant was prone to hide, as he hid when the Carrolls were after him. And the president did not make any difficulties. He thought the revised plan L'Enfant unveiled suitable for engraving and asked L'Enfant to see to it. As for the issues L'Enfant raised in his letter, Washington sent Jefferson and Madison to Georgetown to confer with the commissioners on those as well as other problems.

*   *   *

After meeting with L'Enfant in Philadelphia, Jefferson and Madison went south. They found Baltimoreans "better humored" toward the Potomac capital, preferring to have the government there than in Philadelphia. So much for one of L'Enfant's charges. They arrived in Georgetown on September 7 at two o'clock. "As soon as horses could be got ready," Jefferson reported to the president, "we set out and rode till dark, examining chiefly the grounds newly laid open, which we found much superior to what we had imagined." So much for L'Enfant's complaints about the chaotic lumbering.

On the 8th they met with the commissioners, who were "preadmonished that it was your desire that they should decide freely on their own view of things," Jefferson reported. No matter, they "concurred unanimously in . . . every point with what had been thought best in Philadelphia." L'Enfant gained two points. The commissioners increased the down payment on the lots to one fourth and agreed that the landholders had to provide boundary lines of their property before the sale of lots. The commissioners were against postponement of the sale and opined apropos of L'Enfant's suggestion of a loan that it was "Doubtful if a loan can be *proposed,* without previous legislative authority, or *filled* till a sale shall have settled something like the value of the lots which are to secure repayment."

As for going forward with the canal, bridges, and wharves, the commissioners decided the projects "must wait for money." But to fulfill the president's promise that the public buildings would be begun in the summer of 1792, the board agreed that "the digging earth for bricks this fall is indispensable. Provisions of other materials to depend on the funds." As for the design of the buildings, they decided to offer a medal for the best plan submitted. Jefferson agreed to draft a prospectus for the contest.

The commissioners and Jefferson also discussed L'Enfant's plan. Quibbling with the particulars was up to the president, but they agreed that a post road should be marked on the engraved plan that took the easiest-to-build route between the sites of the Capitol and president's house and on to Georgetown. The old post road ran along a ridge a mile north of the heart of the new city. They also wanted the soundings of the Eastern Branch included, and, other than the president's square and Capitol square, none of the other public squares would be designated on the engraving even though L'Enfant had designated all of the sites on his plan. The engraving also had to have a name on it. To no one's surprise the commissioners decided to name the capital city Washington and the territory Columbia. As for streets, those running east and west would be designated by letters, those running north and south by numbers.

Finally, since the public would be buying building lots in October, the board endorsed building regulations that, by the provisions of the deed of trust with the proprietors, the president would have to promulgate. Several years later, when a rule regulating the height of brick houses on the avenues of the city was under attack, Washington disclaimed having had any strong feeling on the matter. Jefferson and, of course, L'Enfant did, and both agreed that the height of buildings had to be regulated, and, to insure elegance and safety, all houses had to be of brick or stone. Recent fires in Philadelphia and New York prompted the banning of wooden houses.[1]

While the board dispensed with the concerns of the president as relayed by the secretary of state, Ellicott cooled his heels outside the office. He expected to be told exactly which lots to survey in preparation for the October sale. He had no faith in L'Enfant's ability to get it postponed, but he did have an idea that served L'Enfant's vision and also made sense economically. Since the lots around the public buildings would be much more valuable once those buildings were completed, Ellicott thought those lots should not be sold in October. He suggested selling lots near Georgetown and on the Eastern Branch because what made those areas attractive, a trading town and a good harbor, were in place. And he thought lots on the outskirts of the town, good for "meadows, pastures and large gardens," should be sold in October. To Ellicott's amazement, the board merely took the idea under advisement and did not tell him which lots would be put up for sale.[2]

They were that busy. Apart from dealing with Jefferson, they had to try to bring to a close their major project of the summer, figuring out a fair but quick way of gaining titles to Hamburg and Carrollsburg. They wrote a memorial to the legislature of Maryland seeking sanction for their scheme to give lotholders in Hamburg and Carrollsburg lots in the new city in exchange for their old lots. And while they had the legislature's attention, they wanted the power to license retailers of liquor; to make rules regarding the earth dug out of wells, cellars, and foundations; and to license wharves. For the convenience of lotholders, they wanted the authority to set up a registry of deeds in the city and to make the commissioners' certificates of sale as good as deeds. And most important, given the grandiose vision of the city all concerned had, they wanted the Maryland legislature to pass a law enabling foreigners to buy land within the District of Columbia. Tacked on to the end of the memorial was the gentle reminder to pay the commissioners the $72,000 that the state promised but that the state treasurer had decided could not yet be paid.[3]

The day after the September 8 meeting the commissioners wrote to L'Enfant informing him of the city's name and the system for naming streets. They ordered 10,000 copies of the engraved plan, for which Ellicott would soon send river soundings and the post road route. And they asked him to inspect the bricks made by a Philadelphia craftsman named Le Brunt and, if they passed muster, see on what terms the brickmaker would move to Washington in the spring.

Ellicott also sent L'Enfant a report on the commissioners' meeting, confessing, "I expected some directions from them respecting the different places where the lots should be laid off but received none; on that head I am at a loss." Otherwise Ellicott saw no clouds on the horizon and flattered L'Enfant with the observation that Jefferson and Madison "appeared well pleased with the plan of the city and the country which it concerns." A few days after writing that, the confusion in the city took a tragic turn. A tree being felled to clear a street fell on and killed Walter Hanson, one of Ellicott's assistants. He left a widow and four children.[4]

*   *   *

In Philadelphia, L'Enfant was not shy about showing off his plan. With Congress not in session, he principally socialized with Philadelphia's French community. On September 1 Victor Dupont, who had just arrived from France, noted the "general admiration" for the plan's "grandeur, magnificence, and novelty." L'Enfant also talked up the approaching sale to Dupont, predicting that immense sums would be raised, since several foreign capitalists were planning to enter the bidding wars with Americans.

L'Enfant used French colleagues in Philadelphia to engrave the plan. He asked Stephen Hallet, who in 1786 was one of the three architects listed in the Almanack Royale of Paris, to reduce his plan to a smaller scale, which the engraver Pigalle would use. But anxious to get back to the city, L'Enfant didn't wait around to supervise those two gentlemen.[5]

Back on the Potomac, L'Enfant found some new arrangements in the work force that pleased him. Andrew Ellicott's brother Benjamin had come, and they took an instant liking to each other. Andrew noted in a letter home that Benjamin stopped carousing and chasing women. L'Enfant got a lot of work out of him. Benjamin's helping his brother allowed Andrew's assistant Isaac Roberdeau to become L'Enfant's right-hand man. And Valentin Boraff, hired in July as commissary of the work force for $1 a day, was working out well. And unlike Andrew Ellicott, both Boraff and Roberdeau responded to the military metaphors that L'Enfant liked to use to describe how he planned to build the city. Boraff was eager to help lead the "right flank."

Only one decision the board made in his absence really hurt L'Enfant, and, to rectify it, he went to Mount Vernon when the president arrived there for a short vacation. He had expected to design the public buildings. Washington recognized the injustice that had been done and had the board rescind the order authorizing a contest for the designs. In getting the board to rescind its order in deference to L'Enfant, the president did make clear to the architect that he still had to operate under the direction of the board. Jefferson's reaction to canceling the design competition is not known, but he filed away his ideas on the requirements for the president's house and "Capitol," as he called L'Enfant's "Congress House."[6]

Thanks to a $20,000 line of credit from the state of Virginia, the board could give L'Enfant orders to do more than just perfect his plan. Stuart and Carroll met in late September to celebrate the good news. (The president had just appointed Governor Johnson to the Supreme Court. He was still on the board but too busy to attend all of its meetings.) They ordered L'Enfant and Ellicott to dig the clay needed to make three million bricks, half to be made near the Capitol and the half near the president's house. The commissioners authorized L'Enfant to hire 150 men, and to do "such other work connected with the post road and the public buildings as he shall think most proper to have immediately executed." The commissioners would soon regret having included that last clause.

Troublesome as the Carrolls were, L'Enfant could luxuriate in the attentions of other proprietors. Davidson gladly paid his subscription to the Georgetown Dancing Assembly. Although not a handsome man, L'Enfant had already won the sobriquet "a favorite with the ladies," and Georgetown was eager to see him perform.

He perfected an ability to make greedy men feel good by contemplating the future of the city. William Prout came to the city, along with his nephew just over from England; L'Enfant regaled them with the glories of the city. "Uncle has got fixed on his land," nephew William Huston wrote home, "the Royal Exchange, the Town House or Guild Hall, the National Bank, the State House, three markets, three capital squares with many other elegant buildings. . . . All the houses in one street shall be built the same height and that all the Capital Streets is to be 160 feet wide, two rows of trees on each side of the street. . . . Every person says it will be the finest city in the world. My uncle's land, the person who has laid out the city says, is in the best situation." And there would be 10,000 men working in the city the next summer.[7]

George Walker celebrated L'Enfant's achievement in another article, "Description of the City of Washington," which appeared in the *Maryland Journal* of September 30, 1791. Writing as "A Spectator," he began lauding the site, "exceeded in point of convenience, salubrity, and beauty, by none in America," but soon lionized the man. "The plan of this city, agreeably to the directions of the President of the United States, was designed and drawn by the celebrated MAJOR L'ENFANT; and is an inconceivable improvement upon all other cities in the world, combining not only convenience, regularity, elegance of prospect, and a free circulation of air, but every thing grand and beautiful, that can possibly be introduced into a city."

After a detailed description of the plan, the flattery continues: "Among the many fortunate circumstances which have attended this country, during the present administration in government, the residence of Major L'Enfant in America, at this time may be considered as one of the most material.—The plan he has now produced, and which is happily adopted, exhibits such striking proofs of an exalted genius, elegance of taste, extensive imagination and comprehension, as will not only produce amazement in Europe, but meet the admiration of all future ages; having therein so happily combined the beauties of situation with general convenience, and, at the same time, effectually guarded against those inconveniences which arise in other great cities." Needless to say, the city "will grow up with a degree of rapidity hitherto unparalleled in the annals of cities, and will soon become the admiration and delight of the world.''

Walker was careful to praise those features upon which depended the value of the land he had bought. ''The Eastern-Branch is one of the safest and most commodious harbours in America, being sufficiently deep for the largest ships, for about four miles above its mouth; while the channel lies close along the edge of the city, and is abundantly capacious. . . .''

Walker did have a particular animus motivating his essay: the continued agitation in Philadelphia to repeal the Residence Act. Walker argued that Congress had no power over the funds for the public buildings and so could not stop their construction. But more important, given the history of the process, ''The repeal of a law, therefore, so grossly to violate public and private faith, would not be mentioned in a Congress of fiends met in Pandemonium, far less in the general legislature of these United States, whose tenacious adherence to public faith prevented their altering the funding-law last session when proposed.'' That was a neat hint to the North that if it reneged on the compromise of 1790, the funding law would be in jeopardy.

Finally, Walker took L'Enfant's side in the matter of selling lots, admonishing the commissioners: ''With regard to the sufficiency of the funds, now obtained, for the public purposes of this new city, it will, in a great measure, depend upon the management of the sale of the lots ceded to the public. If they are sold off gradually, as money may be wanted to those who will actually improve them in a reasonable time, the fund will be productive far exceeding the most sanguine calculations that have been made upon it.—For the lots remaining on hand will rise in value, in proportion as the growth and natural advantage of the city, as is evident in the most trifling town and village in America.''[8]

9. Worth Above One Hundred Thousand Pounds

Despite Commissioner Carroll having sent a group of Irishmen over, Ellicott and L'Enfant informed the commissioners that they were unable to hire 150 hands. The inability to get those hands was not viewed as a crisis, because the task at hand was not really building but selling the city. In October 1791 the anticipation of a flood of buyers put the labor problem on the back burner. "We cannot forebear expressing our anxiety," the commissioners wrote L'Enfant and Ellicott on October 6, "lest matters should not be prepared to answer the expectations of the public."[1]

A major cause for anxiety was that no engraved plans had come down from Philadelphia. On October 3 L'Enfant wrote to Tobias Lear, the president's secretary, pressing him to check up on the engraver Pigalle. Lear did, and Pigalle said he had just got the copper plate for the engraving. Lear wrote to L'Enfant and to Washington, who was then at Mount Vernon and who had already asked Lear for a copy of the printed plan. Lear did not give up trying to get the plan printed. If some were in hand by the 14th of October there would be time enough to get them to Georgetown on the 17th. On the 9th he set off to see Pigalle again and bumped into Attorney General Edmund Randolph, who joined the secretary in his mission. The Frenchman had had the copper plate for almost a week but, to the shock of Lear, had done nothing, claiming this time that the draft of the plan that L'Enfant had left with him was too small and inaccurate to work from. And Hallet, who made that draft, excused it because L'Enfant had taken his large plan away before he had finished.

To make matters worse, not a few gentlemen were coming to Lear expressing interest in the sale of lots and asking for copies of the plan. He lamented to Washington that they "express disappointment at not having a plan." Ever resourceful, Lear got the allegedly unusable draft of the plan Pigalle had and showed that to potential buyers. As if that were not bad enough, Lear had to deal with the rumors spread by those intent on keeping the capital in Philadelphia. It was said that a man would be a fool to buy at the public sale because "the proprietors of lots would undoubtedly dispose of their lots after the sale at a much lower rate." Lear argued that that made no sense at all and opined to Washington, "I have no doubt but the opinion is propagated here to discourage persons from attending the sale." Indeed, rumor had it that L'Enfant was to design the president's house in Philadelphia. The only good news Lear could report was that Congressman Page of Virginia planned to take a coachful of people to the sale and that the French minister would visit the president and join him at the sale.

The president was in no mood for bad news. Lear had already informed him of a major embarrassment. Congress had adjourned to the fourth Monday in October, and Lear had thought that meant the last Monday, which happened to be the 31st. Much too late he realized that the fourth Monday was actually the 24th. So the president, along with Jefferson and Madison, could stay only for the first day of the sale scheduled to last three days. The president felt so pressed for time that he wanted Lear to meet him in Baltimore with a draft of his annual message. The president's reaction to the avalanche of bad news was to grump suspiciously about the "mistery attending the Engraving of the Federal City which I do not comprehend. It appears somewhat singular, that the incorrectness of the Plan should not have been discovered till now, when Major L'Enfant was detained many days in Philadelphia to prepare and fit it for the purpose." L'Enfant was then only a few miles from Mount Vernon, but the president did not interrupt the busy major to clear up the mystery.[2]

*   *   *

Ellicott managed only to divide ten squares into 40-by-100-foot lots. All were just northwest of the site of the president's house, roughly in the area formed by 17th Street, L Street, 21st Street, and H Street. The commissioners gave no reason and contemporaries left no speculations on why those lots northwest of the president's house were offered for sale first. Judging from the lay of the asphalt there today, the land offered for sale then was dominated by a ridge that ran along I Street from 17th to 21st Streets. That area is more than 70 feet above sea level, 20 feet higher than the White House grounds. North of K Street was a dale through which a small creek ran, forming a small swamp between L and M Streets just east of 19th Street.

On the 16th the commissioners divided those squares with the original proprietors, generally taking every other lot. All was in readiness. The day of the sale dawned with two presidential proclamations, one authorizing the commissioners to sell lots and the other giving the terms and conditions of the sale, including building regulations. Brick and stone outer walls had to be parallel to the streets but not all in a line with other houses. Jefferson had found cities that required uniformity of blocks boring and lobbied for this provision. The house could be no higher than 40 feet and, on the avenues, no lower than 35 feet. The commissioners' agent had to supervise the building of party walls. There were several shall nots: "No vaults shall be permitted under the streets, nor any encroachments on the foot-way above by steps, stoops, porches, cellar doors, windows, ditches or leaning walls nor shall there be any projection over the street, other than the eves of the house, without the consent of the Commissioners." One rule recognized reality: with the permission of the commissioners temporary wooden houses could be built for workmen. Clearly these proscriptions only corrected some intrusive building practices that irritated lovers of communal order. And no one objected to them. The chief topic of conversation that October 17 was the weather.[3]

* * *

Thomas Lee Shippen, the scion of a rich Philadelphia family, timed his return to his Virginia plantation and law practice to coincide with the sale of lots. Shippen left not a few chatty letters, but his October 18 letter to his wife says little about the sale. He stayed with friends in Alexandria and testified that on the day of the sale the worst storm he had ever experienced struck the area. The storm defeated the commissioners' plan to hold the sale on the very squares that were to be auctioned. Instead they and the prospective buyers, an ample crowd, retired to Suter's inn in Georgetown.

The president, secretary of state, and James Madison were there until they had to press on to Philadelphia, but the French minister stayed to see what happened. The president huddled briefly with L'Enfant, not to discuss the sale or plan, but to hear his side of the dispute over Carroll of Duddington's house. The house was almost finished, but in his later recollection Washington did not recall L'Enfant having told him then that it had to come down. And with the president gone L'Enfant defied the commissioners and refused to show his copy of the city plan. Walker and Davidson supported L'Enfant, and the commissioners decided not to embarrass the proceedings with a row. Bidders had plats of the squares to look at, but to figure out how the squares fit into the overall plan of the city they had to rely on L'Enfant's verbal description. Many there did not bid at all, explaining they were interested in lots elsewhere in the huge city.[4]

James Gilchrist, who had come down from Philadelphia, was the biggest buyer, spending more than $1,000 for four lots. Jacob Walsh from Boston bought five lots. Nicholas Kirby from Baltimore bought three lots. Here were men who had more in mind than merely building their own mansion next to the president's. Indeed, Walsh represented Samuel Blodget, a young Bostonian who made a quick fortune in London off the India trade. Thomas Lee Shippen bought only one lot. He told his wife to tell his father, who he was sure would be shocked at the purchase, that he bought it for his son. Clearly, Shippen was not seduced into thinking fortunes could be made overnight in the federal city.

More familiar buyers were Samuel Davidson's brother John, an Annapolis merchant, and former Governor Thomas Sims Lee of Frederick, Maryland, who that summer had offered to sell 400 acres of "heavily timbered" land within the district north of the city. He was also a past director of the Potomac Company, and his wife was a member of the Digges family, which was related to the Carroll family. George Digges, who lived just down the river in Prince George's County, paid the highest price, £150, or $400, for one lot.

Daniel Carroll's brother Henry from Baltimore bought a lot. Francis Cabot, who hailed from Massachusetts but was then a

Georgetown merchant, bought a lot on his own account and then teamed with Peter Casanave, Notley Young's son-in-law, to buy another and, with L'Enfant choosing the lot, bought one for Lear, the president's secretary. The most notable purchaser of all was L'Enfant, who rather enjoyed the sale he had argued against. He bought lot 30 in square 127, which faced east on 17th Street between H and I Streets.

On the 19th the commissioners called a halt to the sale when interest flagged. After the sale the commissioners revealed that the high bids on four lots were actually made in the interests of the commissioners to prevent the lots from going for too low a price. All told, thirty-one lots were sold at an average price of $265, not a huge sum altogether, but what speculators were interested in was the increase in the value of the land. To judge from a letter Samuel Davidson wrote to a Rotterdam merchant from whom he hoped to get a loan, the proprietors were pleased with the sale because it did establish a going price for lots that made them all seem rather wealthy. "To calculate by a partial sale made of a few of the Public Lots in October last, . . . my property in the city is worth above One Hundred Thousand pounds"—$266,000, which was nothing to sneer at in those days.

The public sale also spawned private sales. Standish Forde, on his way from Philadelphia to New Orleans to make contacts with merchants there, stopped off in Georgetown and bought £1,075 worth of lots from that syndicate L'Enfant had worried about. He explained to his partner, "I expect they will turn out to good profit," since he bought at a lower price than the public sale. But the syndicate made a tidy profit, selling for $80 an acre what they had bought for $18. Finally Blodget's agent, Walsh, bought the farm north of Pearce's called the Gleanings for $36,000.

Tench Coxe, assistant secretary to Hamilton at the Treasury, was already overextended in land elsewhere. So he offered to trade other lands for land in the capital. After the October sale, James Lingan, one of the Georgetown merchant-proprietors, turned him down. "Those sales," he explained, "have raised the expectations of those who hold property . . . , and I do not think an exchange for other lands could be effected with any of the present holders at this time."

Indeed, rumors abounded that proprietors such as Carroll and Peter turned down sizable offers for lots.

The renown of the sale grew the farther one got from Georgetown. "The united states began their sales on Monday last," Prout wrote to his brother, "and their land sold for 1,000 pounds per acre and people came from all parts of America to purchase and several europeans made considerable purchases, so that my prospect is something more than mere imagination. My land would sell at present for upwards of 100,000 pounds." Philadelphia's *Gazette of the United States* reported that "there have been at least 1,200 lots sold" by the proprietors all over the city.

The French minister Ternant, who liked the site of the city, estimated that based on the sale the Treasury would be enriched by about $4 million. Evidently, he talked to L'Enfant, because he reported that to finance operations in the spring the city would get a loan.[5]

*   *   *

Although he left the sale, Washington was so interested in it that at five the next morning in Bladensburg he dashed off a note to David Stuart asking for the results as soon as possible. In his annual message he noted that ". . . as there is a prospect, favored by the rate of sales which have already taken place, of ample funds for carrying on the necessary public buildings, there is every expectation of their due progress." Privately, however, Washington and Jefferson were clearly disappointed with the results of the sale.

The administration was not interested in establishing a price for lots to entice money from bankers. It wanted money without strings to defeat the machinations of Philadelphians who wanted to make the temporary capital permanent. Jefferson prodded the commissioners and Ellicott to get the lots along Pennsylvania Avenue from the Capitol to the president's house ready for sale. In a November 21 letter to Ellicott, Jefferson expressed the concern this way: "It is excessively desirable that an extensive sale of lots in Washington should take place as soon as possible."

The commissioners were not entirely pleased with the sale either and decided not to have another sale "till we see that the plate is in circulation and the work so far compleat that every body may have a chance for the object of their choice and no way leave cause of complaint that the whole circumstances are not fully before them." L'Enfant and Ellicott told them that those conditions could be met by the middle or end of June at the earliest. The commissioners worried in their October 21 letter to Washington that that was a bad time. They wanted the next sale earlier "because of the ideas strangers have of coming to the southward so late as July."

And the commissioners hinted at more problems with L'Enfant. They had "several intimations" that "the business" would be "resting more on us than heretofore." They wanted to nail down L'Enfant to "a clear understanding of the terms on which [he] renders his assistance." They suggested a fee of £600, but "Maj. L'Enfant desired to be excused from entering on the subject for the present." The commissioners asked the president to prod L'Enfant to come to terms. This apparent disdain for money was not new. L'Enfant had refused $750 and some land offered by the city of New York for his services in designing Federal Hall as inadequate.

Even when the commissioners offered L'Enfant the plum assignment of designing the public buildings, he was coy. He promised to do it, the commissioners explained to Washington, "as soon as he finds himself enough disengaged—He can have recourse to books in Philadelphia and cannot have that assistance here." The commissioners sensed what was the matter. L'Enfant did not want to take directions from them—not a shovelful of clay had been thrown up as directed a month earlier. The men L'Enfant hired were given other tasks. And L'Enfant himself was more interested in getting Georgetown lotholders to agree to the creation of a causeway leading from the foot of Georgetown across a shallow bay to hook up with a grand bridge to be built across Rock Creek's channel at K Street.[6]

10. Chicane & Raise Opposition

L'Enfant thought the sale "middling good considering the excessive badness of the weather," and was pleased that the sale gave the property a value, which was "essential to facilitate a loan." Still, he objected to all of the lots fronting one square being sold with no guarantee that the purchasers would build. The lots would remain "for ages unimproved." Ameliorating that drawback was the limited number of squares involved and the relative unimportance of the site.

He shared those impressions with Lear, knowing he would pass them on to his boss. He defended his not having shown the plan. Lots sold went at higher prices than they would have if the buyers could have seen how those particular lots fit into the whole scheme of things. "The care I took to prevent the exhibition of the general plan at the spot where the sale is made," he explained, "must convince that enabling individuals to then compare the situation offered for sale with many others apparently more advantageous would have depreciated the value of those lots that sold the most high."

He did realize that his trick upset the commissioners, but he hoped they would realize the benefit of not having had a plan at the sale. Not that he approved of Pigalle's performance. He asked Lear to help the president understand how much L'Enfant regretted that lapse. The engraver should return the $30 advance he got. Meanwhile, the engraving had best wait until L'Enfant could get to Philadelphia so it could be "completed with that accuracy necessary to make it a map worth sending abroad. . . ."[1]

L'Enfant seemed very much like a man who had his cake and ate it too, and the commissioners resented it. David Stuart complained to the president that L'Enfant's behavior was perverse. In a long reply, Washington agreed but allowed that such behavior was not unusual in talented men who seemed to "invariably be under the influence of an untoward disposition, or are sottish, idle, or possessed of some other disqualification, by which they plague all those with whom they are concerned." He thought L'Enfant's talents and taste undeniable. No man who was available "was better qualified," and the president understood that L'Enfant would be "tenacious of his plans as to conceive, that they would be marred if they underwent any change or alterations." So Washington thought there was nothing personal in L'Enfant's perverseness. "His pertinacity would . . . be the same in all cases and to all men." Which is not to say that he supposed that L'Enfant would interfere with the selling of lots.

He had Lear write to L'Enfant reiterating "that he must in future look to the commissioners for directions. They having laid the foundations of this grand design, the superstructure depended upon them; that I was perfectly satisfied his plans and opinions would have due weight, if properly offered and explained. . . ." Just as he assured the commissioners he wanted L'Enfant, he had Lear assure L'Enfant that he would appoint the same three men as commissioners. He informed the commissioners of the lecture administered to L'Enfant and begged them to prepare the lots along the Grand Avenue from the Eastern Branch to Georgetown for sale. He thought it important "to accommodate the two great interests of Georgetown and Carrollsburg."[2]

*   *   *

Back on the Potomac, friction subsided as the commissioners and L'Enfant worked together to get building stone. The board sent L'Enfant to Aquia, Virginia, 20 miles downriver, to purchase quarries. With typical dispatch L'Enfant purchased a ten-year supply of stone from a man named Gibson. On Friday, November 18, commissioners Stuart and Carroll met and approved that agreement. They also asked him to purchase the quarries of George Brent, a northern Virginia gentleman whose brother Daniel was married to Commissioner Carroll's sister.

After adjournment, L'Enfant approached Stuart and told him that he had written to Carroll of Duddington, "informing him that his house must come down." Stuart told him that he "hoped he wrote him in an accommodating manner." L'Enfant said he had and feeling in his pockets said he was sorry he had not the letter with him. Stuart said if Carroll refused, L'Enfant should bring the matter to the board at its next meeting, the following Friday.

On getting L'Enfant's letter, Carroll protested to the president and rode off to Annapolis to get a court order barring L'Enfant from touching his house. L'Enfant dashed off his own letter to the president and on Tuesday sent his men to tear down the house, which, although not occupied, had four walls and a roof. He instructed his men to use "some of the principal people who had worked in raising the house to the end that every possible attention be paid to the interests of the gentleman as shall be consistent in forwarding the public object." L'Enfant himself rode off to Virginia to look over more quarries.

The demolition did not go unnoticed. As soon as they heard about it, Carroll and Stuart ordered it stopped. Carroll of Duddington even reached the scene in time to flash a court order. Then L'Enfant came back and ordered his men to continue, and like good soldiers, Roberdeau, Benjamin Ellicott, and company did not stop. The surveyors did not think much of the Carrolls, joking that old Daniel knew exactly how the house of his nephew fit into the plan but could not tell the difference between the Capitol and the president's house. L'Enfant offered an explanation to soothe Carroll. If the street was shifted to save his house, then the Young mansion, the house of his aunt, would have to come down. Carroll rode off to find the sheriff, in vain. Anxious to avoid a lawsuit at that early stage in the city's development, the board quickly promised Carroll compensation. They had more trouble satisfying Uriah Forrest, the most politically powerful of the proprietors, who demanded to know if L'Enfant could pull down any house or was under the control of the commissioners.

*   *   *

Daniel Carroll was a few years younger than L'Enfant and, scion of the most prominent Maryland family, as proud as L'Enfant. He wanted to increase his wealth through land speculation and so had to appreciate the value L'Enfant's plan, with its canal through his

lands, gave to his city lots. But L'Enfant was trifling with him. So
he didn't take the stakes along the future New Jersey Avenue
seriously. He was not impressed that he would be living six blocks
from the Capitol of the rising empire. He planned a country estate
with a pond stocked with fish. As he told the president, when his
house became inappropriate to the character of the city, he would
tear it down.

L'Enfant's motives seem transparent. Here was a house wall in
the middle of an important avenue leading to the Capitol. To let it
stand would invite other transgressions, making a mockery of the
plan for the city. But the timing of L'Enfant's assault on Carroll's
house interjects some Machiavellian smoke into his pure intentions.

L'Enfant recalled that Commissioner Carroll had told him some
weeks before that if the matter of his nephew's house came before
the commission, he would disqualify himself from participating in
the decision. Ergo, it was pointless to lay the matter before the
commission on November 25 because Commissioner Johnson was
in Richmond, Carroll could not participate, and there had to be two
commissioners to make a decision. By bringing up the matter of the
house while Johnson was away, L'Enfant could prove why he could
not rely on the commissioners for direction.

*   *   *

On November 28 Washington replied to the letters from Carroll
and L'Enfant under the assumption that the house still stood. He
exhibited little patience for Carroll's position. The young man
agreed that if the house was a nuisance it should come down. Since
the wall was in the street it was a nuisance. And it made no
difference that other houses were in future streets. They, Washington observed, had already been built and were not, like Carroll's
house, still unfinished. Washington offered Carroll two alternatives:
pull down the house and the public would pay for rebuilding it
elsewhere, or finish the house, occupy it for six years, and when it
was then demolished be recompensed only for the walls standing as
of November 1791.

Washington sent L'Enfant a copy of the letter he sent to Carroll and advised him to keep cool: ". . . It will always be found sound policy to conciliate the good-will rather than provoke the enmity of any man, where it can be accomplished without much difficulty, inconvenience or loss." If Carroll chose the first alternative Washington recommended letting the house stand through the winter so materials would not be lost, then relocating it in the spring. In closing, he noted that it was "exceedingly to be wished" that he would complete his engraving of the city.

Yet Washington understood that L'Enfant needed some correction. The architect's reply to Lear, which is now lost, was impertinent. Washington sent the correspondence to Jefferson, asking him to draft a letter of admonition to L'Enfant that would speak to him "in decisive terms without losing his services," which "would be a serious misfortune. . . . He must know, there is a line beyond which he will not be suffered to go. Whether it is zeal,—an impetus temper, or other motives that lead him into such blameable conduct, I will not take upon me to decide—but be it what it will, it must be checked; or we shall have no Commissioners."

Then came news of the demolition. Washington's first reaction was to try to head off a lawsuit. He had Jefferson, in consultation with Madison, draft letters to all concerned. He told Carroll that "what has been done cannot be undone," and that "it would be unfortunate in my opinion, if disputes amongst the friends to the federal city, should arm the enemies of it, with weapons to wound it." As for L'Enfant, Jefferson drafted a letter for the president and opined that it might be "too severe." But the mild letter of correction that Lear wrote merely got a "go-by" letter in reply. Clearly, Jefferson told the president, L'Enfant "will not regard correction, unless it be pointed."

Washington signed the letter that "strictly" enjoined L'Enfant "to touch no man's property without his consent, or the previous order of the Commissioners." He still wanted L'Enfant on the job but only "on condition that you can conduct yourself in subordination to the authority of the Commissioners, to whom by law the business is entrusted, and who stand between you and the President of the United States—to the laws of the land—and to the rights of its citizens."

There followed a kinder admonition that Washington added to

Jefferson's draft: "Having the beauty and regularity of your plan only in view, you pursue it as if every person & thing were *obliged* to yield to it; whereas the Commissioners have many circumstances to attend to, some of which perhaps, may be unknown to you; which evinces in a strong point of view the propriety, the necessity, and even the safety of your acting by their directions."

*   *   *

Anticipating a harsh reaction by the president, the friends of L'Enfant overreacted. Most of the proprietors, including Forrest, who had at first chastised the commissioners for letting L'Enfant do what he did, signed a letter supporting L'Enfant's position and demanding that any money used to pay Carroll damages not come from the funds earmarked for the improvement of the city.

That support fueled L'Enfant's arrogance. While expressing his regret to the president, he noted the commissioners' inability to act because Commissioner Carroll would have to disqualify himself. And then he rubbed it in: "There was no more necessity for applying to them than there is to call for their sanction in cutting down a tree." As for causing alarm, all the proprietors except those connected with Carroll "have evinced their satisfaction of the justice of my conduct." To the president's insistence that he heel to the commands of the commissioners, L'Enfant asked for "a line of demarcation between his [L'Enfant's] office and that of the Commissioners." L'Enfant called the president's bluff: he had been asked to plan the city, lay out the streets, divide the squares, design the public buildings, and supervise their construction, so what were the commissioners to do other than continually get in his way?

"His aim is obvious," Washington told the commissioners. "It is to have as much scope as possible for the display of his talents—perhaps for his ambition." Washington sent L'Enfant's letter to Jefferson for his observations. Jefferson had had his fill of L'Enfant. He took a legalistic look at the dispute over Carroll's house and concluded that in point of law the house was not really a nuisance because L'Enfant's plan had not been officially approved by the president: "Mr. Carroll is tenant in common of the soil with the public, and the erection of a house by a tenant in common on the common property is no nuisance. Mr. Carroll has acted imprudently, intemperately, foolishly; but he has not acted illegally." Jefferson ridiculed the supposed necessity of demolishing the house. A "person must know little of geometry, who could not, in an open field, designate streets and lots, even where a line passed through a house, without pulling the house down."

As for setting a line of demarcation between L'Enfant and the commissioners, Jefferson observed that by the act of Congress the president's only power was to appoint the commissioners. But the deed with the landholders required the president to lay out the town. So the president could draw such a line, but Jefferson thought it was not necessary and would be dangerous ". . . to give him a line where he may meet with the Commissioners foot to foot, and chicane & raise opposition to their orders whenever he thinks they pass his line."

That said, Jefferson could only recommend yet another pointed letter: "I confess, that on view of L'Enfant's proceedings and letters latterly, I am thoroughly persuaded that to render him useful, his temper must be subdued; and that the only means of preventing him giving constant trouble to the President, is to submit him to the unlimited control of the Commissioners. We know the discretion & forbearance with which they will excercise it."

The upshot of it all was not even a pointed letter but a brief lesson in the law that gave all power to the commissioners. Washington explained to L'Enfant that he had got some of his early instruction from the president and secretary of state only because Commissioner Carroll could not act as a commissioner until his term as a congressman ended.

L'Enfant got away with tearing down the house. On December 18 the president suggested to the commissioners that to make the "curb" placed upon him easier to bear, they should give L'Enfant "pretty general and ample powers for *defined* objects, until you shall discover in him a disposition to abuse them." Then Washington turned psychologist, continuing: "His pride would be gratified and his ambition excited, by such a mark of your confidence." Not to mention the president's pride in this dynamic young man: If "he should take miff and leave the business, I have no scruple in declaring to you (though I do not want him to know it) that I know not where another is to be found who could supply his place."

Washington even forgave L'Enfant for not showing the plan at the sale, trusting that it arose from "a conviction of the impropriety of developing his design to the public before they were matured and approved." This did not prevent Washington from trying to save some embarrassment. On December 13 he sent the copy of the plan Lear got from Pigalle to Congress to inform them of progress in the federal city. It was hung up on the speaker's chair for members to look at.

Any salutory effect the president's words had on the commissioners was lost when they learned that L'Enfant had told a number of people that he would never take directions "from men so ignorant and unfit as the commissioners."[3]

The dispute with L'Enfant did not cloud anyone's vision of the city's future and the need for work to commence on a major scale in the spring. On November 26 the commissioners gave Francis Cabot $1,000 and asked him to scout New England for men, materials—especially lime—and investors. He was to apprise gentlemen in New England "of the advantages which the Potomac offers to them in a commercial point of view." It was an ambitious mission, but his principal service was as a lobbyist. On his way north he stopped to gauge the mood of the colleages of his brother Senator George Cabot.

What he heard from congressmen disturbed him. The city's enemies were "not only numerous but potent." He pointed out the commercial advantages awaiting New Englanders on the Potomac and presented himself as living testimony "contradicting the prevailing idea that the situation was unhealthy." The chief marplot was Representative Egbert Benson of New York, who said he wanted to abort the capital on the Potomac before too much money was invested in it. However, old colleagues told Daniel Carroll that if Benson did indeed try to repeal the Residence Act, it would not really be the city he was after "but some other damnable design." The North wanted the South to fund more debt.

The only good news Cabot relayed was that Samuel Blodget, who "has a reputation of considerable property and . . . enterprise," planned to form a large land company in the city. And Cabot found something out about brick making: "Burning them [bricks] properly is the greatest art, moulding them the next. They pay here for an overseer of the burning from 10 pounds to 15 pounds per month—a good man can be procured at 15 pounds." Molders came at half that, and bricklayers would go south for 9 shillings or a dollar and a quarter a day.[4]

*   *   *

L'Enfant had no use for brick makers. He wanted the public buildings to be stone. The highest priority was a barracks for twenty men at the quarry site in Aquia Creek, so men could "at once" bring stone to the city. Once he was in Philadelphia he would decide on exact dimensions, but until then he wanted the largest stones, sound and free from stain, brought out. When severe weather came the men could clear out the rubble stone.

In the city Roberdeau was to use a crew of fifty men to build barracks for 600 or 800 men in four areas of the city: near the Capitol, the president's house, and the mouth of Rock Creek; and between the Capitol and the president's house, where the market was to be. David Burnes, who owned much of the land in the last position, had promised to sell timber from the surrounding forests at 8 shillings a cord. At the same time, "Axe-men must also be kept in constant employment in cutting down and clearing timber from the streets that are now run and where ever the individual proprietors will agree to preserve the trunks of trees, these trunks must be [laid] . . . on the side of the street so as to leave free passage."

The diggers were to work up on Jenkins Hill, leveling the square being prepared for the Capitol. Although he had yet to unveil his designs for the buildings, L'Enfant did stake out where they were to be. Wheelbarrows were needed, and Roberdeau was to introduce any person willing to make 100 to 200 wheelbarrows to the commissioners. Indeed, all the commissioners were good for was to sign checks. If Roberdeau needed money he was to go to them, "but if they were absent or that in the execution of the this order some delay should appear," L'Enfant instructed, "let nothing interfere with the work; it must be pursued without interruption."

As he prepared to leave, L'Enfant's mind, if not his body, was all over the federal city. He promised to mark out the square "eligibly situated" at the foot of 17th Street where David Burnes wanted to build his new house. He authorized Burnes to dig in the streets if he needed more clay for bricks, offered to design the house, and volunteered the public's money to ornament the house and grounds.

Meanwhile, across the Tiber, Notley Young's mansion, so long the cynosure of all eyes, ran afoul of the plan. L'Enfant wrote a polite note to Young and informed the commissioners of the problem. Since the house was at the end of a street, it did not have to be removed for seven years.

Christmas Day seems to have been the last day L'Enfant conducted official business in the city. He left Roberdeau a note to give to the commissioners telling them that he had left Roberdeau in charge. He discovered that he needed some more surveying notes to help complete his map in Philadelphia. Andrew Ellicott had already left the city to see his family for the holidays, so L'Enfant asked brother Benjamin "to delineate on paper all that had been done in the city" and send it to Philadelphia where it would be "the basis of the drawing of the remainder."

L'Enfant was in a hurry to leave, not only because of the president's impatience but also because Thomas Johnson was expected shortly to make a full board, which might countermand his orders. A week after L'Enfant rode out of town, Thomas Johnson rode in.[5]

1792

11. I Will Suffer Death

Johnson saw in an instant what L'Enfant was up to: running up expenses to force the loan he wanted. The first money from Maryland, $9,000, was in hand, and if they acceded to the wishes of L'Enfant, not to mention Ellicott, who left a bill for $2,000, the money would be spent in less than a month. And L'Enfant seemed to be doing nothing really necessary. Not a shovelful had been thrown up, even though by the building practices of the day throwing up clay so it could be exposed to night frosts was deemed the only thing best done in the winter. Carroll, who confessed to having a bad case of nerves, was the commissioner closest to the scene, but he had done nothing to correct L'Enfant.

As Isaac Roberdeau told the story, he was in Alexandria on January 1 when he heard that Johnson had arrived in Georgetown. He went to the city the next day and waited for the commissioners to meet so he could deliver L'Enfant's letter putting him in charge and lay the plans for the winter before them. Days passed and on the 6th he decided he had to go to the quarries in Aquia Creek where workmen were being assembled. He had hired a "master-workman" at £6½ a month and expected a foreman from the city to shortly bring twenty-five workers out to build barracks.[1]

On the road to Aquia Creek, Roberdeau met David Stuart on his way to Georgetown. According to Roberdeau, Stuart told him "that the commissioners were about to meet and that my presence was necessary; also that Mr. Johnson and himself were of opinion that *all the hands,* except a few to build barracks, must be discharged until the spring." Since the decision had already been made, Roberdeau decided not to attend the meeting but pressed on to the quarries so that he would not be forced to disobey L'Enfant's orders. The commissioners told a different story. While Roberdeau was in Georgetown, Carroll and Johnson told him not to leave because they wanted him to attend the commissioners' meeting.

On Saturday, January 7, the commissioners met, fired the men hired for the winter, and ordered Roberdeau not to trespass on the quarries. They wanted an end to all of L'Enfant's arrangements: no more men getting wages and chocolate butter for breakfast. They would make contracts that paid men for work done, period. They forbade Roberdeau from entering into any engagements for the commissioners and ordered Boraff to entrust all the tools his men had been supplied with to a Captain Elisha Williams. And the commissioners promptly sought the president's sanction for dismissing men digging ditches "which may correspond with Maj. L'Enfant's designs respecting the Capitol and Palace, but we do not conceive there is certainly enough of the adoption of unprepared plans to warrant the cost of digging long, deep, wide ditches in the midst of winter which if necessary at all might be done much cheaper in any other season." They claimed they would "truely lament . . . the loss of Major L'Enfant's taste and professional abilities," if it came to that, "but we owe something to others which cannot be given up."

Adding to the board's bad humor was a note delivered that day from Notley Young protesting that when he gave up his land for the city he was under the impression that the plan would leave his home in "the spot I delighted in." And while the city was being laid out he received assurances that his house was not in jeopardy. He told the tale about L'Enfant telling Carroll that his house had to go to save Young's mansion. It was evident that with a slight alteration of the plan L'Enfant could have preserved both houses and saved the city considerable expense. Young thought L'Enfant's explanation for changing his mind—that the street it was on could not be altered because it was near a fountain that relied on a spring—was outrageous. Although the spring was flowing now, when the city was built up and pumps sunk to supply water to houses, the spring would dry up, leaving the fountain "as a monument of mistaken expense." Carroll of Duddington was badgering the commissioners with the £550 bill of the builder of his ill-fated house. L'Enfant's assault on Young's house could cost the commissioners £15,000.

*   *   *

Boraff rode all that night to the quarries to tell Roberdeau that if work continued they would be "liable to prosecution." The very horse that Boraff rode was under the commissioners' orders to be sold. They claimed it had been bought at the public's expense. Rather than hazard the horse, Roberdeau let Boraff return to the city on his own horse so he could tell all workers to report to work despite the commissioners' orders. Roberdeau would follow by stage. The two men swore their loyalty to L'Enfant. Work would continue until L'Enfant countermanded the orders he left them with.

On Monday, January 9, Boraff not only rallied his men but made another contract for bread to feed them. However, he had to see the commissioners to settle the pay for his workers. The commissioners were not amused at his rebellion, threatened him with a lawsuit if he persisted, and fired him.

On the evening of January 9 Roberdeau arrived in Georgetown intent on putting the commissioners in their place. The son of General Daniel Roberdeau had spirit and, as Stuart noted, was completely in awe of L'Enfant. He dashed off a letter to L'Enfant opining that with Benson's motion about to be brought before Congress it made no sense to stop all work in the city. It was not an inapt argument, but even Roberdeau admitted that when he finally confronted the commissioners he went too far: "The agitation I was thrown into was inconceivably great—I rushed into the Commissioners' apartment and vindicated my conduct most strenuously . . . , unfortunately I was thrown off guard and insulted them in a public and indecent manner." Nonetheless they promised him a half hour on the next day, the 10th, to present his arguments for continuing the work L'Enfant wanted done.

At that meeting he apologized for his rude behavior and left a letter that offered sound arguments for continuing the work L'Enfant had ordered for the winter. He reminded the commissioners that the lack of barracks for workers had hampered work the previous summer in the city. And if the hands were dismissed, the lumber on hand would rot, and quite likely the stakes marking the lines of the streets "will be thrown down or otherwise destroyed." As for the work on Jenkins Hill, the sooner the ditches were dug, the sooner the foundation could be laid.

Roberdeau's contrition moved the commissioners, and they offered to continue working with him provided he obey their orders. They asked him to turn up clay at the president's house. It seemed as if Daniel Roberdeau's son was just about to heed the commands and advice of his father's old friends, but then in a matter of a few hours he returned to his principled, or obstinate, ways. Stuart later hinted that Walker and Davidson were the devils who got Roberdeau's ear, convincing him to resume his rebellion. Indeed, Davidson loaned £60 to keep the workers supplied with food.

Roberdeau delivered a letter on the evening of the 10th swearing his fealty to L'Enfant and warning that throwing up clay at the president's house might interfere with L'Enfant's plans. In a short letter bringing L'Enfant up to date on developments, Roberdeau made this stirring declaration: ". . . You may be most sure that I will suffer death rather than fail in any respect knowing your Honour as my Friend and superior Officer to be much concerned."

L'Enfant's troops were well drilled and refused to quit work. Assured by Roberdeau that he would personally reimburse him, Boraff continued to pay and feed the workers. When the commissioners adjourned and retired to their respective country homes, Roberdeau ordered the men back to work digging foundation ditches on Capitol Hill.

However, they did not work alone. Before leaving, the commissioners had ordered Captain Elisha Williams to hire men to build twenty huts to house workers in the spring, to guard the survey stakes in the city, and, of course, to throw up clay. Williams saw Roberdeau's men at work and alerted Commissioner Carroll. He sent express riders to Abingdon and Frederick. On the 18th the commissioners reassembled, took a writ of trespass out against Roberdeau, and had the sheriff serve it.

While in the custody of the sheriff, Roberdeau penned a justification to the commissioners. "Nothing could be farther from my wishes than to afford you unnecessary trouble, or anxiety," he informed them. He was only doing his duty to his only superior, L'Enfant, whose latest order was that no man should dig clay, "as there is enough turned up for the use there will be for it."

*   *   *

The worst snows since 1773 made discussion about work in the city moot, but the gossips of Georgetown did not sit idly by. And the commissioners braved snows to track them down. The commissioners, it was said, had accepted bribes of £5,000 to abort the development of the city. Cabot had gone to New England to get the payoff for them. Speed was essential in order to improve the chances for the passage of Benson's bill to repeal the Residence Act.

And that was not the only infamous story. When L'Enfant had gone to purchase the quarry from George Brent at the behest of the commissioners, he found that Brent had learned from his kin Carroll the highest price the commissioners would offer, thus defeating L'Enfant's attempt to save money for the city. Several proprietors who had signed the letter supporting L'Enfant had been persuaded to sign after hearing the tale about Brent.

The commissioners narrowed down the source of the stories to Walker and demanded that he reveal his sources "so that the shame of malicious detraction may be fixed and stamped if possible on the wicked authors." Walker replied on the day he got their letter, January 21. The story that so shocked, he explained in a jeering manner, originated as a jest given as a group of gentlemen shared a bottle in Georgetown just after the workers had been dismissed. "One of the company in a jocular manner observed that, if the Commissioners had been paid by the Eastern people, they could not act more in their interests" at a time when Benson was about to present his motion. (As it turned out, he never made one.)

As for the quarry, Walker enclosed a statement that almost gave the commissioners what they wanted. He said that he learned of the story at a meeting of gentlemen in either Davidson's counting room or at Suter's tavern. And the source of it was "Major L'Enfant or one of the company." Walker refused to retract that story, and if any commissioner wanted satisfaction, that is, a duel, he was ready.

Instead Carroll got his side of the story to the people who counted. He sent a January 23 affidavit to James Madison in Philadelphia in which George Brent attested that "I never received from Mr. Carroll either *directly* or *indirectly* or from any other person the smallest intimation of the price the Commissioners were disposed to give" for his quarry. So it was his word against L'Enfant's.

The winter meetings in such an unhappy place succeeded in

making Commissioner Johnson ill, and on his return to Frederick he found even more sickening revelations. Abraham Faw, who had helped Johnson and the Potomac Company by supervising channel clearing on the Maryland side of the Potomac, told Johnson that he had been in Georgetown when the commissioners were disciplining Roberdeau and happened to converse with that gentleman. He vowed not to take orders from the commissioners and said that before he and L'Enfant would submit to their orders "they would go to Pennsylvania that they had offers from thence and could be employed when they pleased."

Johnson copied Faw's statement and sent it to his fellow commissioners and probably to the president. At the same time Faw wrote to the commissioners offering to take L'Enfant's place, indicating, of course, that he would follow the commissioners' instructions.[2]

*   *   *

In recounting the dramatic turn of events in the city since the demolition of Carroll's house in late November, it would leave a misimpression to imply that, with commissioners and proprietors so suspicious of each other, and Congress threatening to repeal the law establishing the city, all concerned anxiously held their breath. On January 2 Samuel Davidson bought the 500-acre farm neighboring his, and three days later he sold it to his brother John, the Annapolis merchant. An added charm to this farm was an orchard on a little ridge that ran between K and L Streets overlooking 14th just north of a copious spring.[3]

12. Astonishes Me Beyond Measure!

When L'Enfant arrived in Philadelphia in late December, the president asked him to get the plan of the city engraved as soon as possible. L'Enfant was impressed with the need to counteract the negative feeling about the city in Philadelphia. He had the *Gazette of the United States* publish his written explanation of the plan so critics could at least be silenced with such descriptions as "Church . . . intended for national purposes, such as public prayer, thanks giving, funeral orations, etc., and assigned to the special use of no particular Sect or denomination, but equally open to all. It will be likewise a proper shelter for such monuments as were voted by the late Continental Congress for those heroes who fell in the cause of liberty, and for such others as may hereafter be decreed by the voice of a grateful Nation."

Such a church could be built in any city, but L'Enfant clearly gave the impression that his plan had been determined after a close study of the terrain. The squares to be controlled by each state were "such that they are most advantageously and reciprocally seen from each other and as equally distributed over the whole City district, and connected by spacious avenues round the grand Federal Improvements and as contiguous to them, and at the same time as equally distant from each other, as circumstances would admit."

But the description was not the plan, and he did not exactly bend over his maps to prepare something suitable for engraving. He enlisted Benjamin Ellicott to do it, freeing himself for more important things, such as talking with foreign ministers about the sites of their residences. His highest priority was obtaining a loan for the city. He talked to the two men most knowledgeable about such matters, Alexander Hamilton and Theophile Cazenove, both of whom were his friends. The latter had been so impressed with L'Enfant the previous May while investigating the Potomac navigation project for his clients, that his one regret on that score was that L'Enfant was not in charge of that project, too. Both Hamilton and Cazenove had received word that Dutch bankers were eager to loan money to prosperous states such as Maryland and Virginia for development projects.[1]

To demonstrate the need for a loan, L'Enfant prepared a long report for the president. He knew that was the last thing the president wanted. He wanted the plan engraved and the buildings designed. But L'Enfant argued that since he was advocating an entirely new system to defeat the enemies of the city, a presidential decision was needed. In his letter accompanying the report he painted a bleak picture of the current situation: no money, not enough materials, and no available labor. With "the neiborhood of the city offering no kind of resources at least none to be depended on," men and material procured from a distance would be more expensive. For work to begin on a major scale soon, additional funds were needed and could be had through "a loan, which is offered from Holland." The key was developing all areas of the city at once. His plan placed the whole city in a delicate balance. Actions at one end might cause problems at the other. "To organize a machine so complicated & to insure regular action in all the parts demand coolness and Resolution."

The accompanying report described the work 1,070 men should do in the coming building season: 150 men to complete digging the cellars of the two principal buildings, lay the foundations, and then terrace the grounds; 300 men to wharf the banks of the Potomac where the canal was to begin and then dig the canal to Capitol Hill—that should take four months, then they could work on the canal from Capitol Hill to the Eastern Branch; 230 men to grade the parks and streets; and 110 men to build bridges and aqueducts. He wanted the complete infrastructure of the city well on its way to completion before the Capitol and the president's house were raised above the ground.

The remaining 280 men were the teamsters, brick makers, wheelwrights, blacksmiths, sawyers, stonecutters, and their assistants needed to supply the other workers, all to get a daily ration of two ounces of "chocolate sugar butter," as well as a pound of beef or pork, a half pound of flour or corn meal, a half pint of spirits, and soap. As for the supervisory team, L'Enfant wanted seventeen overseers, a head carpenter, a head mason, a draftsman, a surveyor (who he thought should be Benjamin Ellicott), and a "director general'' with two assistants. The only mention he made of the commissioners was that since they worked without compensation no money had to budgeted for their salaries. Not that he finally suggested what the director general should receive by way of compensation. He left the salaries of the supervisory staff blank.

As for materials, he specified everything but the number of bricks. All that added up to a bill of $300,000. He concluded his report by describing the million-dollar loan and how it would support operation through 1796. The total expenditures to that date he expected to be $1,074,110.51.[2]

*   *   *

On January 7 Jefferson tried to arrange a meeting with L'Enfant to get an assurance that he would work under the commissioners, and Jefferson was not amused at the story in the *Gazette* that designated squares in the city for various purposes. As late as the 14th, L'Enfant had still put off the secretary of state. Then letters came about the dismissal of L'Enfant's workers. Washington sent the file, which also included new testimony on the destruction of Carroll's house, to Jefferson, noting, ''The President has not read the Papers, nor is he in any hurry to do it.''

L'Enfant was suddenly in a hurry to see Jefferson. He insisted that the commissioners had no right to fire his workers. Jefferson retorted that the commissioners had all executive power in the city. On the 17th, L'Enfant sent his long report to the president, who gave it, without comment, to Jefferson. And Jefferson gave the president drafts of letters for his signature supporting the commissioners. Apropos of L'Enfant, the president wrote that he might be useful ''if he could be brought to reduce himself within those limits which your own responsibility obliges you to prescribe him. At present he does not appear to be in that temper.''

In their letter, the commissioners had mentioned their hope that, once in Philadelphia, Judge Johnson would take time off from court business to meet with L'Enfant. Washington liked the idea and hoped Johnson ''may be able to let him see that nothing will be required but what is perfectly reconcilable to reason and to a due degree of liberty on his part."

Jefferson, of course, suggested that the president read about the contretemps with Roberdeau. He did, and, in a handwritten note to Jefferson, his temper blazed: "The conduct of Majr. L'Enfant and those employed under him, astonishes me beyond measure! and something more than even appears, must be meant by them! When you are at leisure I should be glad to have a further conversation with you on this subject."

Jefferson had got the impression that L'Enfant was going to quit. Indeed, in recalling his meeting with Jefferson 19 years later, L'Enfant said that it was then that he realized it would be impossible to continue in the federal city. The president was not ready to give up on L'Enfant. While he did nothing to encourage the rebellious artist, he asked Jefferson to find out L'Enfant's intentions. On February 1, Jefferson reported that he had learned that after their unsatisfactory meeting in mid-January, L'Enfant had written to Roberdeau instructing him to keep workers on the job which Jefferson thought "shows he means to continue himself." (During this period L'Enfant began to suspect that his mail was under surveillance.)[3]

*   *   *

Everything hung fire in anticipation of Johnson's arrival in the city when the Supreme Court convened, but he got sick again and posted a letter instead, which has not been found. On the same day L'Enfant wrote to the president defending Roberdeau and accusing the commissioners of pursuing "trivial disputes," and subverting "order and discipline," thereby demonstrating a "disinclination . . . to facilitate the prosecution of the business in such a manner as to enable me to engage in it anew." He would have to "renounce the pursuit unless the power of effecting the work with advantage to the public, and credit to myself is left me." His and Johnson's letters depressed the president. "I wish the business to which these letters relate," he wrote to Jefferson on February 7, "was brought to an issue, an agreeable one is not, I perceive to be expected." On the

9th he learned that George Walker was in town and asked Jefferson to see if he could help.

Walker conferred with L'Enfant over the weekend of February 10, reporting to the president on Saturday and Sunday. He did not come away with "a line of demarkation between the Commissioners and himself." All Walker could extract from L'Enfant was the retort that he had already written a letter giving that line. A perplexed Washington searched his files and found nothing to answer his purposes.

He soon got another shock. Andrew Ellicott checked with his brother and found that no progress had been made on the engraving. Benjamin claimed L'Enfant would not give him access to the definitive map. Andrew promptly informed Jefferson and the president, who promptly summoned Jefferson and Madison for a "family dinner" after which they could "try to fix on some plan for carrying the affairs of the federal district into execution." The solution to the problem with the plan was simple. They trusted the Ellicott brothers' familiarity with it and with the lay of the land would allow them to do a credible job without L'Enfant's assistance.

Andrew Ellicott took over the task and promptly suggested that some changes be made in L'Enfant's design. On the 15th the president summoned Jefferson for another meeting to discuss those changes. L'Enfant learned about the changes inadvertently. A magazine publisher asked L'Enfant for a copy of the plan, and L'Enfant sent him to Ellicott, who said that the plan was almost ready for the engraver. That shocked L'Enfant into checking up on what Ellicott was doing, and the shock became severe.

In a February 17 letter to Lear, L'Enfant fumed: "This draft to my great surprise I found in the state in which it now is, most unmercifully spoiled and altered from the original plan to a degree indeed evidently tending to disgrace me and ridicule the very undertaking." He insinuated that even during the surveying Ellicott had given examples of inattention to the plan and the propensity to suggest ideas that "would tend to destroy that harmony and combination of the different parts with the whole." And L'Enfant could see how the changes made would gratify "two or three individuals." L'Enfant warned that Ellicott's rendition was inaccurate and that Ellicott refused to give it up so he, L'Enfant, could correct it, which had been the original idea of involving Benjamin. Together they were to have corrected and completed the map.

Ellicott was quite proud of the changes he had made. He boasted to the commissioners that "the plan which we have furnished, I believe, will be found to answer the ground better than the large one in the Major's hands." Since the state of L'Enfant's plan at that time is not certain, it is hazardous to suggest exactly what changes Ellicott made. To judge from later complaints from proprietors, he halved the public reservation north of the president's house, diminished the size of Judiciary Square, and realigned some of the avenues. Jefferson made sure the national church and other such designations were not put on the map. Public land was marked, but only the president's house and Capitol squares were designated.[4]

Angry as L'Enfant was, the president still thought the problem manageable. L'Enfant could review Ellicott's rendition and make changes that might reconcile him to it. Provided they were not "productive of unnecessary or too much delay," he asked Jefferson and Walker, "had he not better be gratified in the alterations?" As he bent over backward to accommodate L'Enfant, Washington was shocked to hear from Walker that L'Enfant was showing plans of the public buildings to others. Washington directed: "The Plans of the buildings ought to come forward immediately for consideration."

On February 22 Jefferson tried again to get L'Enfant to agree to obey the commissioners, with one subtle difference. Jefferson began by stating, "The circumstances which have lately happened have produced an uncertainty whether you may be disposed to continue your services there." L'Enfant noticed the new line.

"I am not a little surprised to find that a doubt has arisen in the mind of yourself or the President of the uncertainty of my wishes to continue my services there"; he taunted them, "the motives by which I have been actuated, during the time I have been engaged in it, the continual exertions I have made in its promotion, the arrangement for this purpose which I lately handed to the President, indeed every step I have taken, cannot but evince most strongly how solicitously concerned I am in the success of it, and with what regret I should relinquish it."

He reiterated that he had always tried to conform to the president's will and secure the friendship of the commissioners: "I courted it, I sincerely wished it, knowing that without a perfect good understanding between them and myself, whatever exertions I should make, would prove fruitless." But what treatment had he received from the commissioners, "men so little versed in the minutia of such operations?" When they condescended to ask his opinion, they usually did just the opposite "and appear rather to have endeavored to obtain that knowledge from me the more effectually to defeat my intentions."

He then listed the commissioners' mistakes. They wanted a smaller city. Conspiring with Andrew Ellicott they changed boundaries to suit certain proprietors. They refused to cooperate with Peter in building a wharf, "conceiving that this improvement would be injurious to the Carrollsburg interest." They defeated the canal "under the influence and intimidated now by the Georgetown opposition." They stymied his efforts to get a bridge built over Rock Creek. "Constantly misled by the allurement of parties, or through jealousy of all measures not originating with them, with a temperament little addicted to business . . . involving themselves in contentions and disputes . . . to create dissention with the principals concerned in the execution and encourage mutiny among the people." They could not even arrange for money and materials. They paid Notley Young to build barracks that L'Enfant could have had his men do more cheaply.

As for their obsession with the public buildings, "I rest satisfied that the President will consider . . . that erecting houses for the accommodation of Government is not the only object, nay, not so important an one, as the encouragement to prepare buildings at those principal points, in the speedy settlement of which depends the rapid increase of the city. . . ."

L'Enfant's way was the only way: "nor must it be expected that anything short of what I proposed will answer that purpose or warrant success." He reiterated the purity of his intentions: "the determination I have taken no longer to act in subjection to their will and caprice is influenced by the purest principles. . . ." Then he did not exactly offer his resignation. "If therefore the law absolutely requires without any equivocation that my continuance shall depend upon an appointment from the Commissioners, I cannot nor would I upon any consideration submit myself to it.''

It was pure L'Enfant but more smoothly written because Roberdeau had posted bail and joined him. Jefferson sent the letter to the president, who reacted calmly. He asked that Madison and Attorney General Randolph review the correspondence and that they all meet at 8:30 A.M. on the 27th. On the night of the 26th he sent Lear to the major to see if he "absolutely" declined to act "under the authority of the present Commissioners." To Lear, L'Enfant said "that he had already heard enough of this matter." When Washington heard of that, he felt insulted. And Lear reported that L'Enfant "declared unequivocally that he would act on no condition but the dismission of the commissioners or his being made independent of them."

On the next day Hamilton, L'Enfant's patron, met with Jefferson and the president. A draft of the letter Jefferson wrote to L'Enfant is in Hamilton's hand. Jefferson offered him a last chance to repent: "It is understood you absolutely decline acting under the authority of the present Commissioners, if this understanding of your meaning be right, I am instructed by the President to inform you that notwithstanding the desire he has entertained to preserve your agency in the business, the condition upon which it is to be done is inadmissible & your services must be at an end."

L'Enfant wrote back to the president, hammering away that the system was wrong and that the city was doomed no matter who took his place. "Permit me also to assure in the most faithful manner that the same Reasons which have driven me from the establishment, will prevent any man of capacity . . . from engaging in a work that must defeat his sanguin hopes and baffle every exertion."

The president gave up any hope of retaining the services of the man he had so counted on. His last letter to L'Enfant cut through all the verbiage and summarized L'Enfant's failings: "Many weeks have been lost since you came to Philadelphia in obtaining a plan for engraving, notwithstanding the earnestness with which I requested it might be prepared on your first arrival. Further delay in this business is inadmissable. In like manner five months have elapsed and are lost, by the compliment which was intended to be paid you in depending *alone* upon your plans for the public buildings. . . . These are unpleasant things to the friends of the measure, and are very much regretted."

L'Enfant, usually so quick to defend himself, sensed that the president had had his fill. But he did not think the battle lost. He waited for Walker, who had just left Philadelphia, to bring forth a crescendo of protest from the proprietors in Georgetown.[5]

13. Punctilios

Jefferson called on Walker but found he had left for Georgetown. So he sent a letter after him trying to set the tone of what he should say to his fellow proprietors. He was sure Walker had seen enough of L'Enfant's temper "to satisfy yourself that he never could have acted under any control, not even of the President himself." Jefferson was "persuaded the enterprise will advance more surely under a more temperate direction; under one that shall proceed as fast and no faster than it can pay." Noting that five months had been lost because L'Enfant had not designed the public buildings, Jefferson closed his letter wishing "yourself and the inhabitants of Georgetown to be assured that every exertion will be made to advance and secure the enterprise."

On the same day that he wrote to Walker, March 1, Jefferson wrote to Commissioner Carroll asking him to have a board meeting as soon as possible after March 11 by which time "you will receive from hence such general ideas and recommendations as may occur." At the top of Jefferson's agenda was advertising for plans of the buildings. Ellicott would arrive in three or four weeks "to finish laying out the ground." And Jefferson asked Carroll to drop the case against Roberdeau. But before the board met, George Walker rallied his fellow proprietors to the defense of L'Enfant.

Walker feared that his $25,000 investment was in jeopardy unless L'Enfant was back on the job. As a result of his report, twelve proprietors—all of the principal ones save L'Enfant's enemies Young and Carroll—signed a petition urging the reinstatement of L'Enfant and lauding "his unwearied zeal, his firmness (though sometimes perhaps improperly exerted, in general highly useful), his impartiality to this or to that end of the City." The petitioners hoped that the commissioners could be persuaded "to accommodate to his views," and "in things really in his province (and in which from his Scientific knowledge and approved Taste, He would be most competent to Decide) he would be left without control." Walker—who, to maintain a semblance of neutrality, did not sign the petition—added that he was "sorry to discover such a want of confidence in the ability of the Commissioners" and worried that there would be a "public investigation" if L'Enfant was not rehired.

Walker was mindful that L'Enfant also had to be persuaded, so he and the petitioners reminded him that "the whole powers of your whole mind, have been for many months entirely devoted to the arrangements in the city, which reflect so much honor on your taste and judgment." They hoped that if the commissioners left him control of "all those things in which you would wish to be uncontrolled," he would "stand less on punctilios" and return to the fold.[1]

*　　*　　*

The letter to L'Enfant was never delivered, which made L'Enfant nervous. Anxious to get something down on paper, he sent a letter to Georgetown explaining why he resigned. Noting his "zeal" and "sacrifice . . . to secure a public good," he recalled "the obstacles" placed in his way by proprietors, the commissioners, and doubters throughout the nation. He had proved to the proprietors his impartiality by bearing down "those petit alurements of the jealous and intrigues of a few self conceited interested individual opposers." To defeat the far-flung enemies of the project, he had thought big, hoping "the immensity of the intended operations" would engage "the national honor in the success" of the undertaking. To defeat the commissioners, he had tried to overawe them, hoping that "a great display of the variety of operations persuing to render them more cautious of the ill consequences of an injudicious interference."

The commissioners remained the problem, which did not surprise him: "I wondered not at their confined ideas of the nature of an undertaking so wholly novel. They doubtless wanted object with which to compare those operations I proposed and deficient as they must be in knowledge requisite for a general management of them." He did his best to put up with their incompetence, shrugging off his defeated plans and the extra labor, and "glorying on the contrary at the opportunity to testify my zeal for the business." And devotion to the president obliged him "to sacrifice all personal considerations to the attainment of his favorite object." But finally he realized that "under the present system of management it is impracticable to effect that establishment in any manner answerable to its object."

L'Enfant began to betray ambivalence for the undertaking. It was hard enough "to change a wilderness." But to effect it "in a country devoid of internal resources and distant from the mass of population from whence hands as well as all materials . . . are to be procured must appear to all an undertaking attended with such various difficulties and inconveniences as almost to amount to an impossibility to effect it—particularly without any provision of funds from the united government, enough to make progress not confined to a congress house or presidential palace." All had to be in readiness "to raise the local worth to real estimation."

L'Enfant pitied the proprietors. He alone could pull it off, but the commissioners would put the operations in the hands of a "mechanical conductor" instead of someone with ingenuity, a "common builder" rather than an architect. He opined that even if his plan were carried out, property values would not reach the expectations of the proprietors. Indeed, "the high rate of your demands to purchasers" and "a reluctance in some of you to part . . . with your property, . . . will most probably disappoint your purpose by preventing many from taking a chance with you in the improvement of it." He cautioned them to make sure every sale required the buyer to improve the property. And he held out the hope that with "an immigration of wealthy speculators" pledged to improvements, the "firmness" of the proprietors in opposing changes might save the plan.

And the plan was already in jeopardy. L'Enfant finally gave some clue as to what had been going on in Philadelphia for the past two months: "I cannot disguise to you that much has already been attempted by the contrivance of an erroneous map of the city about to be published, which partly copied from the original has afterwards been mangled and altered in a shameful manner in its most essential parts, apparently with a design to injure or to mortify me, but more especially to the discredit of the establishment." He would be compelled to publicly oppose the changes. "A regard to reputation will in this case necessitate me to a disclosure of facts in evidencing which to the world the treachery may alienate the confidence of intending purchasers." And he pointed out how the changes would harm the proprietors. His diagonals were in jeopardy, and "the suppression of any of the transverse avenues changing their direction or connection with other streets" would be detrimental to "the interest of the most remote situations." As much as the president wanted him, he could not serve in a system in which "dishonor must await the end."

In a March 8 letter to David Stuart, the president characterized L'Enfant's complaints this way: "he found matters were likely to be conducted upon so pimping a scale, that he would not hazard his character or reputation on the event, under the controul he was to be placed."[2]

*   *   *

During the whole crisis in Philadelphia the commissioners did not meet. Each had decided independently that if L'Enfant stayed, he would quit. But when they heard of L'Enfant's fall they were not overjoyed. They were still saddled with L'Enfant's plan. Stuart wrote to the president worrying that the public square surrounding the president's house was too large. "It may suit the genius of a Despotic government to create an immense and gloomy wilderness in the midst of a thriving city," but certainly not the American government. Plus funds were too short to give so much land over to gardens. Johnson wrote to Jefferson worrying about how buildings would fit in the angles formed by the diagonal avenues, and he wondered if the plan as rendered by Ellicott was really accurate.

The president set about restoring the morale of his commissioners. He began by agreeing completely with their suspicions of L'Enfant: ". . . in proportion to the yieldings of the Commissioners his claims would extend. Such upon a nearer view, appears to be the nature of the *Man!*" And he would never work again in the city. The president directed their attention to the task at hand, warning them that "it has been observed by intelligent and well informed men . . . that the whole success of the Federal City, depends upon the exertions which may be made in the ensuing season towards completing the object." If no progress was made, enemies were ready to kill the project.

Writing to Stuart, the president chastised L'Enfant but thought the architect should get a fee of 500 guineas. He also defended the plan. "The doubts and opinion of others with respect to the permanent seat have occasioned no change in my sentiments on the subject. They have always been, that the plan ought to be prosecuted with all the dispatch the nature of the case will admit, and that the public buildings in size, form and elegance, should look beyond the present day." He wanted no changes in the president's square since "it is easier at all times to retrench, than it is to enlarge a Square." And any changes in the plan would open the door to more changes, "which might perplex, embarrass and delay business exceedingly."

This letter was Washington's last bit of business for the day, and it kept him up beyond his customary ten o'clock bedtime. True to his reputation, Stuart, in his letter, gave Washington a frank report on the machinations of Walker. Trying to calm the waters, the president could recall only Walker's early contributions to the effort. He knew keeping the friends of the city united would be difficult, but he reminded Stuart that the real enemies of the city were in Philadelphia.

"More than once, you will remember, I have given it to you as my opinion, that it would be by by-blows and indirect . . . that attempts would be made to defeat the Law. To sow the seeds of dissension, jealousy and distrust are among the means that will be practised. There is a current in this City which sets so strongly against everything that relates to the Federal district, that it is next to impossible to stem it."

Philadelphia engravers were dragging their feet. He asked Jefferson to see if Blodget could get the plan engraved in Boston. He fumed to his secretary of state: "The Engravers say *eight weeks* is the *shortest* time in which the Plan can be engraved; (probably they may keep it eight months). Is not this misteriously strange! Ellicott talked of getting you to walk with him to these People. The current in *this* City sets so strongly against the Federal City, that I believe nothing that *can* be avoided will ever be accomplished in it."[3]

*   *   *

Samuel Blodget had a quizzical, almost comical look to his face. In March 1792 Washington and Jefferson took him very seriously. They were making notes of what had to be done in the federal city and could see that L'Enfant was right in one respect: a loan would be needed. Their list of things needed to be done that summer included the cellar of both the Capitol and the president's house, the foundation of at least one of those buildings, a bridge over Rock Creek, the post road, the canal, and wharves. Plus they wanted as much brick, stone, lime, plank, timber, and other materials stockpiled as possible. Jefferson also readied the advertisement soliciting designs for the public buildings to compete for a 500 guinea prize. And recalling representations made to him when he left Europe that many skilled workers were available, Jefferson suggested and Washington agreed that "Germans and Highlanders" should be brought over to work in the city.

Blodget offered a scheme that would put $50,000 of a $500,000 loan in the commissioners' treasury on May 15 and that would be a handsome supplement to whatever Virginia and Maryland could contribute. He would raise the money by selling warrants, secured by publicly owned lots valued at $100 each, to investors in Boston. The interest on the $500,000 loan, when it was filled, would amount to $30,000 a year, which could be raised by selling 100 lots at $300 each. Blodget was sure, given the fever for stock speculation then raging, that the warrants would sell quickly. He scheduled $50,000 payouts to the commissioners for May and November 15 and four $100,000 payments in 1793 and 1794. The commissioners would not have to begin repaying the principal until May 15, 1800. All told, interest and principal would "absorb" 2,216 lots, or about a quarter of what was available to the public. For every $100 loaned, $142 would have to be repaid, but the investment of $468,000 would raise the value of the lots more than 42 percent.

Jefferson sent the details for the commissioners to approve, and he hoped the loan would counteract the enemies of the city who would "take advantage of the retirement of L'Enfant, to trumpet an abortion of the whole." With the money from the loan, "the works may be pushed with such spirit as to evince to the world that they will not be relaxed." Jefferson felt so good about the prospects that, along with the list of things to do and get, he sent down a proposal submitted by an Italian sculptor, Giuseppe Ceracchi, for a massive monument to the heroes of the American Revolution.[4]

*   *   *

Feeling that they had restored momentum to the development of the city, the president and secretary of state were taken aback by the proprietors' petition. When Jefferson showed it to him, the president flared: "no farther movement on the part of Government, can ever be made towards Majr. L'Enfant without prostration, *which will not be done*." The president recalled the insult to his secretary and then hammered the major once again. "No farther overtures will *ever* be made to this Gentn. by the Government; in truth it would be useless, for in proportion as attempts have been made to accommodate what *appeared* to be his wishes, he has receded from his own ground." To get his job back, L'Enfant had to apply to the commissioners.

In his letter to Walker, Jefferson toned the temper down: "the retirement of Majr. L'Enfant has been his own act. Nobody knows better than yourself the patience and condescensions the President used in order to induce him to continue. You know also how these were received on his part." Jefferson admitted that L'Enfant's employment had been deemed "useful, . . . but that the success of the enterprise depended on his employment is impossible to believe."[5]

14. 'Tis I Fear Too Late

Commissioners Carroll and Stuart met in Georgetown on March 13, 14, and 15, almost two months after their last meeting. They wrote thanking Washington for vindicating their stance against L'Enfant despite the "dirty reports with which we have been assailed." And they were sorry the president had to suffer the typical L'Enfant treatment. Carroll, however, did agree with L'Enfant on one point. Greedy proprietors were slowing progress. "The exorbitant and unreasonable expectations of some," he wrote to Madison, "particularly D. Carroll of Duddington at one end of the city & Robert Peter at the other, may check in a degree the public good & do prejudice to themselves. . . . This inordinate & blind passion may cramp us." But Carroll was over his case of nerves. Long attuned to the increasing value of Maryland property, he gleefully noted the land boom taking place in and around the federal city, with $200,000 worth of private land sales since January 1791.

The commissioners got down to work and were agreeable to all the suggestions from Philadelphia. They accepted the terms of the loan and ordered the building design competitions to begin, with entries due by July 15. They notified L'Enfant that his services with the city were at an end and sent him 500 guineas (about $2,500) and an offer of one lot. That in addition to the $600 fee and $300 for expenses already paid, they thought, compensated him royally. As for the list of things to do that Jefferson had sent down, they would eventually move on them all, but at that meeting they agreed to solicit proposals for a post road and a bridge over Rock Creek. Meanwhile Captain Williams was to do what Roberdeau wanted to do back in January, build huts for workers at the quarries. A wharf at the mouth of the Tiber depended on the delivery of logs. Brick making waited for brick makers. A final decision on the damage to Carroll of Duddington's house had to await an estimate on how much of the material from the damaged house could be reused. They liked the idea of foreign workers and asked Jefferson to amplify the scheme, but they put off a decision on Ceracchi's monument.

As they broke up to go home, they missed having someone in charge. In their letters to Philadelphia they suggested hiring a superintendent and remembered a Charleston architect that the president had mentioned. If he would not do, they asked Jefferson to advertise for a superintendent. As for salary, the president could decide. And they were worried that Ellicott would not return because of a dispute over his fee. Stuart knew of another surveyor, James Dermott, who had done some work in Alexandria, and hired him to at least divide squares. But building the post road required someone who knew where it was supposed to go. So progress in the city was on hold until Ellicott arrived. The wait was so painful that when Roberdeau returned on March 19 to face trial, the commissioners not only dropped legal proceedings against him but hinted that he could have his old job back.[1]

*   *   *

L'Enfant refused the 500 guineas and the lot, taunting the commissioners: "Without enquiring of the principle upon which you rest this offer, I shall only here testify my surprise thereupon, as also my intention to decline accepting it." He asked Roberdeau to pass that message on to the commissioners' treasurer, William Deakins. "He made no answer," Roberdeau reported, "but looked amazed that a man would refuse money when so generously offered him by people in such high stations.''

L'Enfant did not want to accept compensation that might be construed as an admission that the commissioners had hired him. And he did not want to relinquish his rights to future claims on the commissioners. At that time he still held out hope that a mutiny by the proprietors would get him back on the job, in which case he would want royalties on engravings of his plan, and a percentage of all money spent on the project rather than a flat fee for his work.

Roberdeau brought L'Enfant's letter to the proprietors with instructions that they should present the letter to the commissioners. Roberdeau reported back to L'Enfant that Jefferson's letter "has met general disapprobation from them." The proprietors were not "insensible of the True cause" and would hurry an answer to Jefferson as well as L'Enfant. Roberdeau was not about to proclaim victory, but he seemed somewhat optimistic that all would be well: "I am sure, that no exertion in them will be wanting, to form such an arrangement as will be consistent to your wishes and insure the success of the undertaking. They are all extremely anxious for your return justly conceiving that every thing is at stake as it respects those measures immediately necessary to retrieve the injuries done to the reputation of the establishment. The anxiety on all hands is really great and under a due sense that every exertion should now be made to insure that success which nothing but a new system can insure." Even the commissioners were "ignorant as they must be of any mode to pursue their future operations, however sanguine the letters they may receive from Philadelphia, to cheer their languid spirit." They would capitulate if they could do so with "any kind of honor." Samuel Davidson expected L'Enfant would be back in charge by the summer.

Walker did not, however, follow L'Enfant's orders. He decided L'Enfant's letter was too impertinent. He had advice from Cabot, who was back in Philadelphia, that it was possible to save the situation if no one's position was hardened. Since the commissioners would have to agree to L'Enfant's reinstatement, it made no sense to pass on L'Enfant's insults.

In their reply to Jefferson the proprietors hastened to agree that it was unthinkable that L'Enfant should return independent of the commissioners or that the commissioners should be dismissed. But a way had to be made for L'Enfant to return to the city without having to kowtow to the commissioners. They pleaded with Jefferson not to insist that L'Enfant ask the commissioners for reinstatement. Then they tried to impress L'Enfant with how harmless and helpless the commissioners were. The law required them, and "however unequal they may be to the task of rearing the city," it would not be prudent for the president to fire such "men of respectable character and connections." So they hoped L'Enfant's "good sense will point out to you the impossibility of the President's offering you such terms as he might himself think your merits entitle you to — and that your zeal to promote the city, together with your knowledge of possessing the entire confidence of the bulk of the proprietors will induce you to accept such as it is possible to give."

Uriah Forrest wrote the cover letter to L'Enfant, coupling effusive praise with a suggested line of demarcation between him and the commissioners: "the estimates of men and money shall be laid before the commissioners, who shall grant or reject, but when once granted you are exclusively to direct." Forrest understood the president would agree to that and did not doubt that "the commissioners will cheerfully acquiesce."[2]

*   *   *

On March 24, three days after the proprietors sent off their second round of letters, all the major Philadelphia papers began running ads soliciting designs for the public buildings in Washington. L'Enfant never betrayed his reaction, but Roberdeau gave vent to his distress. " 'Tis *I fear too late*," he lamented to L'Enfant. "Every thinking man here does not scruple to condemn very cordially this proceeding, but it was out of their power to prevent it — and I knowing the effect it will have upon you can but lament that a little more judgment has not been exercised."

In late March Walker went back to Philadelphia. If he did see the president and secretary of state once again, it did not register in those gentlemen's voluminous papers. On April 1 L'Enfant gave Walker a letter to be shared with the proprietors. It was a rarity from L'Enfant, brief and noncontentious. He thanked them for their support and assured them of his regret at the accumulating circumstances opposing to an accommodation. . . .

"I do not stand upon punctilio," he replied to their earlier insinuations as he continued gracefully, "nor am actuated from motives of pride or disregard or of enmity toward any of the primary managers of the business, but that I have been wholly determined from a conviction of an impractibility to effect the undertaking begun under a system of direction which must perpetuate misunderstanding amongst the parties concerned."[3]

*   *   *

L'Enfant did not publish his letters to the president, secretary of state, and proprietors. The delay in engraving the plan forestalled any public attack on it. And L'Enfant had the prospect of another job. The Society for the Promotion of Useful Manufactures planned to build a manufacturing city at the Passaic Falls in New Jersey, complete with a system of canals. Alexander Hamilton, the chief organizer of the project, recognized that no man was more qualified for supervising the project than L'Enfant.

For the moment, however, friends of that enterprise had to hold their breath until the financial collapse of William Duer, one of Hamilton's collaborators in the enterprise, sorted itself out. Back in January speculators marveled at the amazing rise in stock prices, especially in New York. Although some attributed it to Hamilton's funding plan putting so much money in enterprising hands, Hamilton himself recognized it as a dangerous bubble being pumped up by Duer, who was extending credit to mechanics and others who had no business risking their savings on stocks. Duer himself owed money to many, including the government. Citing his tight situation, Duer begged Hamilton to forgive repayment awhile longer. Hamilton decided that he could not do so in good conscience. Duer failed and with him many of the great and a dangerous number of the small men of New York City. The master speculator barely escaped with his life when a mob went after him. With Duer's fall, stock prices fell throughout the country. Those who did not fail became cautious.

On March 21, the same day the proprietors were making another attempt to reconcile all warring parties, the president dashed off a plaintive note to Jefferson: "I hope Blodget does not begin to hesitate concerning the loan." Indeed he had. As Jefferson informed the commissioners: "The temporary check on the price of public paper, occasioned by Mr. Duer's failure, induces Mr. Blodget to think it will be better to postpone for a few days the opening of the loan proposed, as he thinks it important that the present panic should be so far over, as to enable him to get through it at once, when proposed." Blodget, however, assured Jefferson that the May 15 payment of $50,000 would be made.[4]

15. People Are on Tip Toe to Come

"One would imagine half the labourers in the country had collected to make proposals for removing the obstructions in the post road," Roberdeau reported to L'Enfant. Not one of the would-be contractors was "respectable," and the hangdog look of the hayseeds helped turn embarrassment into farce. "They generally wished to know what the obstructions to be removed were, whether trees cut down, or stumps grubbed up. . . . As I heard N. Young observe that being without a plan of the city, the commissioners were at a loss to determine where the said post road positively lay, . . . permitting those obstructions peaceably to remain until a future day when they can find them."

Ellicott had still not arrived, so the commissioners postponed the contract for the post road, but they wanted a Baltimore builder,

Leonard Harbaugh, to submit a proposal for a bridge over Rock
Creek. These proceedings likewise amused Roberdeau: "But as he
[Harbaugh] knows neither the dimensions of the one intended nor
the particular kind of all the various sorts of bridges that might be
built, he readily acknowledges that it is not a simple matter to give
an estimate of the expense or a draft of the work coinciding with
their ideas. This also will be a difficult point to settle in as much as
the majority are accustomed to see bridges little superior to beaver
dams. . . . By all this you cannot but conceive in how ridiculous a
point of view the conductors of this business must appear."

As he left the meeting in Georgetown Roberdeau cast a sad eye
across Rock Creek. Bad weather dampened any inclination on his
part to cross over, but from what he could see, the city "at a
distance wears but a gloomy aspect. I hear some new houses are
built and a few holes dug — and that they are at a loss for more
work."

The meetings lasted for another two days, and Roberdeau remained at his post, still reporting no Ellicott: "by this evening he
was positively expected, the stage has driven by and — mortifying
to think of — no Mr. Ellicott; all the hopes and longing are in a
moment destroyed. . . ." The commissioners did know where some
streets were, and they saw clay from Davidson's property thrown
up in one. So the commissioners sent him a note asking him to
desist. Davidson replied with spirit that the clay was turned up "at
the request of a gentleman, who I once considered your equal in
authority and now your superior in judgment." He notified them
that he intended to make bricks, and "in the mean time you may
take your remedy."

Roberdeau did not even mention to L'Enfant that the commissioners had dropped their suit of trespass against him. But that did not
make hanging around any more inviting. When the commissioners
left town so did Roberdeau, returning to L'Enfant and a young lady
he was courting, just in time to see the cornerstone of the president's
house in Philadelphia laid on May 10.[1]

*   *   *

Needless to say, the commissioners took a different view of their performance. Their excuse for not accomplishing so much was the continued absence, not of Ellicott, but of Thomas Johnson. This time he was not sick himself; his mother-in-law was. Not that they did not think they were getting things done. For one thing, their character as a governing body had changed because of the legislation passed last December by the state of Maryland. They now had the power to grant licenses and on March 27 William Venable got the first liquor license in the city. They also granted licenses to two smiths and a baker.

In a March 30 letter to Jefferson they gave every appearance that they were on the move. Advertisements soliciting plans for the public buildings had been sent to Boston, Baltimore, Charleston, and Richmond. To give a spur to development between the two buildings they decided to build a "commissioners' house" — 50 by 40 feet — near the church square, on the ridge above Pennsylvania Avenue. They ordered slate from Boston to cover it. Agreement had been reached with Carroll on the reconstruction of his house. Soon Ellicott would arrive, as well as the man they hired to run the quarries and the man from Baltimore who would "superintend the making of bricks." And they signed a contract with Harbaugh for a bridge.[2]

*   *   *

The Federal Bridge was the first permanent structure to be built by the commissioners, and they wanted much more than a beaver dam. A magnificent stone arch was the chief feature of Harbaugh's design. At its midpoint the 60-foot span was 20 feet above high water. On pedestals atop sat ten stone urns, and sixteen bas-reliefs of fish lined the outer sides of the bridge.

Harbaugh had built the first apartment building in Baltimore and a stone arch at the courthouse there. Although he had not built a bridge, the commissioners were quite confident of his ability. Indeed, they thought he could build the canal and supervise the construction of the public buildings. It was not building the bridge that daunted the commissioners but a legal problem. Their powers ended at the borders of the city of Washington, so they did not feel comfortable spending public money to build the causeway needed to connect the Georgetown waterfront to the bridge.

Rock Creek was a considerable tributary then. Ships with twelve-foot masts commonly sailed up it. Its channel was 300 feet wide where it was to be bridged at K Street. It ran close to the Washington side; the shore there was made up of rocks, and there was a steep bank. But on the Georgetown side there was an area about 1,300 feet wide that was covered with water during spring floods and high tides. As summer wore on low tide would expose the bottom of the river. Speculators in Georgetown had not been unmindful that the area could be turned into firm and valuable waterfront property. A 1,300-foot causeway could run from the higher ground of George-town to the bridge that would span a 60-foot channel. On both sides of the causeway firm ground could be easily made, and L'Enfant had got the landowners on the Georgetown side of Rock Creek to agree to give up half the newly made lots to the public. Selling those lots would help raise money to build the causeway, if it was legal. So first the commissioners deferred the whole project to the president. The agreement with Harbaugh even stipulated that the president could make any changes.

The president was not pleased with such deference. Desperate to get some order into the way the city's affairs were conducted, he had Jefferson instruct the commissioners to carry on without his further advice. That said, Jefferson reported that the president thought the price for the bridge, $8,645, too high, and although "he has hardly time to attend to any details, he thinks that if you were to reduce the foot ways of the bridge to 6 feet each, and make the carriage way 26 feet, it might be better."[3]

*   *   *

No one was more nonplused at the proprietors' love for L'Enfant than Ellicott. When he finally reached the federal city on March 31 he wasted no time in quizzing them. Some acknowledged "that their desire for the restoration of Major L'Enfant arose from a wish to dispose of their lands the ensuing season: and expected, that his extravagant plans, added to his great confidence, and mad zeal, would be highly favorable to them." At the same time they realized that, with "his ungovernable temper," he would soon have to be dismissed.

Ellicott hoped to be the man who could once again get the commissioners and proprietors working together. But the man who had changed L'Enfant's plan was not popular with proprietors, especially since the board pressed him to make more changes. With the arrival of Johnson on April 9, the board renewed their attack on the plan. Finding Ellicott agreed with them, they asked him for a letter that they could pass on to the president. Ellicott wrote that he thought there were still too many diagonal avenues and too many squares. His major complaint was the site of the Capitol: "This last defect is so obvious, that I do not remember to have met with one person, who did not immediately see it, when on the ground."

The site was too close to the edge of the hill. To the east 20 to 30 feet of earth would have to be dug away so there could be a view. With the building on the side of the hill, the foundation "may be doubtful." Finally, on the edge of the hill the ascent to the building would be too steep for convenience. He suggested moving the building 600 feet to the east and "cutting away a small part of the side of the hill." He assured the commissioners that making the changes "will not delay the execution of the plan more than three or four weeks." And he noted, as an added fillip, that "such a change in the plan will save Mr. Notley Young's house, the value of which is far beyond any expense that can attend making the alteration." Ellicott assured them that the changes would not affect the engraved plan; "the plate will convey an idea of the work sufficiently exact to any man living."[4]

*   *   *

As such gumption in the board indicated, Johnson was back running the show. That was bad news for Giuseppe Ceracchi. The Italian sculptor might have wowed Philadelphia with his busts of twenty-seven prominent Americans from Washington on down, but Johnson looked askance at the planned monument. The statue of

Washington surrounded by and surmounting eleven statues of dem-
igods did not bother him; the price, 20,000 guineas, or almost
$100,000, did. In a way Johnson welcomed the extravagance of the
proposal. The trouble with L'Enfant was that although his plan
called for fountains and statues all over the city, he had cunningly
confined his activities to opening his avenues. As much as Johnson
hated all those avenues, it was with difficulty that he could argue
that New Jersey Avenue should not be cleared of houses in its way.
Yet, as both Johnson and L'Enfant must have known, the more
avenues L'Enfant opened the more necessary became the fountains
and statues that were to fill the vistas opened by those avenues.

Johnson wanted the priorities of the commissioners dictated by
common sense, not by the plan. The equestrian statue was one of
the major, if not the major, focal points of the plan. Yet in 1800 it
would accommodate no one and serve no useful purpose. Johnson's
pleasure in negativing the idea was no doubt diminished because
L'Enfant did not propose it, but it did allow him and his fellow
commissioners to establish the new common-sense approach to
developing the city.

"We are of opinion that in the application of the funds, we ought
to class our work, into necessary, usefull, and ornamental, preferring them in that order," they explained to Jefferson. They sent
back Ceracchi's proposal. If it was really needed, "the whole nation
should contribute to defray the expense of the monument."

Jefferson, however, did not give up so easily. He argued that
although it seemed at present a low priority, it would take only a
small advance to set Ceracchi at a work that would take four or five
years even to begin. Since it was "pretty certain that the equestrian
statue of the president can never be executed by an equal workman," he wondered if it might be wise to make the commitment
now since by 1795 funds should be plentiful or Congress might be
persuaded to fund the monument. Jefferson always seemed to light
up when he was able to avoid the realities of the federal city and
view the site as a canvas on which to replicate the aesthetics of the
old world he so admired. The commissioners did not see the light
and did not change their mind. Ceracchi's friends asked Congress
to bankroll the project, but the sculptor returned to Europe empty-
handed.

Johnson also came down heavy on Jefferson's pet idea of the moment, the workers from Germany. He pointed out to those in Philadelphia that they were out of touch with what was going on in the federal city. "The situation of things here is very different from what we expected, or you perhaps have any idea of. People are on tip toe to come from all parts, we might probably have 2,000 mechanics and labourers here on very short notice. We think therefore, there is no occasion to import people from abroad unless stonecutters of whom there are but few and their wages high, of them indeed 20, or 30 from Scotland are desirable & we wish them introduced." Then, three days later, the commissioners informed Jefferson that the Scottish stonecutters were not needed either. Suter, the tavernkeeper in Georgetown, had a relative from New York who could supply all they needed.

Johnson also persuaded his colleagues that no superintendent was needed. Joseph Clark, the architect supervising construction of public buildings in Annapolis, wrote offering to design and build the public buildings. But Johnson pointed to Harbaugh as "a modest well tempered man . . . able to be very useful to us." Captain Williams had "given us much satisfaction by his activity and attention in the little we have to do." And Williams was cheap, agreeing to act as supervisor of the work force and commissary for £250 or $650, a year. Those two men should be able to supervise laying the foundations of the public buildings and build the 50-by-24-foot temporary storehouse the commissioners wanted on the president's house square.

Another virtue of Williams was his ability to handle slaves. In his work with the Potomac Company Johnson had found slave labor necessary to provide "a useful check" and keep white workers "cool." Before adjourning, the board resolved "to hire good labouring negroes by the year, the masters cloathing them well and finding each a blanket, the commissioners finding them provisions and paying twenty one pounds a year" ($55) to their masters.[5]

16. A Handsome Bridge Is Erecting

The Jefferson papers generated during that year of increasing political strife with Hamilton present a curious contrast. The words are
full of pessimism for the future of the union. Yet the sketches of a
Capitol show the effort to convey a grandeur suitable for a nation
pretending to empire. There is evidence that Jefferson even anony-
mously submitted a design in the competition for the president's
house. And by the end of 1791 he had set the French architect
Stephen Hallet to work on a design for the Capitol.

The president shared the same weariness of politics and anticipation of the buildings, though he did not make any sketches. He did
make a show of his impatience with changing the site of the Capitol
or the plan of the city. The president countered the common-sense
commissioners with better sense, "the expediency of fixing the
public opinion on the thing as stable & unalterable." The hill to the
east should stay, "since were it to be dug away, private buildings
would as effectually exclude prospect from the Capitol, except
merely along the avenues." He was sure that Young's house was far
enough away to save it from having to be removed "for years to
come." And he did not want the principal buildings farther apart;
he wanted them designed and built.

The talk of buildings and the loan turned some heads. After
coming down from Baltimore for a visit, William Prout left a glowing
account of the city that spring. "There is a great number of hands
engaged in making bricks and clearing streets, building bridges. . . .
The President has borrowed $500,000 for carrying on the public
buildings. . . . I can any day sell it [his city property] if I was
inclinable, for 50,000 pounds." Of course he was writing to his
brother, who did loan him $1,000, but Prout needed more to pay off
Slater and set up stores in Georgetown and the federal city.

Actually, Harbaugh was off getting cranes to hoist stone for the
bridge. The only building going on was for a lumber shed along the
Tiber below the site of the president's house, "at the place where
the fishermen were." The loan was not working out thanks to the

crash of stock values. Jefferson had to advise the commissioners to trim their sails: "You have certainly heard of the extraordinary crush which has taken place, here at N York and Boston, of persons dealing in paper, & of goods merchants and others who had dealings with paper-men. It has produced a general stagnation of money contracts, which will continue till it is known who stands and who falls, during this crisis, Mr. Blodget thinks it prudent to suspend proposing our loan, & indeed we think so too. This will oblige you to keep back some of your operations."[1]

* * *

In the view of most proprietors the commissioners had already succeeded in keeping back operations. In a letter to L'Enfant, Uriah Forrest painted a bleak picture of the city: "We are doing nothing to the purpose, at least nothing that I can either see or feel — there are some little differences between the agents of the city and Davidson. Burnes too is quarreling with them, & with some cause, but all would be healed, and things go on well if you would return to the direction. I am well acquainted with your obstinacy, though you term it proper firmness, and I would endeavor to reason and persuade you here, where I am sure you would be more welcome than ever."

Burnes's quarrel with the commissioners arose because, despite the supposed value of his lots, he faced an unmanageable debt. Stoddert's sweetener the year before had not made Burnes solvent. He needed that £25 an acre for his land taken by the public, or "my family may starve and my person be imprisoned." Creditors were after him and he had no means to pay them. He had sold eight of his twelve slaves, and his farm had been "rendered useless" by the public streets cut through it. He had a point. The board agreed to divide two squares with him so he could get paid for land the public took, and advertise the divided lots for sale. He took L'Enfant's advice and offered a discount to buyers who would build immediately.

Samuel Davidson strained to make a point. The land he had bought was essentially a working farm surrounded by wood lots.

The outhouse of his farmhouse was, he thought, in an inconvenient place. He wanted to move it temporarily into what was to become one of the public streets. The same day the commissioners threatened to take him to federal court for digging in the streets, he did his best to make a mountain out of a dung hole: "Foreign to my idea and contrary to my wishes," he wrote to the commissioners, "I find all power within the city of Washington is, either impliedly or in reality, absorbed by you. Under this impression, I have most humbly to solicit your kind permission in removing — at my own cost and charges — the little house commonly called a necessary house — now in a very inconvenient place on one of my lots. . . ."

The commissioners had no sympathy for Davidson, Burnes, or Forrest, which was a mistake. The shine land speculators liked to put on things became spattered with the mud of discontent. Davidson was soon engaged in trench warfare. Ellicott needed to dig a ditch to drain the newly cut post road which ran along the ridge just north of Pennsylvania Avenue and then along K Street. He asked permission from Davidson to run the ditch through his property. Davidson not only refused but he justified his refusal in a letter to the president of the United States, no less. Of course, the bulk of the letter was a lamentation over the dismissal of L'Enfant and the incompetence of the commissioners: "To every proprietor the fact comes home with peculiar force, that since the conducting the business has devolved on the commissioners alone, all public confidence in the object is lost. The proprietors retrospect its late situation in comparison with its present, with the most poignant sorrow; since they now perceive a total abatement of disposition in individuals to speculate in the property. . . ."

That was not venting spleen enough. Davidson demanded that the commissioners recompense him for damage done to his land, for "cutting down timber out[side] of the public streets — burning my fences and wood after being cut and corded at my own expense."

George Walker had a momentary flush of optimism when he heard that Johnson had resigned, but it was only a rumor. Given the lack of confidence in the city, Walker decided he could not sell lots. He needed money so he asked L'Enfant to arrange a mortgage for his land with Cazenove, the Dutch bankers' representative. Of course, he did not expect anyone to value the property as city lots. "It should only be calculated at the price of plantation land."

Just at the peak of the building season, when Walker must have dreamed of summoning carpenters and masons, he placed an ad soliciting a married man to oversee his farm at 6th Street and Maryland Avenue Northeast. Walker soon learned that the lot of a Washington farmer was not easy. "Straggly white persons and negroes" were robbing his orchards along the Eastern Branch. He placed an ad warning all that his two brick makers would be laying for trespassers.

Building was giving way to husbandry. Davidson refenced his land and sowed it with oats. To defuse the complaints by Burnes, Davidson, Young, and no doubt others that the streets interfered with their agricultural pursuits, the commissioners directed Ellicott to designate those few streets that really had to be kept open. In all others the proprietors could reap what they sowed.

Leave it to Roberdeau, who was back to see his parents in Alexandria, to all but announce the death of the federal city: "I have been in the city but once since I arrived here," he wrote to L'Enfant on July 2, "every thing is apparently at a stand. Indeed I conceive that I am convinced the day of Judgment is at hand. The confidence of the people here is destroyed. Few now believe the success of the establishment, and none are willing to interest themselves in it."[2]

*   *   *

In mid-May the president made a quick visit to Mount Vernon, and that allowed Tobias Lear his first opportunity to view the lot he had purchased in the city. He had been through the area before, but that purchase prompted him to view the city "with an eye to the purpose for which it is now designed." He liked what he saw. After noting the discontent of the proprietors, he opined, "The thing is progressing steadily and properly." And he informed a friend in his hometown of Portsmouth, New Hampshire, that he planned to make his future in the federal city. "The streets are already cleared," he wrote, ". . . and a handsome bridge is erecting to connect it with Georgetown."

Accompanying the president, he went up to Little Falls to see how work on the canal there was progressing. All seemed to be going well. He "was not a little pleased to find them in such forwardness as to ensure the completion of that great object within two years. . . ."

*   *   *

The president's impressions of the city during that trip are not known, but the main topic of discussion by the board after he left was getting German workers. This time the commissioners decided that having Scottish and German workers may "eventually be usefull, perhaps almost necessary." They told Jefferson that they would arrange with some Scottish merchants to bring over stonecutters from that country and asked Jefferson to use his contacts to get a hundred Germans. They would pay passage for single men in return for sixteen months' labor from skilled workers and twenty months' from unskilled. It was not so much the need for workers that prompted the board to give in to the president's yen for emigrants as the desire to impress emigrants that the federal city was a good destination.

The president also asked them when they planned to sell lots again. It was a touchy subject, since copies of the plan still were not available. They decided on October 8. They also did all they could, at a time when the designs were not even agreed on, to forward the construction of the public buildings. They signed contracts with two brick makers for two lots of 180,000 and 300,000 bricks to be made at the president's house. They had not forgotten the canal; they asked Ellicott to survey its route between Tiber and James creeks. They also tried to placate restive proprietors. They finally settled with Carroll for his house, paying him £1,679 ($4,466), and agreed to divide the two squares he owned which lay just east of the Capitol square. Not only did they pay Davidson for his land, but they contracted with him to supply sixty cords of wood to the brick kilns at the president's house square.

And this time they informed Ellicott promptly of what had to be done before the October sale. They wanted every bidder to "be able to procure their fancy as to any part of the city." They authorized Ellicott to hire more men to get the surveying done, but Ellicott did not have enough surveying equipment, an item always in short supply in the new country. Ellicott wrote to Jefferson that he thought the commissioners had "conducted their business with judgment, and firmness."

*   *   *

Leonard Harbaugh came up with an excellent way to celebrate the Fourth of July: officially lay the foundation stone of the bridge over Rock Creek, which Harbaugh began calling the Federal Bridge. At noon on July 3 he sent the commissioners his ideas for a proper ceremony to which they gladly acceded.

"First, the plank sweep, that at present stands over the place on which the bridge is to be erected, will in the morning be ornamented with the American flag, and other insignia proper for the occasion, after which, the undertakers, mechanics, and workmen employed thereat, will appear in procession furnished with their respective implements, at W. Suters Fountain Inn — precisely at eleven o'clock a.m. from whence they will expect the honour of conducting you [the commissioners] (accompanied by as many of the respectable inhabitants of this City as may favour us with their presence) to the eastern buttment of the bridge, where the ceremony is to be performed by the gentlemen Commissioners in placing the foundation stone in a place that will be designed for that purpose; after which a written discourse will be read, suitable to the occasion and lastly the procession will return to W. Suters in the same order as is above described, where the ceremony is to be concluded."

There is no record of what actually transpired on the 4th, and most likely Harbaugh's ceremony went off without a hitch. But before he left Suter's Fountain Inn, Commissioner Stuart received an intimation of trouble ahead. The man he had hired for the surveying department, James Dermott, was deep in his cups. He approached Stuart, whom he had never met before, and told him that there were inaccuracies in the survey of the city. As far as Stuart had seen, all Dermott had been doing was overseeing the slaves cutting trees to open the streets, a task for which Stuart thought a European like Dermott ill qualified. Still, he told him to present such information formally to the commissioners, which Dermott, not wanting to be fired by Ellicott while the commissioners were away, did not do.[3]

17. The New Appendage the Dome

The Federal Bridge was an imposing improvement laying to rest the insinuations that nothing was being done in the city. When the president came to the city on July 17 to review the designs submitted for the public buildings he admired the progress of the bridge and was gratified to learn that it would be completed in the contracted time, the end of August. The commissioners did not disturb the president by sharing the contents of a letter they had just received from George French.

The year before, French had impressed the commissioners with his proposal to build the Washington canal. Now he was alarmed that the bridge as designed was too small. It forced the creek, which had a natural channel of 300 feet at that point, into an artificial channel of 60 feet. During floods the level of the water behind the bridge would be higher than the level of the river above Little Falls, which would cause dangerous currents in the river. And flooding behind the bridge would ruin lots and perhaps make the creek harder to navigate.

His solution was to build a bridge with three arches, not one. He showed how such a bridge would use less material, allow for a more gradual ascent to the Washington side of the bridge, and be more aesthetically pleasing. As planned, the embankments heaped up at the ends of the bridge prevented a full view of the arch. With three arches, no matter from which angle one viewed the bridge, one would see at least two full arches.[1]

Harbaugh was not able to dismiss French's objections out of hand. The matter would have to be investigated. Making up somewhat for this possible snag in the bridge was the arrival on the scene of another builder and architect who, like Harbaugh a few weeks before, promised to be just the man the commissioners were looking for.

*   *   *

James Hoban seemed destined to have an effect on the federal city. The Dublin-born architect and builder, who was only thirty years old in 1792, made such an impression on his patrons in Charleston, South Carolina, that they alerted Washington during his Southern tour that Hoban was just the man to design and build the federal city. Even before the design competition was announced, the commissioners were interested in finding out more about the Charleston architect in hopes that he could replace L'Enfant. Hoban must have got wind of the commissioners' interest in him. He took a packet ship to Philadelphia, arriving sometime in May. He met with the president, who in turn gave him a letter of introduction to the commissioners. Once there, he impressed the commissioners with his diligence in planning the president's house.

Several designs for the Capitol and the president's house came to Philadelphia, and they did not appeal to Washington. He wrote to Stuart on July 9, "If none more elegant than these should appear . . . , the exhibition of architecture will be a very dull one indeed." Waiting for him in Georgetown were entries much more encouraging. He reported to Lear that he "found at Georgetown many well conceived, and ingenious plans for the Public buildings in the New City: it was a pleasure indeed, to find, in an infant Country, such a display of Architectural abilities."

The president and commissioners did not hesitate in their decision on the president's house. They awarded Hoban first prize, and, impressed that he had "been engaged in some of the first buildings in Dublin, appears a master workman, and has a great many hands of his own," they hired him for $1,500 to supervise the construction of the building. The only snag was that Hoban's winning design did not fill the space allotted for the building by L'Enfant. They asked him to increase the dimensions of his building by one fifth. The president would return shortly to pick the exact site for it.[2]

The Capitol was a problem. Hoban did not submit a design and no one design stood out. The president found some value in five of the fourteen designs submitted. Stephen Hallet must have felt he had a lock on the prize, since Jefferson was encouraging him. Hallet's neoclassical design, called the "fancy" design by the commissioners, was so patently expensive that the commissioners shied away from it. The architect revamped it, and his simpler design clearly was the favorite when the entries were reviewed on July 16 and 17, but it was not deemed good enough. (Most of what he submitted for the contest has been lost.) Leonard Harbaugh took time off from the Federal Bridge to submit a design, now lost. Some elements of it won favor. For a while the commissioners toyed with the design of Robert Lanphier, a builder in nearby Alexandria, but the design did not distribute the rooms properly and seemed unworkable.

Designing the Capitol was more challenging than designing the president's house. There were no prescriptions for the latter, but in announcing the contest for the Capitol, Jefferson had specified a brick building with a conference room, where both houses could meet together, a representatives' chamber that could hold 300 people apiece; a Senate chamber of 1,200 square feet; attendant lobbies to both chambers; twelve rooms, each of 600 square feet, for committee meetings; and clerks' offices to be half as high as the committee rooms. Part of the problem was that Washington felt Jefferson had not asked for enough. For example, he wanted an office for the use of the president.

Just after the president left Georgetown on July 18, a design (now lost) came in from George Turner, a judge in the Northwest Territory, present-day Ohio. The commissioners found "something in it striking and agreeable," and they sent it off to Mount Vernon. But they evidently knew it was not a winner for they informed the president that they had invited Hallet to come to Georgetown to work on improving his design.

Washington wrote back on the 23rd that he was "more agreeably struck with the appearance of" Turner's plan "than with any that has been presented to you." But it had defects. Then, in a long letter, Washington showed a fair understanding of the architectural problems involved and presented some ideas on how to solve them.

He thought the pilasters, or the columns built into the outer walls, should "be carried around the semicircular projection at the end." He questioned specifying 41 feet as the elevation of the upper story. If it had to be that large to preserve the proportions of the building, the space should be cut in half to provide for more committee rooms, "of which there appears to be a deficiency." Turner's plan introduced the idea of a dome above the central conference room, which Washington seemed to like. "The Dome . . . would, in my opinion, give beauty & grandeur to the pile; and might be useful for the reception of a Clock — Bell &c."

What Washington really wanted was a combination of Turner's plan with Hallet's: "Could such a plan as Judge Turner's be surrounded with Columns and a colonade like that which was presented to you by Monsr. Hallet (the roof of Hallet's I must confess does not hit my taste) — without departing from the principles of Architecture — and would not be too expensive for our means, it would in my judgment, be a noble & desirable structure." All that said, Washington added the disclaimer that he had no knowledge of architecture and thought the commissioners "should (to avoid criticisms) be governed by the established rules which are laid down by the professors of this art."

Soon after Turner's plan came another that interested the commissioners. The designer was none other than Blodget, who at the same time was supposedly raising the first installment on a $500,000 loan for the city and supervising the engraving of the plan of the city. His letter accompanying his design of the Capitol breathed all the confidence of a young man who was certain to be a millionaire as soon as the economy improved. He was a self-taught architect, but so was his Boston chum Charles Bulfinch, who developed into one of the nation's leading designers. Blodget tried to interest

Bulfinch in joining him in making a design, but Bulfinch declined. His rendezvous with the Capitol was some thirty years away, when he succeeded Benjamin Latrobe as architect of the Capitol.

In his letter Blodget identified a model for his work, the Maison Carée in Nimes, France. But he diverged from the model and explained why: "My deviations from the maison qurie a Nimes in the four principal projections were deemed essential to accommodate it to the new appendage *the Dome.* I have robbed it of its corinthian capitals, to heiton this chef d'ouvre, in its place viz. on the columns that beam up the dome. . . ."

He condescended to give a short lesson in architectural taste: "I hope I shall be pardoned if I remind you that *full elevated columns* and the Dome has been admired *by all* ever since they were invented, *so say all* the modern connoisseurs. Therefore I hope no new fritters will take the place of noble ancient grecian and Roman *principles,* the results of the experiences of ages."

To save on expenses he thought the dome could be made of wood, and he had been told that "the clay of Maryland does not make *substantial* Brick." So he preferred that the outside of the building be made of stone. (The commissioners would retort that Maryland clay made excellent brick but that they had already decided that the buildings would be faced with stone.) Then Blodget lectured the commissioners on expenses: "If we should be *too sparing* in the instance of the Capitol, all our lands & the loan *will stick on hand* and the city will be delayed of course. (To prove what I have said) I have shown my Plan to a number of gentlemen & they beg'd leave to exhibit it at a public office, poor as it may be compared with others you have received. Its magnitude occasioned the sale of a number of my lots — & several offered donations toward erecting it, till I told them it was only one of many from which the commissioners were to choose."

As a postscript Blodget asked the commissioners to view his drawing from a distance of at least three yards and in good light. The commissioners did, and they were pleased. They asked Blodget to make a more finished design.

*   *   *

The commissioners maintained a good humor about Blodget's other projects. Proofs of the Boston engraving came to Philadelphia without the soundings of the Eastern Branch so essential to attract commerce. As for the loan, Blodget finally deposited $10,000 to the account of the commissioners. It was all his own money. No one wanted to invest in the city, Blodget thought, until the public buildings were begun. Fortunately, the commissioners had money enough; Maryland and Virginia were still paying regular installments on the $72,000 and $120,000 they had promised. (In late June, however, the governor of Virginia alerted the commissioners that fighting Indians in the western reaches of the state had priority, which meant payments to the city could be delayed.)[3]

* * *

On August 2 Washington came up from Mount Vernon to decide exactly where the mansion designed by Hoban should be. Hoban himself was down in Charleston wrapping up his affairs there, and getting his hands. Washington found that with the small building he faced a dilemma. For a better sight line with the Capitol, the building would have to be true to the south edge of L'Enfant's outline. But then the diagonal avenues would not seem to line up properly. Again showing his deference to the plan, the president brought up the building to L'Enfant's north front.

The commissioners could at least take some comfort that they would not have to bankroll the monstrosity of a building that L'Enfant had staked out. At their August meeting, however, no doubt encouraged by the president's enthusiasm for Potomac navigation, they did confront one of the more ambitious elements of L'Enfant's plan. They sent ads to the newspapers soliciting bids for the digging of a canal from the tidewater of James Creek to the tidewater of the Tiber.

Ironically, it was his genius with canals that made L'Enfant such a prize acquisition for the manufacturing city at Paterson, New Jersey, where he had begun work for $1,500 a year. Expressing "a high opinion of the solidity of his talents," Hamilton assured his fellow directors of the project that no man was better at conveying water than L'Enfant. The "efficacy and solidity" of his plan "ought to outweigh considerations of expense if within any reasonable bounds."

"Efficacy and solidity" were not the order of the day in the federal city. There was "a difference of opinion whether the flux and reflux of the tides between the Eastern Branch and Tiber would be such as to prevent the water from stagnating in the canal." No record remains of who trusted the tides and who advocated that water be brought down from the higher reaches of the Tiber to keep the canal filled. The upshot was that the commissioners decided to make the canal one sixth of the intended width by way of experiment, 15 feet wide at the top, 12 feet at the bottom, holding two feet of water at common low tide.

Patrick Whelan won the contract to cut the canal. His men were then building the causeway to the Federal Bridge, and the commissioners had no reason to believe that a man who could build a long dike would have any trouble digging a long ditch. Certainly Whelan was no L'Enfant. The Frenchman had planned to have 300 men digging the canal. The commissioners called for thirty hands. Whelan talked them down to fifteen.

Even with such a modest cut, each party was careful to calculate the advantages. The commissioners had Harbaugh, who still had their confidence even though it was decided to redesign the bridge along the lines French suggested, estimate the amount of dirt to be removed from the mile-long cut: 21,760 cubic yards. They felt safe in offering Whelan 16 pence for every cubic yard removed. Whelan got $300 to pay for removing stumps, and then they argued over rocks that might get in his way. The commissioners said there were none; Whelan was not too sure. The commissioners agreed to pay extra but left the price undetermined. L'Enfant had promised a canal in four months. Whelan promised a large ditch in nine, by July 1, 1793.[4]

18. Are We Never to Get Clear of L'Enfant!

Collen Williamson, a sixty-five-year-old Scot, boasted of having 500 years' experience in masonry, since he had converted "four old castels" into "the modren stile." He arrived that August, and the commissioners hired him for £400 to "superintend" the stonecutting and other masonry work, which entailed hiring stonecutters, inspecting their work, and paying them. They sent him out to the quarries, because the only stone to be laid at the president's house that fall would be the ceremonial cornerstone, which would be done during the October sale.

Men might have come on tiptoe for work, but the only things doing in the city were the bridge and the ditch that might become a canal. Work on the canal began without ceremony because the project was so tentative, not from a fear of the low ground between Tiber and James creeks during the hottest and muggiest time of the year. Although James Creek did form a marsh along its banks where the tides of the Potomac came up it, the ground between the creeks was, on average, five feet above common high tide. And the marsh was not menacing enough to prevent the founders of Carrollsburg from projecting their most valuable lots over it. What swamps there were in the city were beyond the first ridge in the hollows between the post road, or K Street, and the hills beyond. What small swamps there had been south of the road — and in court records an eyewitness remembered that in 1772 Burnes's father had one of his slaves cut down a hickory "in deep snow," and about 40 yards from the hickory was "a small branch and a swamp" — had long ago been turned to farmland, for such bottomland was always considered the most fertile.

No one quarreled with the observation that the city had good natural drainage. The weak point in that respect was the land where the diggers worked, with Capitol Hill to the northeast and the easy slope of Young's plantation to the west. Both slopes were still wooded, but water was liable to collect in the valley before the

James, a rather lazy creek, could drain it. If the experience of a kid playing with puddles in the sand was any guide, a good ditch between the creeks that would flush with the tides might make the area bone dry even before commercial development of what were certain to become valuable lots once the canal was finished. Meanwhile no one, in that day when swamp air was considered the source of most fevers, suspected that low ground of being unhealthy.

In early September Andrew Ellicott came down with a "violent fever." It was almost certainly malaria. Ellicott did not associate any environmental factor with his disease. Mosquitoes were not even suspected back then, but modern doctors could not conclude that he had to have been nipped by a mosquito breeding in a nearby swamp. The clearing and "improvement" of land, especially the sloppy way Americans went about it, left innumerable ruts, ditches, and stump holes in which mosquitoes could breed. Mosquitoes are quite resourceful, having been shown to thrive in the drainage ditches dug to drain malarial swamps. And since mosquitoes have a range of a mile, a poorly managed construction site can be the source of contagion for a whole city. Ellicott got some comfort when he learned that the fever was pervasive that summer, not just in the federal district but throughout the Potomac region. Some thought it the most "sickly" autumn in memory. George Washington alerted those planning to visit him at Mount Vernon of the prevalence of disease.[1]

*   *   *

The commissioners sent out no alarms. They wanted people to come to the October 8 sale. Things were looking up and they did not want fear of fever to ruin it. The sale would be unlike that in the chaotic fall of 1791; prospective buyers would see the cornerstone of the president's house laid, work on the canal commenced, and a stockpile of building materials along the newly built wharf at the mouth of Tiber Creek. And Ellicott promised to have a hundred squares ready for division into salable lots.

Unfortunately, no decision had been made on the design of the Capitol. It was not for want of trying. At the end of August the president again came up from Mount Vernon and with the commissioners looked over the designs of Hallet, Turner, Harbaugh, and Blodget. Working under the direct supervision of the commissioners, Hallet had the inside track but had difficulty shaking the first impression he had given of being prone to design an expensive building. He unveiled a plan with columns five feet in diameter and fifty feet high. The commissioners asked how much it would cost, and it was back to the drawing board. The president asked the thirty-two-year-old Frenchman "many questions regarding my theoretical and practical studies," Hallet reported to Jefferson. Hallet begged the secretary of state to help dispel suspicions and lamented, "I would wish they could have given me more liberty."

To get the extra rooms the president wanted, the commissioners sent new specifications to those whose plans were still under consideration. In their letter to Blodget, they tried to match his eloquence by giving their vision of what the Capitol should be: "Tho limited in the means, we are determined to embrace a Plan which may from the extent, its Design, and Taste do credit to the Age. . . ."

By showing their charming side to Blodget, the commissioners were not really trying to flatter his artistic genius. It was his money, and the money of his friends, that they wanted. In the remainder of the letter they painted a very bright picture of the future: "The Affairs of the City are rather in a pleasing Train and a pretty extensive sale the 8th October in many hands for the purpose of improving will enable us to step boldly next Season as to realize every friendly wish. . . . Your presence at the sale would be very cheery."

Notices of the sale were placed in newspapers throughout the country, and they did not go unnoticed. From Paterson, New Jersey, came the cry of touché. Alluding to a "good deal of talk" coming from Virginia, L'Enfant wrote to Hamilton on September 17 that "a little account" of the progress made on their Paterson project in two months, where "fifty houses are now about digging," would contrast "with the wonderfull Increase of and progress made since one year at the grand City." That, L'Enfant noted wryly, might "be of some effect for the grand sale of lots announced for october." Then he hastened to add, "You [will] not for this suspect me of hill [ill] wish to any. . . ."[2]

*   *   *

To judge from a note Ellicott dashed off to his wife on October 10, the sale was a madhouse: "I have been so busy for two weeks past that I have scarcely had time to either shave or comb my hair, and do not expect one minutes leisure before next Sunday [the 14th]."

Although the surveyor was too busy, the salesmen were not. The commissioners admitted attendance was low. Worse still, many who attended were bargain hunters who planned to buy only if the prices plunged. The commissioners had a strategy to upset those vultures. They asked for and received from the president authorization to make private sales, that is, deals without bids. In those private sales they would offer bargain prices if the purchaser agreed to build promptly. In the public sales they would do all they could to keep the prices above what lots went for the year before.

Congress did not convene until the first week in November; still, the president stayed only for the first day of the sale. No foreign notables observed it. The British minister, George Hammond, visited the president at Mount Vernon in late September, toured the site of the federal city, but did not stay on until October 8. In his report home he merely noted that "preparations were then making for erecting some of the public buildings and avenues cut through the woods for the purpose of forming the streets." Around the same time Hammond visited the Society for the Promotion of Useful Manufactures' project in New Jersey. That rated a three-page report and a warning that British craftsmen were being lured to bring over the latest techniques of British factories.

The first square put up for sale was due east of the president's house, bounded by F, G, 15th, and 14th Streets. The winning bidder for the first lot was the man who originally owned the land, David Burnes. The bargain hunters must have been nonplused to see it go for $533. The previous high price for a lot had been $400. William Augustine Washington, the president's nephew, Thomas Beatty of Georgetown, William Coughlan of the city of Washington, James Hoban, and Pierce Purcell, a master carpenter Hoban had brought up from Charleston, teamed up to buy lots in the square, at prices

from $266 to $333. Everyone thought purchases by mechanics —
Williamson and Harbaugh bought lots in other squares — a good
sign but waited for Blodget and his friends to invest new capital in
the city. Blodget bought here and there and called the federal city
"the darling object of my life." His friends kept their peace.

Steaming at the whole proceedings was George Walker. On the
first day of the sale he gave a long letter to the president complaining
that the commissioners were favoring the Georgetown interests. All
the lots divided and sold in 1791 were near Georgetown. Construction was about to begin on the president's house, "while at the
place for the Capitol only a few solitary stones are to be seen, with
a few bricks lately made in a hurry, as if intended to hoodwink the
proprietors, by keeping up some small appearance of an intention
to build."

Walker was sure that a conspiracy was afoot to leave the east side
of the city unbuilt: "The preceding facts have naturally given rise to
a suggestion, that has long existed, but now gains considerable
belief, viz that the commissioners are entirely led and directed by
Colonel Deakins, with some other influential gentlemen in Georgetown, and that, there is a secret intention of giving every encouragement to the Georgetown end of the city to the ruin of the other."

Walker demanded parity. If a bridge were built over Rock Creek,
one should be built over the Eastern Branch. The president's house
and the Capitol should be built at the same time, "storey for
storey." And since the sale in 1791 offered only lots west of the
president's house, the sale in 1792 should offer only lots east of
Tiber Creek. Instead, the most eastern lot put up for auction was on
6th Street Northwest.

To satisfy Walker, the board offered the square at the southeast
corner of the Capitol square, but they also got Blodget to bid on
behalf of the public, which he did to the tune of $3,648. Blodget
then convinced the commissioners to let him keep the square by
offering to make up for the low price by building "a handsome
building" on it in the coming summer.

Then, as in the year before, after two days of bidding interest
flagged. The only sale on the 10th resulted from a plaint by Samuel
Davidson. When he saw the engraved plan he was shocked to see
the shrunken president's house square. The square, as L'Enfant

had planned it, would have given Davidson more money and more lots fronting the president's house. Davidson pointed out the discrepancies to the commissioners, only to have Johnson growl, "God damn it, are we never to get clear of L'Enfant!" He pressed the board to put the square earmarked for lots up for auction, claiming that they were showing favoritism to the eastern end of the city by virtue of their selling a whole square to one buyer. The commissioners offered the square, and Davidson bought it so no one else could develop it while he pressed his case to get L'Enfant's design of the area made official. It cost him $5,440.

With the bidding done, one of the vultures struck. Standish Forde, who had purchased private lots the year before, offered to buy 500 lots at £35 ($93) each. The commissioners rejected the deal because the price was low and Forde did not specify what lots he wanted. On the 13th all who remained in the city laid the cornerstone of the president's house in accordance with Masonic rituals. Collen Williamson tapped in the stone, and then it was off to Suter's tavern in Georgetown for feasting and toasts.

In the report they made to the president on the 13th the commissioners set up the tally of sales: forty-five lots sold separately at an average price of $244, bringing in almost $11,000. Adding to that the forty-eight lots sold in two squares, the whole sale brought in just over $20,000, which should raise $5,000 immediately in down payments. Prout readjusted the value of his lots to £120,000. The commissioners were encouraged because the prices of lots held firm. That and the sales to mechanics who would soon build also encouraged the president, but he wished more lots had been sold. Then Blodget's friends made their move.

They had not bid because they wanted to look around, not only at the city but at the work on the Little Falls canal. Stuart reported to the president that they "expressed the highest satisfaction" with the city and canal. Then, on October 22, John Templeman bought three lots near the president's house. Five other Bostonians bought too. Blodget even sold one of Burnes's lots to Templeman and cheered to Burnes, "I give you joy on the gain of a new citizen who will be of great use to us in the future."

Needless to say, the commissioners broadcast those sales far and wide. "As they are all men of Large Property," they reported to

Jefferson, "and from the Eastward, we consider it as the most Valuable Sale yet made."[3]

19. Our Sawyers Have Dwindled Away

Blodget and all of the Bostonians left at the end of October. One, John Templeman, promised to be back in the spring with his family to take a house in Georgetown and begin improving his Washington lots. Blodget, of course, expected to be back too. The young Bostonian impressed everyone in the city. Benjamin Stoddert wrote to the president ruing the system that required commissioners only meeting a few days a month to make every decision relative to the city. He begged the president to see that a superintendent was put in charge and cited the delays in changing the design of the Rock Creek bridge as just the latest example of the high cost of slow decision making by the commissioners. Stoddert thought Blodget should oversee day-to-day operations and even sell lots, reporting "it is the opinion here [that] he would be able to sell more lots in a few months, that the commissioners would in a year."

The president did not object and reminded the commissioners that he had long wanted a superintendent. The commissioners were agreeable. Blodget was not an architect but had "a very pretty taste for it." He had "fertility of genius" and a good temper and knowledge of accounts. He would be much better than L'Enfant. Blodget was also coy, wondering if it might be better for him to tour the country in the summer to sell lots. That would also allow him to carry on some schemes from his fertile genius that were not doing

so well, a "universal tontine" in Boston and an insurance tontine in
Philadelphia, whereby pooled resources of the participants were
divided among survivors at the end of a stated period. Blodget, who
had five children by a late wife and had just married the daughter of
the provost of the University of Pennsylvania, did not think he could
afford merely to collect a salary.[1]

*   *   *

There was not much to superintend in the city anyway. Hoban
was having no trouble calculating the materials needed in the coming
year to build the first story of the president's house. Meanwhile the
carpenters he had brought up from Charleston, including five slaves,
Peter, Tom, Ben, Harry, and Daniel, built temporary houses on the
president's house square where they and Hoban would live. Hallet,
who seemed to have won the Capitol design competition by default,
diligently worked at perfecting a design, though when William
Thornton, a friend of Judge Turner, begged an indulgence to submit
a design late because he had been in the West Indies when the
contest was announced, the commissioners granted it. Thornton
was a clever man, having won the design competition for the Library
Company of Philadelphia building in 1789, but he was not a professional architect. Ellicott seemed to be slow in his surveying but had
an excuse. The president had asked him to prepare a map of the
whole territory for that session of Congress. Other than some clay
diggers stealing wood from Carroll of Duddington, the only trouble
spot was at the quarry, but Williamson was handling that.
    Although there was plenty of stone delivered and ready to be
delivered, and Williamson had fifteen men to polish it, the stone had
been improperly quarried. Williamson reported that most of the
men there were no good and urged that liquor sales be banned from
the perimeter of the quarry. The commissioners faulted Wright, the
man in charge, for not using slaves to keep down costs. Wright
defended his performance with the plea "Has there not always been
stone ready?" The commissioners ordered twenty-five slaves hired
at £15 a year each to work in the quarries. On January 1 they fired
Wright and put Williamson in charge.[2]

*   *   *

Ellicott had to determine the size of the government reservations, for which the proprietors stood to get £25 an acre. With sales of lots slow, the proprietors, who had once had visions of easy money, got impatient with Ellicott's progress. When the breaks did not go their way, they were quick to remind the commissioners that L'Enfant said Ellicott's map was inaccurate. Burnes caused the biggest headaches. To satisfy his claim on the public, Ellicott had to survey the president's house square, Judiciary Square, church square, and the reservations for the bank and mint at the foot of Capitol Hill.

That was work enough, and then what was he to do with Market Square, which, he reminded the commissioners, "extends considerably into the water" of Tiber Creek. Burnes, with creditors still at his door, asked the commissioners to guess the amount of land the public would take, pay him, and then settle up when the exact surveys were made. He calculated that the public took eighty acres of his land, worth about £1000, or $2,666. At first Ellicott determined that Burnes had fifty acres wanted by the public, then, after more haggling, he determined it was seventy acres. The commissioners paid him for eighty acres.

At the same time Burnes was making his plaint, early November, George Walker was still raising cain on the other side of town. He informed the commissioners that he was going to Europe to try to sell lots. Since some Europeans might see the advantage of settling on the Eastern branch, he begged the commission to instruct Ellicott to divide some two dozen of those squares. They did. So in the midst of one job, Ellicott had to move his equipment, which was considerably heavier than today's surveying equipment, three miles to the other side of town.

And then Carroll of Duddington summoned Ellicott two miles in another direction, to South Capitol Street, where Carroll wanted to build "several small brick houses" on the back of his lots which he hoped one day would answer as kitchens. (He wanted to set an example to buyers because he was soon to put lots up for sale with the proviso that the buyer had to build within three years.) Ellicott had to divide the squares around South Capitol and P Streets. All the while he was pressing on with his map of the federal district and the ongoing survey of the streets. He ate breakfast by candlelight and worked to sundown, often skipping other meals. Since his work on the map of the district took him as much as eight miles from his office in the old Slater house, which he rented from Prout, he tried to compress his platting of lots into the weekend. Every Monday morning his crew in the camp would be awakened as Ellicott returned to them before sunrise.

The commissioners, eminently practical men, were not impressed and finally decided that Ellicott's problem was that he was a stargazer, a mathematician, and not at all like the surveyors they knew, who surveyed land not to square earth with the heavens but to alert friends of opportunities for, and themselves dabble in, land speculation. On December 10, in a long letter to the president in which he lauded Blodget, Hoban, and Hallet, Stuart confessed that "we are in the dark as to everything which concerns" Ellicott's department. All they knew was that it was expensive. They kept as good an eye as they could on Ellicott and found that "he was up [at work] by starlight" but it all seemed "to little purpose." Stuart suggested that if Jefferson sent "some hints" it might get Ellicott cracking, since the surveyor considered Jefferson "a great mathematician and a good judge of the kind of business he is engaged in." (George Washington was indeed a surveyor but was much more the speculating kind than the mathematical kind.)

Ellicott's response was to withdraw into a shell. On December 14 he wrote to his wife: "I begin to dislike the whole place and have become too ill natured to associate with any beings except my four assistants. . . . I eat alone in the office, to which I confine myself as closely as a Bear to his den in the winter."[3]

*   *   *

In contrast to the bearish Ellicott, Hoban was bullying the commissioners with frequent and copious communications. The Irishman exuded know-how and was eager to build, if not buildings, at least an empire. Since Williamson had not brought masons from Scotland as promised, Hoban offered to get them from Ireland.

Citing his experience in working on the Royal Exchange, New Bank, and Custom House in Dublin, he offered to get Irish masons, four or five bricklayers, and a pair of sawyers. Then he directed the commissioners' attention to the materials he would need. Well acquainted with various sources of material and prices, he knew he could get slate at Charleston for the same price as Cabot could in Boston, and the Charleston slate was better. Meanwhile, he talked with a stonemason in Georgetown about cutting nearby Potomac slate. He needed 60,000 feet of plank but it "must be clear plank, what is understood by clear plank is, not three [k]nots in a plank large as a man can cover with his thumb, which is the quality I have described and expect to get." Then he recommended that they get an ongoing source for nails and that they buy any "seasoned stuff" — wood, that is — that might come to Georgetown. He submitted a four-page list of material needed including a 100-pound bell "to regulate the time of the workmen."

The commissioners promptly solicited bids for supplying planks, brads, and nails. Thanks to a suggestion from one of the buyers at the recent sale of lots, they were hot on the trail of a nearby supply of wood. W. A. Washington offered them about 500 acres of timber-land near the Potomac that could supply all their wants. They authorized Hoban to look into it but surrounded with forests as they were, it was not unreasonable to think a local stand might do. Hoban found some good poplars along Rock Creek and good white oaks and poplars not far from the Eastern Branch. But in both areas the land was "much broken," making it too difficult to get the timber to the city. Then he toured W. A. Washington's land in Westmoreland County, Virginia, and liked what he saw. There was enough timber there to supply all the lumber needed for the public buildings.

The president's nephew owned much of the land called White Oak Swamp and offered to buy the land of his neighbors and generally manage the axe-men and carpenters. He thought it best to have the logs squared on the spot and then floated up the river on "lumber wheels." He advised the commissioners to decide before Christmas because the slaves they would need as axe-men and carpenters were hired out at the first of the year, and after that it was difficult to get any.

The commissioners wanted to move fast and get the timber cut during the winter. But purchasing 300 to 500 acres might steal some of the money they needed for work on the public buildings, their primary goal. So they asked W. A. Washington to buy the land for them with the understanding that they would secretly give him half the purchase price now and the remainder later. As for the slaves, they agreed with Washington but wanted him to hire them by the month because after the trees were cut, which they thought would take a few months, they would not have any need for those slaves.

Sometimes, on paper at least, the development of the city seemed to accelerate. But amid all the talk about a flood of lumber coming up the Potomac, the sawyers working at the president's house preparing the lumber already there were drifting away. "Our sawyers have dwindled away," Hoban wrote to the commissioners on December 1, "from three pair, to two, and from two to one pair, and now there is none. Mr. Sandiford is now sick and his hands all dispersed. He has sent to inform me he has got no hands, and intends to saw no more; it would be necessary to take some steps to get a sett of sawyers, . . . as the pitt is in complete order, and sawyers work to advantage in all weather." The commissioners placed an ad in the newspapers.[4]

*   *   *

While the workers on the scene slowly drifted off, bad news came from Europe. Skilled workers were not eager to come to the federal city. It is not surprising that Virginians and Marylanders of the revolutionary generation thought workers could be drawn from Europe as easily as water from a well. In the early 1770s economic forces in England and Scotland caused a flood of emigration to America, and many leaving were skilled workers. The most popular destination was the Chesapeake Bay area. Twenty years later economic conditions in Europe had changed. But the men who had spent the past twenty years winning a revolution and organizing governments failed to notice.

The commissioners were keenest on getting Scots and entrusted a Georgetown merchant named John Laird with the task of bringing them over. On November 15 Laird sent the commissioners a copy of a letter he had just received from Glasgow: with "great demand and building going on in all the towns. . . . It is our opinion good men could not be engaged to go to America unless they were assured of near double the wages they get here."

With Washington and Jefferson still keen on getting German workers, the commissioners dutifully sought the help of a Dutch correspondent who had led Jefferson to believe, some years ago, that he could indenture a good number of skilled workers from the Palatinate states of Germany. Van Staphorst wrote back to the commissioners that skilled workers seldom were enticed; only common laborers were available. Besides, the system was conducive to lawsuits. Van Staphorst's firm had been involved in one for years and so wanted nothing to do with the business.

The commissioners accepted the bad news, but not so the president. Their failure to get workers from Scotland and Germany, he wrote, "fills me with *real* concern; for I am very apprehensive if your next campaign in the Federal City is not marked with vigor, it will cast such a cloud over this business and will so arm the enemies of the measure, as to enable them to give it (if not its death blow) a wound from which it will not easily recover."

He offered to find someone in Philadelphia who would go to Germany to get workmen, earning a guinea for every one he got. Noting the turmoil in France, where revolution was coursing to terror, he suggested that Hallet be sent there immediately to bring back skilled workers in the spring. He noted that George Walker was about to go to England and Scotland and had offered to do anything he could to help the city. To that last suggestion the commissioners hurried back a loud no thanks. Asking Walker for help would give him "signs of approbation and confidence that we do not feel."

Jefferson also set to work to tap a supply of workers. He called on a Major Traquair, a Philadelphia stonemason, and asked him how hard it was to get skilled workers from Scotland. Traquair was sanguine that his agent could get some. And Jefferson had an idea. Since Traquair was "a capital stonecutter," the commissioners could invite him to Washington to talk about importing workers and then "he might on the sight of the place, be induced to move all his hands there."

Then, six days later, on December 23, Jefferson sent down more encouraging news. He had had a chat with two congressmen from Connecticut, Pierpoint Edwards and Colonel Wadsworth, who claimed there were 500 to 1,000 house carpenters in their state looking for work, "their wages 2/3 of a dollar and to be fed." Masons, however, were scarce, though they did mention "one Trowbridge." But Jefferson "could not find that he had ever done anything higher than stonesteps."

The commissioners sweetened their offer to emigrant workers and sent the new enticements to Traquair, hoping he could get them fifty masons by the spring. A worker agreeing to come would immediately get 30 shillings to pay the expenses attendant to leaving England. The commissioners would pay passage and retain half the weekly wages until the passage money was paid off. In some cases a wife's passage would be paid. Wages would be the same as what others already in the country with similar qualifications got. And as proof that wages would never decline the commissioners pointed out that with "the expenditure of 2,000,000 dollars in the course of eight years there is no probability of any considerable decline of wages."

That done, they wrote to the American consuls in London (Johnson's brother Joshua) and Dublin, and, through the American consul in Bordeaux, they wrote directly to the city fathers asking them to send skilled workers. The Frenchman Hallet thought the letter to Bordeaux was a good idea. The commissioners did their best to chime in with the ringing revolutionary rhetoric they thought was rampant in France. They introduced themselves and described their position as "an honor that swells our ambition to express in some degree the stile of our architecture, the sublime sentiments of Liberty which are common to Frenchmen and Americans. We wish to exhibit a grandeur of conception, in Republican simplicity and that true elegance of proportion which corresponds to a tempered freedom excluding Frivolity, the food of little minds."

Burdened though they were, the commissioners could still sing.[5]

1793

20. Neither Credit, nor Reputation

George Walker realized that fighting the commissioners would not sell his lots. In late November he pressed American capitalists to rescue his investment. William Bingham high-hatted him, claiming "property at such a distance is attended with considerable inconvenience in the management." Walker had better luck with John Nicholson, the comptroller of Pennsylvania who had a knack for seeing that state issues of valuable loan warrants and land grants all wound up in his own hands. Walker sold two squares to Nicholson, and he rightfully expected the thirty-three-year-old speculator eventually to buy more.

In a January 14 letter to Nicholson, written just before he left for Europe, Walker tried to lure him into more purchases by emphasizing that a speculator did not necessarily have to be on the scene to profit from improvements. The proceeds from the sale of public lots would do away with taxes, since "there will be money sufficient to pave almost all the streets." He did have to report one snag. Ellicott had not had time to divide Nicholson's squares. That was bad news for a land speculator such as Nicholson, who was about to send an agent to Europe to peddle his many holdings. Walker rather minimized the difficulty. In fact, the accuracy of Ellicott's work had been called into question, perhaps by Walker himself.[1]

In late December, a letter from a "Citizen of Columbia" appeared in the *Maryland Journal*, published in Baltimore. With much sneering commentary, the author accused Ellicott "of being a weather cock species," "of errors in your department," and "of not doing equal justice to both ends of the city." Ellicott could not shrug off a charge that he had made errors. And he was flustered because he could not look to the commissioners for vindication, since they had complained about the expense and slowness of the survey.

In a fit of temper, he offered to resign as of May 1 and voiced his

frustrations because of the extensive plan and "its extreme com-
plexity." "Those intimately acquainted with such business" would
understand that no delay in the survey was caused by "want of
exertion." Then he offered a gratuitous impertinence worthy of
L'Enfant: "If it had been in my power, to have willed the City into
existence, I should certainly have done it, but as the exertions of
man are confined by narrow limits, and nothing compleated but by
progressive labour, I have had to pursue the track trodden by all the
human race."

In their reply the commissioners admitted that they were not
experts in the field but reiterated their concerns with the expense
and slowness. They did not accept his resignation and hoped that
he could finish the surveying before the summer. That sounded
gentlemanly enough, but it got on Ellicott's nerves. In a reply
dashed off the same day, Ellicott was furious: "That you should
pass a general censure on work which, you say, you do not understand, and great parts of which I am sure you never saw, is to me a
most extraordinary circumstance!" He then suggested that the
commissioners themselves had been the cause of delay, and he
threatened to vindicate himself "as publicly as possible." Ellicott
insisted on charging the dispute with emotion, recalling his assistant
who died in 1791, "one of my oldest, and most valuable friends."
He would not accept imputations that his work had been in vain,
and he announced he would quit on May 1.

Uriah Forrest heard of the dispute and quickly wrote to Philadelphia begging the president to prevent another disaster brought on
by the commissioners.[2]

*   *   *

That the commissioners' relations with Ellicott, whom they had
so eagerly awaited back in March, had turned so sour was probably
made more palatable by the arrival of the new savior. At their
January meeting the commissioners hired Blodget as superintendent
of the city at a salary of £600 ($1,600), payable in cash or city lots.
Blodget met with the commissioners, and, before they could tell
him what his duties were, he unveiled a new scheme to benefit the

city: a national lottery to finance the construction of a grand hotel. If that worked well, Blodget wanted to follow up with a second lottery to build several elegant mansions, and then a third lottery to build "thirty inferior houses." He claimed to have the president's approval. Lotteries were an acceptable and popular way of raising money. The commissioners liked the idea, though it was mutually agreed that it would be exclusively Blodget's affair save for any authorization needed from the Maryland Assembly.

Blodget had discovered a way in which he could help the city and still tend his schemes in Boston and Philadelphia. When he visited those cities to further his tontines, he could also sell lottery tickets. Indeed, once Blodget got the commissioners' approval he hurried back to Philadelphia where his insurance tontine was reconstituting itself as the Insurance Company of North America. Although the commissioners would have preferred having the man destined to have day-to-day control of the city at least stay in the city until their meetings were over, they sent his job description after him.

And they shared some of their managerial wisdom. If all the masons they had summoned from Europe came, they would get too many masons. But without "plain stone cutters . . . we shall be at a stand." So Blodget was to feel free to hire some on his own. As for carpenters, they had enough. Hoban was after a good Philadelphia brick maker. And then they alerted the Boston-bred Blodget to the blessings of slavery: "we may have a good many negro labourers, none so good for cutting before the surveyors and none better for tending masons. Captain Williams tells us he could not have done without them this summer; they were a check on the white labourers. . . ."

On returning to Philadelphia, Blodget advertised the particulars of his lottery, which was novel in two respects. With a projected sale of 50,000 tickets at $7 each and with a top cash prize of $25,000, the lottery would be the largest yet attempted in the United States. And the grand prize, "1 Superb Hotel with Baths, out houses, etc. etc. to cost $50,000," introduced a new style of grandeur unknown in a land dotted with taverns and inns. The total amount of awards, $350,000 — to include 15,000 $10 prizes — equaled the projected revenue from the lottery. The goal was merely to finance the construction of the hotel. In the same ad Blodget offered $100 for the best plan for the hotel. The drawing would begin on the 9th of September. Blodget signed the ad as "Agent for the Affairs of the City."

Meanwhile, he was selling lots: his own, the public's, and Burnes's too. The commissioners said they would confirm any sale Blodget made, if they were not too extensive, and provided no lot was sold for under £50 ($133) and no lot on an open square sold for under £100 ($266).[3]

*   *   *

The threat of a dispute in the newspapers between the commissioners and the city's surveyor alarmed the administration. Jefferson wrote back promptly trying to cool off Ellicott. He was sure the dispute was "without a fault on either side." Ellicott's work was "slow from its nature; and it is not wonderful if the Commissioners should think it too much so." In any event Ellicott should not bring the matter before the public since it would injure "the expectations built on the city." The president replied promptly to Forrest. Agreeing with his observation that quarrels among the friends of the city would do more harm than the actions of its enemies, he urged Forrest to persuade Ellicott to keep the dispute out of the newspapers.

But the call to battle proved irresistible, helped immeasurably by the ease with which the newspapers of those days allowed gentlemen to try to embarrass each other. Articles written under a pseudonym were the rule, and a style replete with wit and innuendo was encouraged. The idea was not so much to get at the truth as to get at each other, using accepted models of satire and invective.

Ellicott decided that James Dermott, an assistant he had laid off for the winter, was the source of the charge that his work was inaccurate. While drunk, Dermott had bragged that he would get Ellicott's job. Writing under the name "Chronicle," Ellicott attacked him in the Georgetown newspaper, not directly but with allegory.

Chronicle attacked "Judas," who sought to deceive "Thomas, David, and Daniel" by impugning the accuracy and completeness of the work of "Balaam." After warning that Judas was a drunk not to be trusted, Chronicle accused Judas of passing his mistakes off as Balaam's in an effort to get the top job in the city. Then Chronicle got very nasty and accused David and Judas of conspiring together to ruin Balaam, alluding also to some work Judas did for David to help out with an inheritance.

David Stuart knew who David was and had sharp words with the surveyor. The attack by Chronicle smarted. He wrote to the president on February 10, "Feeling myself much hurt at the insinuations against me, I gave him [Ellicott] my opinion of the author and his coadjutors in the strongest terms." But he forbore from responding in the newspapers. He told the president that was because he thought it useless, since Ellicott "had not much regard for the truth."

Meanwhile, Ellicott sought to defend himself in a more respectable manner and got his assistants, Isaac Briggs and George Fenwick, to attest to his diligence. He wrote again to the commissioners calling for an investigation, which he was sure would establish that the delay had been caused not by lack of his exertions but rather by lack of equipment, and that discontent with his work had been fomented by a few proprietors who still held him responsible for the dismissal of L'Enfant. All this was very depressing, and he bemoaned his fate in a letter to his wife: "Neither credit, nor reputation will ever be the lot of a single person, who enters into their service. I dislike the place, and every day adds to my disgust."

His honor was at stake. Under his own name, in the *Maryland Journal,* Ellicott dismissed charges of inaccuracy as ridiculous save for a trifling one along the Eastern Branch. Stuart decided to get to the bottom of it, found Dermott in Virginia, and asked him for charges in writing. Ellicott also decided to get to the bottom of things. He checked the plats and found that there were mistakes. The dimensions of some of the squares were wrong, but those numbers were not in his hand. He suspected Dermott of miscopying the numbers. At the same time he noticed that there were papers missing from his office. He decided Dermott stole them to deny him the documents that would prove the accuracy of his original survey. He asked the commissioners to force Dermott to produce the missing maps and notes. Unfortunately for Ellicott, Dermott did not act like a cornered rat. He wrote to Ellicott offering to be at his service. Ellicott saw him and called him "a scoundrel and a thief."

In that February 10 letter to the president, Stuart hoped that Dermott was wrong, that the survey did not have large inaccuracies. But with Ellicott seeming at wits' end and Dermott calmly cooperating, Stuart expected the worse. Then, when Ellicott left the city for his winter break with his family in Philadelphia, Dermott or a friend replied to Chronicle.

Yes, Judas "has taken drink extraordinary at times," but he did it in public, with companions. Balaam had "a *separate* store" of liquor. And he was amused that when Chronicle listed Judas's shortcomings he did not mention "whoremonger and adulter," for Balaam was familiar with the ways of both. As for Balaam's record: "Judas never told the lye to Thomas about the proof-sheet plan; nor did he except by direction, deceive Daniel in keeping up a show in laying off the canal, neither did he tell David and the rest that there was more done by the middle of summer, with the fewer hands employed than there was done the whole preceding year with nearly double the number, and in nearly the same instant, say those men were not able to work because they were not well fed and had no chocolate." Ellicott's role in the dismissal of L'Enfant was remembered, and how he cheated the proprietors in his survey of Judiciary Square. As for the mistakes in the survey, Ellicott knew there were mistakes, knew that Dermott knew, and tried desperately to correct them and cover them up. "A precaution was taken to keep him [Judas] away from the *November Correction.*"[4]

*   *   *

No one in Philadelphia in January 1793 described Blodget in action. But to judge from what he sent to the commissioners, he was a familiar beast: the tireless promoter. Why, if buyers were not satisfied for any reason, he would buy the lots back.

"I have no doubt of making as many sales as will be prudent," he wrote on January 26, "for I tender *to all* my obligation *to receive again for my own private a/c* any or all lots that may be returned by the purchaser *on any dislike that may occur* within ten years from the date of contract. 50 lots are sold already *on those terms* (the particulars of which I will send you) in which I believe I am very safe as they are chiefly to sanguine, monied, influential men *just such as we want.*"

Otherwise, he was signing lottery tickets, and "the prospects for the sale is *much flattering.*" And he was making arrangements to assure the credit of the brokers who would sell the tickets around the country, "for if a single faux pas is made so as to retard the lottery we can never gain credit for another and I hope for one annually."

In the letter he sent down a week later, he crowed to the commissioners: "sure I am that our city gains ground with the public every moment." For that he thanked a final decision on the design of the Capitol. In a January 31 letter the president asked the commissioners to break the news to Hallet that "the Doctor's plan may be prefered to his." If Dr. William Thornton had been a doctor of architecture the sting would have been less, but this naturalized American born in the Virgin Islands and educated at Edinburgh was a doctor of medicine, and not a very notable one at that. His major claim to public notice was for his activities to organize a society to send slaves back to freedom in Africa. And his latest claim to fame was a treatise on elements of written language, which he sent to the president and secretary of state.

To design the Capitol he consulted books on architecture, found models he thought would do, and took what he needed from each. Returning to Philadelphia in November, he had an opportunity to talk to the president and Jefferson, see some of the losing designs, talk with their designers, and come up with a winner. (Of course Hallet, the only man still in running, also talked with the president and Jefferson and also saw the losing designs.) In January he showed Washington and Jefferson a drawing of his idea. Like most of the other entrants Thornton designed the Capitol in three parts, but he added another element to the central portion which would house the conference room. To the east of that room he put a large vestibule, a grand entrance to the building where the focal point under the dome would be a statue of Washington. The exterior of his building, featuring small corinthian pilasters and columns, and a small but higher dome, seemed so light and elegant compared to the massive-ness of Hallet's design. Thornton's elegant central portico reached out to the viewer, while Hallet's recessed central courtyard seemed threatening, dominated as it was by a low, heavy dome. Thornton's taste in drawing and his disinclination to bother for the moment about whether his design could actually be built facilitated his winning the prize.

Washington lauded "the grandeur, simplicity, and beauty of the exterior, the propriety with which the apartments are distributed, and economy in the whole mass of the structure." Jefferson thought the design "simple, noble, beautiful, excellently distributed, and moderate in size." The commissioners would have to delay any final decision for one more month, when Thornton would come to Georgetown with his design. Washington and Jefferson had no doubt that the commissioners would be as enthusiastic as they.

The commissioners had some good news too. The Federal Bridge was finished and meeting "the general approbation of the public." Then, just when they were feeling good about their ability to manage public works, Hoban shocked them by estimating that the cost of his design of the president's house, enlarged by one fifth, would be about $400,000. They sought the president's further advice. At the same time they complained about the money they were losing, personally.

They told the president that they were tired of working without compensation. He suggested $1,000 for past expenses and in the future $6 a day for each day's meeting plus expenses, the same as congressmen got. Carroll accepted the per diem. Stuart wanted to quit no matter what the compensation. Johnson demanded $1,000 a year as his price for staying on. The thought of losing Johnson stunned the president into seeking the advice of his Virginia brain trust: Jefferson, Madison, and Randolph. The question was, "what sacrifice to retain Johnson."[5]

The judge however reconciled himself to getting all expenses paid, past and future, and a per diem. To get a salary, the president insisted, the commissioners would have to live in the city.

21. The Next Field for Speculation

Burnes also took a winter trip to Philadelphia. In a letter to the president, Stuart had characterized Burnes as "a weak and trouble-some man." But he knew how to go for the jugular. On his way back to the city he dropped off an exchange of letters between himself and L'Enfant for publication in the *Maryland Journal*. Burnes's part of the exchange was a blend of his particular beefs: lands to be made by filling in the Tiber were rightfully his, surveying was slow and inaccurate, and as for the commissioners, "The insolence of office was never possessed in a more eminent degree than by their worships," with "their cringing meanness."

L'Enfant ignored the litany of wrongs and refrained from attacking the commissioners except to say that liberality toward the original proprietors was essential for the success of the city. Then he attacked the engraved plan as "no more than a fallacious imitation of the real plan, too widely different from my original design. . . . I cannot help lamenting at the circumstances, seeing the consequences of imposing upon the public must be the total failure of the scheme, already too much disgraced by the very expedient of making prosecution of so extensive and complicated a work an allurement to mere speculators."[1]

*   *   *

Thomas Johnson was eager to get at Ellicott, but the surveyor's wife was sick. So as the commissioners met, a week's worth of stages from the north rolled into town without Ellicott. It was not a happy week. Blodget, the superintendent, did not show up either. Thornton did, but despite all the rave reviews for his design for the Capitol, the commissioners were not bowled over. The layout of the rooms, they reported to the president, was "much to our satisfaction" and the exterior "striking and pleasing." "On the whole it gains our preference. . . ." Then came the qualms: too many small rooms and too many of those without a source of natural light, and, more important, no estimate of expense. Thornton added touches to the buildings that did not make it seem cheap. He wanted Italian marble for the columns, and statues of Hercules, Ajax, buffaloes, and Indians. He boasted that if "the external be magnificent," then Congress would see to it that the inside of the building was furnished to match. That building had to be grand, the commissioners agreed with the president, but the United States, not just the commissioners, had to bear some of the risk, given "the uncertain state of our funds."[2]

By week's end, Ellicott still had not come. They ordered his assistant, Fenwick, to remeasure the squares that Dermott said were inaccurate. Fenwick found errors of up to 100 feet. On some squares reported to have been divided he could find no markers. The commissioners were aghast. "Mistakes of distances might now and then happen accidentally," they informed the president, "but we can imagine nothing to excuse the certifying work as done, when it had not been done, when confusion and embarrassment were so plainly to follow from it. We shall discharge Maj. Ellicott, if he has not already discharged himself." They would resurvey the work as quickly as possible and with a chain, "making as little noise as we can" so as not to upset proprietors, buyers, and prospective buyers.

Before they posted the letter on the 12th, Ellicott, his assistant Briggs, and brother Benjamin rolled into town on the stage at eight o'clock in the evening. The commissioners, who were eager to adjourn their meeting and go home, were on him in an instant. They wrote a letter informing him of the inaccuracies and asking him to stop all work until he could prove, in writing, "that these things have not happened from any reprehensible cause."

Unfortunately, before they could deliver the letter, Ellicott fell asleep, fatigued by his journey. In the morning the commissioners peppered him with more letters. He replied verbally that he would comply with their wishes but that where he was staying, at proprietor Prout's house, east of the Capitol square, there was no pen or ink! The commissioners were not amused and in venting their anger made a tactical error. Dashing off a short note, they reiterated that verbal explanations would not do and insisted his written explanations come "as soon as possible, for our stay here grows extremely irksome.'' Ellicott shared that note with Uriah Forrest, who began thinking hard of commissioners irked at staying in the city they were supposed to be building.

Meanwhile, Ellicott taunted them by claiming that written explanations "will be a work of *time*; which at present is of too much importance, to be wasted in an inquiry *that will eventually be found too trifling,* to need one moments attention." He invited them to come to his office, where, with his papers at hand, he could give them a satisfactory verbal explanation. The commissioners would not give in, fearing, as they recalled later, "that he would talk whole days of altered stakes and altered figures and trifling inaccuracies but he was too cunning to commit himself in writing."

Distressed by his continued impertinence, the commissioners fired Ellicott and marched to his office and demanded all papers and instruments relating to the surveying. Uncowed, Ellicott came right back, accused Dermott of stealing many important papers, most notably L'Enfant's smaller map of the city, and offered "to procure a search warrant, & examine his trunks." "This," Ellicott recalled, "the commissioners strenuously opposed, out of tenderness, as they alleged, for Dermott's character."

But the commissioners did quiz Dermott before the next day and had the pleasure of informing Ellicott that Dermott "has shown no signs of concealment of any papers, he acknowledged his having the possession of Maj. L'Enfant's old draft without any hesitation, and has given it to us, and without request another paper or two."

Ellicott let Uriah Forrest give his side of the story. Dermott had purposely entered erroneous figures on the plats of the city and then bided his time until revealing them could most damage Ellicott's standing with the commissioners. Proof for this explanation rested on two arguments. The mistakes were entered on the plats months ago. Why had Dermott waited to reveal them? And then there was the matter of character. Ellicott's reputation was unassailable. Dermott was a drunk.

Forrest also argued the expediency of not impugning the survey, which was about the only thing accomplished. Maryland and Virginia had given over $100,000 to build the public buildings and had nothing to show for it except "a few solitary stones." And he asked, "Are we to lose another year without anything being done to purpose?'' The enemies of the city would rejoice to see another man of high reputation dismissed from his job.

Forrest bluntly accused the commissioners of reacting less to the facts, which indeed they denied Ellicott a right to establish, than to Chronicle's attacks on them in the Georgetown newspaper. He scored the commissioners for the arrogance of their plea that ''the place had become very irksome'' and for their disinclination to talk with anyone who they feared might differ with them. Forrest had waited through two of their meetings for an opportunity to address them, to no avail.

The commissioners promptly informed Forrest that they acted ''on a very different state of facts than he [Ellicott] has communicated to you.'' They told him they had laid the facts before the president, and only he could change their minds.[3]

*   *   *

The bickering in Georgetown made no impression in London. It took a while for news to cross the Atlantic, and in London people were still feeding off the excitement engendered by L'Enfant. His boast that 10,000 men would soon be working in the city gave rise to a report that 7,000 men were already at work there. George Walker arrived in London in March and was not about to deflate current reports and expectations. Once again he put his pen to the service of the city and wrote a circular designed to interest British investors. He hit the usual chords: he celebrated the ''convenience, salubrity, and beauty, [exceeded] by none in America, if any in the world''; enumerated the springs, the ''inexhaustible mountains of excellent freestone'' a few miles below the city; lauded the harbors; and made the city sound like it was in the commercial center of the country — ''upon the great post road,'' ''upon the best navigation,'' ''in the midst of the richest commercial territory,'' ''commanding the most extensive internal resources.'' The locks at the Great and Little falls would be finished at the end of the summer. Undoubtedly, the city ''will grow up with a degree of rapidity, hitherto unparalleled in the annals of cities, and will soon become the admiration and delight of the world.''

Of course he continued to give credit to his friend L'Enfant, and he wrote as if the purposes for which L'Enfant designated the various squares were still operative. The states would control fifteen squares; the Marine Hospital would be where Massachusetts met Georgia Avenue; the General Exchange would be on the Eastern Branch at 8th Street Southeast; the City Hall would be where G Street Southeast crosses the canal, which would be 80 feet wide and 8 feet deep; and he noted where there would be bridges over the Eastern Branch. All of those improvements were on the east side of town, where Walker's property was. He took great pains to point out that the soundings of the Eastern Branch given on two recent engravings were incorrect. Where the map showed 12 and 18 feet of water there were actually 35 feet. As for the other side of town, he mentioned only the equestrian statue south of the president's house and embassies along the Mall.

Walker did not imply that any of those things had been completed. He reported accurately that when he left the city most of the streets had been run, the squares divided, the canal only partly dug, and the materials for the building provided, and he stretched the truth only when he claimed that "last summer several private houses were erected, and a great many proprietors of lots were preparing to build in this ensuing summer."

He took pains to explain why so few lots had been sold so far. His explanation was ingenious: "The grants of money made by Virginia and Maryland, being hitherto sufficient, few of the public lots have been sold." He assured buyers that there were enough lots to be sold so that all improvements in the city, including streetlighting, would be paid for, obviating the need for high taxes. And he pointed out that those who bought lots were not required to build.

Walker was not out to lure immigrants. He was after speculators. He reminded them of the "immense fortunes . . . amassed in America within these three years past, by the National Debt and Bank Stock appreciating to their full value, as well as by the rapid rise in the value of back lands." Washington lots were to be "the next field for speculation, . . . and there is every probability of their being run up to an enormous price, as soon as the public buildings are considerably advanced." The next public sale was to be September 17, and demand "will be considerable, as the monied men in America have now turned their attention to that great national object."

Walker left Davidson in charge of his property. A week after Walker wrote his glowing assessment of the city's future in London, Davidson wrote to John Nicholson, "The affairs of the City of Washington, are now almost at a total stand; arising from a number of causes, generally ascribed to the inattention, incapacity and misapplication, of the present commissioners. It is said that the President will be here about the 5th or 10th of next month, when a general investigation of facts, is expected to take place."[4]

*   *   *

All was not at a stand. Blodget came down for the tail end of the March meeting with news that he had hired a master brick maker, Jeremiah Kale, for $50 a month. Clay and wood were ready at the president's house; all that was needed to make bricks was sand, which men began carting up from Tiber Creek. Hoban noticed that the carters had to make a wide detour to get around the fence that David Burnes had put around his fields in the autumn. The path used went through the wetter part of Burnes's fields, necessitating that the carts take only a half load of sand. Hoban calculated a savings of £3 a day if the carters could take a direct route from the wharf on the Tiber to the brick kilns.

And beyond Burnes's fences sprouted a few wooden shacks bent on enticing the carters, brick makers, and men at work building a brick barracks for workers on the president's house square. In early April the commissioners put an ad in the local papers threatening to pull down the wooden buildings in the city where "spiritous liquors" were being sold. At least, there was a sense of purpose and sobriety at the quarries. On March 25, Collen Williamson reported thirty-four men working there, sixteen of them "good hands." These were not slaves because Williamson noted that they had been threatening to quit. He thought they should get a raise to $7 a month and should be fed their daily rations even on days when they were sick.[5]

*   *   *

The lame-duck session of the second Congress ended on March 3. The third Congress would not convene until the fall. The president needed about three weeks to dispose of the matters Congress left him with, and then he returned to Mount Vernon for a few weeks. He knew what was in store when he reached Georgetown. In a letter that is now lost, Ellicott demanded that he redress the unjust actions of the commissioners. Jefferson wrote back saying the president declined to interfere in matters between the commissioners and their employees. That made Ellicott only more righteous. "Has a man in public service, tho' under the direction of the commissioners, no recourse for vindication from calumny, and oppression, but in an appeal to the candid public?"

The president did not exactly give Ellicott a meeting. The surveyor bent the president's ear as he rode from the site of the commissioners' meeting down to the landing where he would take the ferry across the Potomac. Stoddert had already urged Washington to reinstate Ellicott. Because the commissioners had not given Ellicott a chance to present his case, and the man causing the trouble, Dermott, had not been hired by him, Washington broke his rule and more or less told the commissioners to reinstate Ellicott. He assured them that he had told Ellicott "in stronger terms than ever, that I would not interfere between the Commissioners and characters subordinate to them; and that it was to *them,* and them *only,* he was accountable for his conduct; because it was with them, & them only, I could or would communicate in future." He also chastised the surveyor for conduct "not respectful" to the commissioners as was "always expected by the employer, from the employed." Washington asked "whether an accommodation, under all circumstance, is not to be preferred to an open breach, and a newspaper justification which will inevitably follow."

Sensing the imposition he was making, Washington continued the letter with a description of how he had scolded Stoddert after that proprietor dared to ask him to overrule the commissioners: "My reply was, that I would support the Commissioners; — that it was painful to me to see such interferences of the Proprietors, who, in my opinion, had no more to do with the conduct of them, (farther than to receive their dues according to contract) — than a citizen of the state of Georgia, or New Hampshire; — and, moreover, that they appeared to me to be acting the parts of suicides to their own interests, as far as their conduct could affect it.''

Stoddert knew how to handle the president's temper. The president closed the letter by noting, "To all which he acquiesced." Of course, Stoddert got what he wanted, the reinstatement of Ellicott. And the spirit of accommodation carried over to other problems. The president verbally directed the commissioners to accede to the wishes of Notley Young and shrink the public appropriations on his land to what was absolutely necessary for a fort. He ordered the land designated by L'Enfant for the "marine pillar" laid out in lots.

On receiving the president's April 3 letter, the commissioners wrote to Ellicott. For the record they confessed that they did not understand why he could not respond to allegations in writing. That said, they gave him until the end of the week to make an explanation in any form he wished. The upshot of that was that Ellicott resurveyed two squares using the instruments he had always used. He showed how the measurements were the same as those in his original notes. Then he showed that the wrong figures were put on the plat of the city, written in the hand of Dermott.

The commissioners rehired Ellicott to make the president happy. To Ellicott's disgust, the commissioners did not fire Dermott. They ordered him to remap and lay out lots in Hamburg and Carrollsburg in preparation for a June sale. Given the commercial pretensions of the city, the Carrollsburg lots, at the confluence of the Potomac and the Eastern Branch, were deemed as valuable as lots next to the Capitol.[6]

22. In a Very Ticklish State

On April 8 Collen Williamson and a handful of masons began setting the stone for the first story of the president's house, according to Hoban's original dimensions. Their progress astounded even as practiced a critic as Isaac Roberdeau. On May 30 he reported to L'Enfant that the stone was "almost above ground" and the masons "industriously pressing forward." The spring brought new masons to help carry on the work, including George Blagden, an Englishman sent down from Philadelphia by Traquair. Blagden proved to be an excellent mason. Such progress caught the commissioners by surprise. They had planned to use brick for the interior walls of the first story of the house. Williamson convinced them that since stone and mason were on hand the walls should be stone inside and out.[1]

As gratifying to the board was Blodget's activity. He marked out his hotel at 8th and E Streets Northwest and began bringing stone up the Tiber for its foundation. At 120 by 60 feet, the building would be larger than any inn in the country. Blodget also marked out a site for a national university up on his own property, north of where Massachusetts and New York Avenues intersected. The university was not on the plan, but the president had mentioned the need for one in his first message to Congress. Appreciating such decision, the board asked Blodget to pick sites for the bank and exchange and to evaluate the site of the Capitol. Once again, there was a meeting of the minds that the Capitol should be moved farther up the hill. Blodget, Thornton, and Hoban all agreed; the commissioners so informed the president, hoping that because "the idea seems not to be disapproved by Mr. Blodget," he might give in. The president did not.

Blodget did not press the issue, nor did Thornton, who went back to Philadelphia. None of the new men had the obsession and passion for the grounds that L'Enfant did. Thornton disclaimed any interest in superintending construction of his building. Not answering the commissioners lingering doubts about how much it would cost, Thornton obliged them to ask Hallet to look over the winning design and estimate its cost. Indeed in his written description of his plan, Thornton noted that to decide exactly how thick the walls should be "the architects may be consulted on the subject." And Blodget, despite the ease with which he sited buildings, had an abiding passion for more abstract schemes.

He convinced the board that the lottery was going so well that another lottery was in order. This time he wanted to finance the building of two town houses, worth $30,000 each, "to give an elegant specimen of the private buildings to be erected in the City of Washington." The lottery would award $400,000 in prizes, topping the record awards of the hotel lottery. The commissioners approved and warned him of a new Maryland law taking effect in June which required special legislation for lotteries. Never one to miss a trick, Blodget placed ads for the second lottery and sold a few tickets before June.

Things were going so well that word from American consuls that workers could not be had in Europe did not worry the commissioners. They did not schedule a May meeting. Blodget could handle everything until June, when they would finally exchange lots in the old speculative cities of Hamburg and Carrollsburg for lots in the rising metropolis. Only the most inveterate complainer could find fault with the progress of the city that spring. Davidson fussed that the city jogs "on very much in the old dull stupid stile. . . . The commissioners stand their ground, with all the firmness and effrontery of old bauds." Yet even he had to admit that progress at the president's house and hotel showed a "degree of spirit."[2]

*   *   *

Then the Federal Bridge began to fall down. By June 17 the foundation piers had sunk "almost 3 feet," opening the arches and crushing stone, which began to fall off the bridge. Roberdeau told L'Enfant the bridge would not last a month. The commissioners would admit to the president only that it was "in a very ticklish state." They were "rather" inclined "to believe it cannot be saved."

At the same time, Hallet, so often criticized for extravagance, gave a convincing critique of Thornton's design for the Capitol. It was beyond the means of the commissioners, would take too long to build, and in several particulars was not architecturally sound. Hallet recast Thornton's design to answer the objections. Hoban and Blodget both agreed that it was an improvement.

Finally the commissioners had to put off integrating Hamburg and Carrollsburg into the city, because proper surveys of those areas were not ready. Ellicott blamed Dermott; notes had been "clandestinely taken out of the office . . . last March." The commissioners still put more trust in Dermott. The Irishman at least bought some lottery tickets, showing more than purely mathematical interest in the city. Indeed, realizing that his heart was no longer in the city, Ellicott left, entrusting the continuing survey to his assistants, brother Benjamin and Isaac Briggs. That, however, did not end the foul with Dermott. They could not help but end their first report on their surveying by bemoaning the numerous corrections they had to make because of the "deliberate, nefarious designs" of Dermott.³

* * *

The problem that alarmed the president was Hallet's critique of Thornton's design. During a quick trip to Mount Vernon after the death of his plantation overseer, he stopped in Georgetown to confer with Hallet and Hoban. He asked them both to go to Philadelphia to confer with Jefferson, whom he wanted to decide the dispute with "the aid of any other scientific character." Washington felt personally responsible for Thornton's design and in a letter to the commissioners excused the evident mistake he had made by blaming it on his lack of architectural knowledge and his haste to placate the Carrollsburg interests, who did not want to see the Capitol delayed any longer. Not that he did not think haste was still in order. He told Jefferson, "The case is important. A plan must be adopted — and good, or bad, it must be entered upon."

Jefferson handled the situation masterfully. To keep Thornton from feeling victimized, he sent him "the five manuscript volumes in portfolio" in which Hallet explained his objections. He also asked Thornton to bring two experts in building to the meeting with Hallet and Hoban. Lengthy though they were, Hallet's manuscripts have not been found. To judge from a draft of Thornton's defense, Hallet objected that Thornton's design would take too long to build and could not support a dome. Hallet accused Thornton of admitting in conversation that the building would take forty years to complete. Thornton agreed that it might take that long to complete all of the "ornamental parts," but the building could be ready to receive Congress by 1800. He pointed to the Escorial in Spain, which he said took only six years to build, and it had 14,000 windows and 1,800 pillars. [It actually took twenty-one years to build.] As for Hallet's worry that not enough workers could be put to the job, Thornton retorted that with war in Europe, "any number of workmen" could be procured from there.

Hallet attacked Thornton's dome for not having columns placed properly to support it. Thornton retorted that that was an error in the drawing, not the design, and any builder would see that the columns could be adjusted to answer the objection. Unfortunately for Thornton's position, his major defense against other objections was along the same line, that they could be easily redesigned, which of course was what Hallet had done. Jefferson and the builders Thornton invited had to conclude that Thornton's drawing was unworkable. As Jefferson explained to the president: some intercolonnations were too wide to support stone architraves; a colonnade in the middle of the conference room obstructed the view, and, if it was removed, the ceiling would collapse; a crucial floor could not support itself; a stairway was so low that members would knock their heads; galleries for spectators in the Senate chamber blocked windows needed for light; and several committee rooms did not have enough light and ventilation.

Hallet met one major defeat himself. In his redesign, he eliminated Thornton's portico, returning to the recessed courtyard he had always favored. Hallet pointed out that after climbing the grand stairs into the portico, one would have to go downstairs to enter the House and Senate chambers. Jefferson didn't mind that and found the portico "a very capital beauty" and refused to accept that change. With the portico preserved, Jefferson thought Hallet's redesign merely "preserved the most valuable ideas of the original and rendered them susceptible of execution, so that it is . . . Dr.

Thornton's plan reduced into practicable form." Moreover, "the reformed plan would not cost more than half what the original one would." Jefferson had one of Thornton's builders estimate the cost of the building (which has been lost).

The president blessed Jefferson's decision and instructed the commissioners to use Hallet's revision with the portico restored. Hallet was to design it so that it would answer his own objections that it stole light and air from the wings of the building where Congress would actually meet. Hallet returned to the city and marked the outlines of the Capitol, not an easy task. The trees had been cleared but the side of the hill had not been leveled, and the area for the south wing was rather undulated.

Carpenters built a house for Hallet on the square, as well as barracks for the laborers. By the beginning of August "a considerable force" was "digging at the Capitol." One of the slaves so employed did not remain anonymous since he ran away on September 3. His name was Jacob, and he was five feet eight, with a cast on a broken thigh. His owner feared he was running away to Virginia, where his mother lived.[4]

*   *   *

Meanwhile, the Federal Bridge held. Tobias Lear was about to quit his job as the president's secretary and try to make his fortune as a merchant in the city of Washington. Although he found the plight of the bridge "too true," that did not diminish his faith in the city. Indeed, he bought lots at the mouth of Rock Creek, just below the teetering bridge, bragging to the president that "upon every consideration [the lot] is thought one of the best in the city for the purposes of navigation and extensive communication."

Lear's faith in the city encouraged the commissioners, and Blodget seemed to devote all of July to boosting the morale of the city and commissioners. With the bridge and Capitol in doubt, he encouraged the board to prepare the Mall, and they informed Carroll of Duddington that it was "very desirable that many ornamental trees should be left in the mall with taste." They would buy the trees from him once the Mall was designed. Then, on the Fourth of

July, Blodget laid the cornerstone of the hotel. His press release claimed 1,500 people attended and feasted on ox to celebrate "the most magnificent building in America," which would have an assembly room measuring 40 by 60 feet.

When Blodget returned to Philadelphia, he latched onto all news favorable to the city and sent it back to the commissioners. War between France and England would bring a flood of immigrants, and "our commerce will flourish and greatly enrich the whole union." The "affair of the bridge," he reported, was little mentioned. "The beauty of the President's house has done away the effect of this slight negative to our progress." And L'Enfant's dismissal from the works in New Jersey "for mistakes and a Quixotic invention, . . . has confirmed the public in your opinion of this eccentric gentleman." Indeed, he had been dismissed because, as the directors lamented, he refused to confine himself to the "essential instead of what is ornamental." L'Enfant did quickly find a new job designing and building Robert Morris's Philadelphia mansion, which was to be 160 feet long, with walls 5 feet thick. Blodget assured the commissioners that Morris already wanted out of the contract with L'Enfant.

Blodget failed to send one piece of long-awaited news, that the men he had sold lots to had finally paid for them. And all of his encouraging words might have sat better with the commissioners if the superintendent had been in the city he was supposed to superintend. Blodget excused his absence by saying it was "unavoidable unless I would risk disappointment in the affairs of the lottery." And by staying in Philadelphia he could talk up the September sale of lots. Blodget did get down for the board meeting at the end of July, and he was armed with a good idea, a census of the city.[5]

The sickness in the city the previous September had not gone unnoticed up north, just as it was well remembered by those in the Potomac valley — quarry workers demanded and got a half pint of whiskey added to their ration between August 1 and September 15. Blodget thought there was no better way to prove a healthy city than by counting the number of healthy people in it. On August 12 newspapers reported that there were 820 people in the city, "and for the last six months there has not been a death of either man or woman taken place." Most inhabitants were not natives. They were "artists in the different branches of building and from the different parts of America and Europe." The report made it seem as if they had come to a spa: "the climate agrees with their constitutions, and they enjoy in this city equal if not superior health to what they have experienced in any part of the continent."

* * *

The commissioners went home after their August 2 meeting without the gloom they bore in June. Williamson had just about built the walls of the president's house as high as they could safely go in one year, and he and his men could be moved over to get to work on the Capitol. Then, just when the commissioners settled back on their farms, came well-founded intimations that large blocks of lottery tickets remained unsold in Boston and Philadelphia. Meanwhile, Richmond had run out of tickets, and agents were charging more than the $7 face value.

Johnson had the sharpest reaction to the news. Although the commissioners had had nothing to do with the lottery beyond giving their permission for it, the "commissioner's jacket laid aside," he told Stuart, "I should be sorry in the conduct of the lottery or anything else which concerns the city done by whom it may," were it not a success.[6]

23. This Second Paradise

The fates dealt Philadelphia a harder hand. On the 1st of September William Vans Murray, a congressman from the eastern shore of Maryland, rode into a city in panic:

"Every body out of the way!" he exclaimed in a note to a Philadelphian who had fled the city for fear of yellow fever. "A more timid city I think never existed. Fewer die than I expected but those who live . . . to one person are more frightened than I thought possible. The Banks of the Potomac look up, I think, when the citizens themselves desert their beloved city."

It was an unkind cut against a city at the beginning of an epidemic that would kill more than ten percent of its population. Its last yellow fever epidemic had been in 1762. In that era, when it was thought environmental factors caused disease, it had been assumed that improvements to the city had banished such tropical scourges. But in the late summer of 1793 Philadelphia supported both the virus that causes yellow fever and the *Aedes aegypti* mosquito that spreads it to humans. No one suspected mosquitoes. Some doctors blamed French refugees from Haiti for bringing the disease and dockside filth for spreading it. Before he decided on a regimen of bleeding and purges, Dr. Benjamin Rush simply advised people to flee. Unlike ague and fever, yellow fever was not something one got used to. It too often claimed its victim within five to seven days, complete with yellow skin and sometimes black vomit.

The rest of the country sent aid to Philadelphia but shunned its refugees and goods. Quarantines by cities to the north and south forced the stage lines to stop service to Philadelphia. Refugees setted in makeshift camps outside the city. The rich, of course, were excepted from any rude treatment. President Washington left the city on September 10 and passed with usual honors to Mount Vernon. He left, mind you, not out of fear for himself. He would as soon have left a week later as planned, but Martha insisted. After he left, the federal officers remaining conducted business outside the city, save for Alexander Hamilton, who came down with the disease.[1]

*   *   *

The commissioners of Washington announced to the world that their city was "remarkably healthy." They invited all to come for the ceremonial laying of the Capitol cornerstone, the drawing of the lottery, and the public sale of lots. They assured a lottery drawing by inspiring a consortium of Georgetown merchants to buy up all unsold tickets. They explained this measure candidly in another newspaper announcement, noting that they would allow the consortium to sell tickets for more than $7 as the lottery continued. Along with that announcement was one signed by Blodget agreeing to the arrangement.

In the late eighteenth century lottery tickets formed a part of many speculators' portfolios. Each ticket had to be drawn individually to ascertain its prize. It was not something done in a day, or even a week. As weeks passed and the drawing continued, speculators calculated the value of undrawn prizes and remaining tickets and consigned tickets for resale to brokers. Lottery investments were not merely made to help the city, with trust in one's luck. Before the consortium was formed to buy up outstanding tickets, Benjamin Stoddert had already bought 1,070 of them. William Deakins handled ticket sales in Georgetown, selling $25,000 worth to only fifty-five gentlemen. Seven, other than Stoddert, bought a hundred or more tickets.

It seemed so easy to make money on the lottery that Blodget was not run out of town. Indeed, the gentlemen of Georgetown were eager listeners as Blodget explained other schemes for concentrating capital that allowed for mutual profits: a bank and a tontine. On being chartered by the state, the Bank of Columbia would open up subscriptions at $100 a share to a maximum of twenty shares for each subscriber. Then it would issue bank notes and make loans, giving priority to those that benefited the city.

The Washington tontine offered shares for $100, with only $10 to be paid initially, the rest on request of the directors of the tontine, who would be elected in May 1794. The money raised would be invested to improve lots sold to the tontine by Stoddert and Lingan (at half price). Dividends would be paid from the income generated by the property. When enough shareholders had died off so that the number remaining equaled the number of properties owned by the society, then the property would be divided by lot to those survivors and the tontine dissolved. Blodget got the agency to sell shares for the tontine in Washington. The other agents in the United States were generally the same as those who sold lottery tickets.[2]

Blodget's greatest piece of salesmanship led to his downfall. He raved about the investment potential of city lots to James Greenleaf, a twenty-eight-year-old Bostonian said to have made a million speculating on the American debt with money loaned by Dutch bankers. The scuttlebutt among Dutch bankers was that he was going to purchase lands in northern New York made very cheap by the fall of Duer and his friends. He returned to the United States on April 29, 1793, leaving behind a Dutch wife, the baroness daughter of a prominent banking family, and one child, and taking with him, he thought, the commitment of Dutch bankers to bankroll his speculations. The administration recognized his importance by appointing him consul to Amsterdam.

By July he was in Philadelphia conferring with the administration. He asked to be excused from returning to Amsterdam until the spring of 1794. Although he bought lots on Greenwich Street in New York, he was so impressed with talk about the federal city that he agreed to back Tobias Lear's mercantile venture. He joined Lear and his other backer, former Senator Tristram Dalton of Massachusetts, in an equal partnership that was formalized on September 3. He also began imbibing Blodget's frothy talk.

In a letter he wrote after he and Greenleaf became bitter enemies, Blodget described how overjoyed he had been when he met his "old esteemed friend and fellow lodger in London, whose reputation in Amsterdam I had exerted myself to establish when he was unknown and myself a merchant of some note on the Exchange of London." When Greenleaf was in Philadelphia, they dined every night together, and Blodget proposed they "unite" their "interests" in two speculations: Georgia lands and the "improvement of the City of Washington." Right away, Blodget recalled, Greenleaf was "eager to embrace" both schemes.

As for the speculation in the city of Washington, Blodget explained that although the commissioners had turned down offers to buy large blocks of lots at low prices, they were about to be audited because of pressure from Uriah Forrest. The money from Maryland and Virginia was running out. Individual lots sold well, but the board needed a large infusion of money and more private housing built in the city. Blodget was not Greenleaf's sole source of information or inspiration. When he approached the commissioners,

Greenleaf did not go armed with a letter of introduction from Blodget. In late August Lear drafted a letter from the president introducing Greenleaf to the commissioners and lending presidential support to Greenleaf's proposals for building houses provided he could buy lots "upon such terms and conditions as may correspond with his interest in the undertaking," which is to say the president sanctioned selling Greenleaf a large number of lots. The president assured the commissioners that Greenleaf would impress them with his means. "He has been represented to me as a gentleman of large property and having a command of much money in this country and Europe." Lear's draft of the letter included intimations that Greenleaf could obtain a loan for the city, but Greenleaf, Lear, or the president crossed that out.[3]

*   *   *

When Greenleaf arrived in the city that September, the dream that lots sold at public auction would raise enough money to build the public buildings was not quite dead. The September 17 sale had been advertised for almost a year and had been touted as the time when big money would finally drive the prices of lots through the roof. It was not to be. Of the eighteen buyers over three days of sales, three — Davidson, Stoddert, and Carroll — were old proprietors no doubt trying to keep prices in their neighborhoods high. Seven of the buyers could not be represented as exciting new money boosting the city. They included Blodget, Lear, Hoban, Dermott, and George Washington. The president bought four lots at First and U Streets Southwest, along the Eastern Branch. Most of the other action was around the hotel and near the Capitol. Of the other eight buyers none bought more than two lots.

The president later claimed that his purchases were unplanned. But he well knew what Greenleaf intended and understood that the introduction of big money and concerted development would soon increase the price of lots. George Washington was not cheap and not a miser, but he liked bargains, especially in land. He did not plan to reside on square 667 in Carrollsburg. According to his calculations that was to be the commercial hub of the emporium on the Potomac of which he had long dreamed. For his city residence he had his eye on square 21 near Hamburg, on Peter's hill at 25th and E Streets Northwest, overlooking the Potomac. He toured the area with Blodget and told him he wanted to buy. Thus, as he often noted later, his purchases in Carrollsburg and Hamburg showed that he had the interests of the rival sections of town at heart.[4]

*   *   *

   The commissioners decided to make more of the cornerstone of the Capitol than they had that of the president's house. A long dispatch in the Boston *Columbian Centinel* described the ceremony. To judge from its lead — "On Wednesday last one of the grandest Masonic processions took place, which, perhaps, ever was exhibited on the like important occasion" — Blodget probably wrote it. The ceremony began at ten with Masonic lodges of Maryland and Virginia meeting on the banks of the Potomac to receive the president, who crossed the river accompanied by a volley from the artillery on the shore. At the president's house square a procession was formed. The city surveyors were at the head, and the president led Lodge 22, of which he was a member, at the rear. Masonic regalia — Bibles on cushions, wands, truncheons, jewels, corn, wine, and oil — made up much of the procession, but the commissioners, "their attendants," stonecutters, and mechanics also marched, along with a band, down the post road to Capitol Hill.
   The only reminiscence of the ceremonial parade, made in 1847 by a man who had been a boy at the time, described one major snag. Since Tiber creek was high, covering the rocks one usually crossed over, it took some time for everyone to navigate a "rude bridge formed of a single log." At the Capitol the front of the procession formed a cordon through which "the grand sword bearer led the van" followed by the president. Everyone else followed in reverse order to the southeast corner of the site of the Capitol, where they formed a circle facing west and "stood a short time in silent awful order." Then the artillery, which had filed a safe distance away, fired a volley.
   The plaque commemorating the event was unremarkable save

perhaps for listing as architects Hallet and Hoban. The president laid the plaque on the cornerstone accompanied by "awful prayer," Masonic chanting, and artillery volleys. The Masonic grand master, Joseph Clark, delivered the oration, which was more like eleven ejaculations of praise and optimistic projections punctuated by eleven artillery volleys. For example, after marveling at the work accomplished by masons from but two states, he gushed about what would be accomplished when all fifteen states sent masons to the city, bringing "an universality of individuals, like innumerable hives of bees bestowing their industrious labor on this second paradise." And that happy thought, the press report noted, was followed by "Volley From the Artillery." Then the company retired to "an extensive booth" and enjoyed 500 pounds of barbecued ox until fifteen rounds from the artillery signaled the end of the festivities.

As soon as the ceremonies ended, the auction began again. After the lackluster showing of the second day, negotiations with Greenleaf must have begun in earnest. But there was still one more public occasion to divert the assembled: the drawing of the lottery began on the 23rd. Even with the purchases of the consortium, Blodget could not guarantee that every ticket was sold. He had to take back "several thousand tickets" sold in Philadelphia because of legal considerations and "the prevalent sickness in that city." But only a few hundred tickets were drawn that day. He could return to Philadelphia, where his wife was recovering from yellow fever, and transmit a satisfactory account of the ticket sales before the next drawing. "You may rely," he wrote to the commissioners, "that every thing shall be arranged with care and exactions so as to secure your honor and my own." The president was good-humored enough about the goings-on that on the 25th he sent a ticket to the young son of Tobias Lear as a gift.[5]

24. Men of Spirit with Large Capitals

Greenleaf knew that Johnson was the commissioner to reckon with, and he took advantage of the judge's yen to be richer. He asked Johnson about his holdings upriver and did not dismiss his glowing description of good crops, plentiful coal, and easy transportation once the river was opened. He not only bought 15,000 acres of Johnson's Frederick County land for £5,000 but also offered to form a partnership to develop Johnson's entire 30,000-acre tract. Then they turned their attention to the federal city.

Greenleaf offered to buy 3,000 lots for £25 a lot and build ten two-story brick houses of 1,200 square feet every year until 1800, provided he could pay for the lots in $28,000 installments over seven years. In addition, he would loan the commissioners £1,000 a month, or another $32,000 a year, at six percent interest, the loan to be secured by the commissioners' lots, valued at £25 each. The commissioners agreed to the low price, with the proviso that Greenleaf not be allowed to pick lots along the rivers or in Carrollsburg, and that the buyers of lots he resold before 1796 had to build on every third lot. Greenleaf submitted to those conditions as long as he could buy lots along the canal for £25. He intimated that he hoped to include Robert Morris in the deal and, if so, did not want him to be required to build on every third lot. The first payment and loan would not begin until May 1, 1794, so both parties knew there would be ample opportunity to revamp the contract.

When Blodget heard those terms, he offered to pay £30 a lot in four years and also to improve the lots. He was sure three Philadelphia partners, including Standish Forde, whose offer of £35 a lot had been turned down the year before, would join him. The commissioners, leery of Blodget, appreciated having a speculator on hand rather than three in Philadelphia. They signed a contract with Greenleaf.

Greenleaf signed the agreement with the commissioners on September 23. On the 25th he bought the Frederick County lands from Johnson. On the 26th he made an agreement with Carroll of Duddington. He offered to buy twenty lots from Carroll that were next to the site of the Capitol, but Carroll replied tartly that he would not take "four times the sum we have talked of." He would sell his lots surrounding Carrollsburg. Greenleaf bought 220 lots there, for £30 ($80) each. Carroll agreed to invest the purchase price in improvements there. And Greenleaf agreed to make £3,000 worth of improvements in two years. Greenleaf also took a fancy to the highest spot on the point formed by the confluence of the rivers. Carroll sold him twenty lots there, at South Capitol and N Streets, on condition that Greenleaf build twenty brick buildings in three years. If he failed to do so, he would pay a £100 penalty on each lot.

Since the commissioners had denied it to him, he concentrated on buying waterside property from the proprietors. Greenleaf all but closed a deal to virtually buy out Notley Young, who owned the land west of Carrollsburg along the river, got forty lots from George French and Peter Casanave along Rock Creek, and began negotiations to buy a large farm on the east bank of the Eastern Branch.[1]

To prove that he was not just a speculator, Greenleaf regaled the commissioners and proprietors with news of a newly invented machine to mold bricks. If the commissioners had not already given up on Williamson's idea to make the public buildings all of stone, the promise of cheap bricks tipped the scales back toward interior walls of brick. Freestone would only front the walls of the public buildings. Greenleaf offered to bring machines to the city and share them. The commissioners placed an ad for "a great number of mechanicks in the building line, especially brickmakers, who will be able to carry on their business on a large scale." They were wanted "on private as well as public account, early next Spring." Greenleaf sent copies of the ad to his brother-in-law Noah Webster asking him to get it inserted in the Hartford, New Haven, and New London newspapers.

Washington, who had seldom let a major action by the commissioners pass without some carping, greeted news of the contract with pleasure, telling Lear that although Greenleaf got "very advantageous terms for himself, and I am pleased with it notwithstanding on public ground; as it may give facility to the operations at that place, at the same time that it is embarking him and his friends in a measure which, although [it] could not well fail under any circumstances that are likely to happen, may be considerably promoted by men of Spirit with large Capitals.''[2]

*   *   *

Not that, with its new source of funds, the board was going to go easy on querulous proprietors of little capital. When Burnes bought lots at auction, the board deducted the full price of the lot from what it owed him for land taken by the public. Burnes protested that he should have advantage of the easy terms of payment all other buyers had; the board could hold back no more than one fourth of the money due for lots bought at auction. The board disagreed, and Burnes got Luther Martin, the best lawyer in the state, if not the nation, to file a suit in chancery court. Burnes also sued Hoban and the commissioners for trespass — carts carrying sand had damaged his crops.[3]

*   *   *

The epidemic that some thought also cinched the Potomac as site of the capital threatened to make the whole issue a political football once again. The fever in Philadelphia did not show any signs of abating. Congress was in recess until the 1st of December, and if the past was any guide the fever should be over by then. But what if there should remain questions about the safety of the city? The president sent letters to his advisors asking if he had the power to convene Congress in another city, and, if so, which city that should be. But in back of the Virginians' minds was the fear that moving out of Philadelphia might reopen the whole issue of the seat of government.

Once Jefferson left the country house he was staying in for home (much to the relief of James Madison, who ''had long been uneasy for your health amidst the vapors of the Schuylkil''), Attorney General Randolph was the Virginian in the administration closest to the malignancy. While the president, Jefferson, and Madison combed the Constitution and statutes, Randolph followed the rumors: "I am satisfied that there will be great maneuvering about the place of congress for next session," he wrote to Madison, explaining that New York had it in mind to set itself up as the only spot available. He added, "A precedent, too, is much wished by some, for violating the compact concerning the final residence, by shewing the powers of congress over the temporary."[4]

*   *   *

After their busy September, the commissioners had a short respite. They were back in Georgetown in mid-October faced with a file of angry letters from the surveyors. While Dermott was picking and choosing lots to buy on his own account, Isaac Briggs and Benjamin Ellicott were finding the man's presence more and more insufferable. The arrangement whereby they surveyed the city and Dermott divided the squares had never pleased them.

Their monthly reports of September and October degenerated into compendia of reasons why squares should be divided by the surveying department. They claimed Dermott had lost the confidence of the proprietors and doubted Dermott's ability to manage a division of any square that was in the least irregular. They warned that division without reference to the relative altitude of the ground would lead to a situation in which "water, instead of retiring to the center of the square, may issue through the alley into the street." With the surveying almost done, the new task at hand was determining the grade of streets and the proper level of squares so that each builder would know "how deep they ought to lay their foundations and where they ought to place their first floor." Finally, Briggs recalled when Dermott had begun destroying the survey. Back in the summer of 1792, he had been running the center line of East 1st Street, but could not find a stake at one intersection. He mentioned that at the camp, and Dermott said it was there and described the spot. Briggs found it, ran the line, "and when much work had been done from the said line, as a basis, the said stake upon examination was found to be several feet from the point originally intended."

At their October 17 meeting the commissioners replied to two months' worth of vituperation against Dermott by giving him their full support. "Some of the imputations thrown on Mr. Dermott, we are satisfied, had no foundation, others went to his prudence as a man, with which the business of the city has no connection." If Briggs and Ellicott could prove that Dermott did indeed "maliciously remove the stakes," the commissioners would listen. As for the suggestion that the proprietors did not care for Dermott, obeying the whims of those worthies "would be acting on a rule that would operate farther than you probably foresee."

The commissioners went so far as to say why they liked Dermott. He had "the merit with us of discovering some errors which have been rectified, and others, which embarrass us, because we cannot of our own power rectify them; a total silence on this head in every other quarter shews inattention or concealment." Andrew Ellicott had been guilty of that silence. In conclusion, the commissioners reiterated that they were in charge and that if anyone did not like how they ran things, he could leave. In a postscript, they put off the issue of leveling the city until another day.

Briggs dashed off a reply defending Andrew Ellicott's work and denied that Dermott corrected any errors. Once again, Briggs tried to define what a scoundrel was for the benefit of those who did not understand that they had one in their midst. Last winter Dermott had "declared that he had put the affairs of the city into such a train, that they should never be set right again and some following events have proved his declaration too prophetic."

Johnson finally put an end to the bickering by badgering Briggs about a reported inaccuracy in his survey of the canal. Briggs gave the commissioners the choice between himself and Dermott. "Then, by God, Mr. Briggs," Johnson roared, "we wish to have nothing more to do with you." That, however, did not end the bickering for good. Benjamin Ellicott was saved by a fever from doing anything rash. He was too indisposed to do more than sign his name to Briggs's letters. He apparently did not think of quitting with Briggs, and to take up the slack, his brother Joseph joined the surveying department. The feud with Dermott would continue.[5]

Otherwise the meetings went quietly. Hoban presented a list of what he would need in the spring: more freestone, planking, and mahogany. His earlier estimate that White Oak Swamp would provide the timber for all of the public buildings was off. They needed a large quantity of white oak and yellow poplar for the Capitol. And of course they needed clay to be turned for bricks. Hoban worried about losing skilled stoneworkers and recommended they be offered employment at the quarries after work ended in the city for the season. The commissioners placed ads in newspapers soliciting what Hoban needed. They worried about having enough slaves for next year, authorizing Williams to hire forty.[6]

Before the month was over the auditors, Alexandria and Bladensburg merchants picked by the president, submitted their report. Two days of checking convinced them that every expenditure was backed up with a voucher (all since lost). Total income amount to £63,000: £30,000 from Virginia, £27,000 from Maryland, and £6,000 from the sale of lots. Expenditures amounted to £50,502, leaving a balance of £12,500. More than half of the balance was cash in hand. Anticipated revenue included £89,568 from the sale of lots, most of that to come from Greenleaf, and £15,000 from Virginia. The latter sum might be difficult to get.

The commissioners thought the auditors vindicated their performance. They were confident of the future, telling the president they could get loans from Maryland and Virginia banks "to keep us in credit till May, even if Virginia should disappoint us; and then Mr. Greenleaf's payment and loan, . . . coming on, things may be pushed with vigour a year longer."

Not that they gave up on Virginia. Soon a new approach to the Virginia statehouse would be essayed. It is not certain who noticed that Governor Henry Lee, who was notorious for being short of ready money, held extensive timberlands along the Potomac with just the white oak and yellow poplar that Hoban needed for the public buildings.[7]

25. A Proselyte to the New Jerusalem

Greenleaf decided to make New York his base of operations, even moving his literary brother-in-law Noah Webster to the city so "our dear Becca [his sister] will be lodged like a little queen." Then he set out to woo Robert Morris. James Kent, Greenleaf's lawyer, described his renown in the fall of 1793: Morris "at the age of 56 has now all the enterprising speculation of youth. He is said to own 6 million acres of land. He purchased upwards of 4 million of back lands in Georgia the other day for a trifle. . . . He has more men under his patronage and moneyed influence than any other man in the union. Had he lived during the period of Athenian Liberty, he would have had the honor of the Ostracism."

Greenleaf wanted a partnership with Morris because he was in a hurry to fill out his investments before he took up his duties as consul in Amsterdam. In New York Greenleaf could treat with Duer's creditors for New York lands. Morris already had the Georgia lands Blodget talked about. And of course the more land Greenleaf could amass the more eager Dutch bankers would be to invest. They would not be interested in loans of £1,000 a month. Indeed, through his son, who was in Europe, Morris had learned that the Dutch bankers were looking for another one or two million acres much like the Genesee lands he had packaged and sold them in 1792. Trusting the rumors that Greenleaf already had an unlimited line of credit with Dutch bankers, Morris was interested in what Greenleaf had to offer. As always, he was in a hurry, and thanks to the March 1793 financial panic in England, in which he lost a half million dollars, Morris was short of ready cash to keep the installments on land he had bought and down payments on land he had contracted to buy.

His failure to get a bank loan had forced Morris to try to raise money by land companies. The latest was a package he and John Nicholson put together to settle French refugees from Santo Domingo along the Susquehanna north of Harrisburg. Selling shares in the Asylum Company was a quicker way to raise money than actually selling land to settlers. The money raised from investors could finance basic improvements to the area, which meant tracts could be sold for higher prices. But investors felt strapped for cash, and shares sold slowly.[1]

Although the cash-poor Morris needed Greenleaf more than Greenleaf needed him, Morris had managed to make himself the pursued and Greenleaf the suitor. In July and August Greenleaf had written him several letters asking for a conference. Morris put him off for several weeks, replying that he was too busy closing deals for Georgia lands. By October there was enough agreement between Greenleaf, Morris, and Nicholson to send Sylvanus Bourne, a young merchant Greenleaf and Morris trusted, to Amsterdam bearing the deeds for 500,000 acres in Pennsylvania and Georgia that Morris and Nicholson already owned and the agreement of sale for Greenleaf's 3,000 Washington lots.

Morris showed only moderate enthusiasm for Washington lots. Young Greenleaf, however, was a good salesman. In a November 9 note Morris signaled his surrender: "I perceive that we shall agree for the lotts and of course I must become a proselyte to the New Jerusalem. Mr. Nicholson was here yesterday and being himself a proprietor of two squares, he rejoiced to find that I was engaged." Greenleaf not only got Morris to join his Washington speculation but sold him half of his investment, 1,500 lots, for £35 a lot. As Morris later explained, Greenleaf was so certain that large sums would be forthcoming from Amsterdam that he felt it foolish not to be agreeable. This was especially so when Washington lots promised to sell more quickly than Georgia lands, thus servicing the loans and allowing the money to be used principally to buy more backlands and establish a monopoly. The money men of Europe, eager to make millions in America, could then call only on Morris, Nicholson, and Greenleaf.[2]

Anticipating success with Morris, Greenleaf sent Lear to Georgetown in mid-October with a letter to the commissioners asking them to sell 1,500 more lots to him through Lear and to take a part of the Dutch loan he was about to get. The commissioners responded immediately as if they were flattered and flustered. Citing the "magnitude" and "novelty" of joining three private gentlemen in a foreign loan, they begged off but indicated they would not be averse to upping his monthly loan to £2,000 secured by lots valued at $140 each — more than twice what Greenleaf had just paid for lots. They also indicated they were willing to sell him more lots at their next meeting, in December.

Shortly after intriguing the commissioners with the prospect of more sales, Greenleaf asked for the deeds to the lots he had already agreed to purchase so that they could be more easily mortgaged. The commissioners had only offered certificates of sale that included the proviso that the improvement agreed to had to be made or the lots would revert to the possession of the commissioners. They assured him that "a short conversation will finish this business not merely to the satisfaction but to the pleasure of us all."

The reassurance they had in store for Greenleaf was an act shortly to be passed by the Maryland Assembly codifying their scheme of the sale. The law would declare that a certificate of sale was "sufficient and effectual to vest the legal estate in the purchasers, . . . without any deed or formal conveyance." In tandem with that, the Maryland law would give them the power to sell lots at auction if the purchaser failed to make payments or improvements. The commissioners simply thought it prudent not to lose control of 3,000 lots to Dutch bankers on the chance that Greenleaf went bankrupt.[3]

William Prout had bragged that his Washington land purchase had been the talk of the country. While he was setting up his Washington store and relieving the pressure to pay Slater by marrying Slater's daughter, Greenleaf made the deal that indeed became the talk of the country. Theophile Cazenove passed on rumors of Greenleaf's activity to his Dutch employers. He had heard that Greenleaf had already hired a man for £1,000 to manage his business in the city. In addition, he had given the same sum to an inventor who had a machine that could make a prodigious number of bricks.

Indeed, on November 16, Greenleaf signed an agreement with Apollos Kinsley of New York taking a half interest in his brick machine. On November 30 he hired a Philadelphia builder, James Simmons, to plan and build houses in the federal city for £1,000 a year for three years. He also offered Dr. Nathaniel Appleton, the husband of Greenleaf's older sister Sarah, the job of managing his Washington property, for $1,500 plus expenses, including what it would take to educate his children. He was a consumptive with a decided bent for literary gossip. Brother Greenleaf evidently felt that a southern climate and outdoor work supervising builders might do him good.

Appleton was quite enthusiastic about the pay, but he worried in a letter to Noah Webster. "Do you think the climate would probably agree with my health, which is always poorest in the months of Augt & Sept? Do you think me competent to do what would be expected of me — would it not be a constant round of great fatigue of body & mind? Do not Bro. James's prospects depend very much on the *contingency* of that place being the seat of Governt at the time proposed? Would not that contingency be problematical in case of the disgrace (if that is possible) or the demise of the present President of the U.S.?"[4]

*   *   *

Even with a death count on its way to 4,000 and the city still deserted, none of the president's advisors thought the president had the power to save Congress from having to meet in Philadelphia. They would have to meet there and then retreat, preferably to Germantown, where Washington decided to make his quarters until Philadelphia was safe.

In a November 2 letter to Madison, Jefferson described the scene. With the arrival of every politician the intrigue over where to move became more intense. The battle lines were being drawn between Lancaster and New York. Germantown, despite previous billing, could not handle the crowds. "According to present appearances," Jefferson wrote, "this place cannot lodge a single person more. As a great favour I have got a bed in the corner of the public room of a tavern: and must so continue till some Philadelphians make a vacancy by removing into the city. Then we must give from 4 to 6 or 8 dollars a week for cuddies without a bed, and sometimes without a chair or table."

To the relief of everyone, there was no new cases of fever reported after November 2. Everyone was amazed and gratified by how quickly the city came back to life, and there was "a general fumigation of houses, apparel, bedding & c . . . , by order of the Corporation."[5]

*   *   *

While Philadelphia recovered from yellow fever, the fever of speculation increased in the federal city. Even Blodget protected his own investment by taking the line that despite the low price Greenleaf paid, the schedule of improvement meant that on the whole the sale increased the value of city lots. Standish Forde tested the waters by sending an offer to Burnes, which elicited the reply that Burnes would negotiate only in person, not by letter, and that he wanted $300 a lot, over four times what Greenleaf paid. Forde's agent, however, noted that Burnes sold more cheaply for cash "as his necessities require."

Greenleaf's price brought others to the commissioners. Peter Casanave, the Spanish merchant who married Notley Young's daughter, also offered improvements in return for an extensive purchase of public lots. The commissioners put off Casanave, waiting to see further proposals from Greenleaf.

Even Judge Johnson had the itch to speculate. In October the president asked him to become the secretary of state when Jefferson resigned at the end of the year. Johnson turned down the request; for that matter, he wanted to leave the Supreme Court and the board. He told the president he wanted "to avail myself of the moment which I saw and has almost past away to benefit myself by the rise of the city to which a long friendship for Potomack and every exertion in my power in its favor fairly intitle me." He announced his intentions to the world in a manner designed to startle the likes of Samuel Davidson and George Walker, who had long thought that Johnson was out to abort the embryonic city: "I wish to change my property in this part of the country," ran his ad in the *Maryland Journal,* "for property in the Federal City." He offered his 850-acre plantation on the Monocacy, including 1,500 apple trees, a gristmill, a sawmill, a tanyard, and a glasshouse; 1,700 acres on Bush Creek; his Bush Creek forge and mill, 260 acres of surrounding land, and "several good negro foremen"; and 20,000 acres of land "westward of Cumberland."

Johnson's old friend George Washington understood a 61-year-old man's yen for a change. He too was planning to sell much of his landholdings and even rent the fields around Mount Vernon, preferably to good farmers coming directly from England, so "that the remainder of my days may, thereby, be more tranquil and freer from cares." Of course, proximity to the future "emporium of the United States" made the price of his lands high. A prospective buyer of his 300 acres along Difficult Run near Great Falls was told, "Nothing short of a very high price would induce me to sell. . . ."[6]

*   *   *

Only one thing kept Johnson on the commission: the lottery. Since his name was on the prospectus of the scheme, he, as well as David Stuart, who also wanted to resign, felt obliged to see the fiasco to its conclusion. Despite the wish of the commissioners that the lottery simply be over and done with, the wheel, as it so often does, took on a life of its own. George Washington was often the recipient of solicitous letters from the kind of folk who did not have a prayer of getting any favors. On October 16 a self-described "Georgetown ticket seller" tried to find a niche through the good graces of the president. He bragged about his services to the community, which included reselling tickets in the Washington hotel lottery, "to enable," as he put it, "those worthy gentlemen who are heavy ticket holders to sell more speedily to such advantage as to reimburse themselves for the losses they have already sustained."

Blodget's luck held out, because after a little more than a month of drawing tickets the grand prize and cash prizes of $10,000, $15,000, $20,000, and $25,000 remained in the wheel. Around Christmastime a Boston merchant was emboldened to sell a hundred tickets in the hotel lottery at public auction, all tickets "warranted undrawn." Not surprisingly, not a few adventurers smelled a fix. On December 9 a New York City ticket seller wrote to the commissioners to complain about the delay of the business. His customers suspected "that you and your agent are leagued to make a mockery of the people by unnecessary delay & protraction, to enhance the value of the tickets. . . . More doubts have arisen amongst the poorer people whether you intend to pay the prizes.''

Blodget would have smiled at such accusations. He and the commissioners were still at odds with each other. Indeed, much of the city of Georgetown was keen to get at his throat. Uriah Forrest led the charge with a letter, now lost, to the president, who promptly passed it on to the attorney general. Forrest evidently accused Blodget of not paying prizes. Attorney General Randolph passed the complaints on to Blodget, who retorted, ''I go rapidly in the payment of prizes tho not quite so fast in the collection of moneys due to me, yet this shall occasion no delay on my part. . . . In a short time it will appear that no lottery was ever better paid in this country than ours, & this will secure success to future lotteries without which the city will never go on with spirit.''

With less bombast, Blodget explained to the commissioners that owing to the deaths from yellow fever in Philadelphia, it would take longer to collect from those people who had bought tickets with a personal note payable in sixty days and had since died. Blodget would dip into his own funds, if necessary, to keep up prompt payment of prizes drawn. A note he held on Morris and Nicholson, of all people, was past due. Morris promised payment in a week. To date, Blodget had lost about $1,000, but he was confident he could make that up through sales of remaining tickets at higher prices. He urged the commissioners not to panic and increase the number of tickets drawn each week, for a slow drawing allowed initial purchasers of large amounts of tickets in Boston to sell their tickets at a profit as lottery fever grew.

As for the business of superintending the city, Blodget must have known that his days in the employ of the city were numbered. The president himself had made it clear verbally that his idea of superintendent was not a man who was often out of town and whose primary task was saving a lottery that had little relation to the public business. Still, Blodget kept his chin up and announced, ''I am making every preparation in my power to do *something* in the spring.''

What comfort that might have given the commissioners was dispelled when Blodget revealed that he had engaged vendors for "several thousand tickets in the next lottery." The wheel of the first lottery finally revealed the $25,000 winner, an Alexandria merchant named Young. Blodget could pay him only $4,000. Given that record, the commissioners were not amused at his selling tickets in another lottery involving the city. Carroll told him to do nothing until it was cleared with the commissioners. Once Judge Johnson got to Georgetown, the letters to Philadelphia were not so pleasant. If Blodget advertised the second lottery as in any way associated with the commissioners, they would publicly disavow it.[7]

26. It Cannot Fail

Greenleaf, Morris, and Nicholson signed partnership papers on December 10 that bound them in joint purchases of lands for five years. They were equal partners save that "in consideration of his more productive connexions in Europe," Greenleaf was allowed to make his payments twelve months late. Also, Greenleaf was authorized to sell Morris's and Nicholson's lands when he went to Amsterdam. The agreement recognized that Morris and Nicholson had the contacts to make even more extensive purchases in Georgia. They would make down payments trusting that Greenleaf would deliver the money from Holland to complete the deals.

On the 12th the three speculators signed a document making them equal partners in Greenleaf's speculations in the federal city and giving him control of the partnership's interests there. Greenleaf pledged to use his own resources to commence development. Although developing Washington was Greenleaf's project, Morris had advice. (Nicholson was distracted by an impeachment trial. He planned to resign from the office of Pennsylvania comptroller, but his honor was at stake.) Morris thought it would be a pity to spend the resources raised in Holland, which could better be used to expand their holdings elsewhere, on property that should be able to support itself. In a matter of days Morris cooked up the Columbian Society.

Morris calculated that with 1,000 subscribers who pledged to give $500 each at the rate of $50 a year for ten years, they could build eighteen houses a year for ten years. From the rent and sale of the houses and interest accruing on the accumulating funds, he calculated that the society would make $1,323,080 for distribution to its subscribers. In 1795 a subscriber with one share would get $2.88. In 1807 one share would get $1,323.08. Over the life of the society one $500 share would earn $1,323.08. Almost 200 houses costing $2,400 each would be sold.

In his instructions to his builder, James Simmons, Greenleaf had something much more elegant in mind, but he was excited enough about the Columbian Society to explain it to the president before he left for Georgetown to meet with the commissioners. His meeting with the president was not a mere courtesy call. Greenleaf offered to trade land across the Eastern Branch for the parcel on the city's shore due east of the Capitol, designated for the Marine Hospital. He softened the president up by getting him to agree that contagion spread from hospitals so they had no place in a city. The president informed Carroll of what Greenleaf had said and added, "I am inclined to that opinion," but of course such matters, he informed Greenleaf, properly came to him through the comissioners, who were not enthusiastic. By turning the area into building lots, the original proprietors would have a claim to half.[1]

*   *   *

Greenleaf took his lawyer, James Kent, with him to Georgetown. Kent kept a journal, but although he was privy to the negotiations with the commissioners, he did not record any of that. His remarks were about the passing scenery and commercial possibilities, very much echoing what he was using as his guidebook, the pamphlet just published by Tobias Lear entitled *Observations on the River Potomac — the Country Adjacent and the City of Washington.*

Lear himself had just shipped off for Europe to drum up business, and his *Observations* outlined the commercial advantages of the Potomac just as he had so often heard George Washington describe them. Kent wrote of his stay in the federal city on the blank pages of Lear's pamphlet. In a sentence he deflated Lear's pretenses: "The *Avenues* are all cut thro woods, & these, together with the basement stories I have mentioned, & here and there a house & hut scattered, being *excepted,* this city, so splendid already in the exaggerating tales of fame consists of *woods, swamps, & naked hills* of apparently thin sandy soil."

Not that Kent argued with Lear's characterization of the city as healthy. (Lear's wife had just died of yellow fever, so Lear would not have taken threats to health lightly.) Kent described Baltimore as "low & marshy, & was formerly unhealthy." The banks of the Schuylkill River were "low & marshy & far from being inviting except at high water." Washington, by contrast, was a succession of charming vistas.

Greenleaf and Kent stayed in Georgetown for nine days and dined with Forrest, Stoddert, Notley Young, and John Mason. The dinner with Forrest was not at his M Street house but in his new country seat Rosedale two miles north of Georgetown on a hill that commanded "a fine view over the city and down the river." Stoddert's mansion, Halcyon House, on what would later be called Prospect Street, afforded not only a view downriver but one upriver, which Kent thought as dramatic as the view on the Hudson looking north from Poughkeepsie. And then from Young's house they had "a fine view down to Alexandria & even to Mount Vernon." Finally, Mason lived on the large island in the middle of the Potomac, which added "much to the beauty of the view" from Georgetown.

Kent did not mention having dinner with the commissioners but did remark on the usual carping against them: "They are accused by some of being very injudicious with their plans, and incompetent to the task." He heard about the bad bridge and their "cutting a canal before the city is begun." Kent was quick to note that his boss, Greenleaf, would soon make such bad times a distant memory

— getting $7.50 a day plus expenses made Kent think highly of his client.

Kent was more enthusiastic about the city than Lear was in his pamphlet. The president's house was "½ mile from the river on a hill yielding a gentle declivity to the river & commanding a fine view for several miles down the river." The stone was "greyish white free stone handsomely polished." The building itself "presages to be the grandest & most elegant palace in the world." The hotel, which like the president's house, had only a basement, was built "on a plan elegant and capacious." As for the other public building, he noted "the ground chalked out for a most magnificent capitol." And he found ground chalked out for a "national university."

The major point of Lear's pamphlet was the song that George Washington had been singing about the Potomac since the 1770s. Indeed, Lear began at the beginning: "Early in life General Washington contemplated the opening of this river, from tidewater to its source. . . ." Kent, who was hardheaded enough to be selected as a law professor at Columbia University, could not help but sing right along. Since the advent of Greenleaf, "the rise of the city in value and importance is now inconceivably rapid. . . . He may be deemed the principal founder of the city, a city which presages to rise with such rapidity, elegance and grandeur." Especially with the assistance of Morris and Nicholson, "it cannot fail of a rapid growth in size, beauty, wealth and greatness." His return to New York did not sober him up. He wrote to his brother: "The federal city must in time be the greatest mart of commerce in the U. States."[2]

*   *   *

Perhaps the enthusiasm about the city was so infectious that it lured Andrew Ellicott back. He was not welcomed. When the commissioners convened on December 17 they promptly notified Ellicott that they did not want him and viewed his leaving in July as his resignation. They could have left it at that, but they could not resist adding, "as we had not your services in the season when they might have been most useful, we will not add to our establishment in winter." Ellicott replied that he had not resigned; his absence was only temporary, and he had returned because the work yet to be done required the use of his transit. The commissioners were right back at him: "if we meet with any embarrassment for the want of one we must add it to the list of chagrins we have met with."

That they relied on two of Ellicott's brothers to carry on the surveying did not give the commissioners pause. They wrote to them on the 17th allowing that "it is a delicate circumstance with you" and hoping that they would stay on the job. They, in turn, held their fire. None of the Ellicotts ever explained why, but with the money of Morris and Nicholson, for whom the brothers had worked, pouring into the city, they must have decided that their family would be counted as damned fools to walk out en masse just at that moment.[3]

*   *   *

The commissioners' only regret was that Morris had not come down with Greenleaf. Greenleaf relayed a personal message from the great man: he wanted to settle one of his sons in the city. The commissioners gushed, "It will be very pleasing to us that you should amongst other friendly acts to the city place one of your sons here. . . . Let us expect Sir in the favorable season to see you here, we have no doubt your visit would afford you pleasure and confirm your resolution perhaps enlarge your views to improve on the most delightful spot in the United States."

The commissioners had good reason to dote on Morris. He bought the same number of lots as Greenleaf, 3,000, for 50 percent more, £35 instead of £25. Not that Morris had reason to feel taken, since Greenleaf split the difference so that both of them would pay £30 ($80) for each lot. With the prospect of the first $68,000 installment on May 1, Greenleaf persuaded the commissioners to postpone the monthly loan until January 1795. But the provision the commissioners dearly wanted, the agreement to build a set number of houses each year, remained. Both Greenleaf and Morris would have to build ten houses a year for the next seven years, a total of 140 brick houses at least two stories high. In addition, the speculators agreed to take half of their lots northeast of Massachusetts Avenue, the outskirts of the city.

The one snag was over deeds to the lots. Greenleaf almost got what he wanted. The commissioners told the president that they were amenable to taking the personal security of Greenleaf, Morris, and Nicholson as assurance that the provisions of the agreement would be fulfilled. In return for their bond, the commissioners would give them deeds to 1,000 lots. They sent a copy of the bond to the president for his approval.[4]

The deal made, Greenleaf helped the board with other problems. The Aquia quarries were not working out happily. In a mid-November report Hoban worried that not enough stone would be on hand by the spring, that it cost too much, and that "a large proportion" of it was so poor it could not be used. Thirty-eight loads totaling 1,350 tons had come upriver that year, but the remaining stone was of poor quality. Then a bit of prospecting on the public grounds in the city uncovered a stratum of foundation stone southwest of the president's house square leading from the rock that jutted out in the river and bore the intriguing name "The Key of All Keys." And at Mount Vernon some stone the president had known about but thought too soft was examined and found suitable. What was needed was a man to develop the sites. Greenleaf promised to find one, and the commissioners could let Greenleaf buy some of the stone.

As every other man wanting to buy land in the city learned, Greenleaf was special. Blodget's friend Templeman was trying to buy a parcel along Rock Creek large enough for his warehouse and wharf. Despite Blodget's assurance that lots could be purchased cheaply if Templeman promised to improve, the commissioners refused to sell nine lots for less than £900. The going rate was what Lear paid, not what Greenleaf paid.[5]

*   *   *

In justifying the deal with Greenleaf and Morris to the president, the board looked at the big picture. In December 1793 not a few Americans expected the United States would be involved in a war with Spain, England, or France by the spring. The commissioners thought the deal was a valuable hedge against the uncertainties of war. Their fear of unsettled times and commerce hampered by belligerents "weighed much with us" as they signed the contract. The deal would "enable the prosecution of the work even in a war, in which event we should be, without this contract . . . almost still."

The commissioners had to meet briefly on Christmas Day because they had been so busy the past weekdays that they had not settled accounts, including their own expenses. Johnson, Stuart, and Carroll gave themselves respectively £291, £279, and £318. (They had learned expense accounts could make work seem much easier.) Then they repaired to the festivities.

Given the small population in Georgetown and the empty spaces in the federal city, it is easy to imagine a kind of frontier Christmas with oven the great folk looking plain and ruddy around their Madeira at Suter's. The New Yorker Kent was there and found that "on Christmas Eve there was great finery at Georgetown all night. I observed the same to a degree in Phil[adelphia] on New Years Eve."

Georgetown outdid Philadelphia in the matter of show! Here indeed was the Metropolis in the making.[6]

1794

27. The Finesse and Cunning of a Quotidian Friend

As news of Greenleaf's and Morris's deal spread among speculators in Philadelphia, considerable attention focused on Greenleaf. Blodget tried to make the most of it. Trumpeting it as evidence that "the business shall not lag," he peddled subscriptions to the newly organized Bank of Columbia. But others were leery. Theophile Cazenove, heretofore the man in America with power to influence the investment decisions of Dutch bankers, gave Greenleaf credit for stimulating the Potomac region, which was good news for Cazenove, who had pushed Potomac Company subscriptions onto his clients. But he noted that "it was said" that Greenleaf had "unlimited credit" with Dutch banks. Cazenove did not believe it. Greenleaf's speculation did not resemble a scheme laid out according to "Dutch principles." He was sure the speculators were still trying to raise money.

Within three weeks Cazenove was proved right. Morris unveiled the European version of the Columbian Society, intending to raise $1 million by selling 2,000 shares at $500 each. Cazenove grew suspicious of such a proliferation of money-raising schemes and did not believe Morris's assertion that the domestic version of the Columbian Society had already raised $250,000. Indeed, he told his clients that a scheme cooked up by Forrest and William Deakins to sell $150,000 worth of shares to speculators based on the development of 1,000 lots "appears to me to be more solid than that of Mr. Greenleaf."[1]

If he had been candid, Greenleaf would have had to agree. Forrest and Deakins at least had solid title. Some of their squares had been divided, so they knew which lots were theirs. Greenleaf only knew that he would eventually pick 6,000 lots. And he suffered a setback in his quest for deeds. The president submitted Greenleaf's bond to his Virginia brain trust. Jefferson, Madison, and Randolph all agreed: "the commissioners ought not to abandon the legal title to lots sold."

Then Greenleaf had some luck. Jefferson retired on December 31 and Edmund Randolph, hitherto attorney general, took his place as secretary of state. Although he lacked Jefferson's knowledge of architecture and acquaintance with the great cities of the world, Randolph was much closer to the president and had more knowledge of and no antipathy toward banks, loans, and debt. Like Morris, Randolph was hurt financially by a bank failure in London in 1793. Of course they were in different leagues — Morris lost a half million dollars and Randolph lost $2,252.50 — but they played by the same rules.

Randolph got the president to agree to giving Greenleaf deeds to 1,000 lots, but he had to finesse it. In a January 19 letter he explained to the commissioners that the president was sure Greenleaf and Morris would fulfill their obligations, "but in so important a trust, as the amount of the purchase, he does not conceive himself authorized to approve a departure from the common mode of retaining the legal title until payment." That seemed to close the matter, but he added "that every facility short of abandoning your hold, should be afforded to the objects which these gentlemen have in view. Indeed he has no objection to your going as far as their proposal now enclosed," which was that they give titles to 1,000 lots.

Adding to the commissioners' confusion was a letter from Greenleaf adding to Randolph's scheme. Throughout the life of the contract, the partners would have the deeds to 1,000 more lots than they had actually paid for, making it easier for them to make sales and get loans. In practical terms it meant that as of the May 1 payment Greenleaf would have deeds to 2,000 lots. He only needed 1,000 more to have the security he thought he needed for a loan of two million guilders, or $800,000, with each lot valued at £100, or $266. The commissioners were amenable but cautious until they could be sure the president agreed.[2]

Meanwhile, Greenleaf set himself to ensuring that the brick machine would accompany the first wave of workmen he sent to the city. He revamped his agreement with Kinsley from a fifty-fifty arrangement into one in which for $2,111.50 he would have exclusive rights to license use of the machine in Maryland. By the end of February he got the inventor himself to agree to go to the federal city and set up his machine. His other immediate service for the city was to do what he could to get rid of Blodget.[3]

*   *   *

Blodget's most committed opponent was Johnson. "Mr. Blodget will not be useful in the affairs of the city," he told the president. "He wants judgment and steadiness. I cannot think of leaving him to a successor. We all wish to part from him and that quietly." Never a great fan of Blodget's, the president completely turned on him after Greenleaf told him that Blodget was selling tickets to the second lottery for Georgia land. That, the president told the commissioners, was "the worst detail in Mr. Blodget's conduct." The president promptly directed the secretary of state to tell Blodget to "suspend all further proceeding" with the lottery. In a long reply to Johnson, the president excoriated Blodget at length. Blodget did not even approximate Washington's idea of the superintendent always on the scene. "At first I was at loss how to account for a conduct so distant from any of the ideas I had entertained . . . , but it appears evidently enough now, that speculation has been his primary object from the beginning."

When Randolph informed him of the president's order, Blodget suspended his second lottery until he could clear up the misunderstanding. For, he assured Randolph, a misunderstanding it was. Commissioners Carroll and Stuart had told him "they would not consent to any responsibility in a future lottery, but how could this affect *either of those in existence*." Needless to say, that bit of sophistry did not amuse the commissioners.

Blodget blamed his troubles on Greenleaf and almost challenged him to a duel. Instead he gave Randolph a four-page history of his affairs with Greenleaf. He recalled how he first got Greenleaf interested in the city but then was shunned after the September sale. It was then that the commissioners turned sour on the lottery. He explained something of the Georgia land business. Greenleaf had come to him ostensibly to buy 10,000 tickets in the second lottery to sell in Holland. Blodget told him about "a Georgia speculation which I had partly compleated to great advantage for tickets which I hoped would make amends for my losses in the first lottery. From this moment he began to rail at the lottery and he and Mr. Morris have it in contemplation to get this bargain from me by a defeat of my second lottery." He tried to impress Randolph with the enormity of such perfidy: "think of being reduced by the finesse and cunning of a quotidian friend to sacrifice my reputation and by a retrograde maneuver to blast all my spirit for successful and useful enterprise."

Blodget hurried to the federal city, not to argue but to go the extra mile. He offered security to guarantee payment of the prizes in the first lottery, including the square next to the Capitol, the farm he owned that was just north of Davidson's farm, and 7,160 shares he owned in the Insurance Company of North America, which he valued at $40,000. He also let Johnson rewrite the prospectus for the second lottery. In Blodget's first prospectus the commissioners were credited as sponsors of the lottery, Blodget was listed as agent of the city, and the lottery was billed as being held so "the commissioners will be enabled to give an elegant specimen of the private buildings to be erected in the city of Washington." Johnson's prospectus stripped Blodget of his title and eliminated all mention of the commissioners except one. They would choose and swear in the "24 gentlemen" who would manage the drawing. And arrangements for securing the lottery were spelled out.

The lottery did have elements designed to melt the hearts of the commissioners and the president. With the $400,000 raised by the sale of 50,000 tickets at $8 each, six "magnificent" dwellings would be built in the city. "Two beautiful designs are already selected for the entire fronts on two of the public squares; from these drawings it is proposed to erect two centre and four corner buildings, as soon as possible after this lottery is sold, and to convey them, when complete, to the fortunate adventurers." The six top winners would get not only the houses, valued from $5,000 up to $20,000, but also cash, $5,000 for the sixth prize and $30,000 for the top prize. In addition, any surplus from the 5 percent deducted for printing or from prizes unclaimed would "be made a part of the fund intended for the National University, to be erected within the city of Washington."

The commissioners even had kind things to say about Blodget in their report to Randolph. The causes for keeping him from the federal city were "no altogether within his control." He offered the security voluntarily, and "he tells us, and we believe truly, that he has already paid off a great many of the small prizes." The commissioners felt "relieved and easy on the present lottery which tho' it has occasioned anxiety to us has, we are satisfied on the whole been useful in bringing the city into the general view and contemplation." As for the second lottery, Blodget had brought it forward "rashly," and they would have nothing to do with it, but if done properly "so as to obtain public confidence it might be useful."

All those nice words did not, however, add up to an extension of Blodget's contract as superintendent. Blodget pressed the commissioners to write a letter of dismissal that would do him "as little injury as might be." The commissioners obliged. They cited the time the new lottery would take and the unlikelihood of his moving to the city as the reasons for dispensing with his services. They left open the possibility that they might ask for his help on certain matters later on. Actually, as Commissioner Stuart later wrote to the president, all three thought that "it was unfortunate that we ever had any connection with him in any way."[4]

*   *   *

They felt the same way about Andrew Ellicott. To the commissioners' consternation, they had not got rid of him. He stayed in the city with his brothers and "worked like so much leaven on the surveying department," Immediately on being told not to resume his work, Ellicott set about trying to build a file on the chicanery of Dermott. He wrote to Briggs to get his testimony about the removal of stakes, which was the one crime that, if it were proved that Dermott was responsible, the commissioners could not ignore. Then there was the theft of L'Enfant's and other maps. Since the commissioners had declined to punish Dermott for his taking them, the Ellicotts plotted to take the matter to court. Joseph Ellicott placed two ads in the Georgetown paper signed by brother Benjamin: "SIX DOLLARS REWARD: STOP THE THIEF!" ran the headline, which was the typical way aggrieved parties attracted attention to a horse thief. But the ad referred to a "plan of the City of Washington, given in trust to me by Major L'Enfant. The person formerly suspected for this infamous conduct was a certain James Mac-Dermott 'alias' James R. Dermott, who has since acknowledged the theft. He is a native of Ireland, well made, about five feet ten inches high, has a remarkably red face, an impudent brazen look, dark-coloured hair, which he commonly wears tied behind. Whoever will take up the said thief, and commit him to any jail in the United States, so that he may be brought to condign punishment, shall receive the above award, from Benjamin Ellicott."

That ad was dated January 19, 1793, to give the illusion that the pursuit of Dermott had lasted a year! In the same issue a letter to the commissioners from Benjamin dated January 19, 1794, appeared. In this Ellicott described the alleged theft and noted that Dermott admitted it and that the commissioners in turn admitted having received the map. Ellicott threatened to prosecute. The commissioners wrote Benjamin a short note chiding him for his public letter. "It would have been at least as decent and effectual" to merely ask them for the map he wanted.

The brothers appeared before the commissioners, and, according to the commissioners, "Joseph said the letter was not to be justified, that his brother was sorry for it, and would make any concessions the commissioners required." But the commissioners had had their fill. On the 28th they sent another surveyor, George Fenwick, to the Ellicotts ordering them to give Fenwick their papers, to inventory everything, and to vacate the house they occupied. As the commissioners told the president, they were tired of the Ellicotts' "want of industry" and "total absence of probity and honor."

The commissioners opined that the mere laying out of the city was virtually done and that the next stage called for men of greater ability than the Ellicotts. ". . . Leveling the city and marking out the proper drains," they wrote, "approach so quick that a man of real abilities in that line will be soon wanted." They had a man in mind, a friend of Thornton, Major John Rivardi. He had visited the city with Thornton, "made a strong impression," and seemed "not a shewy man but . . . one of those characters who maintains the ground he has gained."[5]

28. Ticket 37531

The only workers the commissioners seemed comfortable with were slaves. They were pleased when Williams rented six more than the forty they had authorized. Maryland and Virginia had more slaves than any other region in the country and diminishing reasons to keep them as tobacco farming gave way to wheat. So when William Beall in Georgetown hired out Davy, Frank, and Newton, and Ignatius Boone, on the east bank of the Eastern Branch, hired out Moses, Charles, and Jacob, and the five Brent sisters in Virginia, Elizabeth, Eleanor, Jane, Teresa, and Mary, each hired out one slave, Gabriel, Davy, Henry, Nace, and Charles, they counted themselves lucky that they could make $56 a year on field hands they no longer needed.

The responsibility of feeding and bedding down the slaves did not give the commissioners pause. They provided pork or beef, whichever was cheaper, and shad in season. The staple of the slaves' diet was cornmeal. The commissioners hired a cook, Jane Short, at the same annual rate they paid for slaves. As for room, each slave got floor space in a barracks.

Although no one ever alluded to the slaves being happy in their work, they were not chained. Freedom did not necessarily lie north of the Mason-Dixon line. Slavery was still legal in New York, emancipation gradual in Pennsylvania. If slaves did not show up for work, Williams made no hue and cry. He merely marked them absent, and their masters accordingly got less money. And although slaves had no trouble perceiving that they were the drudges in the operations, not a few white laborers worked under the same conditions, ate the same food, and received the same pay — which, of course, they could keep themselves, but they were usually hired by the month.[1]

The commissioners' relationships with other workers were problematic. On the one hand, they were forced to be paternalistic, keeping skilled hands at a reduced wage during the winter when there was little work. They had to provide housing because there was virtually no housing in the city. In barracks more properly termed tenements, they had Hoban bed three men in a room. On the other hand, they did not want to return to the days of chocolate butter. Housing workers was a necessary evil, not an opportunity to mold a work force with some esprit de corps. Workers above the level of laborer fed themselves. The commissioners made clear that they even wanted to cease being paymasters. They wanted to contract for work and pay for what was done rather than the time spent doing it.

Hoban was quick to use the commissioners' yen for economies to secure his control of operations in the city. The relationship of the commissioners to their top men was rather confused. They hired Hoban to supervise construction of the president's house but had Williamson supervising all masons, who that winter worked in sheds near the work site preparing stone that would be set in the spring. They hired Hallet to supervise construction of the Capitol, but not until he finished designing it. Until then Hoban was to supervise work at the Capitol. Hoban did not let his momentary command go for naught and decided to use it to diminish the power of Williamson.

Intimations by Hoban that masons were often idle convinced the commissioners that it was time to put labor on a more economic footing. In late January an ally of Hoban's named Cornelius Mc-Dermott Roe submitted a proposal to do the stonework at a fixed price by the amount of stone actually laid. The commissioners took it under advisement. One indication of the deference paid to Hoban was that in February a stonemason from Norwich, England, named Dobson, "eminent in *monumental stone work*," came with a letter of introduction from a Baltimore merchant, who added that "he will not interfere with our friend Mr. Hoban's views."

Hoban's intrigues were not petty. Having a part in designing and building the two greatest buildings on the continent excited men's ambition. With not much more than a plan and a few cleared streets, L'Enfant had been able to walk away from the city. But with work actually begun and Morris and Greenleaf promising to invest heavily, even Thomas Johnson had second thoughts about leaving the commission. He had stayed on to finish with Blodget's lottery. Now obviously aching to cement the board's and his own relationship with Greenleaf, he stayed on because, as he told the president, he could think of no man as a replacement. (David Stuart, who had little ambition, told the president he still wanted to resign and thought finding a replacement would not be difficult.)[2]

*   *   *

Andrew Ellicott found renouncing any further part in building the Metropolis rather difficult. His ostensive reason for writing was to give the president the complete map of the district. So large and elaborate was this work that there was not paper large enough on which to print it. It would have to be specially made. That said, Ellicott added that he could only hope the map was "sufficiently correct," since his field notes had been "carried away from the office," and the commissioners had done nothing to help him retrieve them. For that reason, even though he was "one of those with whom the City of Washington may be said to have originated," he did not want his old job back. "No man's reputation can be safe when in the power of men" like the commissioners, who were incompetent to judge his professional work and offered him no redress to competent judges.

Ellicott did not descend to specifics. He was content with the martyr's lot. Time alone, he told the president, would reveal "the injustices which I have experienced." But he could not resist hinting of evil consequences ahead. Those injustices "will not only at some future period be manifest, but perhaps sap the foundation, and injure the whole business of the city in its infancy." All that said, Ellicott then praised his work: "I think it my duty for your own satisfaction to assure you that the accuracy of the work is infinitely superior to anything of the kind heretofore executed." But that superiority was in spite of the commissioners. Their meddling was so foul that Ellicott feared his successor would be unjustly charged "with ignorance and neglect" when he tried to carry on his work in the city.

Ellicott concluded his twists and turns by reminding the president that when he took the job in the federal city for the good of the union, he left other work that could have secured him "ease and independence." At that moment he was hoping to publish a map of the United States. Some respite from surveying would aid that endeavor. He had just heard that Tristram Dalton had resigned the office of treasurer to the mint, and he asked for the job, since "the business in the mint can[not] possibly require so much time as to preclude an attention of two or three hours every day to the completion of the map."

The president found the message of the letter quite clear. Ellicott's silence could be obtained in return for an appointment to another job. And Ellicott had the courtesy to enclose a sample of what he might have to publish. Back in June 1793, he, brother Benjamin, and Isaac Briggs wrote at length of their grievances against Dermott. Out of respect for the busy president, they had not sent it to him then, but at last it was time for the president to hear the whole sorry tale of Dermott's "want of veracity, gasconading cowardice, habitual drunkenness and disorderly conduct when intoxicated [which] had become proverbial in Georgetown."

The president sent the whole file down to the commissioners, not to elicit the commissioners' side of the story but merely to let them see "the temper of, and tendency of his views; and what may be expected from his representations to others." The bulk of the president's letter dealt with the more congenial topic of his purchase of lots in the city. The commissioners were unable to react so coolly. Smelling a newspaper war in the making, they sent a 21-page letter to the president much as if to give the general a chance to review their arsenal before they roared to counterattack "so many untruths artfully combined." In a nutshell, the commissioners told the president that they were confident that the accusations against Dermott were designed to excuse a mistake the Ellicotts and Briggs had made, which had thrown the survey off a few inches or many feet, depending on the area in question. Throughout the seemingly endless rounds of acrimony, Dermott had always been frank and cooperative, the Ellicotts and Briggs always secretive and "dodging." They assured the president that when the lines of parallel streets began diverging, they would know who to blame.[3]

*   *   *

In January a French engineer, James Blois, came to the city to make topographical maps for Greenleaf, who would pay Blois until the Frenchman proved that he was worthy of public employment. Greenleaf was so obliging that the commissioners took pains to oblige him. As they ended their January meeting, the commissioners reported, as usual, to the president and secretary of state. They also reported to Greenleaf. After recapping their latest efforts to corral the lottery, they let him know they were looking out for his interests. The commissioners agreed to hold twelve waterside lots for Greenleaf so two Baltimore merchants could not buy them.

This deference was not without an ulterior motive. The commissioners needed $16,000 in April to make the payments into the new Bank of Columbia that would make them charter members of the institution. Since Greenleaf and Morris were scheduled to pay them $68,000 on May 1, the commissioners wondered if he could not anticipate the sum and get the portion needed to them by April 10.

Between February and May Greenleaf's partners were just beginning a spree of land speculation unparalleled in its scope: 46,000 acres in Greenbrier and Montgomery counties, Virginia, for £1,153; 30,000 acres in Kentucky for £100 down; 20,555 more acres in Virginia bought from James Beckley, clerk of the House of Representatives for $5,151.59; another 30,000 acres in Montgomery County, Virginia, for $4,000; 79,015½ acres in western Pennsylvania for $13,161.25; 602,005 acres in Washington and Effington counties, Georgia, for $100,334; and 20,000 acres in Russell County, Virginia; 43,026 acres in Montgomery County, Kentucky; 79,015 acres in Kanawah County, Virginia; and 663,928 acres more in Georgia. In every deal the price was under 50 cents an acre and on easy terms. For example, for one tract of 761,020 acres each of the partners had to put down only $8,400. Greenleaf was not a silent partner in all the buying. He negotiated the deal with Beckley and even asked President Washington about his western lands.

Given that orgy of buying, Greenleaf did not begrudge the commissioners the advance they wanted. And Greenleaf expected to be in Washington on April 10. The board postponed the matter of the deeds until then and suggested that on his way from New York to Washington, Greenleaf confer with the secretary of state and president and finalize an agreement. Then when he got to the city he could join the commissioners in the big job they had before them: deciding which 6,000 lots should belong to Greenleaf and Morris. All parties already knew care had to be taken. The president himself worried that Greenleaf might take the lots on square 21 that he thought he had spoken for. The commissioners assured him that they had "not only his [Greenleaf's] promise, but his wish that we may dispose of the ground you may chuse let it be more or less. . . ."[4]

*   *   *

While the city eagerly anticipated the influx of Greenleaf and his money, not a few citizens worked up a frenzy that winter as Blodget proved a prophet. His slowly drawn lottery did become interesting. By late January the top prize, the $50,000 hotel, remained in the wheel. Seven-dollar tickets were selling for $12.50. The consortium holding most of the tickets boldly upped the resale price to $14. Two days later the ticket winning the hotel was drawn from the wheel. Georgetown felt cheated. The gentlemen holding ticket 37531 lived in Philadelphia.[5]

29. Candor and Sincerity

Not everyone understood what the spring of 1794 was to mean for the future metropolis. Captain Ignatius Fenwick had the audacity to direct his hands to sow corn on the lands he leased from Carroll of Duddington. The commissioners told him to stop so "that part of the city may be open to disclose its attractions to strangers" (Greenleaf was going to build near there). The only crop Fenwick could sow, they said, was oats, which would not "be productive of so great inconvenience." Corn was "certainly improper and injurious to the interest of the public and individuals."

James Simmons, Greenleaf's builder, had already made his beachhead on Notley Young's land on the point formed by the Eastern Branch and Potomac, just west of Fenwick's farm. Simmons had his men dig a cellar at 6th and N Streets Southwest and build a wharf into the Potomac as soon as the weather would permit. His was not the only activity in the city. Hoban was building Lear's warehouse on Rock Creek. Pierce Purcell, Hoban's partner, went back to Charleston, chartered a sloop, and brought back porter, brandy, and gin to sell at the tavern he was building just east of the president's house, to contrast it with Blodget's massive building, it would be called the Little Hotel. Thomas Johnson, Jr., the board's new secretary and no kin of the commissioners, bought a lot at 13th and G Streets Northwest for £100. Even George Walker was stirring northeast of the Capitol. He had returned from Europe with a contract to sell six squares to the Dutch banking house of Wilhem and Jan Willink. To serve his own mansion at Maryland Avenue and 6th Street Northeast and the lots the Dutch bought, Walker prodded the commissioners to get the road from Bladensburg to Walker's property in shape for carriages. And on the other side of the point, at the end of South Capitol Street, Lewis Deblois, a Boston merchant backed by John Nicholson, began building a wharf and store.[1]

But there was no doubt in anyone's mind that the center of building would be where Simmons had landed. Alarmed at Greenleaf's preference for the eastern half of the city, Stoddert wrote to the commissioners asking to see the "contract," they had made with Greenleaf, which he had heard reserved for the public "all Carrollsburg, half of Hamburg, and your choice of 150 squares." Stoddert wanted to counsel the commissioners on their choices so that another "company . . . possessing resources equal to that with which Greenleaf is connected" could participate equally in the "improvement of the city." Which is to say, Stoddert was desperate to find out what Greenleaf was up to and channel his money closer to Georgetown.

*   *   *

The board had reason to look for even more investors in the city. Their treasurer, Deakins, reported that the treasury was bare. Beginning February 1 the commissioners' bills were being paid at the sufferance of the Bank of Maryland in Baltimore. Notes totaling $18,000 had been honored by the bank but had to be reimbursed in sixty days. Assuming that monthly expenditures during the building season would be $10,000, Deakins estimated that the commissioners needed $82,000 to continue the work through November. He did not expect any money from Virginia, and none of the delinquent purchasers of lots had paid up. In response the commissioners asked Deakins, who was the cashier of the new Bank of Columbia, to arrange a loan for the city from the bank. They would get Stoddert's money — he was a major investor in the bank — from that channel, not from his "company," a tontine, which smacked so much of the scheming of Blodget.

They had reason to hope for some savings in labor costs. The commissioners signed a contract with McDermott Roe to proceed with the stonework at the Capitol on a piecework basis. Williamson's men, working for wages, would go back to the president's house. As for other work, the Federal Bridge still stood, but in case it should fall they had George French build a cheap wooden bridge across Rock Creek at M Street. They did not improve the road to that bridge yet, and they gave up work on the canal. Whelan found the going tougher than he had thought it would be and had to dig deeper than 12 feet. The commissioners agreed to pay him for the extra labor but did not hint at his actually turning the ditch he had dug between Tiber and James creeks into a working canal, which would have necessitated considerable work on the two creeks, not to mention protecting the portion dug from runoff, which would soon silt it up.

One job was almost done, and done well. The board was quite pleased with the two men doing the surveying. George Fenwick and Thomas Freeman were competent, and "if they should meet with unexpected difficulties we have no doubt but they will apprise us of such with candor and sincerity." Unfortunately, leveling the city was beyond them, and the man the board wanted for the job was unavailable — preparing for war, the War Department assigned Major Rivardi the task of supervising the construction fortifications to protect the harbors of Baltimore, Alexandria, and Norfolk. (Major L'Enfant got the job to fortify Philadelphia harbor. By mid-June shippers were complaining that L'Enfant's plans were too elaborate and would interfere with shipping.) So the commissioners asked John Vermonnet, who had been soliciting the job, to come up with a proposal for leveling the city. The commissioners were in no hurry. Putting the job off preserved their resources.

But obviously, with work about to begin on the president's house and Capitol again, the board would face heavy expenditures. They faced them with confidence. Greenleaf would soon be at their side.[2]

* * *

Greenleaf began the building season in Philadelphia, getting excused from having to return to Amsterdam to take up his duties as consul. He did not want to resign because without that office all his property in Holland would be taxed at two percent. He suggested that Sylvanus Bourne be appointed vice consul to act in his absence, and that is what the administration did. Greenleaf also got administration approval for his plan to get deeds to Washington lots. With Greenleaf expressing interest in buying his western land, the president looked kindly on the speculator. The president offered to sell Greenleaf 9,744 acres along the Ohio and 23,216 acres along the

Kanawha for £32,960, or £1 an acre. Tutored by Morris and Nicholson, Greenleaf was expecting to buy western lands for about three
shillings an acre, but there's no evidence that he was fool enough to
blurt that out to Washington. Instead, he strung the president along.
Greenleaf also bought one of the Carrollsburg lots that Thomas
Johnson had been buying up. He paid Johnson £150.

At its April meeting, held at Greenleaf's convenience, the board
gave Greenleaf what he wanted. Even Stoddert decided to try to
work with Greenleaf, coming up with a public-spirited competition.
He and other proprietors would build twenty houses between Rock
Creek and the president's house from the bridge along the post road
and Pennsylvania Avenue, if Greenleaf also built twenty houses
there. Greenleaf was game, provided he had to build only ten houses
that year. Stoddert replied that all the houses should be built that
year, but since not enough clay had been dug, he agreed with
Greenleaf and asked for the aid of his brick machines, "which I am
happy to hear are likely to succeed soon." Stoddert thereupon
made a contract with a local builder, John Henderson, to build six
houses on Pennsylvania Avenue between 21st and 22nd Streets.

Greenleaf began lining up contractors, knowing well that Simmons could not build the houses he was now obligated to build:
twenty to fulfill the agreement with the commissioners, twenty in
two years to fulfill the contract with Carroll, and ten more that year
to fulfill the gentlemen's agreement with Stoddert. On May 8 he
contracted with William Lovering, who had just come to Philadelphia from London, to build ten houses. Lovering was to hire
workmen, get materials, and receive an eight percent commission
on the cost of the buildings. On May 16 Greenleaf contracted with
Joseph Clark of Annapolis, the freemason who had given the speech
at the cornerstone ceremonies at the Capitol, to build twelve houses
for the same commission. At first the builders were to concentrate
their work at the point. He also found a man to take care of the
quarries the commissioners wanted developed. William O'Neale,
then working in Pennsylvania, agreed to go down and work the
quarry in the city and the one on Mount Vernon for $60 a month
from Greenleaf, plus expenses and the pay for three to six workmen.[3]

* * *

On the heels of Greenleaf came Blodget, not with, as promised, a complete accounting of lottery prizes paid. Blodget lamely explained that he could not bring redeemed tickets for fear that, as the commissioners later recalled, "their edges might be fretted, which would prevent an accurate comparison if forged tickets were produced." Back in January he had assured the commissioners that he had already paid out $40,000 in prizes. That April he assured the commissioners that he had paid out $45,000 or $50,000, but, of course, he had no proof and had another $100,000 to pay.

The best the exasperated commissioners could do was to extract a promise from Blodget to submit his transactions to auditors the commissioners would name and to provide more security if those auditors deemed it necessary. The commissioners enlisted George Taylor, a State Department clerk, and Richard Harrison, a Treasury auditor. They begged them to be tough, enlist the aid of the president if needed, and institute a suit in federal court. Above all they were "not to permit any evasion to permit [the audit] from being completed as soon as may be and to advise us of the state of things by every post for this cursed business lies very heavy on our minds."[4]

* * *

There was enough life in the city to attract a priest and two more doctors. Reverend Anthony Caffry bought two lots at 9th and F Streets Northwest at a special price, £40 a lot, on condition that he build a church. When the carpenters finished building temporary wooden shacks for workers, they built a hospital for the sick slaves and other laborers on Judiciary Square. The doctors, Cornelius Coningham and John Crocker, both solicited the job Dr. Worthington had had for the past two years, caring for sick workers. The commissioners decided to open bids for the job, asking all three what they would charge for one year caring for forty-six "Negroes and such white men as we have generally paid the doctor for attending." Worthington offered to do it for what he had gotten before, 20 guineas. Coningham, who was also thinking of building a brewery along the Potomac near Georgetown, asked the commissioners to set the price but wanted surgery paid for separately. Crocker was just so glad to be a doctor in the Metropolis of the future that "small compensation" would do. Always mindful of saving money, the commissioners gave the job to Crocker for £25 a year, a savings of about £17.[5]

30. They Go Spread Disaffection

Taylor and Harrison immediately got into the spirit of the chase. They banged on Blodget's door and found he was not there. They treated the lottery-weary commissioners with rumors that prizes were being paid in tickets in the new lottery, some prizes were being paid "with cash at a discount," and Blodget had gone into hiding. Harrison warned the commissioners to be sure that if they did not physically possess the insurance company stocks held as security, they take measures "to prevent a transfer of them." But soon enough Blodget arrived and charmed the two bureaucrats. He had two clerks making out lists of prizes paid. He welcomed an examination of the tickets and he promised to come up with whatever additional security was needed. "He has promised and is apparently anxious," Harrison wrote to Commissioner Carroll, "to have the business adjusted as speedily as possible."

Then, on May 9, the new ad for the second lottery made its first appearance in a Baltimore newspaper. The commissioners saw red because by omitting one word Johnson had asked to be included, the ad implied that the commissioners did have something to do with the second lottery. "There is no fixing him," the commissioners lamented to Randolph, and they foresaw the endless horror: lottery number two and then "another and another." They wanted to assure the public that they "have given no countenance to the publishing or carrying on this lottery nor will have any thing to do with the conduct of it." And they suggested the lottery did not "comport with the laws of the state."

Having just received $45,000 more in security from Blodget, Harrison and Taylor and even Randolph thought such a disclaimer too harsh, especially after Blodget agreed to print a letter assuring the public that the lottery was undertaken at his "own private risque" and that the commissioners had nothing to do with it. That counsel came too late. The anxious commissioners had their disclaimer printed in Maryland newspapers.[1]

*   *   *

If the commissioners could not fix Blodget, nor could the masons fix the commissioners. As McDermott Roe's men began doing piecework at the Capitol, Williamson's masons calculated that rather than representing a savings, the pieceworkers were getting paid more for an equivalent amount of work. So they petitioned the commissioners for higher wages. For his part, Williamson was just as upset as his workers, not at the pay but at someone else interfering with his masons. He made verbal protests to Johnson and made it clear that unless the situation was cleared up to his satisfaction, he would quit.

The judge was not the man to smooth tensions. So on the next day, May 7, Commissioner Carroll wrote a soothing letter to Williamson inviting him to bring his grievances to the next board meeting, on May 17. The board asked Williamson to supervise McDermott Roe's masons, but they gave short shrift to Williamson's men: there would be no raise, and "we have not the smallest apprehension but your places will be immediately filled." Indeed, Hoban began telling masons who would not switch to piecework to pack up and leave, which they did. Williamson blamed "the papists" Hoban and Carroll for trying to open the way for "a passel of Irish papists."

As masons packed up their tools and families and left the city, the proprietors looked on with alarm. Stoddert wrote in horror to Carroll, the commissioner whose plantation was closest to the city, that fifteen masons "have already gone off in very great disgust, . . . and twenty some odd more are going. These men where ever they go spread disaffection to the city among the mechanics, & it will be found very difficult if not impossible to get tradesmen to carry on the business. The tradesmen who arrived at Norfolk, destined for the city, have stopped on their way, some at Alexandria & some at other places. Some who had come to the city have gone back. Those men who went off a few days ago, have already published in the Baltimore paper, a warning to tradesmen, how they came to the city, where they represent the usage as very bad. The report of such men will have more effect upon the minds of mechanics than every thing that can be said in contradiction from authority the most respectable."

To save the day, Stoddert tried to take matters into his own hands. He found that while all the grousing was going on at the Capitol, only four masons were working at the president's house. He checked with Williamson, who allowed that there was work to be done there, but he would not rehire masons without authority. What angered Williamson was that despite the board's ruling, Roe's men would not follow his orders, and if he tried to discipline a man, he simply rejoined McDermott Roe's crew. Moreover, as a way of economizing, piecework was a failure. The masons getting wages earned £16 a month; the pieceworkers got £17. The whole discreditable affair cried out for investigation by the commissioners, whom Williamson viewed as akin to a court of law.

The commissioners made it clear to Williamson that their sympathies were with Hoban and McDermott Roe. They were happy to hear his complaints but they made him aware of what those gentlemen had been going through: "We are well informed that there are several of those who were at work at the Capitol who have issued threats against Mr. Hoban and Dermott Roe, and that the latter has been for his own safety compelled to take out warrants against them." All of this was happening during the formation of the so-called Jacobin Clubs, which the forces of order feared wanted, at best, to involve the nation in the French war against England and, at worst, to bring the principles of the bloody French Revolution to America. Farmers in western Pennsylvania were mounting protests against excise taxes, which officials would soon label a rebellion. So the three conservative commissioners were eager to do their part to enforce order. They told Williamson, "We can never countenance a riotous and disorderly conduct."

The times were such as to fortify their resolve, but the real strength of the commissioners' position was demonstrated by another letter they received during their June 7 meeting. After attacking McDermott Roe for shoddy workmanship and attacking Hoban for dismissing hands who did not accept the piecework arrangement, four masons offered to do the work on a piecework basis for slightly more than half the price. The commissioners promptly directed Williamson to make a contract, provided the masons had not been riotous or disorderly. The commissioners, however, paid no heed to the masons' warning that "McDermot Roe's [work] is totally unfit for such a building, and must be undone or the House [the Capitol] will be ruined." They kept him and his men on the job.

Hoban began to take some pains to discredit Williamson, reporting that scows sent to Aquia to bring up stone found none to pick up. The masons who switched to piecework at a lower rate complained that they had no stone. The board summoned Williamson and asked him to "urge more vigourous exertions from the hands" at the quarries. Williamson had little control over Aquia, where thirty-five quarriers were on the roles but absenteeism was such that fifteen of them missed more than ten days' work in July.[2]

*   *   *

In trying to decide which masons were working more economically, the board asked Hallet to help. The French architect was still working on drawings and models of the Capitol and was mindful of his next task, supervising the construction of the building. He too wanted Williamson out of the way. He came up with a figure that Williamson thought impossibly low for his wage workers. The Scot retaliated by casting doubt on the plans Hallet was drawing up. Hallet would tell masons what to do but would not show them the plans. The commissioners were curious about what Hallet had been doing and asked for copies of his plans. That was on June 7. On the 23rd Hallet deigned to discuss the design with the commissioners. Did they agree that the first story should be one foot higher? Did they like the idea of two cellars for the east side of the building? The commissioners merely reiterated their desire to see the plans and a list of materials needed.

Unlike L'Enfant, Hallet did not let matters fester. He told the commissioners that he thought of himself as the principal designer of the building and principal supervisor of the work. The next day, June 26, the commissioners responded in writing. He had no authority, they told Hallet, to change Thornton's design without their and the president's permission. As for supervising the work, that was Hoban's job, and they reminded Hallet that they had told him last fall to communicate with and take direction from Hoban.

Hallet replied on the 28th, letting the cat out of the bag. As he made models and drawings and tried to get his revision of Thornton's design to work, he did not think he was endeavoring to save Thornton's design. "In the alterations," he wrote the commissioners, "I never thought of introducing in it any thing belonging to Dr. Thornton's exhibitions. So I claim the original invention of the plan now executing and beg leave to lay hereafter before you and the President the proofs of my right to it."

The commissioners acted swiftly. They sent Williamson and a witness over to Hallet's house on Capitol Hill demanding "several drafts and essays of drafts of the divers parts of the Capitol on distinct sheets or pieces of paper numbered from 1 to 15 inclusive. . . ." Hallet allowed that he had those drafts and refused to hand them over. In response, the commissioners fired him and asked him to vacate the house on Capitol Hill. They also wrote to Philip Key, a noted Maryland lawyer just setting up shop in Georgetown, asking him to institute a suit in the county court to force Hallet to deliver the plans. They warned Key that "we expect he will run out all process before he will give up the papers."[3]

*   *   *

Joseph Hodgson, who aimed to make hats, came to see the lot he had bought on that rainy auction day in 1791. Dermott took him to it and informed him that according to the records in the surveyors' office the lot never belonged to the commissioners. What was worse, Hodgson found it in "a low sunken situation." He had been assured "by a person who I was told was Major De L'Enfant, that it was in a good situation."

The commissioners could take some comfort that more important newcomers noticed nothing amiss. Former senator Tristram Dalton, who came to the city to join his new partner, Tobias Lear, and his daughter, who was married to Lewis Deblois, found the city "more than equal" to his expectations which had been built up by the descriptions of the president and Greenleaf.

With stone short, the symbols of activity that spring were the brick kilns that were sprouting up all over the city, even before the brick machine got into gear. And it was thanks to Blodget that bricks were in thick supply. Patrick Kale, whom Blodget sent to handle the brick making, was proving to be a gem. "There is at present as many bricks made as will finish the principal story of the President's house, and six kilns more will complete the business," Hoban reported, "and from the management in that department I hope the six kilns will be burned early this fall."[4]

*   *   *

Blodget took exception with how the board took exception to his second lottery and in June published a letter reminding people not to send their letters inquiring about the lottery to the commissioners. All the commissioners were doing was handling the security for the lottery, if they had not already transferred it to the Bank of Columbia. Of course the commissioners would advise on where the elegant houses to be given as prizes were to be built, and they would set up an account for the money going to the national university.

When the commissioners read the ad they were flabbergasted. They had received no letters inquiring about lottery business, and they had seen no security for the second lottery, not to mention any money for the national university, which they promptly explained in a letter to the Philadelphia *Gazette* to which they coupled their May disclaimer. And they lamented the announcement of a third lottery that had appeared in an insert to the *Gazette*. The newspaper war was on.

Blodget suggested that much of the confusion arose because two commissioners were resigning and thus loath to get involved with a second lottery. He claimed that he had "requested them to transfer securities to the Bank of Columbia" consisting of 1,000 lots in the city of Washington and $40,000 in other property. As for the suggestion that he had no authority from the commissioners for the lotteries, he invited the public to see "original letters, in my possession."

Two days later, Blodget placed another letter in the *Gazette* in which he made public those letters from the commissioners. He began by making clear that Johnson was the object of his scorn: "Whatever unworthy motive may have misled Messrs. Johnson and Co. to the wanton attack on my plan for improving the Federal City . . . ," Blodget wanted the truth out. He recalled the letters the commissioners wrote to him in January 1793 after an express from Annapolis had assured them that the lottery was not contrary to Maryland law. Commissioner Carroll had noted that "the important effect from this, as well as for future lotteries may be evident." Then Blodget recalled that he had first advertised the second lottery in May 1793 to get around the new Maryland law that regulated lotteries begun after June 1793. The commissioners were aware, said Blodget, that he had sold tickets to that lottery before June to get around the new law. And then, in January 1794, Johnson himself wrote the ad for the lottery. Blodget rued that "he has so soon forgot a child of his own."

He had no trouble with the commissioners, Blodget continued, until the sale to Greenleaf. The commissioners ignored his and other proprietors' objections to the sale. He resigned in disgust, but the importuning of "some respectable proprietors" induced him to continue to "act as an occasional agent" for the city. He quoted from the January 27 letter from the commissioners giving their sentiments in favor of the second lottery. In addition, Johnson drew up the bond and mortgage for the security. Therefore, Blodget asked in so many words, what was the problem? Did Johnson doubt his own legal acumen? If the commissioners did not want to hold the security, Stoddert, the president of the Bank of Columbia, would. At the end of the letter there was some good news for the commissioners. Blodget denied that there were any plans for a third lottery.[5]

*   *   *

On his way home to Mount Vernon, the president made an inspection tour, not of the city, but of the locks and canal at Little Falls, which was the problem spot. That link in Potomac navigation was at first to have been completed in the fall of 1792, then the spring of 1793. Floods and shoddy materials had put back the work. Harbaugh had been called in to replace timber with stone. Finally all the pieces were in place but the puzzle was not solved. The president was unable to offer any advice. On his way there his horse "blundered and continued blundering until by violent exertions on my part, to save him and myself from falling among the rocks, I got such a wrench in my back, as to prevent me from mounting a horse without pain."

When the recuperating president turned his attention to the city, two things were on his mind. He wanted more land on Peter's Hill; indeed, he told the commissioners he wanted "the *whole* square, that I might have space enough for my plan" of building. And he wanted Johnson to remain a commissioner. He had heard from Greenleaf that Johnson planned to move to the city. If that were the case, why not become both commissioner and superintendent, with a commensurate salary. The other two commissioners could receive less and convene only when needed.

Johnson was flattered and proud of what he had accomplished. The commissioners had just closed the books on satisfying any claims the lotholders of Carrollsburg and Hamburg might have on the new city. And he had just worked through a long negotiation with three Georgetowners, Deakins, Casanave, and Thomas Sims Lee, who claimed the land formed by the Rock Creek causeway. Johnson sold them the public's claim to the land for £5,000. "I have the satisfaction that we have had fewer disputes on them than might have been expected under all circumstances," he told the president, but he was weary of the job: "I do not know of any event which would induce me to stand the mark of calumny and gross abuse as I have alone for near three years past."[6]

31. No Lands . . . at Any Price

The Columbian Society met on May 27 in Philadelphia to elect Morris its president and Greenleaf's assistant Appleton its secretary, and to put some prominent land speculators on the board. Not a few held stock in the society because that was all Morris could pay them with for the time being. At the same time, Morris was offering Washington lots for $300 each with the condition that if after five years the buyer was not satisfied, Morris would buy each lot back for $400, plus five percent interest. A month later he had to withdraw the offer because it violated state usury laws.

That spirited activity to get cash arose because no word had yet come from Sylvanus Bourne who they had sent to Amsterdam to get a loan. To support their continuing purchases of backlands, Morris and Nicholson (who survived impeachment) needed money. They were unable to pay their share of the $68,000 installment to the commissioners that had been due May 1. Greenleaf authorized them to write checks on his account, which would be covered by the money Bourne had undoubtedly raised.[1]

While Greenleaf bolstered the courage of Morris and Nicholson, Appleton pressed on to the city, where he found the brick machine famous. "The constant crowd of spectators makes it necessary to erect a fence," he reported to Greenleaf on June 23. But the machine still did not work. Greenleaf had already hired James

Macomb of New York for $1,250 a year to go to Washington and improve and run the machine and undertake "other mechanical operations."

Bricks were not needed yet. The first houses built on Greenleaf's account, designed to house workers, were made of wood. These included an 18-by-30-foot edifice suitable only for slaves, made by nailing planks to stumps left in the ground. Carpenters built three large tenements, one as big as 57 by 24 feet, several modest houses of 450 to 500 square feet, and several two-room shacks of less than 200 square feet. Three houses had adjoining kitchens. Lovering's men built a carpenters' workshop, 72 by 20 feet, with adjoining sheds and a sawpit in the middle of 4½ Street SW, (actually this was the fourth street west of South Capitol Street, but since after it crossed Pennsylvania Avenue it ran into Judiciary Square bisecting the block between 4th and 5th Streets, it was called 4½ Street). With the workshops in the street, when the elegant brick buildings went up nearby and the street was opened, the workshops would have to come down.

When Greenleaf arrived in the beginning of July he found Simmons's brick house at 6th and N Streets Southwest rising and the wharf finished. Lovering had begun a group of three brick houses between 6th and 4½ Streets fronting south on N Street, and he planned four more on that street. All the houses, including Simmons's, were 30 feet wide, 40 feet deep, and three stories tall. Clark had taken longer to get going, having arrived in June with his family and the boosterism expected of the state's top Freemason. He joined Leonard Harbaugh to form the Architects and Carpenters Society of the Territory of Columbia, which planned a special meeting and celebration at Semmes's tavern in Georgetown on the Fourth of July. At the end of June, Appleton had marked out eight houses for Clark to build facing north on N Street between 4½ and 3rd Streets. Greenleaf, however, decided to spread the houses out because, as Appleton later explained, "if the houses had been all in one street, reports would have said, the city makes no progress." Foundations were dug for four houses on P Street and four on the west side of 4½ Street between N and O Streets.

Telling the contractors what to do was not Appleton's only worry. The land Greenleaf had bought from Notley Young and the commissioners had seven tenant farmers. Greenleaf instructed Appleton to give them two-year leases on condition that they "would attend to horticulture," sow grass seed where possible, raise no tobacco, and "raise barley, oats and rye instead of Indian corn." Corn already sown was allowed to be harvested. The seeds for the garden, grass, and new crops would be provided gratis. Appleton, however, took an instant dislike to the tenants. Doubting that they would have any knack at horticulture, he gave them only one-year leases. Only in the case of a Mrs. King did he have a little heart, offering to take butter and garden vegetables in lieu of $30 rent, for which she used to give 1,000 pounds of tobacco. She had a son and daughter who were both deaf.

Although they labored far from the public buildings, Greenleaf's men could look across James Creek and see Deblois's crew building a wharf and store five would-be blocks away. Deblois brought a crew of men from Boston that included a blacksmith, painter, baker, and carpenters. They had not progressed as much as Simmons and Lovering had. Deblois complained of a "tedious spell of rainy weather which has prevented our doing any thing to speak of."[2]

*   *   *

James Blois, the Frenchman Greenleaf had sent to the city back in January, had a disturbing report. He looked at the hills and the slope and width of the streets and saw a disaster in the making. The city needed a drainage system to save it from becoming a swamp or sea of mud, but none was in place or planned.

Greenleaf brought the matter immediately to the attention of the nearest commissioner, Daniel Carroll. The problem was not unfamiliar to the commissioners. They had one man about to report on it and still were encouraging Major Rivardi to come and level the city; but Carroll probably had to admit that the commissioners hoped the whole problem of drainage could be managed without spending any money. When Stoddert had asked about the level of Pennsylvania Avenue where Henderson was to build six houses, the board told him not to worry since any water forming there would drain easily into the hollow just north of the avenue. Greenleaf was so insistent about the problem that Carroll sent expresses to Johnson and Stuart summoning them to a Fourth of July meeting to discuss drainage with Greenleaf and Blois.

Any written report Blois made is lost. John Vermonnet, the man the commissioners had studying the problem, tried to rise to the occasion and submitted his report on July 5. The only thing definite in it was the price to be paid to Vermonnet, £4,000. For the rest Vermonnet offered some general strictures that indicated nothing more than that he had some grasp of the effects of gravity on water. The commissioners declined his services.

Uncertain of the cost or who could do it, the commissioners did not budge from their position that they could not afford drains. They sympathized but argued priorities: "You cannot be more strongly impressed than we are," they wrote to Greenleaf on the 10th, "with the utility and propriety of early entering on large drains judiciously laid out and strongly secured. The comfort, health, and lives of many depend on the cleanliness of the city and purity of the water besides many subordinate advantages. But set to build a city without funds what can we do? We are obliged to rank things according to their necessity and after ranging them to examine every step of our progress for fear of falling—we are too poor to enter on a work of this magnitude and expense."

In reporting on the problem to the president, they doubted that they had the legal power to use public funds to build drains. The commissioners did go so far as to allow builders to dig drainage ditches in front of houses, up to five feet wide, without the approval of the board, provided they were lined with stone within a year.

Blois also pointed out the need for bridges over Tiber and James creeks at 7th and at N Streets, respectively, to connect Greenleaf's lots to the rest of the city. Greenleaf offered to foot the bill if the commissioners' workers did the job. The commissioners promptly instructed Williams to get to work on the N Street bridge. The road from Greenleaf's wharf to the Tiber bridge presented some difficulty. Although the land was high enough and "dry," there was "a very bad place near Goose Creek which will cause great expense."

As reward for Blois's labor, Greenleaf also got the commissioners to promise him a job. The commissioners allowed that Blois's topographical maps of the area were the best they had seen, but for the moment they felt they had no money to spare during the building season.[3]

*   *   *

Greenleaf turned his attention to deeds. He decided the only way to get all of the deeds he needed was to make the commissioners partners in the loan Bourne was negotiating in Amsterdam. This time the board leapt at the chance to get an infusion of a little over $250,000, which Greenleaf expected in a matter of days. The board of course had to get the approval of the president and required ample security to be placed in the hands of the secretary of the Treasury. The commissioners informed the president that "the effects of expending 300,000 pounds on public and private buildings in the city must be so certain and extensive that our motives cannot be mistaken." They naively assumed the full amount of the loan would be spent on the city whose lots secured it.

Finally Greenleaf turned his attention to lots. With the original holders of Carrollsburg placated, the commissioners had a number of lots in that area just east of where Greenleaf was building. He offered to buy fifty-nine. The commissioners agreed to sell thirty-one for £100 each, deeming "the property of too much value to extend the sales further."

Greenleaf pondered the offer and turned his attention to Rock Creek. Stoddert and Johnson led him by the hand. Stoddert decided that the better way to get Greenleaf to build near Georgetown was to give him full control of squares just as Young had done. Then he would not have to wait for the laborious process of dividing squares into lots to see which were his. Stoddert and his partner Forrest offered to sell Greenleaf 34 acres in the city, or most of the area through which Pennsylvania Avenue passed, save for six lots they had already sold to others. They wanted £35 sterling for every 5,265 feet, the size of the standard lot. A pound sterling was worth about $4.65 so that was $161 a lot, twice what Greenleaf had paid the commissioners, but Stoddert agreed to be paid in checks payable in London, two thirds in twelve months and the rest in eighteen months. Finally Greenleaf would take over Henderson's contract for the six buildings and agree to build five more. Greenleaf made the deal.

Johnson's interest in the area was more limited. He fancied the lots along Rock Creek just above the Federal Bridge. Greenleaf picked the square Johnson wanted as his own and then gave the commissioner a letter pledging to hold the property "subject to your disposition." Johnson could have bought the lots from the commissioners, but Greenleaf gave a better price and easier terms.

Greenleaf achieved his goal of forming a virtual monopoly in city lots. James Lingan informed Standish Forde, who was still trying to buy more lots in the city, that he knew of "no lands . . . in the city that can be purchased at any price."[4]

*   *   *

For all he had accomplished in his July visit, it is likely that Greenleaf was not the talk of the town. He had to compete with the formation of a horse brigade, a slave auction, a court decision in a ten-year-old land case, and with the ongoing newspaper war between Blodget and the commissioners. Of course a slave auction in itself was unexceptional in a Southern community, but Edward Burrows was probably the first to sell human flesh in the federal city. He chose to do it "near the Hotel" and offered three males aged ten, thirteen, and nineteen; a mother with son and daughter; and three females aged twelve, fifteen, and seventeen.

The decision in Burnes's suit against Dick Goosequill, the tenant of Carroll of Duddington whom Burnes had ejected, reverberated in a community so obsessed with landownership. Burnes won the suit and maintained his hold on the eastern line of his property. Although Carroll of Duddington's forebears had been in the area since the late seventeenth century, they had returned a portion of their tract to the state, deeming it waste and unproductive and thus not worth paying taxes on. It was that land that Burnes's father added to his farm, and no resurvey by Carroll could take it away from Burnes's son. Damages won from the court, 25,849 pounds of tobacco, were not that important. The possession of such valuable land was. Among proprietors Burnes's good fortune inspired speculation on other possible suits. Stoddert sparred with Samuel Davidson over the line between their property. Probably in jest, Stoddert threatened to "take the President's house" from Davidson on the basis of an old Pearce will. And literally within hours angry letters began passing between the two.

Though nothing came of the wrangling, the style of counterattack employed by Davidson deserves rehearing. He wrote Stoddert on July 25: "Late last evening, I received a note as coming from you—which if from any other character I should consider it scurrilous, illiberal and unfounded; but being for some years past in the habit of reading and judging you reverse to what you write or say on general topics, I have reason to be well satisfied with this mark of your politeness to and friendship for me; I am only surprised, . . . that you did not introduce the words fool, blockhead, ass, terms to which you are prone, and which would render your polite note complete. . . ."[5]

Of course that was a private correspondence, but in *Commissioners v. Blodget,* newspaper readers had a ringside seat and awaited the commissioners' reply to Blodget's two letters attacking them. On July 11 the commissioners gave their recollection of events and warned Blodget, "If you are determined to go through with No. 2, we advise you to pay up or lodge in some bank to the amount of all prizes for which you are chargeable including the Hotel, which is at a stand for want of money to carry it on. . . ." They defended their deal with Greenleaf. Recalling that Blodget had been sometimes for, sometimes against it, they insisted all now saw its wisdom: "for there are we believe more than 800 mechanics and labourers employed on public and private account in improving the city and if the contract had not been made, our operations would have been languid indeed."

In conclusion, they mocked Blodget's contention that he had resigned in disgust, recalling how he begged them to soften the letter of dismissal so it "might do you as little injury as might be." They scorned his protestations of "zeal in the interest of the city" and added that they never had any expectation, contrary to his claim, of calling on him for further services.

A few days later, July 22, Blodget published his rebuttal in the *Philadelphia Gazette.* It actually seemed to clear up the mystery about the security for the second lottery. Since the first lottery was paid off, Blodget expected the security held for that to serve as security for number two. And the lottery was virtually paid off. His ads begging ticketholders to come forward attested to his eagerness to complete the payment. As for the unfinished hotel, "no one can have real cause to complain of any momentary delay. . . ."

The dispute had gone too far to let his reply rest with merely clearing up what might have been a genuine misunderstanding. Blodget ridiculed the commissioners, going so far as to suggest that the commissioners did not transfer the security as an excuse for clinging to their jobs: "I am told your retaining those securities from the bank is a mere pretext to remain in office after you have so often promised to resign."

He defended his record as sales agent for the city by printing their letter asking him not to sell any lot for less than £50 and pointedly asking them why they did not follow that rule. He suggested that that was why they tried to keep the particulars of their major sales secret. Finally, he promised to be in Washington soon and ask more questions about their sales.

The commissioners drew up a reply, making it short (their expert in adversarial relations, Johnson, had to go home to tend to his sick wife). Then Greenleaf wrote to them from Philadelphia that no reply was needed: "The last publication of Mr. Blodget has made the kind of impression that it deserved, & has in a great measure deprived him of the suffrages of the very few who thought well of him, and as he has really sunk to a degree of insignificancy far beneath your notice, I sincerely hope that you will allow yourselves to suffer no further anxiety on account of any thing that relates to him."

Unsaid was that continuing the controversy might allow Blodget to continue attacking the deal with Greenleaf.[6]

*   *   *

The president was kept apprised of the commissioners' busy July. News of the loan through Greenleaf and the battle with Blodget did not merit comment. What bothered him was the drains. He thought the commissioners had the power to make them and that they were needed. If funds could be had they should be made. Greenleaf told the secretary of state that he would "construct them at his own expense and for his own profit." Randolph looked askance at that and warned the commissioners to provide for the public taking the drains, "upon paying the principal money expended."

Randolph did raise a legal question about the loan from Holland: under the laws of Maryland, could the legal title of the public lots given to Greenleaf for the mortgage be transferred without notice being given to the commissioners? By way of apology for asking the question, Randolph hastened to add that "no question can be entertained of the integrity and honor of the gentlemen with whom you have contracted." The legal query went to Judge Johnson, who agreed that Randolph had a point, and if that point was not made moot by the expected news from Holland that the loan was completed, the agreement should be amended.

About the time Johnson wrote that, news arrived from Amsterdam. The loan had "in part succeeded. . . ."[7]

32. Elbow Room Indeed!

The president left Philadelphia for Germantown on July 30 to "avoid the heat." Once again, the commissioners convened at the beginning of the sickly season to authorize more spirits for the hands. On August 4 the commissary at the Aquia quarry bought 31 gallons of whiskey for the thirty-five men working there. Then there was the problem of getting the stone from the quarries to the city. Earlier in the season William Smith, whose boats brought the stone up, rebelled at being paid by the load. The commissioners tentatively agreed to pay him $4 a ton and advertised for bids to do the job by the load. Three weeks passed, and they had to give the contract to Smith for $4 a ton.

And once the stone reached the city, at a wharf either on the Tiber below the president's house or on the Eastern Branch below the site of the Capitol, not enough of it got to the masons. It took six slaves two days to unload one "shallop load." And then it took eight slaves three days to put that load on the drags. No one has left a record of how long it took for horses to pull the stone to the work sites. The slaves used to move the stone had to be taken off other work. The commissioners directed Williams "to keep the yearly hirelings at work, from sunrise to sunset, particularly the negroes." Exertions paid off to the extent that the first story of the president's house was completed that August, "all stone in and out, four feet below ground and 12 feet above it."[1]

With the commissioners having trouble finding building materials, the men from Massachusetts brought their own. In a valley still largely covered by trees, there was no lumber available. And in a state, Maryland, that led the nation in the production of iron, there were no nails, though two nail factories were being built in the area. As Tristram Dalton traveled home to Newburyport to get his family ready for the move south, he tried to arrange to send nails but could not find any ship in Philadelphia bound for the Potomac. He shipped 240 tons of New England timber to the city to be used to build wharves for both Deblois and Lear. Using that timber and the Massachusetts men Deblois had brought down with him, Dalton calculated, would save plenty. "Perhaps we shall never be able to build it on better terms," he told Greenleaf. Appleton waited for supplies of lumber, iron, mahogany, saws, and two cambooses, or open-air cooking ovens, to arrive from New York. To solve the problem of his workers' spirits he bought a two thirds share of Coningham's brewery for $2,700. The brewery on the Potomac shore southwest of the president's house could also distill whiskey, make vinegar, and raise hogs for bacon on the waste.[2]

*   *   *

Sylvanus Bourne was the first to get an inkling that all was not to go the way Greenleaf planned. Bourne did get the firm of Daniel

Crommelin and Sons to offer a loan, which was not surprising since they had made quite a bit of money fueling Greenleaf with $1.3 million for speculations on the American debt. However, Bourne had to settle for six percent interest instead of the five percent Greenleaf expected. The other bank charges were no bargain either: two percent douceur, a half percent brokerage, two and a half percent commission, and two and a half percent commission on the interest paid. Also, Dutch loan brokers and other Dutch bankers refused to buy a share of the loan. The loan had to be filled by subscriptions on the part of the individual Dutch investors. The success of the loan, the banker attested to Bourne, was "utterly uncertain."

Greenleaf had forewarned Bourne to expect the six banking houses that Cazenove represented not to buy up the loan because one of them, Stadnitski, had been disappointed in an attempt to speculate in the city in 1792. Indeed, Cazenove had kept up a running stream of disdainful comments on Greenleaf's speculations, and Stadnitski had been rebuffed in an attempt to buy Potomac Company stock in March 1792.

But the fundamental problem was that it was not a good time to raise money in Holland. Bankers tried to lower the expectations of those looking for money by describing the "dullness for all sorts of loans here" and "the present critical situation of the politics in Europe." The situation was the war between France and England, with Holland right in the middle. The Dutch government sided with the English, but much of the Dutch mercantile community, including the bankers handling loans for the United States, were for the French. Of course sentiment did not cloud the eyes of bankers looking for the best deal, and the huge loans being negotiated by the Russian czar drove up interest rates and required "enormous premiums or douceurs" from anyone who wanted a loan. Despite the tight market, Willink and Van Staphorst managed to fill a subscription for a loan to the U.S. government in early 1794. They attributed the success of the loan to the fact that the war front had reached the Dutch frontier, alerting everyone to "the great superiority of credit the bonds of the United States merit over those of every European state." In his May 9 letter to Greenleaf, Bourne did not intimate that the war would affect subscriptions to the loan one way or the other. (Save for what appears to be a Freudian slip in a postscript: Bourne recommended that Greenleaf send a model transfer form for reconveying mortgaged lots "in case the war is not finished," when he meant to say, in case the loan is not finished.)

Bourne's letter was not upbeat. He wrote it the day after the loan was publicly announced and subscriptions to it opened, so he had no hard figures to report. All he could say was that "favorable sentiments of it appear but we can say nothing certain of it at present." That said, he recommended that Greenleaf separate the deeds of the 3,000 lots into three separate deeds of 1,000 each "so that in case the whole loan should not be effected, an immediate retransfer to you can take place."[3]

That letter reached Greenleaf on July 25, just after he left Washington. On the next day, Greenleaf wrote to the commissioners informing them of the six percent interest, which he blamed on "the opposition made by the employers of Mr. Cazenove who were disappointed in their speculation in the city." That was not the explanation Bourne gave. Nor did Greenleaf betray any of Bourne's pessimism, writing instead "that the loan had in part succeeded and promised fair for the residue."

To some of his partners Greenleaf maintained the pose of assurance. Dalton replied to a letter, now lost: "I congratulate you on the success of your loan in Amsterdam. Elbow room indeed! May you be ever fortunate in all your concerns." To his partners in what was rapidly growing into ownership of six million acres, Greenleaf gave an unvarnished report on matters, and they felt a tad squeezed.

To judge from the July 28 letter that all three of them wrote to Bourne, Morris and Nicholson joined Greenleaf in an act of faith. They informed Bourne that they would begin writing checks based on the assumption that the loan subscription would be filled and that he would have ample funds to cover them. They based their confidence on Crommelin and Sons' association with the loan, "as we well know that their credit and respectability is such that the said loan will undoubtedly fill under their influence."

The trouble was that the doubts of the credit of Messrs. Morris and Nicholson were such that those being paid by them with bills due on Greenleaf's account in London were not about to cherish them the way Morris's notes were cherished in 1780. These bills did not become as good as gold. As $600,000 of them flooded the market, in the main to pay off past debts of Morris and Nicholson, banks began discounting them beyond the customary amount and quickly passed them on to London for payment.

Morris, the most experienced of the speculators, sensed trouble. Greenleaf agreed that Morris should write to Bourne encouraging him to sell or raise money on Georgia lands:

"Mr. Greenleaf is so sure of your success in filling the loan on the Washington lots, that he has drawn largely on you. . . . Mr. Greenleaf is gone to New York, but Mr. Nicholson was here this minute and agrees with me that if any thing should unexpectedly happen to prevent the filling of that loan you must make these Georgia lands a substitute and at all events raise money upon them, either by loan or sale to answer the purpose for Mr. Greenleaf's bills must be paid. We expect however that the loan on the lots is already subscribed. . . . "

In the letters the partners wrote to each other, worries and suspicions began to seep in. To Greenleaf, Morris betrayed his recognition that all might not be well in Amsterdam: "Our engagements already made go to an immense sum and unless those resources which you hold to our view when we first engaged, can be realized, we had all best to hold on. On the contrary if you can point out and establish the funds, we will in that case go any lengths, well knowing that by extending the purchase the chance of profitable resales is increased."

Nicholson had even darker thoughts. During a brief visit to Georgetown he got the impression that the partners' operations there were being paid by bank loans on the partners' stock in the Bank of Columbia. Worrying that Greenleaf was not putting any real money into the operation, Nicholson called for a settling of accounts. Morris suggested stopping operations in the federal city.

Greenleaf's response to Morris is lost (as is Morris's letter to him), but an August 16 letter to Nicholson bristled with shock and indignation. By Greenleaf's account, Nicholson was $20,362.65 in his debt, not including the "very considerable" amount of cash being expended for improvements in Washington. "I *insist* that some one should be sent by yourself and Mr. Morris to the federal city who should investigate everything. . . ." And then he came to the defense of the city and his honor: "As to stopping operations at the fed. city, . . . I will never consent to it, as it would bring a disgrace & shame upon me I should sink under. The operations commenced shall continue even if I am left *alone* to bear the burthens." He felt "annoyed beyond measures" and wrote "that a speedy change must be made in all our operations."

Greenleaf himself gave a hint that the loan was failing. He tried to wiggle out of putting up the security required by the commissioners for the lots to be held as mortgage. Since the loan was not yet filled, it would ease his operations not to tie up so much money, and he could advance more money to the commissioners. The commissioners told him to confer with the secretary of state. Greenleaf was in Philadelphia but avoided Randolph.[4]

*   *   *

Like not a few newcomers to the city, Appleton was optimistic: "It is almost certain that from the efforts now making by the large proprietors of the land here that as soon as the river navigation is open, a settlement will take place & will in all probability progress with a rapidity unparelled [sic] in America, should the climate prove healthy," he wrote to Noah Webster. Appleton did agree with Webster that the commissioners, by being "slow & *inefficient,*" had "greatly retarded the public operations." Appleton suspected them of having "deranged the finances," and he thought "the public may have been defrauded by unprincipled agents and undertakers, [and] by dilatory & unskilful workmen." But he expressed a hope, doubtlessly universal in and around the federal city, that two new commissioners would change all that and give "new vigor & order" to the public concerns in the city.[5]

Johnson and Stuart finally quit. The judge did not even make the last meeting because of the sickness of his wife. Stuart, who had always thought himself most expendable, found he had to stay on longer than Johnson to keep a quorum. The president offered new commissioners a salary of $1,600 a year, but they must reside in the city. Two Marylanders the president first asked to take the job refused. Governor Thomas Sims Lee decided that the city was too attractive an investment opportunity to burden himself with public office in it. Senator Richard Potts dearly wanted to be appointed the collector of the port of Baltimore and held out for that job.

The president did not lack for others to choose from. William Deakins recommended a Baltimore lawyer named Gustavus Scott, said to be "clever in his profession and a man of industry and affable manner." Back in 1789 General Otho Williams had knocked him out of consideration for federal appointment, citing his disloyalty during the war and "intemperate love of litigation." But Williams was dead, and the president appointed Scott. The man replacing Stuart need not be a lawyer. The president's old Virginia friend Ferdinand Fairfax wrote an effusive letter in praise of William Thornton. Others urged John Davidson, Samuel's more prominent brother, for the job. The president offered the job to his former private secretary, Tobias Lear.

No one knew better than Lear how painful making appointments was for the president, but he had just got back from Europe with "a valuable cargo of goods" and a line of credit with the Dutch banking house of Willink. He took a week to think the offer over and then on September 5 refused, explaining that he had to get his business arrangements settled. At the president's request, Lear quizzed the proprietors about Thornton and found that they thought him "a very sensible, genteel and well informed man, ardent in his pursuits; but liable to strong prejudices and such I understand is his prejudice against Hoban that I conceive it would hardly be possible for them to agree on any points where each might consider himself a judge." The president could find no better man.[6]

33. A Happy Change in the Board

Edward Vidler, a stonecutter, placed an ad that August in the Georgetown paper offering to make tombstones. It was timely for, as George Washington put it, the ague and fever was "uncommonly rife." It killed at least one child at Mount Vernon. In late August the partners sent $10,000 down to Appleton, but it gave scant comfort to the consumptive from Boston who had just caught the fever. Malaria can be bad enough for a healthy man to handle. After surviving the first round of chills and fevers, he had a relapse that sent him from Greenleaf's Point, as it was now called, to Georgetown "for the benefit of change of situation." He stayed with Templeman in "one of the most pleasant houses in the place," but recovered only enough to board the stage for Philadelphia.

The yellow fever spared Philadelphia but not Baltimore. A call to arms, however, diverted attention from the unhappy city. The militias of Maryland, Virginia, New Jersey, and Pennsylvania mustered to put down the whiskey rebels in the west. A brigade from Washington marched under generals Uriah Forrest and John Davidson. The *Times* of London did not let Englishmen forget about the fever. It and the quarantine that accompanied it were important to shippers, but the powers that be in England were mindful that such headlines might help stem the tide of emigration to America at a time when war with France called for every hand.

War in Europe made the New World so much more attractive. A professor at Geneva, a friend of Jefferson and Adams, wrote to the vice president proposing that the whole faculty of the university flee their French conquerors and set up a new university in America. He asked if the federal city would be a good place for such an establishment. (Adams received the letter in November and passed it on to the president, who worried that a university conducted in French would not do. He thought that except for "useful mechanics and some particular descriptions of men or professions," there was no need to encourage emigration.)

In London, John Trumbull, the artist, then serving as a secretary to Special Ambassador John Jay, learned from Joshua Johnson that an architect-builder was needed in the federal city. He had no trouble getting George Hadfield, whom Benjamin West thought was the brightest young architect in the country, to agree to go. So high was the regard in which Hadfield was held that Trumbull thought the fact that he had never supervised any major building project should not disqualify him. Trumbull wrote to Tobias Lear and his brother, the speaker of the House (who passed the letter on to the president). Washington and Lear forwarded the letters about the young man to the commissioners.[1]

*   *   *

In mid-September Greenleaf took a break in negotiations to buy lands near New York's border with Canada and journeyed to the federal city. The two new commissioners were on hand, though, not yet having received his official commission, Thornton did not sit with Carroll and Scott at the head table when they convened on September 15.

To his credit, Greenleaf warned the commissioners not to expect any money from the Dutch loan. Writing of himself in the third person, he warned that "the public works should not thro' the want of funds be arrested or even retarded in their progress." He offered "all the assistance in his power towards furnishing what funds may be wanted, tho' from the constant calls for money to face his own immense engagements, he is not without the apprehension, should some of his resources fail, that his power may occasionally fall far short of his wishes." Lest that sound too discouraging, he assured them that he would go to Amsterdam shortly and raise a $1 million loan, which he would split with them.

Thanks to Greenleaf, the partners had paid the $68,000 due that year, and the commissioners seemed unable to believe that Green-leaf could no longer help them out of a tight spot. They asked for an advance on the installment due on May 1, 1795. Greenleaf, however, could pay only with notes payable on May 1, and he wanted another transfer of 857 lots to the partners immediately. He agreed to help get the notes cashed "whenever his means would allow," provided the commissioners drew on him only when they needed money. All this amounted to was giving the board a negotiable note due in May rather than having them rely only on the partners' contractual obligation to pay. This was not an idle redundancy, since courts could force payment for such notes more easily than they could enforce the contract. The commissioners wrote to the secretary of state that they were disposed to make the deal, given the "exhausted state" of their funds, which boded ill for carrying on operations next spring. They believed that by making the partners' failure to pay up in May "more fatal to their punctuality as merchants & consequently to their credit," they made eventual payments a certainty.

Until the administration approved those arrangements, the only hope for new money was Virginia. The commissioners wrote again to Governor Lee, who was off leading the army massed against the whiskey rebels. At the same time Stoddert, president of the Bank of Columbia, told the commissioners that they were already $26,000 in debt to the bank, and the directors had decided to draw the limit at $40,000. Furthermore, the directors thought it essential that, "if not for the security of the bank, for their reputations' sake, . . . you should give the bank the right of receipt [of] the $40,000 due from Virginia."[2]

The financial straits of the commissioners were not bruited about, so the joy attending the arrival of Scott and Thornton was undiminished. In a November 6 letter to the mayor of Cork, Ireland, Samuel Davidson cheered, "A happy change in the board of Commissioners have lately taken place; there are at present near fifty handsome houses, on private account, far advanced, and next spring an active and effective campaign is expected to commence therein: At present there is not the most distant doubt entertained, but that there will be ample accommodation for the reception of congress by the time appointed."

Problems were confronted and new ideas welcomed. William O'Neale, the man Greenleaf hired to get stone, was asked what improvements could be made in the process. He suggested that a dock be made where the drags could be brought right up to the shallops bringing stone so that the stone would not have to be unloaded on the wharf before being put on the drags. Anticipating the efficiency of the assembly line, O'Neale argued that with that arrangement, "one part of the work would drive the other and no time for sculking; less hands employed and less uses for them in this business, as one wheel of a mill moves all must follow."

Dr. John Crocker took Commissioner Scott aside and pointed out that if the garden south of the president's house was going to be ready in 1800, measures must be taken as soon as possible "to get a suitable collection of trees, shrubs & plants, the various productions of this and other countries." Then he turned to the more pressing business of caring for the public workers. The nurse at the new hospital, Cloe Leclair, needed twelve blanket rolls, the only remedy for chills induced by malaria. Worse, the hospital was not fit for use during the winter, there being too many gaps in the plank walls.

When the commissioners adjourned on the 19th, they did not all leave the city. The president positively required his two new appointees to live in or near the city. Thornton stayed in Georgetown to make arrangements for bringing down his family. Pleading that he had unfinished business in Baltimore, Scott did leave. But commissioners would no longer complain about how irksome it was to stay in the city.[3]

*   *   *

Worries about the loan did not cause Greenleaf to stint in his building at Greenleaf's Point. To satisfy Nicholson, he totaled what had been spent on building—$47,271—and promised Simmons, Lovering, Clark, and Henderson a share of $10,000 every two weeks until the building season ended.

Before heading north and perhaps to Amsterdam to face his financial crisis, Greenleaf helped Hallet. Alarmed that work was not continuing on plans for the Capitol, Greenleaf took it upon himself to pay Hallet £400 a year to continue making designs until the commissioners should rehire him.[4]

The gap in Greenleaf's operations in the city was the loss of Appleton. Greenleaf hired twenty-five-year-old William Cranch who was engaged to his sister Nancy. Cranch crossed paths with Appleton in New York and found the business he was heading for "to be much more extensive" than he expected, including taking "charge of all the immense negotiations of Mr. G—control all the cash, pass all accounts, oversee the bookkeepers, &c &c." He reached the city in mid-October and promptly assured his mother, "You have been misinformed with regard to a fever's raging in this city. There is no prevailing disorder here at present. There have been some people attacked with a bilious fever; and many have had the fever and ague. The number of deaths has been remarkably small considering the number of workmen here and considering their mode of life, their imprudences, and their bad provision." Citing the fall fevers as far north as Newburyport and the death of his uncle in Haverhill, both in Massachusetts, not to mention yellow fever in Baltimore and New Haven, he thought the federal city rather healthy.

He was gratified that Greenleaf had assembled an impressive administrative staff of two Frenchman: Lucat, a bookkeeper, and "Mr. Henry, who is a kind of secretaire oeconomique, whose business is solely to study to oeconomize the business, to suggest hints for improvement, and to systematize everything." Simmons had handed over his building for Lovering to finish so that he could supervise all the builders. Cranch also got a house rent-free, which would be ready by March, three horses at his disposal, and $1,500 a year.

Fortifying Cranch's optimism was his awe of Greenleaf. "He does not lose sight of the principal use of wealth which is the general diffusion of happiness," Cranch explained to his father. "No man ever contemplated in theory a more benevolent use of wealth than he is actually practicing. He seeks virtue and genius wherever it can be found in indigence, and brings it out into view." Cranch spent a few weeks in Washington, then Greenleaf summoned him to Philadelphia. There Cranch saw the man in action. "With all this vast business upon his hands, he is perhaps as methodical and accurate a man in his accounts as any in the world, and has an energy and decision in his negotiations which I have never before found in any man." Later, Cranch would recall, "For weeks together I have known him not to allow himself more than 2 or 3 hours of rest in the 24."

While in Philadelphia, Cranch spent an evening with his uncle,

Vice President John Adams, who in turn sent a report of their "sensible and worthy nephew" to his wife: "[He] gave me a particular account of the vast projects of Mr. Greenleaf. His sawmills in Georgia, his iron works on Hudsons River, his forty or an hundred houses building in the Federal City &c &c &c. But among the rest I was sorry to hear of his opening a loan in Holland, though only at four per cent, to enable him to make payments to his workmen. I am apt to suspect speculations upon credit, tho sometimes they may be successful. I however have always placed my glory in moderation not having spirit enough to undertake, nor understanding enough to conceive great projects and enterprises."[5]

34. Not an Ounce of Butter

As the president rode to Carlisle, Pennsylvania, to be closer to the troops massing to quash the Whiskey Rebellion, he heard that Scott did not really intend to move to the federal city. He promptly had Secretary of State Randolph inform Scott that that "was extremely unfortunate as the President promised much to himself from a quorum at least being on the spot." Finding a house in Georgetown, much less the city of Washington, was not quickly done. Thornton had to move a wife and mother-in-law, Scott a growing family. Despite frequent trips north, both men managed to keep a quorum in the city through December.

The old board had left much to do. The Federal Bridge was still standing, but the Georgetowners who had just bought rights to the causeway, among them the board's treasurer, Deakins, decided it would be foolhardy to pay for the land formed behind the bridge as long as the bridge was in such a doubtful state. So Scott negotiated an arrangement to replace the middle arch with a drawbridge to answer complaints that with its sinking foundation, the bridge threatened to block boats going up Rock Creek.

As for that other public improvement that had been languishing, the canal between Tiber and James creeks, the new board ordered the surveyors to ascertain how much had been dug so that the contractor could be paid off. One indication of what a half measure the desultory digging (which had cost almost $5,000) had been was that the commissioners asked the surveyors to suggest what could be done with the dirt piled up next to the ditch.

They got help in procuring slaves when Deakins sent over one John Slye, who already had a crew of thirty. The board still advertised for more to work "in the brick yard, stone quarries & c." for "generous wages." Scott and Thornton were both slave holders. Scott bought "Negro Thomas" on moving to Georgetown for £112 from Davidson, who had bought him but six days earlier for £80.

Not surprisingly, the usual proprietors spoke up to see whether the new board would be in any greater hurry to pay them £25 an acre for lands taken by the plan. Only George Walker, who had moved northeast of the Capitol site with such high expectations, sounded nasty: "It must be a matter of astonishment to you to observe that while almost the whole of the Georgetown end of the city is platted and divided with the proprietors, scarcely anything is done this way."[1]

Commissioner Carroll did not forget Blodget. He pressed his colleagues to sue to force Blodget to pay off the lottery, but Randolph thought that with only $12,246 left to pay, it made no sense going to law. There was also the matter of square 688, right next to the Capitol square, which Blodget had got cheaply by promising to build. He had done nothing; Carroll did his part to get a lawsuit going, signing an affidavit explaining the conditions under which Blodget had bought the square. Ironically, the move to reclaim square 688 from Blodget added a snag in the relations with Greenleaf.

By and large, the board gave Greenleaf what he wanted: 857 lots for notes payable May 1. Greenleaf obligingly cashed a $12,000 note for the board, money it desperately needed. But Thornton and Scott also looked over the old agreements and discovered two things: the loan of £1,000 a month, which had been superseded on condition that the commissioners get part of the Dutch loan; and the stipulation that purchasers of Greenleaf's lots improve every third one. So they asked that the £1,000 loan begin January 1 and that in the deeds to be mortgaged to Dutch banks, the improvement clause be included. They also worried that participating in the new $1 million loan Greenleaf wanted to raise would require them to mortgage so many lots that they would have very few left to sell.

They had one favor to ask: they wanted him to get workers from Europe who could be shared by the commissioners and Greenleaf, especially "a number of men who have been bred to cutting and laying free stone," obliged to work for two to four years at not more than 30 guineas a year, plus food, board, and passage, 55 guineas for men with families minus the food but with the use of land northeast of Massachusetts Avenue for gardens. They added, "We see no means so likely to check the exorbitant prices of building as the arrival of a number of tradesmen and laborers at the city of Washington, and this check will be more effectual if a proportion of them are under terms of service for a time. . . ."

Greenleaf waited a month to reply. To him, putting the improvement clause in the deed of the lots mortgaged was laughable. The Dutch bankers had spied that clause in his agreement with the commissioners and had Bourne specifically exempt them from it. Greenleaf pointed out to the board that it made no sense to jeopardize a loan to improve the city. More alarming to him was their cutting back the loan. To be of interest to Dutch bankers, the loan had to be large. He pressed them again and in reply they completely dropped the pretense of cooperation, telling him in a November 3 letter, "We do not conceive ourselves authorized to make the public answerable for the contracts of individuals."

Then the board got a shock that made them realize how much they depended on Greenleaf. On November 16 the Bank of Columbia would no longer cash any bills, for them or anyone else. Deakins had to go to Baltimore to try to get Greenleaf's note cashed. They tried to catch Greenleaf before he went to Europe asking him to: ". . . mark out some productive recourse for our present needs. The business of the city never called for assistance more than at this moment, and we trust your attention to this subject.''[2]

* * *

Deblois's autumn began happily enough. William Prout gave him two lots in each of the three squares on the east side of 8th Street Southeast between the square formed by North Carolina and South Carolina Avenues and I Street, on the high ground north of what would become the Navy Yard. All Deblois had to do was build a brick backbuilding on each lot within eighteen months, which he was doing at a cost of about $500 each. It bears noting that Deblois did not tell Nicholson about the deal with Prout. As for his and Nicholson's store along the river, he was expecting an infusion of more goods to sell.

His father-in-law, Tristram Dalton, had liquidated most of his estate in Newburyport, Massachusetts, and packed "furniture, 100 doz. [bottles] of old wine, plate, linen, & in short almost all their little family matters," plus $1,000 worth of goods for Deblois, including candles, "370 odd pair shoes, soap, cheese, butter & c." into the *Mary,* bound for Georgetown. She burned in the lower Potomac. All was lost, and it was insured for only $1,000. That was melancholy, but what Deblois really needed was money from Nicholson to cover the purchases he had been making. When a draft for $9,000 arrived, he rushed it to the Bank of Columbia only to be told that since the bank was carrying $60,000 in notes of Morris, Greenleaf, and Nicholson, it did not want to cash any of Nicholson's notes.

A week later Deblois had to fire most of the men he had brought down with him from Massachusetts since they were "expecting more from me than I think the business will afford." A common ploy to induce workers to pioneer a new development is to get them in debt to the company store. Instead, Deblois owed them $2,000, which he begged Nicholson to send down in notes he could cash. He had $100 to his name and still had not finished his warehouse and store. He moaned to Nicholson on November 17 that he had "not yet taken twenty dollars being so much cluttered and pinched for room."

While trying to secure what he had, Deblois worried to Nicholson about preparing for the future by ordering wood for burning bricks and stone for foundations before prices went up in the spring. That said, before closing the letter, Deblois looked around him and let out with this lament: "I begin to be a little discouraged. Mr. Dalton is thinking of building near Georgetown. Lear has, I believe hired out one of the new houses near the bridge & in fact no one comes near me. My family are all very well altho' we have suffered many inconveniences, for a week together not an ounce of butter in the house, & till lately not a place to make a fire except in kitchen, but now we have our stores in order & shall soon get comfortable."

Then, on December 6, a whirlwind blew down "a large frame building 25 feet by 50 feet which was nearly finished" and two half-finished buildings. Deblois had to scramble to protect his goods, estimating the damage at $300. Then one of his checks bounced because Nicholson failed to cover it. He gasped to Nicholson: "I was thunder struck and very much mortified; it has hurt my feelings so that I know not how to turn myself, I never had a note of mine protested before & I am truly grieved for you and much mortified myself."[3]

*   *   *

Deblois's struggles at the end of South Capitol Street did not make a dent in the general perception that the federal city was a place of opportunity. General Walter Stewart, a friend of the president, heretofore disappointed in his speculations in Pennsylvania lands, came to Georgetown and began his new campaign to become rich. First he set up his brother from Dublin in Georgetown as a merchant. Then he shopped for lots, explaining to the commissioners that he had rich friends in Europe who would resettle, "provided it can be done with a prospect of convenience." Stewart asked for "ten or twelve squares" on "the lowest terms."

Stewart wanted waterside lots near Lear's wharf and nine squares between there and the president's house. The commissioners considered them "among the most valuable in the city." After explaining to Stewart that they had earlier decided not to make any more extensive sales to one person, they relented in his case and offered the upland squares at eight cents a square foot, which worked out to almost £11,000 ($30,000), which worked out to about £175 a lot, considerably more than the £30 Morris and Greenleaf agreed to pay. As for waterside lots, the commissioners wanted $16 for every waterfront foot, which worked out to $4,100 for those Stewart wanted.

Those sums took Stewart's breath away, and he returned to Philadelphia. Greenleaf offered him lots at five cents a square foot. But the president advised him "not to haggle" at the commission ers' price. And so, on December 4, within a month of beginning negotiations, Stewart agreed to buy the two waterside lots and three upland squares. "The difference of price which I give you compared to what I pay the other gentlemen," Stewart remarked in closing the deal, "I should not have agreed to by any means, but from the confidence I place in the advice and opinion of the President, & I trust I shall not have to repent of my purchase." The commissioners immediately offered the hand of cooperation, instructing Hoban to send Stewart a list of workmen available in the city. In turn, Stewart promised to try to get stonecutters from Ireland.

The visit of George Parkyns, an artist touring the country to "render the scenery of America more generally known in Europe" through his aquatint engravings, rekindled the hope of a flood of workers from Europe. He solicited patronage to publish his works, which would encourage immigration to America. He asked the commissioners to let him establish an art school with a foundry and exhibition space, to fill a whole square on the north side of Pennsylvania Avenue between 4½ and 6th Streets Northwest. The commissioners were amenable to helping Parkyns. Thornton became quite excited because Parkyns agreed to teach him how to do aquatints, but the square he wanted was "already disposed of." Parkyns still promised to return in the spring to capture the scenery. Not that potential emigrants were getting any bad reports of the city. The *Virginia Gazette* in Richmond reprinted a London article that claimed the city was progressing rapidly. The president's house was "completed," and the Capitol "covering in." In a letter to the editor that appeared soon after, a "Washingtonian" was amused at "this novel mode of procuring information from London of what we are about in this city." "Please to let us know, in your next, from the same authority," he gibed, "whether our Famous Brick machine has succeeded. . . ."[4]

35. God Knows What a Weight

By November 25 Greenleaf knew that all the notes he, Morris, and Nicholson were sending to London and Amsterdam for Bourne to cover would bounce. Bourne reported the loan subscription had been open several months, and Crommelin and Sons had been able to credit Greenleaf's account with a mere $20,436. The partners wanted to pass $600,000 on that account. With a French invasion of Holland imminent, Greenleaf advised his partners to stop passing those notes until he got to Holland to rectify the situation.

Morris and Nicholson had more experience than Greenleaf in such matters, having faced a similar crisis in May 1793. Knowing that appearances counted for a great deal, Morris told Greenleaf that he "must not embark" to Europe as planned on December 10 and "that things must not be done in a *'hurry scurry'* manner." Greenleaf bristled at the suggestion that anyone could think of him as a scoundrel running out on bad bills and insisted, "I must go, & shall go *immediately* to Europe." But he did not because a few doors down from his house in New York City an eccentric nabob, as wealthy Britons leaving the India service were called, had just moved in.[1]

Thomas Law came to New York in August 1794, bringing with him a sizable fortune in pounds sterling. At the age of seventeen he had gone to India, where his family had a record of distinguished service, and he rose to become one of the top bureaucrats in the British East India Company, the chief civil authority in the state of Bihar, and the architect of a new system of land tenure that made Indian land vendable. He left the East India service for reasons of health, and quit England for America because of a lawsuit and his objections to the war with France. The suit arose from no wrongdoing on his part; he held surety for a loan of £10,000 to someone who, though able, refused to repay it.

That is how he eventually described his career. But when he was a thirty-eight-year-old single man in New York, he left this impression with Madame de La Tour du Pin, who was then an exile from France: "He was a brother of Lord Landaff, and when still very young had gone to India as Governor of Patna, or something of that kind. He was there fourteen years, and married a very rich Brahmin widow, by whom he had two sons, who were still children. His wife had died, leaving him a considerable fortune. He returned to England, but grew bored and decided to come to America and use part of the money he had brought from India to buy land. His intention was to discover whether this new nation merited the esteem he was ready to give it. . . . He had created for himself an imaginary America, and was unwilling to give it up. He was an idealist, but witty and cultivated, and both a poet and an historian." She also recalled his eccentricity: "when preoccupied with an idea the house might have collapsed without his lifting his eyes."

She met Law in Albany, New York, while he was on a tour to Niagara Falls with Talleyrand, a former and future foreign minister of France then trying to make a fortune in America. The cynical Frenchman did not fall for the rich widow story and saw Law as a paradigm of former East India bureaucrats who, positioned to tap the lucrative trade between India and the West, all left India rich. Talleyrand was scouting land for speculative purposes. Law went along for the ride. No properties interested Talleyrand, but Law almost bought land around Fort Stanwix along the Mohawk River that was involved in a dispute between owner and tenants. Law envisioned building a thriving city around the fort, but moved on.

Back in New York City Law met Greenleaf, who regaled him with stories of "the New Jerusalem." The idea "of promoting a city in whose success . . . every citizen was interested" appealed to Law. Soon he was full of Greenleaf's "vast idea; it must be verified by every emigrant to the westward—every rising town; every new vessel in America wherever it may be, must advance the Metropolis. That is the center—there all the rays must come to a point—Persons in Boston, New York, Baltimore, Philadelphia, Charleston, Pittsburgh, must all have an interest in Washington City."

Law bought lots site unseen and did not haggle over Greenleaf's price of five pence a square foot (which, for his own edification, Law translated into a whopping £907 an acre), but he took the precaution of reserving the right to get his money back plus interest if he did not like the land once he saw it. He asked Greenleaf to pick the lots and stipulated that the final price be no more than £25,000. But he was dealing with a rather good salesman. Greenleaf talked Law into buying 2,400,000 square feet, the partners' interest in sixteen squares, for £50,000. Someone suggested that he buy up the notes of Greenleaf, Morris, and Nicholson, which were selling at a sizable discount, and use those to buy the lots. Law told Greenleaf that he knew that would be wrong. Greenleaf did not mention the requirement to build a house on every third lot within four years. The agreement Law signed contained that clause, but Law did not read the agreement before signing it.

Once the ink was dry on the deal, Greenleaf broadcast it far and wide, for what better antidote was there to the poison being spread about his credit. Cranch at least was a believer. "In the course of next year," he told his parents, "we expect a capital of a million pounds sterling to be laid out in the city by foreigners. A beginning was this week made, and Mr. G sold about 1/13th of his property in the city for more than $180,000. . . . In the course of 3 years, he must without dispute be the richest man in America."[2]

In his letters to the commissioners, however, Greenleaf did not hint that the deal was impending, though the commissioners must have sensed that something was up. He no longer argued that the building stipulation did not belong in a mortgage. He attacked the stipulation per se as absurd, since it would cramp his operations and prevent the improvements the commissioners wanted. Once the deal with Law was done, he thought of Europe again and asked for the deeds to 2,000 lots for a $1 million loan. The commissioners were not at all accommodating, insisting on the improvement clause and not changing their minds about the loan.

It did not help Greenleaf's chances of getting relief that the commissioners were at the same time toe to toe with Blodget, who had come to get Hoban to finish the hotel but was soon vehemently defending his right to the square next to the Capitol square, improvements or not. He accused Carroll of trying to undo the deal so Greenleaf could pick the square, and then he ridiculed Greenleaf's improvements, "houses which were to have been built to favour the residence of congress being thrown at such a distance from the public buildings."[3]

*   *   *

The state of Virginia became the scapegoat for the money shortage that threatened progress on the public buildings. It paid another $4,000, but $36,000 was still due. On November 25 the commissioners sent a memorial to the Virginia General Assembly informing them that "the necessary materials . . . cannot be purchased in sufficient quantities for the next season without full payment of the Virginia donation." That want was more than inconvenient; it led to the "injury" of the public buildings. Finally, any retardation in the progress of the public buildings "very deeply" affected the only remaining source of funds, the sale of lots. If Virginia did not give and the buildings did not progress, land prices would drop and the nation would have an embarrassment on its hands.

In reality, the commissioners did not wait on Virginia but proceeded to solicit bids for the materials needed next spring. They announced on November 21 that until December 15 they would "sit every day to attend to proposals for contracts." They were even low on bricks. Thomas Peter, proprietor Robert Peter's son, who had married one of Martha Washington's granddaughters the past summer, asked for 30,000 bricks, which he would replace in the spring, for houses he wanted to build on K Street near Georgetown. The board made inquiries and found that they could not lend any. The only thing that seemed to be in somewhat sure supply was timber, since they had "12 to 13 thousand solid feet" slowly heading up the Potomac from Governor Lee's plantation, only six months late.

Scott negotiated the contracts and approached them with more sophistication than Johnson had. First, he got the board out of the quarrying business. The contractors could use the public's quarries. Delivery of stone would no longer depend on the judgment of an employee but on the specifications of a contract stating exactly how much ashlar and bill were needed. The major new wrinkle in the contract was that the contractors were obliged to see that the stone was delivered to the work site. No more, the commissioners wrote to the president, would their "laborers" be "perpetually called off from their several employments to assist in unloading and hauling." The board even sold its scows and carts that had been used to haul stones and bricks. They made two contracts, one with Cooke and Brent at Aquia and one with a Chopawamsic quarier farther down-river. All told, they contracted for 5,500 tons in 1795 and 6,500 tons in 1796 at a price, they boasted, "at least 7/6 [$20] per ton less than it has hitherto cost us."

As for laying the stone, they tried to push the cost of that labor down by contracting with the Englishman John Dobson to show up the feuding Irish and Scots. Dobson knew what the commissioners wanted to hear. "I do not make my estimate," he wrote on December 7, "from the present high price of labor but depend greatly on your advancing sums of money that would enable me to procure men from England that would work at moderate wages." The contract set out the price for twenty separate operations, from two shillings nine pence for plain ashlar inlaid to ten shillings for the ashlar casings of the circular molds on cornices. Dobson had asked for ten shillings a foot for most of the fine work, but the commissioners talked him down to eight shillings for architraves and most molding.

Stonework for the season was stopped on December 6, and not only because the walls had to be covered. Once the first story of the president's house was completed, workers moved over to lay the foundation of the Capitol. But work could not go on at the Capitol because there were no plans. With the foundation completed, the commissioners had Williamson line the water well and drains with stone and asked him for his thoughts on the basement. The old Scot replied that he did not even know there was to be a basement.

Learning that Hallet had drawn up a plan without a basement so that the pilasters and columns would rise from the ground rather than from another story above the foundation, Thornton grew alarmed. As he explained to his friend Trumbull, as a commissioner, he had "an opportunity of correcting some wilful errors which have been fallen into, by those jealous men [Hoban and Hallet] who objected to my plan, because I was not regularly brought up an architect."

In winding down the work for the winter, only the payroll for laborers really shrank. Williamson had such an eye out for his masons that anticipating a vacancy at Hallet's house on the Capitol square, he suggested it would do for "eight or ten stone cutters . . . under the greatest necessity." At the president's house, where inside work could be done, Hoban refrained from wholesale dismissals, and sixteen of the eighteen white laborers returned to work on the 29th. Hoban and Purcell's five slave carpenters continued to work along with the fifteen white carpenters at the president's house. There was one free black working for the commissioners, a measurer in the surveying department named Jerry Holland, who was deemed by Freeman to be "justly intitled" to the top wage offered to hands, $8 a month, because he was the "best hand in the department," one white man excepted. The commissioner paid Holland $5 a month.

Even with outside work stopped, the fields of the city were not empty. Davidson let forty-six head of cattle spend two weeks fattening up on his meadow. The dearth of activity worried champions of the Potomac. Where was the shipping that was to have filled the harbors?[4]

*   *   *

Greenleaf did not leave for Europe as planned on December 10. In the agreement they had signed the year before, Morris and Nicholson had let Greenleaf have a year to reimburse them for purchases of backlands. The day the grace period ended, Nicholson demanded that Greenleaf pay his share, and with a check payable in

three days. "I am mortified beyond measure," Greenleaf retorted
on December 26, to pay "a presumptive balance due on an unex-
amined and unapproved account, and without previous notice,
approbation or permission, is unquestionably *wrong*." At the same
time, Greenleaf had to cover $56,379.71 worth of Nicholson's notes,
pay $20,250 down payment on New York lands for the partners, and
reimburse $15,000 in cash for expenses in Washington. Plus "God
knows what a weight," Greenleaf wrote, "I have to encounter of
protested bills from Europe for which I have benefited hardly the
drop of the bucket." Greenleaf turned to Morris for relief, which he
got under protest. "You call your disappointments cruel and so they
may probably be," Morris retorted, "but remember, other people
suffer cruelties in pecuniary matters also, and I feel mine as much
at this time as you can."

Greenleaf pleaded with them to stop the pressure so he could go
to Europe. He told Nicholson, "Our very salvation depends on my
being in Europe." Instead of forcing him into the "hands of the
Jews," his partners should "do everything in your power to facilitate
my departure and procure for me that state of credit which would
enable my friends to return my protested bills back upon me in
London and save the disgrace and damages arising on them."

Morris had a better idea: the North American Land Company.[5]

*   *   *

The canal around Little Falls was to have been completed in the
summer of 1793. In December 1794 Lear looked at the locks and
could not understand what was amiss. "There has either been a
strange delay of the business," he wrote to the president, "or an
uncommon miscalculation of the time it would take to finish it."
Not only was the gate to the locks not working, stockholder subscriptions had not been paid, the company needed almost $100,000
to complete its work and its charter had to be renewed by the
Maryland and Virginia legislatures. Virginia's disinclination to pay
the final portion of the grant to the federal city boded ill. Lear asked
the president to write to delegates.

The president declined to intervene; his office precluded it, and
he did not know the members. He still believed in an inevitable 15
percent return on capital once tolls were collected. "No speculation
to which money applied, will be more productive with so much
honor and so little risque." Then he kicked himself. Most of his

fellow stockholders in the company "probably never bestowed a thought on the subject." The president did what he could. At a pre-Christmas reception, the president took Robert Morris aside and asked when William Weston, a visiting English expert working on Morris's Pennsylvania canal, could visit the Potomac.[6]

1795

36. The Foundation of Immense Profit

The president did not bother Morris with his reaction to the sale to Law, though it was much on his mind. It grieved him to see private interests make so much money which could have been applied to public good. Commissioner Carroll took the heat. In a January 7 letter Washington recalled how he had "yielded" his assent to the first sale to Greenleaf "because matters at that time seemed to be in a stagnant state, and something was necessary to put the wheels in motion again." Still, he thought the price of the lots too low. His "repugnance" to the second sale was greater. It was not necessary, and it was evident that Greenleaf was "speculating deeply—was aiming to monopolize deeply and was thereby laying the foundation of immense profit. . . ."

He was "opposed to any more *large* sales, if there be *any other* resource by which money can be obtained to carry on your operations." The commissioners had disposed of more than half of the public lots, and not a fourth of the money needed to build the public buildings had been provided. Then he got to the point, Greenleaf's sale to Law. "Will it not be asked, why are speculators to pocket so much money? Are not the Commissioners as competent to make bargains?"

Characteristically, once his anger was expressed, Washington backed off and continued with the optimism that befitted the leader of the rising empire. "The business, I conceive, is now fairly on its legs—to sell therefore by wholesale faster than is indispensably necessary to keep the machine in proper motion will, probably (as property is rising there), be deemed impolitic." But the old refrain fell flat. He closed with a recognition that sacrifices had to be made in the near future, so he wished "to see the force of your means directed toward the capitol."

In reply Carroll gently reminded the president of his complicity in the large sale to Stewart. He did not defend the two sales to Greenleaf but noted that because of the sacrifices made by the public in the sale it was "fair game" to charge Greenleaf for "adjacent improvements." The public also owned valuable water-side lots and indeed had just sold some at £6 a waterfront foot to James Barry, a merchant from Baltimore. It was true that not enough lots remained in public hands to easily finance all that had to be done, but even if they had ample funds, they would be hard pressed to get everything done. A loan was needed to support operations for that year, since Greenleaf could not be counted on.

As for the sale to Law, Carroll merely accentuated the positive. The immense profit made "may contribute toward making Messrs Morris & Greenleaf punctual in their payments." And Law did have to build on every third lot. One hundred and sixty-five houses built in the next four years would increase land values, and some of them had to be near the Capitol, where no proper house had yet been built. Carroll's last point was that the sooner Morris and Greenleaf sold their property "the less is to be apprehended of their keeping down the value of the public property," as they had tried to do in the negotiations with Stewart. All in all, Carroll thought the sale to Law "favourable to the city."[1]

*   *   *

Carroll shared the president's letter and his reply with his colleagues. Both letters helped shape the all-inclusive report on the state of the city they were preparing. The board pulled together the accounts of the various departments and their projected expenditures. Elisha Williams, who hired the slaves, submitted the briefest report. In 1794 he had hired thirty-seven slaves by the year, twenty-six black and white laborers by the month, seven slaves to work with the surveyors, and six to work in the quarries. Three overseers ran the crews (with the imposing names of Slye, Hardman, and Mudd). It was an easy matter to project his expenses for 1795: a hundred slaves at $60 a year, 13 cents a day each for subsistence for 365 days, amounting to about $5,000 for the year, plus $800 for four overseers.

Hoban made the reports on the expenditures at the president's house and Capitol, and to the regret of historians he claimed that the vouchers for expenses were so "blended" that it was impossible to itemize expenses. After an expenditure of £42,000 ($117,720) the first story of the president's house was almost completed. (The cost included all the temporary buildings to house workers and supplies.) It would take two months to get that principal story ready for the joists to hold the next floor. Twenty stonecutters were currently working under Blagden. Hoban gave a detailed estimate for the expense of completing the stonework for the building, laying the wooden frame for the roof (no decision had been made on the roofing to be used), and completing one fourth of the carpenters' work for the whole building. That would cost £15,300, or a little over $40,000, and require those twenty stonecutters to continue work aided by thirteen laborers, twelve carpenters (aided by five slaves), six sawyers, and a blacksmith. The making and laying of 725,000 bricks would be contracted out.

As for the Capitol, Hoban estimated that £20,000, or some $53,000, had been expended; again, blended vouchers prevented strict accounting. That sum included the cost of "temporary buildings such as carpenters hall, lime house, stone shed and some few others for workmen." The Capitol itself was nothing but foundation. Much material on hand, including 250 tons of foundation stone at the wharf and Lee's timber harbored downriver, was included in that £20,000 estimate. Twenty stonecutters were then working at the site. No estimate of further expenses was made because no detailed plans for the rest of the building had been prepared.

In coming up with an estimate of expenses for 1795, the commissioners had a major frustration. The building they had plans for had to be put on the back burner. And for the Capitol, instead of hard estimates they had a scapegoat, Hallet, whose "capricious and obstinate refusal" to deliver up plans "occasioned some difficulties." Hallet, who was still in the city, finally shared his plans, and on January 21 begged to have his old job back. He was somewhat apologetic, confessing that, given his large family, "nothing less than madness could have induced me to act in such a manner. . . ." But the board had already decided to hire the Englishman Hadfield, who had been recommended by John Trumbull.

The commissioners' estimate of expenses for 1795 was $100,960, including $34,000 for stone and $54,000 for personnel. The figure did not include bricklaying, sand, planking, nails, and carpenters. It was thought best to get a better feel for how much wood would be around before hiring more carpenters. And items that canceled each other out were not put in the estimate. The income from the sale of lots would cover the payments to the original proprietors. Funds assessed from lot owners would pay for leveling the city.

As for income in the coming year the commissioners had due: the second $68,571 of seven annual installments from Morris, Greenleaf, and Nicholson, $32,000 in loans from Greenleaf, and $36,000 from Virginia. There was $6,864.26 cash on hand. They were uncertain about the loan from Greenleaf, and the best advice from Virginia was that the $36,000 would not be forthcoming without resorting to some extraordinary expedients entailing the purchase of land warrants and state-owned tobacco, which the treasurer of Virginia offered to do for the commissioners for a three percent commission. To make up the shortfall they could only sell lots or their bank shares. The bank shares were "merely nominal, never having been paid for except by a bank credit." They had fewer than 5,000 standard lots, four-fifths northeast of Massachusetts Avenue, which would probably sell for £25 a lot. As for the others, their recent sales were for $465 a standard lot off the water and $16 a foot on it. Both prices were too low, and "nothing but dire necessity ought to induce us to sell at those low rates, except on single lots and for the purposes of immediate improvements."

Just a year after Judge Johnson told the president that the sale to Greenleaf and Morris and the prospect of a Dutch loan assured the completion of the public buildings, the new commissioners had bad news: "to you, Sir, we owe the confession of this melancholy truth, that the remaining funds of the city at the present prices of property must fall very short of accomplishing the great and necessary objects in view." And that was assuming that the canal was not finished and that the Capitol was built only as far as required for "the immediate accommodation of Congress," which is to say, both houses of Congress could sit in one wing of the Capitol.

The solution was a loan, because completion of the public buildings would raise the price of public lots, and with a loan, bargain hunters would be denied. "Could the idea once be done away that the public must sell," the commissioners wrote, "it would have a most happy effect." The loan would allow improvements that would "more than double the security to the lender, [and] add in an equal degree to the Riches of the Borrower." A loan would "strengthen the public opinion & add perhaps four fold to the value of the property on hand."

The commissioners did not minimize the consequences if they should fail: "Should any unexpected incidents prevent the public buildings from being prepared in time for the reception of Congress, how deep would be your [the president's] and our regret. Such an event might ultimately shake the dignity, honor, and peace of the union." The president had heard the argument before, from L'Enfant. His response to the "gloomy" report was to ask the board to send one of the commissioners to Philadelphia to negotiate a loan.[2]

* * *

To supply their needs in the short run, Scott met with the directors of the Bank of Columbia and assured the board a line of credit until May, when Greenleaf's notes would be paid. The commissioners immediately tried to save money. On January 16 the masons at the president's house were given two weeks' pay at the rate of eight shillings a day instead of ten. They were told that would be their new wage for the year. The skilled workers of the city tried to fight back. An ad summoned the "architects and artificers in the different buildings in the federal city" to meet at Bond's tavern. A number of masons at the president's house laid down their tools in protest and petitioned the commissioners, arguing that "advertisements in our countrys of the great wages and good usages we were to receive & many of us on account of our political principals as good republicans have crossed the western ocean to serve the United States as mechanics." The protest scored one point. Carroll had promised them they would get ten shillings a day until notified otherwise. So the board gave them the two shillings they were docked, but refused to go back to the old wage. Hoban was allowed to fire the masons who laid down their tools. When the dust settled the crew of thirty-two had been cut to twenty, the monthly labor cost for masons cut from $944 to $510.

However, there was a sudden unexpected expense at the president's house, possibly occasioned by the labor strife. Clotworthy Stephenson, a factotum for Hoban and thus quite possibly his hatchet man, found that his gelding was stolen. Ten laborers were put on night watch at the president's house square, fortified with three fourths of a gallon of rum supplied by the city. By the 21st a culprit was apprehended and placed under the guard of twelve men at the square, fortified by the rum plus a gallon of cider. At the end of the month a permanent night guard of six was in place.

*   *   *

The commissioners' cash flow problem did not depress the value of lots. The board looked to Rock Creek as a source of funds. Harbaugh agreed to pay £1,200 damages on the Federal Bridge (in two years) and build a drawbridge to be funded by the payments from the claimants to the land formed by the causeway. The residue of the payments, some $5,000, forthcoming once the drawbridge was complete, could be used for other projects. And noting the interest in the area, Scott thought Water Street, which was to be built to serve all docks in the emporium, could be extended north of the bridge up Rock Creek. The lots along it could be sold as waterside lots. No one had told him of Johnson's interest in the area. While crossing the bridge with Johnson one day, Scott mentioned the idea. Johnson happened to be in town to purchase the lots just north of the bridge from Greenleaf.

Johnson thought so little of Scott's idea that he completed the paperwork transferring Robert Peter's share of the square to the board so Greenleaf could pick it and sell it to him. The board signed the papers, and then, to Johnson's astonishment, Scott and Thornton ruled that the square in question had waterside lots and therefore Greenleaf could not buy them for $80 each.[3]

37. Cash Now, to Lay in My Wood

Greenleaf also used the winter lull in building to render accounts and project expenses, or rather he had Cranch and the "secretaire oeconomique," Henry, do it. That refugee from Santo Domingo was also trying to interest the commissioners in his plans for leveling and beautifying the Capitol grounds, telling them that he paid "daily a tribute of admiration to its majestical, rich, agreeable and diversified prospect." The commissioners were not impressed.

Henry lived on Capitol Hill, Cranch at Greenleaf's Point. Almost daily, letters passed between them. They determined that, based on those almost finished, houses of 1,200 square feet cost $5.50 a square foot. With forty houses to build by the end of the year, they decided Greenleaf's obligations that year for building and attendant operations would cost $142,925. Clark could finish the eight houses that he had covered, build the shells of four to six houses on O Street Southwest and begin six houses at 17th Street and Pennsylvania Avenue, near the president's house. Lovering was to finish the interior work of the seven houses at the point that were as yet just shells and build three more houses there. Henderson was to build six houses at 19th and Pennsylvania and finish the six houses at 21st and Pennsylvania.

Greenleaf also had to build twenty houses on the lots he bought from Carroll. Cranch and Henry thought of a way to get out of the contract, which called for two-story houses on South Capitol Street. Since the streets leading to the Capitol were so important, the commissioners might consider them avenues and thus require the houses on them to be at least three stories high. Ergo the contract with Carroll had to be modified. And there was another reason not to build there: "The lots there are so beautiful and well situated that they will always be *valuable* without buildings on them." The idea was to get the contract rewritten so as to require only that a certain number of houses be built on the land originally owned by Carroll, thus "in effect get rid of the contract with him, by merging it in that with the commissioners."

If that worked, Henry argued that it would be best to build houses up West 3rd Street to connect the point to the Capitol. Cranch nipped that idea in the bud. That ground was "low and wet," and the canal divided 3rd Street "lengthwise for a considerable distance." The easternmost street that would serve was 4½ Street. But Cranch preferred making the "communication" with Pennsylvania Avenue up 7th Street. And Cranch did not feel the point was isolated, especially once bridges across the Tiber at 7th and 4½ Streets were completed. There was also a plan for a ferry across the Eastern Branch from Deblois's wharf at South Capitol and P Streets. Packets to Alexandria would leave the same wharf. Several proprietors were "in agitation to establish a day stage from the Point to Georgetown by the way of the Capitol." So confident was Cranch that traffic would make its way to the point that he proposed turning one of Lovering's houses into a hotel.

But for the moment all of Greenleaf's men had to look for savings. Henderson claimed he could bake bricks for half the cost by using coal instead of wood in the kilns. There was enough clay dug up to make two million to three million bricks. If the brick machines could be brought to their potential, they could make bricks more cheaply than anyone. Of course, Clark and Lovering did not have to buy bricks from them. Cranch chafed at the autonomy the architects had. He could not force them to scale back and make their houses more economical. The commissioners, however, might have to buy Greenleaf's bricks. Mitchell, their contractor, was already complaining about not having enough wood and slaves to get the job done.[1]

*   *   *

Cranch and Henry had no inkling of the extent of Greenleaf's financial predicament. Deblois began getting some idea of the sad state of Nicholson's finances. His operations across James Creek were considerably smaller than what Cranch was trying to fathom, but like Cranch, he had no money. On the second day of the new year, Deblois told Nicholson that if he wanted to build in the spring, he needed "cash now, to lay in my wood, lime, stone & c., which can be done at least one quarter cheaper than I could purchase in the summer.'' He pointed out that Lear and Company had just bought a cargo of lime ''at less than cost and charges by having the cash to pay for it.'' And he was eager to buy timberland south of Alexandria that was for sale.

Deblois was willing to make sacrifices. His wife would agree to give up the promised brick house and live one more year in a wooden house so that the brick one could serve as a tavern, for ''one is very much wanted here.'' Doing that required more money. Another thing limiting the attractiveness of coming to the point was that Deblois did not have enough goods to sell. When folks were obliged to go to Georgetown, ''they get all there.''

No money was forthcoming. On January 19 Deblois tried again. This time he revealed his arrangements with Prout and tried to appeal to Nicholson's yen to expand. So pleased was Prout with what Deblois had done on the six lots given to him in the summer that he offered him three lots on the southeast corner of 8th Street and Pennsylvania Avenue Southeast for £100 for all three, only one third down, and on condition that one brick house of 50 square feet be built that year. Deblois, who thought the location excellent for ''a large boarding house with rooms for public meetings, drawing rooms, & c.,'' offered Nicholson half the lots if he financed the construction of the building. He had at his command $100. He needed $3,000 in a hurry. That sum, he told Nicholson, would be the best assurance that the rumor that Nicholson had sold his interest in the Washington speculation to his partners, thus leaving Deblois high and dry, was not true.[2]

*   *   *

If Deblois needed $3,000, Nicholson needed $300,000. Morris and Greenleaf needed as much. Of course, then as now, those who carried such a heavy load of debt succeeded as few others in living the good life. In the midst of all his financial uncertainty Morris was still the premier host of Philadelphia. ''I dined yesterday at Mr. Morris' whose hospitality is always precious,'' John Adams wrote to his wife on January 29, ''a company of venerable old rakes of three score years of age, drinking Madeira, talking politics till almost eleven o'clock.''

Adams had no notes coming back from London unpaid. To those who did, Morris explained that ''the invasion of Holland by the French has put a stop to the negotiations of Mr. Greenleaf's agent & will probably defeat his measures, in which case the bills will come back [unpaid], indeed I have been fearful of this event ever since I knew of the progress of the French armies, altho' a good many of the bills had been accepted before Mr. Bourne became alarmed. Mr. Greenleaf will be here the end of this week, and if he has any good intelligence I will communicate it to you.''

The partners were not in a panic. Bourne sent word that subscriptions for a $400,000 loan at five and a half percent interest had been opened with a Rotterdam banking house. Morris and Nicholson recognized that Greenleaf was a rather good salesman. Not only had he closed the deal with Law for Washington lots, but three weeks later he sold 144,000 acres of New York land for a shilling more than he had paid for it a few months before. Samuel Ward, a seasoned New York speculator, joined him in that deal and found Greenleaf ''a good fellow, well informed and ready to communicate all useful information.'' Greenleaf even hired the once master speculator William Duer, still under house arrest, as an advisor.

While Nicholson was arranging to use 50,000 acres of Pennsylvania land to pay a $50,000 debt, Greenleaf was negotiating with Law's friend William Duncanson, another East India trader, who wanted to buy Washington lots, as did an agent for David Scott, ''the great Bombay merchant.'' Rather than attack Greenleaf, Nicholson tried to tap the same mine, offering to help Law's East India friends exchange rupees into pounds at an advantageous rate. The days of looking askance at the Washington property were over.

Back in August Morris seemed to think more highly of Georgia lands than Washington lots. Now he was having a change of heart. Like the commissioners, he decided that the failure of Greenleaf's loan had little to do with the value of Washington lots. The art of being Robert Morris entailed having a reason beyond his control for every failure to make good on a note, and a recent sale that promised a turnaround. The sale to Law was his good news that winter. To his land agents he had to admit that "large quantities of land from all the southern states are hawking about at New York and this place and offered at very low prices. . . ." So Morris concocted a plan to consolidate all the partners' other land operations, holding the valuable Washington lots in reserve as security.

Although he would protest to complainers that his and Nicholson's notes were "as good and secure as any paper in the world," Morris realized their names on a note lessened its value. So he created a scheme that took his name off the paper. The six million acres he owned with Nicholson and Greenleaf became the capital for the North American Land Company, and the 50,000 shares of stock the company offered would, Morris hoped, stand as security for loans and be valued as payment for debts. The partners would unveil the company in late February. That January Morris won the commitment from his partners not only to give their share of the land to the company but to ante up security assuring investors three annual dividends of six percent.[3]

*   *   *

The president too was making plans. In a January 28 letter to the commissioners, he offered to contribute his fifty shares in the Potomac Company, which the state of Virginia had given him and which were worth $22,200, to endow a national university in the federal city. He regretted that "the youth of the United States should be sent to foreign countries" for their education and worried that they would be "too early prepossessed in favor of other political systems." He wanted a plan for a university adopted "by which the arts, sciences, and belles-letters could be taught in their *fullest* extent." He hoped to bring youth from all sections of the country and thus contribute to the removal of "prejudices, which might perhaps sometimes arise from local circumstances."

Washington made his donation contingent on concrete plans being made and hinted that the commissioners should get to work on them. On February 18 they responded with glowing praise for the president's sacrifice to promote "the most engaging subject with which the human mind can be impressed." As for any plans, they revealed that Commissioner Thornton had long been thinking of such an institution and would soon bring his plans to fruition.

The man actually putting plans for the university on paper was Blodget. Wearing his architect's hat, he was touring the studios of the artists of Philadelphia with the engraver Parkyns enlisting support for the Columbianum, or National College for the Encouragement of Painting, Sculpture, Architecture and Engraving. That January a working group of sixteen artists drew up plans of instruction.

The Italian sculptor Ceracchi returned that winter and immediately signed up to teach at the Columbianum. He soon had a letter soliciting subscriptions of $30 a year signed by the president and some sixty national leaders, all for his national monument. The idea was to raise $30,000, which would finance the construction of the monument, and then the federal government would buy the monument back, reimbursing the subscribers. No less than the four members of the president's cabinet served as the managers of the subscription so the Goddess of Liberty could descend "in a car drawn by four horses, darting through a volume of clouds, which conceals the summit of a rainbow.—Her form is at once expressive of dignity and grace.—In her right hand she brandishes a flaming dart, which, by dispelling the mists of Error, illuminates the universe; her left is extended in the attitude of inviting the people of America to listen to her voice.—A simple pileus covers her head; her hair plays unconfined over her shoulders; her bent brow expresses the energy of her character; her lips appear partly open, whilst her awful voice echoes through the vault of heaven, in favor of the rights of man.—Her drapery is simple; She is attired in an ancient chlamys, one end of which is confined under her zone,—the rest floats carelessly in the wind; the cothurnus covers her feet."

Oblivious to all those grandiose plans, the Reverend George Ralph came to Capitol Hill to start a boarding school.[4]

38. Give a Spur to the City

Johnson returned to the city on February 8. On the 10th, the commissioners sold a lot, in the square he thought he owned, to Uriah Forrest. On the 12th Johnson threatened a full-scale newspaper war and lawsuit if the commissioners dared to sell lots in his square. And he complained to the president. The board discovered in their minutes that they had indeed awarded the square to Johnson. That was so shocking that it called for an investigation, that included a list of "interrogatories" directed to the secretary. He answered them even though he expected he might "be called upon to give testimony in a court of law or equity." Hearing that, the commissioners promptly asked Luther Martin to represent them. The proceedings were wild enough to undermine the already frail health and unsteady will of the senior member of the board, Daniel Carroll, who had tried to help his old colleague Johnson. On February 19 he sent his resignation to the president pleading poor health.

The former Supreme Court justice was not above making his case directly to the commissioners in a series of long, rather snide letters. After all, it was he who had made the agreement with Greenleaf and had been with Greenleaf when the speculator chose the square as his own. There seemed to be a basis for compromise. Forrest replied to Johnson's threat of a lawsuit by offering to trade his lot for any other in the city of comparable value. But the commissioners would have none of that. Scott called Johnson "the Tom Thumb Hero of Frederick standing in Greenleaf's shoes," but not in official letters, of course. In a February 21 letter to the secretary of state, the commissioners underscored the importance of increasing the number of waterside lots, which were selling for $16 a waterfront foot, a far cry from the $80 Greenleaf had to pay for each lot. "If Mr. Johnson should prevail in the question which is pending it may make a difference in our revenue of about 20,000 Dollars which we shall never submit to but upon compulsion."

Johnson won valuable allies for his cause. In a February 22 letter to the president, former commissioner Stuart promised much to say on the matter when the president returned to Mount Vernon and allowed that "the commissioners are in my opinion in an error and have acted with too much precipitation."[1]

*   *   *

Speculating on the price of lots became the all-consuming passion of ambitious men in the city. Dermott became Stewart's agent to buy lots. In a February 26 letter he chided the general for not moving fast enough to buy lots on Pennsylvania Avenue Northwest between 24th and 26th Streets, noting that such "tardiness has deprived you of property for which you could now double your money on." Dermott had other ideas and tips. A lot at 20th and Pennsylvania had sold for £101, "but the purchaser would be glad to sell." He also touted lots near the hotel, not telling Stewart that that was where he had invested, and the squares along Pennsylvania Northwest from 7th Street to the Capitol. "From my situation," explained the man who divided lots for the commissioners, "I have, with assistance, in my power to make some money; therefore am desirous to be concerned in this property, . . . as I can dispose of it again immediately."

Scott had to take a hard look at the city, not only because he was a commissioner. He had to settle there. He knew he would get the best deal from Greenleaf. As for the good of the city as a whole, he saw that the commissioners, the proprietors, and Greenleaf were working at cross-purposes. Greenleaf was selling by the square, which detracted attention from the commissioners' sales of individual lots, which were bringing good prices, 16 to 18 cents a square foot, well above the 5 cents Greenleaf charged for lots in bulk. The other proprietors were not selling at all, "the ideas of the value of their property being highly visionary." Looking at the situation that way, Scott was less sure a loan was the answer. If all of the public's lots were tied up to secure a loan, the proprietors could combine to drive prices beyond the reach of buyers. Better than a loan would be for Greenleaf to divide his squares and market his lots individually. That, Scott discovered, was the "evil." "Until the immense fund of lots at market in the hands of Morris and Greenleaf are divided and subdivided so as to get out of public view as a known object of sale, our lots will not bring their value. . . ."

His colleagues allowed that last observation to go into their letter to the secretary of state, but not without reiterating their concern that the city was in desperate need of funds. Carroll had expected to go to Philadelphia to raise the loan but was sick and resigning. Scott's sentiments against a loan disqualified him. Thornton was well known in Philadelphia, and although he had no experience in such matters, the board assumed the loan was a done deal. The president and secretary of state had had a month to arrange it.

On reaching Philadelphia, William Thornton caught a bad cold, and he found nothing had been done to get a loan, save that Randolph had determined that if a loan could be obtained, it would be "impregnated with usury." Scott ascribed that to bankers getting wind of their troubles. "We are in distress," he explained to Thornton, ". . . and must expect to be preyed upon." There were two consolations. The distress "thank God [was] not of our own creation." And "the future prosperity of the territory" meant they were able to manage a loan at "even 8 or 9 percent, provided we have a good breathing spell" before repayment "and our finances are conducted with system and economy." With no loan in the works, Scott urged on Thornton and Randolph his idea that a small loan, $100,000 for one year, would do. The greatest evil would be to tie up too many lots.

Thornton set out to procure a small loan in Philadelphia but received little encouragement. And it made no sense to bother the London money markets for a pittance. Randolph advised that "it would be best to have all the money as soon as we can get it." He wanted a $400,000 loan for six years. The upshot of it all was that Thornton enlisted Richard Wells, a good friend and cashier of the Bank of North America, to forward the necessary information to one of his English correspondents, who in turn would sound out the bankers of London.[2]

*   *   *

In late February Thomas Law set out for the "New Jerusalem," stopping on the way to see the president, who was "very kind and attentive.'' Law told him that he hoped to spend the remainder of his days in Washington. But on that trip he spent only ten days. He liked the situation of the lots Greenleaf had picked for him (five carpenters sent from the president's house had finished the bridge over the Tiber in the nick of time, and Hoban sent the $1,028.33 bill to Greenleaf). Furthermore, Law made a good impression on those in the city. Scott wrote to Thornton that Law had "been a good deal in company and appears to me to be a polite, well bred, sensible man." In addition, Law's friend from the East Indies, Duncanson, was with him and eager to buy.

Law asked for deeds to the lots he had bought and ran into trouble. Having no funds to actually pay the commissioners for the lots, Cranch asked the commissioners to oblige by giving the titles and taking a mortgage as security for payment. The commissioners refused. As they put it to the secretary of state, if Greenleaf was getting four times what he promised to pay for the lots, he could jolly well "let the public participate in the benefits resulting from a ready money payment."

In a March letter to Greenleaf and his partners, Law asked for an explanation. In response to that complaint, both parties signed a new agreement on March 10. Greenleaf and company agreed to give Law "a good and sufficient mortgage" on the lots they did own until they could provide the titles to the lots Law had bought. Law also got all the partners to accede to his right to choose any lots, within ninety days, that had not already been sold. Law relinquished his option to back out of the deal after eighteen months. Greenleaf convinced him that that "would go abroad and give a spur to the city."

That contretemps did not deter Law's sidekick. After a week of looking around, Duncanson decided to buy up to £20,000 worth of lots in the same squares where Law would pick his lots. The three cash-poor speculators should have been feeling on top of the world, given the sale to Duncanson, the commissioners' confidence in getting a loan, and the opening of stock sales in the North American Land Company, as well as other odd harbingers of more sales. For example, a French India trader named Le Guen sent out feelers through Talleyrand that he was willing to trade 270,000 pounds of India cotton worth about $120,000 for lots in the federal city. But such a phalanx of good tidings hardly made a dent in the gloom surrounding the speculators, who simply could get no cash. There was a scarcity of money "as was never experienced before," because, Morris thought, of timid bankers and "the extensive shipments of money which have been made to Europe, the East and West Indies which exceeded anything of the kind in former years."

Law recognized all the symptoms of impending bankruptcy, but only in Morris. He wrote about it to the increasingly desperate Greenleaf. "He borrows at a dreadful interest, and sells disadvantageously like a desperate gambler to recover what he has lost. He has I know great resources, but no fortune can support his constant drains."

So desperate were the three partners that they fought over Duncanson's payment. Greenleaf returned to New York, leaving Cranch behind to collect Duncanson's check and bring it to New York. Morris got wind of that and told young Cranch that he wanted his part of the £20,000, as did Nicholson, and until then would withhold Greenleaf's shares in the North American Land Company. Cranch backed down and allowed Morris to hold it until Greenleaf sent down his authorization that it be divided into thirds and distributed to each partner. None of the partners even thought of dutifully advancing a portion of Duncanson's money to pay the commissioners for the lots they had sold to him. Greenleaf split the money. He could not turn his back on the land company, which promised so much. (Duncanson's check bounced, but he eventually made good on the payment.)[3]

The land company's capital was to be the six million acres of backlands the three had bought for an average of about a third of a dollar. Valuing the land at 50 cents an acre, the three partners split 30,000 shares worth $100 a share, thus giving themselves an instant and handsome profit. But the bylaws of the company forbade them from selling out. Each of them had to maintain a ten percent interest in the company, and, in selling the shares they controlled, they could not sell for less than $100. The penalty to be assessed against them if they cheated was $100,000.

Those who would settle the lands got a deal too. The individual who sold land was in a hurry to be paid. The company would always have its agent nearby to collect installments, so the company could give easy terms. A settler could buy a 500-acre farm at \$2 an acre by paying \$67 a year plus interest for fifteen years. The agent would be nearby because each tract the company opened for sale would be first settled by "some smart active intelligent young man of good character and connections" ("plenty of such are to be had," Morris claimed). The company would make out well too. "The farms will in the first instance sell for two dollars per acre . . . ," Morris explained to prospective stockholders, "and when 30 to 50 families are fixed on this tract the price may be raised to three and four dollars per acre, and as the settlement progresses, the price keeps advancing until it amounts beyond what I dare at this time to name lest you might suppose me extravagant in my ideas." He based the estimates on sales in the Genesee tract he had sold, which was being developed in the same way. Land bought for \$350,000 had sold for \$657,965.34. He estimated that the neighboring tracts were now worth \$2.5 million.

Morris expected that after three or four years dividends would be larger than six percent and at the end of the fifteen years it was likely the original capital invested would gain ten times as much in return. He only briefly alluded to the prospect that with such healthy dividends the shares were "good objects of speculation"; that is, they would be publicly traded at well above their par value of \$100 each. Those who bore the brunt of the hype saw through it rather easily, especially if they compared notes. The one thing they all had in common was that Morris owed them money. His hope was that they would take shares instead of cash.

The Washington lots the partners owned were not a part of the North American Land Company. But the futures of those lots and the company were linked. If money were raised by one, it would go to support the other until both enterprises were well established. In hyping the company Morris did not forget to hype the city. He told correspondents of the partners' "deep and promising" interest there, noting the sales to Law and Duncanson at five pence a square foot and alluding to a possible £40,000 sale at six or seven pence. He bragged that "single lots sell at 8d, 9d, 10d & 12d per square foot according to circumstances and position so that you see we shall wind up well especially as the purchasers are obliged to build a house on every third lot."[4]

*   *   *

To make ends meet, Deblois had to borrow $300 from one of his joiners, a "mortifying" experience. Because he was not getting money from Nicholson, Deblois said his operations in the federal city were falling apart. His workers took goods out of his shop in lieu of payment, and "when they know I have taken ten dollar in shop they are here like hawks after their prey ready to devour me for it." Having lost credit in Boston, New York, and Philadelphia, he could not restock his store. Those were "heart breaking circumstances" for a family so far away from all their friends and "3 miles from a doctor or any one that can assist us in sickness of which we have had a great deal thro' the winter." Unless Nicholson gave him $1,500 in a week, when he had to pay back Colonel Deakins, he would lose all credit in Georgetown.

A week passed and nothing came from Nicholson. "Oh! my dear sir," came the cry from the federal city, ". . . I am distressed to death, mortified and cast down to the earth. . . . I hope yet you will not let me sink—Death would be preferable to the horrid state I am in. . . ." Five days later, on March 25, Mrs. Deblois, the daughter of a former U.S. senator, wrote to Nicholson. Her husband was in bed with a violent fever that struck him down when no letter came from Nicholson in the Friday post. "Let me entreat you for a few moments to think of my situation watching my best friend in I fear a dangerous illness, in a strange place with three female infants, my case is deplorable. . . . I never saw such gloomy days."

Nicholson's rhetoric could rise to the occasion: "My distress for your situation is extreme. . . . I cannot describe my feelings for your case—but let it not sink you—we both shall soon see happier days. I have a negotiation a foot that must relieve me; yours shall follow as quick as the post can ride with it." But next day followed a more detailed excuse. The payment of $200,000 from Havana for a shipment of flour to France was past due since September. A few days later he sent the suffering family $1,350 and promised another $2,000.[5]

39. Hauling Pork to the Capitol

While in Philadelphia, Thornton was not about to miss the opportunity to unfold his vision of the city to the president. Not surprisingly, his chief concern was the Capitol. With the foundation laid, it was evident that it sat too low on the hill. And he wanted to make sure Hallet's plan, which did away with the basement, had not won over the president. Moreover, he had an idea how to level the city. The surveyors could make a book showing the intended level of every street, showing exactly how much earth had to be removed and where it could be used as fill. The proprietors he had talked to liked the idea and thought, with such a definitive guide, they would gladly defray some of the expense of grading the streets. He also had ideas about selling lots. But after dinner with the president, Thornton was so impressed with his burdens that he only brought up the issue of raising the foundation.

Thornton began his March 12 letter to the president by describing how he had gone over the ground east of the Capitol "with a very accurate instrument" and found that the levels taken by Blois were accurate. The ground was 17 feet, 8 inches, above the level of the foundation. At two shillings a cubic yard, it would cost £36,205 to remove all that earth from the Capitol square. By raising the foundation ten feet, however, the cost of removing the necessary ground would be £12,311. Thornton quoted estimates given by Hallet and Williamson for raising the foundation ten feet and came up with his own middling estimate of £7,400. To raise the foundation would save £16,494.

After laying the numbers before the president, Thornton cited aesthetic reasons. Keeping the building so low "contravened" the reason for placing it on an eminence. Only the top of the building would be visible throughout the city. Although it was true the other two commissioners were against raising the foundation because the expense of leveling the hill could be postponed, Thornton argued that it would "fall very heavy on a future day" and scare developers away from nearby lots. ". . . It would be a matter of universal condemnation were we to sacrifice so noble a monument of splendor, for the sake of so trivial and time saving consideration.''

Thornton let his colleagues know what he was up to, and Scott and Carroll presented their case to the secretary of state. The foundation was already ten feet deep and had cost $60,000, and raising it would be expensive and time consuming "in a country where money will not always command labor." As for removing the hill, it would soon disappear, since "the quantity of bricks wanted for public use together with those wanted by individuals would daily lessen that inconvenience." Anyway, it was "high time to know" what the president wanted, for they were "embarrassed very much whilst things remain in their present state of uncertainty." Were they to build Thornton's basement or Hallet's first story?[1]

*   *   *

The president put off any decision until he saw the situation himself on his way to Mount Vernon in April. But the problem with Thomas Johnson could not wait. Johnson had unabashedly set out to charm the president, pledging his fealty to his friend's dreams, for "the success of the city has now become important to your reputation," and "I tell you that I take the same interest in your success and honor as in my own." On March 4 the president wrote to Lear asking him to find out what people were saying about the dispute. On the 6th he wrote to Johnson ruing that the dispute had arisen and declining to get involved. Then he asked Johnson to recommend someone who could replace Carroll on the commission.

Lear's report to the president on the 8th endorsed Johnson's position. "It seemed to be a generally received idea that the lots on Rock Creek could not be conceived as water lots in the common acceptation of the term water lots *as applied to the city*." Only lots accessible to large ships were waterside lots. Lear also recalled that in October 1793, the commissioners had given him the strong impression that Greenleaf could select lots along Rock Creek. Lear begged off giving a fuller report because he was about to tour the river with the expert on canals, Weston. In his next letters Lear talked only about the canal. Weston found some of the workmanship "clumsy" but thought the locks at Little Falls would work and that the work at the Great Falls' locks could be completed in two years with no difficulty. That good news, combined with the new discipline among shareholders inspired by an auction of thirty-seven delinquent shares, promised to shore up the company's finances.

The Potomac, more than ever, seemed destined. The president took pains to remind the commissioners to enlarge his holdings on Peter's Hill.[2]

*   *   *

The roads to the federal city were crowded that spring, but the sculptor Ceracchi was not one of the travelers. He told the president he was unhappy with the management of the subscription to raise funds for his monument, likening the "malicious ignorance" attacking his project to the trials Galileo and Columbus had to endure. Senator Cabot had told him "the great project must absolutely fall for want of support." Elias Boudinot, director of the mint, had called it a "most foolish attempt." Ceracchi challenged Boudinot to explain why he signed the subscription letter and got the discouraging reply that "he did it as many other gentlemen, only to encourage my feeling." The artist recoiled at such moral principles. Meanwhile, the managers had not distributed the subscription letter, and Ceracchi had been told that Attorney General Bradford, one of the managers, had been heard to echo the opinion of Boudinot. "Certainly this," the artist raged, "is an opposition that would abate the courage of a lion." He begged the president to use his influence to "disperse the clouds that conceal the truth."

Others came to the city borne on clouds that concealed the truth. In March a group of English immigrants was persuaded by a dockside land agent to go to the federal city instead of Philadelphia. The latter city was "overstocked with immigrants. . . . Its situation, he said, in point of climate was very unfriendly to an European constitution . . . , that even Americans, who were natives of other states, most certainly avoided the dreadful spot from a knowledge of the certain destruction which accompanied the numerous malignant fevers so generally prevalent in and round Philadelphia." The federal city had cheap land and high wages. "Its very climate is grateful to Englishmen, and seems to invite them to partake of its salubrity; if we may judge of the uninterrupted state of health they enjoy after once feeling its invigorating influence."

Others were able to use the city's reputation as a boom town to practice more happy deceptions. One of the Bowies of nearby Prince Georges County, Maryland, offered a $40 reward for the return of two slaves, Clem and Will, "who were last seen on their way to the City of Washington with their broad axes and some other tools, and were believed to be in the city." Another planter advertised a $10 reward for John, who escaped from southern Virginia by claiming that he had a pass and that "he had hired his time for the year and was going to the federal city for employment."

This did not imply that the federal city was a safe place for blacks. But the widespread knowledge that a large number of slaves were working there made it seem plausible that blacks would legitimately be on the road bound for the city. Slaves such as Cogo and Richard Bowman found life there uncongenial enough to run away, but not necessarily too far. The latter was thought to be "lurking about the borders of the City of Washington." He was to be returned to Joseph Clark, the builder, and so, probably, was one of the slaves rented on Greenleaf's account.[3]

Working conditions in the city were made worse that winter by an outbreak of smallpox. The commissioners had their doctor inoculate ten of the slaves working for Slye. The cost of the treatment, $2.30 each, was deducted from what the slave earned for his master. That preventive, by giving the recipient a mild case of the disease, kept men off the job. When Deblois got enough money from Nicholson to finish building the tavern, his joiners "were obliged to get inoculated . . . , which will put back the house six weeks at least." Needless to say, local newspapers did not breathe a word of the smallpox epidemic.

The stream of building materials, which, by contract, were to begin streaming to the city in the spring, met some snags. William O'Neale, who was quarrying stone out of the public grounds along the western edge of the city, agreed to deliver 500 tons a month, but one of the scows the commissioners sold him had so many holes in it that large amounts of stone fell out next to the wharf and had to be removed. The scow sank in the Tiber. As that floundering was going on, John Mason rebelled at the new contract. He refused to sign unless the commissioners accepted the stone at the wharf, since he felt he had no control over the men he had to hire in the city to unload and haul it.

As the building season approached, the commissioners sent out their annual search party for lime. Hoban found none. To their consternation, wood too was still a problem. Hoban's man Stephenson went south to check on Henry Lee's lumber and found two rafts of 22,000 square feet (6,000 less than Lee was to have delivered in June 1794) lodged in the inlet formed by Jotank Creek on the Virginia side of the river across from Port Tobacco. The lumber down at Stratford Hall that Lee said was ready to be rafted up was uncut.

The commissioners asked Lee to have the rest of the timber contracted for ready for delivery by April 10, not that Hoban was going to wait for it. He asked the commissioners to advertise for 120,000 feet of flooring plank 32 feet long, 6 inches wide, and 1½ inches thick. On March 12 Hoban signified that it was time to begin outside work. He asked the commissioners for permission to hire someone "to ring the bell regularly." Carters began "hauling pork to the Capitol" to feed the slaves.

What was supposed to be different that building season were the work habits of the commissioners, since it was widely known that the president expected them to earn their $1,600 a year by being on the scene to supervise the work. Thornton did buy land in the city and Scott bought an estate one-quarter mile north of it, and not far from Rock Creek. But it would take time to build houses. They did set up office hours: three days a week, Thursday, Friday, and Saturday, from 9:00 A.M. to 2:00 P.M. "and as much oftener as the business required." And they moved their office from Georgetown to a building next to the Little Hotel at 14th and F Streets.

When he required the commissioners to reside in the city, the president had expected them to actually supervise the work in about the same way he managed his plantations when he was at Mount Vernon, namely, by riding around and seeing that the overseers had the work crews diligently doing their assigned tasks. Only Carroll had shown any predilection for going about to see what the workers were doing, but he was leaving the board. Given his interest in the Capitol, Thornton should have been a frequent visitor, but to be on the scene underscored the embarrassing fact that he had little idea how to actually build his plan or even provide detailed drawings of the work. Scott was by nature a wheeler-dealer and spent a busy spring cutting deals. Hoban told him what had to be done on the grounds: a fence 500 by 800 feet around the Capitol work site protecting the "carpenters' shop, stone cutters' shed, sawpits, lumber yard, store house & c." with three gates ten feet wide; a barracks for workers at the Capitol; and a horse to hoist stone at the president's house. Scott okayed the requests and set about raising the money. Scott sold a barracks at the president's house to Davidson for $2,000 and sold the house Hallet had occupied to Reverend Ralph for $2,400. Hadfield, who was to supervise construction at the Capitol, had no family and so would not need a house. Scott relished selling lots, getting a price of 18 cents a square foot from James Barry, the Baltimore merchant who had been looking at property for a year and was persuaded by Thomas Law. Barry was an East India trader, too.

Given their ordinary business, the commissioners had little time to spare for touring the work. That spring they had two extraordinary problems, finances and Johnson's suit. The Bank of Columbia refused to cash a Greenleaf note for $27,619, which necessitated reminding the bank's directors of their January agreement. Stoddert had learned to distrust Greenleaf's notes, since he realized the ones he had sent to London would come back protested. Scott managed to get money for the board but not before coming to some understanding with Stoddert and Forrest that it might not be a bad idea to declare Greenleaf in default and reclaim his lots. The idea also appealed to Scott because by getting rid of Greenleaf he got rid of Johnson, the other headache that spring.[4]

Johnson was back in the city in March prepared to fight. He insisted the commissioners divide the square so that he would know where lay the land he had bought from Peter. The commissioners refused to divide until the president decided if Water Street should run through the square. Johnson made the delay seem as detrimental as possible to himself and the city. He wanted to bring his farmhands to the city to improve his lots, but with any more delay he would leave them in Frederick to plant crops. He warned them not to convey his lot to Forrest: "an executive officer subjects himself to an action and charges if he exercises his office to the wrong and injury of a private person, a point that perhaps you and I may have occasion to look into." They should not "plunge into new absurdities," but he was sure they would. "If a man finds himself in the mire, 'tis best for him to look about before he takes another step lest his next may be deeper and at last his unavailing struggles so sink him entirely; but I have no expectation but you will plunge forward." The commissioners disdained replying to "personal abuse and invective," as they informed the president; "those distinguished by nothing but the purity of the language and the keenness of the satire are carefully preserved among the archives of the city, for the benefit of learned posterity, and to be laid before the public when necessary."

The president, however, got his own dose of Johnson's wit. After averring "that they or I must retreat and it is not usual with me to give up the ground I have taken," he passed on a homily: "It is mortifying that an old man almost crossed the stage, cannot quietly quit it without having kicks at behind personified in young men; however some times, instead of the old fellow's falling on his nose, the blade kicks so wanton and high that he falls on his back himself and draws on him the contemptuous laughter of the spectator. May such strokes never reach you or your humble servant."[5]

40. Partiality, Knavery, and Utter Ignorance

That April the city awaited the arrival of the president and Greenleaf. The commissioners were eager for instructions regarding the Capitol and for vindication of their fight with Johnson. The employees of Greenleaf wanted money to continue their work. But instead of those main men, Thomas Law and Norton Pryor came to town. Not that friends of the city were not pleased to see both. Law's quick return signified a satisfactory arrangement on his part with Greenleaf and Morris. Norton Pryor was one of three men who had won the hotel in Blodget's lottery. His arrival promised the rapid completion of the hotel.

Hoban, who had supervised construction of the hotel, gave Pryor a tour of the $15,000 worth of work done and thought $9,000 more would completely enclose it, with windows. The commissioners assured Pryor that they had an eye on Blodget, who was still struggling to pay off prizes, and would cooperate with him "in taking the most effectual measures to compel the finishing of the hotel."

As for Thomas Law, it took only two trips to the city for him to decide on what the fate of the city depended. He wrote to Greenleaf and Morris and urged them to get the president to understand that "the Eastern Branch can alone make the city. . . . From the moment that some conclusions are formed respecting wharfs, warehouses, &c. that city take its rise and a rapid one." The route of the branch of the canal that ended at the foot of New Jersey Avenue had to be changed so that it could avoid a 40-foot-high hill. "The President upon seeing the ground would at once perceive the necessity of the alteration." Although Law himself did not buy waterside lots, he formed a virtual partnership with James Barry, who had.[1]

*　　*　　*

The North American Land Company was undergoing a rocky birth and was not bringing in money or much paper from creditors. Nicholson hit on the idea of securing a domestic loan secured by the deeds sent to Holland, but not used. Greenleaf scotched the idea by warning that under their instructions, Bourne may have sold lots reconveyed to him by the bankers.

Nicholson was the antithesis of Greenleaf. The Bostonian was primarily a salesman. The Pennsylvanian was a manipulator adept at tinkering with lands, stocks, bank notes, mortgages, and, most of all, accounts, squeezing as much profit, or at least credit, out of them as he could. Discouraged in his attempt to wrest more income from the arrangements Greenleaf had made, he turned his attention to decreasing expenditures on the Washington property. At last, Nicholson began to feel that he was striking gold. After calculating that the partners had spent not less than $120,000 there, he asked Morris, "What have we got for our money . . . ?"

Back in July he had impugned Greenleaf's management of the property based on scuttlebutt from the federal city. Now he could analyze reports generated by Greenleaf's employees. One third of the money sent to Cranch was unaccounted for; the salaried employees were a waste. Nicholson hired a man of his own to see what was going on in Washington. This was Adonyah Stansburrough, a Dover, Delaware, tanner, for whom a promise of financial backing for a tannery was a good enough fee.

Greenleaf did not appreciate Nicholson's pressure. He was having trouble finding the money to carry on the Washington operations because he was forced to pay the bills coming back unpaid from Europe, almost all for the comfort of Morris's and Nicholson's creditors. To end the pressure and get full command of the only property held by the partners that was raising money, Greenleaf offered to buy out his partners' interest in the city. Nicholson countered with his own proposal to buy Greenleaf and Morris out. Needless to say, both buyers wanted liberal terms of payment. Nicholson offered no more than six percent on their investment in the city until the property began to raise money. The man in the middle thought both offers unrealistic when the problem at hand was raising money to pay the next installment of $68,000 due May 1. Morris blamed Greenleaf for the predicament because the money paid by Law had gone into the maws of his other creditors.

Greenleaf did press his friend Law to help by raising money in London to stop the bills from coming back. Law persuaded Duncanson to buy another $64,000 worth of Washington lots to be paid for by friends in London, provided they agreed, at six cents a square foot. (They didn't.) Greenleaf's only other negotiation was with a Georgia speculator, Isaac Polock, who offered to trade 731,000 acres of Georgia land for lots and houses valued at $20,000. Greenleaf asked for cash instead. Polock countered by offering the notes of David Allison, who had sizable claims on Morris and Nicholson. That would help. They made a tentative agreement to be finalized in Washington.[2]

*   *   *

When the president arrived in Georgetown, Johnson made the shrewder moves. He had filed his suit a few days before, so that he would not be in the position of having to accede to a presidential wish to keep the matter out of court. He also arranged for Stuart and Carroll to meet with the president and support his claim.

As they conferred with the president about raising the foundation of the Capitol—he put off a decision until his return in a few weeks—Scott and Thornton avoided talking about the dispute. Then they heard about his meeting with the old board. They amassed every scrap of paper they could on the dispute, put it in a packet, and sent it hot on the trail of the weary president, who had at last reached Mount Vernon. The heft of the file depressed the president. The cover letter accused his old friend Johnson of "partiality, knavery, and utter ignorance." The president sent it all back, saying he had not read any of it and pleading that since the dispute was in litigation, "it is unnecessary for me to express any sentiment thereon." He regretted that the dispute had not been settled, "as good rarely flows from disputes—evil often."

It is safe to assume that Scott and Thornton did not breathe a word about Johnson when the president joined them for a day, April 27, on his return trip to Philadelphia. They all agreed to raise the foundation six feet. The president was not impressed with his new commissioners. Not only were the disputes demoralizing, but the board still was not supervising the work. He explained the problem to Alexander White, the former Virginia congressman whom he wanted to replace Carroll on the board. The only difference between the old and new board was that the old one met once a month, the new once or twice a week. "In the interval the old resided at their houses in the country; the new resided at their houses in Georgetown." The new board had shifted to getting work done by contracts and piecework but relied on others "to see to the performance."

The changes were for the better but, the president thought, "by no means apply a radical cure to the evils that were complained of," nor did they justify a salary of $1,600.[3]

*   *   *

Hoban decided not to suffer through another building season with Williamson, who, apart from being anti-Catholic and anti-Irish, kept harping on keeping bricks out of the public buildings, literally trying to turn them into the castles he claimed to know so well. Williamson in turn did not care for the new contract Roe's and Dobson's crews worked under. Men paid by the perch, he calculated, were making 18 to 20 shillings ($2.50) a day while doing less than men working by the day for 9 shillings. The pieceworkers hid the ease with which they made their money by "sporting away time." Roe also brought more slaves to assist the masons, fourteen slaves for eighteen masons. Williamson complained to Scott, demanding all masons work under him. Scott humored him but had no inclination to undo the contracts that, he had told the president, saved money. Roe explained the seeming inactivity of his men by pointing out the lack of stone, claiming 137 labor days lost in April. Furthermore, there was no direction. They needed an architect to tell them "the just thickness of each wall, also the latitude of the doors and windows," and so on. The board gave Williamson his notice, but not without thanking him for his work. They hoped the old man would be content to spend his days in his house off the president's house square merely viewing the great work around him. They placed Hoban in charge of all masons in the city.

Williamson was in no mood to retire quietly. He ridiculed the board's putting an Irish carpenter in charge of stonework—next they would be asking Hoban to make shoes!—and accused the board of impugning his professional ability, which gave him cause to demand an investigation. They summoned Clark, Lovering, and Henderson to form a board to hear Williamson's grievances, taking care to assure them that they thought Williamson had carried out orders to "the best of his faculties" and had always been "decent and proper." The board cited the old man's "inability to carry on

large works and . . . inability to keep the workmen at their labor and
duty.'' The three-man board agreed that he was just too old for the
task.

*   *   *

On his return to Philadelphia, the president got a long letter from
Mrs. Hallet. Her husband did not want his old job back even though
the plan of the Capitol was his and no one could superintend its
construction better. She begged the president only to pay their debts
as compensation for their considerable suffering, ''I shrink still at
the remembrance of three children torn out of my breast by death
here, on this very spot. . . . The exhorbitant price of any kind of
provisions in this retired place; a heavier rent for a house in the
woods than we should have paid in Philadelphia for a more decent
and more comfortable one; . . . who can rise and object that
mismanagement, pleasure or ostentation in the midst of the woods
far from all society have brought us to this cruel situation?''

She wanted $550, enough money to return the family (two children
survived) to Philadelphia and pay off their debts. The commissioners in turn were unmoved, explaining to the president that they had
given Hallet $250 more than called for merely out of regard for the
suffering of his family.

By mid-May the commissioners bragged to the president about
how ''rapidly'' the Capitol progressed. The only cloud on the
horizon was trouble in delivering stone and bricks. The Chopawamic
quarry turned out to have bad stone, so they offered Cooke and
Brent, who ran the Aquia quarries, a premium to get out more
stone. Cooke and Brent asked instead for an advance to build three
vessels that could carry 100 tons of stone each. The board stayed
out of the shipbuilding line, sensing rightly that Cooke and Brent
would build the ships themselves. They had just cut into rock of the
highest quality, which gave ''a tolerable prospect of a sufficient
supply of stone.''

Their brick supplier, Mitchell, worried about his ability to make
the bricks the commissioners ordered. Again, labor was the crux of
the problem. A set of slaves he had hired cheaply would not do. He

hired an experienced slave from Deakins for four shillings plus a half pint of rum a day. That added up to $20 a month for one slave, and Deakins was upping the rental to five shillings a month in June. The commissioners refrained from soothing the nerves of suppliers with more money.

Their own nerves became frayed when the expected payment from the partners did not come. Greenleaf sent a note for $28,333.33, his third of what was due, which Deakins said could be cashed only in New York or Philadelphia in twenty-five days. The board did not appreciate the partial payment nor the delay and expense of getting the money. "The affairs of the city are too seriously alarming to admit of delay," they told Greenleaf. If not paid in real money by May 25, they would "use every means which legally can be used to compel payment." And for good measure, they told Blodget that if the money to complete the hotel was not forthcoming in twenty days they would sue in chancery to foreclose on his property that they held as security.[4]

*   *   *

After a general meeting to rally support for the monument fizzled, Ceracchi gave up. He told the president of the "plot which is now hither against the Trionfe of Liberty and the success of the Federal City." Noting that he had lost $25,000 in the enterprise, he informed the president that the busts he had made could no longer be considered donations, and he sent a bill for Washington's, $1,500 and $812 for the pedestal.

The president offered to pay for the bust but protested that he had never been told what it would cost. He reminded the artist that "the United States are just emerging from the difficulties and expenses of a long and bloody war and cannot spare money for the purposes of these gratifns. and ornimental figures as in the wealthy countries of Europe."

Before departing, Ceracchi bewailed the "pernicious" plots that showed that "immorality is practiced by the gentlemen in the highest station." Then he rose triumphantly above them: "I am disengaged by this American infatuation, from which I am now delivered as from a poisonous monster which possessed my senses." He went to France.[5]

41. The Workmen Assembled Clamourous

Lear went to New England that spring to arrange for shipments of lime, timber, and salted meats to his wharf in the federal city. In New York, he conferred with his backer Greenleaf who confessed that he could contribute nothing to the company. As for the checks coming back unpaid from Europe, Lear wrote that he was assured by Greenleaf "that he had sent on more than enough [money] to face everything that might be in his name," and as for those used for payments by Morris and Nicholson, if they "should not be provided for by them, that he shall make any sacrifice to take them up."

Back on the Potomac, Lear was gratified to see a boat with a hundred barrels of flour go through the Little Falls locks, and the public buildings were going on "briskly." However, "almost every private building" was "at a stand," with "great numbers of workmen" leaving. The only sign of progress was Barry preparing to build a wharf along the Eastern Branch and Duncanson laying out the grounds for his mansion above it. The slump in private building did not alarm Lear. Blaming it on the ill effects of Greenleaf's and Morris's speculations elsewhere, he told the president, "Whenever a sober state of things shall again take place, I am persuaded that the tides will flow here as rapidly as the most sanguine well-wishers to the establishment could desire."[1]

Deblois, the veteran merchant, was not so cool. The only thing his backer Nicholson could offer in support was a bill of lading for a ship bringing the $150,000 to $200,000 he expected as payment for a shipment of flour. The idea was that Deblois would wave that around town and get instant cash. Deblois mentioned it to Commissioner Carroll, who thought it worthless and lectured Deblois, who dutifully passed the gist of it on to Nicholson: "Mr. C. was very much alarmed that you should trust to so slight prospects of providing for payment of your note, indeed he was much in dread of the consequences, & feared they would be very serious to you and the Company." Deblois got the impression that "the commissioners . . . mean to push" Greenleaf and company.

That boded ill for the future, as if present operations were not grim enough. Deblois had "brickmakers, masons, joiners & c. doing little or nothing for want of money; I cannot discharge them for want of cash to pay them off, I cannot employ them for want of funds to push on." By the end of May the situation had not improved. Alexandria merchants, burned by the failure of a ship chartered by Nicholson, attached the ship and its goods. Fearing that their next step would be to attach his own effects, Deblois begged Nicholson to settle accounts between them.

Nicholson was not disposed to panic. He was confident that money was on its way, and he sensed that he had the upper hand in his struggle with Greenleaf for control of the Washington property. Deblois was important in his plans, so rather than close accounts with the long suffering merchant, he opened new vistas, dubbing him the man in charge of all building in the city (once Nicholson took control of everything). He passed on encouraging words—Law had a high opinion of Deblois. As for paying the commissioners, Greenleaf should have paid with the money he got from Law and Duncanson.

Nicholson refused to admit he had no credit. He had just bought out (not with cash) Morris's share of the Asylum Land Company, which he calculated was worth $500,000. For a London banker he listed fourteen sources of income: three ships on the high seas; money the French government owed him; two large checks to him that, so to speak, were in the mail; and eight agents in Europe or on their way to sell his lands or shares in the various land companies

Nicholson had large stakes in. One of the agents was James Tate, "famous for his cure of cancer." If all that seemed too nebulous, he owned half of an "excellent furnace" on the banks of the Potomac, with ore and coal "in plenty." With a little encouragement, he could ship pig to London.

Morris, most likely because of his friendship with the president, was more upset at their inability to pay the commissioners. He tried in vain to get Alexandria and Baltimore merchants to sell shares in the land company. He tried in vain to collect early on some ship insurance due him. He was left with trying to shame Greenleaf into paying the whole installment: "You must work up the whole sum and I shall credit my part against what you owe me on the land account." Nicholson calculated that Greenleaf owed them both $104,698.84 and so informed Greenleaf, who was unmoved. In May, Morris managed to raise $7,000, which he sent to Greenleaf for payment to the commissioners, and then he let Greenleaf draw on him for the payment, provided Greenleaf pay him back as soon as possible. Morris did not want to lose the property, still viewing it as his ace in the hole. On June 1 he wrote to his son William, who was selling lands in Europe, that they had sold Washington lots "to the value of 100,000 pounds and the price is risen greatly." However, he could not instruct William to sell because he was not sure which lots belonged to the company. Only Greenleaf knew enough to actually sell.[2]

*   *   *

Greenleaf was not ready to lock horns with Morris and Nicholson. Not that avoiding them in Philadelphia showed any lack of courage. Going to the federal city without money to pay his workers was an act of courage in itself. He did take the precaution of persuading Law to go with him and hoped to close the deal with Polock. On his arrival, Law recalled, "the workmen assembled clamourous for arrears of pay." Law offered a loan, which Greenleaf refused on the spot but took up when he got back to New York. He wanted money to pay creditors who would thereupon loan him more money. Work in the city was not as important as that, and the nucleus of his operation, two relatives, Cranch and Samuel Eliot, and three French refugees, Henry, Blois, and Lucat, he could trust implicitly. He set them to investigate "the unfair demands" of the contractors and workers. Clark especially seemed to ask far too much, $72,000, than his eight unfinished houses warranted. Greenleaf had already paid him half of that and suspected Clark owed him money, not vice versa.

Despite not paying his workers, contractors, and suppliers, including Carroll of Duddington, who had sold bricks to Clark and Lovering, Greenleaf still impressed everyone to whom he did not owe money. He told all about Polock buying the six houses Henderson was building and was much in the company of Law. They joined other Capitol Hill proprietors in forming a subscription to build a hotel next to the Capitol. Work on the building began immediately. Lear informed the president that Greenleaf and Law proposed "very extensive improvements on the Eastern Branch, at the place where the canal is to enter, and some measures are taking to carry them into effect." Lear was only mildly suspicious. "But they *talk* of doing a vast deal more than can possibly be accomplished this season." However, "the situation is eligible and their plans so far as I have heard of them, good."[3]

Greenleaf used the wharves to get the commissioners' minds off his inability to pay them. To a degree it worked. After he left the city, the president tried to reestablish the chain of command and get the commissioners back to implementing the plan. The secretary of state wrote that the president wanted them "to fix the places for the bank, exchange, the judiciary, mint and other public institutions." Around those "points" the other buildings in the city would be gathered. All those sites had been designated, save the mint, which the board thought could go just north of Pennsylvania Avenue at the foot of Capitol Hill, where the Tiber's waters would be available. Then the board moved on to what was important. Greenleaf, Law and Barry wanted warehouses along the river. Barry calculated that he could save five percent in loading and unloading his ships. Restrictions would drive shippers to Georgetown and Alexandria. The commissioners asked the president if the developers should be accommodated.

To divert complaining workers, Greenleaf helped establish a

newspaper at the point. Thomas Wilson's *Impartial Observer* breathed not a word about the misery there. It broadcast ads for a new tavern, a dry goods and hardware store, and a school opened by John O'Connor, propagandist for the Potomac back in 1790. James Simmons not only lived in the first completed house, the large brick one at 6th and N Streets, but imported furniture from Philadelphia to sell to those moving into neighboring houses (if they were ever finished). Most important, the *Impartial Observer* ridiculed Blodget's announcement that he would soon commence drawing the second lottery. It explained that he meant on "All Fool's Day." Wilson published this news item: "It is reported that a Great Agent has lately been to Laputa, and obtained a patent from the King, granting him the sole privilege of erecting buildings by beginning at the top. This is thought by many fortunate, as he never yet could do anything by beginning at the BOTTOM." Blodget was the rascal ruining the city, not Greenleaf.

To stop ridicule of the hotel and get the commissioners off his back, Blodget came to town and promised to pay the board $16,000 to be used to finish the hotel. That satisfied the commissioners, though when reporting the good news to the secretary of state, they assured him they would stay on Blodget's case until he actually paid. That left Blodget with the legion of adventurers in the second lottery to satisfy. A number of them formed a syndicate to buy tickets in an effort to force Blodget to begin the drawing.[4]

*   *   *

Thomas Johnson came to town hoping that with Greenleaf there as well as the newly appointed commissioner, Alexander White, his problem could be solved. White was too busy clearing up his legal business in Winchester, Virginia, and before any meeting of the minds could take place, Johnson heard that Forrest had actually seen a draft of what Scott and Thornton had sent to the president. Johnson asked to see it. They refused. The president soon heard from both parties. In a letter to the board, which he sent to the president, Johnson got personal: "the more intercourse I have with you the less I wonder at the confusion so obvious in your letters and conduct. One [Scott] has an empty space to fill up with ideas on trusts, equitable interests and legal titles; the other [Thornton] a still harder task, he has his head to clear of the lumber which crowds it to make room for what is correct."

The dig at Thornton was a rather neat reminder of the trouble the amateur architect had in arranging the beams in the Capitol so that rooms could be used without everyone bumping their heads. Scott's and Thornton's response was to return the letter with the following explanation: "We conceive it peculiarly indecent in you, having been in public life, to offer insults to us as servants of the public; more especially as decent language was returned by us to all the disgraceful epithets of your former letters. We are willing to attribute the whole of your conduct to a derangement of mind, which we lament, and therefore consider you rather as an object of pity than of resentment. We return your last letter, and refuse all further communication till a return of reason point out the propriety of using at least the language of a gentleman."

Scott decided to strike at the root of the evil, asking the man defending them against Johnson's suit under what conditions Morris and Greenleaf should get deeds. Luther Martin opined that not one lot should be conveyed until all conditions of the sale were fulfilled. "Shall M & G have a liberty to select the best of the lots, pay the 30 pounds for each of them, and claim a conveyance of those lots so selected? It appears to me that this would be as absurd as for a person who should contract for a thousand acres of land at a certain price per acre to select a few acres of the best land and on paying for those acres to claim a conveyance thereof."

Scott and Thornton promptly suspended all further conveyances to Greenleaf and gave him sixty days to pay the May installment or face default. ". . . Those gentlemen think," they excoriated the partners to the secretary of state, "their funds can be better employed than by complying with their engagements with us. If we were disposed to grant indulgences and the affairs of the city would permit it, which they will not, these gentlemen would come with very ill grace to ask it."

The board's attack somewhat backfired. Rather than pressure Greenleaf to pay so he could get titles, Law demanded the commissioners give him titles, or he would appeal to the president. And

Law promised Greenleaf that he would build houses to take up the slack. Greenleaf did with the commissioners what he was doing with so many creditors dunning him for payment on his bounced checks. He agreed to complete the payment with notes due in thirty, forty-five, and sixty days. Looking to the time when payment would fall due, he had Cranch open negotiations for mortgaging lots to the commissioners in lieu of cash payments.

Then good news came from Holland. Bourne reported that the Rotterdam loan was going well.[5]

42. The Motley Set We Found Here

Into that happy land sailed the *Two Sisters,* bearing workers for the federal city. To judge from the tally of the customs inspector at Alexandria, the ship carried only fifteen passengers. Only four brought tools with them. Samuel Moodey, for example, had "one chest tools, one trunk, one bag wearing apparel, one hat box, one bed and bedding, one gun & &." No employers from the federal city were on hand to greet them. The interesting cargo was "an electrical machine" complete with an "aurora borealis flask," wire with feathers, spoon for spirits, and a pyramid. The latest fad to ease the pains of modern life had landed.

Letters published a year later in *Look Before You Leap, or a Few Hints To Such Artisans . . . Desirous of Emigrating to America . . . Particularly to the Federal City of Washington,* an anti-immigration pamphlet printed in London, showed that the newly arrived workers did not like what they saw. After expressing shock at the anti-British attitude of the press, Moodey described Alexandria as "one of the most wicked places I ever beheld in my life; cockfighting,

horse racing, with every other species of gambling and cheating.''
He estimated that there were forty to fifty billiard tables in town and
heard that the Protestant church had services once a month.

He was soon in the federal city, and it was no improvement: ''at
present the heat is almost intolerable, the market being obliged to
be kept at 4 in the morning, the meat killed at 12 at night, and all
liquors are kept in water. As to what we have been told in England
respecting the City of Washington, it is all a mere fabrication . . . ,
not *40 houses* in the *extensive* metropolis.'' He compared the terrain
to ''Sutton Colefield,'' which the editor of the pamphlet described
as ''an extensive barren waste near Birmingham.'' It bears noting
that the editor, who was trying to discourage workers from leaving
England, probably did not print any portion of Moodey's letters that
might have been favorable to the city. Moodey got work with a
contractor at the point who worked for Hoban on Barry's buildings.[1]

*   *   *

The prospect of having to supervise workers almost prompted
Alexander White to back out of his appointment to the board. After
he accepted the job, the president wrote to the former congressman
criticizing Scott and Thornton for not supervising the work. That
worried White. He wrote back, ''Idleness can only be prevented by
an accurate knowledge of what labourers ought to perform.'' The
president did not want to lose his man and assured White that he
need not be ''skilled in the principles of architecture'' nor have
''any particular knowledge of work.'' Care had to be taken to
prevent ''imposition'' by contractors and ''when day wages are
given (which in all practicable cases ought to be avoided) to have an
eye that the overlookers of them are diligent.'' White took the job
but was not eager to ride around at the mercy of 150 to 200 workers
whose thirst was so voracious that the board directed Captain
Williams to make a weekly report ''of all persons who retail liquor
without a license.''[2]

In late June masons at the Capitol were strung out from the wall
of the north wing, along the wall of central section and along the
wall of the south wing. They were laying 300 feet of stone, the like

of which had never been seen in the United States. Then part of the foundation wall on which the workers were laying the freestone collapsed. News of the "accident" spread quickly to Philadelphia. Hoban and Blagden investigated and concluded that there was bad work in the foundation walls that had to be taken down. Fearing that reports of the problem would be "exaggerated," the commissioners took pains to "state the thing as it really is" to the secretary of state. By taking one foot of the bad foundation walls down and "laying large bond stone," workers would make the walls "perfectly secure." None of the work in the north wing was suspected, so the stonesetters could begin laying the freestone there again in the next week.

The commissioners did not mention the name of the offending contractor, only saying that he had worked on the building from the beginning and that there was no suspicion "of any foul play." They had dismissed the contractor and his men and planned to hire "a better set" in a few days who would work under a person "constantly" employed "to see every course of stone or brick as it is laid." Actually, there was no such happy denouement. Almost all of the work that had been done that season had to be taken down, a loss of $1,264 worth of work in the north wing and $1,470 in the south wing. And no one accepted liability. McDermott Roe's men, who it was thought did the work, disclaimed any responsibility, blaming it on other workers, who in turn claimed to have heard McDermott Roe tell his men to lay the wall without mortar.

Randolph's reaction was to gently remind the board that the president had encouraged them to pay closer attention to the work, not that he meant to insinuate that they had not paid "due attention . . . to the running up of the walls of the Capitol." "But," he continued, "it may happen in some other instance, that a similar fatality may take place, which might be prevented by the watchful inspection of the commissioners." It was not so much "professional skills" that the commissioners had to bring to the subject, "but, the artists, being conscious, that they are animadverted upon by persons of activity and authority, will not venture far upon improper conduct." While he had their ear, Randolph passed on a question from the president, "whether the board can by meeting once or twice a week only, accommodate in due time all their business."

Randolph also enclosed a letter to the president from Collen Williamson (which has not been found) to show them "what anxiety there is to animadvert on the commissioners." And he enclosed a "very inauspicious" letter from Wells, who was trying to arrange a loan for the city in England.

In their reply, the contempt Scott and Thornton had long felt for the men building the city poured forth: "Those not acquainted with the motley set we found here, and who from necessity have too many of them been still continued in public employment can form no adequate idea of the irksome scenes we are too frequently compelled to engage in." They protested that even if they had been on the scene every day, it probably would not have prevented "the scene of villainy." The men at fault, especially McDermott Roe, had property in the city, and so could not be capable of "a cool premeditated and deliberate act of villainy which in its consequences might have occasioned the death of thousands." The commissioners reassured Randolph that work was continuing in good order. That day, masons "commenced setting the freestone." They did not mention that only ten, not the thirty they had there before, were at work under Blagden, who moved over from the president's house, getting a $1 a day raise, which brought his pay to $3.63 a day.

That, combined with the failure to get a loan in England, forced Scott to think that building one wing of the Capitol by 1800 would be job enough. In desperation, Thornton came up with an idea to get obedient and cheap masons: buy "50 intelligent negroes" and train them to do the stonework. Two or three experienced men could be induced with a wage of up to $4 a day to train and supervise the slaves. As an incentive for the slaves, who would only get room, board, and clothing, the commissioners would give them their freedom in five or six years.

Although nothing came of the idea, it highlights how uncomfortable the commissioners were with free labor. They preferred workers who could make no demands and who were beholden to them for everything they knew. Periodically, men came bearing other substitutes for free labor. The commissioners were unmoved by "a machine for carrying and raising earth." They were a little leery of machines, since the brick machine still had not reached potential.

Harbaugh rigged up a sawing machine, but "a proper person to attend [it] has been wanting. . . ." They did have four men and a horse attending a machine to grind lime and a few cranes to lift stone.[3]

* * *

The Philadelphia banker Wells passed on some rather damning extracts from his London correspondent who confidentially sounded out four bankers on the possibility of a loan. Those gentlemen saw through the commissioners' effort to fob off remote lots as security. Nothing in the proposal induced "a belief that this remoter part of a very extensive plan will soon, if ever, be wanted for building." But even if the security were proved to be "unexceptionally ample," the loan would not fly in England. Repayment depended on Congress actually moving to the city, an idea "*here* represented, not to be very popular in any of the states northward of Maryland." Finally, investors were making six to eight percent on English and American public securities, so why should they invest in anything riskier?

The commissioners wrote to Stoddert, the president of the Bank of Columbia, alerting him of the failure of the English loan and the deficiency of between $40,000 and $50,000 in the payments from Morris and Greenleaf. "To guard against the hazard" of work on the public buildings stopping for want of funds, they wanted a loan of $20,000 for 120 days.[4]

* * *

Among the partners a realization dawned that stopgaps in their affairs would no longer do. "A doleful letter" came from Bourne. The Rotterdam loan petered out, and the little money raised had to be used to cover other debts. The end of the vaunted partnership to corner American backlands on the strength of a Dutch loan secured by Washington lots was at hand. In late June Greenleaf again offered to buy Morris and Nicholson out. They invited him to come to

Philadelphia to talk it over. The contentiousness of their past
meetings was gone. They were that bad off. Greenleaf could raise
money to pay off the bills coming back from Europe only by turning
to moneylenders, who charged up to five percent interest a month.
Morris was sorry Greenleaf was "obliged to pay through the nose
to obtain the use of money." Something had to give, so Greenleaf
"offered to buy or sell the Washington lots at a price & on terms
which he named." Morris thought that "manly" and at first concluded to sell. Then he and Nicholson talked it over and bought
Greenleaf out. Morris explained: "It was more likely that the lots
would command money to pay our debts than Mr. G's paper."

That decided, they arranged the deal so that each party seemed
to come out of it stronger financially. They valued the Washington
property at almost $2 million so that Morris and Nicholson paid
Greenleaf $681,904 for his share, payable in four annual installments
through 1799. But the $318,501.71 Greenleaf owed to the North
American Land Company covered the first two installments. The
only pressure the transaction put on Morris and Nicholson was to
raise money to pay the commissioners and continue building in the
city. Greenleaf was released from those demands and had almost
$400,000 more in Morris's and Nicholson's paper, payable in three
to four years, to use to secure loans.

All three claimed they were trying to keep the best interests of
the city in view. Morris wrote to Cranch that hitherto he had trusted
the Washington property to Greenleaf's "care and attention" but
found that it was "in disgrace and distress." Now that he had
bought out Greenleaf, and once things were put in order, that would
never happen again. Greenleaf assured worried retainers that the
federal city "has not, nor ever will cease to be very dear to me."
Nicholson wrote to creditors in Georgetown that he and Morris
would look "personally" to the affairs of the city, beginning "by
discharging those arrears which remain unpaid."

Each of them knew too well that his first priority had to be to save
his own skin. Greenleaf wrote to Nicholson that he had covered
$34,100 of the $205,555.55 worth of Greenleaf's bills that Nicholson
used. Now, however he was so pressed that he had to "*rely solely*"
on Nicholson to pay the rest. He urged Nicholson to forget about
the city and worry about the "more pressing" problem of "retiring

my engagements for your bills." It was not the city's progress that worried Greenleaf. "I fall, tho' in the midst of wealth," he warned, "a victim to our common cause—& my fall will give a blow of the most fatal nature to operations which begin now to wear a pleasing aspect and to promise the most happy issue."

Nicholson replied promptly with a plan suggested by Morris "by which I can be able to meet my engagements for the bills." It all depended on mortgaging some Washington lots. Nicholson had the same priorities as Greenleaf. Money raised on the city property would not go into the city but to retire old debts. As for Morris, while promising to pay the commissioners "within a week or ten days," he instructed Cranch "to avoid as much as possible incurring any expenses or debt."

Of course, to the world Morris sounded a fanfare. "The city of Washington will rise faster than any city ever did," he wrote to one of his land agents in England. ". . . My son William is to settle there, and I can now turn my attention, and going to bend my force to the building and improving there. Lotts that may now be purchased for 5d, 6d to 9d per square foot will soon get up to the double and treble of these prices, and houses built there sell instantly for ten per cent advance on the house and 100 per cent on the lott, so that I recommend to you and your friends to take an interest there in time. . . ."[5]

43. To Cavil at Trifles

Greenleaf left New York to live in Philadelphia, in part to avoid his creditors, in part to be closer to his former partners, now so in debt to him, and there was a Miss Allen he was interested in. A resident but a few days, he bumped into the secretary of state and explained why he sold out. He blamed the "commissioners" who "have constantly and will continue to oppose every obstacle to my operations in the city. . . ." His major beef was that both Scott and Thornton had bought property on the Georgetown side of the city so that it had become "for their *personal* interest to promote . . . that part of the city" and thwart plans to improve the Eastern Branch and open trade with India. (Thornton must have found that rather boorish, since he bought several lots near Georgetown from Cranch.)

Randolph insisted that Greenleaf make the charges in writing. Greenleaf demurred, and Randolph "explicitly informed him that he must either give me under his hand his charges against the commissioners or request me in writing not to mention them to the President." Greenleaf made the charges. The commissioners dismissed Greenleaf as a "malignant slanderer" trying to divert attention from his inability to meet his payments. Greenleaf, in turn, defended his performance. Property values in the city had risen in some cases "eighteen fold." He and his partners expended "upwards of $150,000 for the past year, a sum fourfold what was ever contemplated by your predecessors as necessary to the fulfillment of my contract. . . . If therefore the strict letter of the agreement has in some instances been deviated from, the spirit of the agreement has been attended to, and I know too well the intention of the President to believe he placed you where you are to cavil at trifles." Greenleaf left head high, and those he left behind tried to keep from sinking.

Law was back in New York and, before learning of Greenleaf's selling out, complained to him about the commissioners. He had taken a ride around the city with Scott and was shocked to find that the commissioner did not know the difference between Pennsylvania and Maryland Avenues. The accident at the Capitol did not surprise him. Hoban had lived next to the president's house while it was being built, whereas the commissioners sold their house next to the Capitol to a clergyman. They ought to be required to live there. He passed along the conclusion of Dr. Crocker, who worked with the commissioners: "They do not possess minds sufficiently enlarged to promote the real interests of the city if they wished it." In closing, Law begged Greenleaf to get a decision on the wharves and deeds to his lots.

In reply, Law got a "Dear Mr. Law" letter from Greenleaf's clerk. He was devastated. "I made a common cause with you," he replied, "& hatred and malice will persecute me. The change is compleat as any in France. The Jacobins will persecute the Moderees. Pardon me if I hurt your feelings. You must be conscious that mine are lacerated." Forsaken, Law begged Greenleaf for deeds and a statement that Law had five and a half years to fulfill the building clause—the four years the commissioners required plus the eighteen months' grace period he had relinquished under pressure from Greenleaf to give "a spur to the city."

Greenleaf replied promptly with a long, tender letter. "Imperious motives" and "absolute necessity" forced him to do what he did. He had "been actuated by pure & honorable principles' and would have never made the bargain if he "conceived" it would injure Law and Duncanson. He would gladly interest himself in Law's operations if requested. And of course he promised him the deeds. Those of Notley Young's lots he had. He would send deeds of Carroll of Duddington's lots as soon as he completed payment for them on September 26.[1]

Cranch got the news just after drawing up several contracts Greenleaf had wanted: John Frost to run four brick machines; O'Neale for three years of quarrying; Henderson for $13,384 to finish the six buildings on Pennsylvania Avenue for Polock; and Lovering to supervise all future building for an annual salary of $1,500. Contractors working at a percentage had proved wasteful. Clark rendered a bill for eight brick and fifteen wooden houses of $72,097.46. His eight percent fee amounted to well over $5,000.

Morris, who knew and liked Lovering, kept that contract in effect. He knew Cranch's uncle and so kept him, urging him to sell lots and pay the commissioners. He kept Henderson at work, hoping Polock would pay him, and fired Simmons and the Frenchmen. Not that those still working got paid.

Deblois was overjoyed at Greenleaf's fall. He hoped it would cripple the new hotel being built on Capitol Hill, which as of July 22 only had its cellar dug. Greenleaf had been a major backer. Deblois's own tavern, built on Prout's lots at Pennsylvania and South

Carolina Avenues, was about to open. His gang of twenty men had
built it that summer, taking much of their pay out of Deblois's store.
His laborers got a pound of pork, a peck of meal, and two loaves of
bread a week. Nicholson had not paid him much, but enough to
keep his credit good. He could stock his store and tavern, which
was to be run by an experienced tavernkeeper up from St. Marys,
Maryland, attracted to the area because he could send his children
to the school just opened by Reverend Ralph on Capitol Hill.
Nicholson's man checking up on the city was impressed only with
Deblois. Stansburrough agreed that the partners had lost thousands
on the contracts with their builders but thought Deblois "an active
strong man, and of business, economy, judgment and I think sells a
great deal of merchandize at a very good advance. . . ."[2]

* * *

The president was facing the crisis of his second term, the
ratification of the treaty with Britain negotiated by John Jay. The
issue divided the nation as the Senate met in special and secret
session to ratify it. The president had no time for most federal city
problems. He excepted the problem with Johnson, deciding Johnson
could see the commissioners' letter to the president provided they
had put it in their official records. In his letter to Johnson the
president again regretted that the dispute had arisen but put no
pressure on Johnson to end it.

After the Senate ratified the treaty the president reached Georgetown on July 19, met with the commissioners the next day, and got
home to Mount Vernon that afternoon for dinner. The commissioners had not agreed on regulations for wharves, so he looked over
the proposed site for the mint and approved. The commissioners
explained their foremost problem. The president wrote to Randolph
asking him to call on Morris and Nicholson and press them to pay
up. If they did not, "valuable workers" might leave the city and
"such a cloud" would be thrown over the city that "would be
susceptible of such magnified and unfavorable interpretations, as to
give it a vital wound." The commissioners needed $12,000 a month
for building and they had not begun that part of the work which

required expensive materials. The president did not mention the threat of selling their lots to make up the arrears. He merely wanted them to pay some, if they could not pay it all.

The board gave Cranch until the end of July to get authority to give up lots to guarantee the eventual payment of the May 1 installment. Failing that, they would advertise enough of Morris's and Nicholson's lots for sale to cover the May installment.[3]

*   *   *

On the Fourth of July, just as he had promised back in December, Thomas Freeman and his surveying crew quietly completed the resurvey of the city, which is not to say Freeman looked on the experience with equanimity. The maps generated by previous surveyors "could not be relied upon," and his own work seemed in hazard because people were constantly monkeying with the stones marking the squares. He noted the threats posed by farming and cutting roads "indiscriminately," and by the "wilful acts of evil or weak minded persons." If care was not taken, he warned the commissioners, the whole survey would be undone within three years. The commissioners found a Maryland law that allowed them to fine anyone who moved a boundary stone 5,000 pounds of tobacco, with the informer getting half.

There were too many new people in the area. Georgetown expressed its anxiety by forbidding slaves and indentured servants from congregating. No more than five could be together, and the penalty for transgressing the new rule was up to thirty-nine lashes for the slave and a £5 fine for the master. Over in the federal city, Carroll of Duddington complained to the commissioners of the behavior of their laborers. The commissioners promised an "inquiry" and "to bring the offenders to justice."

The proprietors met and discussed petitioning the Maryland legislature to establish a police force for the city. The board's police powers were limited. Thomas Peter was about to move his family into the city. Although he was far away, at 25th and K Streets Northwest, he did not appreciate the goings-on in a wooden house on the president's house square rented by Hoban to a group of ladies. The commissioners agreed that such a nuisance had to go. Betsy Dunako (or Donnato) was summoned before the board "for keeping a riotous and disorderly house" where "persons harbored by you have committed violent assaults of others passing quietly by." She appeared with her landlord, Hoban, and all agreed that the house should come down within a week.

In other matters the board controlled, it had been remiss in establishing regulations, even such obvious ones as that forbidding dumping. It rectified this oversight without much trouble but continued to agonize over wharves. Scott and White wanted to accommodate merchants. As White put it, "the subject of wharves is one which I of all men know the least," but the "object is to promote the growth of the city, by rendering it agreeable to mercantile characters; to accomplish this I would sacrifice beauty to utility." However, they had a healthy fear of replicating the fever-inducing filth attendant to docks in Philadelphia and New York. So they allowed warehouses on wharves, but to prevent a wooden city from growing out over the water, there could be only one chimney per warehouse for the counting room, and every 300 feet of wharf had to be followed by 60 feet of open space for the free circulation of air, or, if the ground around the wharf was filled in with dirt, for a street. The end of the wharf had to be unobstructed for 60 feet. And the wharf could not block the channel on one end or obstruct a street on the other.[4]

*   *   *

But fevers did not need crowded wharves. It did nothing but rain the last week of July. On the 30th storms turned violent and did not stop for several days. The storm or storms wreaked havoc from Virginia to Pennsylvania, carrying away bridges and whatever else could not escape to high ground. Compared with the damage along swollen smaller rivers, what happened along the Potomac near the federal city was slight. The Federal Bridge did not fall, though Harbaugh probably thanked the stars that he had dismantled much of the superstructure, selling the marble slabs that would be of no use on the drawbridge he was about to begin.

Nevertheless, overflow from the Tiber and surrounding rivulets and gullies got in the way of commuters. Three masons who boarded near the hotel were tired of walking up and back to their work site at the Capitol three times a day. They found it "so injurious to our health" that unless they got lodging on Capitol Hill, they would quit. In the river below Georgetown, the receding waters so increased the size of the mud banks there that Thornton became convinced that in time sediment coming downstream would turn it into solid ground. He paid the $7 it took to make a claim on unoccupied land, calculating that there were upward of 60 acres in the making. But soon the tides amply concealed the bonanza.[5]

44. At As Little Expense As Possible

Blagden inspected the latest stone brought up from Aquia and calculated that 30 tons was bad. Stone from farther downriver was worse. One third was too soft, too coarse, not scrabbled, or irregularly shaped. And it sat by wharves already clogged because, as one supplier complained, "for the want of proper tackle," the crane unloading stone at the Eastern Branch wharf was "wholly inadequate."

Other materials that could not be used littered the grounds. The carters blithely "lumbered the Capitol yard" with "bad bricks." Mitchell blamed it on the bad carts supplied by the commissioners. A raft of timber came up the Potomac, and on inspection Hoban found it "by no means of the dimensions necessary." If he could not deliver one third of the timber contracted for in six weeks, the commissioners told Henry Lee on August 10, they would buy their timber elsewhere.[1]

*   *   *

The president cut short his visit to Mount Vernon. He was not getting enough information about the public's reaction to the Senate's ratification of Jay's Treaty. He had another surprise waiting for him when he got to Philadelphia. The New Englanders in his cabinet, Treasury Secretary Wolcott and War Secretary Pickering, presented evidence that Randolph had sold state secrets to the French minister. The president did not dismiss the allegations out of hand. Randolph had been talking about retiring eventually to practice law in the federal city, but his retiring under a cloud did no good for the federal city. The president had no one in his cabinet he could trust to handle the city's affairs.

That August the commissioners needed Randolph's good offices to clear up the mess they had made regulating wharves. The president approved the regulations, but the man who really counted, Barry, did not. The merchant told them that with those regulations his wharf, on which he planned to spend $20,000, would be next to useless. Thanks to the rule that 60 feet of open space had to remain between the last building on the wharf and the water, ships would unload into his warehouse in four feet of water. With Randolph gone, the commissioners' letter about the problem sat unanswered until the president saw it a month later.

Morris needed Randolph to help deflect the dunning notices from the commissioners. He could tell Cranch only to try to prevent the repossession of any property by assuring the commissioners that "probably this will be the only time that we shall ever be in arrears and it shall not be of long continuance." If the commissioners persisted, Cranch was to warn them that they would incur "heavy damages." Legally, Morris noted, he and Nicholson had paid their May installment with Greenleaf's check. The trouble was the commissioners could not collect on that check. Thus they could not get relief through the mechanisms provided for in the agreement itself. They had to go to court and get judgment for the collection of a bounced check. By the time they had managed that, the arrears would be paid.[2]

To pay the arrears, they needed to raise money on the property.

When Lovering came to Philadelphia to see what they wanted, they sent him right back to finish all the buildings he, Clark, and Henderson had begun, twenty-one brick houses in all, and make them tenantable as soon as possible. In addition, he was to begin twenty houses to fulfill the contract with Carroll. He was to do all that "in as short a space of time and at as little expense as possible," by contracting the work out to reputable men who were to understand that Morris and Nicholson "expect also to be indulged with as much time for making the payment" as possible.

They told Cranch to sell lots, "for it seems almost time for the City of Washington to support itself." And if that did not raise enough money to pay workers, Cranch should go to the Bank of Columbia for advances, giving security and promising that the money would be spent only on buildings in the city.

That was a nice sentiment, but at that moment Nicholson was using Washington lots to secure a number of financial transactions of no direct benefit to the city. As he told Greenleaf on July 28, "the lots are my sheet anchor," and he was desperate for the deeds to them. He used what he had to secure a purchase of wine from the firm of Harrison and Sterret, which he paid for with bills due in twelve months. In turn, he used the wine as security to raise cash for Greenleaf. Then he used lots to "liberate" the mortgage of a farm he thought he could sell. Nicholson even offered the tavern Deblois built plus fifteen other houses and lots, which he valued at $52,000, as security for overdue debts.

To bolster courage in the city, the partners bragged about deals in Europe. Their first check to Lovering was a note payable in London, which they assured him he could "draw with safety" because once it reached London their land agents would have made enough sales to cover it. No one in Philadelphia fell for that. They paid Cranch with the same dubious notes. Morris frankly explained that he did not worry about the young man because he assumed Greenleaf had paid him well. These were trying times for Cranch. Someone stole a saddle, bridle, and his "small spanish, shaggy lap dog, white, spotted and fawn color." When he asked for money from brother Greenleaf, he got a letter back from his French clerk assuring him that "tho he is engaged in numberless occupations and his mind is oppressed by a thousand disagreeable thoughts there is scarcely a moment but he thinks of you." And relief was on the way. Greenleaf had just bought 13 million acres of Yazoo lands, between Georgia and the Mississippi, and sold 6 million "yesterday." It contained the "most charming situations in America" and would make $500,000. "So you see, there is no cause to complain." But the clerk enclosed no cash.[3]

*   *   *

In September Theophile Cazenove wrote a thorough evaluation of the federal city for his clients. He raved about the beauty of the plan and showed how the Potomac was intimately connected to the Ohio and Mississippi. For good measure, he noted the "airy and healthy" situation of the city, its abundant supply of good water, and the ease with which it could be defended from attack by water. Then he killed the city with numbers. The public buildings were not the problem. He thought the president's house, Capitol, and even the hotel were well on schedule. The trouble was so few houses in such an expanse. Cazenove hired Hallet, who was still in the city, to count the number of brick houses already built. He counted 54 in a city that had 29,000 building lots. There were only 23 brick houses under construction. That there were almost 350 wooden houses did not count because by the regulations they were temporary.

Cazenove had more telling numbers. The city was six times larger than Philadelphia as planned, twelve times larger than Philadelphia's actual size. Philadelphia, with 50,000 people and 7,000 houses, was 112 years in the making. And it had better real estate bargains than the federal city. For £225 one could buy a lot between 4th and 5th Streets (counting from the Schuylkill) on which one could build twelve houses; that was £19 for each house lot, much cheaper than the £100 for a house lot in the federal city in areas as far from the Capitol or president's house as the Philadelphia lot was from the center of the city, near the Delaware. The same was true in New York, where one could find land that was a better bargain than in the federal city, which was "at present only a forest and wasteland."

Opening the Potomac would not make any difference. Georgetown, with 500 houses, would take all the business, and Alexandria had rich merchants and industrious people. Then it was doubtful that the government would move to the city. There were "several causes" which might lead to a "dissolution" of the union. And suppose Congress did move to the city in 1800. Congressmen did not buy houses but lived in boardinghouses during the session. Cazenove was confident that "at that time and for a long time after the transition, one would still find land at as cheap a price as at present."[4]

* * *

When the president heard enough encouraging news to convince himself that the nation was not about to come asunder over Jay's Treaty, he hurried back to Mount Vernon. Of course he wanted to go there but he also had not made any arrangements to stay in a house outside of Philadelphia during the sickly season. Thanks to the rainy summer, August and September were uncommonly bad. At the end of August the rich took their children out of New York City. Soon yellow fever drove many more out. Malaria ravaged the whole country. In Philadelphia Dr. Rush bled ten members of his family, often twice a day, even a six-week-old baby, who "was . . . thereby rescued from the grave."

The whole state of Maryland, it was said, was more sickly than usual. No characterizations of the state of health at the federal city remain, but no one bragged on it. The carpenter from the *Two Sisters*, Samuel Moodey, died on Greenleaf's Point. Collin Reed, who did blacksmith work for the commissioners, died, as did Thomas Wilson, who printed the *Impartial Observer* at the point. In early October Mitchell stopped making bricks on Capitol Hill because his crews were "generally sick with the ague and fever, intermitting fever and fluxes." In late October one of the rising leaders of the city, secretary to the commissioners and postmaster, Thomas Johnson, Jr., died.

At the beginning of August, Daniel Carroll overcame his nervous distress to write some lengthy "reflections" on the city, but before sending them off to the president, he felt so miserably sick that he let them lie. In mid-September Carroll was still alive (he would die next spring), and the president was passing through on his way to Mount Vernon, so he sent the letter to him. He touched on some other concerns—that there should be only one commissioner, the necessity of finishing the House wing of the Capitol first, the placement of the executive offices, and the renewed effort to get immigrants to come directly to the city—but in the main Carroll was obsessed with the lowlands of the city, as if the incessant rains were playing on his already shot nerves. Leveling the city should be attended to "without delay." "I am sure," he added, "it is unnecessary to say a word on the importance of" building sewers. Something also had to be done with the tentative canal between the two creeks. "The banks by falling in at different places may occasion ponds of stagnated water to be left in several parts of the canal, and render the city unhealthy." He thought a common drainage ditch had to be bricked in at the bottom of the canal immediately.

It is probable that those ruminations on the lowlands were the heartfelt valedictory of a dying commissioner, but his nephew was rather keen on completing the canal and thus opening up much of his property to its full potential. At the same time, William Duncanson tried to wring some personal profit out of a small stagnant marsh at the end of East 9th Street. After setting himself up at Deblois's Eastern Branch hotel on Pennsylvania and 8th Street Southeast, near his almost finished house at 7th and South Carolina, he set out to find himself a waterside lot and found what he wanted just down the hill along the Eastern Branch. He asked the commissioners the price and offered "to bank out an inlet thereon" with the proprietor of that square, Carroll of Duddington, "which will much improve the health of the city thereabout."

                              *   *   *

George Washington probably had more first-hand experience in ditching swamps and banking inlets than anybody connected with the city. But he did not get his hands muddied with such problems. At the same time that he got the letter from Carroll, a more alarming missive came from Scott, explaining that the work in August and

September had been paid for by loans from the Bank of Columbia on the private credit of the commissioners. Repayment of the loans had to begin on October 5. If Morris and Nicholson did not pay any of their arrears by that time, all work on the public buildings must stop. The president promptly sent Scott's letter to Morris and endorsed its dire warnings: "Everything at the capitol seems to progress as well as can reasonably be expected under the embarrassments which have been encountered—But without the aid required in Mr. Scott's letter, the whole must be at a stand, at the time he mentions;—the workmen *must* be discharged;—and, more than probable, the most valuable of them will be irrecoverably lost. Whilst the buildings will be left not only in a stagnant state but in a hurtful situation;—involving consequences which are too obvious to need enumeration."

Morris replied promptly, expressing his "mortification," and said he had "some faint hopes" that Law would help pay the arrears. Then he excused his late payment with an assertion that made the commissioners' jaws drop: "However I was not until the receipt of your letter acquainted with the necessity there is for supplying the commissioners with money, and imagined that a little delay was not of any *real* importance."[5]

45. Pray, Pray Send Me Some Money, or I Shall Die

Back in the autumn of 1793 Morris had urged L'Enfant to stop work on his mansion rather than expose workers to yellow fever. In the autumn of 1795 Morris scolded L'Enfant for not finishing the house as promised. He rued the day he gave in to his better judgment and let L'Enfant load on expensive marble. The house he was renting, for £1,000 a year, had just been sold. Indulging "genius" was one thing but, he chided the architect, "Had you executed my intentions instead of your own, my family would now have an inhabited house instead of being liable to be turned out of doors." (Morris was not about to move into his old house, which the president was renting.) In reply, L'Enfant said he lacked money to continue the work punctually. Morris assured him he could have what money he needed, to the tune of $1,800 to $6,700 a month.

To his new batch of creditors Morris made his want of money seem shocking, and he blamed the general scarcity of money or the French invasion of Holland. But to old friends the truth had out. "I am in as great want of ready money as ever . . . ," he lamented to Gouverneur Morris. Yet times were bad. Treasury Secretary Wolcott was not sure how to manage the government's finances. Foreign loans were impossible and domestic capital already pledged. Banks "multiplying like mushrooms" issued too many bank notes, keeping prices high so exports were crippled. As for developing the country, "Usury absorbs much of that capital, which might be calculated upon as a resource if visionary speculations could be destroyed."

The best that can be said for Morris was that he did not panic. Urged by a friend to sell land at any price and raise the sums to restore his credit, Morris recalled the times people had told him that no one would buy land at the price he was asking "and yet purchasers (American citizens) have unexpectedly arisen and taken them off at high prices and for ready money. . . . My whole time is now spent upon ways and means and in seeking purchasers—you shall see by and by that I will shine out in full lustre, and then I quit work in this world." Yet embarrassments continued to accumulate. The "malicious . . . misrepresentations" of a Philadelphian, who claimed it was "a bubble," stopped the sale of land company shares in London.

Morris tried to raise $10,000 to pay the commissioners by importuning Law. But despite Morris's offer "to make a return of services and kind offices" and his pledge of "honor" to pay the money before it was due, Law refused him help. Law and Duncanson took a proposal from Nicholson to secure a loan for $36,000 with Washington property valued at twice that, plus interest and a two and a half percent commission, more seriously, but they shrank from making another deal until they got titles to the lots they had already bought.

On October 1 Morris told the commissioners that they would hear from him on October 5. They did, but got no money. He told Cranch, "By all means keep Mr. Lovering's men at work for we expect soon to raise money to pay all off." That expectation was based on a scheme to sell lands he had contracted to buy from the state of Massachusetts secured by $140,000 worth of debt certificates. If the lands were sold, he could reclaim the security.

Although in the short run the speculators felt rather pressed, their confidence in the land company and Washington lots remained. They looked to Morris's son-in-law, James Marshall, brother of the future chief justice, to save the day. He set out for Europe authorized to sell stock and property and raise loans. They wrote several long letters explaining what could be done with Pennsylvania lands, land company stock, and Washington lots. They wanted Marshall to sell or raise loans on 4,000 Washington lots, the 2,000 Bourne had available to secure Dutch loans and 2,000 owned by Morris and Nicholson. Since they were not certain where the money raised by the Amsterdam and Rotterdam loans had gone, Marshall had to find out. If subscriptions were no longer being received, he was to buy out the loan so the lots could be used to secure a loan "in Antwerp, London, Paris, Germany & c & c." Or the lots could be sold. Morris thought it "probable" that Marshall could get an advance of money from a London banker who would then sell the lots. He suggested Marshall get a copy of the Columbian Society plan to build houses in hopes that Europeans might subscribe to it, or he could cook up "any other plan" to raise money.[1]

*   *   *

Morris might have known the president, but Nicholson knew storekeepers, tavernkeepers, tanners, button makers, bakers, and the like, who could be induced to do things without cash. The tanner Stansburrough could get his hands on a considerable stand of timber along the Eastern Shore of the Chesapeake. An English storekeeper named William Prentiss came up from Virginia offering to build houses in the federal city with an advance of goods in lieu of cash.

It was an offer Nicholson found difficult to resist, especially when his latest from Deblois began, "I am really mortified at your not being able to help me to some money. . . . pray, pray send me some money, or I shall die. . . . I have hardly enough to keep my store going ten days. . . . It is death to be so dunned and harassed, ten times worse than the fever and ague." Yet reports from Deblois showed how successful a store could be. Since opening it, he had sold 540 gallons of French brandy, 1,132 gallons of rum, 110 gallons of Madeira wine, and as much Lisbon wine, plus brown sugar, loaf sugar, molasses, cheese, and bacon, not to mention supplying "the neighborhood with beans and potatoes out of my garden all summer."

Nicholson did not send money to Deblois. He sent Prentiss to build five double houses and asked Deblois to spare what materials he could, let workmen have temporary houses, and let Prentiss rent a wharf and the large house that Simmons had been living in (reserving "the long room on the south front and the chamber above" for when Nicholson and Morris visited). Prentiss promptly commenced digging cellars for a double house along N Street between 3rd and 4½ Streets, agreeable to Nicholson's wish "of connecting the Point with the Eastern Branch." Deblois accorded grudging cooperation while reporting, "people here laugh at the idea of Prentiss's building new houses for you, when you and Mr. Morris cannot supply funds to finish those that ought to have been finished some months since and many have it in their mouths that your property here is to be sold to pay the commissioners. . . ." Moreover, Prentiss was building in the wrong place, for "the Point must sink." What really hurt was Nicholson supplying Prentiss with goods for a store.

Nicholson did not want to lose the services of Deblois, so he offered to buy the squares Prout had offered to Deblois and agreed to try to cash checks Deblois sent him. Deblois still asked for cash, $1,200 to $1,500, but decided he would be a fool to give up on Nicholson just yet. Trusting Nicholson would cash his checks, he wrote to Boston "to get credit for coffee, chocolate, candles, soap, beef, pork, butter, shoe leather and many other articles" that were cheapest in New England.

For a man who had no cash, Nicholson did very well, but he could not barter with the commissioners. Morris and Nicholson offered to mortgage lots back to the commissioners, redeemable on paying £30 for each, if the commissioners gave Duncanson and Law titles to the lots they had bought. The commissioners were loath to give up any leverage. They needed money.[2]

* * *

On September 27 they were in a state of "indignation and grief," for "the hour" was fast approaching when all operations would have to stop for want of funds. They had to raise $30,000 to $40,000 to keep going until mid-December. "Various expedients have been discussed," they told the President, "nothing bearing even the appearance of efficiency has occurred." They decided they could not carry out their threat to sell Morris's and Nicholson's property until they had the opinion of the attorney general. All they could do was ask Morris and Nicholson for money.

No money came from Philadelphia so they sold some Bank of Columbia shares. They would lose six to eight percent of their original investment on the deal, but it was the only way to keep work going through December 1. As for the long term, the commissioners drew up a memorial to Congress asking for a loan and passed it on for the president's comments and approval. On his way back to Philadelphia on October 12, the president conferred with the commissioners and agreed that White, the former congressman, should go to Philadelphia to shepherd a loan through Congress.

Otherwise the board tried to carry on business as usual, concealing as best it could its desperate financial situation. The commissioners had their usual bad news. Their lawyer, Philip Key, settled the 1793 case with Burnes out of court for $940 plus costs. Bringing it to trial would have caused unpleasant notoriety for the board. Dobson, the Englishman who contracted to do stonework at the Capitol, absconded owing at least $2,000. The board had to pay his eight hands. The quarries kept sending up the wrong stone. Blagden went down to tell them to send bill, not ashlar, only to report, " 'twas a little mortifying to be informed that two of the vessels were just loaded with that kind we so much abound in. And it was by mistake." On the good side, another quarry was opened, with stone "well adapted" for moldings, cornices, corners, and friezes. The Capitol was back on track, footlocks to get workers up on the walls ordered, and enough barracks were ready for the winter. There was such activity that in mid-October, when Uriah Forrest was clued into their financial situation, he was shocked. Before, he had thought only that "the finances of the city were not in so flourishing a state as its friends could wish," not that they were "deranged."[3]

*   *   *

On private account, Law and Barry took up the slack. They moved into Duncanson's eight-room mansion, which had an outside kitchen and a greenhouse. Duncanson's sister made the place comfortable. Law hired Hallet to contract for a million bricks and build three double houses on New Jersey Avenue just up from Barry's wharf. Law also hired one of the city surveyors to reroute the canal and prepared legislation to authorize private development of the canal through a lottery, and he joined a group attempting to get legislative authority for a bridge over the Eastern Branch.

Barry asked that the recently approved rules be contravened so he could extend a wharf at the end of New Jersey Avenue out over a bay thus preventing it from being filled so Georgia Avenue could run from the planned fort south of the Capitol to the planned riverfront entrance to the city east of the Capitol. Not only did the commissioners waive the rules, but they expressed their gratitude for "his large scale improvements." That is, Scott and White did. Thornton protested the decision in a letter to the president, arguing that the wharf marred the plan of the city. The wharf was almost completed by the end of October and Barry prepared to fill contracts from Portugal and Spain for Potomac wheat.[4]

*   *   *

Before sending him to America, John Trumbull gave George Hadfield some good advice: "be particularly careful to cultivate their [the commissioners'] good opinion and to avoid any circumstances that may thwart their views or give them offense." That said, Trumbull set about painting a sobering picture of the rude new world. "As you will probably find but one person, L'Enfant, in America your equal in knowledge in your profession, you will of course see much to criticize but give the least possible pains to others."

Years later Thornton would claim that Washington asked him to restore the design of the Capitol by eliminating the changes Hallet had gotten Jefferson to approve back in the summer of 1793. But Thornton had done little to make the design all his own. In November 1795, over a year after Thornton became a commissioner, Washington remarked that "the present plan is no body's, but a compound of every body's." Although Thornton had difficulty designing interiors that were buildable, his exteriors were more credible, save for his dome. Washington also complained in November that the dome had been eliminated, which Thornton blamed on Hallet. But evidently Thornton was still tinkering with it, shrinking it until it looked more like a cupola. When Thornton gave him a tour of the site and reviewed the plans, Hadfield saw walls three and a half feet above the foundation and a plan with Hallet's interiors and Thornton's exteriors, with various versions of the dome. The young man sensed that he could still make his mark by redesigning the building.

But a few weeks on the scene, Hadfield informed the board that the building as planned had "defects that are not warrantable in most of the branches that constitute the profession of an architect, Stability, Economy, Convenience, Beauty. There will be material inconveniences in the apartments, deformity in corners, chimney and windows placed without simmetry and no economy of space." He did allow that he was sorry to offend, but since the public would hold him responsible he had to speak his piece.

The board not only sent Hadfield's letters but Hadfield himself to Philadelphia to make the case to the president. Thornton could not be spared at that trying time, so they dispatched Hoban to defend the plans Hadfield thought so bad.[5]

46. Miscreant Junto of Gipsies

Uriah Forrest, who had served in the preceding Congress, did not like the city's chances of getting a loan. The Republicans aimed to defeat Jay's Treaty by not funding it. Congress would be too embroiled in politics to lend money to the city. If a loan failed to pass, everyone, "especially foreigners," would take defeat as an indication that Congress really did not intend to move in 1800. Forrest had another idea: the commissioners should ask the state of Maryland for money. The state held $200,000 worth of U.S. debt certificates that paid six percent, enough to support the state government. Forrest was confident that the state legislators, a majority of whom he thought "friendly to the City of Washington," would lend the principal if they could be assured that the commissioners would faithfully pay the interest. He was able to allay the suspicions of several legislators by pointing out the large number of lots still held by the public and the rise in the value of lots.

Scott and Thornton liked the idea and sent Forrest's letter to the president. White turned Forrest's reasoning around and argued that if an attempt to get a loan from Maryland failed it would jeopardize his effort to get a loan from Congress. He remembered how Northerners tried to use Baltimore's opposition to the Potomac to split the Maryland congressional delegation in the debate over the permanent residence. "Should it appear that such division still exists," he warned the president, "it will revive their hopes." In addition, the amount of money to be had, $200,000, was not enough.

The president was on the same wavelength. Before he got White's letter he approved an application to Maryland, only if the commissioners were "fully assured (as far as possible) of success." After reading what White had to say, he did not change his mind but warned that Baltimore, "despite its flourishing state, cannot view the progress of the federal city & inland navigation of the Potomac, without perceiving the ultimate effect. . . ." He left the decision up to Scott, who knew the ins and outs of Maryland politics, but suggested that "his visit to Annapolis could be covered by any good pretext."

Scott went to Annapolis before he got that presidential advice, but he anticipated it. He told those he buttonholed about a loan that he came as an individual not authorized by the board or the president. Publicly, he said he came to urge the state to invest $14,000 in thirty shares of Potomac Company stock. He soon got the impression that Forrest's idea of getting the state to lend the debt certificates would not go. The state bureaucrats, whose salary came from the interest, "would clamour loudly." By November 13, after the assembly had been in session but a few days, he thought the dispute over the plan of the Capitol rendered his attendance "absolutely necessary at the city."[1]

*   *   *

Before going to Philadelphia, Hadfield explained in writing what was wrong with the plans of the building. He backed off from his broad charges. What had been built would not have to be redone, and what he wanted done would be cheaper than what was planned. Like Hallet before him, he went after Thornton's basement. He thought it odd that the entrances to the legislative chambers were in the basement, thus rendering the grand stairway up through the columns of the portico "useless." He did not feel that a basement was needed to elevate and support the main floor. That could be accomplished by making the columns six inches larger. In addition, the basement added a weight that he feared the foundation could not support. That said, he was willing to carry on the current plan if he got "drawings of all parts of the building inside and outside."

Thornton also drafted a letter to the president. He thought it had been made clear that Hadfield was to come to execute "plans already made." Therefore he could not "but express astonishment at some of the young man's observations." He admitted that he and Hoban had found defects in the distribution of the interior rooms but had corrected most of them. He recognized that some small defects remained, and, given young Hadfield's "genius," he was amenable to his exercising his talents to come up with "small alterations."

As for the basement, he had found that the legislative chambers would "be only in just proportion" with "a basement of 20 feet" upon which the columns could be mounted. In addition, since only one wing would likely be completed by 1800, and both houses would be required to sit in it, the library on the first floor of the north wing had to be a full-sized room rising above the first story. Its entrance would be on the first floor so the portico entrance would not be useless after all. It also had to be more than one story high or else it would be extremely long, 90 feet, for the elevation.

Doing away with the basement also did away with the arcades along the sides of the chambers on which the columns would be mounted. Thornton admitted that he was not thrilled with arcades, but without them there had to be columns so large that they would get in the way. And arcades would be a unifying feature throughout the building. On the main floor a system of arcades would emanate from the portico and from the galleries of the chambers, and "the object in the center, contemplated as its grand ornament, would appear throughout to great advantage." This was the statue of Washington.

Thornton cited Roman and British buildings that had basements. He even cited Hallet's use of an attic to solve the same problem as evidence that elevation and space could not be obtained without something either above or below the columns. And since keeping the mass of the building below the columns made it seem light, a basement was the best solution. Finally, he did not see how eliminating the basement could save expense, because stone for it was on hand.

The president talked with Hadfield and Hoban individually and together with the plans in hand. His chief worry about Hadfield was that he would leave the job after a year or ask for an exorbitant salary once his year's contract ran out. So he extracted a promise "to stick by the building until it was finished." Hadfield assured the president that he "means no change in the interior of the building of the least importance." The president begged insufficient knowledge to decide the dispute over the basement. He told Hadfield about all the "changes, delays, & expenses as have been encountered already" and did not want any more unless necessary. He told Thornton that if Hadfield was a man of "science," "character," "industry and arrangement," and "his proposed alterations can be accomplished without enhancing the expense, or involving delay, . . . I should have no hesitation in giving it as my opinion that his plan ought to be adopted." But the decision was left up to the board.

Hadfield did not give up the fight. With the aid of Blagden, he made a list showing that his changes would save about £5,000. As for the issue of the defects of the current plan, he stood his ground that the drawings given to him by the board were inadequate. Thornton responded with a note informing his colleagues that Hoban said he could work with those drawings. And Hoban joined Thornton in the opinion that Hadfield's plan "could not be executed so as to secure stability to the building." Citing that and the inability of Hadfield to prove to their satisfaction that the current plan was "capitally defective," and discounting Hadfield's estimate of savings as not being precise enough, the full board rejected Hadfield's plan. However, to Thornton's regret, Scott and White did not put Hoban in charge. The board ordered Hadfield to put "as many men as possible setting freestone." Hadfield obliged but added that what was really needed were the drawings.[2]

*　　*　　*

The commissioners' call to get as many men setting stone as possible did not arise from any infusion of money but from the desire to get as much done before work would stop from lack of funds. They maintained a grim sense of humor about it. In an October 27 letter to the president they hoped for "the friendly aid of a good frost which if not very late indeed will be very convenient to save our credit." That is, they could dismiss laborers without owning up to their empty treasury.

On November 2 Morris sent an apologetic letter to the commissioners explaining that he did not send money because the person who had promised money to him had not delivered. "I have been endeavoring ever since to obtain money but it seems as if every person here was as much in want as myself."

In the federal city, the commissioners were not the only people

who wanted money from Morris and Nicholson. Cranch sent up
disturbing reports. Not only were individual workers demanding
payment, but they were threatening to unite in their demands.
Morris told Cranch to keep the workers at their jobs. As for money
to pay them, "you will hear from me in the course of this week."
The workers met, and it was resolved to petition the state assembly
to allow Morris's and Nicholson's land to be sold "to pay us our
just demands for Services rendered."

Nicholson was not ashamed of the role he had played in building
the city. He replied to the unpaid workers through Deblois. He
emphasized that the people who employed them, Clark, Lovering,
and Henderson, should pay them. He had never seen an account
from those gentlemen nor had he seen Greenleaf's accounts. He
had no idea who had been paid what, but he did know they had
spent $144,000 and it was widely reported that they did not have the
"worth of our money." "There is a deficiency somewhere, and
until I can receive the accounts I never can consent to admit any
balances [due]." That said, Nicholson offered to pay workmen for
"personal services" to save their families from distress and left it to
Deblois to forward such personal accounts.

This fiscal rectitude was somewhat disingenuous on Nicholson's
part. Deblois had told him what a mess the accounts were in: "Such
has been the borrowing & lending, buying & selling & shifts obliged
to be made for want of money that it was impossible to attend to
regular accounts." Deblois saw the handwriting on the wall. With
numbers Nicholson would prove that he did not owe Deblois a thing.
When he asked that their affairs be closed and final accounts drawn,
the merchant threw himself on Nicholson's mercy; any money
would do, but he had to send some immediately. That very day he
had asked his clerk, whom he had not paid for nine months, to lend
him two or three dollars. Nicholson took time out from his latest
vain schemes to raise sums to pay Georgia land taxes, North
American Land Company dividends, and the growing number of
speculators who waited for payments on hundreds of thousands of
dollars' worth of his paper, to preach to Deblois: "Where you have
one demand against you, I have at least 900, yet I call in the aid of
reason, and do not let my mind be unfitted for business at a time
when it ought to be fitted. . . ." No money came with the lecture,

only an account showing that he had given Deblois more than the $4,000 to $5,000 originally agreed on.[3]

*   *   *

One person did manage to get under the skin of Morris, if not quite Nicholson: the aggrieved wife of Joseph Clark. She wrote to those gentlemen from "a poor hovel" in Baltimore where she lived "without money, property, or credit, with an helpless husband, whose intellect you have deranged, by your vile treatment, to insanity; with seven small children, white and colored, and two old faithful servants, and no means to procure them food." The last money had come from the sale of her furniture at "that island of bubble, deceit, horror, poverty and desolations vauntingly dubbed Greenleafs Point." Joseph Clark had been "there beset, insulted and threatened with his life by a *hired* banditti." The "hired french fellow, a mutilated aristocrat, a french poltroon, miscreant ruffian," even insulted and abused her when she was alone in her own house.

She explained her tardiness in writing: "I have long expected an opportunity to address you in person, as your reporters, on Baneful Point, have yelped for many months, ye were all to be there to pay your *arrearages*. Had you come I would have your eyes and cars witness the woes you have overwhelmed me with, in defiance of all opposition of the numerous miscreant junto of gipsies, french poltroons, dolts, delvers, magicians, soothsayers, quacks, bankrupts, puffs, speculators, monopolizers, extortioners, traitors, petit foggy lawyers, ham brickmakers, and apostate waggon makers."

Morris confessed that he "was never so astonished in the course of my life" as he was on receipt of Mrs. Clark's letter. He explained that he had had nothing to do with Clark, that it was Greenleaf's affair, but that he was willing to contribute to a fund to relieve the woman's distress. Nicholson was not so sensitive. He informed Mrs. Clark "that there were irrefragile proofs" and her husband's "own confession of frauds in his dealing for us." He left it to Greenleaf to "review the matter."[4]

47. To the Grinding Mill

Alexander White left Georgetown for Philadelphia on December 3 accompanied in the public stage by five Southern congressmen. From the stage window they could see an impressive mansion. The walls of the president's house were six feet from the eves. White could add that most of the windows and doors were ready to put in, as well as flooring plank. He asked the congressmen "what sentiments the eastern members appear to entertain of the Federal seat." He was told "that if their sincerity could be relied on," they meant to come to the Potomac in 1800.

In Philadelphia he met with the Virginia delegation and told them why he had come. They opined that the South was sure to support a loan, and that while the Eastern members "could not consistent with their avowed principles" obstruct such a proposal, they might "find pretexts for refusing a grant of money." White said that although a grant was most desirable, guaranteeing a loan would do. He asked that his intentions be kept secret until "the sense of the known friends of the Potomac could be collected."

It also gave White a chance to see what he could do with Morris and Nicholson. For fear of not appearing "congressional," he wanted to finish negotiations with them before Congress got down to business. His idea was to get them to agree to pay monthly installments and let the board sell their lots when installments were missed. On his first day in the city he took "family dinner" with the president, who was not encouraging. He had sent a letter asking Morris to pay up and had "not seen or heard from him since."

White tracked him down. Morris was ever ready with excuses and told White of his "great uneasiness," "the exertions," and "a hope" that in ten days he would pay White $10,000. White asked the financier how he would like making smaller installment payments throughout the year. Morris said he liked the idea but would have to consult Nicholson.

White then called on Nicholson who invited him to dinner the next day. Where Morris had expressed only a hope, Nicholson boldly stated that arrangements had been made to pay $10,000, and then he did not wait for White to press him for more. He asked White how much the commissioners needed before May and how best to divide the installments. Sensing a trap, White was careful to emphasize "that nothing less than paying up the arrears" would do and that an extra $10,000 by April 1 "would enable us to open the business next summer," and thereafter they would expect $10,000 a month. White "endeavored to impress on his mind by the strongest terms I could command, the necessity of rendering the payments of these installments absolutely certain."

White was not so thrilled with those first meetings that he did not check up on the speculators. He reported what he heard to Scott and Thornton: "from the best account I have been able to obtain of the inconveniences of Morris and Nicholson I much doubt their ever complying with their engagements."

The loan or loan guarantee from Congress was more important than ever. White conferred with the two most influential members of the Virginia delegation. William Giles showed "no small displeasure at the style of the buildings especially the President's house" and informed White "that the spirit ran so high in North Carolina that no countenance could be expected from that state." The "spirit" of course was republicanism, the vehement disdain farmers and philosophers felt for the extravagances of the Federalists. But Giles was well known as a blowhard. The opinion of James Madison was more chilling. He opposed the application to Congress, because Northerners, no matter what they said, would cause trouble once the bill came to the floor.

White was not disposed to entertain Madison's fear of Northern trickery. He opened up to Senator Baldwin, who represented Georgia but had lived most of his life in Connecticut. Baldwin had "no doubt" the Northern members would support a loan. Between Madison's fears and Baldwin's assurances, White told his colleagues, "it is impossible to attain absolute certainty. Shall I proceed on probable grounds? To form an opinion even of the probable event will be more difficult and more tedious than any one accustomed to transacting business with large Republics can conceive." Soon after writing that, White wondered if the city could scrape by on cash due from other than Morris and Nicholson and be saved "perhaps from final ruin by the advances of its friends of such sums as may be absolutely necessary till debts can be collected or property sold for reimbursement."[1]

*   *   *

Friends of the city proved they could unite their resources to aid one public works project. After vigorous lobbying by Forrest, Lear, and Law, the Maryland Assembly subscribed to forty shares of Potomac Company stock. The hope was that Virginia would do the same. But if work were to continue, there could be no doubt, so a meeting was called at Georgetown and the remaining shares taken up, to be relinquished if Virginia subscribed. The money was in hand to hire Captain Christopher Myers, who the president thought was the man to build the Great Falls locks.

When they ran out of money on December 10, the commissioners went quietly to the Bank of Columbia for a $10,000 loan. After the new year most salaried employees agreed not to draw their pay until the financial crisis was resolved. The board continued contracting for supplies. Scott used his own credit to provide advances. They kept the usual number of men at work during the winter: twenty-five stonecutters, fifteen carpenters, and twenty laborers at the Capitol; twelve stonecutters, thirteen carpenters, and ten laborers at the president's house. Each month they had to pay the stonecutters $1,350, the carpenters $600, and the laborers, whose masters were paid quarterly, $100. By not drawing their own pay, the commissioners freed $400 a month. And the city did progress. Financed by Blodget, Hoban's crew finished the roof of the hotel, which, on completion, some found to be "really a very handsome brick building."

Proud though they were at keeping operations going, Scott and Thornton were not comfortable. If suppliers were not paid soon, Scott would be placed personally "in a very unpleasant situation." The owners of slaves they rented expected payment. "Should the masters meet with difficulties in obtaining the wages of last year, at the very moment we are advertising for 120 laborers for next year, we shall certainly go into the market with a bad grace." So eagerly did they want a loan that they told White to tell congressmen that if they thought the president's house too extravagant, the law did not preclude them from using it for another purpose, one that "the most stern republican" would think suited its size. Far from the scene of action, the issue seemed to them to be simply one of national faith. "We think there can be no danger from the Eastern members," they wrote to White. "They called loudly on National faith when the funding system was under consideration, and we hope the same cry from another quarter may be heard."

As for Morris and Nicholson, raising $5,000 "could not be a matter of difficulty . . . , tho to us it really is." The speculators got "every benefit resulting from the contract"—lots to mortgage and sell—and the public got no money. They wanted White to lay the contract "before eminent counsel" so measures could be taken "as will compel a performance of the contract."[2]

*   *   *

White joined Madison for a private dinner with the president. White could not dispel Madison's doubts, so the president took him aside and tried. Later, another Virginia congressman, Richard Brent, opined that Madison would actively support the measure. So White kept buttonholing members. True, they met only from eleven to three and dined from three to five, but the rest of the time they were always visiting. Too often he found them "in large companies" so that while he hardly ate or slept he had been able to talk to only thirty-eight of them.

In the pitch he gave he used none of the rhetoric or plaints his colleagues passed on to him. He was careful not to imply that the city was desperate. The public lots were worth a million and could be sold to finance the buildings. But if the lots could be held, they would be more valuable and "the city will be so improved as to afford eligible accommodations for congress and all their followers, and much property remain for the use of the U. States." Bringing too much property to market "at this time, it will fall a prey to speculators as too much of the city has already done. The buildings will drag on heavily."

Most of the members he talked to got the point. No one breathed a word about repealing the Residence Act. Some wished "with all the appearance of sincerity" that Congress could move immediately. But everyone advised not even to mention a grant of money. As for guaranteeing a loan, "they have pretty generally observed that they see no impropriety in it, but that the thing was new, that they would consider it, and give me their candid opinion when they had made up their minds." White was encouraged and felt "a degree of confidence that a loan may be obtained."

His confidence in Morris was fast diminishing. On Christmas Day he "asked him to make an immediate advance of the $10,000 so often promised." No sooner than next week, said Morris. White pressed him for $6,000, even $5,000, by the next post. Morris "paused awhile and said he would try, and that he would inform me by two o'clock." White then went to deliver the latest desperate letters from Georgetown to the president. They spent two hours together, but even the president could think of no way to get money immediately. "If he had money he would freely advance it," the president said of himself and then added to the gloom, saying he had "lost all expectation of money from Mr. Morris." The notes of Morris and Nicholson could not raise five shillings on the pound, but suing them "would afford no immediate relief," so he "thought best to suspend coercive measures at least during the dependence of the business in Congress." It was up to White "in the mean time to use every effort to obtain something by fair means."

Nothing came from Morris but an invitation to dinner on the 27th. His host took him aside and said "he had got unexceptional notes, . . . and that he would go early in the morning to the grinding mill (as he calls the brokers office) and get them discounted in time to go by the post if possible." White kept his letter open till that time, and Morris delivered $4,000, but not in a form White could readily send to Georgetown. They were bills payable in March. White decided to try to get them cashed in Philadelphia. The form of payment so disappointed White that he wrote on New Year's Day that he doubted he would be able "to wrest anything more."

White was decidedly glum that holiday. Just after he became confident in the ultimate success of the measure, members came back to him and expressed a wish "to keep it out of sight" until the major issue that session was decided: whether to fund the British treaty or to accede to the wishes of Madison and kill the treaty by not funding it.[3]

*   *   *

Then came a mixed blessing—a major sale that highlighted the value of Washington lots. But the commissioners got no money out of it. The Coombs family's title to the farm that stretched from their farmhouse at Massachusetts Avenue and 6th Street Northwest up the hill east of Blodget's farm, was in such doubt that back in 1791 they had not been considered proprietors. But in 1794 they got clear title. In October 1795 an area land dealer named William Bayly bought the 150 acres for $37,000 and turned around and sold it to the New York merchants Comfort Sands and Dominick Lynch for $42,000. Bayley revealed that the sale was on rapid payments, $8,000 down and $20,000 in fifteen or twenty days. Scott and Thornton asked White to approach Lynch and Sands about buying the public half of the Coombs tract.[4]

1796

48. The Ground in General Being Hard and Gravelly

Morris and Nicholson did not send all suitors from the federal city away empty-handed. William Prentiss was not oblivious to the tavern talk that his employers were broke and that judgments were being obtained against them in Philadelphia courts. Since September he had "one house covered in and a second up one story." For about $650 he had bought a building for a store at the point and added an addition for "wet goods," a place to sell booze. He bought another store near the hotel. He calculated he had spent $6,000 and had got only $2,784 worth of goods from Morris and Nicholson. What hurt most of all was that the lumber promised from Stansburrough never arrived. So he went to Philadelphia to get his due. Of course he got no money from Nicholson, only £500 credit with a Philadelphia merchant. It kept Prentiss's store going during the winter, enraging Deblois. Workers trying to dun him for back pay kept up their snarls, fueled by Prentiss's rum.

Cranch would just as soon have been spared the added labor that Morris's and Nicholson's way of doing business without money entailed. His wife had their first child, a son, on January 11. Dr. Frederick May, who had just come down from Cambridge, Massachusetts, delivered the child, helped by two women neighbors, who admired the doctor's "tenderness and delicacy." Parson Ralph, whom Cranch thought "the only decent clergyman in this part of the country," came down the hill to baptize the boy. (Perhaps in a run, for his boarding school was too successful. He had eighteen students and two assistants living with his own family in six small rooms. Noting that his neighbor Dobson had vacated a larger house built by the commissioners for workers, he asked to be able to rent that.)

Cranch spent a day with wife and baby and then it was back to the accounts. His headache of the moment was Henderson, who was waiting for payment for the houses he had been building. On Henderson's being satisfied depended Polock's being satisfied, on which depended $34,000 for Morris and Nicholson, albeit much in suspect notes. Of course, putting the accounts in order did not mean that they would actually be paid.

About the only people paid that January were the slave owners. The commissioners paid them $902.13 with money lent by the Bank of Columbia, secured by the commissioners' private credit. Times were good for slave owners. The commissioners wanted 120 slaves for the coming year. Mitchell, the man supplying bricks for the public buildings, wanted to hire forty.[1]

*   *   *

Nicholson could picture the future of the city. He contracted with George Parkyns to make a dozen prints of American views, including several of the federal city. Now he wanted a book that would contain plats and descriptions of every square in the city. He told White that he would soon send a draftsman to the city. Morris was also upbeat, telling White he did not want to pay in $10,000 installments, "if I could command money I would rather pay the whole at once, and I am pretty confident there never would be another failure on my part." White suggested that by selling his Genesee lands Morris could save his Washington property. "He said," White reported to his colleagues, "he intended to settle two of his sons in the City of Washington, and said much in favor of its future prospects, but insisted that the Genesee was equally eligible; that he had settled one son there, who would not change situations for any part of the world."[2]

*   *   *

On January 6 White reported to the president that he was confident that Congress would pass a loan guarantee. White challenged

Madison's suspicions of the Northern members. They were friendly toward the city. "Many had said unequivocably that they wished to remove" to the Potomac, "that they would do anything in reason to promote it." White did, however, warn the president that several leading members saw trouble ahead if Republicans monkeyed with the treaty with Britain. "Some went so far as to say" that if the House did not appropriate money to carry the treaty into effect, they would "consider the government as dissolved and never act more under it."

The bill funding the treaty could not come forward until the signed copies of the pact arrived from London. White thought that to hold back the loan bill until the treaty was funded only tied two issues together that were not related. The president turned devil's advocate. White wrote that he "had near an hours conversation with him, the affairs of the city were viewed in every light, and he requested my opinion in more decided terms than in so important a business I could on a sudden give." The president asked White to dinner the next day.

When White joined a large company of congressmen for dinner, the president took him aside and said that his message endorsing the loan guarantee had been prepared. In the message the president tried to deflect criticism of the scale of the public buildings, deeming them "consistent with the liberality of the grants [from Virginia and Maryland] and proper for the purposes intended." And he touched on that early assumption that federal money would not be needed, writing, "I have no doubt, if the remaining resources are properly cherished, so as to prevent the loss of property by hasty and numerous sales, that all the buildings required for the accommodation of the Government of the United States may be compleated in season without aid from the Federal Treasury."

On receiving the message on January 8, the House sent it to a select committee chaired by Jeremiah Smith of New Hampshire, who informed White that the committee would meet on Monday. As if that were not enough to gratify White, on Saturday Morris gave him two checks totaling $2,850 endorsed by John Hall, a Georgia land dealer. A cryptic note accompanied the payment: "put one at the Bank of the U.S., one at the Bank of Pennsylvania, but do not let it be known to any person whatever, of where you received them. . . ."

*   *   *

When the committee met, White was ready. To finish the president's house "in an elegant style," he told them, would cost $88,690.66. The work to date had cost $97,329.83. As for the Capitol, it would cost $75,141.45 to finish the north wing. Work so far had cost $78,035.29, which included the foundation for the whole building. White did not mention the bad work that had to be taken down. For good measure he listed the materials on hand: 1,994 feet of freestone prepared, 440 tons in the rough, 267,618 bricks, 4,750 bushels of lime, 7,000 feet of prepared timber, and 11,000 feet unprepared.

White hoped that would slake the congressmen's thirst for numbers, since he had no estimate for finishing the whole Capitol. He did his best to minimize it. Since the south wing was just one large room, it should cost less than the north wing. The central portion, the grand vestibule, might yet be covered with a dome, but if not, "it will consist only of an arcade twenty feet high, and ten feet wide; and over that, a colonade sixteen feet high," topped by a cupola. He estimated the whole building would cost less than $400,000.

The executive offices would cost $100,000, as would a building for the judiciary. As for the streets, "filling up some gullies or ravines near the capitol and paving Pennsylvania Avenue from thence to the President's house is all that is necessary . . . , except clearing of stumps and grubs, and perhaps, in a few instances, leveling, previous to the removal of the government, the ground in general being hard and gravelly, will afford an easy passage, until the city becomes populous."

As for income, White noted that purchasers of lots, including Morris and Nicholson, owed the city $378,191, to be paid in five roughly equal installments. Not that, but sales from lots would pay off a loan. The public still owned 4,694 lots, of which 1,694 were choice lots. The average value of lots sold since 1791 had been $285. So the commissioners held property worth $1,337,790, plus 3,500 front feet of waterside property at $16 a foot worth $56,000. White added that he had "no doubt" that "if the public buildings can be carried on without immediate sales," the whole could be sold for $2 million "even before the government removes."

White gave the committee copies of accounts, cost estimates, and the plan for the Capitol. He had only a copy of Hadfield's design, which he showed to the committee anyway. Everyone liked it but a congressman from North Carolina, who brought up all the commissioners' "misconducts" and expressed "great displeasure" at the style of the buildings. None of the other members responded, and the North Carolinian said "as they had gone so far he was willing to finish them." The committee chairman took the account of expenditures home, which generated some questions. By the next meeting, on the 16th, everyone was agreeable to guaranteeing a $500,000 loan, enough to finish the Capitol and president's house, erect buildings for the judiciary and executive offices, and pave some roads. The committee would meet on January 18 to formally approve the report.

White was ecstatic. With a surge of energy, he looked forward to clearing up other matters. He would offer the public half of the squares Lynch and Sands had bought for $50,000, one fifth down and then $10,000 a month. Reacting to the criticism of several congressmen who contemplated building in the city, he asked the president what he thought about waiving the requirement that buildings be three stories on the avenues. He informed his colleagues that the president "said he was no wise attached to these regulations."

Then the committee chairman heard a report that Andrew Ellicott said it would cost 500,000 guineas (almost $1.4 million) to finish the Capitol and 300,000 guineas to finish the president's house. Impossible sums. The chairman asked more questions about the commissioners' bank stock, the money to be paid to the original proprietors, what had to be done to the streets, and so on. White got the chairman to call Ellicott before the committee but not before talking himself with Ellicott. "He gave me a very friendly reception," White reported to his colleagues. Ellicott based his estimate on a design of the president's house, which had three stories. White continued, "In a long conversation he said many things favorable to the city—though I found he reprobated much that had been done—and had imbibed much of the prejudices of the day. I believe however his appearance before the committee will not be injurious."

Ellicott gave the committee a favorable report on the city. However, the more members talked over matters, the more they talked about changes, such as having the central portion of the Capitol finished to house the judiciary. Nevertheless, the committee report sent to the House on January 25 betrayed no itch to redo plans. The report gave a figure of $140,000 a year for the next five years to complete the buildings. Morris and Nicholson and others who had bought lots would pay $40,000 a year, leaving a deficiency of $500,000 for the next five years to be covered by loans. The committee assured the House that sales of lots could meet that deficiency but that it would "be a wanton sacrifice of the public interest," and Congress should "cherish these funds [lots] so as to make them productive of the greatest public utility."

*   *   *

Troubling White was some nagging from the federal city. Thornton had a particular peeve, warning White not to show Hadfield's plan. That might cause trouble in the future. He sent his own plan up. But the big problem was that the committee was talking about too small a loan guarantee. The amount of money to be guaranteed should be left up to the president; just a half million would not do. It had to be emphasized that the lots would be worth ten times their present value in 1800. And they liked the building regulations. The prices of lots on the avenues will be so high that none "but the wealthy will in general build."[3]

49. Ward Off Evil Until That Era Arrives

White did not leave it to the House to print the committee report. He had it, his own report, and the memorial from the commissioners printed, and he made plans of the city and the public buildings available at the clerk's table. Still, White feared he probably did not have enough facts on the table to prevent opponents from finding some pretext for delay. He pressed his colleague to send up an estimated cost of completing the Capitol, and he asked the heads of the executive departments to specify what they would need. The Treasury secretary wanted twenty-nine large rooms; the secretary of state five rooms with board-lined, unplastered garrets for the patent models. White had no idea if those requirements could be accommodated in a $100,000 building, but he made it seem as if someone was working on the problem.

While waiting for the House to take up the report, White called on Morris. No bank had as yet cashed the notes Morris had given him. The funds financing his mission nearly depleted, he begged "a few thousand dollars." Morris thought he could let White have $3,000 within the week but "would make no more promises." Then the speculator astounded him by suggesting that if the commissioners did get a loan, they advance money to Morris and Nicholson to finance *their* buildings, taking improved lots as security. White managed to keep a straight face, reasoning that if Morris proposed such an arrangement it would at least open negotiations toward a new agreement. White's colleagues were not so calculating. When they heard what Morris had suggested, they wrote to White, "One would have thought that common modesty would have forbid his making so insulting a proposition." They worried that his making it was a strong indication that he had no intention of paying his arrears.[1]

*   *   *

Troublesome as the commissioners were, Morris and Nicholson had two bigger problems, Carroll and Law. To keep the lots they had bought from Carroll, they had to pay him £6,000 and build twenty houses by September 26. To prove to other potential buyers that they indeed owned the lots they offered for sale, they had to persuade the commissioners to give Law the titles to the lots he had bought. With the loan bill about to pass, they did not want to lose lots because the value of the property would "be much increased."

To reassure Law, they mortgaged the houses at the point to him to serve as a guarantee that they would give him titles. About two thirds of the lots Law bought had been owned by the commissioners, the rest by Carroll. So they tried to use Law to pressure the commissioners and Carroll to make it easier for the partners to get the deeds. Law saw some reason to pressure the commissioners. They had received almost $100,000 from the partners (mostly Greenleaf), and Law did not like the board. Their latest reply to his request that they open New Jersey and Pennsylvania Avenues for carriages was that their workers were too busy. In the middle of winter!

However, Carroll had got next to nothing from the speculators. With each succeeding visit to the federal city, Law became less the speculator and more the proprietor, joining forces with Carroll in organizing the Washington canal lottery. The best Law could do was suggest that Morris and Nicholson give some lots to Blodget, who had to build prize houses for the second lottery, for which the drawing still had not begun.

Cranch handled the negotiations with Carroll, who was as adamant as ever. He would convey no titles without a payment of at least half the purchase price, $8,000, plus interest, and, as to the twenty houses on South Capitol Street, he would "unalterably abide by the contract." Morris and Nicholson played hardball too, instructing Cranch to withhold the $8,000 unless Carroll agreed to place the titles to the twenty lots they had to build on in escrow and also agreed to give Law and Duncanson titles to the lots of his they had bought. They also insisted Carroll make the improvements required of him in the contract. Carroll was not intimidated. He would convey titles once the houses were built and the lots paid for.

If he did not fulfill his end of the bargain, they could take him to court. Moreover, they owed him $1,400 for bricks.

Morris and Nicholson made peace with their builders. Nicholson suggested to Deblois that Duncanson arbitrate their dispute over accounts. Morris sent Lovering $500. Building those twenty houses might be the only way to save themselves from having to vie with a Carroll in a Maryland court.

*   *   *

Law did not let the trouble over the deeds weigh him down. On January 19 he sent a plan to retire the British national debt to an English friend and added that, as for himself, "I hope to obtain the heart of Miss Custis the President's grand daughter. I mean to set up an Agency for India at Washington City." So busy was his pursuit of Eliza Custis (he was then proving to David Stuart, her stepfather, that he was worth a little over $250,000 and could settle £10,000 sterling on Eliza) that Duncanson became the point man for the canal committee, on which Carroll, Young, and Deblois joined the two nabobs. Duncanson, like Law and Barry, aimed to trade with India from Washington. Just as Law found Barry to help bankroll his Washington business, Duncanson waylaid James Ray who had stopped in New York on his way back to India.

Duncanson pressed the commissioners to take sections of the canal route so they could be more certain of its cost. One expert opined that as planned it would cost $3 million. The committee wanted to know if the commissioners had the power to deviate from the plan by narrowing the canal. Duncanson wanted the new canal engineer, Myers, to look over the route and "to ascertain whether locks will be necessary to retain a certain quantity of water for health—to prevent the fatal effluvia that exhale from mud and filth when the tide is out." The commissioners offered their full cooperation, since, after all, it cost them nothing, and encouraging the fever to build canals, which was sweeping England and America, to spread into the city provided relief from some rather tedious goings-on.[2]

They accused the constable of not prosecuting people caught

stealing their lumber. When David Burnes heard that the board was thinking of knocking down his fences that crossed Pennsylvania Avenue, he asked to be forewarned so he could "be on the spot to take the legal measures for prevention and indemnification." Cooke & Brent and Mitchell, suppliers of stone and brick respectively, grew restive with their contracts.

The river remained opened that winter, hardly good news for the commissioners. The schooners *Quarrier* and *Contract* and the sloop *Peggy* brought up 142 tons of stone from Aquia in late January, but the days of liberal advances to their best supplier were over. The commissioners refused to pay any more until all of the stone was moved from the crowded docks to the work sites. The quarriers complained that they were hauling as best they could, considering the hill they had to haul over and "the badness of the roads." They needed $600 on the $1,428 the commissioners owed them. The board relented. Then Mitchell complained that he was losing money on the brick contract, wanted out of it, and needed the $2,000 owed to him. Thanks to a short-term loan from Deakins, they could pay Mitchell $968, and they renegotiated his contract to a million more bricks at $6 a thousand (a 50-cent increase).

Then, to get the money from the men who had bought the causeway, they had to begin work on the drawbridge. So they advanced Harbaugh $600. The money came from another bank loan.

The only bright spot on the ledger was a purchase of waterside lots by William Prout. He bought some of the public's portion of the waterfront on his original holdings for $3,866, $16 a waterfront foot. Prout had established a market, open every Saturday and Wednesday, at that end of the city near his store and hoped to profit from its inevitable expansion.[3]

*   *   *

On February 3 the House formed a committee of the whole to discuss the committee's report on the loan. In two days of debate only two members spoke in opposition. Both thought it was evident from the commissioners' own report that the city had resources enough to complete the buildings without the help of Congress.

Zachariah Swift, a Federalist from Connecticut, also challenged the premise on which the loan was based. He opined that the lots would not increase in price and consequently the government would eventually "be obliged to make good the whole loan."

Since he was from New England, Swift's opposition alarmed White. After the meeting he sought him out, had a "long conversation," and reported to his colleagues, "I believe [he] will in the future be silent." The other opponent was from New Jersey and thus deemed irreconcilable. Off the floor, members wished for a cap on the interest to be paid, and many thought the guaranteed sum too high. "Friends of the city" thought it best to give in and agree to leave both the interest and sum to be guaranteed blank. Thus amended, the report was approved, 57 for and, White thought, no more than 30 against. The committee had authority to draw up a bill, which the committee chairman asked White to do.

Anticipating that a cap of six percent would be placed on the interest, White asked his colleagues if they could get a loan at that rate. Then he warned that "some gentlemen speak of 200,000 dollars only." He wanted to know how "warmly" he should contend for more.

Scott and Thornton had got a report that the Senate was unfriendly to the loan, so a few weeks after having argued that the president should determine the interest rate and dismissed $500,000 as too small a sum, they changed their minds. They were confident they could get a foreign loan for less than six percent, and they recognized that limiting the interest rate the government paid to six percent was a good policy. As for the sum to be guaranteed, they instructed White to take whatever he could get.

"The day may come," they wrote, "when the public counsels may be more enlightened and better able to see and to pursue the true interest of their country and the sum proposed may ward off the evil that Era arrives." Such stoicism was prescient, for Congress had yet to really bare its teeth.[4]

50. A Field for Cavil and Declamation

"Mr. White seems to entertain no doubt of a favorable issue to his Mission," the president wrote to Lear on February 15, "but it goes (as everything else does) slowly on."

To speed it up, White wrote a bill and personally got it approved by enough committee members so the chairman could present the bill without having to convene his committee. All seemed to be going well, but then the chairman decided he did not like White's draft and wrote his own. Still, the bill did not come to the floor. Chairman Smith joined the crowds hearing arguments before the Supreme Court on the efforts of Virginians to get out of paying their prewar debts to British merchants.

White did not express it, but in the back of his mind must have been Madison's warning that New Englanders like Smith would find some sneaky way to defeat the loan. On February 21, Chauncey Goodrich of Connecticut wrote to the governor of his state that he was against the loan because it was "an expenditure under a disguised form." City lots would not defray the whole expense. But he did not think the loan could be defeated in the House. He left that up to the Senate. All the House could do was "lessen the sum."

On George Washington's birthday, the House voted by 48 to 34 to postpone the western lands bill and take up the loan. A problem cropped up immediately. In his version of the bill Smith required that all unsold public lots in the city be conveyed to the president. Swanwick, who represented Philadelphia, contended that the United States, by virtue of owning the lots, would be obliged to complete the public buildings. The next speaker, Nicholas of Virginia, was drowned out by sounds "of cannon and beating of drums" from the street in celebration of the president's birthday. Nicholas favored the loan, but subsequent speakers did not come to the aid of the president's city. Opponents of the bill set out not to defeat the measure but to recommit it. Swanwick claimed he would rather grant money to complete the buildings than place all the lots in the hands of the president. He did make a telling critique of the bill's premise. If the growth of the city depended on commerce, it was better to sell lots, not hold them out for higher prices, which "would be the obstacles to settlement." But the debate centered on who really owned the land and who should control it: the commissioners, the trustees, or the president.

White wrote to his colleagues asking exactly who did own the land. Debate dragged on for three days, and, as it did, criticism of the extravagance of the buildings began cropping up. Williams of New York averred that the buildings were "much too magnificent, . . . more so than any palace in Europe: they would cost a million of dollars more than calculated." Dearborn of Massachusetts said more information was needed about the buildings. White wrote to his colleagues that "the change of the plans seemed to have few advocates" and that he "did not anticipate any great countenance of the preposterous scheme." But the economizers in the South could not resist the call. Giles said he had been to the city, and the president's house "was much too magnificent," though he was all for a Capitol on a "grand scale, and fitted for the Representatives of a great and free people."

The House voted to recommit and placed four new members on the select committee. But the House had not done with the city. Dearborn moved to have the committee also "inquire whether any, and what, alterations ought to be made in the plans of the buildings. . . ." Murray of Maryland tried to stem the tide, arguing that changes at this point would only increase expenses. But Bourne of Rhode Island and Giles of Virginia both thought the buildings fair game. Swanwick blessed the alliance of economical Yankees and Virginians, observing that he had been in the city and "found plans had been frequently changed."

Murray must have looked longingly at his Federalist colleagues for aid in beating back this attempt to make the government go cheap, and at least Sedgwick of Massachusetts rose. In the 1789 debate on the residence bill he had predicted that a Potomac capital would mean a death sentence for every Northerner who went to it. In 1800 he would say that he had always thought putting the capital on the Potomac "unfortunate." In 1796, however, he said that the only ground for complaint would be if the buildings were too small.

"Even if they were more splendid than European palaces," the House, "should be grateful for them." The House did not agree, and the resolution passed 42 to 38.

White was stunned. "What shall I say when I am asked for an estimate of the expenses of the Capitol?" White asked his colleagues. "What a field for cavil and declamation when it is said that the plan of such a building was accepted without any knowledge of the costs." He begged for an estimate and for information to use against the economizing Virginians. "Do not Jefferson's letters show that both plans were examined and improved by him? That circumstances would shut the mouths of some," like the member from North Carolina who said "he would vote any sum that was necessary to pull down the President's house and to build one on a proper scale."

The first meeting of the committee did nothing to relieve White's anxieties. The members "came to no resolution and their conversation consisted principally in starting difficulties." Sitgreaves of Pennsylvania argued that under the deed of trust, lots could not be mortgaged. Then the committee looked over the plans of the Capitol. Straining to keep down expenses, White contended that the building would be only 26 feet high from the foundation wall. The members rightly saw that it was more than twice that high. The committee adjourned, not to reconvene, White feared, until he had information about the land and plans. He wrote again begging for information, adding "there are men who do not scruple to say, the commissioners designedly with hold the real state of affairs. Indeed so many unpleasant circumstances have attended this business, that I can with great truth say, the last two months have been the most disagreeable periods of my life." Then the signed copy of the British treaty arrived on March 1. The president would soon ask that it be funded. White heard that some proponents of the treaty wanted to postpone action on the loan bill, thus holding it hostage until the treaty was funded.[1]

*   *   *

The delay got Robert Morris's dander up. In the face of any foot-dragging other than his own, he was always the bold man of action.

He described the situation to James Marshall: the bill "hangs at present in a committee owing to nonsensical and bombast[ic] speeches. These things you know must have their course. Many private houses will this year be built in that city whether Congress lend them credit or do not. I have just agreed with Mr. Barry of Baltimore to build ten, five for him and five for me. Mr. Law, Mr. Duncanson, Mr. Nicholson, Mr. Barry, Mr. Pollock, myself and many others are going at it in earnest."

Actually Barry had not agreed to join him in building houses to satisfy the contract with Carroll. He was still considering Morris's proposal. Also unreported was news that the partners' one sure purchase was in jeopardy. Notley Young had always been amenable to whatever Greenleaf wanted. When Morris and Nicholson took over, he continued to cooperate by accepting their notes due in six months for the September 1796 installment of $13,739.20. As usual, when the time for payment of the notes approached, Cranch asked if they could be extended. To Morris's sorrow, Young said no. "March is a dreadful heavy month to us," Morris lamented as he added one more payment due.

The only good news from the city was that a carpenter had offered to finish one or two houses and take his payment in lots. Morris prodded Cranch to hurry that carpenter on and rent or, preferably, sell the houses. Morris authorized Cranch to sell all the lots he could. At the same time he told White that while the bill was pending in the House he would not sell lots, but once it was passed he would sell one hundred and raise all the money needed. White got in the habit of trying to call on Morris every day to pester for payment. They good-naturedly argued in circles. White reminded Morris that even if Congress approved the loan, funds were needed immediately to prepare for the coming building season. Morris retorted that "if Congress sustained the loan it would enable him to comply with his agreement." Morris did have one new idea. If the commissioners would convey titles to Walter Stewart, Morris and Nicholson would assign to them Stewart's debt of $23,000, of which $5,000 was due immediately. White liked the idea, suggesting to his colleagues that "it is our business to keep every man in a good humor who wishes to improve the city and I believe General Stewart is of that number." Still, White asked the attorney general if the commissioners could sell Morris's and Nicholson's lots to make up their arrears.

White's other efforts to raise money were also frustrating. Lynch and Sands declined to buy any public lots. Even if they had wanted to buy, the sale would have been complicated because Morris and Nicholson had not yet chosen all of their lots and could have claimed lots in those squares the New Yorkers wanted. Another of White's ideas did not pan out. The New York brokers March and Bleeker were amenable to trying to sell Washington lots but not while congressional action on the loan was pending. The most tangible nibble he had was from a Philadelphia builder named Cook who wanted to build a row of houses near the Capitol and asked the price.[2]

*   *   *

Back in the federal city, the marriage of Law and Miss Custis became the occasion for the commissioners to solve one problem. They gave titles of public lots to Law in return for lots reconveyed to them by Morris and Nicholson, enough to give Law about a third of the lots he had bought in December 1794. Law dropped them a note as he went off to the ceremonies in Virginia: "I will drink to your health. You made me quite happy yesterday." Law's energy, after all, was keeping private building going. Other forces seemed to be scattering.

As a wedding present to Law, Morris and Nicholson rented the best house at the point to him. Prentiss, who had just moved in, threatened to leave the point despite having dug and bricked in two cellars there. He calculated that Nicholson owed him $3,200 for work on four houses and for buying two stores. If paid in goods, he wanted "linens, callicoes, and summer articles." Deblois's tavern-keeper failed, and his baker threatened to move to Alexandria or back to Boston. The only thing Nicholson could spare to help the tavern was some art prints, made by a company he owned, "much suited to a new and improving city."

Others not connected with the speculators were having a hard time. George Walker offered to sell his coachman Aaron and another slave, Ned, a copper still, a cider mill, feathers for a bed, and shore facilities for fishing, and to rent his house and its gardens, just "¼ mile from the Capitol on Maryland Avenue which is now the Post Road." Walker was nursing a resentment over the way his squares had been divided with the commissioners that December. He was convinced they had taken more than they were entitled to and had taken the best lots.

As for the public works, even without money, the commissioners made some moves. On March 5 crews hauled the crane from the Eastern Branch wharf to the Capitol, where it was hoped its hoisting of stone would be more appreciated. On the other end of town, carters began bringing rock chips, "spalls", to the president's house, where they could be used to make level ground to facilitate making the frame for the roof. Through March and April the small crews at both buildings did not miss a working day. With another building season coming, even old Collen Williamson felt the sap rising. He wrote to the commissioners asking for work, on the chance that "by this time you have seen some part of carrols and hobans cloven foot" and come to realize that Williamson was "not an Irish vagbond" but was adept at "archectry" and making "weighty buildings." The commissioners declined his services.[3]

*   *   *

Scott and Thornton sent documentation to Philadelphia to show that the commissioners held "legal estate" of the lands owned by the original proprietors and that they had agreed to reconvey a portion to those proprietors. They argued that Congress should not change the legal arrangement but should keep the property in the hands of the commissioners to simplify the division of squares and adjudication of disputed lines. The property could still be pledged to the loan, save for 300 lots they thought should be left free for sale to foreigners and those who promised "immediate improvement." Even before White sent down his alarm, Scott and Thornton sent up an estimate (since lost) for completing the Capitol, formed by Hadfield. They downplayed its significance, since "the prices of everything have been rising for three years past, and will continue to do so until times are more settled."

They found Jefferson's letters supporting the buildings and sent them up. They took the criticism of the president's house with equanimity and deflected any suggestion that the judiciary be in the Capitol by acceding to any congressional wish that it be placed in the president's house. They only wanted the change made soon, since it would mean the house would have "to be finished in a different style." They were so agreeable to change because "we are very anxious to obtain money from any quarter and on almost any terms being entirely at a stand for want of supplies." The Capitol was a different matter. Thornton explained to White that the height of the building was 50 feet and that "it would be destruction to alter one stone." The bad news from Philadelphia at least did not panic Thornton into embracing any offer from the builder Cook. Thornton thought Cook's buildings "destitute of taste and loaded with finery." He quoted a price of 20 cents a square foot for lots, which scared Cook away.[4]

*   *   *

The committee met at seven o'clock on the evening of March 10 and, encouraged by the presence of Attorney General Charles Lee, White did not inflict the "maze" of Maryland laws pertaining to the city on the committee, fearing that the assembled lawyers "never should have got through them." Lee calmed the committee. From Alexandria, Lee was no stranger to the federal city, and he assured the committee that the commissioners had legal title to the land. Under his guidance, the committee reported a bill that authorized the commissioners to obtain a $300,000 loan at six percent interest and required them to sell, under the direction of the president, such lots as were needed to raise the money to pay the interest and principal of the loan. If, once all of the lots were sold, the loan was still not repaid, then and only then, and only for that amount, would the United States be liable. The bill also assured the original proprietors priority in payment for their land and released any who bought lots from liability for repaying the loan. The committee also reported that "no alteration can with propriety now be made in the plans of the public buildings."

White was quite pleased, even rationalizing the reduction of the sum to be guaranteed from $500,000 to $300,000. The extra votes the lower sum would bring to the measure, by showing broad support for the city, was worth the $200,000 lost. Despite the treaty debate taking up most of the House's time, he hoped he could get the loan bill debated and passed during "the intervals."[5]

51. T'Other Side of the Gutter

As the debate over funding Jay's Treaty dragged on, White compared his unhappy fate to that of the American hostages held by Algiers. Some had languished for ten years. But those lucky souls were about to be freed with Senate ratification of a treaty that paid $800,000 in ransom. White saw no end in sight and worried that Thornton and Scott would further extend the commissioner's private credit to get money from the Bank of Columbia. Although he "contemplated with pain" the state of the city, if there was no money the work must stop. He told his colleagues he could not hazard his personal credit "to an amount which at this advanced period of my life may eventually reduce me to a state of indigence. . . . There is no reason that we should risk our private fortunes for promoting a public institution in which the money lenders [Bank of Columbia] are at least as much interested as ourselves."

Scott and Thornton tried to cheer up White with the assurance that "in no winter since the commencements of the city has more been done with so little means." With only $18,000 in income since January 1, the board had continued to amass $50,000 worth of stone,

brick, men, and their rations, and had increased their debt only to
$40,000. Lumber was in short supply, but that was the result of "the
complete failure" of Governor Lee to deliver; lime was also short,
but it always was. All that elicited only more gloom from White,
who felt "a regret inexpressible at the crippled state of affairs which
prevents our making the most of what is done." The board tried to
distract him by siccing him on Blodget. Only $30,000 had been spent
on the hotel, whereas $50,000 had been promised. Appalled at how
literal the board could be, Blodget insisted he had done enough.
Knowing little of the history of the business, White dropped it.

He did keep up the pressure on Morris to arrange matters with
Stewart. But Stewart wanted titles, and the board refused to give
them until payments were completed. On March 22 the attorney
general finally rendered his opinion, which strengthened the commissioners' position. He opined that they were right to withhold
titles until the fulfillment of the terms of sale, that they could sell
Morris's and Nicholson's property to make up their arrears, and
that Morris's legal theory was wrong. Payment with notes subse-
quently protested was not a proper payment. That prompted Stewart, who owed the board for public lots, to stop taking advice from
Morris and Nicholson. "Knowing the want of money that prevailed
in the city," he sent $5,000 and pledged to settle any balance when
he got down to the city.[1]

*   *   *

On March 24 the House passed a resolution calling for papers
pertaining to the treaty. That did not end the debate, but it had to
pause while the president pondered the request. White contacted
five Virginia and Maryland congressmen, prodding them to bring up
the bill, and then, when White thought it was finally his turn, he
found none of his men on the House floor. He hurried to Brent's
lodging, got him to the House, but too late. A long discussion on a
disputed election was in progress. On the morrow White's day
dawned.

The strategy of the friends of the bill was to take advantage of the
general feeling that too much time had already been spent debating

the loan. They contemplated no grand speeches. By lowering the sum to be guaranteed, limiting the interest rate, and disavowing any congressional responsibility beyond making good the loan, they felt they had brought a sizable majority over to the bill. In contrast to the 1789 and 1790 debates on the seat of government, the loan bill did not really matter to most members. The chairman of the committee that reported the bill, Jeremiah Smith, sent not a few letters to friends that session about congressional business. He did not mention the federal city bill. Nor did Joshua Coit, the man who rose to attack the federal city.

Coit claimed he was not against Congress going to the federal city, but he took pains to prove that it "was a mere speculating bubble." The city had too many rivals nearby to become a great commercial center, and only "two or three hundred houses, at the utmost extent" would be needed to house congressmen and all their "connexions and appendages for many years." The commissioners had already spent almost $400,000 to what seemed "no purpose,": half of the president's house and only the foundation of the Capitol had been built. The best way to get the commissioners to use money more wisely was to get them to live within their means, "but if the public treasury was once opened he should expect many future applications and heavy ones on the public treasury for those buildings, which, he feared, would be a lasting monument of the pride and folly of his country."

After protesting that he had not planned to speak, Nicholas of Virginia rebutted Coit by pointing out how cheaply 4,000 lots could be sold to raise $300,000, but better than any arguments from a Virginian, a Connecticut Federalist, James Hillhouse, rose and argued that, reduced to $300,000, the bill "was now on safe ground." "He was under no apprehension that the United States would even be called upon for a single shilling," and the Congress should not stand in the way of making it easier to complete the buildings.

With victory well in hand, Rutherford of Virginia rose to urge a big majority in favor because "the minds of the people were drawn towards the Federal city, and property would advance in price." Such bragging was counterproductive. Swanwick of Philadelphia took the floor. He was rich, flamboyant, and overextended in real estate. He had had his fill of federal city hype: "No sooner was it announced that government was to go to this new city at a certain period, than the cry was immediately raised that commerce would flow into it from all quarters; that it would become the center of all the property in the union; that ambassadors would build great seats there; that it would be everything that fancy could picture as delightful. What was London, Paris, or all the cities of the earth compared with this city! . . . Speculation now, however, being in some degree flat, it must be raised by the present bill. . . . And it will be asserted that the United States will take up this city as the Czar Peter took up St. Petersburg." And Swanwick gave a primer on speculation. "If the lots ever would be of value, it was now; for, in matters of speculation, the more uncertainty there was, the greater room there would be for conjecture and calculation." Once the city became home to congressmen eager for short sessions, it would be found, "that much of the speculation which had been founded on the great prosperity of that city, had been founded in error."

The friends of the city were ready for Swanwick. William Vans Murray of Maryland intoned that the federal city "was founded on nothing airy but to the mind that could think lightly of the sanctity of public faith; nothing groundless, unless to those whose interests led them from a fair calculation of those immense advantages that unite themselves in the center of the union, on one of the noblest navigable rivers in the world." Murray pointed to the windows from which could be seen Swanwick's Philadelphia property, which included a circus, or theater. He could not believe someone "so excellent a judge of good speculation, of commerce, and of city property" could think the federal city an airy speculation. "It must have been in the moment of poetical indulgence, and been determined in the cast of characters he meant to assume in the debate, to give us "T'other side of the Gutter," which he understood was an excellent dramatic thing, as it was played in the gentleman's own circus."

The eighteenth century lapped up such displays of wit. Swanwick knew he had to respond with good grace and somehow disarm the insinuations that the envy of Philadelphians motivated their opposition to the federal city. Isaac Weld, an English traveler who was in

Philadelphia during the debate, characterized the opposition in just the way the friends of the city wanted. He wrote that opponents wished "to crush the City of Washington while it is yet in its infancy, because they know, that if the seat of government is transferred thither, the place will thrive, and enjoy a considerable portion of that trade which is centered at present in Philadelphia, Baltimore and New York."

Swanwick rose and claimed that Philadelphia was "indifferent about the removal of the government. It would not take one cubit from her stature, nor from the value of the land to which the gentleman from Maryland had alluded on " 'T'other side of the Gutter.' " To prove there was no envy of the Potomac, he even held up the fiasco of Philadelphia's version of the president's house as an object lesson of what would happen in the federal city. That house was to have cost £20,000, "but nearly twice that had been asked for since, and the house was not yet finished." He closed by predicting the federal city would come again to Congress for money. The House passed the loan guarantee bill by a vote of 72 to 21.[2]

*   *   *

On the morning of the House debate a rumor spread that Nicholson had just made a sale worth $900,000. After passage of the bill, White sought out Morris and learned that a buyer in Hamburg, Germany, had indeed bought a great deal of Pennsylvania lands, but—and there was always a "but" hanging on news about Morris and Nicholson—the money would not be available until July. White passed the news on to Scott and Thornton but banked on the passage of the loan bill. He anticipated early Senate approval, and while it was pending he would try to get a small loan in Philadelphia. He suggested they check out "a Dutch house in Baltimore" that was said to have money to lend. He reported that Duncanson passed through Philadelphia saying he had sent gentlemen interested in Washington lots to the city.

Scott and Thornton were on the same wavelength, suggesting an immediate loan of $60,000 to $70,000 paid in monthly installments of $10,000 or $12,000. That, along with Morris's and Nicholson's

May payment, should see them through the current building season. Then property values might rise so high after the loan bill was signed by the president that no other borrowing would be necessary. At the moment, however, they had only $1,300 in their treasury, not enough to pay the work force at the end of April. As for Nicholson's big sale, they steeled White against giving Morris and Nicholson any grace for their May payment based on it. He was to tell them that if they did not pay by May 2, some of their lots would be sold. In light of that big sale, however, they were amenable to accepting notes of sixty or ninety days if they were well endorsed and negotiable with the understanding that no lots would be conveyed until the notes were paid.

Although the relief felt by White, Scott, and Thornton was evident, to judge from a letter Samuel Davidson wrote, the proprietors were downright jolly. Announcing incorrectly that a loan had been granted, Davidson informed his uncle in London that he would "now laugh at the man who would offer me less than $100,000" for his city lots.

Desperate as they were for cash, the commissioners would not sell cheap. Henry Lee came and offered to buy 100 to 300 public lots for $300 a lot. Able to get him up to only $350 a lot, they stopped negotiating. Then Dermott sold a lot next to the Capitol— by his own estimation "the best lot in the City of Washington"—to Senator John Brown of Kentucky for £600 ($1,600), and the surveyor-speculator thought that was a bargain price. He could have sold it for £800. In a letter to Stewart, Dermott characterized the mood in the city: "We are here in suspense about the fate of our bill in the Senate. Applications for lots are many and the prices are in my opinion intolerably high, considering that the best property is already selected."[3]

*   *   *

While those who lived in the city could hardly take their eyes off ground worth from $300 to $1,600 for every eighth of an acre, the English traveler Isaac Weld could not get over the trees. "Excepting the streets and avenues, and a small part of the ground adjoining the public buildings, the whole place is covered with trees." Weld swallowed all the talk about the Potomac and had no trouble foreseeing "thousands of vessels" in the Eastern Branch "sheltered from all danger." He thought the president's house "undoubtedly the handsomest building in the country," far superior to the one in Philadelphia. He estimated that 5,000 people, mostly "artificers," lived in the city, and, given the "numbers of strangers . . . continually passing and repassing through," city lots offered "an extensive field for speculation." All that said, there was simply not any city. "Were the houses that have been built situated in one place all together, they would make a very respectable appearance, but scattered about as they are a spectator can scarcely perceive anything like a town."

Yet that spring a sensitive soul yearned to escape from the supposed city and find solace in undivided nature. William Cranch spent the winter "poring over accounts," finally closing Greenleaf's accounts, "learning the tricks of the world and the deceitfulness of mankind, and qualifying myself, by experience, for doing business for myself on a sure foundation." For all of Cranch's labor, Greenleaf offered no money. (His Georgia speculation had made $800,000 on paper, then the Georgia legislature voided the sale because the legislature that had made the deal had been bribed.) Instead, Greenleaf let Cranch use a 2,200-acre estate across the Eastern Branch. Theophilius Holt had just opened a nursery along the Eastern Branch, advertising seeds from London, including "Large Cattle Cabbage, White Norfolk Turnip, Swedish Turnip and White Dutch Clover," and Cranch became a good customer. He rowed his friends across a wide river to a one-story house "which would make one of the most enchanting villas in the world." He showed off "the labor of my hands—my beautiful orchard, my peas, my melons, my grapes, my wheat and rye, my cabbage and lettuce." He was most proud of his orchard "of the choicest kinds of apples such as Newton Pippins, Golden Pippins, Golden Rennets, Spitzenburgs &c-, & a few fine pears, peaches & cherries & grapes." There all was well, save that for fifty-seven days there had been only one small rain shower.[4]

52. When the Present Gloom Blows Over

On March 31, the day the loan bill passed the House, White called on Senator John Henry of Maryland, a friend of the city who "stands well with the Eastern members." White wanted to know if the measure would be delayed in the Senate. Henry quizzed his colleagues and assured White that the bill would be approved but that there was a majority for postponing consideration until "the fate of the British treaty is known." Four senators, whose votes he relied on to pass the bill, were for postponement until the House acted on the treaty.

White, himself a friend to the treaty, thought such a delay was "preposterous." And once Potts, the other Maryland senator, returned, he vowed to push for floor action. The bill was read in the Senate on April 1 and referred to a committee composed of Henry, Henry Tazewell of Virginia, and Rufus King of New York. White's first task was to get the bill out of committee promptly without any amendments attached. It was slow work. White got to the room where the committee was to meet early, Henry came on time, King a quarter hour late, and at half past the hour White went looking for Tazewell. He found him in his lodgings "in the hands of his barber." Once the committee finally convened, White explained the House bill, but before they could come to any decision the Senate went in session and off they went. Henry promised to tell White when they would meet again.

He did not. The next day White went to the Senate but Henry was not there. Off to the solon's lodgings he went and found him still in bed. Henry had heard nothing to change his opinion that until the treaty was acted on by the House, nothing would happen in the Senate. White had to hear it for himself and managed to talk to two of the four senators Henry had cited as crucial. They would not specifically link the loan to the treaty, but they gloomily averred that "if the treaty is not carried into effect there will be an end to the Union," which of course meant there was no need for a federal city. Still, on April 8 White tried to stir up some action. He went to the Senate and asked King and Henry when the committee would meet again. They did not say and intimated that White would not need to attend anyway. White got a serious hankering to go home and sought the president's sanction. The delay in the Senate was just the half of it. House members who had supported the loan guarantee were going out of their way to make clear that they did not support the way the city had been run. White found it no joy to be the only commissioner on the scene.

*   *   *

Some progress on other fronts did not make his sojourn in Philadelphia any less frustrating. Theophile Cazenove told him that a $200,000 loan could be obtained in Europe at six percent interest with a douceur to bring the actual interest up to seven percent. He thought he could even advance $10,000 or $12,000 on the loan himself once he got the necessary papers. White ran Cazenove's terms past the president, who was agreeable provided a douceur was agreeable to the law.

But Cazenove was not so encouraging that White could stop putting pressure on Morris and Nicholson. In a letter the president read and approved, White reminded them that the mere passage of the loan bill did not give the city the money that it desperately needed to get building going again. He suggested that they immediately advertise a sale of some of their lots to raise money, which would be easier and less embarassing than if the commissioners did it themselves. He told them that he learned from Blodget that Greenleaf had obtained an opinion that the commissioners could not sell lots to make up arrears, but he challenged that opinion with that of the attorney general.

Morris summoned White to his countinghouse and disavowed Greenleaf's legal strategy. He "would prevent a sale by honorable means" and not "dispute" with the commissioners or "have recourse to chicanery." As for the arrears, he made a counterproposal. They would sell lots "immediately," provided that the commissioners would give titles to purchasers on their paying $80 per lot. Since after January 1, 1796, purchasers of their lots did not have to improve, there was no reason to withhold deeds. White was agreeable.[1]

*   *   *

Perhaps White was too nice, for while his ticklers only seemed to give Morris an excuse to chat with the amiable Virginian, the threats of Carroll of Duddington steeled Morris and Nicholson to action. Morris's hope that James Barry would come to the rescue did not pan out. Barry decided Morris would not be a reliable partner. Their backs to the wall, Morris and Nicholson made a vow, as Morris informed Cranch on April 12, "to disappoint Mr. Carroll's expectations of getting back the 20 lots." Morris promised "to spring a mine for this purpose."

The commissioners had nothing to spring. They did their best to keep "up appearances and the spirits of our people" by attending the office at least two days a week as if they had money to spend. All they had was $1,300, not enough to pay the carpenters and stonecutters at the end of the month. By mid-April a tone of hopelessness began to imbue their letters to White. Yet they simply could not believe that the purported friends of the government would forsake them if the House defeated the treaty. Passing the bill hurt no one, while rejection "will be attended with ruin to thousands, who will owe their destruction to their faith in government. . . . When the present gloom blows over, which probably it will do in no long time, the city will remain the only martyr to the follies of the day."[2]

*   *   *

White's plans to head home were short-lived. The president would not allow it. White's business was too well known, and if he left, it would be taken as an admission of defeat. Besides, when the Senate did consider business again, someone had to be there to push the city's bill. Not only did White agree to stay, but once again he was enthralled with the majesty "of that man whose abilities and virtues have rendered him so conspicuous in Europe as well as in America." White took the president's advice to seek out King and find out his "real sentiments."

King said he "had no aversion" to the loan, no objection to the capital on the Potomac, and no objection to promoting it, but "in the present state of things the bill ought not be acted upon. That he did not expect this would influence the votes of any man or mean to use it in that way." The stalemate in 1796 was not a reprise of that of 1790. "But if the British treaty should be rejected, no matter by whom brought about, it would place us in such a state, that he should think it improper to engage in any enterprise either of a public or private nature or to pass any laws except such as were necessary to keep up the form of government."

White lamented to Thornton that having the two houses of Congress at loggerheads made for as inefficient a government as was had under the confederation. As for disunion, White refused to utter "such sentiments" for fear of "familiarizing the idea of dissolution in the minds of the people." Here was a man more disposed to despair than deals. "My spirits sink when I see the season passing away which might have been employed to so much advantage had it not been for the preposterous policy of the Senate."

Then, on the 22nd, the committee reported the bill, and the Senate considered it on the 25th. Ross and Bingham of Pennsylvania ganged up against it. But it survived a motion to recommit by one vote, only to be postponed by one vote. White went home with a cold and toothache and spent all of the next day in bed.

He managed to write two letters. Trying to take advantage of adversity, he insisted to Morris and Nicholson that postponement of the bill was tantamount to rejection, and he pleaded, "Tomorrow when I state to my colleagues the above disagreeable intelligence, you will [can] enable me to console them with assurances" that their May installment would be paid. No assurances were forthcoming.

*   *   *

At last the House was talked out. Madison knew his majority, which he had once thought to number twenty members, was dwindling. Public opinion had decidedly swung in favor of the treaty, and commercial interests in every state saw to it that the members knew it. The Federalists alarmed the public that rejection of the treaty meant war, and they made that alarm hurt by virtually suspending commercial business, causing, the president thought, a decline in the price of flour just when Southern farmers were bringing it to market. Then, in one of the greatest speeches in the history of Congress, Fisher Ames of Massachusetts brought such eloquence to bear on that theme as to bring tears of joy to the eyes of his friends and long looks of dejection to the faces of Madison and his allies. Still, Madison thought the House would reject the treaty, at least at first.

It did not. By the tie-breaking vote of the speaker, the bill to fund the treaty survived weakening amendments and passed by three votes. A deal over the city loan did not enter into the vote. None of the members from northern Virginia, whom White would most likely influence, voted for the treaty. Two Marylanders flip-flopped on the issue, but Samuel Smith and Gabriel Christie represented the Chesapeake area and had never shown any affection for the federal city. Pressure from commercial interests, Smith admitted, prompted their reversal. The Maryland member representing Georgetown voted for the treaty, as he had long said he would. In a letter to Jefferson, Madison blamed the "Philadelphia brokers" who were "like a highwayman with a pistol demanding the purse."

White bestirred himself and returned to the Senate. That body, having done little for a month, had a full agenda, but members were not about to rubber-stamp anything. Ross and Bingham offered amendments to every paragraph of the bill, but all were rejected by a 16 to 9 vote. Then King offered an amendment making clear that the United States was not liable for completing the buildings. That too was rejected, but as the Senate adjourned for the day King threatened another amendment. White was seething and took cold comfort in Mason of Virginia's goodbye. He was so sure the loan bill would pass that he was heading home. White was "incessant" in seeking out King's allies and urging them not to cripple the city with such a negative imputation, especially when no federal help would be needed. Then he sought out King and, after "a very pointed discussion of considerable length," got him to withdraw his amendments and support the bill, which passed 16 to 7.[3]

*   *   *

On April 27 Thomas Twining, the young scion of a family of tea merchants, crossed Rock Creek, setting out to find his friend in India, Thomas Law. The day before, the stage from Philadelphia had deposited him at the Fountain Inn in Georgetown. With no carriage available to take Twining to Law's house five miles away on Greenleaf's Point, the landlord lent him a horse and he set out after breakfast.

He "crossed an extensive tract of level country somewhat resembling an English heath," then "entered a large wood through which a very imperfect road had been made, principally by removing the trees, or rather the upper parts of them, in the usual manner." He was likely going east on K Street. Then he reached New Jersey Avenue, which "assumed more the appearance of a regular avenue, the trees having been cut down in a straight line." Not a house was to be seen. A half mile down the avenue he "came out upon a large spot, cleared of wood, in the center of which I saw two buildings on an extensive scale, and some men at work on one of them." He was at the Capitol and the roofed-in but unfinished Capitol Hill tavern.

He had been led to believe that there was more to the city. Instead, he saw "on every side a thick wood pierced with avenues in a more or less perfect state." He thought the Capitol promised to be grand and "walked through several of the lower apartments, and saw the halls designed for the representatives and senate," all unfinished and "encumbered with building materials." The masons were civil, answered his questions, and pointed out the road to Law's house.

"After going about three quarters of a mile through a silent wilderness, I found myself upon a trackless plain partially covered with trees and brushwood." He saw no houses, so he continued "to explore my way through the thickets, keeping my horse's head rather towards the right to gain, if necessary, the Potomac, whose banks I might then follow." Then he spotted a carriage "issue from the forest beyond the plain, . . . making for a small bridge, which I now discovered for the first time, considerably to the right of the point for which I was making." Twining set his horse toward the bridge, hoping to intercept the carriage there, but the carriage was on a road. Twining's progress "was almost stopped, and was soon likely to be quite so, by the bogginess of the land as I drew near a small stream that I found running along the bottom."

The carriage crossed the bridge, "escaping," but then veered to the right, heading for the woods Twining had just left. Twining spurred his horse to the high ground, hoping to follow the road the carriage was on. He made it just before the carriage passed. It proved to be Law's, sent to pick up Twining in Georgetown. The coachman tied the horse to the back, they recrossed the bridge, "passed through the forest I had seen, and a second plain beyond it, and reached the banks of the Potomac. In a few minutes more we arrived at Mr. Law's where I had a most cordial reception."

Twining's confusion demonstrated how distant all the disparate parts of the city were despite five years of cutting trees. To one coming down from Capitol Hill, Law's house at 6th and N Streets Southwest was still hidden by trees. The masons evidently sent Twining down Maryland Avenue, and he mistakenly kept veering to the right toward the low ground formed by the Tiber in what was to become the Mall.

Once in Law's care, Twining's suffering was over. He spent a day with the Laws and joined them and Miss Wescott, a poet from Philadelphia, in an excursion by boat to Alexandria, where he was struck by "the vast number of houses" being built. Law talked up the federal city as only Law could. "As we stood one evening on the bank of the river before his door," Twining recalled, "he said, 'Here I will make a terrace and we will sit and smoke our hookahs.' " Twining "deeply regretted this delusion." That someone with the talents and family connections of Law was content with "the clearing of ground and building of small houses amongst the woods of the Potomac" was baffling.[4]

53. The Supineness of the Many Wealthy Men

Before leaving Philadelphia, White went over city affairs with the president, who agreed that "no further indulgence ought to be granted" to Morris and Nicholson. He also touched on the buildings—there should be a slate roof on the president's house, a marble staircase was too expensive, and he preferred that such matters no longer be left for his decision. He thought work on the executive offices should not begin until the two major buildings were virtually finished. Told that Deakins, the board's treasurer since 1791, wanted to resign, the president did not think a replacement was needed, with the commissioners living in the city.

White mentioned the speculators who would descend on the city now that the loan was guaranteed. The president lectured him on the evils of speculation. Lots should be "sold in small quantities to such as mean to improve." And Washington insisted on zealous rectitude in fulfilling the spirit of the law guaranteeing a loan. Not only should the proceeds from sales go to pay off the interest on any loan, but any excess income should be invested in government bonds to be set aside "to indemnify the government" against any possible loss arising from its guarantee.[1]

*   *   *

Passage of the bill raised expectations in the city but not the level of activity. Richard Forrest, who was trying to give the city the good hardware store it lacked, held back from increasing his stocks until the bill passed. Then the bill passed, and there was no run on his store. First things first: carpenters wanted a raise. Six who had worked at the Capitol through the winter cited the "great advance in the prices of all manner of provisions, . . . and consequent terms of boarding," and their "numerous tools, which required "continual repair." They politely asked for more money now that the city was no longer in a "precarious state." The board gave no raise.

When White reached the federal city in mid-May, he found no one working and everyone angling for the money to come. Led by Law, the proprietors around the Capitol were circulating a petition to require that the new money be spent there and that the commissioners live there. Scott and Thornton, meanwhile, refused to hire new workers until they had money in hand. "Chagrined" to find the city still stagnating "at this critical period when the eyes of the world were drawn afresh to the city by an event considered as favorable to it," White called a meeting and attacked "the supineness of the many wealthy men interested in the city." After considerable discussion, they agreed to advance $12,000 to $20,000 so the board could get work started on the walls of both buildings. To quiet the disgruntled eastern-side interests, the commissioners agreed to give "considerable preference" to the Capitol by putting a large number of men to work there. On Monday, May 23, work on the walls began.

The issue of the commissioners' residence struck White dumb. He had not had the time or money to move. Scott knew the agitation was aimed at him. He had bought and begun expanding an old house, called Rock Hill, which was on a hill beyond the city limits, much nearer to Georgetown than the Capitol. Alarmed that the petition would still go to the president, Scott wrote to him dismissing it as arising from the misunderstandings of the excitable Law. Scott's letter crossed one from the president, who himself was getting worked up about the issue. George Walker was in Philadelphia and doubtlessly shared his grievances with the president. The president reminded the commissioners that "it is said" that if they had lived in the city defective walls at the Capitol would never have been put up. He wanted them to live as close to the public works as possible "because they would have it so much more in their power to scrutinize all the movements of men & measures which are under their control, than it is possible to do at the distance of two or three miles by periodical or occasional visits. Being on the spot & seeing everything that occurs, they would be better enabled to systematize the business & have it conducted with greater economy."

When the president read Scott's letter, his temper flared, and he snapped back in a prompt reply that he knew no more of Law's "sentiments, . . . than I do of Tippoo Sahib's." The president reminded Scott that the reason new commissioners were appointed was to get men who would reside in the city; that "the remarks which were made during the discussion of the Guarantee Bill, even by its friends (not so much in, as out of the house)," underscored "the indispensable necessity for close attention" to the city's business; and that not until the commissioners resided near both public buildings would the "jealousies" between each end of the city "subside."

Scott found a defender in the retiring Deakins, who wrote to the president that the residence of the commissioners "cannot be an object of so much consequence as to cause the removal of good men from the office." He lauded Scott as "equal to" any commissioner who had served. He assured the president that after the expense Scott had put into his new house, he would not move to the city. But he was too valuable a man to dismiss. He seemed to have "a perfect knowledge of the value of work and materials." The contracts he had made for the public were made on "much more favorable terms" than those made by private individuals.

Scott and Thornton replied to the president in an official letter. "Unthinking persons" had made those allegations about negligence leading to the defective work at the Capitol. In reality, "if they had visited and walked over the walls three times a day it would not have been possible to prevent imposition where men are resolved to practice it." Furthermore, they could not find accommodations in the city because the proprietors had built so few. White wrote his own letter and took the same tack. He had been too busy to move, and he would once he had time to buy a few lots and money to build.[2]

* * *

Under fire, the board fired back at the east siders. An adversarial relationship remained throughout the summer. Reverend Ralph and James Barry, who fancied themselves as doing so much for the city, bore the brunt of it. Ralph taught school, preached at a Capitol work shed every Sunday, and set out to get the Episcopal church to do something in the city. He also thought he had made a bargain to buy a forfeited lot at its original price. The commissioners demurred. Ralph had to admit that only one commissioner, Scott, had made that agreement, but nonetheless he protested that he did not appreciate being treated like a greedy "speculator on the public property."

Barry was doing so well in Baltimore that it was he who supplied the cash so Law could live the life befitting his wealth. He rented a "negro coachman" for Law for $50 a year and bought a piano and a set of Pleyel sonatinas for $165. For the city, he paid for the ads for the canal lottery, which, with a top prize of $20,000, was to gross $175,000 and net $26,250 for the canal. Some Baltimore merchants joked at his belief in the city's commercial potential. Barry told them he believed in it because George Washington told him so. To help the commissioners, Barry continued to buy lots, and he offered to let the board use his wharf for the public works without charge until 1800. They returned his letter with some alterations. Barry was miffed that his letter was changed, miffed that he did not get a letter answering his, and thoroughly fed up with the legalese that infected all business with the board. That alteration in his proposal, which he supposed in "city language" would be called "amendments," said the wharf must be "returned in status quo." Barry refused to "wrestle" with legal phrases, though he had to admit that he had "never yet met in Washington the literal language of quid pro quo." All he wanted was the wharf back "in good and complete order and the water there cleared and not shoaled." Sarcasm was not the way to the board's heart. In reply they blamed Law for the alterations in Barry's letter and left the wharf matter for face-to-face negotiations.

Law himself was always pestering the board about something. On June 1 he demanded that they stop allowing temporary houses on the Capitol square, for they destroyed "the intended uniformity and are ultimately a loss of labor, time and money as they must so soon be removed." He threatened to bring the matter to the president's attention. Law never missed a chance to remind the board of his special relationship with the president.[3]

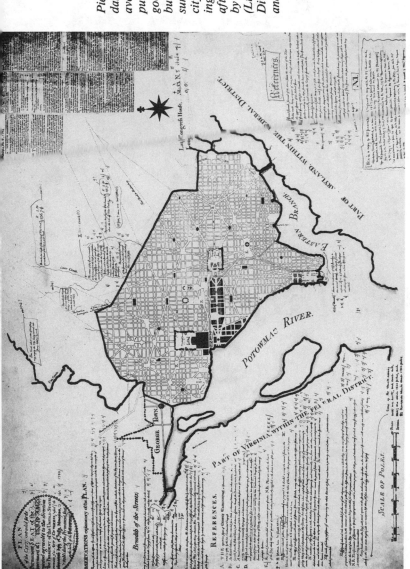

Pierre L'Enfant's plan, dancing with diagonal avenues and large public places, made a good first impression, but those who had to survey and build the city found it a maddening blueprint even after it was simplified by Andrew Ellicott. (Library of Congress, Division of Prints and Photographs)

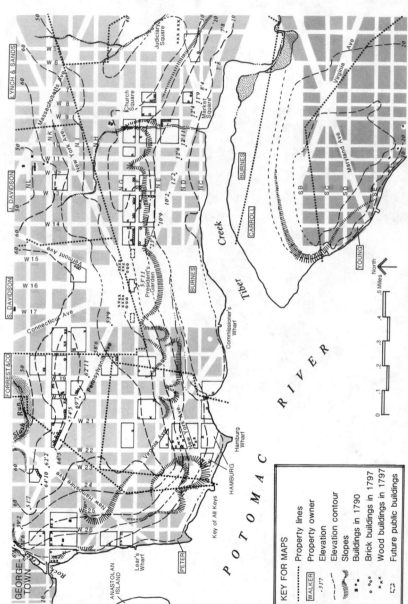

POTOMAC RIVER

GEORGE TOWN

ANASTOLAN ISLAND

Lear's Wharf

Key of All Keys

HAMBURG

Hamburg Wharf

Commissioner's Wharf

Tiber

Creek

BURNES

CARROLL

BURNES

YOUNG

PETER

Rock Creek

Slash Run

Connecticut Ave

Vermont Ave

Pennsylvania Ave

New Hampshire Ave

Virginia Ave

NEW YORK Ave

Massachusetts Ave

New York Ave

President's Garden

Church Square

Market Square

Judiciary Square

Maryland Ave

Virginia Ave

LYNCH & SANDS

J. DAVIDSON

S. DAVIDSON

FORREST & CO.

W 5
W 6
7
W 8
W 9
N K
10
N I
N H
W 11
N L
W 12
W 13
W 14
W 15
W 16
W 17
W 19
W 21
W 22
W 23
24
W 25
W 26

N G
N E
N D
N C

S B
S C
S D
S E

North

0   .1   .2   .3   .4   .5 Miles

KEY FOR MAPS

WALKER	Property lines
.317	Property owner
	Elevation
	Elevation contour
	Slopes
	Buildings in 1790
	Brick buildings in 1797
	Wood buildings in 1797
	Future public buildings

© Stephen Kuter

© Stephen Kuter

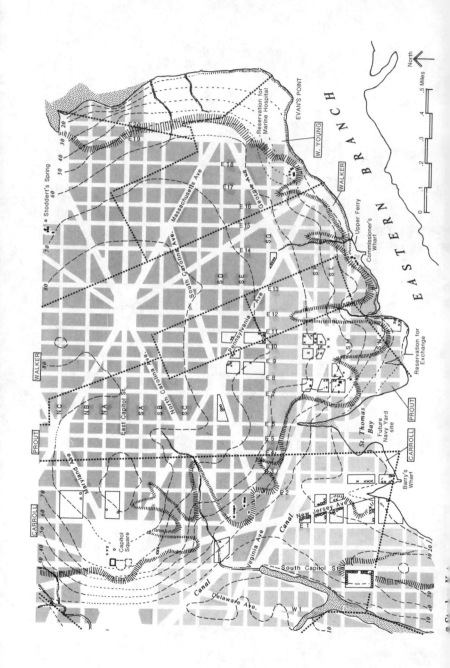

young Thomas Johnson by C. W.
Peale. The dominant commissioner
was eventually mystified at why he
did not get rich off the city. (Library
of Congress, Division of Prints and
Photographs)

Benjamin Stoddert, whose inexhaustible effort to profit on the
federal city resulted in penury.
(Library of Congress, Division
of Prints and Photographs)

Daniel Carroll of Rock Creek, an
engraving after a portrait by John
Wollaston. The commissioner was
so unnerved by the task at hand
that it ruined his health. (Library
of Congress, Division of Prints
and Photographs)

William Thornton, architect, by
Robert Field. This commissioner—
the designer of the Capitol and a
practiced in-fighter—was miffed
that he did not become governor of
the District. (National Museum of
American Art, Smithsonian Institution, Catherine Walden Myer Fund)

In 1792 Samuel Blodget came to save the city. His loan, lottery, and other efforts to sell lots created many headaches. Washington and the commissioners soon rued the day they met the man, but his intrepid optimism continued to inspire his fellow proprietors. This copy of a damaged John Trumbull original shows Blodget in his Revolutionary War garb. (Yale University Art Museum)

Andrew Ellicott, with his two brothers, surveyed much of the city and apparently did much of it wrong. (Library of Congress, Division of Prints and Photographs)

This portrait by Lewis Clephan, who painted most of the public buildings, seems to have captured the beguiling innocence of Leonard Harbaugh, whose buildings and bridge had a propensity to burn or fall down. His winning virtue was that he was the cheapest builder in town. (Collection of the Museum of Early Southern Decorative Arts)

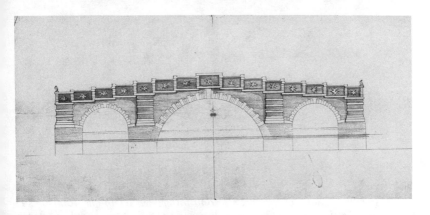

Leonard Harbaugh originally designed a bridge with one arch to span Rock Creek. A critic worried that one arch would be unstable. Harbaugh built a bridge with three arches which became so unstable that the middle arch was taken down and a wooden drawbridge substituted. (National Archives)

UNITED STATES LOTTERY.

Permission of

By THE COMMISSIONERS,

Appointed to prepare the Public Buildings, &c. within the City of WASHINGTON, for the reception of CONGRESS, and for their permanent residence after the year 1800.

SCHEME OF THE LOTTERY, No. II.

For the Improvement of the

FEDERAL CITY.

1 A magnificent dwelling-house,	20,000,	and cash	30,000,	are	50,000
1 ditto	15,000,	and cash	25,000,	are	40,000
1 ditto	15,000,	and cash	15,000,	are	30,000
1 ditto	10,000,	and cash	10,000,	are	20,000
1 ditto	5,000,	and cash	5,000,	are	10,000
1 ditto	5,000,	and cash	5,000,	are	10,000
1 Cash prize of	-		-		10,000
2 ditto	5,000 each,	are	-		10,000
10 ditto	1,000,	are	-		10,000
20 ditto	500,	are	-		10,000
100 ditto	100,	are	-		10,000
200 ditto	50,	are	-		10,000
400 ditto	25,	are	-		10,000
1,000 ditto	20,	are	-		20,000
15,000 ditto	10,	are	-		150,000

16,739 Prizes.
33,261 Blanks

50,000 Tickets, at 8 dollars, are — 400,000

an Opportunity will be afforded

By this lottery ~~the commissioners will be enabled~~ to give an elegant specimen of the private buildings to be erected in the city of Washington.—Two beautiful designs are already selected for the entire fronts on two of the public squares; from these drawings it is proposed to erect two centre and four corner buildings, as soon as possible after this lottery is sold, and to convey them, when complete, to the fortunate adventurers, after the manner described in the scheme for the Hotel-lottery.—A net deduction of five *per cent.* will be made to defray the necessary expences of Printing, &c. and the surplus will be made a part of the fund intended for the National University, to be erected within the city of Washington.

☞ ~~The drawing will commence on Monday the Twenty-second of December next.~~

~~JANUARY 18, 1794.~~

add what is in Manuscript.

~~S. BLODGET, Agent~~

~~for the affairs of the city.~~

354

The prospectus of Samuel Blodget's second lottery with Thomas Johnson's corrections. At the time it was the largest lottery in U.S. history. It did not prosper. Six years after it was announced, three years after tickets were drawn, Blodget encouraged players to exchange their winning tickets for Washington City lots. Most speculators wrote off the tickets and lots as completely worthless. (Library of Congress Manuscript Division)

This rendition by George Parkyns of the Georgetown waterfront was painted in 1796 when the artist was all afire about building an art school on Pennsylvania Avenue. An avowed propagandist, Parkyns aimed to make things look good. Robert Morris, who knew the Georgetown of old, thought the port was going downhill as local investors speculated in Washington City lots. (Library of Congress, Division of Prints and Photographs)

VIEW of the SUBURBS of the CITY of WASHINGTON.

One of William Thornton's many designs of the Capitol, probably made after he had vanquished Hallet and Hadfield. It shows the portico that helped win the design competition and the basement which professional architects could not abide. (Library of Congress, Division of Prints and Photographs)

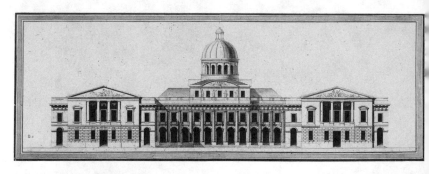

One of Stephen Hallet's many designs for the Capitol which highlights elements he especially favored: no basement, no portico, and a recessed courtyard to make it easier to light the legislative chambers in the wings. (Library of Congress, Division of Prints and Photographs)

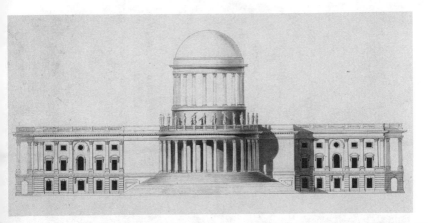

Probably inspired by criticism that he did not know how to light the building properly, William Thornton revised his design to let the sunshine in. As funds were lacking to complete the south wing of the building, much less the dome, this rendition was an academic exercise. (Library of Congress, Division of Prints and Photographs)

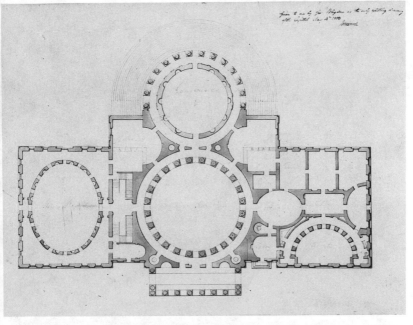

When Benjamin Latrobe took over at the Capitol in 1803, this was the only drawing of the Capitol, a legacy of William Thornton's inability to make correct drawings. Thornton's nemeses, Hadfield or Hoban, probably made the drawing. (Library of Congress, Division of Prints and Photographs)

William Birch's "View of the Capitol," painted in 1800, shows the just completed north wing. The workers in the foreground are probably a conceit of Birch's as the commissioners, nearly out of money, had long since fired their masons and were straining to get the interior plastered and painted. (Library of Congress, Division of Prints and Photographs)

An 1803 Nicholas King drawing looking west from just below the ridge above Pennsylvania Avenue. Blodget's Hotel is to the right; the Treasury and White House are in the distance. By 1803 locals called the bushy ravine just beyond the hotel "the marsh," at which the hunters in the foreground seem to look on eagerly. (Library of Congress, Division of Prints and Photographs)

James Greenleaf by Gilbert Stuart. Not a few speculators attributed their bankruptcies to his guile. Yet to the end he viewed himself as a victim of rapacious partners and he managed the legal system to keep his pretension alive for over forty years, much to the detriment of the Washington property he claimed. (Library of Congress, Division of Prints and Photographs)

Robert Morris had to be coaxed into investing in the capital he had done his mightiest to locate on the Delaware River. For his pains he wound up in Philadelphia's Prune Street Debtors Prison. (Library of Congress, Division of Prints and Photographs)

One of the better selling engravings in the 1790s, this portrait by Edward Savage of the Washington family helped wed the man to the city. On the table lies the L'Enfant plan. However, for those who could not stomach the capital-to-be, another engraving substituted a map of the United States. (Library of Congress, Division of Prints and Photographs)

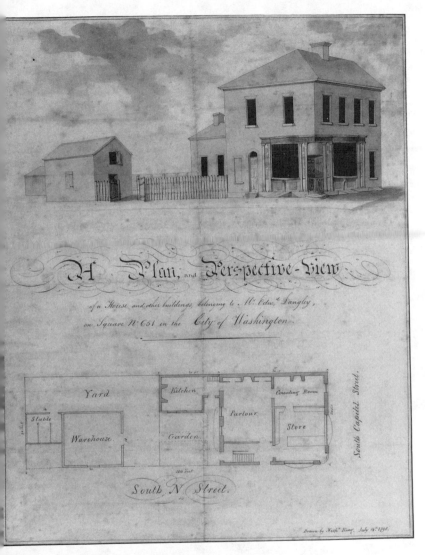

A Plan, and Perspective-View

of a House and other buildings belonging to Mr. Edward Langley,

on Square No. 651 in the City of Washington.

Yard

Stable

Warehouse

Kitchen

Garden

Parlour

Counting Room

Store

South Capitol Street.

100 Feet

South N Street.

Drawn by Nicholas King, July 14th 1796.

William Lovering's storefront design of the twenty buildings built for Morris and Nicholson in the summer of 1796 invited merchants like Langley to buy, as well as saved bricks. Daniel Carroll, original owner of the land, sued to claim the buildings, and ensuing legal complexities helped turn the block into the city's first slum. (The Winterthur Library: Joseph Downs Collection of Manuscripts and Printed Ephemera)

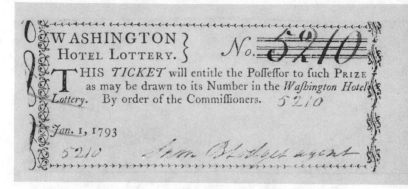

One of the 50,000 tickets, originally selling for $7 each. Near the end of the drawing in early 1794, undrawn tickets sold for $12. Prizes ranged from $10 to a $50,00 hotel which, as it turned out, was never finished. (Library of Congress Manuscrip Division)

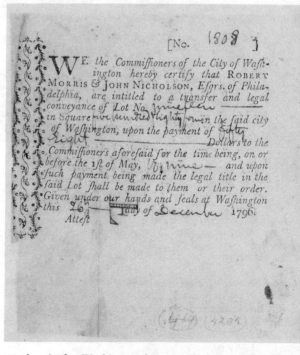

John Nicholson expected scrip for Washington lots to save his and Robert Mor ris's fortune. Square 534 lay just southwest of the Capitol and, at $58 to be pai in two and a half years, should have been a bargain, but lawsuits cast doubt o all the scrip. (Library of Congress Manuscript Division)

*   *   *

That spring it was business as usual for the board: suppliers were failing them. While Henry Lee was in town trying to speculate in lots, he also promised wood. The commissioners might have laughed in his face, but the men they relied on to make up for Lee's failing, Parrot and Blake, were themselves failing. On May 3 the commissioners warned them that if the oak contracted for was not delivered they would sue. A man named Alderson who had promised plank came up short. So the commissioners fortified a Captain Robert Sutton with seven slaves and five gallons of whiskey and for twenty-nine days he scoured the Potomac for any of Lee's timber that might have been harbored in various coves. He came back with ninety-two logs and a bill for $142.50. Each slave earned an extra 45 cents a day for every Sunday and holiday he had to work. Whether the slave or the master pocketed the change is not known.

The commissioners discovered another reason to stick with Lee. The price of everything was rising, and they could not contract for timber at a better price than they had got from Lee in 1794. Much as they wanted to, they could not maintain the price they were paying for stone because their quarries were becoming exhausted. They sent Blagden down to investigate, and he wrote a detailed report with his usual rugged charm. The only rock remaining that was easy to get to was "of a most nigged churlish nature." About 100 to 200 tons of good stone was covered "by a considerable quantity of earth." By early June the board had a new contract for 1,300 tons of stone from other quarries, which meant it was more expensive.

Their problems with building materials, although a cause for concern, did not constitute a crisis. As the carters who had to negotiate wharf areas clogged with stone well knew, laying in supplies was quite the specialty of the commissioners. It was the most tangible way to demonstrate their will to get the job done, and White let them know how impressed congressmen were to learn of the extent of material on hand. On May 18 Hoban submitted a progress report on work at the president's house designed to impress the next Congress. In the main it was merely a list of the woodwork and stonework in various stages of completion. Some turgid description—"the mahogany for the doors is cut out and seasoning"—was buried in a sea of numbers detailing the state of some 958 tons of stone. There were also 84,000 feet of lumber, 2,000 bushels of sand, 600 bushels of lime, and 170,000 bricks on hand.

The report did not mention the man who began working on the walls on May 23. In August the payroll for bricklayers and masons was half that of the year before. The commissioners were trying to do more with cheap unskilled labor. In August the number of white laborers, hired by the month to supplement the slaves, swelled. These were not the same old hands. Of thirty-seven laborers at the Capitol only seven had worked for the city in 1795. The overseers were also new. Jane Short, "public cook," provided some continuity. She was still on the job and had received a raise to £75 a year. Ten slaves rented by the city did get a bonus of sorts from the commissioners. They bought each a pair of shoes from an itinerant cobbler for $1.66 apiece. It was no sacrifice, since the board charged the masters for the shoes.[4]

*   *   *

The short-term line of credit afforded by the proprietors got work on the walls going again, but the board still needed a bank loan, preferably not from the Bank of Columbia. The trouble was that interest rates everywhere were higher than six percent. New York money commanded two and a half percent interest a month, and in London between 12 and 20 percent annually. That left Amsterdam. White did not follow through with Cazenove after Scott told him Robert Gilmore, a Baltimore merchant, had command of Dutch money. Scott explained that the board needed at least $120,000 for the present year, and that amount "may be all that is wanted," as sales of lots might provide for "all future wants." Gilmore told the board what to send to Willink. The board reported to the president that Gilmore gave them "every reason to suppose that our endeavors will be successful." Well briefed on the continued chaotic state of things in Holland, which had just been proclaimed the pro-French

Batavian Republic, the president thought it "not unlikely" that the application for a loan "will be unfavorable."

The commissioners asked the president to enlist the aid of Secretary of the Treasury Wolcott in getting a short-term domestic loan. The president agreed but was pessimistic: "I much question whether *any* of the banks in *this* city are to be relied on for a loan—the reason for this, needs no explanation." Undaunted, the board wrote to Wolcott on June 20 alerting him that upward of $100,000 may eventually be wanted from the bank. In case neither Amsterdam nor Philadelphia proved good, they applied to the Bank of Columbia. They owed that bank $42,000, so they asked for a further line of credit up to $58,000 at six percent, which they needed in four equal monthly installments beginning August 1, when the fillip from the proprietors would run dry. They would repay the loan in six months with the proceeds of the Dutch loan. They asked the bank to defer its decision until the Bank of the United States reached its decision on a loan to the city.[5]

54. Myriads of Toads and Frogs

Cazenove made a quick trip to the city in mid-May to check on some concerns of Dutch clients. One had been assigned several city lots by creditors of Nicholson. And the others, who, on Cazenove's advice, had bought Potomac Company stock, were wondering about the long promised dividends from tolls. Cazenove took one look at the federal city and the locks at Little Falls and then went back to Philadelphia. To clients who did not own lots in the city, he advised not to speculate in city lots. To clients who did own lots, he reported that he believed lots would sell for 5 to 20 pence a square foot.

Since, however, the original proprietors had done little and speculators had spread buildings over 7,000 acres, the best he could say
of the city was that "one has the plan of a beautiful epic poem of
which none of the cantos have been written." At least he could send
a glowing account of the Potomac. He went around Little Falls in a
boat with sixty barrels of flour. All was "in good order" and profits
soon to come.

Of course Cazenove gave his opinion privately, but it was so
widely held that the *Washington Gazette*, the new newspaper at
Greenleaf's Point, sought to demolish it with statistics. If five people
lived on each lot, and with twenty lots in each of 1,246 squares, the
city could house 124,600. In New York 1,000 houses were being
built a year, and, given the advantages afforded by the Potomac and
the seat of government, the city would grow as quickly so that by
1820 the whole ground would be covered. So "poor Mr. L'Enfans"
would soon face the "reverse" of the present complaints and be
"censured for sacrificing so much ground to the public
purposes. . . ."

Exaggeration was the order of the day that summer. With the
election of 1796 approaching, not a few editors held up the federal
city as an example of the administration's extravagance, quite in
character with the party that preferred government by the few, if
not a return to monarchy. The *Boston Independent Chronicle* reported that the kitchen of the president's house was so large that
the Senate could meet in a chimney corner. It wanted the $2 million
to be spent there by 1801 to be used instead to finance roads and
canals. The *Charleston Gazette* added that "only the name 'Washington' led people to acquiesce in such extravagance."[1]

*   *   *

The president came to the city in mid-June. The only extravagance he saw was yet another plan for the Capitol. Still insisting
that the design was unbuildable, Hadfield unveiled a new one (since
lost), which, two years later, Thornton characterized as another
attempt to steal the design from him. "As the building could not be
reduced from three to two stories," as he had wanted to do in

October, "it had better be changed to four stories." The president, Thornton recalled, "heard of those attempts, so incongruous in themselves, with astonishment."

Hadfield was hurt by the president's disapproval, and he gave notice. Rather than have him around for another three months, the board asked him to leave immediately and offered to give him passage back to England. Hadfield left the city, briefly. He thought better of his rash act, came back, apologized to Thornton, and got his job back. Thornton claimed that he got Hadfield to admit that his objections to the plan were "prompted by ambition, . . . and that though he had declared the plan not executable yet he assured the board it was and he would faithfully execute it, and at all times advise with Thornton." Needless to say, Thornton could not abide the young man, but Scott, the most powerful commissioner, liked him.

The design of the Capitol did not worry the president. The lack of housing did. Scott and Thornton bowed to his wishes and on June 25 the rules requiring houses of brick or stone and houses of 35 to 40 feet in height on the avenues were suspended until December 1, 1800. All wooden houses built before then "shall be considered as lawfully erected." In promulgating the new rule in newspapers throughout the country, the president even admitted a mistake. The old rules "have been found, by experience, to impede the settlement in the city, of mechanicks and others, whose circumstances do not admit of erecting houses of the description authorized by said regulations." While the lines of all streets and avenues had been run, in most areas the avenues had been opened first.

The president also saw no reason why some avenues could not be properly graded. The board finally asked for bids to grade New Jersey Avenue between Barry's wharf and the Capitol. The president once again took the commissioners to task for not moving to the city. Why should others live near the Capitol, "if those whose particular duty it is to be there, and to set an example, hang aloof and fix the attention another way."

Scott had another exchange of letters with the president, which finally cleared up the misunderstanding. Scott thought he was authorized by the secretary of state to live as far away as Georgetown. The president said that what he had meant was that he could live in

Georgetown until accommodation was ready in the federal city. He rued that the old board had never carried through a plan to build a house for the commissioners between the two public buildings. Actually a house had been built and then sold to a baker.

One old conflict was resolved. Johnson came to town when the president did, hoping to salvage a deteriorating legal position. With his old ally Greenleaf gone, and Morris and Nicholson in disrepute, even his friendship with the president could not get him his lots unless he admitted he was wrong. So he agreed to ask Morris and Nicholson to relinquish the lots along Rock Creek. Then he would buy them from the commissioners.[2]

*   *   *

Morris agonized over being in the doghouse. When James Marshall sent him the antiemigration tract *Look Before you Leap, or a Few Hints To Such Artisans . . . Desirous of Emigrating to America . . . Particularly to the Federal City of Washington,* which chronicled the disappointments of Samuel Moodey and the other workers on the *Two Sisters* among the "swamps producing nothing except myriads of toads and frogs (of an enormous size) with other nauseous reptiles," and "agues and fevers" deadly even to natives, Morris suggested that some "envious American" out to "ruin any or all of his countrymen" wrote it. But he blamed himself for the accurate allegations in the pamphlet that housing was "deficient" and buildings "at a stand for want of money." He had to admit that the city "has lingered a little in the hands of Mr. Nicholson and myself owing to the want of money. . . ."

When he heard that the new English and Spanish ministers had accepted the president's invitation to visit Mount Vernon, he hung his head in shame, telling Law: "The President . . . will hear all complaints and among the rest those against Mr. Nicholson and myself for delinquency of payment to the commissioners. We lament that such complaints are justified . . . , and are making exertions to remedy and remove the evil, which we hope to accomplish and to appear personally at the city soon."

Morris and Nicholson set about creating a fund of money for

Washington to pay the commissioners and, more important, thwart Carroll. The big sale of the previous month, the 300,000 acres sold in Germany, was not panning out. The partners realized that as long as the war in Europe continued, investors would make too much money there to spare any for American investments. They had to accumulate cash the old-fashioned way, by mortgaging everything they owned. Still, they bragged about a good promise of selling 100,000 acres in Virginia.

In late May Morris gave the battle cry to Cranch. "Mr. Carroll shall not have the forfeiture of ten lots and ten hundred pounds from me . . . ," and he authorized Cranch to draw on him for whatever was needed to build, with a few caveats. Drafts should be "at as long sight as you can," materials "as cheap as possible," the plans "most easy and cheap to execute," and the building contract with Lovering "upon the most economical terms possible."[3]

Nicholson asked Prentiss and Deblois to undertake his share of the twenty houses and try to manage it without cash. Deblois had learned his lesson, complaining that he had to borrow a dollar from one of his workmen to buy butter. His master joiner wanted to get married but—this was the talk of the town—could not because he was unable to furnish a house since Deblois could not pay back all he had borrowed from him. So Nicholson worked on Prentiss, who was in Philadelphia to get payment for work done. All he got was credit at a dry goods store but he did see that Nicholson, despite all the talk about his bankruptcy, still lived the good life, and he promised to raise cash and bring it to Washington. In 1800 a Philadelphia merchant described what it was like calling on the speculator at his house on Race and 7th Streets: "If you wished to see him, you entered a small room adjoining the apartment in which he sat, attended by a single clerk. This antechamber was crowded from morning till night. One by one was admitted to his presence & each must wait his turn. Altho' most of his visitors were creditors and of course not likely to treat him very ceremoniously, he never suffered himself to get out of temper and went directly to the business they came on. . . . From his desk, he continued to write, which he did with amazing facility and correctness and conversed with me at the same time without confusion or perplexity."

The commissioners took heart at the news of the partners' plan to come to the city, informing the president in a June 13 letter that Morris and Nicholson promised "a considerable payment" when they arrived within a week. But the weeks dragged on. On June 27 the partners told Cranch they would be there "certainly" the following week. Finally, they hit on a reason not to come. They noticed that the commissioners had announced in the newspapers that they would finish dividing lots with the original proprietors in September. Since they could not pick what public lots they wanted until they knew which were the public lots, it was best they come later.

It was impossible to delay work on the twenty buildings that had to be built by September 26. By June 24 Cranch had "a great number of hands" digging cellars for Morris's houses. By July 12 he sent up $3,000 worth of checks, which Morris covered, though he complained, "they come rather thick on a distressed man." Nicholson had no credit. So Prentiss agreed to take "4 or $5,000 in rum, sugars, coffee, teas, some wines as port, lisbon, Tenneriff and sherry, spanish and french brandies, molasses & c," and he would try to "make as much payments in dry goods as possible." But all building materials had to be bought with cash, and laborers digging the cellars had to be paid every day in cash, "as it is done by the lower order of people that has nothing before hand." Getting up the "carcases" of all ten houses would cost $22,000. Lovering also agreed to serve as Nicholson's agent on the scene. He advised that if the work was begun after July 8, it would be "madness." They needed cash by then.

There seemed to be no rational reason for the two Englishmen to undertake the work for someone as patently unreliable as Nicholson, but they did it as much to spite Carroll. Nicholson had Lovering demand titles to the lots he was building on. Carroll refused and offered no assistance, leaving town to investigate Kentucky lands instead. Writing to Nicholson of Carroll's "most rigid disposition, . . . glad to take every advantage," Lovering averred, "I shall be sorry if he has his desires." Too far away to house congressmen and too small to make them really desirable homes, Lovering designed eight buildings on N Street and twelve on South Capitol for shopkeepers, with storefronts below and living quarters upstairs. He designed the twenty buildings so that they could actually house thirty families.[4]

*   *   *

The race to finish the houses began inauspiciously with a brutal heat wave. Cranch's thermometer, which was in the shade, read 98 degrees at 2:00 P.M. Irish laborers wilted, and Cranch hired Robert Sutton to bring his crew of slaves in to dig the cellars. With slaves, he avoided any daily outlay of cash to the workers. By getting a head start on Prentiss, Cranch was able to use the foundation stone and bricks stored in sheds for the joint account of Morris and Nicholson. He relied on Morris to supply lime, which was always hard to get, and Morris did not fail him, sending two shiploads down. The hard-pressed Morris urged Cranch to raise as much cash as he could on the scene. Cranch rented nineteen workers' huts to Hugh Dinsley, the plasterer on the point, for $666.66 worth of plastering work. (Morris appreciated Cranch's economizing, which was in marked contrast to L'Enfant, who had Morris howling, "It is with astonishment I see the work of last fall now pulling down in order to put up more marble on my house, on which there is already vastly too much.")

Prentiss began digging cellars on the Fourth of July. (Incidentally, Blodget began the drawing of his second lottery the same day.) By the 6th Prentiss had "15 hands and carts at work and tomorrow shall have many more." Cranch took the sting out of his getting all the stone for the cellar walls by offering Prentiss stone that was at a quarry owned by Greenleaf. By the 11th Prentiss had eight cellars dug but could not commence stonework for want of lime. Still, on the 15th Prentiss assured Nicholson that he had "no doubt" he would get done in time. Then Lovering got very sick with a "rheumatic complaint," and no one would cash the check Nicholson sent down to pay for the work. Already $3,000 in the hole for lime, stone, and labor, Prentiss threatened to quit the city unless Nicholson sent him lime, wet goods, and $1,000. Yet he made it clear he hated to quit. "Mr. Morris's buildings go on rapidly," he told Nicholson on the 22nd, "most of them the floor joist laid. It will be a great mortification to have mine dropped after going this far. . . . I have five gangs making bricks on the spot, 10 to 12,000 a day in good weather." He had 100,000 bricks on hand and calculated he needed only another 170,000.

In the nick of time, just as workers were quitting, money came from Nicholson. Prentiss cheered back, "I now hope to go on with spirit," but even though Nicholson was assiduously amassing cash solely for saving his investments in the federal city, he was always sorely tempted to divert some. On July 12 he wrote Morris, "I am almost wild for the want of $1,410 which are yet lacking" to pay the Asylum Land Company dividends. Throughout August slow payments from Nicholson almost forced Prentiss to give up. On the 5th he was "without $10," and two cargoes of lumber waited to be paid for. On the 8th all was going "extremely well"; on the 12th he reported "next week all will quit"; on the 16th, "Mr. Morris's hands going on well—mine all leaving the works. I kept all going until last night (assuring them Monday's post would relieve me) but some have left, however I shall not wholly give up until Saturday. If we fail now, we fail in any credit forever in this place. . . . Yesterday I had twenty masons at work, seven have left me."[5]

*   *   *

Morris and Nicholson naturally failed to pay the commissioners. The activity on South Capitol Street did not impress them. On July 15 the board informed them that there was "a certain point beyond which forbearance becomes folly and total dereliction of public trust." Given that no payments had been made and that contrary to Morris's promise no special sale of lots was held to pay the arrears after passage of the loan guarantee bill, they threatened to sue if they did not get $12,000 in fifteen days.

The threat of a suit shocked Nicholson into greater exertions to raise money. On the 22nd he offered Thomas Fitzsimons 700 Washington lots to secure a loan of $56,000. On the 27th he sent $4,900 to the commissioners. Fitzsimons failing him, he tried to secure a $160,000 loan from James Jarvis, $40,000 in cash, secured by 535 lots southwest of Massachusetts Avenue. Morris dealt with a usurer named Amaringe in trying to squeeze up to $50,000 in cash out of his various properties, stocks, and promissory notes. But they could not pay. The Board asked a Philadelphia lawyer, Edward Tilghman, to file suit.[6]

55. Shall Be Perhaps Too Rich

The British minister, Robert Liston, and his wife visited the president at Mount Vernon and stayed with Duncanson in the federal city. Mrs. Liston counted one hundred houses and thought the situation "noble and beautiful strangely resembling Constantinople," which had been their last posting.

Benjamin Latrobe was not one of the distinguished visitors the president was expecting at Mount Vernon, but he left the most vivid impressions. The young Englishman had come to Virginia that March and was lining up jobs primarily as a hydraulic engineer. The president dropped his other business and, Latrobe wrote in his journal, "the conversation then turned upon the rivers of Virginia; he gave me a very minute account of all their directions, their natural advantages, and what he conceived might be done for their improvement by Art."

Since Latrobe had seen the Great Dismal Swamp and not the Potomac, they talked about "the Swamp," then moved slowly north. Latrobe told him about silver mines along the James, and "he laughed most heartily upon the very mention of the thing." After canals they talked about crops until the president retired at eight o'clock. In the morning Lear and others joined them at "breakfast . . . served up in the ususal Virginia style, tea, coffee, and cold and broiled meat." Latrobe heard the latest from Great

Falls and the federal city. Then for an hour they all stood on the
steps of the west door of Mount Vernon and discussed the national
university. The president explained the donation he had promised
contingent on plans being made and rued that "there seemed to be
no inclination to carry them into reality." Latrobe thought "he
spoke as if he felt a little hurt upon the subject."[1]

When the president returned to the city, on his way back to
Philadelphia, he had reason enough to be pleased with developments
there. On August 17 Law had a large dinner party for him, amid all
the activity at the point. Not only were the twenty buildings going
up but, houses built the year before were being readied for occupancy. Law's own house at the foot of New Jersey Avenue was
almost completed. A well was dug at the foot of Barry's wharf, and
18 feet under, black mud and reeds from a primordial swamp had
been found. Crews were grading the avenue and even bridging a bit
of marshy ground, which Law paid for in order to perfect that "most
useful street." Most important, up on the hill, fifty-one white
laborers and probably as many slaves were assisting masons in
putting up the Capitol walls with a dispatch that quieted critics,
including the president.

Law had several particular projects which he pressed on the
president: canal lottery tickets, subscriptions to build the eastern
market, and a new machine to hoist stone, which Hallet had perfected under his patronage (and which the commissioners declined
to build). He also campaigned to bring a sense of English orderliness
to the untidy city. "The stumps have so sprouted forth that the
streets are almost obscured by bushes and young trees." He wanted
the board "to levy contributions" from lotholders and keep the
streets clear, for "a stranger will not purchase . . . if he cannot
obtain access to the spot selected." He also thought people should
be allowed to "clear" the Mall "at their own expense." Trees worth
saving "would grow more luxuriantly by the brushwood being
cleared, and not only the eye would be gratified, but vegetables
might be obtained on moderate terms."

Law was wont to brag about how special a city was that promised
such rural charms. Working in Baltimore, James Barry was envious:
"it is happy for you to be out of large towns this season for the
heats are intolerable in Philadelphia and here." Even when the

sickly season caught up with Law, he did not blame nature. "As I lay on my bed after a walk in the garden where I saw the nankeen cotton plant and the bamboo," he wrote to the president from Mount Vernon, where a fever laid him low, "it occurred to me what an advantageous import of seed and plants might be introduced at this period from Asia, but too soon this pleasing idea was discouraged by a doubt where they should be deposited." So Law began lobbying for a botanical garden.[2]

*   *   *

That summer and early fall three new stores opened, William Huston's Eastern Branch Store, Alexander M'Cormick's, and James Sweeney and Company. The latter two were near the president's house. In newspaper ads the stores listed a cornucopia of dry goods, groceries, and hardware. Huston, Prout's nephew, offered "to sell cheap for cash or produce." Sweeney and Company was also a branch of a Baltimore concern and offered "a complete assortment of English, French and India goods." Ladies wanting dresses could come for measurements, and the clothing would be made by the Baltimore store. Soon Ross M'Laughlin, "from London and Dublin," topped that, setting up shop "on Capitol Hill near the Post Office" offering to make "Ladies' habits . . . in the greatest haste and newest fashions." The tavern next to the Capitol square was finished, and, along with the usual amenities, it offered "a shuffle board and nine pin alley."

The apparent boom in the city was fueled by inflation. In Baltimore, Parson Weems sold $600 worth of books, but for "Georgetown and Alexandria bank money," which he found could command only $350 in Philadelphia money. The surfeit of local paper arose in part from the board's inability to raise a loan in Philadelphia. The Bank of the United States turned the commissioners down. Wolcott explained that "the means of that institution are inadequate to the demands of the merchants of" Philadelphia. And so the Bank of Columbia began lending the board $10,000 a month, up to $40,000, to be repaid in sixty days, renewable to six months, and absolutely no longer. Still straining to make a good show for the president in

August, the board ran short. On the day of Law's dinner for the president, the commissioners asked Forrest for $2,000, explaining, "We are run aground and do not wish to break in upon next months appropriation."

Not only did the infusion of outside capital through a loan fail to materialize. Nor did the expected boom in lot sales. Samuel Davidson was once again talking big. He offered to sell all of the square at the northeast corner of the president's house to Wade Hampton, a South Carolina politician and speculator. On August 3 he was dangling the same square before Joseph Covachiche, an agent for Comfort Sands, claiming he had refused $24,000 for the square. "I consider it worth 25¢ per square foot, say $33,750, however $30,000 would carry it." There were nibbles but no takers. From July through September the commissioners sold only two lots just west of the president's house, for $482 and $337, and half of the triangle formed by Pennsylvania Avenue, Georgia Avenue, and 14th Street Southeast, for $1,736.

Sluggish sales did not quench the thirst of those already drunk with speculation. Blodget, who built a house at 14th and F Streets that Thornton promised to rent, insisted he owned square 688 next to the Capitol. Law thought square 688 rightfully his, the only worthy substitute for square 687, which Greenleaf had sold to him but which the commissioners had given to Carroll. Stoddert contended that Burnes's father had never bought 62 acres of Beall's Level and that it belonged to a man named Massey, whose land had been confiscated during the war. Stoddert was in the syndicate that bought Massey's land. Benjamin Odens, who owned land along the upper reaches of the Tiber, claimed three of Burnes's squares near Judiciary Square, as well as one of Carroll's squares.[3]

*   *   *

On August 22 Nicholson got his hands on $17,000, which, combined with $4,000 he already had, was enough traveling money, so he left for Washington before anybody knocked on his door to dun him. He promised to be back September 5 and left it to Morris to pay $17,500 or so in pressing demands, including $2,500 to the sheriff to delay the serving of writs. To excuse his hurrying off, he said that Prentiss had stopped work for lack of money, and without an immediate infusion, all that he had spent on his buildings was "at hazard." Nicholson noted another advantage: "If I am molested by suits I'll let you know." On discovering Nicholson had gone without him, Morris confessed that he had never been so surprised in his life. But he gamely struggled to pay the sheriff before going to Washington himself. It was not easy. "I am sadly plagued for want of money," he wrote to Nicholson. "We must work like *men* to clear away these cursed incumbrances and satisfy the cormorants."

Nicholson came to the city with a plan that took advantage of the high estimation men in the city had of the property around them. Rather than raise cash to pay the commissioners, he would get the local speculators to endorse notes that the partners would use to assume the commissioners' debt at the Bank of Columbia. He would secure the endorsers with Washington lots. The commissioners could not take such security, but true believers would. It was a cashless operation.

By assuming the board's bank debt, the partners would be entitled to the titles of several hundred lots, which they could use to secure the endorsers. For each of those lots Nicholson wanted the board to give him a simple certificate, the size of a bank bill which he called "scrip," each signed by the commissioners, which stated that the lot belonged to the bearer. For those lots the partners had not yet paid for, the certificate would say that for the sum of £30 that lot would belong to the bearer. The partners could then sell those scrips, giving the equitable rights to a lot to others. And since their future installments were spread out over the remaining four years until May 1800, payment on the scrips could be for as long as four years. The first step was to pick lots, draw up the scrips, and have them signed. He had already sent an English surveyor, Nicholas King, to the city to assist in dividing and mapping squares.

As befits a man carrying from $2 million to $8 million in debts, Nicholson's self assurance was colossal. He was also indefatigable. It is safe to say folks in the federal city had never met his like. The wide open spaces of the federal district meant nothing to him. On arriving, he advertised that he would do business at the Little Hotel next to the commissioner's office, any day from 3:00 to 5:00 P.M.,

or at the Union tavern in Georgetown until 7:00 A.M. From 7:00
A.M. to 3:00 P.M. every day he was either out dividing squares or
arguing with the commissioners. Such energy was not sustained by
negative thoughts. He told Morris, "We have an immense property
here and shall be perhaps too rich when we get through our difficulties."

Within three days of his arrival, he gratified the commissioners by
applying to the Bank of Columbia to assume $50,000 of the commis-
sioners' debt, but he began skirmishing with the board on several
issues. Nicholson refused to concede anything. The commissioners
contended they had to divide by squares, that is, the public would
retain all lots in one square and Morris and Nicholson would take
all public lots in another. Nicholson reported to Morris that "the
contract was referred to and discussed and [the point] given up by
them." Morris and Nicholson could pick lots where they chose. The
commissioners argued that no conveyances could be made until all
the installments were fully paid. "We had a lengthy discussion in
which we clearly proved and I believe convinced them we were
right." (Cranch was with him.)

The commissioners were eager to cooperate with Nicholson in
one regard. The sooner the squares were divided, the sooner they
would make a mortgage for a loan. Nicholson discovered that they
were in an even greater hurry than he, so to gain leverage he refused
to agree to choose lots quickly. He and Morris were entitled to wait
"until time should point out the spot most valuable which no
foresight could discover and also determine who are right the
Georgetown or Eastern Branch party." The commissioners were
not beyond finding pressure points either. They acquainted Nicholson with a Maryland law that there was a twenty percent penalty on
payments by foreign checks that bounced, three times the custo-
mery six percent. Nicholson threatened to take the issue to court.
The board countered that the partners owed more than the bank
debt that they assumed, so the board's Philadelphia lawyer was still
continuing their suit.

The upshot of it all was that Nicholson and the man on the board
he usually sparred with, Scott, grew to respect and like each other.
Nicholson did not care for other of his opponents, joking to Morris
that their petty creditors were "around me numerous as the pearly

drops of dew from the womb of morning." "I shall manage them very well," he boasted. He gave no quarter where he had the advantages, even in dealings with Law and Duncanson, who had a mortgage on Nicholson's and Morris's houses until they got all titles to their lots. Nicholson urged the board to include the building clause in the conveyances they gave to them. "These men will find they have a task before them that'll make them sweat," Nicholson chortled to Morris; "thus we turn them over to satan who will butter them if they don't go on" and build.

As for Nicholson's own improvements, Deakins told him that Carroll contended that merely covering the twenty houses would not fulfill the contract. Nicholson was undeterred. Prentiss wrote to him on September 3 that he felt "extremely anxious." He needed $6,000 to purchase shingles, brick, and lime, and he had to pay 120 hands each day.[4]

56. Social Glee

Morris reached the city in the first week of September, and despite L'Enfant's still not having finished his mansion, he congratulated him on his plan. But a few days in the city, he began broadcasting his optimism. To Marshall in London he lauded "the beauties of situation" and found that "the buildings exceed in number and beauty the representations that had been made to me and the value of lots is increasing perhaps too rapidly." He thought that by "the year 1800 the price will be not less than from $1,500 to $3,000 per lot" and regretted having to sell lots too soon in order to pay debts. To Henry Lee, who was no stranger to the city, he toned down his assessment of immediate profits. Progress to 1800 will be "tolerably fast, . . . but in the year 1800 and afterwards, it will increase beyond all example. The people will rush into it from all parts of America and Europe. . . .'' In the meantime for $350 he bought the services of a mulatto, Nat, for seven years, to be his valet, and he prepared to deal.

Being in the city reassured Morris, and his presence reassured ambitious men in the city. There was a way men of a speculative bent could express that reassurance. The notes of Morris and Nicholson, with a nominal value of well over $1 million, had flooded the economy since 1794 and had become objects of speculation. In Philadelphia they sold for 17 cents on the dollar. One bought them in hopes that Morris and Nicholson might redeem them or at least buy them back for more money once they got back on their feet. But with both gentlemen in the city, building houses and showing every indication that they were going to make something of their Washington investment, not a few sensed that they could make a killing buy buying notes of Morris and Nicholson before their value began to rise. Commissioner Scott, for one, began buying them.

William Smith, a Georgetown broker, sensed the excitement and alerted his Philadelphia correspondents. Just a month before he had been pushing shares in the company building a bridge above Georgetown. Those shares were selling for $140, and he was sure they would be worth more. Those shares in turn had eclipsed Columbia Bank shares, Blodget's lottery number two, and the canal lottery as the interesting games in town. On September 14 Smith spread the word that $20,000 worth of M & N notes, as they were called, might fetch $4,000 or more in cash. Philadelphia was all ears. Two days later Smith reported an actual sale, $13,500 worth of notes sold for $2,868.74, 21 cents on the dollar.[1]

Morris and Nicholson did not allude to such transactions, which so patently demeaned their credit. But they too held their own notes. They did not squelch a rumor that they themselves were buying up the notes, for that rumor raised the price and made it easier for them to raise the cash to keep Prentiss's and Cranch's men hard at work on the buildings, which gave such an appearance of being ready on time that they decided to make an occasion out of it. Each anted up $120 for a barbecue for the 200 or so workers. The prospect of such a feast did not make the workers any less mindful of getting paid before completing the work. On Thursday, the 22nd, Prentiss complained, "if we cannot pay, the entertainment on Monday will not have a pleasing effect." Nicholson's roofs were all shingled on the 23rd. Cranch had finished Morris's houses three days before, save for doors and windows (they did have floors and chimneys). All told, Morris spent $19,372 and Nicholson $22,000, though not all in cash.

According to the *Gazette,* which Cranch had helped start, the barbecue came off famously: "We do not recollect ever to have seen a greater appearance of social glee on similar occasion." As for the buildings, not only did they form the first complete block of houses in the city, but it was "the greatest effect of private enterprise of any in the city, and for the time in which they were building, we believe the greatest in the United States." Carroll attended the barbecue, and years later in court testimony Prentiss recalled that he seemed well pleased with the houses. Carroll himself testified that the houses were "done in a very bad manner, many of them to save materials, . . . left with large openings almost co-extensive with the front of the buildings." In retrospect, at least he easily saw through the storefronts.[2]

*   *   *

On September 17 the president sent his farewell address to the newspapers of the nation. He was unmoved by the pleas of Federalists such as William Vans Murray that he "terminate his great career by handing the government to its permanent seat—it would be a fine finish." The president asked the board to send him a list of things that had to be done before he left office in March. They knew that the main thing on the president's mind was the national university. The site had never officially been designated. Of late the consensus had grown to put it on Peter's Hill, where L'Enfant had wanted a fort. Thornton explained to the president that the ground was too high for a fort, and placing a university on the height would "add much to the grandeur" of the city. Left unsaid was that it would be just east of the square the president bought, and Thornton had just bought the square neighboring this.

The site of the executive offices was still hanging fire, and the board suggested that "two handsome brick buildings on the President's square" accommodate them. The visit of the Spanish minister to the city reopened the issue of where foreign ministers would reside. L'Enfant had offered land to the Spanish king, and the commissioners were loath to take it away. But they were in no mood to give up building lots. So they asked the president to give foreign governments land on the Mall for their embassies. Such buildings "judiciously placed and not too numerous, so far from counteracting the original design would add greatly to the beauty and pleasure of the scene and would be the means of bringing the whole into more immediate notice and cultivation."

While the president tried to digest that, the commissioners had a file of suggested improvements to work on. After the barbecue Nicholson's energy could scarcely be contained. On the 28th he offered to build a bridge over the Tiber at Virginia Avenue, opening a direct diagonal road from Greenleaf's Point to Georgetown, if the commissioners would pay for half. On the 30th he sent no fewer than seven letters to the board. He wanted to control landings along the canal and wanted a branch of it to run north of the Capitol. He wanted fire pumps and the declivities of the streets determined and an officer appointed to enforce them. He offered to engrave a new plan of the city and wanted to know the disposition of the public reservations and public building lots. By showing the large number of lots still in the board's hands, he hoped to demonstrate the extent of public resources that could defray the expense of paving, watching, lighting, and watering. He would thus eliminate the need for taxes "and thereby furnish a motive to reside in this place."

The commissioners replied the next day, promising a complete map of the city with all public reservations labeled. They offered to forward to the president any proposal for a canal north of the Capitol, and they informed Nicholson that the canal landings would be public and a road built only on the east side of the canal. As for the officer to regulate the level of houses and streets, they acquainted Nicholson with the vain attempt to get the proprietors to agree on a petition to the Maryland Assembly for a law giving such an officer the requisite police powers. The upshot of the exchange was that Nicholson proved his zeal for improving the city, the commissioners showed how zealously they had carried on the great work, and nothing was done.

The only suggested "improvement" that engaged widespread attention was Nicholson's renewal of Greenleaf's effort to turn the hospital square on the Eastern Branch into building lots. Having just had the site surveyed, the commissioners were keenly aware that they would soon have to pay the original proprietors $5,333.33 for the 80-acre site. If the site were divided into 480 house lots, valued at $200 each, the half belonging to the public could bring in $48,000. The two original proprietors were Prout and Abraham Young, and Young had sold some of his land to the partners. Nicholson, with his usual dispatch, got Prout and Young to join him and Morris in agreeing to turn the reservation into building lots.

Walker, who owned lots nearby, got wind of the change and protested to the president. The site had been marked as a hospital in the plan that L'Enfant showed to Congress and that was "hung up on the Speaker's chair." Although the engraved plans did not show a hospital, they showed a large space for public buildings or gardens. To turn those into house lots broke faith with those who had bought lots on that side of the city with expectations of a large building there. It would be "a glaring violation of public and national faith." Walker also demanded that he get paid for land L'Enfant had designated for a "Historical Column" one mile east of the Capitol.

Thornton also thought ill of relinquishing the hospital and wrote to the president that a hospital should be in the city to be convenient for doctors. That ample space was needed to accommodate a poorhouse, lying-in hospital, vegetables for the invalids, and "extensive walks for valetudinarians." The waterside site allowed sick marines to be brought in without infecting others, and the site had springs for baths.[3]

*   *   *

In mid-September the commissioners got a scare. A group of workers charged that there was bad brickwork at the Capitol. They summoned Allan Wiley, the master bricklayer in charge, who begged off appearing because of the fever and ague. He would come when he was "able to walk without injuring myself." He did not believe the work bad and urged the board to summon Hadfield. The young Englishman decided nothing had to be redone but was less than reassuring. Since they were about to begin on the arcade of the Senate chamber, they needed better-quality work. Bricks continued to be a problem. At the Capitol Mitchell pleaded sickness and loss of money and wanted out of his contract. With all walls almost to the roof, Hoban could assure the board that only 230,000 bricks were needed to enclose the president's house. He had 141,950 on hand and another 50,000 in a kiln. As for the stonework, Blagden estimated all the bill stone needed to finish the finer stonework for entablatures, window sills, pediments, and pilasters in the president's house and north wing of the Capitol at 397 and 877 tons respectively.[4]

Meanwhile, Nicholson was prompting Prentiss to estimate the cost of completing all of the houses not in rentable condition, plus fulfilling his previous contract for five double houses, which meant building three more. Prentiss said he could finish Nicholson's ten houses on square 651, finish the two double houses at the point, finish the houses at the point that Lovering never finished, cover the houses at 21st and Pennsylvania that Henderson had not finished, and build three more double houses on Capitol Hill for $44,000. To obviate some of the need for money, Nicholson as well as Morris sold lots to workmen in return for their finishing houses and building a house on the lots they bought. They negotiated good prices for the lots, up to 25 cents a square foot, which, when they told others, left the impression someone had actually paid that money. Carpenters also occupied some of the South Capitol and N Street houses, paying rent with work. Morris sold the house at the corner of South Capitol and N to Edward Langley at 25 cents a square foot for the lot, with Lovering and Hoban to determine the value of the house, on condition that Langley finish the house in eight months. Langley was allowed to pay with goods from the shop he would open there.[5]

*   *   *

Greenleaf missed the barbecue but was mindful of what Morris and Nicholson were up to. In mid-September, after finding that no titles existed for some of the proprietors' lots he had bought, Nicholson rashly attacked Greenleaf, accusing him of fraud and announcing that as far as he was concerned the accounts between the two men were ripped up. It was a mistake to push a desperate man. In July Greenleaf had offered Alexander Hamilton half his assets if only he would free them from legal entanglements. Hamilton declined the offer. So Greenleaf went deeper into debt, getting advances from a Philadelphia auctioneer, Edward Fox, on $700,000 worth of M & N notes. He secured Fox with what Nicholson had used to secure a defaulted loan from him. And Fox scheduled an October 1 auction of a hundred Washington lots and 5,000 shares of North American Land Company stock.

Nicholson reacted, reminding Greenleaf that he, Greenleaf, had already mortgaged those lots to Law. Greenleaf did not flinch and a newspaper war commenced in the September 29 issue of *Claypool's Gazette,* published in Philadelphia. Nicholson cautioned the public that Greenleaf had "fraudulently or improperly obtained" notes from him. Greenleaf countered with spirit: "The wickedness and impudence of the above advertisement are too glaring to escape the most vulgar eyes." And Greenleaf alluded to the "deep injuries" Nicholson had inflicted on him over the past three years. On October 1 Greenleaf published a longer letter revealing that Nicholson was indebted to him "for the enormous sum of $1,130,077.06." Not only did Nicholson owe him for Washington lots, but Morris and Nicholson had bought out Greenleaf's share of the land company. A quarter of all that had been past due since April 15.

During October readers were entertained with charges and countercharges not likely to inspire confidence in Washington lots. Nicholson accused Greenleaf of selling more lots than he actually owned. Greenleaf explained that in his purchases from some proprietors the number of lots involved was only estimated and that the final price would be adjusted. He boasted that he had paid for all lands he had bought in Washington with cash. Rather than "fraudulently" try to obtain Nicholson's notes, he rued the day he saw them, having sold "$600,000 of the choicest property in New York" to pay Nicholson's protested bills. That said, Greenleaf declined any further public controversy and invited Nicholson to carry it on in a court.

"Reflecting on your late Billingsgate address" was the taunt that began a series of nine newspaper letters from Nicholson to Greenleaf. In letter four he accused Greenleaf of mortgaging Washington lots to get a $28,000 loan from Comfort Sands and then selling that property. Letter five contrasted lots near the president's house and the Capitol selling for $1,000 with the bulk of the lots Greenleaf had sold them, which were worth no more than $200. Letter seven wondered where the money raised on Washington lots in Holland went. Letter eight accused Greenleaf of selling a bad title to the land in the city called the Hopyard. The other numbers attempted to reveal Greenleaf's faulty accounting and prove that in amassing property for the North American Land Company, it was Morris and Nicholson who dealt squarely and Greenleaf who failed to deliver on the money he promised from Holland, which was the immediate cause of Nicholson's financial embarrassments.

At the first sign of blood, the price of M & N notes plummeted. Forde and Reed were major players in that game, and they informed William Smith that the notes "will hardly circulate with us at any price." No time was to be lost, they instructed him on September 30, in selling those notes in Georgetown. Four days later the rumor spread in Philadelphia that Morris and Nicholson had decided not to return to Philadelphia, absconding on their debts. That prompted Forde and Reed to urge Smith to use his "utmost industry in getting rid" of the notes he held on their account.

Nicholson was unfazed; the federal city would save him. He explained to an uneasy creditor: "Of all the situations I have beheld for a site of a city this exceeds. It will now advance most rapidly in a few years will produce a change that men who are not enthusiasts will scarce credit. I count this journey here to have been worth about $1 million to me so much has my exertion with Mr. Morris turned the current of affairs."[6]

57. Mount Your Horse and Come Down Here Instantly

When that antiemigration tract printed in London reached the federal city, the *Gazette* challenged its grim portrait of the city not with facts but with a living legend: ". . . the writer terms it [the city] a mere hobby-horse of the president. If it is a hobby-horse, it is such an one as Constantine rode when he removed to Bizantium, but with this material difference, the new city of the Roman Empire divided that government, while this will unite ours in America. . . ." After the divisive debate over Jay's Treaty, friends of the federal city became obsessed with the city as the symbol of national unity. The men running to become the presidential elector in the district containing Georgetown withdrew in favor of an elector pledged to vote for both Adams and Jefferson. Since electors cast two votes for president, with the second-highest votegetter becoming vice president, the ploy was in order and appealing, for a week. Then, just before the balloting, such neutering of the vote turned enough stomachs that two men entered the race pledged to vote only for the candidates of one party. The Adams elector won.

As President Washington rusticated at Mount Vernon, preparing for his last stint in Philadelphia, he too was mindful of the federal city's importance in cementing the union and thought that the national university would assure it. He had wanted to include the arguments for the university in his farewell address, but Hamilton, who drafted the address, convinced him to put it in his last message to Congress.

The president methodically went through the file of decisions he had to make about the plan of the federal city. He agreed to put the university on Peter's Hill and thought the executive offices should be convenient to the president's house, but he agreed with Walker that no public reservations should be converted to building lots.

The decision also pleased Law, who had left a "jocular" petition for the president at Mount Vernon signed by "Capitol." That neglected building complained about still not having commissioners residing nearby and did not see why the hospital should not be where doctors wanted it, why the university was closer to docks than congressional debate, and why the ambassadors were condemned to the low ground of the Mall, given the mess the canal diggers had made at the foot of Capitol Hill: "if the south side of the canal is as unhealthy as that of the north, the foreign ambassadors will be frequently changed and a prejudicial impression against the health of the city will be made abroad."

When the president headed north, he conferred with the commissioners and Blagden, who was finally to inspect the quarry at Mount Vernon. Before he left the city, Davidson petitioned him to lay out the president's house square as L'Enfant planned it, to Davidson's profit. Otherwise, all seemed well in the city. Scott reported that Morris was "laboring hard to rid us of part of our bank debt." So busy were the workers that when someone wanted to withdraw his two slaves, the commissioners refused: "the public works might suffer by taking away any of the laborers."[1]

*　　*　　*

Morris's charm and optimism went a long way in the federal city. Earlier in the year he had had little trouble winning the friendship of Alexander White. His conquest of Gustavus Scott was even easier; after all, Scott was "a clever fellow." "You have a strong hold on his affections," Nicholson assured Morris, "indeed they all speak of you with rapture." In the fall of 1794 Thornton had hounded Greenleaf. Nicholson found him "faithful as the needle to the pole." Stoddert, the bank president, became their "friend and ally." Nicholson called him "a good boy." Forrest, a state senator, promised to look out for lawsuits and writs aimed at them in Annapolis. They all dined together, drank together, advised each other.

Morris also took advantage of a change he noticed in Georgetown. When he had come through in 1787 arranging for shipments of tobacco to France he had found it a busy port. Not so in 1796. Alexandria had the trade. The capital of Georgetown was all invested in federal city lots. As Morris negotiated a loan, he knew the local capitalists would not forsake him for fear that he would forsake them, but they were not pushovers either. To get Deakins, Duncanson, and Forrest to secure their $50,000 note in the Bank of Columbia, payable in six months, Morris had to pledge the certificates or scrips of just over a million square feet of city property, which he thought worth a little more than $200,000.

When James Barry heard of the arrangement he was appalled, telling Law that he thought the odds "10 to 1 it will occasion the [bank's] stock to fall considerably and be a mortal wound to its credit." Citing rumors of a failure of another American speculator to rival Greenleaf's, Barry was sure a crash was coming. Oblivious to such talk, Morris set about securing another loan from Forrest for $120,000, secured by 334 lots, but the money could be used to support their speculations along the Potomac and in Kentucky.

While Morris dealt with the cream of the capitalists, Nicholson dealt with the dross as he pushed to get all the squares divided, which was "a most tedious business." The proprietors lived "scattered about and the habits of indolence are so prevalent that it is extremely troublesome to bring them up. We have effected more in this way since we came than was done in all the time before since the establishment of the city." On two days in mid-October when there was no one ready to divide, Nicholson explored the grounds. He tried to jump a ditch and hurt his leg so badly that he had to stay off it a few days.

By late October enough progress had been made that Morris could write to several creditors offering them building lots in the city, which he boasted were "the most inviting objects of speculation that offer in the United States; the price rises every year and cannot fail doing so for 100 years to come." "Mount your horse and come down here instantly," he urged another creditor. If he were not satisfied with the property after four years, Morris would buy it back with interest. Nicholson pushed as hard, if not harder, claiming "the property is the first in the world" and quieting the oldest bugbear about the place: "I never knew a finer climate or more healthy situation."

Such was the enthusiasm that even the hardheaded Prentiss was caught up in it. Behind the ten storefronts he foresaw a shoemaker, hatters, blacksmith, and others. "Their work will constantly turn in payments" for the houses, thus "increasing the confidence our late proceedings has established." Very soon, however, Nicholson had no money to spare. By November 1 Prentiss was complaining that he had run out of lumber and lime. The lumber was in the harbor, but he did not have the money to get it on land. He heard the sheriff was after him for payment of overdue notes. On paper Morris and Nicholson were back, but the lack of payments to workers and suppliers was telling. Smith wrote to Reed and Forde that M & N notes "are now become almost bye words in the conversation of all persons and companies, and little you may be sure does it tend to advance the credit of the paper." Notes that had sold for as high as 21 cents fell to 12½ cents at the end of October. Then Isaac Polock saturated the city with the notes, using them to buy everything from city lots to dry goods, at once taking advantage of the gullibility of those impressed by the promises of Morris and Nicholson and punishing the speculators for their refusal to complete the buildings on Pennsylvania Avenue that he had bought from Greenleaf.[2]

*   *   *

The long awaited news from Amsterdam arrived. In their letter to the commissioners the Willink brothers did not give the war in general as a reason for not lending them money, but taxes of "6% of the whole fortune of each individual." Once those taxes were paid in December, they thought they could successfully raise the loan. There were, however, two other difficulties. They needed a description of all lots to be held as security and an assurance that banking charges would be paid despite the stricture that interest and charges not exceed six percent.

The board reminded Willink of "the urgency of this business" and explained that they had not described the property because it was so patently more valuable than the sum it secured and because the loan was guaranteed by the U.S. government. As for bank charges, they had been assured that six percent interest was so generous that it would be sufficient to pay all charges. But they authorized a sum not to exceed one and a half percent of the principal to pay for all fees. Too late Treasury Secretary Wolcott advised them that bank "profits arise from the charges not the rate of interest, that your chance of success is better under proposals for a low rate of interest with high charges. . . ."

They had enough money to carry on operations through mid-December, the end of the building season, but that was the best time to contract for pork, lime, and slaves. They had just made contracts to make bricks at the Capitol. They wanted to buy a stand of timber on the Paint Branch, a tributary of the Eastern Branch. They needed at least $7,000 a month during the winter or their summer operations would be "considerably crippled." Starting in May they would need $11,000 a month. They asked Wolcott to get them $100,000 from the Bank of the United States. If that loan did not succeed, they would ask the Maryland legislature for money. They also asked the president if they could sell squares through respectable brokers in Boston, New York, and Philadelphia and perhaps raise $70,000.[3]

*   *   *

Richard Forrest had begun the year hoping to sell tools to a growing work force. By November he had moved so few goods that he could offer to pay his suppliers only with tickets in either Blodget's number two lottery or the canal lottery. Other men who had expected much saw only emptiness. Law almost gave up. Of the 2.4 million square feet he had bought in December 1794, he had, almost two years later, titles to only 773,122 square feet and that by virtue of Morris and Nicholson having reconveyed some lots to the commissioners. To get his remaining titles, he knew that those gentlemen had to pay their arrears. He heard that they did, and still he did not get titles. On November 3 he threatened Morris and Nicholson with a lawsuit.

Morris genuinely wanted to satisfy Law. Nicholson only wanted to get "this strange inconstant unsteady man" off his back. Law's latest oddities included causing a scene over a £12 debt for lumber, and when Reverend Ralph failed to show at the Fountain Inn to preach, Law shot up and gave the sermon. Law decided to go back to England and solve the world's economic problems. Barry spent several letters trying to reassure Law that "many men envy your situation." If he stayed "on the E. branch, with your sheet anchors about you—your rib—your N. Jersey—your two fine boys, your many other rational and natural pursuits, is there not field enough to fill and gratify the mind," not to mention providing a base so that his "ideas of resources, public debts, funds, lands & c." could be "methodized, extended and disseminated. . . ."

Law gave it a try. He urged the commissioners to raise money by issuing their own six percent notes at $100 each, in effect becoming their own bank and increasing the amount of money circulating in the area. No attention was paid to the idea.

In early November Law and his friend the Philadelphia merchant George Wescott joined Morris, Nicholson, and Duncanson for dinner at the Little Hotel. Wescott recalled that "altho we had drank a cheerful glass, we were not intoxicated." Duncanson, Law, and Wescott left together. Duncanson also lacked titles but trusted Morris and Nicholson, even lending the latter money. When Law "broke out into some degrading expression respecting the city," Duncanson accused Law of aching for titles so he could sell out and go to England. Then and there Duncanson offered to buy Law out for £75,000, 50 percent more than what he had paid, plus a fair valuation of his improvements. Law said he had spent between $20,000 and $30,000 and must have that much in cash. Duncanson ridiculed the idea of paying in cash and assured Law that he would pay the whole in ten years at ten percent interest paid annually, which would provide more than enough for Law to live on in England. Duncanson asked Wescott to bear witness that as far as he was concerned a bargain was made, and the wine had impaired no one's senses.

News of it spread quickly. Uriah Forrest pressed Duncanson to give him a piece of the action. Morris included the tale in his fund of stories about how valuable Washington property was, and Nicholson cherished it as a way to get rid of Law. But within two days of the bargain, Law renounced it.

Then another angry proprietor weighed in. Walker threatened to caution the public not to buy lots. The board had cheated him with a rigged division of squares. Nicholson tried to stop him, explaining how accommodating Scott could be. Law, however, was also in the room and knew exactly how to stir Walker up. He had heard Scott speak in such terms that proved that he was doing all he could to retard the development of the Capitol so "that congress may be forced to hold their sessions in the President's house, and to lodge in and about Georgetown."

Walker published his caution, opening up another newspaper war. Walker tarred the board for "an immense waste of the funds for the public buildings." The board dismissed the charges as "obscure" and Walker as "insignificant." Walker rehashed the whole episode of Johnson's Rock Creek lots. That, he said, was the only way the board could jack up the price of lots along Rock Creek, where Scott had invested heavily. The board replied that getting Morris and Nicholson to renounce any claim to lots along Rock Creek was advantageous to the city. They explored the possibility of suing Walker for libel.[4]

*   *   *

The Bank of the United States refused a loan. It was straining to serve its best customers "at the present moment of difficulty and distress." The crash Barry predicted had arrived in Philadelphia. Scott packed his bags for Annapolis. The board begged the president to send an address to the Maryland legislature. "Without some effectual aid," they warned him, "we shall in a few weeks be obliged to stop."[5]

58. We Are Not Now in Laughing Humor

In mid-November the *Gazette* published an essay that envisioned the great metropolis. Law was the perpetrator if not the author, which caused wry comments among those who knew how close Law had come to selling out. Yet somebody had to counteract Hoban's official report to Congress on the state of the public buildings. The first story of the Capitol was not finished. At the same time, the interior walls of the president's house were done, the exterior walls two feet shy of the roof, twenty-six pilasters were set (with capitals on six of them and the other twenty hoped for in the spring), the joiners' work for the basement finished, "window-frames, sashes, doors, window shutters, base, sub-base, architraves, & c." all "seasoning."

Law described the Capitol-to-be, where "more than twenty streets" would terminate, emblematic "of the rays of light issuing" from the edifice and of the ease of approaching it from all parts of the union. Law credited L'Enfant with placing the Capitol in the center of the union and Hallet with the "masculine and bold" architecture. He described the "court" of the Capitol, where there would be "the altar of liberty" surrounded by figures of young women allegorical of the states. Statues of "illustrious men" and busts of "distinguished men" would be around the portico or in the galleries. The square to the east would be large enough for 50,000 people "on days of public solemnity." There would stand a statue of "the United States assigning to the President the direction of the Federal City," with him "inviting artists from every part of the world, to come and enrich" it.

Law foresaw his other passions. The Mall would be "divided thro" its whole length by a canal, from which will proceed an immense number of branches, intended to water and cleanse the city streets." Some of these branches would be "cascades" issuing from statues representing the major rivers of the nation. Alongside the canal would be alleys 50 feet wide and "two solid clumps of trees each of 200 feet thickness," and two more clumps on the other side of alleys 90 feet wide. On the south side of the garden would be hotels, on the north houses. Houses opposite those would form "a gallery of 25 feet in breadth and about 9,000 feet in length." Entering streets would form "porticos or triumphal arches," creating "a winters-walk the most extensive and splendid in existence. . . . Treasures of objects of luxury and delight will enrich the whole length of this gallery, which, when completely finished, will produce the effect of an enchanted place, rather than that of a line of private houses."

There would be no quays along the canal through the garden, but there would be on the Eastern Branch, where the earth "will be leveled and raised to admit of cellars." Water Street would run on top of those cellars. Fire engines would sit on the wharves, as would shelters for the indigent. Indeed, "the real advantage which Washington must have over ordinary cities, which are mostly built without a plan, will be the multiplication of useful accommodations which may tend to the comfort of the indigent and laborious class of people."

The essay provoked no discussion in the *Gazette*, where there was much too much reality. Slaves were being auctioned on the "plantation" just northeast of the president's house, a meeting was held to draw up a petition to the Maryland Assembly to give the city police protection, and a range war broke out. "An evil disposed person with an ax" cut up some milch cows grazing "on the commons of the city." Property owners wanted livestock penned. After three days of horse races in the city, stallions began running loose on the commons.[1]

* * *

On November 4 Morris received a "very solemn and serious report" from Philadelphia. As the partners quit work the usual tavern laughter left them cold. Nicholson notes in a sketchy diary, "We are not now in laughing humor—domestic attachments threaten." Morris wanted to hurry to Philadelphia to prevent the sheriff from seizing their belongings, but Nicholson convinced him to stay another week until they could secure a $32,000 loan to completely pay off their arrears. They quizzed Scott, Stoddert, and Forrest for leads to new endorsers.

No one outside the coterie of federal city enthusiasts fell for what they were doing. One creditor, especially eager to jail Nicholson, rejected Washington lots because they were encumbered with conflicting claims. In Philadelphia, "all classes of people" doubted their ability to pay their debts. On the evening of November 13 the two friends went over what was left to be done: paying arrears and getting scrips signed by the commissioners; procuring titles for Law, Duncanson, and workers finishing houses; and paying Carroll, Young, and others. The next morning, without fanfare, Morris left, careful to avoid Baltimore, where writs had been issued against him. He traveled through Frederick, York, and Lancaster, did not let falling off his horse slow him down (but took time to find a good cook for a salmon caught while crossing the Susquehanna), and arrived in Philadelphia, "in the nick of time to defeat the malevolent designs" of their creditors.

Scott was "rather amazed" to find Morris gone. The board had just decided that all arrears had to be paid before they would give more titles. Until Nicholson could come up with the $32,000, "all was yet unsettled." Then Forrest found an angel, James Dunlop, another Georgetown merchant. Dunlop walked over what Nicholson was offering him and concluded 1.6 million square feet of it was "not worth the purchase money." To Nicholson's amazement, the rejected lots "lay along the Mall from the Potomac to the Capitol, along the canal, Delaware Avenue south of the Capitol, the prime lots in the city in fact." Dunlop averred that no one would build on such low ground. A delighted Nicholson submissively substituted lots far from the action. He did have to lower the value of the lots he gave, from the $280 agreed to by Forrest to $250.

With "porter water and sugar" at his side, Nicholson wrote to Morris sharing the good news, ruing only his loneliness—well, almost loneliness. A Philadelphia creditor named James Cramond felt constrained to shadow Nicholson so that matters in Washington would not be settled to his disadvantage. Cramond all but slept with him. Missing Morris's valet, Nicholson hired a "mulattoe family."[2]

As news spread of Nicholson's good fortune, Scott was delighted.

Law seethed. Nicholson made getting titles for him his next project, though not out of any respect for Law. Nicholson blamed Law's wife for all the complaining. "You will say I have got her on my back . . .," he joked with Morris, "no matter back or belly or who is on or off, I give her credit for many of the visits I have from him. He comes in full charge and after a little conversation he is reasonable." A few days later Law came in reasonable because Nicholson promised him conveyances. Then Law saw that it included the condition to build a house on every third lot within four years. "He flounced and went wild."

They both went to the next commissioners' meeting, and Law explained that Greenleaf had assured him that he was not required to build. The assembled read the contract he had made with Greenleaf, in which the condition to build was spelled out. Law protested that he had not read the contract before signing it. Nicholson thought such "pitiful evasions . . . ran down his character in the opinion of the board." Law was adamant and vowed not to release the mortgage on Morris's and Nicholson's houses unless he got his lots unconditionally. Nicholson was ready to fight, suggesting to Morris that they give Law the titles with the condition and then sue him for the mortgages.

Nicholson needled Duncanson, who did not object to the building clause, to take Law to task, which almost led to a duel. Duncanson accused Law of "shameful breach of contract" in regard to building and then insisted that Law had legally sold out to him. Law denied that. Duncanson thundered that his honor was at stake. Then, according to Nicholson, "Law wept that he would lay down and die before he parted from his word but he was wedded to the city. How could he justify himself to Barry."[3]

Nicholson enjoyed seeing Law cower, but that did not solve any problems. Carroll also had to give titles so that Law's purchase could be completed. Carroll demanded $13,000 and refused Nicholson's invitations to dinner, complaining that when with Nicholson he felt like he was being "trifled with . . . beyond bearing." Nicholson tried to get endorsers for a payment to Carroll. He failed and finally sent $200,000 worth of his notes to his assistant in Philadelphia in hopes that he could raise $8,000 in cash. The prospect of one day having to pay $200,000 on those notes did not give Nicholson pause. In a letter to London bankers, he recalculated the value of his Washington property and found it was worth $10 million. Meanwhile, Carroll sued, and Forrest told him that there was a writ out for his arrest for nonpayment of a debt. Nicholson sent an assistant out to try to raise bail. Until then he stayed in his room, where the sheriff could not touch him.[4]

*   *   *

In his long letters to Morris, Nicholson tried to paint others as the buffoons. But it was Nicholson that the town was laughing at. "They are here full of anecdotes respecting Nicholson at Georgetown," reported an agent in Baltimore, trying to sell M & N notes, "none of which are to his credit and are all admirably calculated to hasten the destruction of all opinion as to his responsibility. That the bubble will soon burst I doubt not. . . ."

Scott's task was to keep such stories from turning the Maryland legislature against the loan to the city. The president, as requested, wrote a letter asking for the state's help, but Scott did not have an easy time of it. As usual, Baltimore delegates looked askance at aid for the Potomac. Scott calculated that he had a ten-vote majority, but to get the measure passed he had to agree to take only $100,000 instead of the $150,000 requested. Scott got the loan in U.S. debt certificates paying six percent interest. To obtain cash, the board had to sell them, and their current price was almost 15 percent below par. Instead of $100,000, the commissioners had only $79,000.

With money in the bank, the board sent two crews up to the Paint Branch to cut timber. Twenty-one slaves cut timber for the president's house and eighteen white laborers cut timber for the Capitol. All got paid one shilling (13 cents) a day. At least it was a good way to keep warm during a very cold winter, which only Law seemed to relish. The Potomac froze two weeks before the Eastern Branch, another proof of the superiority of the east side of the city.[5]

*   *   *

In his message opening Congress, the president called for legislation establishing a national university in the federal city. The commissioners also sent up a memorial informing Congress that the president would appropriate 19 acres of the public grounds in the city for it. All the board needed was the authority from Congress to incorporate a body to accept donations for the university. They thought no one could object. James Madison managed the bill through a friendly committee. Once it was on the floor, Nicholas of Virginia worried that this was but the beginning of federal support for an institution which would be inconvenient and dangerous. "The further children are from home, by being less under the eye of their parents, the more their morals would be injured." Proponents denied there would ever be a need for federal support and ignored the argument about morals. The next day the measure was brought up early before proponents had entered the House, and without further ado the committee of the whole voted overwhelmingly against it. Proponents scrambled to undo the damage. After several long speeches arguing the innocence of the measure, the best they could do was to get the House—to postpone consideration—and that by a one-vote margin—thus saving the president the embarrassment of seeing his pet voted down.[6]

*   *   *

Philadelphia was not kind to speculators that winter. Creditors had James Wilson, an associate justice of the Supreme Court, jailed. Morris wrote to Nicholson that "notice was given me to take care of myself for unless cash . . . is produced this day or tomorrow, it will be my turn next. . . . I am seriously uneasy for Wilson's affair will make the vultures more keen after me." No one trusted anyone anymore. The president of the Pennsylvania Bank failed and, having illegally spent bank funds, brought many friends down with him. The Washington scrips, Morris found, "will not work yet as confidence is wanting." Only two of almost a dozen creditors showed interest in taking Washington lots. He did save his house and Nicholson's when Reed and Forde took lots in ten squares to secure a $50,000 debt.

Morris did not look forward to the December court term. He was
having trouble raising a few thousand to pay the bail to postpone
having to pay many thousands in debts. He thought he was about to
get a $50,000 loan from a Baltimore house, Barrett and Cohen, but
one of the partners had to go and see the lots. He paid bail in one
suit only to learn that the Bank of North America was about to
proceed against Nicholson, as was the Bank of the United States.
Greenleaf was unable to cover a sizable bill, so it would have to be
faced by Morris.

He fought back with humor and bravado, joking with Nicholson
that his levee was more crowded than the president's and that the
hinges of his countinghouse door were about to come off. "We must
depend on ourselves," he preached, "put the world at defiance and
set ourselves on the front seats of the worlds amphitheatre." The
"hot" time would come just after Christmas, as the court term
ended. He wanted Nicholson there. To avoid writs, Morris advised
him to "cross at the Upper Ferry go to my little villa. . . . You will
find a negro woman and her son there, tell them I am coming order
a fire and send me word. I will soon come and give the needful
information. . . ."[7]

1797

59. Afraid to Show My Face in the Streets

Mrs. Alexander White came from Woodville to see if she could live in the city. She left after three weeks and declared in the strongest terms that she could not. White offered to resign, though he thought he could faithfully perform his duties without his permanent residence in the city. The president forgave White his wife and did not accept his resignation, but he urged Thornton to see that all city officers lived and all city business was conducted in the city. Such measures "would form societies in the city—give it eclat—& by increasing the population, contribute not a little to the accommodation of the members who compose the Congress." To Scott, who had work continue on his Rock Hill house, the president sent congratulations on his getting the loan.

Mrs. White turned her back on the battle of the balls, the latest manifestation of east versus west in the city. The Washington Dance Assembly patronized the Eastern Branch Hotel in Southeast. A rival group soon congregated almost two miles away at the Little Hotel. They named themselves the Washington Amicable Dancing Assembly. The Eastern Branch Hotel was the brick building on 10th Street and Pennsylvania Avenue that Deblois had built and opened, only to see his tavernkeeper walk out. Nicholson hired an Englishman named William Tunnicliff to run it. He also revitalized the bakery Deblois had started two blocks west of the hotel to keep men working on his houses happy with warm bread in the morning.[1]

* * *

The November writ against Nicholson never materialized, but he knew more would be generated at the December court term. So he

hurried to finish dividing squares. The board was at his service, but
Dermott slowed down the work, telling Nicholson that he wanted
"more greasing." Nicholson rued the two lots he had already given
Dermott for a song and cursed him as "one of the damndest
scoundrels I ever knew."

In early January Nicholson trusted that he had finished calculating
the extent of his and Morris's holdings and had most of the necessary information to write scrips for their lots. That done, he made a
room in the Eastern Branch Hotel his castle safe from writs. That
boosted Tunnicliff's business. Law had to admit that thanks to
Nicholson's incarceration, the citizens east of the Capitol finally got
a glimpse of Scott.

Most respected Nicholson's move. Distress was so widespread
that most bought his argument that he had ample wealth in property
that just could not be turned into cash. The trouble was distress was
too widespread. No one gave him bail money. Those who had
money loaned it for five percent a month. No one wanted to place
money at risk at such a time for such a man. "I am like the stricken
Lear," Nicholson wailed to Morris, "avoided."

Not that he felt panic. He had a way of seeing lawsuits, which put
the issue of his debt in the slow judicial process, as actually
enhancing his credit. "I have considered when any man sued me,"
he later wrote his Philadelphia lawyer, "that he gave me a new
credit, and I did not include such within the list of my creditors for
whom my immediate exertions to raise money were to be used." So
he ignored the Philadelphia, Baltimore, and Georgetown merchants
suing him and sought ways to satisfy Carroll and Prentiss, to
preserve the property that would eventually rescue him. Prentiss at
least was reasonable. All he wanted on the $30,000 owed him was
$5,000 in goods for his store, just so he could keep going. And even
if Prentiss got nasty, with contractors Nicholson simply put disputes
into arbitration to buy time, as he had done with the claims of Clark,
Henderson, and Lovering. As luck would have it, Clark went insane,
and Henderson was dying, further putting off any settling of accounts. Lovering, however, was a special case, since Nicholson
liked him and his wife was dying. Nicholson saw to it that he got
$45 in cash.

Failing bail, the only way Nicholson could leave the hotel with safety was by placating the sheriff directly. So he offered him Washington lots as security for his bail. Sheriff Joseph Boone and his brother owned land in the city along the upper Eastern Branch and so could not deny the value of what Nicholson offered. Boone promised to "do everything in my power, consistent with my duty and safety to myself, to make the matter the most agreeable to your feelings." Nicholson felt safe enough not to feel forced to give away too much to raise money from the men who came to "fleece" him. He realized he had made one mistake that fall. By lowering the value of the lots with Dunlop by $30, he had caused others to want lots valued lower still so they could get more of the property.

The vultures hovering were not the men suing him, but Scott and Forrest. Nicholson entertained them with Tunnicliff's best Madeira, kept smiling to hide his troubles, and heard their proposals. Scott offered him $11,000 in cash and $40,000 in M & N notes to be secured by lots, including those mortgaged to Law. The last thing Nicholson wanted were his own worthless notes. "They've ordained to plunder me," Nicholson exclaimed to Morris. "God in heaven what harpies." He refused the offer, but warily. Nicholson worried that Scott would "embarrass" him in his efforts to get Law his titles.[2]

That matter was still hanging fire. Law had collected enough legal opinions to convince Nicholson that the condition to build need not be in the deeds. Philip Key lectured the board for five hours on the topic. As for improvements, Law pointed to thirty houses, including four brick on New Jersey Avenue with 100 inhabitants, as well as Barry's warehouse and wharf. He also threatened them with a chancery suit if he did not get his way, and in that case he would not build at all; "thus the object of a condition to build would be lost by persisting in its insertion." The commissioners did not budge. They could not in good conscience let Law get out of building 151 brick houses. They calculated all the sales Greenleaf, Morris, and Nicholson had made before January 1796. Two hundred ninety-four houses, including Law's, had to be built before 1800, if they stood their ground. So they asked the president to solicit the attorney general's opinion. Law raged to Nicholson that Scott and Thornton were out to destroy the eastern side of the city.[3]

*   *   *

Nicholson's sojourn at 10th and Pennsylvania Southeast was not
the only thing improving the eastern end of the city. James Piercy,
a friend of Duncanson, came to build a "sugar house" where raw
sugar from the West Indies would be baked into loaves. Law,
Carroll, Duncanson, and Nicholson signed on to back the enterprise. The plan was to have a 57-foot-high eight-story factory
standing next to Barry's wharf by late January. But there were no
public improvements on the eastern side of town, and Law learned
from Hadfield that the executive offices were to be next to the
president's house.

Indeed, on January 25 the commissioners sent the president
Hadfield's plans for two brick buildings "slightly ornamented with
freestone to make them correspond with the President's house, to
which they will appear as wings." With interiors "in the plainest
style," Hadfield thought they would cost $80,000 each. The board
suggested laying the foundations in the coming summer and finishing
them once the president's house was covered.

As the news spread, there was an uproar that soon reached the
president. Walker told the president he had learned from a confidant
of Scott about how the commissioner planned to make Congress sit
in the president's house. He begged the president to make the plan
of the city unalterable before leaving office, or Scott "will reign an
absolute Bashaw in the city" and "the Capitol will be kept back."
Walker pointed to the silting of the Potomac above the point to show
the absurdity of pushing Georgetown. "The channel is now filling
up so fast, that there is not now more than 10 feet water at low
tide." Walker even took a house in Philadelphia to personally press
his case with the president."

Law and Carroll wrote to him in the first week of February. "The
idea of those offices," the squire of Duddington wrote, "has thrown
a damp on the spirit of all." He did not want them built on Capitol
Hill. Indeed, he would be against them if they were built at all
because there was not enough money to finish the principal buildings. Starting work on those offices meant abandoning the Capitol.
The pace of work had already been so slow that Carroll thought of

his three brick houses there as "dead on my hands." He had intended to build a boarding house next to the Capitol but now would not lay out one shilling.

Law wrote out of fear of being upbraided "in the year 1800 at Mount Vernon when Congress cannot come to the city." He described how Scott once "amused" the eastern proprietors "by showing the President's house on the map and pointing out where the offices should be & by anticipating the future splendor of that part of the city" with its residences of ambassadors and courtiers. Law warned that Georgetown harbor might be frozen when congressmen came in December 1800. Building the offices near the president's house would mean all the men on the job would come from Georgetown, and no one would live near the Capitol. The president had to act or Congress would sit in the president's house. Law even enclosed a poem on the plight of the Capitol. There is no evidence that Georgetowners were gloating. Some, however, began plotting to steal one charm of the east by bringing Nicholson to Georgetown and to justice.[4]

*   *   *

His self-imposed jail term did not cramp Nicholson's style. He had four horses available to carry messages, and on January 17 put them through their paces sending off no fewer than fifty-six letters to people in the federal city and Georgetown. Particular victims of his zeal were the trees of the city. After hearing from Scott that someone had cut and removed trees from some of his lots, he ordered Tunnicliff to have all trees removed to be used for fencing or firewood. He encouraged his baker to go out and get the treetops for firing his ovens. He wanted all their squares cleared and fenced and put into grass, gardens, or crops, and he encouraged the commissioners to do the same.

As for his buildings in the city, Nicholson began to tire of Prentiss and prepared to do to him what he had done to Deblois the year before. He pledged to set Lovering up with a store to sell wet and dry goods. Not that Lovering was overjoyed at the thought of becoming Nicholson's main contractor. He had still not been paid for work done in 1795, and most of the checks he had got in 1796 had bounced. But he was desperate and responded with an idea to turn the unfinished two-story houses on South Capitol Street into three-story houses at little cost, thereby increasing their value by 25 percent. Unfinished though most of his houses were, it did not crimp Nicholson's efforts to get tradesmen to move in. He encouraged a Philadelphia hairdresser to set up business on South Capitol Street, assuring him, "you are the very man wanted to put this place into buckle curl and trim and powder it off. . . ." Scott wrote Morris that at night the Eastern Branch Hotel was not "as quiet as a mouse," for Mrs. Tunnicliff was seen slipping into Nicholson's chamber.

Nicholson soon had another cause for sleepless nights. After being jailed briefly in Boston, Greenleaf was back in Philadelphia up to no good and even Morris turned on Nicholson. Nicholson's absence was bad enough, but when Nicholson said he could not hurry home because he had to go over Cranch's accounts of Greenleaf's Washington operations, Morris lashed out, "I suppose like the rest of the world I must give up the expectation of seeing you." He was also peeved at getting a letter from Notley Young saying Nicholson had done nothing to satisfy his account. He even blamed Nicholson for trying to saddle the building condition on Law's deeds.

After getting Morris's letter, Nicholson was up at 4:00 A.M. pleading with Morris that he had been up an hour and a half "doing your business and mine." He explained that he would deal with Young once he was finished with Law and that the commissioners had first insisted on the condition to build. All in all, he thought he was doing more good in Washington than Morris in Philadelphia, because he would soon get certificates to lots "above suspicion." Morris apologized, with this caveat: "I have never told you a tenth nay not one hundreth part of what I daily go through." There was the usual dun to meet that day, this time a whopper, $30,000.

*   *   *

A trap was being laid for Nicholson in Washington, and he sensed it. The commissioners stopped signing scrips, citing the number of mistakes constantly being discovered as reason to go slowly and saying they worried that if Morris and Nicholson failed to pay the May installments, scrips sold to others would complicate matters. Then, on February 4, a man claiming to be an associate of a friend Nicholson was meeting with gained entry and served a writ from Montgomery County, which began at Georgetown. Nicholson demanded to see the Prince Georges County sheriff with whom he had an understanding. Then three deputies of the Montgomery County sheriff appeared, among them one of his Baltimore creditors. They said they would take him "dead or alive." Nicholson saddled his horse and rode between them to Georgetown.

That a busy merchant would come 10 miles from Baltimore just to publicly drag a man before the sheriff bespeaks of how appealing it was to men of the late eighteenth century to humiliate their adversaries. Nicholson was a hard man to shame, but that ride between "hell hounds," to be confined in a room to wait for the sheriff, deeply offended him. In an instant the community had to decide to provide the bail or leave Nicholson's fate to the sheriff. Scott was too busy to come. But promised lots as security, others did. "In about twenty minutes," he was free "in a most honorable way." His friends returned to Tunnicliff's for a cold supper.

The episode took the savor out of life in Washington, but at least Nicholson kept his sanity. About to lose in arbitration, Joseph Clark pleaded in a letter to Nicholson that he never cheated Greenleaf, for if he had, "I should be afraid to go to sleep lest my offended God would in that situation with his justice scourge me—and I should be afraid to show my face in the streets lest my offended and injured fellow creatures would retaliate. . . ."[5]

60. A Whole Banditti of Cormorants

"I have known for three years that James was in the path of ruin," Noah Webster wrote to another brother-in-law, Daniel Greenleaf, "converting with astonishing zeal and folly, good property into bad. I knew he was wantonly and deliberately feeding a long train of *whores* and *rogues*. But I could not believe till lately, that he would rob his innocent friends for that purpose."

Webster was upset at Greenleaf for taking money from Boston friends with the assurance that he had the means to reimburse them in Philadelphia. All he had in Philadelphia was a meeting of creditors at which he listed all his assets and liabilities, which he thought proved he was $2 million in the black. To reassure creditors, he assigned almost all his property (he reserved some Washington lots for his Boston obligations) to five trustees who would formulate a plan to raise money on the property and pay all creditors. Any residue would belong to Greenleaf and his uneasy partner of the moment, Fox.

Even Morris had to admit that after Greenleaf bared his books, creditors began to think better of him. Nicholson opined that he was out "to clog" their operations. Regardless, Morris wanted war only "in the counting house, and *not in the public prints*."

*   *   *

As president, George Washington had only one month left in which to bring peace between Carrollsburg and the Georgetown interests, as he called them. In the main he agreed with Walker, Carroll, and Law. He had no enthusiasm for the executive offices and blamed the commissioners' insensitivity for all the worries about the Capitol, which had discouraged the erection of private buildings to accommodate congressmen. He even lectured the commissioners once again on the virtue of taking "their stand in the city, to do it without delay; and as convenient to the important theatre, as they can be accommodated." He even enclosed a list of available houses there that Law had sent him, two owned by the commissioners and one that Dr. Crocker was building. An office in one of Carroll's houses could be had for a lower rent than the commissioners were paying.

The commissioners still did not get the point. The Capitol was their primary object, they replied, but the president's house had best be covered to protect the work done, and the executive offices would be needed before the Capitol "because papers must be on the spot before the removal of congress, and they cannot remove in a day." The president once again tried to make them see the light. The failure of the loan and crisis in the funds required that the public see that the two principal buildings would be finished on time. At present the "public mind is in a state of doubt, if not despair. . . ." As long as there was any doubt about the adequacy of funds, the Capitol must get most of the resources. In 1800 the executive offices "might shift (as they have done) a while longer." He did agree that the president's house should be covered. The commissioners still pressed the president to approve the plan for the executive offices and not leave it to his successor. Work would not begin before next winter. By that time, they promised, with the Capitol 30 feet higher, complaints about its backwardness would be a thing of the past.

Thirty feet was not enough for Thomas Law. He told the president that Hadfield had told him that "he could get the Capitol covered in this season," if the commissioners did not interfere by slowing down the work with "unnecessary ornaments." That complaint moved the president to tell the commissioners to avoid "all carving not *absolutely necessary*, to preserve consistency. . . ." Indeed, such ornaments were "not so much the taste now as formerly."

While that exchange was going on, the president reserved judgment on Walker's charges against Scott. Finally, on February 27, he assured them that on investigation, he judged Walker's charges unfounded. He declared his "real satisfaction" with the board's conduct and said that nothing was "wanting" in Scott, "except residence in the city."

His last official act for the city was seemingly perfunctory. The board sent up a deed describing all the public reservations to be conveyed by trustees to the commissioners on the president's instructions. To transfer the land for streets, he was to ask the trustees to follow an attached plan. What complicated the transfer were the complaints of the proprietors. They insisted the large intersections formed when avenues and streets met were public squares for which they should get £25 an acre. To placate them, the board went so far as to suggest that those areas be "enclosed by handsome palisade, . . . sown with grass, and ornamented with fountains, statues, &c." To save money, they could be ringed with streets 150 feet wide. Thornton described ten such intersections, areas such as today's Dupont Circle, and estimated only 11 acres would have to be bought, at a cost of $736.

The president chose to ignore that controversy. Davidson's claim that the engraved plan cheated him was another matter, since Davidson insisted that the president had made L'Enfant's map the official plan by sending it to Congress in December 1791. The president countered that that plan was sent with the understanding that it be returned for necessary corrections, and those corrections were made. Indeed, he informed the commissioners, no L'Enfant plan ever would have been engraved because "his obstinancy threw every difficulty it could, in the way of its accomplishment."

On March 2, 1797, the president signed the order instructing the trustees Beall and Gantt to convey the public lands. He did not, however, have a map to attach, so he attached one of the printed plans. Dermott had not finished the official map. A new surveyor found out why. Nicholas King, who had come down to work for Morris and Nicholson, agreed to help the commissioners prepare a map showing the public's lots for Dutch investors. To help him along, Dermott gave him "two old torn maps." King thought it strange that "the knowledge of public property to the amount of thousands depends on old maps illy or confusedly colored, or on scraps of paper or a few sheets of paper stacked together almost unintelligibly and scratched upon."[1]

*   *   *

"You think your troubles equal to mine," Morris taunted Nicholson in a letter that probably reached the federal city after Nicholson left, "they probably will be so when you get here, but at the City of Washington it was paradise compared to what it is here." Nicholson sneaked into Philadelphia, never revealing how he did it in case he had to do it again. He came, as he put it, "with my fingers in my mouth," without signed scrips, which ruined a "bold strike" Morris was planning. He wrote to James Marshall, who was to have been his point man in raising money in Europe, accusing the commissioners of a "breach of faith."

On arriving in Philadelphia, Nicholson secluded himself to avoid writs and tried to stop the sheriff from selling some of his Philadelphia property. Morris tried to turn what scrips they had to advantage. The negotiations with Barret and Cohen floundered, but Sharp Delaney had promised to relieve Morris's and Nicholson's debts in the Bank of North America with a loan secured by ninety-six Washington lots. Closing the deal was not easy, for "some devils or other" wrote to Delany abusing Morris and Nicholson and representing the lots "as insufficient security."[2]

* * *

Law came to Philadelphia in despair. "I see and hear of nothing about the city but what is painful and disastrous," he told Nicholson. "If in a day or two I am compelled to state my case, I shall deem myself a sacrifice for others good; I shall be a warning and give admonition. My case is a peculiar one. I came forward first, I have stayed by the city. When I have taken the step of despair after being disappt. in every exertion, I will bid adieu to the city."

Law was on tenterhooks. The attorney general would decide if his deeds had to have a building clause. On February 19 he ruled that the deeds given by Morris and Nicholson to Law did not have to have the building clause, but the commissioners could require Morris and Nicholson to build the houses they had freed Law from building. The board thereupon refused to convey titles until Morris and Nicholson gave bond guaranteeing that they would build those houses. The partners assured Law that they would, but it would take time because they were pressed from all sides. Law still had to get titles from Carroll, who said he would give them if he got $13,000 from Morris and Nicholson.

Law found a Frenchman, Denis Cottineau, who wanted to sell eighty shares of Asylum Land Company stock. Law got him to offer those shares and $13,000 cash, for Washington houses. Morris urged Nicholson to make the deal. Nicholson told Law that he wanted some cash above what Carroll would get. Law was his high-strung self, begging Nicholson, "relieve me from anxiety—do not delay . . .—ask your own heart what claims I have for confidence and forbearance and how I must suffer in mind." But Law refused to pull the wool over Cottineau's eyes. He would not value Nicholson's houses at more than $4,000 each because they would not sell for more than that. Nicholson wanted to sell seven houses for $60,000. An attempt to make a smaller deal with Morris also failed over the value of the properties offered as security. "The fact is," Morris informed Law in a tart letter, "that any two of the brick houses and lots at the Point are worth, nearly if not double the sum proposed to be loaned"—$13,000. Law left for the federal city, leaving Cottineau to fend for himself.[3]

*   *   *

On leaving Washington, Nicholson dubbed William Tunnicliff as his agent in the city. He explained to Tunnicliff that his troubles with Deblois had arisen because of a want of communication. Thereupon Tunnicliff resolved to send up a diary of what he did on Nicholson's business: "Sunday 12th Febr. 1797, Mr. Duncanson called, never was any man more surprised to find you was gone—gone! I cannot believe it." Others that came by were glad Nicholson had made his escape, but Sheriff Boone "was extremely concerned that you was gone. . . . All of us dull and melancholy at the loss of your company." First thing Monday, "a whole banditti of cormorants presented themselves . . . with Mr. Prentiss at the head and chief orator to the whole. He still persists that you owe him mo. and concluded by declaring that he would seize the houses and materials to indemnify himself in short he was very abusive and noisey."

Tunnicliff was somewhat humbled by his importance in the scheme of things, reporting that the last stoppage of bread "was severely felt by many, for on the Monday after you left the baker found the families waiting. Tea things set and ready to begin their breakfasts when lo there was no bread to be had as usual, with tears and the most pitious requests both husband, wife and children all have joined in begging for bread. How can this be denied and how can I proceed long in this supply without I hear from you to effect it." He needed $1,800 from Nicholson, plus $150 a week for bread.

Not all neighbors were to be pitied. The blue cloth out of Nicholson's coach was stolen, as well as seat covers for the hotel. His wife "frets much at the selfishness of the people around us. Their meanness is beyond description." Neighbor Deblois, who lived on the north side of Pennsylvania a little ways down a hill, had done some ditching, which "dams up the water on purpose to accommodate us with the musick of frogs." Tunnicliff cut a drain across Pennsylvania Avenue and was pleased that Deblois's slave Harry ran away, for "poor D. is now fretting his gutts to fiddle strings." (According to the ad offering a $30 reward for Harry's return, the slave, twenty to twenty-two years old, had stolen a considerable wardrobe.)

On March 9 Tunnicliff, who went to Georgetown to collect tavern debts so he could pay the workers, "could get but $10 tho' I was all day at it." His profit from the tavern since Nicholson had gone was not much more than a dollar a week. Yet he was eager to improve. He wanted to use a plow to make a racecourse across the street and a garden around the hotel. His wife planned to whitewash the assembly room as soon as she heard that the prints Nicholson promised were on their way down. Nicholson decided to keep the entertaining reports coming. He sent $522.50.[4]

*　　*　　*

In their last letter to President Washington, the commissioners were optimistic. With most squares divided, if Morris and Nicholson did not pay, the board could sell their lots. "We have certainly better prospects as to funds than for the two seasons past, and every thing promises fair for more extensive operations."

Thomas Jefferson, riding through Georgetown in late February on his way to Philadelphia to be inaugurated as vice president, was told that "there would be few or no private buildings erected" that summer because of the speculation in M & N notes. Men who thought the value of those notes could only go up were being proved wrong, and they could not build. Richard Forrest, whose hardware business did not gel, admitted to creditors that he had sold lots for those notes "at considerably more than they now command."

Jefferson prodded those with whom he talked to "use every exertion," because "it could not be expected that men should come there to lodge, like cattle, in the fields." Privately, he wondered if it might be wise "to apply for a suspension of the removal for one year." That such a suggestion came from one so friendly to the city was sobering indeed, especially when it was widely held along the Potomac that the new president was not friendly.

During the campaign, Adams's nephew William Cranch and old colleague Tristram Dalton assured all that Adams understood the federal city's importance in securing the union. To prove it, they tried to get him to visit the city that summer. Law was in Philadelphia during the transition but only pushed his scheme for a code of laws for nations and arbitration by neutrals to prevent wars. Dalton's wife opened the campaign to get the new president to visit the city by assuring Abigail Adams that it was just the tonic for the fevers nagging her in Quincy, Massachusetts, "as I am sure you would regain your health in the Montpelier of America."

Cranch wrote the day after the president was inaugurated. He thought improvements were "as great as could reasonably have been expected." He characterized the disputes plaguing the city, but thought the only important issue was money for the public buildings. The superiority of the Eastern Branch would resolve other disputes, because the city would grow there. He was harsh on the commissioners. All three were polite with him, but Scott "appears hasty and overbearing." Thornton was also hasty, not firm, "a little genius at everything," and little respected. White was "more mild" than Scott, "more firm" than Thornton, "and more respectable than either." That said, they were "all probably equal to their stations," which "seems to require rather men of business, than men of science." Finally, he told his uncle of the "general expectation'' that he would visit in the spring or summer and offered to accommodate him in his house. He had room to spare.[5]

61. Neither Palitabel nor Constitutional

John Adams was mindful of his responsibilities in ''fostering'' the federal city, but he was not bred to them. Unlike the planters of Virginia, he had no mansion that he was forever building and did not speculate in land. He had a broader experience in Europe than Jefferson yet gave no evidence that it had broadened his sensitivity to architecture and town planning. Unlike Washington, he would not hazard to say what was in or out of taste. His passions were law and politics. Having sat through all the Senate debates on the seat of government and the loan guarantee, he was mindful of the legal pitfalls and political opportunity afforded by the city. Legally, as he put it, the affairs of the city were ''in some sort under my direction.'' Adams well knew that politically, his support for the federal city could gain him Southern friends, but a visit to the city was problematic.

Never one to minimize his sacrifices, he was peeved that Congress did not increase the salary of the president. In an April letter to his wife he gloomily looked at the summer before them, when they would not have the money even to travel back to Quincy. ''You must go for the hot months to East Chester [New York, where one of their sons lived], and keep your house at the tavern and pay your board and I must go to the federal city, that must be my farm in the future and I shall have as much more plagues and less pleasure in it, than I had in the Quincy farm.''

By "plagues" he meant more than disease. Dalton warned him: "Few, very few, are to be found, concerned in this business, whose tales and representations are to be relied upon. This is a country of speculators. Whoever treads this ground must do it with the utmost caution, if he expects to escape impositions and censures. Parties are so wide from each other that their endeavor to serve each their own interests would strangle the child, if it were possible."

Officially, the president handled city matters just as they should have been handled. The day before he took office, the governor of Pennsylvania offered him the president's house in Philadelphia, which was to be finished in a few weeks. Although it would have saved him rent, Adams declined because "by candid construction of the constitution," he thought he could accept the offer only with the sanction of Congress. Thomas Law helped break the ice between the president and the commissioners. He informed the board that he had had a talk with the British consul, who said that the British minister had been surprised that his country was not offered a site during his recent visit to the city. The consul, Edward Thornton, believed his government would build a "handsome" ministry of stone. And given France's withdrawal of its minister in protest of Jay's Treaty, an offer to the British, Law thought, might induce them to build immediately "as a compliment to the late President and as a conciliatory measure to his successor."

A few days after getting Law's letter, the commissioners congratulated Adams on his election and raised the issue of giving lots to foreign countries for their ministries, noting that it was a matter left unresolved by his predecessor. Adams thought the offer of sites should come from the commissioners and wondered about the president's September letter that alluded to a problem with the transaction. That problem, they replied, was whether the commissioners had the authority under the deed of trust to give away building lots. President Washington had believed that since having ministries built would increase land values, the proprietors could not object. The commissioners sent Adams a copy of the deed in trust. He saw that there was no "literal authority" to give lots, but he thought they could be conveyed "for a very small pecuniary consideration."

The feeling-out process continued as the commissioners explained their financial problems to the president. The loan from Maryland would fuel "considerable progress during the present season, but we have no reliance on sufficient funds for the ensuing year." Since there was little prospect of a loan from Europe, they wanted to employ agents to sell lots. Because the loan guarantee law vested in the president the power of selling lots pledged to reimburse any loan, they asked for the president's sanction. Adams readily approved and signaled his trust in the commissioners. "The whole of this business is so new to me," he wrote to them on April 17, "and I have so many pressing avocations that I must repose myself very much on your wisdom and experience."[1]

*   *   *

On March 14 bricklayers began working on the walls of the Capitol again. By the end of the month Patrick Farrell had a crew of ten, with thirty-three laborers, mostly slaves, bringing up the bricks. Work did not bring joy to the city, for just about all who labored thought they were underpaid. Samuel Smallwood, the overseer at the Capitol, griped that his "diet" was "nothing more than salt meat for breakfast, dinner and supper which is neither palitabel nor constitutional and to bye tea sugar and other vegitables out of fifteen dollars [a month] you must reasonably suppose gentlemen will reduce that to a mear nothing. . . ." He wanted $20 a month.

The carpenters working on the roof of the president's house, citing "a considerable expense for tools calculated to answer that kind of work," also asked for a raise. Well knowing that they were the men of the hour, five stonecarvers asked for the same. They were to put up the ornamental capitals along the 350 feet of architraves. And their secretary, Thomas Munroe, citing "the enormous prices here of all articles indispensably necessary for housekeeping" and "a whole years confinement" in the office as a result of the work done by the treasurer devolving on him, wanted more than $1,000 a year. The board gave him $250 more a year, and seven stonecarvers got a 17-cent raise to $1.63 a day. Smallwood got $3 more a month. The carpenters got nothing, for with Morris's and

Nicholson's operations grinding to a halt, there were not a few idle carpenters in the city.[2]

The commissioners were as hard-nosed when it came to supplies. When their supply of bricks ran low, they tried to squeeze more out of Mitchell, who had walked out of his contract to deliver one million bricks. The board threatened to sue if he did not come up with 200,000 bricks. Mitchell said he would try: "When I reflect how much I have suffered on account of the city, above all my health, I feel very much affected should the public works stop."

As for other materials, the board threatened more suits. They gave Henry Lee six weeks to deliver almost 60,000 cubic feet of timber, and Parrot and Blake until the end of the month. Blake, who was Davidson's tenant on the farm northeast of the president's house, replied that Parrot had left town and he knew nothing about the business. Henry Lee came up to the city to view the Washington Races. One of the most charming men of the age, Robert Morris, thought no one more charming than General Lee, and that worthy had no trouble avoiding a suit. The timber was there, after all; it was just a matter of getting it. In trying to avoid the bind in the future, Scott quizzed contacts across the state of Maryland and had several negotiations going to secure another source. As for stone, Scott sent reminders to the Aquia quarrymen on April 21 that the city had "engaged a sufficient number of hands to work up stone as fast as it can be delivered." They had twenty-nine stonecutters at the Capitol, in April 1797, six more than they had had in August 1796.[3]

On private account there was some work going on. A 400-ton ship bound for Havana was tied up at Barry's wharf. Cranch wrote a description of the activity there to the president. There was "a large wooden store" on the wharf as well as a "bake house with 4 ovens" turning out ship's bread, and also a cooper's shop. Near the wharf was Barry's three-story brick house and a grocery store run by his nephew. Preparation to build the sugar bakery was under way. A little farther up New Jersey Avenue, Law had "built 3 respectable houses and a number of small temporary houses." The lots in the area had begun "to acquire a real and permanent value," unlike the speculative holdings of Cranch's failing and warring bosses.

Lovering had gone to Philadelphia and while returning without the means to continue any work, he was impressed with Nicholson's current stratagems which featured a pamphlet listing all the back-lands he owned. He hoped to overawe creditors with the extent of his holdings. "Mr. Lovering called and . . . tells me such news," Tunnicliff wrote in the diary he sent to Nicholson, "that gives my wife and me great pleasure. We sincerely hope that you will triumph over all the Jews that now infest Philadelphia." To effect Nicholson's designs Lovering made a complete description of the partners' property at the point, which could be shown to interested parties in Philadelphia. Lovering described the sixteen brick houses. Of the eight Clark built, the four on the west side of 4th Street (now called Wheat Row) still needed inside work, including carpentry, plastering, painting, and glazing. Only some of the sashes were made. Lovering valued them at $3,776 each. The four houses Clark built on P Street lacked paint and some carpentry work, and Lovering valued them at $6,815 to $7,496. There were three houses finished and occupied. Lovering valued the house on the corner of 6th and N, where the Laws honeymooned, at $10,000. The two houses on the south side of N Street where Cranch and Prentiss lived were worth $8,000 each. The four other houses on that block needed some work. A two-story house (all the others were three-story) on the north side of N Street would be completed in a week. Lovering valued the four houses at $5,500 to $6,000 each. Lovering thought the permanent house at the point, including the wharf, worth $100,839. Lovering thought the twenty-eight wooden houses, stump-cornered shacks, and workshops were worth no more than $11,821.[4]

*   *   *

General Lee's visit for the races gave Tunnicliff his first business since Nicholson had left. Lee and two other gentlemen stayed in the hotel. Some of the workers at the point took a few of Tunnicliff's barrels of beer to sell at the races. He noted all that in his diary, notwithstanding Nicholson's advice to "discourage" horse racing because it would "not promote" the hotel. The main attraction was a match race between the steeds of Ridgely of Maryland and Tayloe of Virginia for a purse of 500 guineas. Near the starting pole, at Mr. Turtle's house, for a fee of 50 cents visitors could see Mr. Salenka and "the Learned Dog" perform "curious & mathematical experiments." Tayloe won the 500-guinea purse. He celebrated the victory by buying a lot at the corner of New York Avenue and 18th Street Northwest for $1,000. Scott, who had bought the lot from Morris and Nicholson, was the lucky seller.

The race may not have been the talk of the season. In early April the Prince d'Orleans of France graced the city with his presence. A week later the Duc de la Rochefoucauld-Liancourt, once grand master of the king's wardrobe, was in town. Scott gushed about the visits in a letter to Morris, and that avuncular man of the world told him to think nothing of it, for "the reputation of the City of Washington is advancing in the world, and it is daily growing more and more the fashion to pay the visit."

Unfortunately for Scott, the cicerone for both visitors was Thomas Law, whose family connections in England made him a suitable contact for these noble French exiles. The prince and his companions, two dukes, spent the night with Law, who tried to help them make sense of the empty spaces by complaining about the Georgetowners' efforts to stymie "his expansion." He also blamed the proprietors for avoiding "communities; they prefer isolation, and each builds on his own property to increase its value." After two days in the city, the prince opined that the disagreements had slowed the city was well as "the speculation and knavery . . . to an extent that no buyer can be sure of his purchase, as the seller's title to the property is always dubious." Yet like Weld, he believed that "if everything already built had been more concentrated, the capital city would by now be quite something, but as matters stand it is nothing."

He had nice things to say. The city was "superbly situated," and although the front of the president's house was "ridiculously small," it and the Capitol were "the best looking, and even, I believe, the only such in the United States." He complimented Morris and Nicholson for building "a group of very beautiful houses" and recorded the rumor that they had cost $200,000. He was even kind to Blodget's hotel, describing it was "a large house without doors or windows on which the word *Hotel* is already painted in bold letter, and of a certainty there is none half so handsome in Philadelphia." Of course he lauded Law's Eastern

Branch. Barry's house at the foot of New Jersey Avenue was "charmingly situated."

Actually the prince was probably slightly bored by all that, having come to America to see the wilderness. What really struck him about the city were the wild peach trees in bloom and the heat, so "oppressive" yet "thorns and haws . . . barely begun to bud." The Duc de la Rochefoucauld-Liancourt was a sociologist, not a naturalist, and planned to travel extensively in the settled parts of the country and write a book about it. Whereas the prince was content to be fed by his hosts, the duke checked to see if everyone else was fed.

Shops in the federal city were "miserably provided, and excessively dear." The six days he was there he saw no butcher's meat, few eggs. "In short," he wrote, "I have not been in any of the obscurist parts of America where I found provisions so badly furnished." Not that he was moved by the evident sufferings of the workers. They were "the refuse" of that class skulking for higher wages. He did credit the stonemasons for excellent workmanship on the public buildings, but he did not admire the architecture and reported that the stone used, which was "extremely white," was not strong enough to survive many frosts.

The buildings got off easy, but he ridiculed the plan. "Judicious and noble" though it was, its "grandeur and magnificence . . . renders the conception no better than a dream." If the citizens "were less occupied with their speculations, rivalry and hatred, they could still form no society." It would take 500 houses to line the avenue between the two principal buildings, and not one was yet built. With $500,000 already spent on the two unfinished buildings and $600,000 needed to complete them, there would be no money left for courts, prisons, churches, pavement, fountains, or public gardens. Liancourt did not hold out much hope for the preservation of the union, so it was "idle to imagine the federal city will arrive at the execution of the tenth part of its plan."

But that did not account for the rancor in the city. For that he blamed a lack of public spirit and the "mischief" caused by the feud between the eastern and western ends of the city, which he thought "irreparable." Pioneer settlements, where everyone could pitch in, worked in America, but in the city the poor were seen as stealing space from proprietors who wanted to sell to the wealthy. "Benevolence" was banished from such a system. Taverns, shops, billiard tables, lotteries, "the means of prodigality and vice" were encouraged. In such a city even the good-hearted Law had to fail. "Every day his obstinacy on the subject increases, continually leading him to new expenses in this vexatious speculation. I fear he will not be as fortunate as he deserves to be."[5]

*   *   *

In mid-March Greenleaf lobbed a shell, restarting the war with Nicholson. He cautioned the public that he claimed all lots conveyed to Morris and Nicholson. Despite Morris's earlier insistence that they avoid one, he and Nicholson readily entered into a newspaper war with Greenleaf. They really had little choice after Greenleaf called into doubt their title to 3,245,385 acres of backland, 6,000,043¼ acres of North American Land Company lands, 2,117 lots in Washington, and 152 squares in the city that he claimed as security for monies due from Morris and Nicholson. The war raged for more than a month. Morris and Nicholson highlighted every shady deal by Greenleaf: where was the accounting of the money he supposedly borrowed in Holland secured by Washington lots? Why did he not return protested notes paid by other means? Why did he imply that they sought to conceal any mortgages held on lots when all encumbrances were properly recorded?

Morris tried to get the commissioners to forget about "Master Jemmy." "You will see what a dressing we shall give him about city lots . . . ," he wrote to Scott. "I believe he now wishes himself with the devil, for all our attacks are so fortified with truth that he cannot slip his neck out of the noose, and we have told the story so dispassionately that he cannot answer in wrath."

Greenleaf answered by suing and getting a court order forcing Sheriff Boone to attach Morris's and Nicholson's property at the point and on South Capitol Street. "We are all confusion," Tunnicliff spread the alarm to Nicholson, "the men are every hour running up to me frightened so that they cannot tell what to do—all is at a stand." "The convulsion of Mr. Greenleaf's attachments," Lovering wrote, "has made every soul uneasy and desponding."[6]

62. You Should Keep up the Price

Greenleaf had Cranch scout Morris's and Nicholson's holdings in the city. They had got scrips for 1,230 lots, and 3,647 lots had already been deeded, so "the commissioners appear to have parted with their power over 4,947 lots." With most of the scrip securing loans and the lots deeded already sold or tied up to secure the Dutch loans, Morris and Nicholson were running out of lots to manipulate. In May, Cranch noted, they had to pay a $68,000 installment to the commissioners and the $80,000 loan to the Bank of Columbia. There had to be a massive sale of Morris's and Nicholson's lots, and when they flooded the market they would be cheap.

Cranch thought that good news. He told the president that he looked forward to Morris's and Nicholson's failure. Those who had loaned them money could sell the lots they held as security in case of delinquency, "so that in a short time a great number of lots will be brought into market, and the price will fall until they get into hands who can afford to hold them." Cranch, however, did not count on his brother-in-law's zeal for ruining Morris and Nicholson.

Once Greenleaf officially signed over most of his affairs to five trustees—Henry Pratt, John Ashley, Thomas Willing Francis, John Miller, and Jacob Baker, all Philadelphia merchants—Morris and Nicholson opened negotiations with them, since the creditors they represented held $1,993,726 worth of their notes. Morris had been thinking of creating a sinking fund to guarantee the punctual payment of the interest on all their debts while they worked out the

438

1797, Spring

land deals that would eventually pay the principal. Greenleaf's trustees might serve to do just that. If the trustees could save Greenleaf's property, they might also save Morris's and Nicholson's.

By claiming Morris's and Nicholson's Washington property, Greenleaf warned the trustees of the hazards of cooperating with Morris and Nicholson. By attaching that property, he hoped to show Morris's and Nicholson's other creditors the way. Cranch served the attachments while two of the trustees, Pratt and Ashley, were in Washington looking over what little property Greenleaf still owned there and, more important, Morris's and Nicholson's vast holdings. The attachments startled them into action because the more they looked into Greenleaf's dealings the less they trusted him. They found that Nicholson's allegations were accurate. Greenleaf had advertised lots for sale, knowing that they were already mortgaged. They had to serve their own attachments to protect their claims from other creditors of Morris and Nicholson who were following Greenleaf's lead.

Judging from Morris's squeals, Greenleaf's attack was quite successful. Until the attachments were quashed, Morris complained to Scott, "all our operations with Washington lots must be suspended." He knew whom to blame. "Jemmy . . . takes great credit with his assignees for having hunted them out the road to those attachments and he is setting as many of our creditors as he can on the same scent." Just as infuriating were the stories going around making Greenleaf out as a victim.

Greenleaf had left a wife and child in Holland. He also enjoyed the company of Miss Ann Allen in Philadelphia. He began consulting lawyers about getting a divorce. Rhode Island had the most liberal divorce laws. Although it was evident that he had abandoned his wife by coming to America, Greenleaf revealed the sordid background of his marriage. He formed a "connexion" with Miss Scholten in 1787, but without having "practiced any of the arts of seduction towards" her. When he came back to the United States in 1788, he got a letter from her saying she was pregnant. He did not love her, but friends advised him that the honorable thing to do was return and marry her. He returned and found that she had had a miscarriage, but she and her family still wanted him to marry her.

He did, and they had a miserable marriage. She had a "violent and ungovernable temper" and tried to commit suicide. They did have one child. Then, at the end of 1792, the chambermaid revealed that the first pregnancy had been a hoax designed to trap Greenleaf. They separated, he agreeing to paying an annuity of 2,000 guilders. The Rhode Island court granted a divorce.

Morris saw the farce as typical Greenleaf chicanery. " 'Poor Fellow' his wife seduced him to her bed before marriage in Holland," Morris fumed to Scott, "and Morris and Nicholson led him into scenes of speculation. 'Poor Innocent' as if it was not known what great pains he took to obtain his wife, and to lead M & N into his schemes. . . . I shall never forgive myself for having been duped and taken in by him "

"The general cry" in Georgetown and the federal city was against the attachments. When someone would return from Annapolis, where the attachments were filed in court, there was a greater crowd around him than when the mail or newspapers came to town. Scott advised Morris and Nicholson to hire Luther Martin and Philip Key to quash the attachments as soon as possible. Since they had only equitable claim on most of the property, Scott thought the attachments could be quashed on the grounds that a court could not award to a creditor property that the debtor did not really own.

Scott worried that attachments would hamper the board if it had to sell Morris's and Nicholson's lots to make up the arrears. Scott had also bought a sizable share of the loan Forrest had given Morris and Nicholson, so the attachments also threatened the security he and his friends had on Morris's and Nicholson's property. "I am not desirous of being rich," he confided to Morris, "but highly so of being easy and independent, and with my present prospects I have God knows too little chance of soon being so." Notwithstanding his fear of being entangled with Morris and Nicholson, he held too many of their notes to give up trying to exchange them and some cash for a loan secured by Washington lots, which were still the things of greatest value in his ken. Morris understood the feeling and assured Scott that once the fate of the attachments was known, they would need Scott's help to service the loan from the Bank of Columbia, and he could then "set in safety and peace on Rock Hill and overlook his *security*."

Scott also reminded Morris of the installment due to the board and begged him to say frankly whether it could be paid. Morris did not say. He hoped Greenleaf's trustees would pay it, on the grounds that it was in the best interest of Greenleaf's creditors to keep intact the holdings of those most in debt to Greenleaf. Morris did offer advice. He had heard from Henry Lee that they were selling lots for eight cents a square foot. That was a mistake. "You should keep up the price for depend on it, they will sell faster at a high than at a low price." Big money was on its way: the current panic in the London money market "will send us some purchasers of city lots therefore look sharp and hold them up." His son William bore the glad tidings of the London panic. "This is the son I intend to fix in the City of Washington," he reminded Scott. "He was bred for the law but has been taking his pleasure for three years in Europe. Shall these plunderers take my city property it will not be worthwhile to fix my son there."[1]

*   *   *

Just half Morris's age, Nicholson was not looked to for sage advice, but to the worries of Lovering, Prentiss, and Tunnicliff he replied, "Affairs in the city will mend as was always the case when things are the worst." But they got worse. After Notley Young attached their lots, Carroll took "legal possession" of all the lots Greenleaf had contracted to buy back in 1793 and 1794. He magnanimously offered to let Morris and Nicholson have the twenty lots on square 651 that they had "partly improved" if they paid him 20 cents a square foot in sixty days. Or to be quite correct he would "convey [the lots] to the different mechanicks to whom you have sold a part of the buildings," adding, "you cannot consider this an exorbitant price as you have yourself demanded 25¢ the foot."

Carroll's action did not improve the morals of such men as Charles McNantz, who was about to put two staircases in two of Nicholson's houses. He calculated that he had done $4,000 worth of work since October; after a $1,200 advance, he had got no more than $150 worth of meat and malt from Tunnicliff. He warned Nicholson and Morris that unless the work was completed, much "will go to destruction." On May 19 Prentiss wrote that one of Nicholson's houses on Capitol Hill being finished by James Hogan had been completely stripped. Hogan had died that winter, and no one was watching. Rumors about the fate of the attachments and the certainty of more increased anxieties in the city. Tunnicliff reported in his diary on June 11 that Lovering had heard that "Ashley and Pratt are now at Annapolis and that every attachment will lay and that nothing but ruin and destruction now to take place amongst us." A deputy served Tunnicliff, as well as Deblois and "twenty more," with attachments. The victims decided an inventory was being taken of all the property for the delectation of Ashley and Pratt. On June 14 Prentiss reported that the two houses next to Hogan's on the Hill were "nearly stripped of all the materials."[2]

*   *   *

For three months a young, ambitious city worker named Isaac Nesmith had tried to prove to the board that he could do more than just drive slaves at the president's house. He could write well and keep books. In early May his persistence paid off, and the commissioners sent him on a mission down the Potomac to find the lumber promised by Thomas Carberry. The young man's reports reveal what passed for business in the late 1790s.

Twelve miles downriver from Port Tobacco, Nesmith began asking folks where Carberry was. No one knew. Eleven miles farther down, at Upper Machodoc, there was still no Carberry, so he could think of nothing better to do than go 30 miles down to Lower Machodoc. On the way he met a man who knew Carberry but said that since "his employment was in the water . . . , finding him would be precarious." Back in March the man had heard Carberry say he had got the timber for the city, then fallen sick, and could not attend to it. Carberry "had lost the greater part of it." No sooner did Nesmith begin looking for others to supply the pine than he bumped into Carberry, who "stated many disappointments and difficulties." Nesmith almost got him to agree to collect what he had, but Carberry pleaded that what he had "lay in such a manner as to require much time to examine and measure it." Nesmith concluded that "from what I have seen and heard of the country" he was afraid the city would not get any pine from there. Meanwhile, down at Stratford Hall, General Lee's overseer had the slaves cut the pine the commissioners wanted, but because of the wet weather it was impossible to move the logs to the river.

It was not by the ongoing comedy of suppliers that the world measured progress in the city, but by how fast the Capitol walls were going up. Twenty-five masons and ten stonecarvers worked from sunup to sundown, six days a week, so that they were paid for 31½ twelve-hour days in one month. No one complained that season of a lack of activity at the Capitol. Inside, there was trouble with the brickwork. Mitchell failed to deliver more bricks, and to keep the work going the commissioners let Hadfield buy bricks on the open market at high prices. Then Hadfield and Patrick Farrell who supervised the brick laying began feuding. Hadfield told the board that Farrell was not obeying orders and Farrell retorted that for no apparent reason Hadfield had "repeatedly" used "the most insulting . . . language and abuse" in the presence of the workers, going so far as to say "he would break all the bones in my skin" and suggesting that he was kept on the payroll out of charity. The board decided not to discipline either man and breathed a sigh of relief that accusations of bad work were vague. Scott and White found one virtue in Hadfield. He learned that the way to their hearts was to save money. Hadfield suggested eliminating fireplaces in the Senate gallery. Thornton thought hard of it but his colleagues outvoted him.[3]

Pointing to their balance sheet, the commissioners could show that in the past six months spending at the Capitol had outpaced that at the president's house, $18,630.35 to $15,734.11. On May 18 the board reported those figures, as required by law, to the secretary of the Treasury. Scott also rode down to Mount Vernon to share that evidence of their zeal for the Capitol with the retired president. Scott was handling a less pleasant matter for Washington, who feared that he was being fleeced out of the Bank of Columbia stock Henry Lee had transferred to him to pay an old debt. Reed and Forde of Philadelphia were the brokers, and they were on the verge of bankruptcy thanks to their speculation in M & N's notes. Adding to Washington's agony was that he took the shares from Lee at $40 each, and they were selling for $33.

Washington must have avoided any discussion of Morris and Nicholson, because after Scott's visit he expressed hopes for the city that had never been more sanguine. In a letter to an old friend he updated progress in and around the city. "An elegant bridge" was "thrown over the Potomac at Little Falls," and the navigation of the river should be completed that autumn. As for the public buildings, the president's house would be covered by the fall and the wing of the Capitol, "with which Congress might make a very good shift," would be ready to be covered by then. Martha wrote to their dearest friend in Philadelphia, Eliza Powel, urging her to get down to the city before the fall because "some of the best lots may be disposed of in the interval."[4]

*   *   *

After feeding those illusions, Scott went back to face a calculation that the board would be out of money by July 1. Newspaper ads cautioning people not to buy Morris's and Nicholson's lots and sheriff's attachments made it more difficult to sell any city property. On May 1 the commissioners auctioned off a few lots on which payments were a year overdue. Two of their employees, Hoban and Munroe, bid up and bought the lots for the public so none would sell for less than their original selling price. The board wrote to Amsterdam again upping permissible charges to two and a half percent, provided interest was no more than five percent. But Dutch money, if it came, would not come soon. Getting payments from Morris and Nicholson was the only way to keep the public works going. They pleaded with them to prevent a forced sale, because "if the lots do not sell it will be injurious to the holders of city property."

Morris and Nicholson saw that as reason for indulgence, which they asked for, assuring the board arrangements were being made. Negotiations with Greenleaf's trustees continued. The snag was Nicholson's desire to retain some city property. After all, the particular demand the trustees had against them was for $2 million, and Nicholson valued the Washington property at $10 million. But the trustees wanted all the property to avoid complications. The partners had little bargaining power and could only trust that when the trustees satisfied the claims against them there would be something left over for them. The trustees got Greenleaf to agree, but the agreement did not end any claims the old partners had against each other.

Despite the lackluster sale at the beginning of the month, on May 31 the commissioners advertised the sale of enough of Morris's and Nicholson's lots on August 7 to raise the $68,000 that had been due on May 1. Three weeks later, Morris and Nicholson agreed to assign all of their Washington property to Pratt, Ashley, Francis, Miller, and Baker who called themselves the trustees of the aggregate fund. That did not free Morris and Nicholson from all connection with the city. The trustees did not assume their indebtedness to their contractors and the Bank of Columbia, and in late June Scott and Forrest went to Philadelphia to hammer out a deal to save their own and Georgetown's credit.[5]

63. The Healthiest Place in the World

Collen Williamson petitioned the president for his old job back, claiming he could have saved £20,000 by using stone instead of brick and by ridding the city of Hoban and his Irish "vagbonds." Tristram Dalton's reports were more coherent and more troublesome: "Great fears, and I believe not without foundation are entertained by many" that there would not be enough money to finish the public buildings. He wanted the president to come and personally investigate.

What Scott told the president when he called on him in Philadelphia is not known, except that Scott's traveling companion, Forrest, bore news of political importance. A letter purported to have been written by Jefferson had been read to Forrest. In the letter Jefferson characterized all the alarms generated by Adams and the Federalists as a cynical attempt to destroy the Republicans by creating animosities against France. Such gossip was the way to the president's heart. He wrote back to Dalton reiterating that the commissioners were "gentlemen of so much intelligence and respectability, that I suppose I cannot do better than to repose myself in their wisdom in general." Their competence as well as the crisis with France, which necessitated a special session of Congress that summer, precluded a visit to the city. "The commissioners must be my eyes and I should shudder at the thought of taking the situation out of their hands into my own."[1]

Scott and Forrest then got down to the business of using Morris's and Nicholson's notes to gain Washington property in the only way Morris and Nicholson would allow, by lending them money. But by the rules of the game, the loan had to be used by Morris and Nicholson to satisfy their debts in the city. So it was not cash but credit at the bank that Scott and Forrest would provide. Indeed, Forrest had been such a generous endorser of Morris's and Nicholson's loans that in return for covering Morris's and Nicholson's obligations at the bank, he wanted some cash.

They had no cash, but "after a good deal of contentions," Morris and Nicholson thought they were on the verge of closing a deal in which Scott would cover $6,000 they had due on notes at the Bank of Columbia and Forrest would cover $4,000, which would relieve the demands there for at least sixty days. As security Scott and Forrest agreed to take land company shares as well as Washington lots.

Scott and Forrest worried that the trustees of the aggregate fund would object to the deal. Morris assured Scott and Forrest that the trustees supported anything that saved the property. Everyone was on the same side. Their assignment of their property, he assured Scott, meant that "the surplus of the aggregate fund"—his residue after creditors satisfied their demands—"will always enliven and give brilliancy to the prospect from Rock Hill." Scott and Forrest called on the trustees, who okayed the deal. Then one of them, John Ashley, let drop a comment that threw the negotiations into jeopardy. He gave Forrest the impression that Morris had intimated that Scott was a welcome caller, whereas Forrest had come along only to dun them. Forrest did not appreciate not being appreciated, and he promptly left Philadelphia without closing a deal. Scott left with him. Morris denied making the aspersions, but Forrest refused to close the deal. Convinced that continuing to service Morris's and Nicholson's loans only put off the day of reckoning, he urged them "to give your assent to the endorsers to sell" the lots held as security. The alternative was for the bank to begin legal proceedings for a sale that would require "an enormous expense of fees and commissions to the sheriff." Scott finally afforded some relief by making his end of the bargain.[2]

The date for the commissioners' sale of Morris's and Nicholson's lots approached. On hiring Luther Martin to defend them against the attachments in Annapolis, Morris and Nicholson asked him if the commissioners had a right to sell their property. In 1795 Martin had told the board that they had the power. This time he found that the law giving the commissioners that power had been signed into law four days after Greenleaf and Morris had signed their agreement with the commissioners. He opined that the commissioners had no right to sell until they went through the usual court proceedings. Before they had assigned their property the partners had cherished the decision, but they were not comfortable when the trustees thought of using it to get a court order blocking the sale. Morris reminded the trustees that by paying what the commissioners needed when they asked for it, the trustees would help finance the public buildings, on which the value of all lots depended. A sale would sacrifice the property since it would sell at a low price. The commissioners also pressed the trustees to help, emphasizing that "so many lots forced at once into market no doubt will have a bad effect, especially if from the present scarcity of money, the lots should not be sufficient to raise the sums called for." Worse than that would be a suit to block the sale. The commissioners offered the same deal they had offered to Morris and Nicholson, $12,000 a month until the $60,000 was paid off.

The trustees were in the midst of creating the mechanism by

which they would satisfy the creditors of Greenleaf. Those with claims would exchange them for a certificate entitling them to relief plus interest to be paid in two installments, on December 26, 1798, and December 26, 1799. Since they were trying to get claimants to come forward, it was not the time to get bogged down in court. They agreed that a forced sale would "give a death blow to the value of the city property." But in their view, that was an argument for the commissioners not to sell. That said, they magnanimously agreed to furnish "the means of carrying on the public buildings." The trustees authorized their agent, William Dorsey, a Georgetown merchant and state legislator, to give the commissioners a $10,000 check payable in seventy-five days, on condition that they get all the conveyances at $80 a lot that $10,000 could buy. The commissioners postponed the sale for seventy-five days, until October 18. Morris cheered from the sidelines and tried to get the trustees to begin paying off the loans from the Bank of Columbia.[3]

*   *   *

George Washington visited the city on July 19 and was pleased with the progress on the public buildings; everyone was. The problem was housing. Thanks to the continuing curiosity of Theophile Cazenove, a census of the houses in the city was taken in July 1797, giving an account of the number of brick houses of three, two, and one stories (35, 81 and 17 respectively), the number of wooden houses of two and one stories (82 and 107), and the number of houses commenced and the number occupied. There was a total of 322 houses, plus twenty to twenty-five small huts. Of those 322 houses, 155 were occupied. The lowest occupancy rate was at the point. There were sixty-six houses at the point, only fifteen of them occupied. Of the thirty new houses on square 651, only five were occupied. There were not that many houses surrounding the president's house, only seventeen, but fourteen of them were occupied. Only the cluster of houses next to Rock Creek had a more lived-in look. There were eighteen houses, all of them occupied. There were eight houses surrounding the Capitol, five of them occupied. Only fifteen houses were being built during the peak of the building season. Eight of those, at 19th and Pennsylvania, were the effort of Walter Stewart, who was dying in Philadelphia.

That rather lackluster reality did not prevent one monthly magazine from claiming that "as for the private accommodations, there are already almost enough for the reception of the members of congress." Law set about to make the assertion true by convincing an Englishman named Edward Gilbert to build a hotel next to the Capitol. But Law insisted on using Gilbert to gain another point. He had Gilbert make the offer on condition that the board move its offices to the hotel. After a month and no reply, Gilbert wrote again pressing them for a commitment. He had friends in Baltimore "who will join him in building a distillery and brewery" next to the Capitol if he should get a commitment from the board. Then Law himself, who the commissioners knew was behind all those propositions, offered to build two town houses at the Capitol for the commissioners' residences. The commissioners finally told Gilbert, "We will remove when we deem it expedient but we deem it an improper subject for negotiations."

Capitol Hill did not prosper. Reverend Ralph offered his house, kitchen, stables, and garden for sale at auction. There were no buyers. Ralph left town, leaving his house for Deakins to sell. Even McLaughlin the tailor, who had set up shop on the Hill, relocated to a spot near Blodget's unifinished hotel, next door to a shoemaker named Delphy.

The commissioners were loath to do anything to relieve the general distress, even though suppliers for the public buildings were hurt by the building depression because they had counted on making money off the private building. The blacksmith Gridley (who had originally come down from Massachusetts with Deblois) complained that despite his contract to do all the public's smithery he was losing money, for in the past five months he had done only $150 worth of private work, most for Scott's Rock Hill house. Gridley worried that his workers were about to sue him.

Prentiss asked Nicholson for payment in "lands or estates in the country." He wanted to take his wife and child from the point and its "noise, distress and confusion." Prentiss left for Philadelphia to confront Nicholson. He made the mistake, however, of going via Georgetown, Delaware, where he hoped to get Stansburrough to release him from the absurd contract that had served no other purpose than to shelter Nicholson from creditors, since Stansburrough had delivered precious little lumber, which was to have been his end of the bargain. When Prentiss reached Delaware, Stansburrough had him unceremoniously thrown in jail for failing to execute the contract. Lovering gave up going to Philadelphia and tried to raise money to return to England.

Tunnicliff made it to Philadelphia and saw Nicholson. For three weeks the tavern keeper begged and cajoled Nicholson. In one letter he prefaced his doleful description of his family's distress by warning Nicholson and Morris of a plot to serve writs: ", , one or both of you bathe every morning out of the house, in that situation an attack has certainly been mediated."

Then after a month of unrequited begging, Tunnicliff served Nicholson with a writ attaching all his movable property in Washington.

Nicholson's rage could not be contained. It was not fair for a man to wage war without first declaring it. Nicholson and Morris promptly wrote to everyone they knew in the federal city, declaring that Tunnicliff was "unworthy of the support and countenance of honest men" and that they hoped "to see the days of his retribution and repentance. . . ." Tunnicliff came home at least with permission to auction off Nicholson's movable property in Washington.

Prout's nephew William Huston showed how low one could go on the plain between the Eastern Branch and the Capitol. In the spring of 1796 Huston gave "himself up entirely to gambling and drink," much to the injury of Prout, who banished him from his store. Huston seemed to reform while working for a printer in Baltimore. Prout gave him another chance, but on a trip to Baltimore to buy goods for the store, Huston lost $70 gambling. Then Prout had to go to New York, and Huston "was gambling in the store every night and used to go to bed at daylight" or sleep behind the counter while the store was open. Banished again, Huston got a job with the newspaper at the point.[4]

*   *   *

The commissioners needed cash. They went to the Bank of Columbia, hoping the "long respite" they had given the bank would induce it to lend $3,000 to $4,000 so that the public works could be carried on through September. The bank agreed to make $3,000 available but "with extreme reluctance." No one else was getting money out of the bank, so the commissioners "cannot calculate on more in the future." The board asked the trustees of the aggregate fund to pay off their $10,000 note as soon as possible. Since a September payment had not come, the commissioners kept advertising an October 18 sale. They even requested a loan from the canal lottery managers so that the public works could continue through October.

On October 3 the board told Hoban and Hadfield to tell the workers that there was no money to pay them. After promising them priority when money came, they asked the men to continue the work and offered the hope that proceeds from the October sale would raise enough money to pay them. They doubted the trustees would pay any more by then, since Philadelphia was in the throes of another yellow fever epidemic.[5]

* * *

There were fevers in Washington, but not deadly ones. Cranch assured his mother that although his neighbor on the point Dr. May had "plenty of business, yet he says this is the healthiest place in the world." Not long after he wrote that, Cranch's wife and two sons came down with long bouts of diarrhea. But even New England harbored such terrors. Amariah Frost wrote from Massachusetts that he could not move as planned to the federal city because his entire family had fearful cases of dysentery, and he had lost one daughter.

People in the federal city had to brag. The *Gazette* offered accommodations gratis to "any genteel family" fleeing Baltimore or Philadelphia. Another correspondent sang the praises of the city as "one of the healthiest spots in the United States." On September 16 a writer in the *Gazette* contended that there had not been one death from fever in the city during the past year out of a population of about 2,000. There were two deaths by consumption, and one each from diarrhea, "cancerous bread," old age, convulsions, and a smallpox inoculation.[6]

64. A Batch of Those Cursed Notes

Sheriff Boone had an uneasy summer. Nicholson had left him with scrips for Washington lots with the assurance that they would satisfy creditors. But one Pennsylvania creditor who had a judgment for $30,000 against Nicholson refused to take the scrip, making Boone, who had not arrested Nicholson, personally liable. Boone was also up for reelection. In September he braved the yellow fever and went to Philadelphia to urge Nicholson to pay the $30,000 or return under arrest, thus ensuring his reelection, which would be a boon to the speculators. Nicholson did like Boone, and Morris soon found that he was a prince among men. He happened to be standing at his window when Boone approached his house. The sheriff took umbrage at the typical surly comments of one of those denied entrance. "That man," Morris wrote to Nicholson, "has feelings that do honor to human nature." In return, the speculators strung him along with promises and trusted the trustees of the aggregate fund to pay him.

Morris and Nicholson lived on promises and joked about it. Morris told Nicholson that the next time he let a Tunnicliff into his house he should make sure it was a female. Nicholson sent his wife's dying breadfruit plant to Morris, hoping his gardener could cure it. Morris replied that the Nicholsons should not count on getting their daily bread from it. While Nicholson adhered religiously to his voluntary imprisonment, not even letting the yellow fever drive him from his

Philadelphia house, Morris felt safe enough to venture out in public, though always with his son as a lookout for creditors with writs. So it was up to him to meet the trustees and press them to do something for poor Boone.

Morris grew to detest some other federal city duns. Law kept sending complete strangers to press his case. Then, to spite the partners for not paying Carroll for Law's lots, Law released his mortgages on Morris's and Nicholson's property to another creditor so he would have better standing in the attachment cases that continued their slow progress through Maryland courts. Morris called that "inimical and dirty conduct." "Although we suffer much and in many shapes by the derangement of our affairs," Morris taunted Law, "yet we have spirit and vigour enough not to suffer injustice tamely."

Good lawyers and a court system geared to protect debtors tamed most creditors. The trustees were to tame the commissioners and save the Washington property, but they did not, so Morris used his considerable charm to try to get them to pay the commissioners. He also continued to woo Scott to get him to give up forced sales. Scott kept pressing the speculators to take their notes, "a batch of those cursed notes," Morris called them, and give Scott lots. Morris characterized the pressure as "another pluck at our feathers" and protested that they had already been plucked clean.

Morris was joking, but John Ashley came to the same conclusion, and he was not joking. He was the trustee who journeyed to and from Washington city, and the more he saw of it, the less he seemed to like it, or at least he gave Morris that impression. Furthermore, talking with Morris did not make the situation any more understandable. At a meeting with the trustees, Morris pressed them to assume all of his and Nicholson's immediate obligations in the city. Ashley asked how much that entailed. Morris did not know. The trustees began to think highly of Sheriff Boone's suggestion that Nicholson return to the federal city and at least be on the scene to sort out the confusion.

The basic problem, the trustees found, was that they could neither sell nor raise loans on the Washington property because of all encumbrances Greenleaf, Morris, and Nicholson had placed on it to raise money. While Greenleaf's attachments could probably be defeated in court, others who had loaned money to the partners had a stronger case. The trustees had hoped Mordecai Lewis, a Philadelphia merchant, would turn his M & N notes in for certificates of the aggregate fund. He asked the trustees to convey 1,250 Washington lots to him instead. When they did not, he sued.

Morris suggested that the trustees try to sell other property held by the partners that would sell at closer to its value than city lots. The trustees were game and advertised some Virginia and Maryland property. No buyers came forward. Morris blamed the yellow fever. Nicholson finally decided $50,000 would restore order and hope in their Washington affairs. Morris pressed the trustees to raise that money through a loan. They were amenable, provided that Morris and Nicholson come up with the 15 percent premium that would have to be paid to the lender. On their agent Dorsey's advice, the trustees did pay $2,089 to the state of Maryland to end encumbrances on a tract on the Eastern Branch thought to be worth $24,473.

Morris took that as a sign that more support was forthcoming, and he tried to cajole the commissioners into postponing the sale. At the same time he hinted to the trustees that the commissioners were eager for some reasonable arrangement to avoid a sale. He had a brainstorm: forget arrears for the lots, what was needed was money for the public buildings. The trustees should lend money to the commissioners secured by the guarantee of the U.S. government and to be paid off from the money raised by the property of the aggregate fund.

He tried to appeal to Scott's ambition. By getting everyone to work together, he would win honors and "the chief magistrate of the City of Washington will become an important station in a few years." So Scott had to keep Ashley "in good temper . . . but if you once get at points all will be confusion and contest. . . ." Getting money from the trustees was not so necessary as the commissioners seemed to think. The U.S. government had a full Treasury, and Congress would be more willing to pay because the yellow fever made them "afraid of staying in Philadelphia and they can never agree to remove from thence to any other place than the City of Washington."[1]

                              *   *   *

To judge from the scene in Upper Marlboro when freeholders from all of Prince Georges County convened to vote for sheriff, voters were in no mood to save the speculators. When the citizens from the city of Washington arrived at the courthouse, a mob accosted them. A William Pollock was felled by "a brick-bat" and killed by "repeated blows after he had fallen." Boone, who was favored by the city, lost. He blamed his having helped Nicholson.

By October 18 no money had arrived from Philadelphia. The threatened court orders to stop the sale did not materialize. So the bidding began on lots at 14th and I Streets, just two blocks from the president's house square. Twelve of the twenty-two lots sold for less than $80, and the buyers were familiar. Dermott bought seven of the lots and Uriah Forrest five. On the next day, of twelve lots offered eight did not get a bid. The total sales for two days amounted to $3,539. Within sixty days the buyers had to pay one fourth and then would have three years to compelete payment. A year before, Morris and Nicholson had tried to make the average price for one of their lots 25 cents a square foot. At auction, the top price was just over three cents.

On the 20th, a letter from the trustees of the aggregate fund arrived, saying the disruption of the fever in Philadelphia had kept them from responding sooner. They indicated that they would pay the $10,000 and make arrangements with Morris and Nicholson to take care of the rest of the arrears soon. The commissioners decided to make some gesture without relinquishing their right to sell the lots. They decreed that until November 3 they would sell only three lots a day. By then they hoped to have the trustees' plan. There were few bidders. The *Washington Gazette* asked how long the "farce" would continue and wondered, "in case the commissioners should convey property to me which they have no legal right to, who is bound to refund?"[2]

The plan of the trustees was only to wait until Morris and Nicholson came up with something of value to secure a loan. On November 2, a day before the new deadline set by the commissioners, the trustees informed the board that they still could not make any more payments. Morris had offered them lands in Georgia, the Carolinas, and Kentucky as security for a loan. They refused it. As Ashley rudely put it to Morris, "The bubble is up." The trustees decided the only holdings Morris had worth anything were Genesee lands, and creditors in New York, where Morris had been declared an outlaw, had already claimed those.   Ashley's words so stunned Morris that he let letters from Scott, Forrest, and the commissioners lie on his table unanswered for weeks. Although he would continue to go through the motions of trying to save his Washington property and pay his debts there, he knew all was lost. At least he went down with a rhetorical flourish. "I wish to God I had the same command of money as formerly," he wrote to Scott; "I would make the City of Washington flourish by my own exertions but the devil of it is that men who use money lose the command of it and it gets into the hands of *hold fast* who never parts with it, unless to squeeze more out of some poor hungry devil or another." To save face, Morris accused the trustees of duplicity, claiming he had made a deal with Ashley only to be told by the rest that Ashley had no power to make the deal. To get revenge, he did what he could to torment the author of his troubles.

Greenleaf had not been inactive while Morris was trying to save himself. He prompted Sylvanus Bourne, who had returned to the United States, to attach Morris's and Nicholson's Washington property on behalf of the Dutch bankers. Greenleaf also ducked creditors by letting the sheriff take him to the Prune Street debtors' prison, from which he petitioned for protection under the state insolvency law. Greenleaf entered jail on the strength of only one small suit, easily satisfied, so he hoped his penance would last but a month or two. Morris got wind of that, dredged up some old debt to him that Greenleaf had never technically covered, and sicced his lawyers on him. The gentlemen of the bar came up with a better stratagem. To get a divorce from his Dutch wife, Greenleaf had claimed citizenship in Rhode Island. Since he was not a citizen of Pennsylvania, he could not take advantage of its insolvency law and post bail for his freedom, but must languish in prison for six months.[3]

*   *   *

The last warm days of autumn were not cherished in 1797. In the federal city the first frost would be reason enough to dismiss most of the workers. In Philadelphia the frost would end the contagion. As in 1793, some doubted that Congress could safely convene in Philadelphia. Unlike the Virginians, Adams did not worry about where to move. The only place that could accommodate Congress was New York. A law passed in 1794 gave him the power to convene Congress elsewhere if the seat of government was made unhealthy by disease. Adams told his advisors that he was not loath to use that power despite "the loud snarling among the inhabitants of the foul dens in Philadelphia" that the decision would occasion. The fever abated in time.

On the night of November 15, the frost along the Potomac was bad enough to justify the board ordering the bricklaying and stone-setting to stop. Workers covered the unfinished walls of the Capitol. Everyone walked away from the work with a sense of accomplishment. The freestone of the outer walls had been raised 36 feet, up to the capitals, and the brickwork inside the walls 35 feet, to the roof. The stone wall stood 57 feet high, the brick 56. The unfinished flooring had been laid in twelve rooms and four of the galleries. At the president's house all the stonework was done save for the balustrade, the party walls were bricked, and chimneys were carried to the roof, which was covered and ready to be slated. The gutters were almost completed, and the inside work was "in great forwardness." In the past six months the board had spent $28,569 on the Capitol and $13,881 on the president's house. Hoban estimated that it would cost $54,783 to finish the president's house. Hadfield estimated it would cost $46,762 to finish the north wing of the Capitol. Only $13,000 worth of stonework at both buildings was left.

Carpenters to do the interior work moved to the forefront and began jockeying for position. Chafing at favoritism shown to Irish carpenters by Hoban and his foreman Pierce Purcell, those who were not Irish raised allegations that Hoban's and Purcell's slaves were getting paid too much, whereas many white carpenters were getting nothing, and that lax supervision of the public stores had led to paint and timber being stolen. In response, the board ordered that "no negro carpenter or apprentice be hired at either of the public buildings." They also fired Pierce Purcell, the head carpenter at the president's house, as well as the man who had charge of the public stores. Collen Williamson was so thrilled at seeing the associates of his rival fall that he wrote to President Adams, describing how Hoban's men had stolen enough material to build five or six houses for themselves. The old Scot attacked the blacks and Irish in general. The ten or twelve blacks drawing wages for Hoban and company could not do the work of two good hands. Because Hoban hired all "the Irish vagbons . . .," there is nothing here but fighting, lying and stealing."[4]

*   *   *

All the fury could not distract the commissioners from their main problem, the lack of money. In November they had $109.76 on hand. On November 9 they stopped the farcical sale of lots, which had raised only $4,539, and gave the trustees two weeks to come up with a payment plan. None was forthcoming, so they informed the trustees of the aggregate fund that they would advertise on January 1 for a sale on March 1, which finally got another $10,000 payment. Not enough.

The board asked the president to renew their power to get a loan from Maryland, explaining that "notwithstanding the most rigid economy our money is entirely exhausted, and we are considerably in arrears to the mechanics and others." In case the loan from Maryland failed, they prepared a memorial that the president could present to Congress. With George Washington in retirement they no longer had to subscribe to the fiction that no federal help would be needed. They argued that a review of the Constitution and several acts of Congress proved that Congress was "bound" to complete the public buildings. Given the war in Europe and "the general distress and depreciation" of property, they had not been able to get a loan in Europe or sell lots. The buildings, "now far advanced, are on plans approved by the late President and they were carried on under his direction. . . . Can Congress refuse to finish them? . . . Even a debate on the subject, would occasion uneasy sensations."

The president did not sign off on the authorization to get a loan. He sent it to his secretary of state with questions, to elucidate some finer legal points, and then forgot about it. He was busy, and every time the federal city surfaced in his affairs it presented some problem. Samuel Davidson sent up a memorial contending "that at this day there is no *real* fixed plan for the City of Washington." Once again he went over how Ellicott diminished the size of the president's house square and contended that the plan being executed "is as variant from the engraved plan, as the engraved plan is from the original." He disclaimed any desire to litigate the matter for fear that that would tend "to lessen the confidence of the public in the stability of everything respecting the city." He asked the president to appoint three men to look quietly into his claim. The president did nothing about that either. The commissioners, however, had to take Davidson seriously because he convinced the trustees, Beall and Gantt, who had held the deeds to the city's land since 1791, not to convey the public lands to the commissioners, as instructed by President Washington, until the rights of the proprietors had been assured.

The noise from the city that did elicit presidential reaction was a series of articles in the *Gazette* attacking him. Their scurrility did not alarm him as much as that they appeared in a city he thought friendly. Indeed, he thought his nephew had some say in the *Gazette*'s policy. Abigail inquired, and Cranch explained that he had only lent the editor some money long ago and that the paper had no standing in the community. Then in a postscript Cranch added that many in the city were not happy with the president. "I have heard complaint made," he wrote to his aunt, "that the President neglects the interests of the city—that he does not answer the letters from the commissioners & c." on December 5 the president authorized the commissioners to get a loan from Maryland or "wherever you find it." If they failed to get a loan he was agreeable to going to Congress.[5]

*   *   *

The commissioners were pessimistic. Other parts of the state had caught on and wanted loans for their pet projects. Such was their pessimism that they looked to Virginia for help. Henry Lee thought that if Jefferson wrote to the governor "perhaps money could be obtained." Lee suggested that if Maryland built a "hotel" for the use of its congressmen, Virginia "would probably do so too." Then, just before Christmas, the commissioners got a present. The Maryland House passed a loan bill with the tie-breaking vote of the speaker. The state Senate then passed the bill without opposition. Scott suggested to his colleagues that they try to sell $30,000 or $40,000 of the $100,000 worth of stock to "relieve the sufferings of our deserving creditors as soon as possible." Scott did not write to the president, but he did share the good news with George Washington.[6]

1798

65. Languishing in a Loathsome Prison

The commissioners had been going out of their way to be service-able to the retired president. When Washington needed a mason at Mount Vernon they sent one from the public works. To encourage Washington to build, they had the square he had bought resurveyed so he got as much land as possible. But building on Peter's Hill next to one granddaughter was made problematic by the importunings of the husband of his other granddaughter. Law tried to lure him to build near the Capitol, where there was such a lack of private buildings. Washington did wish that more buildings had been finished so that if yellow fever drove Congress from Philadelphia they could come to the federal city, and he agreed to subscribe to a tavern Law wanted to build there, but he begged off doing any building himself because he had already spent $22,000, which he had raised by selling his Pennsylvania lands, in reestablishing himself at Mount Vernon.

The city needed Washington to do more than build. With Adams slow to answer their letters, the commissioners looked to Washington for guidance. Even with another $100,000 worth of stock at their disposal, they could not assure enough funds to carry on the buildings through 1798. They still needed a loan from Congress. Yet they had told Adams that success in Maryland would obviate the need to go to Congress. So they got Washington's blessing first and then explained the predicament to the president.

With debts of $36,632.58 for wages and materials, plus interest payments on the Maryland loans amounting to $12,000, plus the annual expenses of the commissioners' office, surveyors, hospital, and so on amounting to $13,176.92, they would have only $22,190.50 left of the $82,000 they could raise from the Maryland stock. That was not enough to continue the Capitol and president's house through the season, not to mention beginning the executive offices, which Lovering estimated with much economizing on Hadfield's design, would cost around $48,000 each. Although $68,571.43 was due them for lots purchased, they could not count on punctual payment. So in six months they would be out of money, with no state legislature in session to bail them out.

Adams was not quick to reply. White left Georgetown on January 20 for Philadelphia but not before writing a note to Washington complaining that he could wait no longer for the president's decision.[1]

*   *   *

For the two men who would gain the greatest glory from the work, Thornton and Hadfield, completion of the north wing of the Capitol would not be an occasion for mutual satisfaction. It would better secure Thornton's claim as architect of the building not to have the trained architect finish it. For Hadfield time was running out to put his stamp on the building.

To prove to all that he had designed the building, Thornton planned to make drawings fit for publication. He told friends about the project, but other matters, such as plans for a steamboat boiler, kept getting in the way. It proved a convenient distraction, for Thornton discovered that there were advantages to having Hadfield make drawings so that he could criticize them, rather than vice versa. To judge from an October letter he wrote to a friend in England, Thornton was very mindful of the malice of trained architects toward him. "I worked day and night at [designing] the Capitol. I finished, and obtained the prize against a world of competitors: some regularly bred architects. I went at once to the highest order— viz. the Corinthian. I was attacked by Italian, French and English— I came off, however, victorious."

With the walls of the north wing of the Capitol almost completed, it was time to plan the roof. Thornton did not hand his colleagues a drawing but expressed a fear that Hadfield might not be up to it and, to make it easier to effect proper drainage, might raise the top of the roof so that it was above the balustrade. The board asked Hadfield for his plan for the roof. The young architect assured them that it would not rise above the balustrade even though he felt that having it a foot or two above would be imperceptible, and "some advantage would be gained in the interior of the building." Thornton asked him what the angle of the roof would be. Hadfield, according to Thornton, said he did not know. Thornton suggested he get a "protactor," and "he knew not was meant."

Convinced that Hadfield was incompetent, the amateur architect insisted that Hadfield had botched the cornices. In his revision of Thornton's design, Hadfield had increased the diameter of the pilasters. When the board rejected his revision, he forgot to reduce the width of the pilasters to the size Thornton wanted, and as a result the medallions were distributed unevenly. The medallions, executed after a drawing by Hadfield, were defective because the rose was too small by an inch and three quarters and thus was "not in proportion recommended by Sir Wm. Chambers in his work on architecture which is admitted to be a work inestimable in its way."

Thornton asked the board to correct the mistakes, which Blagden estimated would cost $1,100. Hadfield also used the good offices of Blagden to justify his handling of the pilasters, arguing that the master mason had agreed that, given the length of the walls, some adjustments had been necessary and some asymmetry inescapable. White and Scott decided against Thornton only on the grounds of cost. Their colleague was not a good loser and entered a "protest" in the minutes, averring that the cornices "will remain forever a laughing stock to architects."[2]

*   *   *

The board reacted to the *Gazette*'s attacks on the president by no longer sending ads to the newspaper. To retaliate, the *Gazette* began a series of attacks on the board in the form of parodies of the Old Testament ridiculing the commissioners: "Book III Chap. 26. 12. And URIAH went unto the three men, and said, sell me I pray ye, a lot of land bordering on the water. 13. And the thing pleased the three men." Then "THOMAS heard what was done, he was very wroth, and he came unto them and cursed, and took the name of the Lord his God in vain.'' In Book VI Scott was held up for scorn: ''And many said that he also had taken of the materials for building the house of the chief ruler and for the officers chosen by the people.'' The commissioners did not reply to the insinuations. When subscriptions were canceled the editor, Benjamin More, retorted that he had not set out to attack the city but only to tell the truth. His last issue came out on March 24.[3]

*   *   *

The ''Old Manuscript'' had also noted the ''famine in the land.'' Only Isaac Polock seemed to have money. At a sale of some of Greenleaf's waterside property at the end of 1st Street West (today's Buzzard Point) and East 10th Street, he bought ten lots for $3,711. But for most proprietors it was still a time for protecting what they had, not expanding. David Burnes and Daniel Carroll prepared for the hard times that winter by placing ads in the newspapers warning people not to take wood from their land. Burnes also warned people ''from hunting with dog or gun,'' which earned him no respect from folks who could not be taught to read, for he soon accused ''Peter, Jonah, Moses and Ester'' of theft and receiving stolen goods.

Dr. John Crocker sold all of his mahogany furniture as well as medicines and vials to pay debts. Prentiss's wife asked Nicholson what she was to do without money and with a sick thirteen-month-old baby and her husband in jail miles away. Other retainers of Morris and Nicholson fared better. Tunnicliff auctioned off more of Nicholson's property and felt prosperous enough to buy a lot next to the Capitol. Lovering managed to earn some money by being hired by the trustees of the aggregate fund to watch the wood on Greenleaf's land across the Eastern Branch. Cranch, who had once planned to turn that land into a farm, studied law. Greenleaf, however, was his sole client.

Noah Webster was still trying to disabuse the Greenleaf clan of their belief in James's worth and character, suggesting that any security he offered for loans was ''mere moonshine.'' Cranch retorted that James ''has been dear to the heart of every one of us, in whose prosperity we have rejoiced, in whose benevolence we have felt pride, and in whose many virtues we have often exalted.'' James was then ''languishing in a loathsome prison.''

Prune Street, however, did not take the spunk out of Greenleaf. On January 18 he asked President Adams for a federal job in Philadelphia. In February he summoned Cranch to his prison room, told the young man that he, Cranch, stood to lose $3,000 to $4,000 on Greenleaf's account, and asked him, when the time was right, to mention that federal job to his uncle.[4]

Cranch had another door to knock on at Prune Street. Morris was too much the man of the world to stay cooped up in his house like Nicholson. Morris tried to work on the sympathy of the sheriff to let him go out without fear of arrest. But with several judgments against Morris, pressure from creditors grew. The only way he could save something for his family was to give up his person. On February 16 Morris was taken to Prune Street, bearing debts which were later calculated at $2,948,711.11.

When Prune Street had been but a threat, Morris had been sure that if confined there he would lose the will to carry on any business. But creditors came banging on the flimsy door of his room, which was not really his. ''I sleep in another person's bed,'' he complained to Nicholson, ''I occupy other peoples' rooms, and if I attempt to sit down to write it is at the interruption and inconvenience of some one who has acquired a prior right thereto.'' He talked with his archenemy Greenleaf only once, and he joked to Nicholson, ''He thinks that a man who gave *nine millions* of property to his creditors ought to be liberated and you will probably think so too as I do, But.''

For the most part he bore up, but then came the men whom he had persuaded to lend him money on Washington lots the year before. They begged more security to keep the loan at the bank from being called. The best Morris could do was offer James Dunlop 33,333 ⅔ acres of Georgia lands and Kentucky lands to Forrest. To his embarrassment, he broke down when Dunlop called. ''My feelings were on the rack,'' he explained to Nicholson, ''and I could not help showing too much of them to him.''

Nicholson maintained a fearful freedom. Around Christmastime he was sure Cranch, Lovering, Tunnicliff, and Boone had sent a special constable after him. Instead, Boone begged an opportunity just "to talk to you thro the window," pleading, "I am miserable and unhappy indeed." Nicholson continued trying to hatch plans to save the day. Morris jeered at him, "My friend you feed hope on the most slender diet of any man I know.⁵

66. Beautiful Warblings Enrapture the Ear

In Philadelphia Alexander White did not expect to pick up where he had left off two years before. He gave up on Morris and Nicholson, did not know if the president would be glad to see him, and realized that only fourteen members of the fifth Congress had served with him in the first. And it was a rancorous Congress. Matthew Lyon, a Vermont republican, spat on Roger Griswold, a Connecticut Federalist, after Griswold asked him if he had won a wooden sword for cowardice during the war. The spraying happened by the fireplace off the floor just before the House convened on January 30. The House was soon embroiled in an investigation and a debate over how to discipline Lyon. Nevertheless, White was encouraged by Federalist control of both houses, and the administration program of taxes, a navy, and a strong central government seemed not incompatible with a grand new capital.

The president, who was expecting White, had a new memorial from the commissioners. He had instructed them to rewrite it so that it would be from them to Congress, not to the president. White did not like the change and argued that it was important to have the president directly involved. Adams countered that the memorial submitted in 1796 was from the commissioners to Congress. He did let White prepare a message to Congress to accompany the memorial. Two days later White called on Adams again and proposed making "a small alteration" to state that the president had authorized the memorial. An argument began. Adams wanted White to send it back for his colleagues to change and sign. White countered that the alteration was not of "sufficient consequence to justify the delay." Adams replied that "while the House was engaged in the business of Lyon" any memorial from the commissioners would meet "an unfavorable reception."

White did not get the president's insinuation and pressed him to state in his message that he had reviewed the memorial and "deemed it deserving the consideration of congress." Adams had a short fuse, and it went off, as he snapped that "he would do what his official duty required of him and no more" and that if Lyon "were not expelled the seat of government would be in New York." Eastern members would not "be tyranized over by Giles and such men." White described that scene to the former president, "I was astonished . . ." but "restrained my feelings."[1]

That the president, even in anger, would hazard the federal city because he disliked the rabble-rousing tactics of Giles was disturbing enough, but then as White began chatting with members of Congress he was stunned to find that Uriah Forrest and Thomas Law had brought their war to Philadelphia. At first he ascribed the amazing misconceptions some members had about the city, such as that "the President's house and the Capitol stand four miles apart," to the traditional enemies of the city. Then he learned that Forrest was retailing the information "that the President's house had been from the beginning . . . calculated for the accommodation of Congress." Forrest even passed around an estimate made by Hoban that it would cost only $12,000 to ready the president's house for Congress.

Law alerted members that Forrest and Commissioner Scott held a mortgage on $120,000 worth of lots near Georgetown. He urged members to thwart self-serving designs by having "a small house erected near the Capitol for the residence of the President" as well as for the executive offices and by "making a judiciary of the President's house." The friends of Georgetown had a counterinsinuation against Law. He was a pro-French schemer who "discouraged persons, some of property, from coming to settle in the city because they preferred another part to that where he was."

Law's shenanigans did not faze White, since he had long ago stopped taking Law seriously. Forrest, however, a former member of Congress himself, gave the impression that he had been sent by the commissioners, and indeed, he had a letter from Scott and Thornton urging him "to expedite your intended journey to Philadelphia as fast as possible, and . . . to interest yourself to forward by every means in your power the objects of Mr. White's mission." White pointedly asked his colleagues what was going on. Meanwhile, he made his rounds of the members and found that all seemed to want to go to the federal city "if they can be accommodated." No one seemed to agree with White's argument that the Congress was obliged to see the public buildings completed. White quizzed the Virginia and Maryland members and found an alarming degree of pessimism. Brent, who had managed the loan bill through committee in 1796, was "much indisposed" to take an active part. Attorney General Lee thought getting a loan impossible. "Upon the whole," White wrote to his colleagues, "if I had expected the difficulties I now expect, I should have been against applying to Congress at this time."

After the "astonishing" interview, the president made a point of assuring White of his support for the city and his high regard for the decisions of his predecessor, which was a timely expression because he had just scandalized the nation by declining an invitation to the Birthday Ball on February 22. He was miffed (although he did not say so publicly) that it was not his birthday being celebrated. Adams had another reason to rethink his damning the federal city to spite Virginians supporting Lyon. The day after Adams had shouted at White, Griswold had caned Lyon.

On February 23 the memorial was read in the House and referred to committee. Citing an estimated cost of $96,792 for the executive offices, $98,545 to finish the president's house and north wing of the Capitol, and a rough estimate of $100,000 for the as yet unplanned judiciary, the commissioners asked that the president be allowed to draw up to $300,000 to complete the public buildings. The sums needed were "too inconsiderable to be felt at the Treasury," which, thanks to Federalist taxes, promised to be full. Moreover, such a commitment by Congress would show its good faith to Virginia, Maryland, and individual citizens who, through grants of money and sales of property, had contributed $774,296.58 to prepare the city for the reception of Congress.[2]

*   *   *

Farrell, the bricklayer, and Hadfied squared off again. The Irishman accused Hadfield of ruining the chimneys. If his lateral chimney flues were not changed, "the principal room in the house will be full of smoke." Redmond Purcell, foreman of the carpenters and brother of Pierce, accused Hadfield of making poor plans and preparations for the roof. Purcell told the commissioners that he had asked Hadfield "whether he intended to have diagonal rafters framed or not, how the gutters were to be regulated, also whether the ceiling joists was to be connected to the roof. . . . His answer as usual was very dissatisfactory, that he expected paper from Philadelphia; that he had to encounter many such affairs since he come to the city, and he would not be hurried to it."

The board gave Hadfield a copy of Purcell's letter, and he told the board that the accusations were false and that he would lay before them the drawing of the roof the next morning. Although he forgave Purcell for his "unprovoked enmity," he thought harmony essential and asked for a new foreman. As the board set about investigating the matter, the *Gazette*'s "Old Manuscript" described the attempt of "the chief artificer in wood" to "hurt" the "overseer," who was an "upright man, and just in his dealings." The artificer made accusations against the overseer and, to back them up, told all who worked for him that "he who is among you, who will not say when he is enquired of by the three men the words which I shall tell unto to him—I will be his enemy, and he shall no longer work on the house designed for the chief rulers."

That did not intimidate Purcell, who threatened to sue the *Gazette* for libel. To show the true colors of Hadfield, who had boasted of being willing to forgive his accuser, Purcell gave the board names of witnesses who would testify that Hadfield had told Purcell that he would be "tied up and whipped and after that turned out of the yard." Hadfield in turn got depositions from men explaining how Purcell and Farrell had spread the rumor that ten feet of wall had to be taken down to fix chimneys and that Hadfield's plan for the roof had been condemned. Hadfield admitted that some adjustments would have to be made to a wall near a beam "but the work of two hours would place it right." The board censured Hadfield for using "improper language."[3]

*   *   *

Scott thought he had solved the lumber problem when Littleton Dennis, the brother of a Maryland congressman, agreed to procure all the lumber the board needed. But the board's habit of ordering supplies in the winter for spring delivery did not suit the Eastern Shore of Maryland. Dennis warned of late deliveries of plank because "our swamps are so wet it is difficult at this season to haul stocks out of them." So Scott fell for the old siren song of Henry Lee and contracted for one hundred stocks of white oak to be delivered in six weeks.

In mid-February there was the annual mishap at the quarries. A ship loaded with 40 tons of stone for both the commissioners and Daniel Carroll sunk in 10 or 12 feet of water just off the Aquia wharf. Blagden needed stone for the architraves and balustrade of the Capitol. Because of the delay, the stonecutters at the Capitol worked only seventeen days in March. Carroll was stymied in his attempt to put the finishing touches on his country estate that filled a whole square six blocks from the Capitol, but not in any streets.

The commissioners were in the unenviable position of wanting to hurry the work, in case Congress should flee Philadelphia, and yet not to spend too much, with their fund so uncertain. Their solution was more slaves. They ordered Elisha Williams to hire ten more laborers, bringing the total crew up to eighty-five. In Philadelphia, White was to get the wage rates for skilled labor there, which they were sure were lower than what they paid, thus justifying a general wage cut.[4]

* * *

Upset by all the talk of the city lacking accommodations, someone decided to make the most of it, lauding Washington's rural character in an article in the *Boston Gazette:* ". . . the trees diffusing their variegated foliage by the banks of the Potowmack, increase the rural scene; add to this, the tuneful echoes of the groves, captivate the attention and add to the delightful scene—the feather'd choristers with their beautiful warblings enrapture the ear. . . ." Other boosters made much of progress at Barry's wharf. Piercy finished his sugar bakery, and in late February a sloop from Baltimore arrived with sugar to be refined.

For the men who had once worked for Morris and Nicholson, there was no spring. "There seems to be nothing but distress here," Lovering wrote to Nicholson on March 30, "nothing to do and all confidence at an end." The price of a ticket in Blodget's second lottery, which continued to be drawn in desultory fashion, rose to $13.18 from its original $8.[5]

* * *

Nicholas King, the surveyor, was joined by his father, Robert, also a surveyor. With ambitions not satisfied by a salaried job dividing squares, Nicholas resigned so his father could take his place. Nicholas passed on his journal, a compendium of the egregious idiocies of the city, to his father. For example, he noted that early in 1797 the board ordered him to survey Piercy's lot, which extended into the water. King asked Scott and White how far it should go. Scott said as far as King wished. King replied that he had not a wish about it. White said it should extend out to the line of New Jersey Avenue. About 60 feet, Scott thought. King then bumped into Dermott and mentioned the instructions. The Irishman quipped, "The board did not for half an hour know their own minds." They had told him something quite different, only 28 feet.

Robert King soon discovered the board's fear of bearing any expense for drainage. Asked to drive stakes into a lot at 12th and F

Streets Northwest to show the owner what level the streets there would be (if they were ever graded), Robert King wondered what was to be done about the creek running through it creating a gully as many as eight feet deep. King identified six squares from 11th and K to 9th and Pennsylvania that had to be divided so that the creek would coincide with the interior alleys, which could then be covered. The commissioners did not react to the problem, having long since become comfortable with the idea that lotholders would solve such problems themselves.

The Kings applauded one change in the surveying department. The new year began without Dermott in it. His dismissal generated no documents which have remained. In a letter he wrote in 1802, Robert King noted that Dermott was dismissed "for misconduct." King then described how he was left "unravelling the bewildered state of the proprietors accounts. . . ." "Much had been committed to memory, and most of the documents relative to the proprietors lines, [had] been taken from the office by Mr. Dermott, who claimed them as his own! Saying that he had taken the references to the proprietors lines in his own time [after office hours]." Adding to the confusion was that Ellicott and his successors had "committed a great number of errors, so that lots cannot be laid out with certainty without remeasuring each square." The official map of the city, as far as the commissioners were concerned was the one made by Dermott who left little documentation of his work.

*   *   *

Late that winter William Deakins died. "Amidst a sordid world," Cranch wrote to his aunt, "he is almost the only man I have met with here whose actions seemed to flow from the impulses of his heart. And yet he was so far engaged in business that he supported almost the whole commerce and credit of Georgetown and its vicinity. He left no children, but he has left a thousand mourners. There was no man in this neighborhood so universally loved and respected."[6]

67. The Negroes Alone Work

The commissioners' memorial had rough going in committee thanks not to the enemies of the city but to its friends. William Craik, who represented Georgetown, proved himself such a tool of Uriah Forrest that he supported only a $100,000 appropriation. With less money available, it would make more sense for Congress to sit in the president's house. Thomas Sprigg, who represented the federal city, urged that the $100,000 be spent to finish the north wing and erect temporary housing for the president and executive offices near the Capitol. Craik, "with great warmth," said that would break faith with the proprietors, and if faith had to be broken, it made more sense to center the government at the president's house, since that building was almost completed. He urged that members be sent to investigate the site.

Rather than get that involved in the dispute, the committee decided it was best to stick with the original plan. They recommended an appropriation of $200,000, in three installments, to finish the north wing, the president's house, and the executive offices. A building to house the five members of the Supreme Court could wait. The committee asked White to write their report. He upped the estimate for finishing the north wing and the president's house to $120,000 and decided $80,000 would do for the executive offices.

White was heartened that the bill was an appropriation rather than a loan but he knew the committee's support for the bill was shallow. Benjamin Goodhue, a Massachusetts Federalist, told White that while Congress was obliged to go to the Potomac in 1800, it was not obliged to stay. Goodhue was thought to be the "oracle" of President Adams. White went to the president once again, not only to ascertain if Goodhue was speaking for him, but to enlist Adams in easing passage of the bill. A number of members warned him that if Congress appropriated money for the city, it would have to say what that money was to be used for "unless the President's sentiments on the subject were previously known." To White's relief, the president made clear that he wanted the big mansion. He did not mind the distances. He "could go a mile and an half whenever his duty required his meeting the legislature." But he thought the executive offices should be near the Capitol for the convenience of congressmen and to "encourage the necessary building convenient to the Capitol." White had learned not to argue with the president, and he respected Adams's power over the New England members. So he felt his colleagues out about going along with the president, if it meant getting $200,000. He hit on the idea of temporarily putting the executive offices in the south wing of the Capitol and making the west side of the center building, the conference room, into the chamber for the House. To soothe Thornton, he argued that "the superb and elegant building will not be finished during the present age unless it is appropriated to some useful purpose."

White's deference to the president's ideas did not surprise his colleagues. Craik had sounded the alarm that White was forsaking Georgetown. Scott and Thornton decried any changes in the plan, telling White that "no true friend of the city" would encourage any alterations. As for putting the executive offices in the south wing of the Capitol, that was unworkable because "the foundation walls of that part of the building have been much questioned, and have not yet been well examined." In addition, the unfinished north wing had already cost $229,223.97. Materials for it had been bought when they were cheap, so the south wing would cost more. To simply complete the present buildings and build the executive offices would cost only $200,000. Davidson and Peter wrote to the president, informing him that back in 1791, before the deed of trust had been signed, President Washington had fixed the site of the executive offices next to the president's house.

George Washington also wrote to White in support of the plan. He thought the proprietors, with their feuding, were among the city's "worst enemies." "Nothing short of insanity can remove Congress from the building intended for its sittings." He confessed that he felt it was "a matter of moonshine" where the executive offices should be fixed. He had put them where he did because the cabinet needed to have daily intercourse with the president.

White was rather peeved at being accused of wanting to change the plan. Meanwhile, however, the House acted just as White wished. The Virginia delegation agreed to unite behind a bill to simply give the commissioners $200,000 to complete the buildings true to the plans of the former president. Giles warned that once the bill passed he would set about seeing that a president would never live in the grandiose president's house.

Despite Edward Livingston of New York comparing the city "to the sandy deserts of Arabia," House passage came quickly, without a recorded vote. Thomas Law took the House action as complete victory. "Washington City must now rise rapidly," he wrote. Scott and Thornton worried White with arrangements for the quickest way to get the appropriated money to the city. They thought getting the tax money deposited in Alexandria and Baltimore transferred directly to the city would be best. They also reminded White of the campaign to lower wages, "as it is high time to take up the subject here." They needed to know how little Philadelphia workers got.

White did not take Senate passage for granted and indeed found opposition "so formidable" that he asked his colleagues if it was best just to take $66,666.66, a year's worth of the money, and leave it at that. On April 2 the Senate took up the bill and promptly amended it to $66,666.66 for one year. On the next day, James Hillhouse, a Federalist from Connecticut, reminded his colleagues of the loan guarantee and suggested that the government merely lend the city $100,000, to be guaranteed by the U.S. government. He preferred that course because "the guarantee bill was particularly guarded so as not to implicate the government of the U. States as being ultimately liable to finish the buildings." Even senators who, the day before, had spoken in favor of a $200,000 grant, liked a loan. The Senate postponed discussion so an amendment along those lines could be prepared.

Back in the federal city, the commissioners were of the "decided opinion" that a $66,666 grant was better than a $100,000 loan that used up their authority to borrow. They were sure they could get a $100,000 loan elsewhere. But that advice came too late to guide White. He thought he had the votes to pass either a loan or a $66,666 grant. Yet he could not be sure because senators would not "gratify" him "so far as to say so." Uncertain that a $100,000 loan could be raised elsewhere, he told friends of the city to support "that measure which they judge most safe." The path of least resistance was the loan, and an amendment to that effect passed 18 to 9. White thought final passage of the bill was assured but not before Pennsylvania's senators, Ross and Bingham, criticized the $100,000 loans from Maryland that were worth only $82,000. "The liberality of that state," White reported, was "held up in a high style of sarcastic ridicule." Some Virginians came up with an explanation of how $200,000 appropriated by the usually stingy House had been pared down to a $100,000 loan by the Senate. Adams's frugality had got the better of him. Since Congress refused to raise his salary, he was loath to occupy a house he could not afford, and so had his minions in the Senate cheapen the bill. Digesting such reports back in Virginia, where he was taking a brief respite from public life, Madison alerted Jefferson to the effect Adams's disdain for the Potomac would have on the upcoming presidential election. His "dislike of the City of Washington will cause strong emotions."[1]

*   *   *

When White returned to the federal city, he quickly patched things up with Scott and Thornton. They had to muster some unity because they were much on their own. Congress did not tell them what to do, and White knew firsthand how dangerous it was to let the temperamental president decide anything. They had to work out a compromise of sorts among themselves. Given his personal stake in the city, Scott could not see the president's house abandoned. White stayed on the board only because of his commitment to the dreams of George Washington. He had no personal stake in the city, nor did he want to have one. Washington had instructed them to devote everything to the Capitol, so that was what White wanted done. Thornton should have been drawn to the Capitol, but his jealousy of Hadfield solved the dilemma. Expansion of the Capitol with Hadfield still around was premature.

The commissioners reached their compromise by pledging to fulfill the last commands of George Washington to complete the Capitol first, with one qualification: they would push on with the executive offices next to the president's house. They so informed President Adams, who graciously bowed to their wishes. They asked for bids on the building to be built east of the president's house which would house the Department of the Treasury. White did worry about finding the funds to complete those two buildings. They had $170,000 assured, less than needed for finishing all of the buildings by any calculation. Scott assured him that money would come from Morris's and Nicholson's lots, especially if the attorney general reaffirmed their right to sell and thus assured buyers of their rights to the property. White had doubts but did agree that money could be saved in their operations. He had come back with evidence that their workers were overpaid.[2]

*   *   *

White learned that masons in Philadelphia made 9 shillings a day. So the commissioners refused to give the customary raise to 13 shillings for summer work. They told the masons they were lucky to get their winter rate of 10 shillings. Twenty-one stonecutters at the Capitol and nine at the president's house, as well as the five stonecarvers, gave notice that they would quit unless paid as they had been the year before. They disputed the figures White had sent down from Philadelphia, complaining that along with the daily wage, stoneworkers there and in Baltimore and New York got a supplement for the amount of work done, measured by the foot, which brought their wages up to the level workers on the public buildings were getting. One of the men at the president's house recalled that the late commissioner Carroll had promised them a month's notice if wages were lowered, which had not been given.

As soon as they got the petitions, the commissioners fired the thirty stonecutters effective May 1 but were not so rash with the more essential stonecarvers. White wrote to his informant in Philadelphia, urging him to send down as many men who would work for nine shillings a day as he could. The board asked Blagden to estimate how many stoneworkers would be needed at each site. Blagden thought sixteen at the Capitol and twelve at the president's house could get the job done. Not that he supported the board's rash dismissals. He began to effect a compromise by persuading the board that no one would leave work paying nine shillings a day to take up the same wage. The board agreed that the new workers should get ten shillings and six pence as a base and more for greater skill. That, at least, was more than the winter wage of ten shillings. They still refused to hire the men they had just fired.

Then word came from Philadelphia that men would come down only after they saw a written offer. On the day that this less than encouraging news arrived, Hadfield alerted the board that the stonecutters wanted "to make an accommodation," which Hadfield thought "wise" to accept, so that work on the Capitol would not be stopped. The commissioners did not fire the workers after all, the workers accepted the new wage rates, and half got 12 shillings or 12 shillings, 6 pence, more than the base and only slightly less than the old rate of 13. The carpenters were already making just 9 shillings a day. To effect savings there, the board decided that 9 shillings should be "the worth of the best" and asked Hoban and Hadfield to dock the rest, trusting that "some cannot be worth beyond half that." No wages were docked.[3]

During this contretemps, a Polish exile visiting the city took more pains than the usual visitor to observe the workers. Julian Niemcewicz noted that the workers began at six o'clock in the morning, had an hour for breakfast between eight and nine, an hour for dinner between one and two, and quit at six. It did not impress him as a hard regimen, and he often saw them "quit their work, come into the little dramshop in order to talk while drinking a glass of grog." He described how the Capitol looked on May 14. "A huge scaffolding surrounded it and all around for a considerable distance the ground was covered with huge blocks of . . . stone, some already cut and polished, others yet undressed. [There were] some sheds for cutting the stone and for working on the roof and the framework, some cabins scattered here and there, a shelter for the workers, two or three small shops for liquor and other articles of prime necessity. The top of the edifice was covered with 200 workers, raising the stones by means of machines and placing the first framework of the roof. All were working in silence."

Minds, however, were racing. Hadfield and Purcell were at it again. Hadfield had just excoriated the men working on the roof, finding "great deficiency in the work. . . . The hips are improperly placed, the rafters are improperly notched to receive the purlines, the trimmers are wrong, &c &c. All which is contrary to drawings and directions." Hadfield feared he would lose time correcting it. The attack on Purcell's crew came at an ominous time for the friends of Hoban. On May 12 the board ordered him to stop work at the president's house on June 9, fire five carpenters, and transfer five others and two apprentices to the Capitol. Realizing that he would be looking for work too, Hoban offered to supervise the construction of the Treasury building, which Hadfield had designed. On the day the Pole viewed the works, Hadfield decided to fight for control of the construction of the executive offices.

Hadfield grasped for too much, and Hoban attacked on all fronts. Robert Aull, one of the carpenters sent over from the president's house, intimated to the overseer of slaves at the Capitol, Samuel Smallwood, that he needed to live in the shed near the works used by the laborer who rang the work bell because there was a "scheme" afoot. Smallwood told Hadfield, who asked the overseer to find out more. For his pains, Smallwood was waylaid by Aull, who hit him several times. Smallwood complained to the board not about the "scheme" but about his "situation . . . how do I know but a certain class of peopel may entice even the blackis to commit depredations."

What was up was another attack on Hadfield's design of the roof. Purcell complained that Hadfield had "some of the best men making handspikes, pins &. . . . 19 or 20 men generally at this work, if continued will not be finished these three months—The expense to the public is at least as 7 is to 1, and part of the work I am certain will not answer the purpose."

Hadfield had fended off Purcell before. But at the same time he was at odds with the board over his design for the Treasury. The board wanted contractors to bid on the job, which Hadfield had anticipated. He came up with a pretext to get the design. Then, when the board asked for it back, he refused, saying he would give up the drawing once he was told "in what manner am I to be concerned respecting the execution" of the building, "as I have a just right to claim what belongs to me as the architect who has furnished the design." White and Scott replied that he had no rights in the matter and that the drawings were the property of the United States. Hadfield countered that although he did the design when asked, doing it was not under his contract as superintendent of the works at the Capitol. The design was his property, and he aimed to acquaint the board with rights of architects "that do not appear to be understood in this country." Then he made a dig at Thornton: "I have long since learnt, that it is possible to be deprived of ones own, for the advantage and reputation of others."

The board gave him notice that when his contract expired in three months he would not be rehired. Then it took up the matter of the roof. Only two men in the city, Hoban and Lovering, were qualified to decide if Hadfield's roof would work. The board asked Hoban to inspect the roof. He replied promptly, at least by Thornton's recollection, that Hadfield's design "could never be finished," and, if carried on further, it could not be changed without great expense. It was "more expensive and not as good as the original plan." The board fired Hadfield and put Hoban in charge.

On May 31, just after Hadfield was fired, Niemcewicz visited the Capitol again, at 11:00 A.M. "No one was at work; they had gone to drink grog. This is what they do twice a day, as well as dinner and breakfast. All that makes four or five hours of relaxation. One could not work more comfortably. The negroes alone work."[4]

68. Oh Well, They Can Camp Out

The policy of David Burnes had been not to talk to any buyer who offered less than $350 a lot, but the death of his son, and his own failing health, prompted the fifty-nine-year-old proprietor to sell off most of his lots. William Dorsey, the trustee of the aggregate fund's agent, formed a syndicate of local men to buy 113 lots for $200 each. Polock bought fifty lots for $250 each. Thornton bought thirty-three lots, and a friend of John Tayloe bought ten for $200 each.

Burnes gave them up to six years to complete payment. He turned his lots into an estate of almost $50,000.

The greatest landowners in the country could not raise a dime. ". . . This constant groping in the dark," Morris wrote Nicholson after walking around the Prune Street garden sixty times, "keeping constantly driving on towards ruin by securing, sacrificing, and tying up property without any other view than endless lawsuits and contests, I cannot give into it. . . . I have often reflected on your method of proceeding and must confess it appears to my mind as clear as the sun that you have or will so entangle all your property that you will neither be able to draw subsistence from it, pay debts with it, or even be able to give or obtain clear title for it."

The commissioners looked to the attorney general to assure them clear title and to defeat the insinuations of the trustees' agent that the sales were illegal. Charles Lee reaffirmed the legality of the forced sales, giving the commissioners what they needed to encourage bidders. The only right those who held scrip had was that they were entitled to all money over $80 raised on each lot.

The commissioners scheduled an auction for September 11, just when they expected the crunch for money to begin. They would be using up the first installment of the Treasury loan just as work was beginning in earnest on the Treasury building. The more money they raised, the longer they could hold the stock from Maryland, which was then selling at such a low price.

The winning bid to build the Treasury was comfortably low. Harbaugh, Blagden, Hoban, Lovering, and Polock all made bids for the building, which was to be 140 feet by 57 feet, 6 inches, two stories with fourteen rooms on each floor, primarily of brick but fronted with enough freestone so as not to clash with the president's house. Harbaugh's bid of $39,511, well under Hoban's $56,000, won. (Not until three years later would Harbaugh reveal that in making his winning bid he had miscalculated the building's length by 7½ feet and so deserved more money for his work.)[1]

Such was their confidence in their finances that the commissioners scorned an offer from Polock to buy more than fifty public lots. At the same time they gave Joseph Nourse, registrar of the Treasury, a very good deal when he came shopping for his federal city lots. The board sold him seven lots near 18th Street and New York Avenue for four cents a square foot on the condition that he build. Thornton protested the favorable deal, but White and Scott did not expect "the register of the Treasury of the United States would build a cottage," and they wanted to encourage other federal officials to build their Washington residences.

Having Nourse build near his future office further solidified the development of the area around the president's house. Scott scored another coup when the minister of Portugal came to select the site for his country's ministry and accepted part of the public land just south of the president's house. The Georgetown interests were in the ascendancy. Then President Adams gave the Georgetowners an unexpected boost by appointing Stoddert to be his secretary of the navy.

At first Stoddert declined, pleading the press of his own affairs, which in the main were his yet unfilled dreams of profiting from the federal city. He finally accepted, not unmindful of the help he could give to the city by being in the cabinet. In one of his first letters from Philadelphia, he left instructions to associates on how to manage matters. Stoddert urged them to take advantage of the improved Potomac navigation and the high price of flour by shipping down as much as possible from Hagerstown. Then they should invest their "gains in lots and cheap but good homes, on one of the Avenues leading from Geo Town to the Prests. House."

He thought houses could be built for $4,000 and then rented for up to $1,000 a year. The important thing was to get Peter, Davidson, and Polock "to aim at one street." "I wish one street would be tolerably built up, . . . to secure beyond all possibility of doubt, Congress forever." If Peter laid out $30,000 in houses his estate would be worth $250,000. By building, Davidson could increase his estate to a half million. He thought it possible even to win Law over to build between Georgetown and the president's house. It was "impossible . . . to build the necessary homes about the Capitol. The members of Congress will not trudge through the mud for miles—I am sure therefore, tho I lament it, that the Prest. House must for a time, be the region of Congress."[2]

*   *   *

Stoddert miscalculated when he thought Law might forsake New Jersey Avenue. Law offered to give away lots to men of means who promised to build. In early May he offered General Washington a free lot near the Capitol plus an advance of $5,000 to commence building. Law feared that at the end of the year Congress would send someone to ascertain if there were accommodations being prepared for Congress. So he suggested that Washington "building one house at this crisis would ensure the rapid rise of the city by doing away doubts." As for workmen, "it is charity to employ them," and they, as well as materials, could be had cheaply. Washington still pleaded lack of funds and explained that he already had lots, a square on Peter's Hill for a residence and lots on the Eastern Branch, for commercial purposes. The land was not far from Piercy, who, on May 23, gave Washington two loaves of "double refined sugar."

In late May the Washingtons visited Martha's granddaughters in the city, Mrs. Peter, who lived on the far west end of K Street, and Mrs. Law, who lived on New Jersey Avenue. At the former house the general was diverted by harpsichord music, at the latter billiards. The Pole Niemcewicz recorded some of his conversation. After Peter and Law "discussed at length the difficulty that there would be to finish enough houses to lodge the members [of Congress], Gen. Washington said jokingly, 'Oh well, they can camp out. The Representatives in the first line, the Senate in the second, the President with all his suite in the middle.' "[3]

*   *   *

The former president did what he could to entice the president to make a trip to the city, inviting him to stay at Mount Vernon. Such a meeting would have been convenient, since Adams was about to appoint Washington to command the volunteer army of 10,000, formed to intimidate France. Appointing Washington was the only way Adams could defeat the machination of those who wanted Hamilton to lead the army. But Adams told Washington that a trip south was "uncertain," and news from those parts kept making it more so. He soon had reason to think the federal city was a nest of intrigue best avoided.

The letter Hadfield sent to the president protesting his dismissal has been lost, but he struck chords that piqued the president's interest. Here was a well-connected young Englishman encouraged to come to the federal city by the son of Adams's friend John Trumbull, and he had been summarily fired. Hadfield requested an investigation and also gave the president his drawing of the executive offices. The president had Secretary of State Pickering inform the commissioners that he "would be much more grateful upon a review of the affair, you should think the public service will admit of Mr. Hadfield's return to the station from which he has been discharged or to some other similar employment. . . ."

In their reply, the commissioners were merciless in their denigration of Hadfield. He was "a young man of taste" but "extremely deficient in practical knowledge as an architect." They suffered him to superintend the construction of the Capitol because they trusted the men under him to check his mistakes. "But when the roof of the Capitol was commenced, his want of knowledge became more conspicuous." Such was Hadfield's incompetence that they expressed their "astonishment that Mr. Hadfield should provoke such an investigation: it is strange indeed if he does not know that it will operate to his prejudice." Thornton collected some evidence of Hadfield's incompetence from Hoban: three floors had to be taken up and the elliptical staircase was at risk of falling.

The president was also reminded of the strained relationship between the commissioners and the proprietors. The commissioners asked the president to redo the official acts President Washington had taken on the last day of his administration to make the plan official. They explained that "in the press of business" the actual plan had not been, as stated, attached to the official act of the president. So they sent up the official plan and asked Adams to make it official. At last Adams was able to understand the intimations Davidson and others had made about the uncertainty of the plan of the city. Besides, there was more trouble brewing.

On May 8 the board gave proprietors five months to clear the remaining trees off their land and stop farming that land for which they had been paid £25 an acre. After that "the commissioners will consider themselves at liberty to fell and remove all trees not marked for public use'' and remove fences. Carroll had 119 acres of public land under cultivation and argued that he should be recompensed for it, have the use of it until the public needed it, and be paid £25 plus interest dating from the first sales of public lots on what had been his property. He also threatened to go to court.

Then, in early July, William Duncanson destroyed any chance of a presidential visit. Duncanson had done no more in the city than finish his house above the Eastern Branch. His commercial affairs with his partner James Ray were in suit, and he no longer spoke to Law. Although he had lost considerably by lending money to Morris and Nicholson, like not a few others, he blamed Greenleaf for his troubles. He had a particular grievance. In the days when he was trying to exchange Indian rupees into pounds, Greenleaf helped but the note Greenleaf gave was never paid. Duncanson sued him for nonpayment. Meanwhile, Greenleaf considered Duncanson in debt to him. He was in the same boat as everyone else who had paid Morris and Nicholson for Washington property that Greenleaf still thought was his. Just before going into debtors' prison Greenleaf assigned to Cranch the right to collect what was owed to him in Washington, which Greenleaf estimated at $300,000.

Cranch still thought the world of his brother-in-law. In mid-June he wrote to the president, urging him to give Greenleaf a federal job, claiming he did not have ''a single stain upon his character as a merchant, or as a man of honor and integrity. . . . The integrity of that man must be sound indeed, who can run the career of speculation, without a blemish.'' Greenleaf melted Cranch's heart when speaking about the injustices done to him in the federal city. After all, he had paid $120,000 to the commissioners and spent upward of $140,000 on buildings, bridges, map, and so on. All he had to show for it were the worthless promises of Morris and Nicholson.

Duncanson was not at all moved by Greenleaf's sufferings, and, as he put it, when the suit was served, he ''punished with my horse whip the insolence of . . . Mr. Cranch.''

By all reports, Duncanson was guilty of a breach of peace. The community blamed his notoriously short temper. Abigail Adams dismissed him as ''a ruffian and assassin'' and lamented that her nephew was ''in the only spot in America where from particular circumstances of local and partial views of interest as it respects the federal city, the passions of individuals are excited and their animosity kindled against each other to the interruption of that harmony and friendship, cordiality and freedom of intercourse so desirable in every neighborhood." It was "the very source and hot bed of dissension."[4]

69. I Do Not Sit Here to Be Interrogated

Only one of the boiling disputes in the federal city resolved itself that summer. Hoban reigned supreme. He built his roof on the Capitol, and while Harbaugh built the Treasury, the board gave Hoban 100 guineas to supervise that work too, which meant he made more than the commissioners, $1,866 to their $1,600. Not that Harbaugh had that big an operation, just a crew of nine stonemasons, nine carpenters, nine white laborers, and "Negro Frank." By August Harbaugh had finished enough of the foundation to warrant an inspection. Hoban did not like what he saw, which brought forth a flurry of attestations of the good workmanship. Harbaugh did "most solemnly declare that I have not the least apprehension of the said wall."

The commissioners asked their most trusted employee, Blagden, to inspect the work along with two other masons. They found the outer walls too weak to support the building because of poor mortar. The inner walls were better, except that stones were placed on edge, which saved stone but weakened the wall. The board congratulated themselves and Hoban for catching the problem. No one, however, checked up on Hoban's crews at the Capitol.

Scott felt sick (cancer, not fever) and repaired upriver to the medicinal springs of Virginia. White did not spend much time in the city either. Thornton busied himself with sending Stoddert ideas for arming the new American navy. The board did not plan to really get back to work until the auction in September.[1]

*   *   *

One man, Nicholas King, did perceive a crisis that summer. Even the board's having hired his father did not forgive their incompetence. Nicholas had hoped to work for Morris up north, but when that fell through, he solicited Robert Peter and became his agent. He showed Peter that his waterside lots were unmarketable because of the board's refusal to determine the city's waterline. On June 22 he wrote to the board on behalf of Peter, explaining that the engraved plan showed square 22, just south of 26th and E Streets Northwest, extending over made ground. There was, however, enough shallow water between firm ground and the channel that another square could be formed. To facilitate development, the commissioners had to strictly define the extent of all waterside property.

Before breaking up for the summer, the commissioners washed their hands of such problems. Once a square was divided, even if it was on the water, they had nothing more to do with it. The flabbergasted King begged for clarification. Looking forward to the arrival of Congress and commerce to the city, King reminded the board of yellow fever, which "has been always traced to the neighborhood of the water." Without "proper regulation, . . . they have been crowded with houses, excluded from air, immersed in filth, and the prey of contagion." He ridiculed the board for allowing Barry to build his wharf on what was to have been an avenue and not even requiring him to build it at a right angle to the shore.

When White came to the city in August, King went to the commissioners' office to quiz him. King asked what were the "bounds" of the city. "Them declared by the President of the

United States," White replied, or so said the memo of the conversation that King made. King asked if the bounds were the high water or low water of Rock Creek. White "did not conceive the commissioners had any right of determining." King asked what was the plan of the city. White bristled: "I do not sit here to be interrogated." Thornton, who was also there and was still claiming all land that might be formed as the Potomac silted up, opined that "there was no such thing as a plan of the city, altho' it was absolutely necessary."

Actually, President Adams had signed the plan they had sent up, thus making it official. The secretary of state had informed them of the president's action, but the plan had not yet been returned. So when King said he thought the engraved plan the official one, White could only say it was not, but he could not show King the plan signed by the president. Thinking he had finally got somewhere, King tried to conclude then that that plan delineated the official waterline. White, and even Thornton, disagreed. It was the plan "no farther than related to the land reserved for the United States government." King told them that he thought there was nothing left to be done but for the proprietors to send a memorial to the president to get him to determine the waterline, "for until it was determined, the property of the city lost half its value, and the health of the future inhabitants was wantonly sacrificed."

Apparently, King's smoking out that there was an official plan other than the engraved plan was news to the proprietors. What Stoddert wanted to hear from Davidson was that he was building houses; instead, he got a worried alarm that the commissioners "have latterly smuggled forward to the President a spurious plan of the City of Washington for his ratification and signature."[2]

*   *   *

King's concern was prescient in one respect. Yellow fever scourged the crowded ports of the East once again. In early August it was reported in Boston. By August 29 people were fleeing New York, and 40,000 had already left Philadelphia; the government went to Trenton. Some people stayed in the cities to show their faith in the theory that the disease was brought from the West Indies and could not spread beyond the filthy dock areas. Elizabeth Wescott, the young woman with a literary bent who had composed a poem as Thomas Law rowed her across the Potomac, was one who stayed, and she died, as did Morris's son William, who was to have made his career in Washington.

Since August 2 there had been 1700 deaths in Philadelphia. New York was losing forty-one people a day to the fever. The epidemic was considered the worst ever. A medical journal intoned, "At present, a constitution of the atmosphere prevails in the United States which disposes to fever of a high inflammatory character. It began in the year 1793. Its duration in other countries has been from one to fifty years."

Citing their city's lack of deaths, boosters of the federal city blamed poor planning for the high death tolls elsewhere. Thornton thought it evident that closed cities suffered the most. "Privies" there were "generally not cleansed for years," houses and "back offices" were crowded together, "and the water from cabbage and other vegetables is suffered to taint the air. . . ." After writing that, he got sick but assured all that it was not the pervasive fever. It was caused "by getting very wet, and remaining so a long time."

The *Alexandria Gazette* boasted, ". . . Whilst the yellow fever stalks with desolating strides in some of the principal towns of the Union, the Federal City, destined at some future day to rival the glory of ancient Rome, bids fair to be secure from the ravages of cities and enjoy from its peculiar situation and construction an envious scene of health." It was not so much the lack of marshes that encouraged this writer to sing the praises of the city's healthy air, as its proximity to coal. "London, since the New River supplied it with fresh water, and the introduction of coal, has ever been exempt from the plague; and the Federal City, at a small expense, can have pure water conveyed to the top of every house, and coal in immense quantities can be obtained at half the price of wood fuel."

The fever convinced John Francis, who kept a hotel in Philadelphia, that in 1800 Congress would not strain to find reasons to stay there. When he fled the fever, he went to the federal city to find a place to board thirty congressmen.[3]

*   *   *

The yellow fever did not engender any boom in Washington lots. Before the sale the board tried to counteract the dire warnings that the sale was illegal by publishing excerpts of the attorney general's opinion. Still, when the auction opened at the Little Hotel on September 11, there were no bidders for the twenty lots offered, and some of the lots were as close to the president's house as 16th and K Streets. Twenty more lots, offered the next day, elicited no interest.

Then, on the 13th, the auctioneer got some high bids. An agent for Joseph Nourse bought four lots at 20th and M Streets for $249, $201, $174, and $305. Former congressman Mercer bought five lots, but cheaply. Then Samuel Eliot, Cranch's assistant, bought nineteen lots, paying as much as $393 for a lot just south of the Mall along Maryland Avenue at 7th Street.

The total sales for the day amounted to $5,794, but the commissioners had to doubt they would ever see much of the money. Eliot was acting as the agent of James Greenleaf, who was then preparing to apply to the Maryland legislature for protection under the state's bankruptcy law. He explained to the board how he, a professed bankrupt, planned to pay for the lots. He would give cash for some and expected, on going over his accounts with the commissioners, to find that they owed him money, which is to say he would prove that the credits they had given Morris and Nicholson for the bridges built over the creeks and for land taken by the public rightfully belonged to him.

To effect his design, Greenleaf needed one indulgence from the board. They required checks vouched for by another party to serve as a promise to complete payment for the lots bought. Since he was applying for bankruptcy, Greenleaf explained that it was "improper" for him to write checks at that moment. Scott, who was back in good enough health to attend some meetings, thought Greenleaf should be accommodated. White and Thornton could see no basis for having confidence in the man and demanded checks properly endorsed. They also sent their own petition to the Maryland legislature, urging it not to free Greenleaf from his obligation to build 140 houses in the city.[4]

*   *   *

Once again Greenleaf was the center of attention in the city, but not primarily because of Eliot's bids. Given the code of honor at the time, Greenleaf could not immediately intervene in an affair that should have been avenged by Cranch. That father of three had thought of challenging his assailant, but he took the advice of his Aunt Abigail to trust in the law and "holy religion."

Greenleaf had no such compunction. On arriving in the city in mid-August, he said in company that he thought Duncanson was a coward. On September 30 Duncanson learned of the remark, and, in short order, he issued a challenge, which was accepted with pleasure. Greenleaf chose his fellow proprietor George Walker as his second. Duncanson chose a former fellow officer in the British army, Presley Thornton. A number of Greenleaf's friends attended, intent on doing what they could to prevent bloodshed.

The seconds made the arrangements. Thornton tried to prevail on Walker to have the men start at fifteen paces and advance to within three to five paces until the affair was ended. Walker insisted on three shots at fifteen paces. The principals crossed over to the Virginia side of river, and their seconds found level—or almost level—ground behind a tobacco warehouse. Greenleaf thought Duncanson was slightly higher, so Duncanson promptly changed positions. At his new vantage Duncanson kicked the dirt to get better footing. Suspecting Duncanson had stepped forward, Greenleaf had the distance remeasured. The first shots were fired to no effect. Thornton asked Walker if the exchange proved to his principal that Duncanson was not a coward. Greenleaf would not admit that. Thornton retorted that they could shoot at fifteen paces all day without effect and that they should shorten the distance. Greenleaf agreed to do so after the second shots. They were fired without effect. Greenleaf agreed to shorten the distance one pace. On the next order to fire, Duncanson's pistol snapped without firing. Greenleaf held his aim when informed of what happened, refused to fire, and asked that Duncanson be given another pistol. Duncanson took a pistol but refused to fire again until he had taken a shot from Greenleaf. The seconds discussed terms under which the affair could be terminated without another exchange of shots, but further discussion only increased the acrimony. Greenleaf demanded apology for a statement Duncanson had allegedly made that he would prove Greenleaf a rascal just as he had proved Law a rascal. But on resuming firing positions, Duncanson refused to aim, insisting that Greenleaf take a shot. Greenleaf threw down his pistol and left the field of honor. There would have to be another "interview."[5]

*　　*　　*

The commissioners continued the auction every Monday through Thursday until October 23. On many days there were no bidders at the Little Hotel, whereupon the auctioneer offered only three lots. The board decided to counteract the alarms spread by the trustees' agents by asking the legislature for another law authorizing forced sales "in words too clearly expressed to be misconstrued." Failing that, they would "not be able to keep the usual number of hands employed during the ensuing summer."

After Greenleaf's unwanted bidding, Philip Fitzhugh bought thirty-six lots for Henry Lee and nine for himself. Like Greenleaf, Lee was bankrupt. The only security he could offer for his note was a "deed of trust of fifty negroes," which the commissioners did not accept.[6]

70. Raised, Boarded, Shingled, and Painted

When Francis came to town looking for a boardinghouse, Thomas Law told him to write to George Washington. Sometime that summer Washington decided to build a large three-story double house on Capitol Hill suitable for boarding congressmen. Law told him that it would cost no more than $6,000, and it would have boarders by the fall of 1800 at the latest. Washington drew up plans for something better than the mere suitable and calculated on spending $8,000 to $10,000 to build it. He reasoned that if ground were broken promptly he might earn income even sooner than 1800.

Not trusting Law to take care of the matter, he asked the commissioners to help him choose a lot and contract for building a house. White sent him maps of the squares around the Capitol, and Washington gave "a decided preference" to lot 16 in square 634, just northwest of the Capitol between B and C Streets along North Capitol Street, which today is parkland between Union Station and the Capitol. Its salient feature then was that it would be near the north wing. But the price of the lot, $1,200, gave pause, and Washington asked White if a lot southeast of the Capitol was on level ground and had a view from there to the Eastern Branch.

He pressed White to answer quickly, "as I never require much time to execute any measure after I have resolved upon it." He wanted the cellar dug and foundation laid that fall. He offered no apology for soliciting such favors. "To promote buildings is desirable, and is an object under the present circumstances of the first importance to the city."

On September 20 Washington toured the area. Law tried to get him to build south of the Capitol, arguing that men doing business on the Eastern Branch would stay there. And if his house joined those being built by Law, Carroll, and others south and east of the Capitol, there would be a neighborhood, which "raises the value of property." Washington took the lot in square 634 and placated Law by subscribing $250 for five shares in his scheme to build a hotel.

The commissioners asked Blagden to make an estimate for the two houses. While waiting for that, Washington performed another service for the city through Stoddert. The navy secretary asked him for a testimonial on the virtues of putting a navy yard on the site reserved for the Marine Hospital along the Eastern Branch. Stoddert asked him to hit the old chords: the resources of the Potomac valley—timber, iron, hemp, and so on—were abundant; the site was convenient, with its springs and creeks able to fill locks needed for launching ships; and, most important of all, the principal shipbuild-

ing yard of the navy should be "under the eye of government."
Stoddert's only worry was that ships of the line drawing 24 feet of
water could not get down the Potomac fully armed.

With the help of Lear, whose mercantile house was virtually
bankrupt and who had been forced to return to his old job as
Washington's secretary, Washington rephrased and embellished
Stoddert's arguments. Once the navigation of the Potomac was
opened, which would be soon, "an abundant supply of the largest
and best white pine trees for masts" could come down the river, not
to mention cheap iron; "the rich bottoms on this river and its
branches" would be an excellent place to grow hemp for ropes. He
gave a long description of the difficulty an enemy ship would have
getting up the river. The channel narrowed at Digges Point, some
eight miles below Alexandria, so that only one ship at a time could
pass. From a fort there, guns could mercilessly rake an enemy. It
was possible the river was too shallow at points for fully armed
American ships to get out, but if this were so, a naval arsenal could
be built downriver.

Then, after celebrating the city as the cheapest place in the
country to build ships, Washington learned that it was not the
cheapest place to build houses. Blagden estimated that he could
build Washington's, with a 9-foot-high basement, two 12-foot-high
principal stories, and a garret 9 feet high, all with front and back
walls 2 feet thick, for $12,982.29. The figure stunned Washington.
He told Thornton that, in the belief that materials were cheap and
wages low, he had drawn plans for "houses of better appearance
than is necessary. . . ." To lower the price, he suggested that he
might have his men at Mount Vernon do some of the work but would
wait until he got Blagden's detailed estimate to make a decision.

The details only frustrated him more. Blagden described the
brickwork, stonecutting, plastering, floors, doors, sashes, shutters,
stairs, surbases, plinths, architraves, cornices, ironwork, painting,
and glazing, but he did not say how much each part would cost.
Sensing the season for digging the foundation and laying in supplies
slipping away, Washington decided not to hound Blagden for the
figures. He told the commissioners to offer the job to Blagden for
$10,500, including commission, but said that he would do the
painting, glazing, and ironwork and supply the lumber himself.

Blagden would not go below $11,000. Washington still thought he was being had, even telling the commissioners that by sending his black carpenters to town he could save $1,000, but he relented. About to go to Philadelphia and New York to check on supplies for the army, he had no time to set up his slaves in the city. From long experience with their poor work habits over the years, he knew they would need close supervision. He signed the contract, grumbling that there was no way he could make more than common interest once the houses were rented. No sooner was the deal struck, however, than Blagden and Thornton began suggesting improvements. So Washington agreed to pay $150 more for a stone frontispiece for the door and another $100 for part of the cellar being vaulted "for the benefit of wine," which the hotelkeeper Francis thought essential. As he headed for Philadelphia, he told Blagden, who had shepherded tons of stone to the public buildings, that if he could not begin the foundation immediately he should at least lay in the stone because it was easier to cart in the fall than in the spring.

At least one man was thrilled with the prospect of Washington's building. Thornton bought one of the neighboring lots and even talked to the general about their party wall.[1]

* * *

Despite his grumbling about expense, Washington had to feel good about the prospects of his building. The north wing of the Capitol was almost finished. The roof was "raised, boarded, shingled, and painted," the gutters "laid and leaded." The balustrade was up on the east front and all the rest prepared for putting up. The chimneys were finished saved for the stone tops. Inside, most of the rooms were ready for floors and for plastering. The fine carpentry remained to be done, including window frames, doors, and staircases. One snag was that no supplier had yet found panes of glass of requisite quality, crown, and as large as the 18 by 28 inches the board wanted. But no problem seemed insurmountable since the money to finish the building was assured.

The commissioners did have their money problems. The stock loaned by Maryland could be sold at only 72.5 percent of par. They hated to sell it. If they could find some money to tide them over until the new year, when the next installment of the loan from Congress would be paid, then they could hold the stock until better times. So they set out to collect old debts. That was painful because debtors, noting the two loans to the city, were quick to suggest indulgences.[2]

One of the most embarrassing cases was the $5,500 owed by Deakins, Casanave, and Thomas Lee for the rights to the commissioners' share of the land formed by the causeway at the mouth of Rock Creek. First Cazenoves had died, and the other two partners postponed repayment until the deceased's estate was sold off to raise money. They did not raise the money expected. Then Deakins died, and it soon became apparent that the man who had been thought to be the most creditworthy in Georgetown was in fact deeply in debt because, his brother lamented, of "unlimited favors to many ungrateful men." To avoid a suit, the only remaining partner, Lee, offered to sell the property once deemed so valuable, thus in a sense paying the commissioners exactly what it was worth, which no one suspected was much.

When the commissioners went after Polock to pay sums overdue on lots he had bought, he castigated them for "injuring instead of encouraging those who embark largely in the improvement of the city." He wondered why they threw "impediments" in his way while others who did nothing for the city got every indulgence.

Going after debts was ill advised because a new state property tax and federal taxes on carriages and houses burdened property owners. Sketchy tax records throw some light on the pecking order in the district. Scott's house was valued at $5,500, Collen Williamson's at $350. Pierce Purcell owned five houses. Law had eight tenants. Notley Young still had the most slaves, sixty-one; Burnes, once down to eight, had twenty-two; Carroll had the same number. Scott had twelve, Thornton only one. There were 259 slaves in the city, 144 of them between the ages of twelve and fifty. Georgetown had 538 slaves.[3]

*   *   *

Once again the cash-poor commissioners kept a sharp eye out for the first frost. After it painted the city on November 12, the board ordered Harbaugh to stop work on the walls of the Treasury. With half the foundation wall up high enough to take the first-floor joist, and the other half up seven feet, the building seemed well on its way. During the winter a small crew would make sash frames, sashes, doors, and shutters.

Not only did the commissioners stop work at the Capitol, but they dismissed masons and laborers. Future stonework would be done by special contracts, and 499 tons of unwanted stone and 30,000 extra bricks would be sold or used elsewhere. They decided they would need to rent only twenty-five slaves the coming year, which meant they could rent out the hospital. Just when they were contemplating that savings, their doctor presented his bill. Back in the spring, Dr. May had taken over as the physician to the public laborers. He suggested that instead of being paid for each of the eighty-five slaves employed by the city, he should get 50 cents a visit. The board agreed. In early November May presented them with a bill for $268.50 covering just half the year. They asked Dr. Coningham to give an opinion on "the reasonableness" of May's charges. He demurred, saying only the attending physician could judge, and he had not done any doctoring since opening his brewery.

To raise money, the board once again tried to get a loan from the canal lottery. It is more likely that the commissioners, well knowing that the lottery had raised nothing, asked for money only to embarrass those frequent thorns in their side, Carroll and Law. Those canal managers had sold so many tickets on credit that they had barely been able to pay all prizes.

The board's last move to save its stock was to go to the Bank of Columbia once again. The bank refused to accommodate the commissioners.[4]

*   *   *

Carroll's latest complaint was that before building three houses facing the Capitol square, he wanted assurances that no buildings would intervene between his and the Capitol. Most of the work

sheds, barracks, and temporary houses were on the southern end of
the Capitol at the head of New Jersey Avenue. Carroll planned to
build at the eastern end of the square on East Capitol Street. The
board said no intervening building was planned. Peeved at any
temporary buildings on the square, Carroll shot back that he wanted
assurance that the board had no right to erect any building between
his and the Capitol. The board refused. Carroll thereupon complained that the surveyor had shortchanged him in measuring the
amount of land taken by the public. He wanted to be paid for the
land taken by the canal, and he objected to the road being placed
around every public reserve, which took land from a proprietor that
the board did not have to pay for. The board countered that it had a
right to build roads and that for 240 yards the canal was to be the
navigable waters of James Creek, and after that it was flanked by a
street on either side. All went to the attorney general, and the board
asked the Maryland legislature to investigate the canal lottery.

There was no respect between the commissioners and the proprietors. Despite the board's order in May, "no wood had been felled
nor enclosures removed," and so much of the public appropriations
were "in constant cultivation" that the board feared "neither grass
nor anything else" would grow on it. The proprietors had larger
issues on their minds, the whole plan of the city. King finished a
memorial attacking the plan the president had just approved, which
King found "different from that laid off on the ground." The
president could still have a proper plan made because trustees, Beall
and Gantt, still refused to deed the public lands to the commissioners in deference to the proprietors.

King accused the commissioners of making such innovations in
the plan that "gentlemen anxious to make improvements are deterred, from an apprehension lest at some future period they be
deprived of that which constitutes their present inducement." The
most glaring recent innovation was letting the Portuguese government build a ministry on the president's house square, an area
designed to be free of building for reasons of health and beauty.
King's major beef was still the indeterminate waterline, and he
warned that if nothing was done "the United States are voluntarily
allowing reservoirs of contagion." He credited L'Enfant's genius
and criticized his successors, especially those after Ellicott. They

had instituted a reign of "dull uniformity" in planning and had clogged the surveyors' office with "several mutilated, unfinished, and discordant plans, which bewilder instead of explaining, and paralyze property to a very large amount, that would otherwise be employed in improving the city." Ten proprietors signed the long memorial urging the president to have an accurate and definitive plan made.[5]

71. His Darling Wish to Kill

When his cabinet colleagues kidded Stoddert about his "selfish partiality for the District of Columbia," he only came back at them with more vehemence. Before Congress convened in November he plied Treasury Secretary Wolcott with arguments why "a long and a vigorous naval war, cannot be carried on by this country without the resources of the Chesapeke, but more particularly of the Potomac." Along the Potomac "the lumber is good and so plenty that it can almost be had for cutting." That year's efforts to build frigates in Northern ports was about to exhaust the supply of lumber in those places. He thought there should be one naval yard for building on the Potomac. He would immediately fortify Digges Point, which would make the Potomac above it the safest place in the union for ships.

In a letter to the president, he made another point. The officers of government, who might have to move to Georgetown as early as the summer of 1799 to avoid the fever, had to be defended from a naval attack. There might be great excitement about the army Washington was organizing, but Stoddert knew a big navy was the "only rational system of defense." The army need only be large enough to keep up appearances for the French and to "cower the Jacobins" at home. Stoddert did do his bit to build the army, going over volunteers from Maryland. John Miller of Georgetown did not fare well. Stoddert scrawled next to his name, "an ignorant & a violent Jacobin."

When the fifth Congress began its third session in November, Federalists and Republicans were back at each others' throats. Congressman Lyon, as well as a number of Republican editors, had been arrested for violating the new sedition law. With a house tax and stamp tax to attack, Republicans tried to arouse the people. The Virginia and Kentucky legislatures asserted their right to resist unconstitutional laws. Major General Hamilton wanted to march the new army into Virginia.

Although his party was ready for war, the president was not. In his state of the union message, Adams began with a call to protect citizens not from the French and Jacobins but from "the alarming and destructive pestilence with which several of our cities and towns have been visited. . . ." Adams did not raise the issue out of any love for Philadelphia. The city did not like Adams, and he did not like the city. Returning without his wife, who was too ill to leave Quincy, he was more peevish than usual. When his son Thomas, who had studied law in Philadelphia, decided to establish himself in the city, the president growled, "I expect the plague will drive him out again. It is undoubtedly here lurking about the city all this winter."[1]

The city turned to science and engineering for salvation. Scientific thinkers, who still made Philadelphia their capital, had been urging a plan since 1797 to save the city by bringing water down from the Schuylkill so city streets could be periodically flushed and drinking water kept pure. After the fever of 1798, more political and business leaders embraced the plan and tapped Benjamin Latrobe, the English engineer and architect who had done most of his work in Virginia, to draw the plans for necessary canals, waterworks, and pumps. Latrobe promised a clean, healthy city for $402,000 and thought he could have the system in operation by July 1st. On February 7th the city council authorized selling $100 shares in a 6% loan to raise $150,000. By the end of the month, $60,000 was pledged. The loan would be paid off by the 6,000 houses to be supplied water.

In his report explaining his plan Latrobe did not discuss the causes of the fever or its deleterious effects on the city. He talked about aqueducts, reservoirs, and steam engine pumps, and it proved just the tonic the city needed. Only toward the end of his long report did he allude to the crisis in the city's self-esteem. By bringing pure water to the city, public baths were possible. Although that might sound extravagant, "it might not be bad policy," Latrobe quipped, ". . . to counterbalance the fashionable inducements which point to the Potomac, by conveniences and advantages which cannot for many years be thought of in a city, which is at present almost destitute of dwellings."

The editor of the *Georgetown Centinel* picked up that gauntlet. Given the federal city's "elevated scite, . . . unrivalled spaciousness of its streets and avenues, the intervals for public walks & c., the variety of natural fountains from which pure water flows, the lively streams which pass through its different parts or wash its borders," it had promise of "a long continuance of freedom from pestilential disease."[2]

*   *   *

The editor ignored Latrobe's gibe about the dearth of houses, but that predicament was only half lamented. An ad hoc committee of three Georgetowners, Lingan, Waring, and Mason, wrote to their congressman, Craik, that, given the fevers of Philadelphia and unreadiness of the federal city, it was time to adjourn Congress to Georgetown. They sent up a report on the availability and reasonable cost of housing and provisions to induce congressmen to come.

Craik explored the possibility of amending a bill giving the president more power to save the government's officers and judges from exposure to yellow fever so that he would be positively instructed to move to Georgetown. But most of his colleagues to whom he mentioned the idea were "violently opposed." Congress had already given the president the power to move the site of congress away from disease. Without opposition, they gave him the power to move the executive and judicial offices. Craik told his Georgetown correspondents that they were as likely to persuade the president to move everything to Georgetown as they were to persuade a majority of Congress, and Craik thought chances were good the president could be persuaded. Trenton had been found "very inconvenient," and Philadelphians had engaged all its rooms for next summer. He had shown the president the information the Georgetowners had sent up about housing. The president read it, endorsed Georgetown as a viable site, and sent copies on to his cabinet.

Craik seemed well pleased with what he had accomplished and in a March 15 letter to the committee cautioned them to keep prices of housing and provisions reasonable. "We must be satisfied to grow rich by degrees and not in our impatience for the golden egg bring on a premature death." That said, he lectured them on the need to improve the streets. The two questions every member asked were, "What is the state of the streets and how are the publick buildings situated with a view to the convenience of walking." Members did not appreciate mud. They did not "quietly submit to those difficulties which they are often satisfied to encounter at home." He urged that Georgetown's streets finally be leveled and that a footpath be laid from Georgetown to the Capitol. If the fever struck Philadelphia that year, the government would move to Georgetown, and first impressions were important.[3]

*   *   *

Washington kept in good humor about his houses during the winter. He incorporated into the design some features he saw in Philadelphia houses and even returned some of the work to Blagden, "although I know it will cost me four times what I could do it for myself." Seeing expenses increasing, he alerted the nephew who handled his real estate to hurry up in getting rents and payments for lands sold. It was his only hope for avoiding a bank loan "at its ruinous interest." In March he sent his nephew to the city and was shocked to learn that despite his instructions nothing had been done on the ground. Careful not to correspond with Blagden, he had Lear lecture the contractor: "Now, bad roads & multiplied excuses may be a plea for the backwardness of the work."[4]

Blagden had other projects. He did leave public employ, but the commissioners still contracted with him to do the $1,400 worth of stonework that Blagden estimated needed to be done. That winter he picked out the stone he needed from the Capitol yard, segregated it, and had the rest formed into "forts." He also picked the men he would hire when the building season began. He continued to oblige the board by inspecting other work. Most worrisome was the evident incompetence of the man making the lead gutters for the president's house. The pump he put in at the Capitol was useless soon after it was finished.

*   *   *

It was to have been a quiet winter at the public works. Masons and bricklayers were dismissed. Elisha Williams rounded up everything that could be sold at the discontinued hospital, as well as "drays, carts, barrows, tools & c." no longer needed at the Capitol and the president's house. The only large crew at work were the carpenters at the Capitol, who were getting interiors ready for the plasterers scheduled to begin work in April. They prepared doors, sashes, and shutters for the building. In previous winters, work had been done in the carpenters' sheds next to the public buildings. Hoban decided to have the work done in the Capitol itself, which could be managed if the windows had temporary sashes and cheap windows to keep out the cold and admit the light. Preparing the Capitol's rooms to serve as workshops also increased the work load, which enabled Hoban to keep more men employed.

In mid-January the board got an inkling of trouble among the carpenters. Thomas Watkins complained that he was fired and another man docked in pay because they refused to join the artillery company of which Hoban was captain. The company, the pièce de résistance of such public ceremonies as Washington's birthday and the Fourth of July, was Hoban's pride. Thornton thought an investigation was warranted, but Scott and White believed Hoban's explanation that Watkins was a bad carpenter and the other man did not have enough tools.

Once again Hoban proved that it was unwise to cross him. After giving his favorites the task of making temporary sashes, Hoban set out to get the contract for making the Capitol shutters and doors even though a cabinetmaker named Joseph Middleton was already doing it. He was no friend of Hoban's clique because he had given evidence that had led to Pierce Purcell's dismissal the year before. Middleton was at Hoban's mercy because it was through him that he was to obtain both drawings and wood for the work. On January 30 Middleton asked for drawings. Two days later the board asked Hoban to estimate the amount of materials, time, and men needed to finish the north wing. He made a great show of activity in coming up with the estimate and ignored Middleton. He did not, however, ignore the Capitol doors and shutters. He had another crew at work on the shutters and had John Lenox, brother of his number two carpenter at the president's house, come up with an estimate below Middleton's.

Middleton had been around long enough to know what was going to happen next. As he and his men sat idle for want of drawings, it was just a matter of time before Hoban informed the board and got Middleton dismissed. In the winter the commissioners never visited the works. Middleton decided to attack first. In mid-February he informed the board that he had no drawings. The board asked Hoban about it, and Hoban assured the board that shutters were on hand so no time was being lost. Middleton waited two weeks and then complained again. This time the board decided to investigate and summoned Hoban to appear before them on March 12.[5]

*   *   *

Just before the intimations that something was rotten at the Capitol, disaster struck on the other side of town. On February 18 fire broke out in Harbaugh's workshop along Rock Creek, where his carpenters were making the architraves, jambs, window frames, and shutters for the Treasury buildings. The fire destroyed $350 worth of material already prepared, as well as almost 5,000 feet of plank worth $145. Harbaugh, his family, and many of his workmen lost all their clothes. The commissioners did not breathe a word of this catastrophe to officials in Philadelphia.

*   *   *

The board took some comfort in the attorney general's backing them in the dispute with Carroll, save that Lee ruled that Carroll should be paid for the portion of the canal above tidewater. Having won most of their points, the board magnanimously allowed Carroll to plant corn that summer. In return, he did not insist on full payment for the land the public took from him. He explained that if he got $4,000 it would help him carry on his building. The commissioners promised to try.

Then they were shaken by the way the president handled the proprietors' memorial. They did not see it until the secretary of state sent them a copy. What galled was that Pickering also enclosed the attorney general's opinion of same. Lee was not impressed with the memorial except that he did think the deed given to the queen of Portugal ill advised. Only Congress could alienate that public land. As for which plan ruled the city, he thought it obvious that all other plans simply had to yield to the plan sanctioned by the president. On the subject of waterside lots, with eight miles of waterfront, Lee believed that "to define universally the rights, manner and distance of wharfage appurtenant to each lot would be a work of difficulty and expense." In his opinion, with so little built on land, few would be eager to "redeem land out of the river." But he forbore deciding the issue until he heard from the commissioners.

In a testy reply to the secretary of state, the commissioners dismissed the memorial out of hand. "Not a single fact can be pointed out to give the semblance of truth to their accusations." Regarding the deed to Portugal, two presidents endorsed the idea and method, but if the attorney general wanted congressional approval, so be it.

The commissioners asked Dermott to justify, in writing, the differences between his maligned plan and Ellicott's map. Drawn once again into controversy, Dermott proved a model of geniality, patiently detailing the problems Ellicott and his successors honestly had in an effort to square the city. As for waterside lots, Dermott noted that he had explained to every buyer what their rights were, and all had seemed contented until Nicholas King came on the scene. "A little time will settle the whole business," Dermott concluded, "and I hope I may live to throw in my mite towards justice and harmony in this place."[6]

*   *   *

Duncanson scorned a challenge from Greenleaf in January, opening a newspaper war to warm readers. Duncanson called for a "court of honor," which he was sure would find that Greenleaf had "acted like a coward or scoundrel." Greenleaf ridiculed the idea and pledged to "baffle any attempt" by Duncanson to regain his honor. Duncanson reminded all that if Greenleaf had been man enough to lessen the distance he could have easily had "his darling wish to kill or be killed."

Drawing out the affair, which everyone knew had begun with the whipping of Cranch, did little to help the young lawyer's self-esteem. "I was not made for a life of brawls and contention," he lamented in a letter to his mother. ". . . Tamely to submit to injury, is to sink into contempt. To resent it with proper spirit is to involve others, perhaps, in distress. The medium is difficult." He could at least drown his sorrows in a growing practice with a sea of lawsuits, almost a thousand of them, that he handled in Maryland courts.[7]

1799

72. Hoban Wants All the Influence Himself

The state property tax was no more than a few shillings a lot, but for such proprietors as Samuel Davidson that amounted to almost £200. Bankrupt speculators had a new fear, a sheriff's sale of their property for failure to pay taxes. There was no worse publicity for the city than the sheriff's list of delinquents in the newspaper at the first of the year.

Amsterdam and Rotterdam notaries held 847 and 480 lots, respectively, as securities for loans to Greenleaf. Lynch and Sands, who were teetering on the brink of bankruptcy in New York, owned 66 acres of city land. Harrison and Sterret, a nearly bankrupt partnership in Philadelphia, owned 132½ lots. They had been ruined by their association with Morris and Nicholson. Standish Forde, who owned 179 lots, was on the brink of disaster for the same reason. His sole consolation for his dealing with Morris was that he got all the marble L'Enfant had larded onto Morris's unfinished mansion. Finally, Blodget owned 187¼ acres plus forty-eight lots for which he owed $312 in taxes.[1]

The man who came down from Philadelphia in the late winter to try to solve the perplexities caused by failed speculation in lots was not strictly one of the absentee landlords. Edward Fox was the Philadelphia auctioneer ruined when he extended himself to cover $720,000 worth of Greenleaf's notes. Fox was not shy of telling anyone about Greenleaf's "villainous and wicked manner," and Greenleaf's presence in the city also attracted him. He feared that his nemesis was trying to thwart the trustees of the aggregate fund and thus ruin any chance Fox had of getting his debts cleared. Greenleaf certainly had stopped cooperating with the trustees, refusing to officially record in Maryland the deed transferring property to the trustees, forcing them to file suit. Fox professed no claim to Washington property, as Greenleaf did, and came just to get cash flowing from it to the trustees and then to his creditors.

Before coming, Fox conferred with Morris at the Prune Street debtors' prison, corresponded with Nicholson, who refused to see visitors anymore, and met with the trustees in their countinghouses. They were glad to see him look into city affairs because they were having doubts about their agent Dorsey. Fox arrived on February 15 and saw in an instant that Dorsey was not the problem. His being sick and in bed much of the time did not help, but Fox told the trustees, "The business is more complex and more intricate than can be well imagined. The claims upon the city property are so various and the number of interests, real or pretended, so many. . . ." The simplest problem was the commissioners' basic demand for money. The real problem was that no money could be raised from the property because of all the other encumbrances.

Fox first worked on Dorsey's inability to battle Greenleaf's attachments and impositions—Greenleaf was even demanding that tenants in the houses at the point pay rent to him—by acquainting Dorsey with all the instruments Greenleaf had signed (along with Fox) relinquishing his claims. Lovering had reported to the trustees that "the negro people at the Point" were picking the property apart. Fox thought all could be put in order. Then he dealt with a claim Francis Deakins had arising from money his brother had lent Greenleaf. Fox convinced Deakins that the trustees were only protecting their right to have the matter examined, and Deakins was amenable to having counsels resolve the dispute without going to court.

The spot where he thought money could be raised was on the farms across the Eastern Branch. He hired Nicholas King to divide 30 acres into ten to twenty lots for "gentlemen's seats," confident that "from the situation of the land," the lots would bring up to $50,000 "in the course of a few months." As for the city property, given a proper map with the trustees' lots colored, it too would sell. Finally, he thought Morris's December 1796 deed to Reed and Forde might be disallowed, freeing up many valuable lots, because those gentlemen had got other security, and, at that time at least, Morris and Nicholson had preserved their property. Despite all the good news, Fox warned that several bills against the property would soon be filed in the state chancery court.

Dealing with Fox was one of the board's pleasures that spring. They negotiated a new schedule for trustees' payments. Instead of a payment every month, the board would accept $10,000 every two months, beginning in June. By November 15, 1799, however, the trustees had to exercise one of two options to prevent immediate sales. If they agreed to pay $100,000 more in monthly installments, all forced sales would be put off until December 1800. If they agreed to pay $50,000 more, sales would be put off until January 1800. Until the trustees agreed to that plan, the commissioners could offer three lots a day for sale.[2]

*　　*　　*

The city's ability to excite newcomers was undiminished. But that spring, even old hands seemed to think something had to give. Nicholas King felt confident enough about the future to begin advertising a full-service real estate agency next to the hotel. He would buy, sell, survey, map, lay off, make perspective views, and draw deeds and mortgages for city lots and country property in the vicinity.

Carroll was advertising for written proposals from carpenters and joiners for a three-story house, 54 feet wide and 40 feet deep, to serve as a tavern. Law was preparing to build several houses along New Jersey Avenue. Not only was George Washington building, but John Tayloe, the wealthy Virginia planter and horseman, wanted to sign a contract with Lovering for a $13,000 house near the president's house. (The English builder was eager for the job but had trouble finding security to give a bond for his work. With $69 to his name, he begged Nicholson for a few hundred acres of Georgia land.) A handful of Baltimoreans, led by James Barry, were investing in the city. That port had been immune to Philadelphia's economic doldrums, and investment in Washington seemed a natural outlet for profit. Walter Brown built a printing office on New Jersey Avenue, and his brother-in-law, William Hodgson, built near O'Neale, across Pennsylvania Avenue from the six buildings. Philadelphians were not exactly too poor to dabble in the city any more. The merchants Nicklin and Griffith got command of lots after a Nicholson default, and rather than sit on them, they sent an agent down to see what could be done with them.

There were some adverse indicators. Dermott was making so little buying and selling lots for clients that he tried to sell nine black women and children, including three girls from six to ten years old. While Carroll and Law were building, Burnes was offering thirty barrels of corn, thirty bushels of oats, and ten pounds of hay for ready cash. Lear and Company gave up all pretense of respectability. To the shock of his partner Dalton, Lear confessed to pocketing payments to the company for his personal speculations.

There was a glut of property for sale. Not only were the commissioners auctioning enough lots to fill a column and a half in the newspaper, but William Prout advertised a sale of forty-one lots to be held at Tunnicliff's hotel on April 9. There were a number of ads indicating varying degrees of distress. Philip Fitzhugh, Henry Lee's partner, decided city life was not for him and offered to sell three frame houses, a post chaise, a phaeton, a thoroughbred mare, four curtained beds, and "one of the best house servants in the United States." William Prentiss, out after eight months in debtors' prison, put all of his belongings at the point up for sale, as did Richard Gridley, the blacksmith who offered feather beds, tools, a milch cow, and a fourteen-year-old Negro girl. He added that his departure was caused by "ungenerous treatment from the commissioners."[3]

* * *

On March 12 Hoban responded to Middleton's charges in a manner implying that he was too big to be bothered. He had not given Middleton drawings because he had just delivered paneling for doors to him. Hoban thought the paneling would keep Middleton busy while Hoban exhausted himself estimating what was needed to complete the north wing. The estimate was "a weighty and intricate piece of business to accomplish," especially since he had no "plan or section of the building to measure or calculate by, nor the parts in detail, all which ought to be put into the hands of the superintendent.''

That was a shot across Thornton's bow, the purported designer of the Capitol. Then Hoban went after Middleton, a mere cabinet-maker who was not qualified for the task, which was evident from the sorry quality of the wood he had bought in Alexandria for the doors. John Lenox would make the doors cheaper anyway. By "what influence" Middleton had got such a contract Hoban was "at a loss to know.''

Hoban overplayed his hand, antagonizing the board just when a concerted attack was made on his empire. The commissioners scheduled an investigation for April 2. In their investigations the board took evidence, allowed cross-examination, and let the person being investigated know what the charges against him were so he in turn could call witnesses. Legal counsel was not customary, but when Hoban asked permission to bring Carroll and Young to view the proceedings the board did not object.

The board called for testimony from thirteen men, including Hoban, Middleton, Purcell, Smallwood, and seven carpenters. Captain Elisha Williams saw to it that the investigation of Captain Hoban took an unexpected turn. Witnesses testified that men were loafing because of lax supervision. It was clearly established "that 14 carpenters for a period of seven weeks or more, did not one third of the work justly to be expected from them, that 13 sawyers for a whole year played the same game, and sashes for temporary purposes have been made . . . which cost the United States little less than fifty cents a light.'' Middleton found someone in the Purcell clique to reveal secrets and hoped the board would not let local custom prevent "Pierce Purcell's negro Tom" from testifying.

Making matters worse, the men marking time were not apologetic. James Tompkins, one of four carpenters fired for not working, retorted in a letter to the board that his dismissal was "a very gross mistake.'' "I do acknowledge that there might have been more work done than was but it was so general that every man in the yard took whatever liberty almost he pleased as the main thing was to keep time. . . . If I am discharged for not doing a full days work every day, every carpenter might be discharged for the same reason.''

The commissioners decided the man most at fault was not Hoban but his foreman, Redmond Purcell, so they postponed further investigation of Hoban and offered Purcell a chance to defend himself by calling witnesses. Purcell replied by letter that he wanted time to prepare his case and that if investigations were continued they might go further than the board wished. He reminded the commissioners that he had saved the public "some thousands of dollars" by getting Hadfield removed. Furthermore, since Elisha Williams had made charges against him, he wanted him called to testify so he could ask him "why he gets three hundred pounds yearly, . . . for doing no great things."

Scott took him aside and warned him to promptly defend his handling of the carpenters. Instead, Purcell wrote a letter attacking Scott. He deserved a fair trial and did not appreciate Scott telling him "in a peremtory imperious manner, that I shall be debarred from some of the right of natural equity." Scott's attitude did not surprise Purcell, who knew Scott was mad at him for exposing "the embezzlement of some thousands of dollars thro the mismanagement of his favorite Hadfield." Such was the litigious maze hamstringing the young republic that when Purcell went to get three builders, Lovering, Harbaugh, and Stephenson, to accompany him to the board meeting and stand up for the rights of builders, all three were off in Upper Marlboro testifying in court.

The commissioners fired Purcell, and, while waiting for the inevitable publication of his abusive letters, they addressed the problem of Hoban. They believed Purcell's dereliction had to be Hoban's responsibility but admitted that "the world" would say they were to blame too. Besides, there were charges against Hoban that had nothing to do with Purcell, stemming from countercharges Middleton had made to Hoban's charges against him.

Middleton began by echoing a complaint made by Andrew Ellicott: "no person can stay long in this employment who will not sacrifice every sentiment which is honorable." There was the carpenter Sandiford, discharged by Hoban for allegedly not having enough tools. Middleton had been in Sandiford's house and seen his chest, and no man at the Capitol had more tools. He was really fired for speaking up too freely. Of Hoban's animosity toward him, Middleton wrote, "Captain Hoban wants all the influence himself and whenever he thinks any person on as good a footing as himself, it raises in him the greatest degree of rancor imaginable."

Middleton let his work stand for itself and brought up instances of bad work at the president's house. If Hoban worried about him getting 15 shillings a day, what about his man at the president's house getting 17 shillings, 6 pence, who spoiled twenty-eight pairs of shutters. A whole set of architraves for the basement had to be condemned "for frivolous pretensions." As for John Lenox, the man Hoban wanted to do the shutters, "the pediment was shingled under his direction and what a piece of work that is." He also spoiled the sashes and frames at the president's house.

Middleton was striking some of the right chords. Early in the winter the board began receiving complaints that the roof of the president's house was leaking. Hoban adamantly defended the work and persuaded the board to pay the contractor. Then there were more complaints of leaks. Checking the roof after "a severe night of wind and rain with all the dormer windows open," Hoban estimated that leakage "did not amount to half a pint in that extensive building." In that same report, Hoban admitted the gutters of the building were not completed. The board pointed out that he had signed off on that work. Middleton had the commissioners check the accounts of lumber and found "a great deficiency." Finally, they chastised Hoban for his March 12 letter, with its "very indecent and even insolent language," which they were "by no means disposed to suffer from you or any other person."

The day after the board invited Hoban to attend an investigation of those matters, Purcell struck again. Commissioner White, who thought his colleagues were straining to find a pretext for firing Hoban, had thought Purcell deserved more than an evening to prepare his defense. Concluding that White was on his side, Purcell wrote a letter to him attacking the commissioner's colleagues. He blasted Thornton as "a fribbling quack architect who smuggled his name to the only drawings of sections for the Capitol ever delivered to the commissioners' office, made out by another man" because the original plan "was not reduceable to practice." Scott, "on a sunny day," might "view the public works for ten minutes." White did not have to share the charges with his colleague. Purcell published the letter and all his other letters attacking the board in the Georgetown newspaper.

Such attacks only steeled Thornton's resolve, and now that he was being tarred by Purcell, he was big enough to offer an apology to Hadfield, who was still in the city, living on South Capitol Street. Hadfield responded by publishing a letter to the commissioners noting that their actions against him deserved investigation, given "the source from whence you have derived your information. . . ." Thornton and Scott replied that although "the malicious falsehoods and malevolent slanders" of Purcell were beneath their notice, they considered it their duty to attest that Hadfield had "acted with the strictest honesty and with great attention to your public duties."

Hoban did not react tamely to being investigated, and he began throwing more of the load of his work onto the commissioners. Deciding the staircases were too difficult for his carpenters, he asked the board what he should do. Then he asked the board to give him "drawings necessary for carrying on" the work at the Capitol. He needed the east entrance staircase, the elliptical staircase, the back staircase, the House chamber, and the Senate chamber, and he needed them in a hurry if the work was to continue. Scott and White looked over the terms of the original advertisement for designing the Capitol and found that the winner was to provide drawings. They asked Thornton to give Hoban the drawings requested.

Thornton promptly excused himself from the task and gave several reasons. He had already given his colleagues and Hoban his ideas on finishing the rooms and was "always on the spot ready to give further explanation." He did not think drawings were necessary since they had decided not to finish the rooms in "a splendid and expensive style," and the superintendent was expected to give the decorative drawings needed for a plain finish. Thornton protested, "If the works now in execution were not considered in many respects as temporary, and in others as only to be partially finished I should be very anxious to supply the drawings. . . ." Finally, to deflect the notion that the terms of the original advertisement obliged him to make drawings, he reminded them that Hadfield had been hired to make drawings, so he assumed it had become a duty of the superintendent.

Hoban made the drawings and made his point. The investigation went forward, but he was indispensable, and no further criticisms of his conduct remain in the record. The accusations, however, continued. "Hoban's party," as it was called in the city, amassed a considerable indictment of Middleton. Two mahogany desks and a tea table were made in his workshop and veneered with the same satin wood used on the doors of the president's house; his "yellow girl" was seen carrying two-and-a-half-inch plank out of the shop; at dusk he was seen handing down from the president's house two-and-a-half-foot-long planks "to his little negroes who carried them away in two baskets" to his shop at Vermont Avenue and I Street. Furniture was seen delivered to the captain of a packet who said he was delivering it to John Chalmers in Baltimore. There was much more, including a cradle made for Thomas Munroe, the commissioners' secretary. But after Chalmers informed the board that he had received nothing, Middleton was exonerated (over White's protest) and completed his contract.[4]

73. Nothing Honorable, Useful, or Decorous

"I am now in the office writing a building contract," Law informed George Washington in an April 5 note. "Your corner stone is to be laid today and I am to attend. My garden is preparing and I am planting poplars. My square is today sown with clover. I am filling in a wharf. I hope therefore to be excused for this hasty scrawl." Law was building next to his own house at New Jersey Avenue and C Street and farther up the hill on Pennsylvania Avenue, just off the Capitol square.

Not everyone could get their juices flowing. Winter simply would not quit. It snowed in the beginning of May. Cranch complained of having to keep fires for "upwards of seven months." On May 1 shivering citizens were cutting the trees growing on public grounds and streets. This was the second growth, and after seeing perhaps too many of the original trees felled, the board decided it wanted some trees to grow in Washington. So the commissioners ordered Elisha Williams to prosecute "with vigor" anyone caught cutting. Williams, however, had no posse of men to keep watch, since the board did not hire that spring. With "only 12 or 14" slaves, the commissioners no longer needed Jane Short, who had cooked for public laborers for four years. They even gave notice to Williams, a mainstay since Roberdeau's rebellion in January 1792. Although "perfectly satisfied" with his conduct, they did not need him after July 1.[1]

*   *   *

Before the trustees of the aggregate fund agreed to the plan Fox had negotiated with the commissioners, they wanted the creditors they served to advance some money. They prepared a report devoid of the hyperbole endemic to reports on real estate, and it was not unflattering to the city. They explained that although they held Greenleaf's lands in Georgia, South Carolina, and New York from which to raise money, the "increasing value" of the Washington lots "may be more relied upon."

They explained the difficulty of ascertaining titles to lots. To begin with, Greenleaf had refused to acknowledge his deed in Maryland. They sued and expected to win shortly. They also discovered "several nice distinctions . . . growing up," which was a nice way of saying that a welter of attachments and chancery suits required good Maryland lawyers and a vigilant agent on the scene because other creditors of Morris and Nicholson "were on the watch." "Every attempt which the ingenuity of opposite counsel and the watchfulness of creditors could suggest have been resorted to" in order to steal property from the trust.

So far the trustees successfully preserved the property and at a relatively small cost. They cleared encumbrances on the Hopyard, spent $4,775 for some of Morris's notes (which saved them from a

$175,000 claim on the property), and spent $10,000 for lots valued at $23,116 and another $10,000 to postpone a forced sale until a payment plan could be devised. Of course, the men who guarded the property had to be paid. Dorsey's salary was $2,000 a year; lawyers Martin and Key had been paid $666.66 and the sheriff another $400 for serving attachments.

Nevertheless, threats to the property were mounting because the gentlemen holding scrip for lots as security for loans would soon exercise options to buy lots as the scrip for one, two, and three years came due. The trustees challenged the legality of the scrip, confident that the property was worth more than the encumbrances, arrears, and future installments. All money paid to the commissioners would go to the public buildings, which would increase the value of the property. Real estate values were depressed enough in Philadelphia that the trustees did not have to belabor their inability to raise money on the Washington property at that time. They reminded the creditors that "as the time for the removal of the general government to the City of Washington approaches, the property in that city will soon reach to its value."

The five Philadelphia businessmen who were the trustees showed no disposition to sabotage the city by bad report, but the creditors, most of them in Philadelphia, had to come up with the money, a five percent advance on their stake in the trust, by May 25, and five percent more payable in three and six months. That would raise the $40,000 required by the commissioners and service the loans from Forrest, Dunlop, Deakins, and Scott, who had bought Duncanson's share of the first $50,000 loan. A rumor spread in Washington and Georgetown that the trustees were even going to relieve the men who paid Nicholson's bail. "Tantalizing" as that prospect was, one of those standing to lose his money wrote to Nicholson that he feared "they are not serious—I wish to God they would do it."

Then, just before the scheduled meetings, the gentlemen of Philadelphia were called to their regiments to go out into neighboring counties and crush a rebellion by German-Americans loath to pay taxes. A week later, on April 22, the trustees held the meeting. Most creditors found the plan acceptable, but assessments were not quickly paid. The trustees asked the commissioners for more time, since they needed "the creditors to go hand in hand."

Beginning March 20 the commissioners had auctioned three lots a day. During March they sold a handful, and only one during all of April. Lots sold for more than $80, but not by much. One lot strategically placed along the proposed canal route on the low ground just southwest of the Capitol sold for $509. The original proprietor, Carroll, bought it. The commissioners gave the trustees until June 1 to agree to the plan. After that they would do their "utmost" to sell the lots.[2]

*   *   *

Burnes died that May, and thanks to his sales the year before to Polock, Dorsey, Thornton, and others, he left a wealthy widow and a very marriageable daughter. The family still owned many lots. The widow repaired the family carriage, getting a new body for $100, and enjoyed her new station in life, the living example that money could be made on Washington lots. The other proprietors girded to carry on the struggle.

On June 5 the board asked the attorney general about suing Beall and Gantt, who still would not deed the public lands to the commissioners. The proprietors had prevailed on Beall and Gantt to offer to deed only those public lands already laid out, thus giving the president, or future presidents, the chance to restore the glories of L'Enfant's original conception. The proprietors also held that the deed should not verbally describe the reservations (which would make suits over conflicting claims more interesting) as had been done in the deed President Washington had wanted executed. The commissioners were flabbergasted. Two years before, Gantt had originally suggested such descriptions.

Meanwhile, George Walker and William Thornton battled over the parcels of land that fell through the cracks of the plan. In applying the engraved plan to the ground, surveyors found that, especially where the avenues met the intersections of streets, oddly shaped, unnumbered tracts materialized. Thornton thought they belonged to the public and wanted them used for "churches, temples, infirmaries, public academies, dispensaries, markets, public walks, fountains, statues, obelisks, & c." There could be no more than eight acres of such land, so to buy it from the proprietors would cost £200, or $532.

Walker thought these tracts should be divided between the public and the proprietors, and if the commissioners insisted on taking the land, which he estimated to amount to some 92 acres, he wanted more than £25 an acre. Land in the city was worth £1,600 an acre, and those lots were perfect for retail stores. It was imperative to save the triangular tracts from becoming "disgusting" open spaces. To Thornton's suggested uses he replied that "infirmaries" were "the greatest nuisance that can be introduced into a city." Walker, a staunch Federalist, wondered "what gods or goddesses" Thornton, a Republican, wanted his "temples" to honor. Scott and White decided to divide the lots rather than pay for them. Thornton wrote to George Washington, trying to get him to vindicate his position.[3]

*   *   *

At the end of May the president's son, Thomas Adams, visited the city. He rode past Tunnicliff's just opened Washington City Hotel and Tavern, which boasted of being "a few yards from the Capitol," with a view of the city, Georgetown, and Alexandria. Adams rode on to stay in Georgetown near his boyhood friend, cousin Cranch. As he toured the city, young Adams missed the nuances: Tunnicliff's old hotel was still locked, with lawyers circling it because Deblois had bought the building at a tax sale; Adams saw George Washington's houses going up, but the general did not tell him about the latest vexations—Blagden needed two $1,000 payments in a two-week period and a Boston glassmaker had sent him someone else's order; Joseph Wheat gave up his tavern at the foot of Barry's wharf to dig clay in the streets; Sweeny filed for bankruptcy and at his store west of the president's house square, a Mr. Allen from New York advertised "a new manufactory of ladies slippers"; William O'Neale offered his two houses at 21st and I Streets Northwest for sale but had no takers; a Mrs. Phillips advertised the opening of a school for girls near Lear's empty warehouse; Collen Williamson probably would have complained, but he was off in Annapolis hoping to get his case for back pay and reinstatement before a court.

The fawning citizens did not go out of their way to point out problems to Adams. He was "bowed and scraped to, & feasted & flattered" so that he "might make *a good report.*" Adams toured the public buildings and thought well of them, believing someone's boast that the Capitol "Might be ready for the accommodation of Congress in a few months." The president's house was "another fine, spacious and magnificent pile."

Much as Adams's guides tried to present the city in the best light, its essential blemishes shone through. As he reported to his parents, "the affairs of that city have been unfortunately managed; the title to a considerable portion of the soil is liable to dispute; private speculation has so interwoven itself with every thing relating to the concerns of the city, that no one, who does not court difficulty and embarrassment will venture to purchase there, and in my opinion a reformation must take place in the plan and entire scheme, or nothing honorable, useful, or decorous will ever result from it."

And no one spoke well of the commissioners. White knew "nothing about the business." "Presumption" was that Scott "used the public materials in building his own house upon the hill." And Thornton's "exclusive merit" was "a pretty taste in drawing." But the true measure of their incompetence showed when White told him they could not finish the president's house "without a supply of money." Adams would not spend a cent more. "Fifty millions of dollars would not suffice to finish and furnish the buildings alone, on the present scale." Locals asserted that a deal had been struck between New England and the South to put the capital on the Potomac in return for assumption of state debts. Adams was not so sure: "if the public faith is pledged, (which I don't believe) for the performance of such a condition, I must think it a misfortune and burthensome to the country." About the only nice thing Adams said about the city was that "the situation of the city is beautiful and by all accounts healthy." Despite poor provisions, once the Potomac was opened he thought there would be "an abundance of every comfort."

His report told his parents nothing they did not already know. "Your account of the commissioners corresponds with what your father has repeatedly heard," Abigail Adams replied on June 15, ". . . but as he has nine plagues, he has been loath to meddle with the tenth, and for that reason has kept clear of a visit to the federal city. Planning buildings has been no part of his education and few persons have less taste for them. If he had displaced these commissioners, those whom he might have appointed would have never given better satisfaction."[4]

*   *   *

Sloops came up the river with laths for the plasterers, but not enough scantling for the carpenters. The commissioners told Dennis that if the scantling did not arrive "in two or three weeks the Capitol will be delayed." And the laths he sent, the plasterers found, were no good. Dennis wrote back describing how busy lumberers were on the Eastern Shore. Only one man would cut the long scantling the commissioners wanted and he charged more. Other scantling was waiting to be delivered "but there is no calculating upon the tardiness of many of these boatmen." As for the laths, he had ordered them from "a professed lath gather" living some distance from him who "says they are the best he ever got before." The board took the expensive scantling and assured Dennis that the "professed lath gather . . . must have egregiously deceived himself, or have designedly imposed on you."

They ordered plaster from Alexandria for shipment to Georgetown, where small boats took it up Rock Creek to be milled by Isaac Pierce, and then slaves had to boil it down. They got a half pint of whiskey for that hot work. With plastering under way, Lewis Clephan, who had done the board's painting since 1792, did not wait for the ceremony of signing a contract to anticipate problems. He alerted the board that there was a shortage of oil in the city, so they had 500 gallons of linseed oil shipped up from Alexandria.[5]

74. The Forerunners of Numbers to Come

Too old to submit to the indignity of the state insolvency law, Morris was counting on a payment from London to make his stay in debtors' prison more pleasant. But a man from Martinique attached it to cover a protested bill endorsed by Morris that Nicholson had used to pay for Georgia lands. Morris was crestfallen. The days of urging Nicholson to join him in prison were long over. It was better to be your own jailer at home. Nicholson took the advice to heart and did not fall for the enticements of Uriah Forrest to come and serve time in Washington, where the sheriff promised to let him move about the city, where he could help Forrest wrest property from the trustees of the aggregate fund.

It was a wise choice. Greenleaf was proving that guile alone could not squeeze a living out of Washington property. He was living off the charity of his brother-in-law Cranch and his sister, to whom it was said he bore a striking resemblance. Cranch went so far as to write to his uncle the president, urging that if White truly was about to be appointed to the Supreme Court of Virginia, then Greenleaf should be appointed to replace him on the commission. No man knew better the system, "or rather want of system which has of late been pursued in that department." As for his past dealings, "misfortunes have corrected his opinions of men, and in some degree contracted the extent of his imagination. He knows well the avenues through which fraud and imposition advance upon us, and the haunts to which they retreat to elude investigation." The president's reaction was to have his wife ask her sister why her son wrote in behalf of such a character.

Few were disposed to go out of the way to help Greenleaf, Morris, and Nicholson. The trustees of the aggregate fund ran into suspicious inquiries about Nicholson. To prove that their plan to pay the commissioners was not designed to make Nicholson's life easier, the trustees extracted more property from him. By the end of May, two thirds of the creditors had agreed to support the Washington property. The trustees let the commissioners in on the good news but did not go so far as to send or promise any money.

On June 3 the commissioners responded by announcing that on August 13 they would begin auctioning off enough of Morris's and Nicholson's lots to raise $180,000. They hoped that would startle the trustees into paying the arrears, but it did not. The trustees did not respond at all. In a July 12 letter the commissioners reminded them of it, saying they "hoped indeed expected to have heard from you in the course of a few weeks." They urged them to pay up so work could begin on the War Department offices, "which will give additional value to your as well as all the other property in the city." Still no money was forthcoming.

Yet the commissioners had some reason to believe that the auction would actually raise some money. With the Capitol virtually finished, and with the good citizens of Philadelphia beginning to move to summer refuges as early as July 1, it was apparent to all that the government would move to the Potomac. The new directors of the Potomac Company were confident that with just $60,000 more they could finish the locks at Great Falls.[1]

* * *

The commissioners received two shocks that July. At the beginning of the month a storm struck the city, leaving many trees "blown down and shattered to pieces." Two horses near Rock Creek were killed by lightning. A lightning strike on Capitol Hill left "a tree torn to pieces" and prompted the commissioners to order lightning rods for the public buildings. The other shock came late in the month. A shipment of glass ordered from London arrived. In the fourteen crates and thirteen boxes most of the panes were broken. The lot cost almost $1,700. What was worse, according to the surveyor Robert King and the painter Lewis Clephan, who had both been glaziers in England, the glass was not London best crown glass but "Newcastle crown of the quality of seconds." The board refused to pay for the order.

Otherwise, work on the Capitol went on well enough. The plasterers were progressing fast enough that on July 3 the board contracted with Clephan to finish the painting by November 18. He was to give the inside three coats at 30 cents a square yard, put five coats of mahogany color on the doors at 66 cents a square yard, and cover the outside with two coats sanded at 27 cents a square yard. The contract did not include the color scheme, but the commissioners had Smallwood supply Clephan initially with 440 pounds of white lead, 200 pounds of Spanish whiting, 12 pounds of Prussian blue, 12 pounds of Turkish umber, 56 pounds of ochre, two and a quarter kegs of red lead, and "one large hogshead of Spanish whiting."

With the north wing almost finished, the board preferred raising petty cash to saving tools for future work. It had Smallwood sell unneeded ropes, carts, barrows, axes, saws, spades, and shovels. Even slaves were expendable. John Templeman hired four slaves to cut timber downriver. Like most of the New Englanders who had moved to the city, Templeman had little trouble adjusting to the use of slave labor, and he had a reputation for treating slaves well. In May an ad for a runaway placed by a Maryland planter explained how Dick, who belonged to Templeman, took Bet, who was pregnant, and her one-year-old child. Dick, the ad claimed, was "a grand villain" who "pretended to have Bet for a wife." The planter suspected they were in Georgetown or Washington city and offered an $8 reward.

Three of the slaves Templeman hired from the commissioners, Clem, Moses, and Jess, belonged to Joseph Queen, who lived downriver. Anthony, another Queen slave working at the Capitol, begged Templeman to take him. "He assures me," Templeman wrote to the commissioners, "that there is a pair of sawyers now at the Capitol, say George and Oliver, who square good and do not want to go below. I hope you will not consider me as troublesome, I write at present as much to oblige the poor fellow as myself. He seems very uneasy at being obliged to stay, when the others are gone to work very near home." Two of the Brent sisters' slaves pressed to join too. The commissioners let them all go.[2]

Harbaugh made good progress on the Treasury building and submitted a list of nine changes in the interior work that seemed sensible. The first put the "water closets or previs" in a more convenient spot. Hoban endorsed the changes. Since Thornton paid little attention to the design of the executive offices, and since

Harbaugh absorbed the cost of all the changes in his contract, the board approved them. With that building staying within budget, the board felt bold enough to begin work on the building that would house both the War and State departments.

On July 23 they solicited bids for the building from the men who bid on the Treasury building. Specifications were the same, save that the foundation was to be ten feet deeper. Harbaugh won the bid again and on August 6 contracted to finish the building by November 1, 1800, at a cost of $39,511. The *Georgetown Centinel* thought such progress worthy of comment and on August 9 reported that the ground for the new building was marked and digging had begun. It welcomed Harbaugh's doing it because the Treasury "appears to merit and meet general approbation." It also noted the "elegant houses" rising near the Capitol and that the completion of the Capitol had been "hastened."

At long last there was a sign of public building east of the Capitol. William Marbury, who had been appointed naval agent, offered to buy white oak, red cedar, mulberry, and pine for a seventy-four-gun ship to be built in the city of Washington. Joshua Humphreys, the government's master shipbuilder, came to take soundings of the Eastern Branch and, to judge from Law's report to Washington, liked what he felt. Humphreys told Law that there were two or three places suitable for the Navy Yard and that he was "glad to find that the bottom is so muddy and soft." Isaac Polock also quizzed Humphreys and came away convinced that the yard would be on his property, which meant, he told the commissioners, that he could finally pay for his lots.[3]

*   *   *

That the commissioners would dare set a date for an auction in August attested to the change in the nation's attitude toward the "sickly season." Back in 1791 the commissioners had been leery of a summer auction for fear that Northerners would not come. But after a succession of yellow fever epidemics on the Eastern seaboard, Northerners were less prone to dismiss the South as the sickly region. Crowded cities, anywhere, became the places to avoid. Even Boston was deemed unfit to visit in the late summer.

Washington was a summer resort. Bishop John Carroll, the late commissioner's brother, left Baltimore and rusticated at Notley Young's mansion southwest of the Capitol. Law marveled at the notables visiting the city that August: Fenno, the Philadelphia editor, was there; the clerk of the House of Representatives came shopping for a lot; and Wignall's theater troupe came to play in Georgetown and Alexandria but enjoyed themselves in the rural city. "Last night I heard Bernard and Darley," Law recounted to General Washington, "and spent a very pleasant evening. There were Thornton the architect, Cliffen the poet and painter, Bernard the actor and Darley the singer, in short several choice spirits the forerunners of numbers to come."

Bernard and Darley did not come to buy lots, but enough gentlemen from Baltimore came to put a sense of anticipation in the air. Blodget, no mean promoter, came to move lots and sensed that the city's hour had arrived. On August 13, the day of the commissioners' sale, he placed an ad offering 150 lots for sale, some surrounding the president's house but most along the southern border of the farm he had bought, flanking P Street Northwest from 5th to 13th Streets, which means they were rather far from the action. He told all "that this is probably the best moment to secure a few lots at a low price." Since his second lottery had been in suspended animation for almost two years, and since the lots he was offering were supposed to be securing that lottery, he offered prizewinners the chance to pay for lots with their winning tickets.

But Forrest was the great actor on the stage of the auction. In the first three days, he had Harbaugh buy 151 lots for him. The plunge was both a necessity and an opportunity. That Morris and Nicholson had used lots to secure loans did not prevent the board from selling them. If another party bought lots Forrest held as security, the Bank of Columbia might force Forrest to come up with more security for the notes he had endorsed for Morris and Nicholson. Since he held scrip for the lots, any money he paid over $80 would be credited to himself. Besides, buying lots cheaply on the west side of town fortified his growing holdings there. If Congress convened in the president's house, he would make much, and he did what he could to bring about that event.

Two gentlemen from out of town came to a board meeting and began talking as if it had been decided that Congress would sit in the president's house. On being corrected, the gentlemen informed the board that Forrest had a letter from Treasury Secretary Wolcott assuring him that such was the case. White dashed off a note to Wolcott, who he was sure had written no such letter, asking him to discredit the rumor so it would not revive "those jealousies and animosities which have heretofore occasioned so much discord" and helped "retard" building near the Capitol, which was "going on with great alacrity." Wolcott replied that he had expressed no opinion though he had rented a house for himself and his family in Georgetown.

On the sixth day of sales, August 22, one of the visitors from Baltimore finally made a move. After buying two lots the day before, Solomon Etting, a merchant, bought 109 lots, paying as little as $38 for a lot just northeast of Judiciary Square and a top price of $181 for a lot near 6th and Pennsylvania Southeast. Total sales that day topped $13,306. Etting then bought two lots privately at 17th and G, just west of the president's house, for eight cents a square foot. Then, in what must have been a genial contest, Etting and Blodget bought forty-eight and fifty-nine lots, respectively, for as low as $31 apiece, along the gully formed by Tiber Creek; to these two buyers went 107 lots for $5,930, or $55 a lot.

In early September the *Georgetown Centinel* was teeming with notices of lots on the block. Carroll offered to sell the lots on which the twenty buildings stood, noting that "the situation is among the first in the city, being very elevated." Forrest announced he would offer 206 lots on Friday, September 27, at the Little Hotel. Acting jointly, Forrest and Deakins offered 113 more lots. The lots were the security held by Forrest and Deakins for their 1797 loan to Morris and Nicholson.

The trustees of the aggregate fund had yet to pay any attention to the commissioners' sale, but the success of the sale and the ads placed by Carroll and Forrest forced Dorsey into action. He gave the commissioners a note for $10,000 and assured them the houses on the point would be finished. He also placed an ad cautioning the public that the trustees claimed interest in the lots Forrest and Deakins were selling.

Forrest retaliated. "I trust the public in general, and the people of this neighborhood in particular," read his ad, which the editor of the *Centinel* placed right below the trustees' caution, "have suffered enough already by certain speculators and swindlers of Philadelphia, to know that not much respect is due to their caution." They were out "to cripple the place." He and Deakins "have the advice of eminent counsel in this state, that our title is indisputable."

Dorsey's note was payable in Philadelphia, so the board could not yet count it as a payment. They continued the auction and felt good about it. In a September 1 letter, Thornton shared the good news with George Washington. "Our late sales have been very productive, and purchases of great extent have been made by persons resident in Baltimore. We shall continue them as long as we find purchasers. The trustees of Morris and Nicholson are going to finish the houses at the Point."[4]

75. With Perfect Safety from Risk

Thornton had been too sanguine. Shortly after he bragged about the sale, interest in it flagged. On paper the sale made $41,000, but whether the major buyers, save for Etting, could pay was doubtful. There was no hope of money from Blodget and very little from Forrest, since their private sales went badly. So the year that began with such hopes for the Georgetown interests ended in gloom. Not only did the president show no inclination to move the government to Georgetown, but with the removal of Congress a year away, the almost finished Capitol swarmed with workmen and the unfinished president's house was deserted. Not only did the order to finish the president's house to suit meetings of Congress never come, but there was not enough money on hand to simply finish it as the president's residence.

Most painful to the men who trusted in the preeminence of the western end of the city was that they were broke. The proprietors near the Capitol were building ten houses in orderly fashion around the Capitol square and down New Jersey Avenue. There were buildings going up in the West End, most notably Tayloe's house, which Lovering began building after the legislature granted him protection under the insolvency act, allowing him to get a bond for his work. But there was not enough building to rival, let alone eclipse, the activity on Capitol Hill. Instead of Stoddert or Forrest stepping in to develop classy dwellings around the president's house, the mover and shaker there was Bennett Fenwick, slave driver. He farmed a tract just northeast of the president's house, dug clay just northwest of it, sold bricks to Lovering for Tayloe's house just southwest of it, and built the tavern just to the east of the Treasury. The commissioners had to channel his grasping for profits, ordering him to stop making clay pits so close to the president's house and to stop planting crops in the streets.

What led to the downfall of Forrest and Scott was their dealing with Morris and Nicholson. Law and Carroll had battled the pair of speculators. Scott and Forrest, however, did not give up. Back in the winter, Edward Fox had suggested using Morris's and Nicholson's lots to secure a loan directly to the commissioners. Then the idea seemed to beg the question. With sales not raising money and most of the public lots pledged to repay the $300,000 worth of loans already raised, the idea was the last chance. Scott would get the board to write the president and get his approval, and Forrest would use the lots to secure a $50,000 loan from Maryland. As for private building, there was still a year to go. Scott and Forrest could not give up; personal bankruptcy was a distinct possibility.[1]

*   *   *

The president was far away in Quincy, so the board gave him ample warning of its need to have his authority to go to Maryland for the loan. But the federal city, as ever, was far from his mind. Those who worked with him most closely did not even think of bringing federal city matters to his attention. Secretary of State Pickering had an idea to save American ports from yellow fever. In place of solid docks that caused the shoreline to silt up and become receptacles of disease-causing filth, the portion of docks nearest the shore should be a bridge so that there would be a free flow of water along the shore. He thought the city of Washington needed such docks because "the Eastern Branch . . . wanting a large head of water will require extraordinary precaution to preserve its depth." Pickering sent his ideas not to the commissioners or the president, but to George Washington.[2]

*   *   *

Washington had other things on his mind. He sent Pickering's ideas to the commissioners. His chief worries were his wife's bad fever and his being obliged to ask the Bank of Alexandria for a loan. By the standards of the day it was a rather conservative proposition. Payment on a sixty-day note for $1,000 was due, and rather than have his money on deposit cover the note, he asked for another sixty days in which to pay. Like any Virginia planter, Washington was no stranger to debt, but being indulged privately by one's agent in London or Philadelphia was one thing. Having the board of a bank say yea or nay every sixty days was scarcely bearable, especially when confusing rules dictated exactly how one had to go about getting credit.

Washington did not entirely blame his houses for draining his pocketbook, but it was the major expenditure on which he was getting no return. His farms, mill, distillery, and fisheries provided something. Although he did not draw his full salary as lieutenant general, he did get some pay, which defrayed the expense of feeding an endless file of would-be officers and their horses. He could look forward only to renting the houses. In July he asked Thornton what the rent should be. Thornton thought ten percent of the expenditure on building was the common rent, but since congressmen were used to less, seven and a half percent plus taxes and insurance would prevent "murmurs." He reminded Washington that "gentlemen of fortune will visit the city and be suddenly inclined to fix here," so the houses would sell easily for $9,000 or $10,000 each, and the proceeds could be laid out in building more houses, "with perfect safety from risk."

John Francis, the Philadelphia hotelkeeper, continued to express interest in the houses through Thornton. Blagden was confident one house would be ready November 1, 1799, and the other by March 1, 1800. Washington told Francis what the terms were and when the houses would be available and hoped a deal could be closed as soon as possible. Francis trusted Washington's "own sense of justice" to fix the rent "as it ought to be," but given the great expense he would incur moving from Philadelphia to Washington, he could not pay rent until he moved to the city on August 1, 1800. Washington countered that they should split the loss. If the houses were ready by March, he would absorb the loss for April and May, and Francis would pay rent beginning in June. Washington even enumerated all the then certain costs of the two houses and the lots they were on, $13,451.31, so Francis could get an idea of what the rent would be. Francis never wrote back.[3]

*   *   *

When Congress arrived in December 1800, the commissioners expected to be out of a job. They decided they could no longer extend credit beyond that date. They wanted lots paid for and houses built by then so they could close their accounts. A lower price made those conditions more palatable. They gave a 50 percent discount on the price of a lot if a brick building was built on it by December 1800.

Private sales by the board did not slacken. Blodget had brought down General Samuel Smith from Baltimore, and the congressman and merchant bought two lots just west of the president's house for five and a half and seven cents a square foot. Captain Thomas Truxton bought just north of Pennsylvania Avenue at 6th Street Northwest for seven cents and a waterside lot along the Eastern Branch at 12th Street Southeast for $10 a front foot. An agent made the purchases for Truxton, the captain of the *Constellation*. His victory over the *Insurgente* in February 1799 made him the hero of the moment. He became the first of not a few navy captains to invest their prize money in Washington real estate.

Truxton's waterside lot was near the Navy Yard. Stoddert, however, had failed in his effort to get Washington the one and only navy yard. Facing an election year, Adams had decided to build six, and Washington got one as long as it could decide where to put it. Humphrey decided to place it at the exchange square on the Eastern Branch between 9th and 7th Streets, provided some privately owned land could be included.

Stoddert thought there would be no problem with this condition since, of the 65 acres wanted, only 25 were what he called "fast land." The rest was covered by water at high tide or always underwater. Prout was willing to give up his share of the grounds in return for equivalent lots, but Carroll was not so sure. He would agree to a trade but under protest. "I am convinced the changing of that which was intended for an exchange into a navy yard," he wrote to the commissioners on August 27, "is depriving the property adjoining of the greatest and most valuable advantages that any other property possesses in the city." This exasperated the commissioners, who, the week before, had fielded a letter from Carroll asking permission to keep the farm he had along the Tiber just north of the Capitol in Indian corn until the early summer of 1800.

Carroll had a habit of walking away when matters appeared to be reaching a crisis. Just as he had gone off to Kentucky when Morris and Nicholson were about to build on South Capitol Street, he went off to the Genesee lands without executing the deed for the square the navy wanted, which caused consternation. Stoddert insisted on clear title to the land before any construction began. The Republicans opposed the naval buildup as a ploy to enrich friends of the government, citing the experience of 1794, when wharves financed with public funds were built on private land.

To Stoddert's chagrin, the commissioners even delayed sending him good title to the public lands. Stoddert complained and the navy agent Marbury went so far as to remind them of the nation's peril. "Delay in the execution of the business will be of very serious consequences to the United States." The board reminded Stoddert that it was the president, not the commissioners, who had to assign the public lands. Finally, Carroll came back to the city, the president returned to Philadelphia, and that bit of acrimony ended.[4]

*   *   *

To be accused of causing a delay had to amuse the commissioners. They reminded the president of their need for his authorization for another loan. Then their contractors seemed to be dawdling. There were too few plasterers, which the board remedied by ordering the contractor Kearney to double his force to twenty men and to use more slaves. Some of the stone laid in the foundation of the war office had to be replaced, but that was predictable. Most frustrating was the inability to get supplies. True to the tracts of its many propagandists, the Potomac valley did supply stone, lime, clay, a little lumber, and certainly enough sand, but it was sorely deficient in the materials needed to finish a building. The board frequently had to send to Baltimore for hardware and paint, and it found that delivery by packet took six weeks.

Window glass was the main problem. They had ordered glass for the Capitol in November 1798 and for the Treasury in January 1799, and they still had no glass. Early spring was their absolute deadline. The board tried to make a cause out of it by proclaiming that it wanted American-made glass. But the only American glassmaker capable of the job, Charles Keepser in Boston, sensed that he was dealing with gentlemen who did not know anything about glass. He explained that crown window glass was made in round sheets with a knot in the middle, and it could not be made large enough for what the commissioners wanted. There was also rolled glass, which came in cylinders without a knot in the middle and which could be made large enough to answer but had to go through a second process "by which it loses part of its brilliancy." That said, Keepser looked over the commissioners' order for the president's house and offered to supply only the smallest panes. There was a man in town who had imported large panes from Europe that were "of tolerable good quality," but they were going fast.

The commissioners were reminded again and again that there was little respect for their undertaking. No one was going to drop anything, let alone everything, and come to their rescue. Not even the president. The secretary of state informed them, at the president's direction, that the attorney general was of the opinion that the board had no power to ask for a loan without specific legislative authority. They promptly protested, though since no one sent them Attorney General Lee's opinion they were not sure on what it was based. They pointed out that President Washington and attorneys general Randolph and Bradford all thought they had the power to negotiate a loan.[5]

76. 'Tis Well

George Washington was sure he could get a painter for less than the $2 a day Blagden's man wanted. Thornton agreed that $2 was too much and that Blagden's man obviously charged so much because he thought Washington was rich. Thornton told Blagden to hire the painters before they knew where they would work. Washington, however, investigated what Alexandria painters charged and found that it was the same price. Thus by degrees he was reconciled to the high price of painters, though he retained a suspicion that the painters' insistence on charging by the square yard, "London measurement," was a ploy to shrink a square yard from its customary nine square feet. He left it up to Blagden to hire whom he wanted and bothered with only one more point on the matter. He wanted sand "dashed" on the last coat of paint just as he had done at Mount Vernon. Still not having heard from Francis, he informed Thornton on October 6 that it "would comport better" with his finances to sell the houses rather than rent them.[1]

But sales were flat once again. Davidson thought he had a deal for lots with Edward Jones, a Treasury Department clerk, but Jones, when he returned to Philadelphia, thought better of it. Other than to procure his own lodging, it made no sense to buy lots with an eye to any immediate gain. It might make sense, however, to invest part of his "children's legacy" in Davidson's lots. Davidson retaliated with one of those sardonic letters he was so good at, telling Jones that he could "not but embrace with pleasure your notification that the said provisional agreement is null and void" and assuring Jones that his "confidence in the value of our city lots is by no means diminished." Davidson turned his attention to building his mansion on a hill, in Georgetown.

The promise of a navy yard at the foot of his property perked William Prout up. "On account of the war in Europe our city has not progressed so fast as was expected until this summer," he confessed, but he assured his brother in England that with the public buildings nearly finished "and grate number of elegant houses . . . building," once the government came in June, he expected to see "every house in this place rented." Meanwhile, his nephew William Huston had got married and seemed to reform. Prout set him up in the store once again, offering him half the profits, "which in a little time would have been something considerable." But Huston started drinking and gambling again. The store was "about two hundred yards from my dwelling house," Prout explained to Huston's father, "where he and myself slept alternately for the security of the goods and the nights he slept there he used to take a mulatto woman with him into the store and his wife at the same time here in my house." Prout kicked Huston out; he got a job with a printer in Alexandria.

Huston had good reason to sleep on the job. Business was bad. Edward Langley put his store at South Capitol and N Streets up for sale. James Blake, who had been trying to sell two houses at 13th and F Northwest, announced he was leaving town. William O'Neale stopped trying to sell his houses at 21st and Pennsylvania and opened his own boardinghouse and general store. About that time a daughter, Peggy, was born; when she became Mrs. Eaton, she would cause half of Andrew Jackson's cabinet to resign. Dermott diversified into helping Virginia planters get back their slaves who had run away to the relative safety of the federal city. Not that the city was a paradise for blacks, especially those working for Bennett Fenwick. He was advertising a $10 reward for another runaway.

Two notables sought refuge under the Maryland insolvency act: Dalton, the former senator, and Cranch, the president's nephew. Cranch had feared he would have to go to jail for debts he incurred on behalf of Morris, "one creditor did everything in his power by threats and bribes to the sheriff to induce him to commit me to prison." Friends saved his property at the sheriff's sale. Uriah Forrest bought all his furniture and books for $513, all of which he let Cranch keep and reimburse Forrest later. (Other bargains put on the block by the sheriff that season included two tracts just northwest of the city called Chevy Chase and Friendship.)

Greenleaf kept trying to prove there was life after bankruptcy. As soon as a Maryland judge forced him to acknowledge his deed to the trustees, Greenleaf offered to work for the trustees. If Greenleaf acted fast, the remaining woodwork in the houses at the point could be saved; if he did not act, even the foundations would be damaged by the weather. Greenleaf offered to manage the property for ten percent of sales and rentals, but he did not give up fighting for his property.

Just after the board finished auctioning some valuable waterside lots to Barry and Blodget, a court injunction arrived forbidding the sale, thanks to Greenleaf. He had bought the lots auctioned back in 1794. Although he had never paid for them, the court, in its leisurely fashion, would hear his case. Meanwhile, the board could not collect the $5,000 for which it sold the lots.[2]

* * *

The president did not respond to the board's arguments against the attorney general's opinion. Scott decided that the solution was to ignore the president. He argued that they needed presidential authority for a loan only when public lots were mortgaged. They were offering Morris's and Nicholson's lots. White would not fall for such sophistry and was resigned to finishing what they could with the $50,000 remaining from the federal loan and the Maryland stock they had on hand. Congress itself would bear the expense of furnishing the buildings, as it had done in New York and Philadelphia. Thornton hated to see a bare treasury just when it was time to add the finishing touches to his Capitol, so the board asked for a loan anyway. White registered a protest in the minutes.

The commissioners did not completely ignore the president. Hoping he would sing the praises of the city in his annual message, they had Hoban write an unusually full report on the state of the work, from the sixteen columns "of the ancient ionic order, two feet three inches in diameter," to the lightning rods. More important, he provided the dimensions of the two chambers, five committee rooms, five clerks' offices, two halls, an attic chamber, and the staircases. The plasterers had three more weeks of work, and the painters had two more coats to put on. The stairs were all prepared and ready to put up. Half the carpenters could be dismissed January 1, and all of the carpentry and joining would be done by February 1.

The executive offices, Hoban thought, were right on schedule. The Treasury walls, roof, and gutter were up. The exterior was painted, woodwork and floors ready to put in. The upstairs was plastered. The walls of the war office were up to street level. All the stone, bricks, and plank needed were on the spot. At the president's house, all the woodwork save for a quarter of the flooring plank was ready to put in. That plus the plastering, painting, and other finishing work would cost, Hoban estimated, $32,480.57, money the board did not have.

The commissioners told Adams they had provided dimensions of the Capitol's rooms so that Congress could furnish them. Since work at the president's house had been suspended, no dimensions need be sent up; the president would be staying in a private house. They assured him, however, that if they collected enough debts, or if Congress provided funds, they would send up the size of the house's rooms so that the president could see that they were furnished. To accommodate other government officials, "a number of houses" were up or begun near the Capitol, and there had been "preparations made by opulent men for building early next season." There were enough houses in Georgetown and around the president's house to accommodate the executive officers, so there was no reason not to move the government to the city. All "will be perfectly satisfied with their situation." The president notified Congress that the commissioners thought the city would be ready to receive the government.

The board put pressure on Stoddert, the oldest booster of the president's house, to raise the money needed to finish it. The trustees of the aggregate fund had still not agreed to the plan negotiated almost a year before. The board asked Stoddert to negotiate with them in Philadelphia and try to get $50,000 or $60,000. Stoddert approached the trustees. He understood what was at stake and used his position as the man in Philadelphia who knew the city best to put all the talk about building near the Capitol in perspective. When Liston, the British minister, asked about suitable housing, Stoddert told him there was none near the Capitol.[3]

Then Liston and his wife toured Virginia, and accepted an invitation to visit Mount Vernon. On their way through the federal city, they were surprised to see houses near the Capitol. They told White what Stoddert had said. White told George Washington. It was not the only bit of perfidy the former president had to contemplate.

On the same day that White wrote, Thornton told Washington about the roadblocks Adams had put in the way of the desperately needed loan. Washington replied promptly, and his anger flashed. He admitted that he had not read the recent laws Congress had passed relative to the city, but "no doubt" ever occurred in his or his officers' minds that the commissioners had the power to get a loan. "But, by the obstructions continually thrown in its way, by *friends* or *enemies,* this city has had to pass through a fiery trial. Yet, I trust will, ultimately, escape the ordeal with éclat. Instead of a *fiery trial* it would have been more appropriate to have said, it has passed, or is on its passage through, the ordeal of local interest, destructive jealousies, and inveterate prejudices; as difficult, and as dangerous I conceive, as any of the other ordeals."

The effort to sabotage Capitol Hill property was a low blow to one who wanted to sell two houses. Washington had seen the buildings on November 9. Neither side was near completion. On November 13 Thornton notified him that Blagden needed another $1,000. Washington did not object but observed, "I fear the work which is not enumerated in the contract with him, is pretty smartly whipped up in the price of it.—I had no expectation (for instance) that a well little more than 30 feet deep, was to cost me upwards of £70." Then, when he tried to get the money from the Bank of Alexandria, he discovered that, "not being well enough acquainted with the rules of the bank," he applied on the wrong day. He would have to wait a week to get it, but if Blagden was in a hurry he could ride out and Washington would borrow the sum from his nephew.

In his reply to White, Washington showed no trace of anger. He merely analyzed the evidence. Liston, the British minister, had no motive for misrepresenting what Stoddert had told him, and what Mrs. Liston was reported to have said "was more pointed": she described "the attempts of diverting the followers of the government from engaging houses in the vicinity of the Capitol." Washington could only trust that "accommodations will be found equal to the demand for them; and altho' (I believe it may be said with truth) that those whose interest it was, most to promote the welfare and growth of the city, have been its worst enemies, yet that matters will still go right."

What makes a man angry need not have anything to do with his death, and the city was not Washington's last peeve. As he rode around his plantation in dreadful weather, he saw a cattle pen so dilapidated that he thought the cattle would have been better off running wild. Then he wondered why, with more than 101 cows, his overseer still had to buy butter. That night, hardly able to breathe or talk through his sore and swollen throat, he recognized death's coming instantly. He had himself bled and followed the doctors' orders, entailing blisters and more bleeding, with no expectation that he would get better. Nothing he said on his deathbed pertained to the unfinished city that bore his name and that showed the imprint of his, more than any other man's, will. His last request was that he not be put into the vault until three days after his death.

He and some old friends, including Robert Morris, had once pledged to live to see the dawn of the new century. " 'Tis well" were his last words, and he died on December 14, 1799.

Washington's death surprised and shocked the nation. On December 19 the House formed a committee of sixteen, chaired by John Marshall of Virginia, to decide what should be done to mark his passing. On the 23rd the committee reported and the House passed a resolution that the government erect a marble monument in the Capitol "and that the family of General Washington be requested to permit his body to be deposited under it; and that the monument be so designed as to commemorate the great events of his military and political life." Then Henry Lee rose to say "one hope is cherished, that whatever is done, will be unanimously adopted. This will be most pleasing to our constituents and most honorable to the character we all honor." The president promptly sent his secretary William Shaw to Mount Vernon to get the family's permission.[4]

Washington's passing did not bring forth an outpouring of support for his city. The Maryland legislature bought 130 more shares in the Potomac Company before he died. After his death the House defeated the loan bill by one vote. Supporters would try again when some of the opposition went home to spend Christmas with their families. Nor did the death of Washington inspire the trustees of the aggregate fund to invest in the city. Stoddert got the board's approval to offer them a cessation of forced sales for a mere $40,000 payment to be given in monthly installments once the building season began. The trustees would not commit. That blow was softened by the Maryland legislature finally coming through and loaning the city $50,000 in six percent stock.[5]

*   *   *

The day after Washington died, someone wrote a description of the public buildings. Here too was part of the legacy the hero had left. The largest room wrought was the Senate chamber, 48 by 86 feet and 41 feet high. The House would sit one floor up in the library, 35 by 86 feet and 36 feet high. The anonymous appraiser counted five committee rooms 30 by 35 feet and 19 feet high on the first story, as well as a lobby, 22 by 38 feet, with a view of the highest ceiling, 56 feet high. Outside the House chamber was a lobby 22 by 38 feet, an antechamber 21 by 45 feet, and a clerks' office 30 by 35 feet. There were offices on the third floor too. All the work was "nearly complete."

The audience room in the president's house was 40 by 80 feet and 20 feet high. The "eliptic" room was 30 by 40 feet. There were two rooms on the principal story 22 by 28 feet, two 28 by 38 feet, and a "private room" 14 by 18. "The north front is finished with pediment." There were chambers upstairs and "apartments for servants" in the basement. The description did not characterize the state of any of the rooms. East of the president's house stood the Treasury, "in great forwardness," with twelve rooms on both first and second stories and eight rooms in the garret story. The war office, on the other side of the president's house, was "begun and will be finished early next year." "The basement of this and all other buildings contain convenient apartments for servants & c & c." Finally, "the number of tenable house (that is of the value of 100 dollars & upwards), by a late return are 570, . . . the number of inhabitants 3,420."

*   *   *

The day before Washington died, Alexander White got caught in a snowstorm on his way to Winchester and decided to wait the storm out in Leesburg. He used his leisure to write to the president, amplifying on the last letter the commissioners had sent to Adams. In that letter, he explained, it had been thought impolitic to say exactly what private houses would be available for his residence until the president's house was finished. White said they were thinking of Tayloe's house, which was "in great forwardness," and two new houses built by Carroll and Law near the Capitol. "Any one of these three," White noted, "is better than the President . . . , as such, has resided in."[6]

1800

77. Large Naked, Ugly Looking Building

On New Year's Eve Martha Washington relented and agreed to give up the remains of her husband. "In doing this," she said in her letter to the president, "I need not, I can not, say what a sacrifice of individual fooling I make to a sense of public duty." Thornton promptly wrote to John Marshall that the obvious spot for a mausoleum was "in the center of the intended dome," which "is the point from which we calculate our longitudes." (If the world accepted Ellicott's recalculations of same.)

Thornton frankly noted that placing the remains there would be "a very great inducement" to finishing the whole Capitol, "which has been thought of by some contracted minds, unacquainted with the grand work, to be upon too great a scale." Small minds would be won over to the project if "the remains of the virtuous Washington render it more dear to them." Aware of how dearly the widow wanted to be entombed with him, Thornton suggested that "in a secret vote" Congress agree to let her bones join her husband's in the national temple.

The remains of Washington would build the Capitol. The idea did not excite anyone in Philadelphia, but White's letter about housing the president, written a few weeks earlier, did. After pondering it Adams finally realized what was happening. He took Stoddert aside and, as Stoddert explained in a January 2 letter to the commissioners, told him that he would not, as White suggested, "take for his residence one of General Washington's houses or Mr. Carrolls, but was determined to occupy the house intended for him." He told Stoddert to have the commissioners furnish, through Stoddert, a plan of the house and "an estimate of the sum necessary, and the time it will require to furnish each room. His intention," Stoddert continued, "is to direct the completion of such rooms as he shall judge necessary for his accommodation, if the whole cannot be finished in time." And then the honest New Englander shone through: "His year in his present house will end in June, and his wish is to remove his furniture at that time to his house in the city."

The temper of Adams would complete the president's house. With the Maryland loan passed, the commissioners readied for work there, ordering all the tenants in dwellings on the president's house square to vacate by February 1 so workers could move in. They ordered 19,800 feet of plank and scantling from Dennis and glass and hardware from London, and they learned from Hoban that the carpenters could be shifted from the Capitol to the president's house in one month.

Scott and Thornton did not ignore White's private letter to the president. In a letter to Stoddert in which they assured him work would begin on the president's house in one month, they expressed shock at White's advice to the president. They held "it to be highly dishonorable to violate that faith which was pledged to the city proprietors when they relinquished their property for a city." The president's house must be built, for the sites of the public buildings were "founded on principles of eternal justice, and can never change nor ought they to be deviated from, but when an absolute and inevitable necessity compels the measure."

White returned to the city on January 14, went to the office, and found the copy of that letter. He dashed off a letter to his colleagues "explicitly" denying what Stoddert said he had written. Then he wrote to the president, quoting extracts from both letters. Reminding him that he had stated facts and not advised anything, he asked the president to send back a copy of the offending letter so he could vindicate his honor.[1]

*   *   *

Relations between the commissioners were not improved when the Maryland Council, which, along with the governor, ran the state, looked askance at the $50,000 loan. In passing the loan, the Maryland legislature called for the personal security of the commissioners, as well as property they controlled as an official board. Already overextended, Scott wanted to avoid such a requirement. He and Thornton offered to so undervalue Morris's and Nicholson's lots as to make them adequate. The governor and the council were not so sure. First, they thought all lots under the control of the commissioners were pledged as security for the loans guaranteed by Congress. Second, they thought the president's authorization was needed. Finally, they put little value on city property. Scott and Thornton were stunned. They had been so confident that their money problems were over that they had sold $6,000 worth of stock to Forrest for a $5,000 note payable in April, even though they knew he was short of cash.

White made it clear to his colleagues that if Maryland insisted on personal security, he would not oblige. Scott pressed the governor and the council to amend their position. White had gone back to Woodville, so Scott could not petition in person. Assuming that doubt about the value of the lots was the chief stumbling block, Scott explained that since they had had the choice of 6,000 public lots in December 1793, Morris and Greenleaf had selected "among the best the commissioners held." The board had the power to resell 1,210 of those lots, and it had "no hesitation in saying, that on a credit of six, twelve and eighteen months, we think these lots will sell to *good* and *responsible* purchasers for more than the original purchase money." At $80 a lot, that amounted to at least $100,000, but they were willing to value them at half that. The stretching Scott gave to the truth—Greenleaf and Morris had not had the pick of the lots, and many of the good lots they chose had already been conveyed to others—showed how desperate he and Thornton were to avoid giving personal bond. Of course, in the letter to the council they gladly offered their bond and expressed willingness to get the bond of others. In a letter to their lawyer Key, however, they confessed giving their "responsibility for the loan is quite an extra official act and by no means pleasant." They would have to raise $50,000 from the sale of Morris's and Nicholson's lots that summer to end their personal obligation as soon as possible.

In the midst of all this, Thornton received word that a sizable check of his had bounced in England. He began having chest pains. When the council still refused to hold the lots as mortgage and asked for the commissioners' personal security, Thornton put the best face on it, bragging to one friend, "They have such dependence on us as to grant it [the loan] under our personal security without involving the city lots—so that we have defeated all opposition, and shall apply vigorously to the completion of the President's house." Thornton was scraping by on his salary, some rents, and stud fees. Although overextended, Scott had more resources, but before jeopardizing them, he called in Uriah Forrest to lend a hand. He agreed to join in the bond, pledging 425 acres of Montgomery County real estate.

Despite Thornton's boasting, taking the commissioners' security was a rather oblique compliment to them, since it reflected an impatience with the endless ballyhoo about the value of city lots. The governor and a majority of the council decided the commissioners would say anything to get the loan they so desperately needed. The state could not abandon the city, but it could at least extract something from the perpetrators of what might turn out to be a fiasco. A member of the council in favor of taking lots as security took a position not much more flattering. If the loan were never repaid, it was still worth it for the state to support the city.[2]

*   *   *

Enough glass arrived from Boston to begin glazing the Capitol. Thornton celebrated by taking his wife with him to the cozier building so she could watch him work. ". . . We staid for some time by a fire," Mrs. Thornton wrote in the diary she began that year, "in a room where they were glazing the windows—while Dr T—n laid out an oval, round which is to be the communication to the gallery of the Senate room."

To judge from Mrs. Thornton's diary, such work was not common. The Thorntons took a week in mid-January to visit their Maryland farm. On their return, the first order of business was to prepare accounts on Washington's houses (now due to be finished in April), since the will was about to be executed. Then much time was spent fielding inquiries about a prize horse, Clifden, that Thornton had imported. On good days they paid visits to the Laws, Peters,

Dorseys, and Polocks, and being at the midpoint between George-town and the Hill, they generally had company. Mrs. Thornton did most of her shopping in Georgetown. She went to a shop on New Jersey Avenue to look for black chintz but thought it "a poor little store—there are too few inhabitants for any business to be carried on extensively." The deepest snow in five years afforded Mr. Thornton the leisure to work on the plans of a house for a lot across the street from Tayloe. Although their landlord, Blodget, put no pressure on them to move, the house was likely planned as a residence for themselves, since she described it as "a house to build one day or other."

The crisis over funds for the building did not seem to make Thornton any more realistic. He urged Stoddert to get Congress to give Adams $100,000 to furnish the president's house. With that sum, the house could be made to "conform to the dignity of his station." "Few of our countrymen have traveled," he preached; "their views therefore are generally contracted. Our country is extensive, our resources great, and our ideas ought to be exalted."

Stoddert filed that communication away and got down to the business of persuading the House Ways and Means Committee not only to furnish the public buildings but also to build footpaths to serve them. He made clear that the commissioners, of whose performance few congressmen approved, need not have anything to do with it. The four cabinet officers could administer the funds.

Adams looked over the floor plan of the president's house Thornton had sent to Stoddert and promptly sent back explicit instructions through Stoddert. "He desires me to say," the secretary wrote, "that there will be quite enough room for him without finishing the large room. —the other part of that floor he is very desirous should be plastered and painted as early as may be, that it may be perfectly dry when he takes possession. About one half the upper story he thinks will be enough, if you should not have time and money to compleat the whole of that story." He would be sending his furniture in June.

Stoddert added that the commissioners had to do something about that "large naked, ugly looking building . . . A private gentleman preparing a residence for his friend, would have done more than has been done; would you not be ashamed to conduct the President to

the house without there being an enclosure of any kind about it."
Stoddert urged a garden be planted in the style of Bingham's garden
in Philadelphia and a stable and carriage house built. The house, he
advised, should be ready by June.

But there were other signals coming from Philadelphia. Abigail
Adams gave her nephew Cranch the impression that the president's
house might not do. Shaw, the president's secretary and nephew,
told Cranch that Mrs. Adams had said she would never come to the
federal city. Cranch assured her that the city was "without any
comparison, more healthy than that of Philadelphia, New York, or
even Boston, and infinitely more agreeable. The situation of the
President's house is high and airy, and is proved to be as healthy as
any part of the world. The views from it are delightful; and the
water is remarkably good." Abigail said Shaw had it wrong. She
would go to the city, but she did admit that she was "somewhat
discouraged from the account of the roads, and from the account of
the President's house which is represented so very large and like to
be uncomfortably cold, situated from all society, without furniture,
for what is contained in this house, 'tis said, will be lost in that. Into
that house the President is determined to go and part of it I hope
may be got ready so as to accommodate him for the session."
Cranch mentioned to Law that if his aunt came to the city, the first
family might want a private house after all.[3]

                                *   *   *

In their official letter to Stoddert, Scott and Thornton pledged
that the president's "directions shall be pursued." They reported
that twenty carpenters were at work in the building but that they
thought the building could not be ready until October or November.
Until then, they could "lodge very safely" his furniture. No mention
was made of the continuing leaks in the roof or of the leaks that had
begun in the Capitol roof.

In an unofficial letter to Stoddert, Thornton gave his highest
priority to the garden. Scott, and White before he left, restrained
his zeal by refusing to appropriate any money for it, but Thornton
"offered to do all in my power in laying out a garden and other

conveniences if my colleagues will only allow me two or three common laborers." For the moment, a foot of snow kept him from inspecting the grounds. This did not idle the renaissance man, who worked on a design for the monument and mausoleum for Washington. He envisioned a rock on which "Eternity was leading him to the pinnacle and pointing upwards ready to take flight, while Time is left below in a posture as if inviting him to stay attended by independence, by victory, by liberty, by peace, virtue, prosperity, and fame." To one correspondent he explained that it was simpler than Ceracchi's design, and he discounted any chance that the artist could return because he had heard that he had been killed in a revolution in Rome. At the same time he worked on drawings of the Capitol. He had yet to fulfill his pledge to friends to publish them, and if the whole Capitol was to be hurriedly completed to accommodate the mausoleum, they might soon be needed.

*　　*　　*

Eighteen hundred was the city's year of destiny, and there was preparation to meet it. Tayloe's house began making a "handsome appearance." (Posterity would credit Thornton with the design, but no contemporary did. In early 1800 Lovering felt so good about the house he was building that he advertised that he had "specimens of building suitable" for the city's angular lots, which, in those days when architects publicly claimed no credit for private houses, seems about as close as Lovering could come to claiming credit for designing Tayloe's house. The designs similar to Tayloe's house, left in Thornton's papers, could very well have been designs for his own house, which was never built, in the lot he owned at the angle formed by New York Avenue and 17th Street.)

Law finished his house on Capitol Hill, Templeman began his first house in the city. In January his slaves began digging a cellar in the lot next to the Thorntons'. Only Blodget, who had been boasting of building, did not seem to be following through. Rumor had it that instead of using $500 to buy scantling, his son took the money north so he could meet other demands to save his father from a sheriff.

Even the point showed some life. No one was building or finishing houses there, but Langley did get a buyer for his South Capitol Street store. Amariah Frost, who in 1796 had bought the lot next to which Washington began building, had to raise money before he could build. He brought rum and cheese down with him from Massachusetts and needed a place to sell it. George Pitt announced that he was "reforming" the upper ferry across the Eastern Branch, promising "proper boats," "good ferrymen," and a tavern at the city shore. All he needed was some financial backers.

An increased demand for slaves was another sign that the depression was over. In addition to the twenty-five the commissioners wanted, Bennett Fenwick asked for fifteen "negro men" and five boys ages fourteen to seventeen. He also solicited contracts for inside work on the three houses he was building near the Treasury. William Lovering was finishing Tayloe's house, and William Lovell, who planned to build around the president's house square, wanted to hire "negro brick makers."[4]

78. Locked up . . . by Mortgages and Judgments

Although various clerks had scouted the city, the first arm of the federal government to make its presence felt was the navy. William Marbury, the local navy department agent, contracted with an Alexandria builder to make a wharf out of logs Deblois supplied. During the winter his men guided logs down the Eastern Branch, and others waded into the cold water to drag them ashore. Stoddert ordered Captain Thomas Tingey, who had just commanded the U.S.S. *Ganges* in the Caribbean, to supervise the construction of a seventy-four-gun ship and also to form plans for expansion of the yard. Tingey reached the city on February 7 and found the site of the Navy Yard covered with deep snow.

Tingey was not one of those navy captains who strained to get back to sea. He was too sociable a being, but he had a captain's typical ambition. So he immediately bent himself to building an empire, even though all he could then do toward that end was write to Stoddert for the first requisite, people to command. He painted the task at hand with sonorous rhetoric: "the indispensable magnitude of the wharf, appears a Colossial and operose undertaking it will of necessity be expensive—a strict attention however to prevent injustice, and misapplied time of the workmen, aided by a laudable economy, and avoiding superfluous appearances may effect much in reducing the account to narrow compass." Then he got to the point: he needed a company of marines to guard the yard; "wanting these the losses by pillage will no doubt be extreme."

That sent, he set about arranging other business. The lackluster results of numerous commercial transactions he had undertaken before and during his navy career had left him considerably in debt to the firm of Willing and Francis. Francis was one of the trustees of the aggregate fund and hired Tingey to be an agent for the trust.

Unfortunately, people moving to the city were looking for lodgings, not lots, and the houses the trustees had to offer at the point were too far from any public building. All the dreams about a commercial capital had come up dull. Living with his niece at the end of K Street, Thomas Johnson was behind payment on his Rock Creek lots and advertising them for sale as "esteemed the best stand in the city for business."[1]

Cabinet officers bringing their families looked for houses in Georgetown. On February 26 Uriah Forrest described the housing situation to Secretary of State Pickering. There were several good houses, but they were "locked up . . . by mortgages and judgments." The best of that lot was the house Dalton had to give to the sheriff. Of what remained, the best bet was Dunlop's house in Georgetown, which had once been used by Stoddert. Pickering could probably get it for $450 a year, but the dining and drawing rooms might be too small. Pickering made no commitment, but

McHenry gave Forrest something to crow about. He engaged the Georgetown house of George French's widow.

With only the Treasury built, other cabinet officers also had to find offices. Two Treasury officials came in April to arrange rentals for all the departments. Forrest could not get them to rent offices in Georgetown. They stuck to the west side of town and looked at the six buildings and Clotworthy Stephenson's house just east of the president's house. They closed a deal to rent Dalton's house and rented Lear's warehouse for $1,800 a year as a good place to store government property. A few brick buildings that looked promising were going up across from the six buildings.

With Wolcott, McHenry, and Nourse in Georgetown, Forrest asked the commissioners to build a bridge over Rock Creek connecting Pennsylvania Avenue to Georgetown so that it would be easier for the cabinet officers to get from their residences to the city.[2]

Law and Carroll had ways to make up for Scott being so close to the Georgetown interests. They flattered Thornton. Law asked for Thornton's help in designing a stable, and Carroll, who, along with his brother Henry, planned to build seven large brick houses that year, asked Thornton to make some plans for them. Law had success in getting important people to stay on his side of town. He lured the Episcopal minister and the president's nephew. Cranch was his lawyer, and with the lure of more work, Law prevailed on him to move to New Jersey Avenue, where he could have a house, an office, and a "pretty large garden" for $200 a year.

With Cranch came his boarder, Greenleaf, unable to buy decent clothing but able to cast a spell over Law. By early spring he was on his way to Philadelphia in the service of Law, to whom he had held out the hope of raising money to pay off the money Law had lent him. Law was that desperate. After all his building, he explained to Greenleaf, "I am pressed for cash beyond belief." Encouraged by Cranch, Greenleaf and Law set out to finally trump Forrest and get the president to stay near the Capitol.

Greenleaf delivered the description of Law's house to Abigail Adams. Law described it as "on the side of an hill" with a "passage to the outhouses" and "the best kitchen in America," formed like a fan 36 feet across, with modern facilities to boil and bake. The house itself had an oval room 32 by 24, a bedroom 21 by 20, an upstairs oval room 30 by 25 "with an European Rumford steel fire place," all told "say 8 bedrooms and an oval sitting room." It had an excellent pump, a stable for five horses, and a good coach house, "warm in winter and cool in summer." George Washington advised Mrs. Law never to let it be sold. It had cost Law $12,000 to build, and he would rent it for $1,000 ($800 if pushed) and move his family into one of his $6,000 houses across the street.[3]

*   *   *

Philadelphians had given up fighting the imperative of legislatures to move to the west. The state moved its capital to Lancaster. But many congressmen were still not thrilled with going to the Potomac. It was a difficult time to stop the move because it was an election year. Adams and Jefferson were squaring off again, and everyone anticipated another close contest. Maryland's electoral votes could be crucial. With such issues as the undeclared war with France, the sedition law, and higher taxes, whether the government moved to the Potomac was not likely to excite most voters. But the candidates were advised to show that they cared for the city. Thomas Johnson assured Adams that a visit to the city would "strengthen and probably extend the favorable sentiments entertained of you."

One of the congressmen supporting Jefferson wrote to White, asking him to find a suitable house where the vice president and nine of his congressional allies could board. White sent a copy of the letter to Law, who began showing it around town. On April 23 Jefferson wrote to Thornton, giving some ideas on arrangements inside the Capitol, his first show of any particular interest in that building since 1793.

Republicans opposed to government spending, however, could not resist attacking the extravagance of the city. In early April Robert Harper of South Carolina reported a bill from the House Ways and Means Committee that would appropriate money for furnishing the public buildings and paving footpaths. A provision to pave the streets did not make it out of committee. On the floor, furnishing the president's house attracted most opposition. Knowing that Republicans would attack furnishing the president's house as unconstitutionally increasing the emoluments of a sitting president, Harper made those funds expendable only after March 3, 1801 (well knowing the Senate would do the sensible thing). John Randolph, a Republican from Virginia, objected that giving money for furnishings was unconstitutional at any time. The speaker observed that the debate was over how much money to appropriate, so just to show his disdain for the extravagance of the building, Randolph moved to insert the sum of $500. The House voted down $20,000 by six votes and then approved $15,000 by 44 to 42. An amendment to strike out the $10,000 for paving got only twenty-one votes. An amendment to give clerks who removed to the city an extra quarter of their salary passed. By a 47-to-32 vote, the House passed the bill. The Senate amended it to allow Adams to furnish his house, and, still mindful of the propaganda about how valuable city lots were, the senators decided to make the $10,000 appropriation for paving footpaths a loan. The House concurred with the amendments.

Henry Lee, back in Congress, worried that support for the city was rather shallow, that many viewed removal to the Potomac as a trial dependent on the behavior of landlords. On April 26, two days after the president signed the bill, Lee wrote a long letter to Carroll explaining how unenthusiastic his colleagues were. ". . . It is not only possible, but may become very probable, that Congress may convene but for a session." That day, "accounts" came to him that "a spirit of extortion" was alive in the federal city. Members could board in the best boardinghouses of Philadelphia for $8 to $10 a week, $3 to $5 for servants. The gentlemen had their own rooms and the servants good beds. "Now we hear that more is already talked of among you and that the rooms are going thru divisions so as to make them uncomfortably small and when tolerably large that two beds are destined to the room. These arrangements will produce discontent." Rumors that some landlords were demanding cash advances did not please members either.[4]

*   *   *

With the coming of spring, the men of the city, at least to judge from newspaper ads, had their minds on stallions. Bennett Fenwick offered Highflyer for an $11 cover charge. At Rhodes's Little Hotel the "lately imported, high bred horse Punch" was available for $20, plus $1 to the groom. Meanwhile, Thornton was offering Clifden's services by word of mouth.

The most stable businessman in the city of Washington seems to have been Theophilius Holt, who had been advertising garden seeds from his nursery on the Eastern Branch since 1796. A heavy snow on March 9 had delayed gardeners, but even before moving day in May, Cranch was busy preparing his Capitol Hill plot, which he found "a good garden spot . . . , peas and beans, cabbages, lettuce, radishes, turnips, cellery, onions and corn" grew "finely."

The commissioners still countenanced such rural pursuits when they were in bounds, but they ordered Smallwood to prosecute those who cut "young trees to make brush fences" for their gardens. Thornton became painfully aware of the cost of cutting too many trees. On March 20 it was finally nice enough to see what had to be done to get the yard of the president's house shaped into a garden. Thornton took his wife along with him, and she recorded his reaction: "it is at present in great confusion, having on it old brick kilns, pits to contain water used by brick makers, rubbish &c &c." The doctor averred if he did not do it with the few hands his colleagues could spare, then "it will not be done at all." His wife added in her diary that she would just "let it be."

As sure as the spring brought the violets, so did it bring shacks near the work sites from whence the enterprising hoped to sell whiskey. The board directed Smallwood to inform all who sold spirits without a license that they would be removed from the premises.

The workers were also cheated out of the pleasure of finishing the buildings in high style. To save money in the short run, the board decided on wooden chimneypieces for the Capitol and the president's house. Marble would come later. Stones for the hearths were to be cut so that when they were removed they could be used for paving. And, as ever, the commissioners had an eye to cutting wages. When they asked a Baltimore correspondent how much paving cost in that city, they also asked about the wages of carpenters and joiners. There had been a slight financial panic in the port cities that spring, and it was as if the board wanted to profit from any resulting depression in wages by cutting their own. When they tried to cut what they paid the man who did their general hauling, Joseph Dove announced firmly that he would not work for less than what he was getting seven years ago, when "one dollar would purchase more than two will at this present time." The board gave in. Only the indispensable overseer Smallwood got a raise to $40 a month.

Stoddert kept riding herd on the board, which is to say, Thornton, who was the only one of the three commissioners in town and able to get around. Many board meetings were held at the bed-ridden Scott's house. On April 19 Thornton assured Stoddert that the plastering and painting of the rooms the president wanted would be done by the end of July. The walls having been up for three years and hence more "seasoned," the plaster and paint would dry quickly. Thornton thought some of the requirements of a gentleman's residence could be readied, such as a temporary stable and carriage house, but "the garden will be a work of much more difficulty and expense than was at first apprehended and we despair of doing anything effectual towads more than leveling some of the ground during the present season."

The board began formulating an excuse for any delay in completing the building: "when it is recollected that it was late in February before the commissioners had any funds to go with the President's house, it cannot be reasonably expected that much has been done." As if it might be of some consolation to the president, the board noted that they were waiting for delivery of building materials from Boston.

Yet Thornton was too much the artist to preside over a job without any touches of brilliance. He could not afford to install Ionic columns in the president's rooms as he had done in the Senate chamber, but he did set out to find the best wallpaper available and welcomed a Baltimore plasterer named George Andrews, who contracted to ornament the architraves and temporary chimneypieces. Colonel Nicholas Rogers, the man in Baltimore whom Thornton asked to get the wallpaper, at least began to immediately raise the tone of the commissioners' correspondence. Rogers invited the assistance of "the many connoisseurs and men of taste that must be collected at the federal city," and himself opined that "the fashion of plain grounds with high colored fanciful, or rather fantastical ornaments, is almost exploded, and I think justly as they possess no real taste, and highly counteract the effects of . . . jirondoles, pictures, and the neat ornaments of an elegant room."[5]

79. I Am Well Pleased with the Whole

Greenleaf managed to put enough doubts about the viability of the president's house in Mrs. Adams's mind that she wrote to Mrs. Cranch on April 17, worrying that while the president still hoped the mansion would be finished in time, she was "for his taking a house, as I fear it would prove his death to go into a house so green and I think the president's house must and will be." Her nephew did not write back recommending Law's house because he admired another house more. He asked Carroll for a description of his. Unlike Law, who thought his nonpareil, Carroll only bragged about the spring that first attracted him to the site back in 1791. It was "one of the best springs in America." He lauded the garden but had to admit that the yard, which included the whole square enclosed by a wooden fence, was "in an unfinished state." He would rent it all for $2,000.

Cranch sent the letter to his aunt and added that Carroll's description did not do his house justice. Its situation was "delightful," the fish pond good and stocked, his springhouse, bath, and smokehouse all excellent. Furthermore, Carroll was about to put up "a very handsome freestone portico" at a cost of $800. Most important, Carroll's house had been lived in and was thus proved healthy. Cranch was not so sure about Law's house; he had "suspicions that a marsh which runs at the foot of the Capitol hill, will render it liable to the ague and fever.'' Carroll's house was farther from the marsh. Cranch quickly added that ''the marsh . . . may be drained at a very small expense.''

With the government about to come to the city, even its enthusiasts began to look at it more critically. The low grounds becoming progressively soggier had been overlooked because it was assumed that once the canal was built, private investors would flock to its banks and improve those areas. In 1800 there was not a cent available to build the canal or even keep the small portion that had been built drained. All efforts to improve were concentrated on the two principal buildings and their vicinity. Of course, no one was alarmed at the low grounds of the rural city compared to the horrors associated with the docksides of New York, Philadelphia, and Baltimore. The president ordered the executive offices to be in operation in the city by June 15 to end forever the annual flight from yellow fever.[1]

*   *   *

While everyone continued to laud the natural advantages of the city, it became popular to fault L'Enfant for what was wrong with it. L'Enfant had come on hard times. Morris's mansion was being torn down. He had loaned Morris his nest egg of U.S. six percent stock and had no prospect of getting it back. With his record of extravagance, he was unemployable. The ostentation of the 1790s was out of favor. He lived with Richard Soderstrom, a Swedish admiral, merchant, consul, land speculator, and crony of Morris who supplied L'Enfant with petty cash. L'Enfant turned to petitioning former employers for payment with typical zeal. He asked the city of New York to pay him for his renovation of Federal Hall. In May he used several thousand words to prove to the commissioners that his plan, if followed, would have redeemed, rather than created, a wasteland, and therefore he deserved a handsome reward.

By his plan he meant more than just his map. He meant his way of doing things: shunning speculators and building the canal and avenues and landscaping all the important gardens and sites before work began on the Capitol and the president's house. The failure of the city vindicated his approach, and because of that vindication the commissioners owed him not only a salary of $8,000 and $37,500 in royalties for the published plan, but $50,000 in damages for the money he lost because he was unjustly dismissed and his plans were not carried out. He arrived at the $50,000 figure by calculating what he never revealed in 1792, that he expected a five percent commission on the million dollars to be expended in building the city.

L'Enfant argued that if George Washington could know the plight he was in, he surely would affirm that because of L'Enfant's "exertions" the city had been made big enough to afford the means to make it rich. He contended that Washington would have recognized that if he had remained in charge, none of the "bankrupts, land and stock jobbers," nor a "swindling scheme of lottery," would have ruined the city. He listed twelve specific grievances, including the intrigues surrounding the engraving of the plan, his name being left off it, his papers having been stolen, and the rewarding of his enemies, "expert agents of villainy." Not only had he been denied the chance to design the public buildings, but those built ruined his plan. The president's house was "hardly . . . suitable for a gentlemen country house wholly inconsistent for a city habitation in no aspect present that majestick of outer ordinance nor inward distribution becoming the state residency of the chief head of a souverain people." The Capitol, rather than being "prety should be of a massy sullen." Both building were "sunk" too low.

If the city had been built properly—and in L'Enfant's view nothing had been done toward that end—the "industrious pedler" and "opulent idler" would have come to the city, especially after yellow fever drove so many out of other cities. "Vast numbers" of them would have settled in Washington. Instead, on viewing the city, they "were disuaded through disgust at the death like aspect of all about it." Even if the commissioners had taken the simple step of themselves building in the triangle formed by Pennsylvania Avenue and the Mall and encouraging others to join them, then after seven years the city would have seemed viable. Now "the work of a century will hardly . . . be sufficient to raise the city of Washington to that splendor and credit which twenty year time may have gained to it, had its establishment been but only prosecuted till this day conformably to my sisteme and plan."

L'Enfant's criticisms were not inapt, but each telling observation was shrouded by vague accusations against "the ill designings" of his enemies, who, if he were "to squash would only stain and infect me." For an unknown reason the May letter was not sent until August.[2]

* * *

Whereas, L'Enfant had expected to have hundreds of thousands of dollars for landscaping and paving, the commissioners at that late date had, at the sufferance of Navy Secretary Stoddert, $9,000 to make footpaths. In mid-April White returned to the city and formed a board with Scott while Thornton was at his farm. They informed Stoddert that the board thought it best to pave with foundation stone. A few days later Thornton and Scott formed a board, and they informed Stoddert that the board thought it best to pave with "good round paving stone" or brick. Both letters were rather hazy as to prices.

Stoddert passed the feeble reports of the divided board on to his cabinet colleagues with the observation that "the subject seems to be little understood in that quarter." Stoddert, however, knew of good stone within three miles of the city, "broad, thin and with joints so even, that they will require little or no hammering." He thought a six-foot-wide footpath between the Capitol and the president's house would not cost more than $4,000. His colleagues agreed to let Stoddert handle the matter and he told the commissioners to get that stone and to pave the distance between the two principal buildings first. He reminded them that the footpaths were for the convenience of Congress and that they should not be thought of as permanent. There should be no delay while streets were brought to planned levels. Ditches could flank the footpaths to keep them serviceable.

The board promised to have the ground prepared that Monday and begin paving the next Monday. They bought stone for $1.50 a perch and contracted for paving at 25 cents a perch, higher than what Stoddert had hoped for. But to express their confidence that the whole way from Georgetown to the Capitol would be paved, they agreed to split the cost with Georgetown for a bridge over Rock Creek at Pennsylvania Avenue, provided the pavement did reach that far.[3]

*   *   *

Stoddert and his fellow cabinet members were too busy to properly supervise the commissioners. Not only were they clearing up the business Congress had left them, but the president decided to shake up his cabinet. State elections in New York did not go well for him. Thanks to the exertions of Aaron Burr in New York City, the Republicans would control the new legislature, which in turn would select the state's presidential electors. Adams blamed Hamilton and took it out on his cabinet, which, save for Stoddert, was more loyal to Hamilton than to him. He fired Pickering and McHenry but kept Wolcott because he did a good job. McHenry thought himself exceptionally ill used because he had just rented a house in Georgetown for a year.

McHenry solved that problem by billing the government for the loss, which was what every official who actually made the move did. High officials such as Joseph Nourse were careful to ask for reimbursement even for the drams of brandy provided to the men who packed his family's belongings. Treasury was the largest department and seemed the most organized, keeping one official in Philadelphia to oversee shipping and sending another to Washington to be on hand to receive the boxes. On Stoddert fell the task of moving both the War and the Navy departments. On May 30 he arranged to close the offices in Philadelphia on June 7, when four wagons would take the public furniture to waiting ships. Papers would go by land accompanied by a clerk. Stoddert himself would leave Philadelphia on the 9th and expected at least two of his three clerks to be in Washington prepared for business on the 15th. Marbury was to have an office ready.[4]

*   *   *

In mid-May Attorney General Lee arrived. Since he had no office, his arrival presented no problems, and he brought glad tidings. The president would arrive within a few weeks to visit the city. His house was not finished, and the commissioners could not say with honesty that everything was in order. The glass ordered from England had not arrived, and on the 27th word came that it never would, "owing to the uncommon size" wanted. The buildings needed 450 panes 18½ by 26½ inches. The commissioners wrote to Baltimore and Alexandria merchants, as well to Keepser, the Boston glassmaker.

Dennis wrote from the Eastern Shore that Chesapeake ships were so busy that it was difficult to find any to deliver lumber to the Potomac. The other problem was the ongoing leaks in the roof of the president's house and the Capitol. They sent Harbaugh and two carpenters, Peter Lenox and Wilson Bryan, up on top of the buildings to see what could be done, not that they worried about the president being disappointed at the level of activity at his house. While they were eager to get six or eight good joiners down from Baltimore, thirty-four carpenters, as well as a score of plasterers, were at work.

The president took the western route to the city, which enabled partisans to greet him in Lancaster, York, and Frederick. On June 3 a reception committee on horseback greeted him at the northwestern boundary of the District of Columbia and accompanied him to Georgetown, where he rested a night before formal ceremonies greeting him. The president rode in "a chariot and four" with his secretary Shaw, "respectable citizens" accompanied him on horseback, and the militia and what few marines had just been recruited for the Navy Yard provided the firepower for sixteen volleys. The city toasted Adams for his policy of "peace abroad and the cultivation of Americanism at home." He congratulated Georgetown for being next door to the city and hoped all "reluctance" to changing the seat of government "will soon be removed."

The ceremonies at Georgetown began at noon. At three the president stopped at Thornton's house, and White and Thornton gave him a tour of the president's house, the Treasury, and the Capitol. He was friendlier with White although they talked mostly about farming. Dalton had warned him that Thornton was a rabid

Republican. Adams spent the night at Tunnicliff's. At noon on the 5th he was escorted from Tunnicliff's to the Capitol, where his old friend Dalton read a brief speech of greeting and he made a ninety-five-word reply congratulating the assembled "on the blessings which Providence has been pleased to bestow, in a particular manner, on this situation. . . ." Afterward he went to dine at Thomas Johnson's, and there a large party was to meet him at tea. Mrs. Thornton reported that not many came, and "the President did not come into the drawing room 'till tea was ready and went immediately after" with Mrs. Cranch, whose husband was attending court in Annapolis. According to Shaw, the president was not that standoffish. He said he was "continually surrounded."

Some of the nation's newspapers reported on the formal reception of the president and his reaction. A Philadelphia newspaper included a letter from the city reporting that it was "impossible" for government officials to get "comfortable houses at moderate rents, or indeed any rents," but provisions were "plenty, good and . . . cheaper than in Philadelphia." Another letter from Washington countered that "every exertion" was being made to provide "comfortable accommodations" for "all classes . . . in the most beautiful situation the United States affords." But no one described the president's tour of the city.

Thornton kept the drawings of the Capitol in his house, and Adams promised to come by and view them at one o'clock on the 7th. Mrs. Thornton's pen was at the ready to record the moment, but the president came late and could not even stop because he was in a hurry to get to General Forrest's for dinner with seventy gentlemen. She hoped to corner him the next day by joining the after-dinner throng at Peter's house. A large crowd was there, but the president slipped away to see Dalton.

After a visit to Mount Vernon and more festivities in Alexandria, Adams returned to Tunnicliff's gratified to find that his new cabinet members John Marshall and Samuel Dexter were there. Marshall, the new secretary of state, had arrived while the president was in Alexandria. Having been appointed only a few weeks before and being habitually haphazard in making personal arrangements, Marshall so despaired of getting a room that his old friend White prevailed on the board to let him stay in a room in the president's house. Marshall never told the tale and wound up spending the night at Tunnicliff's.

On the 13th, with all the official receptions over, Adams finally had a chance to write to his wife. Over the years she had got a good number of letters revealing his anxieties, but in his letter from Tunnicliff's he shared his buoyant mood. "I like the Seat of Government very well," wrote the man who could not bear staying in Philadelphia longer than absolutely necessary, "and shall sleep, or lie awake, next winter in the President's house." He could even joke about his propensity to worry, and he concluded apropos of the city, "all things seem to go on well." In a letter to his old friend Elbridge Gerry, who, back in 1790, had made the last stand against putting the capital on the Potomac, Adams wrote, "I have taken a view of the federal city and the environs as far as Mt. Vernon, and I am well pleased with the whole. I think Congress will very soon be better here than at Philadelphia. . . ."[5]

80. Live Like Fishes, by Eating Each Other

Cranch got back from Annapolis before the president left, and the young lawyer was quite full of himself. "I was opposed by Mason and Kilty two Jacobins, but both good lawyers—I was *alone*—They had the advantage of opening and closing the argument. In one case I obtained a verdict for my client, and in the other, obliged my opponents to withdraw a juror, to pay costs and beg leave to amend their proceedings and to get a continuance." Unfortunately for the city, the case resolved was not one of the many tying up Washington lots. Cranch's victory excused Law from having to make good on a note he had endorsed for James Piercy, the sugar baker who had yet to make any money. Yet the victory was important for Law. As Cranch explained, "The transaction had been grossly misrepresented by his [Law's] enemies." The president did not stay in the city to hear more about the court term in Annapolis. His sudden departure on the 14th surprised even Cranch.

Those left behind did have to sort out the legal perplexities. Thomas Johnson might have averred that he would not testify in cases involving the city because as an original commissioner he would never be free from court appearances, but that did not prevent the present commissioners from suing him for nonpayment on lots. The legal agenda of the commissioners was simple. raise money. They sued Johnson for $906, the men who bought the causeway for $5,545, ex-Congressman Mercer for $420, even McDermott Roe for $1,253 to repair his bad work at the Capitol, and they kept trying to quash Greenleaf's injunction, which would allow $4,573 worth of lots to be sold.

The day before the president arrived they advertised another sale of Morris's and Nicholson's lots. The trustees of the aggregate fund's new agent, Captain Tingey, promised to cooperate. Rather than try to save everything, he convinced the trustees to have him pick out the best lots, pay for them at the rate of $80 each, and sell them for much more. The trustees were persuadable because they lost their suit to prevent Dunlop from selling lots that secured Morris's and Nicholson's loan. On June 30 Dunlop auctioned the 208 lots he held as security for a $40,000 loan. The community rallied to prove that the property was indeed valuable enough to support the loans. Dunlop himself bought $9,618 worth of lots, Scott bought $5,901, Tingey $6,211, Barry $3,359, Chandler $3,419, Thornton $1,382, and nine other gentlemen, including Law, Deblois, Prout, and Templeman, bought the remainder, for a total sale of $34,735.15.

The trustees, however, did not surrender on other legal fronts. They sued for possession of the twenty buildings and contested claims by Law, Duncanson, and others who attached the property. With countersuits, that amounted to nine major suits involving the trustees. Complicating the whole issue were suits by the Dutch, who claimed more than 1,500 lots as security for loans. They were reminded of that claim by the sizable tax bills they began to face in 1798.[1]

*   *   *

Removing to Washington made running the Navy Department more difficult. Stoddert opened his office on June 18 but his papers had not yet arrived. A week later the boxes had arrived, but the clerk who knew where the papers were filed had not. The outfitting of ships was delayed. Further complicating matters was that the Treasury was not yet set up and able to dispense money. Stoddert began feeling a pain in his side that worried him.

In a June 23 letter to the commandant of marines, he lamented that the city "languishes for want of a little spirit of exertion." The only part of his instructions to the commissioners being fulfilled was the construction of a stable for the president. A brick stable for twelve horses and three carriages, costing $1,600, was going up on 15th Street. The commissioners' excuse for not paving a footpath between the Capitol and the president's house was that they did not know the "extent and direction" the cabinet wanted. Meanwhile, the commissioners had paved the least essential part, around the president's house. Stoddert promptly ordered the pavers to stop until he could see what was going on, or rather, what he and his cabinet colleagues could see. The four cabinet officers and three commissioners were overseeing the work of two contractors and a half dozen slaves. On the 23rd Stoddert ordered the board to pave the north side of Pennsylvania Avenue. It was up to the board to determine exactly where. "The exact distance must depend upon the regulations of the city in respect to the encroachments permitted on the avenue for steps, or decoration of any kind attached to buildings." Stoddert observed and added pointedly, "This you can determine, I cannot."[2]

*   *   *

Almost nine years after Washington and Jefferson had urged that Pennsylvania Avenue be opened from the site of the Capitol to the president's house, the commissioners asked their surveyor to report on what had to be done to actually make a serviceable road. For years a portion had been covered by Burnes's corn, another portion by brick kilns and their attendant pits. The first growth of trees was long gone, but bushes were growing everywhere. With gullies coming down from the terrace to the north, anyone could see that care had to be taken to prevent carriage ruts on the avenue from forming a quagmire after any sizable rainstorm.

Robert King, or "old Mr. King," as he was usually called to distinguish him from his son Nicholas, made the report. His last effort to improve the grounds had come to naught. William O'Neale had cut a ditch to drain the area behind his boardinghouse. His neighbor Brown claimed the drain was a nuisance and had it filled in. King warned the board that the same battle would be fought in half the squares of the city unless some rules were made. Nothing upset the board more than unwanted reports from surveyors. King had to be encouraged that the board asked for the report on the avenue.

King found that water from 14th to 10th Streets could be drained by a five-foot-deep ditch down 14th Street, 950 feet to Tiber Creek. Between 10th and 9th Streets a watercourse that had become known as the swamp or marsh presented a major problem. During very high tides water from the creek came up to the avenue, and after storms a stream several yards wide and two feet deep coursed down the hill and over the avenue. King thought a portion of the avenue 370 feet long should be raised at least two and a half feet, and a 300-foot-long ditch, 5 feet deep and 12 feet wide, should be dug to carry water across the avenue and down to the creek, which meant that a bridge had to be built to carry traffic over the ditch. A deep valley near 8th Street could be filled and several gullies near 7th Street could be combined into one drainage ditch to be carried across the avenue. Only a small bridge would be needed. Hollows at 6th and 4th Streets could be handled by laying a trunk for the water to run through under the footpaths and carriageways. Of course Tiber Creek itself had to be bridged where it crossed the avenue near 2nd Street. Usually horses and carriages forded the creek just upstream.

The commissioners' reaction was to worry about the cost. They set slaves to digging and warned the cabinet not to spend all the money for paving, until they were sure how much the drains would cost. Smallwood advertised for six to eight more ditchers.[3]

*   *   *

Treasury Secretary Wolcott arrived on July 1. Thornton greeted him that day with projections that the city would have "a population of 160,000 people, as a matter of course, in a few years." "No stranger can be here a day," Wolcott wrote to his wife, "and converse with the proprietors, without conceiving himself in the company of crazy people. Their ignorance of the rest of the world, and their delusions with respect to their own prospects, are without parallel."

What they had wrought in the city was sobering. The situation of the city was "pleasant, and indeed beautiful," and appeared healthy, "but I had no conception," Wolcott continued, "till I came here, of the folly and infatuation of the people who have directed the settlements." Everywhere everything seemed wrong. "You may look in almost any direction, over an extent of ground nearly as large as the city of New York, without seeing a fence or any object except brick kilns and temporary huts for laborers. Mr. Law, and a few other gentlemen, live in great splendor; but most of the inhabitants are low people, whose appearance indicates vice and intemperance, or negroes." The whole miserable lot "live like fishes, by eating each other."

He could not get over the waste of money. "Immense sums have been squandered in buildings which are but partly finished, in situations which are not, and never will be the scenes of business; while the parts, near the public buildings, are almost wholly unimproved." Of course he was talking about the point, where of "50 or 60 spacious houses," five or six were home to blacks and vagrants, and just a few were inhabited "by decent looking people." He did not see how congressmen could be accommodated unless they crowded into what few houses there were. "There is no industry, society, or business. With great trouble and expense, much mischief has been done which it will be almost impossible to remedy." Vacant land was deemed too valuable to fence and use for gardens.

As for expenditures on the public's account, he had to admit that the Capitol and the president's house were "by far the most magnificent buildings I have ever seen." The north wing of the Capitol was four times the size of the new Bank of the United States building. The external appearance, save where the north wing was to connect to the central portion, was "magnificent." Inside, the height of the Senate chamber struck Wolcott, and he noted the Ionic columns. The room for the House, however, seemed smaller than the one in Philadelphia and more inconvenient. Magnificent though it appeared, on the score of convenience the president's house also did not pass muster. It was still "in a very unfinished state," and Wolcott pitied future residents of a house bound to be "cold and damp in winter" and tolerable only with "a regiment of servants."

Wolcott then turned to a request from Hamilton for evidence of Adams's maladministration. Hamilton did not consider the other man nominated by the Federalists, General Charles Cotesworth Pinckney, as a running mate. He wanted him to be the next president, which was possible if one of the electors voting for the Federalists did not vote for Adams. So while the ditchers opened a drain down 14th Street to the Tiber, Wolcott, working in an office close by, became Washington's first leak.

The political intrigues against the president helped take the shine off the new city for members of the administration. Morale in the federal service was not high. "I have never felt composed or satisfied since I have been here," Jacob Wagner, the chief clerk of the State Department, wrote to his old boss Pickering. "Every thing is mysterious, and every man's conduct and opinions inexplicable. But I suppose at the present crisis, mum is the order of the day." Not a few bureaucrats, as they boarded at Tunnicliff's or in the Georgetown taverns (paid for by the government) and looked for cheaper lodgings they would have to pay for themselves, began calculating how soon they could quit the government. Only Thomas Claxton, the clerk of the House, was given one of the houses the commissioners owned. Deference was due to Claxton, the man Stoddert and his colleagues put in charge of furnishing the Capitol, so he and his large family lived on the Capitol square.[4]

*   *   *

The heat that July even impressed General James Wilkinson, a native Marylander: "The heat here for a few days past," he wrote, "has exceeded my experience, and unhinged all my faculties rational and sensual." The *Georgetown Centinel* tried to make the best of it. "The intense heats of the season," it explained in its July 11 issue, "actually remind us of the immense superiority which the City of Washington will enjoy, even when it shall become populous, over every other city, perhaps, which ever existed, in its numerous open ground and the noble spaciousness of its streets and avenues. These are advantages in point of health and pleasantness which come home to the feelings and for the want of which wealth and grandeur cannot compensate."

Actually, along with the worst heat in memory, the city was exceptionally sickly. No one then remarked on it, but the secret to the city's good health in past years was its lack of people to get sick and spread disease. The city did have wide open spaces, but all the people coming to it were crowding into what little housing there was. The most prevalent complaint was diarrhea. The sickness and heat did not help speed the work on the public buildings, but the board was lucky there were no major catastrophes. The carpenters at the president's house complained they were delayed because the hearths had not been laid. The gutters at the Capitol kept leaking, damaging the walls.

In mid-July Hoban went up to Baltimore to shop for the locks, bolts and other hardware still needed for the buildings. Promised shipments from England had still not arrived. Paying retail prices was expensive, and smiths there had to fashion bolts to suit. Hoban could not come home with what he needed but had to wait for the always unreliable shipments from Baltimore. A hundred large panes of glass were found in Baltimore after someone thought of looking for them in the printing shops. In an ad in a Pennsylvania newspaper a new glassworks in Pittsburgh boasted that it could make glass of any size. The commissioners sent their order. The owners of the glassworks wanted to fill it, but their workers refused to undertake the job because it was too hot outside to slave over so large a job.

News did come from London that glass specially made in Scotland was being shipped from Dublin. Keeser in Boston seemed the most reliable supplier, but he was careful to get payment in hand for work done before he undertook new work. They did hit on one good idea and inquired about a man in Baltimore who covered skylights without using thick glass, which was hard to come by. He used common thin glass covered with a network of brass wire.[5]

Once again the commissioners faced the possibility of running out of money before November. They searched for any savings. Night guards at the public buildings cost $30 a month. They asked Stoddert to spare two marines to take over the duty. They pressed their lawyer Mason to collect on debts for which court judgments had been obtained. "The situation of our affairs requires our best exertions to keep the public buildings in motion," they explained in an effort to rally Mason to the cause, "which we shall not be able to do much longer unless some of our debtors pay." But the law did not so much force debtors to pay as force them to make arrangements to pay. Johnson offered to secure his debt with his Frederick County lands, and the board accepted his offer rather than drive him into the clutches of the sheriff.

The board well knew that the credit of the community had been worn thin. The sweetheart sale of $6,000 worth of bank stock it had made with Forrest back in January was even proving an embarrassment. He had been given ninety days to pay. By the end of July he still had not paid the $5,000 he had promised. On July 30 Forrest gave the board his note to be paid by his old partner Stoddert. The board presented it to Stoddert, and he refused to endorse it. As such frustrations mounted, the board's last hope for an infusion of funds was a good sale of Morris and Nicholson lots. The first $50,000 had to go to pay the state of Maryland, but if the sale actually raised $180,000 the board's troubles would be over. With the city bulging with new people, their hopes were high.[6]

81. As If Time Was to Stand Still

Republican leaders wanted a newspaper friendly to their party in operation in the capital when Congress convened. In mid-August Samuel Harrison Smith, a twenty-eight-year-old writer and editor, came to the city from Philadelphia to buy a house and printing shop. He spent two hectic days and engaged to rent a half-built house on New Jersey Avenue that was to be finished by November 1. A printing office next to it would be ready October 1. (The printing office Brown from Baltimore had built was being converted into an oyster house. Citing lack of support and pressed by the commissioners for payment, Brown went back to Baltimore.) Given the demand for housing that he found in the city, Smith considered himself lucky to close the deal. Somewhat complicating his plans was his hope to marry his second cousin Margaret Bayard before he moved to the city. His brother opposed the marriage and might see that his banker friends in New York did not extend the credit Samuel needed.

Smith's brother argued against not the marriage per se but its timing. There would be no accommodations in the city, which would force Smith to stay with his wife in a boardinghouse. With such unrespectable lodgings, the newspaper would get off on the wrong foot (bad enough that it was Republican). Margaret Bayard would not stand for that. "No one, who removes to Washington," she retorted to her fiancé, "will be exempt from the same difficulties; people of fortune and fashion, if there are no houses, must go to lodgings, and must live in unfinished buildings. This will not be the result of poverty, but of local circumstances, which must affect the rich and the poor."

Although the commissioners and proprietors hoped newcomers would buy lots, the demand was for housing. Always good at sensing how money was to be made, Dermott told the commissioners that he would buy some of their temporary buildings on the Capitol square and move them to lots he owned nearby. That would allow him to vacate his own house next to the Capitol "so as to accommodate a family genteally." He would also buy and move the hospital. He did, however, need liberal terms. No one in the temporary houses, seven on the Capitol square, twenty-two on the president's house square, and six on Judiciary Square, would vacate. Doorkeeper Claxton wanted to move to a bigger house on the Capitol square just vacated by workers and have his assistant move into the house he was vacating. In the small house his large family was "stowed so close . . . as to endanger their health."

The business of the city became boarding. Sweeny's went through another transformation. The store of 1796 with a long list of goods for sale survived bankruptcy, fizzled as a shoe manufactory, hobbled along with mantua making, and finally took in boarders, with some success. Mrs. Sweeny advertised that she was a few doors east of the secretary of state's office. Since Georgetown was near the executive offices, the influx of some one hundred clerks could be accommodated. The unfolding drama was on Capitol Hill. Carroll advertised for men to turn his new buildings into boardinghouses, and in the late summer Pontius Stelle came down from Trenton. While handling government boarders during the epidemics, he had learned about the opportunity in the offing.

When Law saw that the president was not going to take his house, he arranged for the vice president to use it, not exclusively but as one of many Republican boarders. Conrad and McMunn from Alexandria, who had bought lots to build, decided to rent Law's house, the house next to it (which Law also owned), and the stables behind. One house would serve for boarders, the other as a tavern for transients. Law would move his family back down the hill. As for George Washington's house, Francis still had not written back. The executors of the Washington estate waited for a buyer and did not lease the buildings.[1]

*   *   *

One who sorely regretted that George Wasington was not around to dispense his patronage was William Winstanley, the English artist from whom Washington had bought several canvases. He came in late June and spent most of his time with the Thorntons. In early July his boxes of paintings and prints arrived containing his copy of

Stuart's portrait of Washington, plus a Stuart original, three water-color landscapes by Noel, and many prints. Winstanley and Thornton became inseparable. Soon they were painting together and chatting about the bare walls of the public buildings (until they had a row over the price of a lot the painter thought he had bought from his host and Winstanley left town).

The actor-producer Wignell came to the city a month before the usual August opening of his productions and asked the commissioners for permission to build a temporary theater in Blodget's hotel. Although he did not really own the building, Blodget wanted it tenanted, even trying to get the Bank of the United States to put a branch there. (For a while Blodget insisted the bank owned the building since they had a judgment against the bankrupt ticketholders, Budd and Pryor.) The commissioners told Wignell that it had nothing to do with the building, so he started building the theater. Blodget had hoped to come down to help Wignell and everyone else, but creditors had detained him in New York City.[2]

*   *   *

A complication in the commissioners' sale was that they were offering lots Morris and Nicholson had used to secure loans. They could raise only $80 on those lots for which scrip had been issued. The rest of the purchase money would go to the scrip holder. The men who held those lots as security were loath to see them bought by others. Such an event would force them to come up with new security for the loan. Tingey urged the board not to sell scrip lots. But the board needed money and feared being accused of favoritism, since Scott himself held scrip.

The sale began normally. William O'Neale bought a lot near 19th and K Streets Northwest for $86. Hugh Densley, the contractor plastering the president's house, bought a lot near the Capitol for $400, and then Stoddert bought sixty-five lots, all but five for more than $200, seven for $400 or more. On the next day he bought another seventy-six lots, and Forrest bought fifteen on his own account. Forrest and Stoddert were protecting Forrest's security.

The sales were adjourned over the weekend and then came the

deluge, rains so heavy that a mule drowned in the Tiber, four horses in Rock Creek, and many took a Sunday excursion to Pennsylvania Avenue to see the damage done to the new pavement by the "inundation."

When the sale resumed, Stoddert bought thirteen of seventeen lots offered and then the old pattern of a few sales a day resumed, until a chunk Dunlop held as security came on the block. The auction failed to attract outside buyers who could infuse new funds into the city.

The commissioners waited until the end of the month to see if Forrest and Stoddert could come up with some means of payment that promised an infusion of cash. The best they could do was to transfer fifty lots to Scott for $6,269.92 and give that money to the board. In notes totaling $27,533 Forrest tried to pay for lots that Harbaugh had bought for him the year before, and Stoddert offered down payment for his purchases. But each endorsed the other's note, and in good conscience the board could not accept them.

White thought that with economizing, the work could be completely sufficiently. Thornton and Scott, both personally responsible for repaying the $50,000 loan from Maryland, made the case for more help from the government in a letter to Secretary of State Marshall. They needed $25,000 more to see the public works through the building season.[3]

* * *

So touchy were the commissioners that when a master took one of the rented slaves away from the crew at the president's house, they went into high dudgeon, threatening "the most summary and effectual measures" to recover the slave and obtain damages. Yet they could do nothing to prevent their energetic overseer Samuel Smallwood from leaving them to work at the Navy Yard. Labor was in the driver's seat. The carpenters at the president's house, on whom so much depended, petitioned for a higher wage. The board agreed to give nine of the most skilled $2 a day. Meanwhile, the board was at the mercy of wind and seas for the delivery of glass, wallpaper, hardware, and even lumber. They tried to borrow some pine plank from the Navy Yard and had Hoban scour Alexandria and Baltimore for whatever could be used. At the same time, they tried to sell whatever they could no longer use. The plank from the fence around the Capitol went for 75 cents a hundred feet, the four gates for $8 each. In the Capitol at least, the final touches were being made. The plasterers finished, and by September 4 the painters were at work on the Senate chamber. Tingey told Thornton that a carver in Philadelphia could make an eagle for $40. Thornton got the board to order one for the Capitol.

The great battle of the buildings would end in a draw, so the two sides of the city fought over the paving. Stoddert of course approved the Rock Creek bridge, but when Law insisted that an equal sum be spent on footpaths from the principal boardinghouses to the Capitol, Stoddert thought $250 could be spared for walks three feet wide. If the footpaths and bridges over Rock Creek and the Tiber could not be finished for $10,000, the pavement from the president's house to Rock Creek could be four feet wide instead of six feet. This Solomon-like decision went sour when Law insisted that portions of New Jersey Avenue had to be leveled first. The board objected and quoted the April letter from Stoddert forbidding use of the money for leveling. The commissioners also needed more money to pay higher prices for stone, which was the only way to "hasten" deliveries. Moreover, if the footpaths were made four feet wide, or narrower they would be useless. On September 11 the board signed the contract for the 300-foot-long, 18-foot-wide wooden bridge over Rock Creek with Harbaugh, who had sunk over $12,000 in bridges downstream.[4]

*   *   *

James Barry began doubting that the commissioners and the original proprietors had the will to make a city. Long before the city was laid out, the Fenwick family had farmed the Carroll family's land at the point. The death of Captain Ignatius Fenwick changed nothing, as eleven slaves continued to work the farm for his widow, Mary. Her house stood in the intersection of South Capitol Street, Georgia Avenue, and R Street, surrounded by gardens and the huts of her slaves, including one but nine feet square. From his house and wharf at the end of New Jersey Avenue, Barry decided not to follow his friend Law with investments up the avenue to the Capitol but to invest and develop the waterfront between his wharf on the Eastern Branch and the Potomac. In May he asked the commissioners to open Georgia Avenue, the thoroughfare that united his properties. It was a nice way of saying he wanted Mrs. Fenwick and her gardens and slaves removed.

The board passed on Barry's request to the widow, and she complained to Daniel Carroll's mother, who in turn complained to her son. He took up her cause, telling the board that she did not object to removing "real obstructions to any one intending to build," but that the avenue was so wide, folks could pass by without bothering her and vice versa. But if all had to go, she would cooperate as soon as she was paid a fair value for her property. The board summoned Barry and Mrs. Fenwick to attend a meeting. Barry attended, but Mrs. Fenwick did not, and only one member of the board was present. Barry lost his patience. It was "as if time was to stand still" while the building season passed. "Can it be expected," he complained to the board, "situated as I am, surrounded by shades of all colors that I am to breakground by placing a building or improvement with [in] 30 or 40 feet of the hovels and purlieus of this class." The board ordered Mrs. Fenwick to cut back her garden "to allow a free passage of all carriages on the street" and to remove one small building and one hovel that were in the street. Barry demanded that the avenue and streets be completely opened.

The board did show that summer that it could enforce the regulations. Robert King discovered a party wall going up that was only 9 instead of 12 inches thick. The board ordered the wall torn down. Pierce Purcell was caught building a porch on the street. But Mrs. Fenwick and the Carrolls could not be handled so brusquely. Finally, in mid-August, the board sent the order Barry wanted. Carroll dropped the other shoe, insisting that the board remove all the temporary buildings from the Capitol square and drain the clay pits there, "now filled with water and filth and which has and will continue to render the place unhealthy; perhaps many introduce the yellow fever or some other plague equally destructive."[5]

*   *   *

The yellow fever was on everyone's mind. On August 26, two days before Carroll complained, his uncle Bishop John Carroll, who was staying at Notley Young's mansion, wrote a "Pastoral on Epidemic" to the Catholics of Baltimore. He apologized for not being with them as yellow fever ravaged the city, but since 1793 eight priests had died of the fever in the United States, more than could be replaced. He asked them not to request a priest if they had the fever and instead "repent themselves most sincerely before God."

Despite the prevalence of the flux, Washington tried to carry on its tradition as a place of summer resort. The disbanding of the armies specially raised to repel the French brought not a few officers and men from the army that had been camped at Harper's Ferry. A military band entertained the populace. Wignell packed 300 people in his warm little theater in Blodget's hotel to see "Columbus" and "Fortune's Frolic." The Thorntons had so many houseguests that they had to sleep on a mattress in the tearoom.

On September 18 Mrs. Thornton gave her guests a tour of the city. They picked up Dr. Thornton, who could get them into the president's house. Dr. May interrupted the tour. There was an unknown man lying under a tree. No one would take him in for fear he had yellow fever. Dr. Thornton had him brought into the just completed president's stables, where he died the next evening. The doctors decided it was not yellow fever.[6]

82. Bad Paper and Perplexity

". . . We entered a long and unshaded road, which rises a hill and crosses a vast common covered with shrub oak and black berries in abundance. I looked in vain for the city, and see no houses, although among the bushes I see the different stones, which here and there mark the different avenues. Foot paths and roads dissect the extensive plain, which is exactly like the common the other side of the Raritan, only more extensive and more productive of black berries and sweet briars. At last I perceive the Capitol, a large, square, ungraceful white building; approaching nearer I see three large brick houses and a few hovels scattered over the plain. One of the brick houses is the one where we lodge.

"We drive to it. It is surrounded with mud, shavings, bricks, planks, and all the rubbish of building. Here then I am. I alight, am introduced to Mr. Still and led into a large handsome parlor. I seat myself at the window, and while Mr. Smith is busied with the baggage, survey the scene before me. Immediately before the door is the place and whence the clay for bricks has been dug and which is now a pond of dirty water. All the materials for building, bricks, planks, stone and c. are scattered over the space which lies between this and the Capitol, and which is thickly overgrown with briars and black berries and intersected with footpaths. The Capitol is about as far from here as Col. Nelson's from you. Some brick kilns and small wooden houses are seen at or by the scene. About half a dozen brick houses are seen at a small distance. The Capitol stands on a hill which slopes down towards the Potomac, from the bottom of this hill, to the river, extends a thick and noble wood, beyond this you see the river and the scene is then closed by a range of hills which extend north and south far as the eye can reach.

"I had time to take this scene before I was conducted to my chamber. It is about as large as yours. The windows look upon the scene I described. It is a western exposure and as I entered the rays of the setting sun fell upon the white walls. A neat bed with a little counterpane stands opposite the fire place. A toilet is placed between the two windows, a wash table on the other side of the room, a tea table on one side of the fire place, white windsor chairs with stuffed bottoms, red copperplate curtains compose the furniture of this neat and comfortable apartment. I immediately changed my dress, and then sat down by the window. The sun had now set, tho' the horizon still glowed with the richest crimson. A few tears started to my eyes when I gazed on the new scene before me. When I felt that in this place I was a stranger, unknowing and unknown. It was thus Mr. S found me, when he entered. He drew a chair close to me, he pressed me tenderly to his bosom and mingled his tears with mine. They were tears of the purest happiness.''

Mrs. Samuel Harrison Smith had arrived, wearied from the excitement of her wedding and the long journey to her new home. She consummated her marriage, telling her sister 'it was all that my fondest hopes had pictured, all that my heart could require.' And she began a new life. The planners and schemers had not anticipated such rhetoric or calculated that the noncity would charm the sensibilities of a new Romantic age.[1]

*   *   *

The place certainly did not charm Jacob Wagner, the chief clerk at the State Department. On September 23 he wrote to Pickering that ''the conveniences and comforts of this place daily diminish, and the fall is very sickly. Beside the high price and scarcity of manufactured and foreign articles, the produce of the country is not to be had in plenty.'' Wagner ascribed it to the ''poverty and indolence'' of merchants. He trusted enterprising men from other parts of the country would soon come.

Men who had more invested in the city still tried to put a gloss on what the genius of late-eighteenth-century America had wrought. On September 3 the *Norwich* (Connecticut) *Courier* printed an extract of a letter that reiterated the old faith. ''Inexperienced young men'' who had come to the city complained about the loss ''of their former luxuries,'' but ''the prospects of the growth of this infant capital of an infant Empire are, by no means inauspicious. We have *present* inconveniences—our buildings are too few to render accomodations comfortable, but we perceive houses in abundance rising, which gives an happy presage, that soon our rents will be moderated, and the emigrant procure accommodation without extortion.''

Another piece of promotion that made the rounds of newspapers (probably written by Blodget, since it explained that his large unfinished hotel was actually three small, easily finished hotels) boasted of the city's immunity to yellow fever. The illness had been brought to Alexandria and Georgetown but "has never yet been contagious, owing to the high ground, and purity of the air; there being no marshes within the territory.''[2]

*   *   *

The campaign to prove the city healthy was so successful that the president's wife decided to come south to improve her health. Quincy was rather unhealthy that summer. First Abigail thought she had a recurrence of rheumatic fever, then she decided it was the return of intermitting fever. Many neighbors were sick. Cranch's mother was near death. Her son admitted that in Washington there was "a great deal of the ague and fever and bilious complaints and a few cases of dysentery,'' but "no deaths scarcely.'' Cranch himself had "a very threatening attack of the bilious fever, but after fighting it about ten days with calomel, jalap, tartar-emetic, castor oil and bleeding,'' he conquered it, and was "quite hearty.''

Catherine Johnson, John Quincy Adams's mother-in-law, pressed Abigail to come to the city. They had become close through regular correspondence, and then she had visited her that spring in Philadelphia (and her husband, Joshua Johnson, got appointed to run the general stamp office, which sold the stamps the federal government required on all legal documents). In August Abigail wrote that she was almost persuaded to come, since the president "speaks in such flattering terms of the Federal City,'' but with the election uncertain she could not think of coming only to have to go home in March. Then, three days before the president was to leave, he insisted she join him in Washington. Quincy was too sickly and she too indisposed to stay. He needed her, and, as she explained to Mrs. Johnson, she wanted to help make the place "agreeable.'' She could not rush off with the president. It would take a week to arrange their affairs in Quincy.[3]

*   *   *

The election campaign reached no high plain. Hamiltonians spread stories that Adams stamped on his wig when his cabinet did not agree with him. Republicans stuck with the old canard that he favored a monarchy. Federalists were not easy on Jefferson, assuring voters he was an atheist and worse—that he was dead. Colonel Burrows, the commandant of marines, wrote to Stoddert from Philadelphia on July 2 that news of Jefferson's death "stands here uncontradicted."

Other than being an example of Federalist extravagance, the new capital did not enter into the campaign. And with much campaign material to print, culminating in a long pamphlet by Hamilton attacking Adams, in addition to news of a peace in Europe, American newspapers by and large could not spare space even to print descriptions of the new city. The *Georgetown Centinel* was so clogged with election screeds that it had only one brief call to "rejoice at observing the number of buildings which have lately risen or now rising."

The newspaper ads show that all was not well in the city. On August 15 Isaac Polock was advertising seven of his brick houses in the city for sale or rent and offering ten-year leases on his lots to men who could pay for them with carpentry, bricklaying, or plasterwork. A month later the sheriff was selling the same property, plus mahogany chairs and a fourteen-year-old Negro boy. In a mock petition to the editor, some reality got into the *Centinel*'s pages. Tired of the jeers of gentlemen from Philadelphia that their streets were muddy, the residents south of Bridge Street (today's M Street) in Georgetown wanted all to understand that muddy streets after rain "is a natural consequence and that almost every unpaved part of the world is the same state after a shower."

There was one newspaper controversy over work in the city. Marbury dismissed Deblois as supervisor of building at the Navy Yard, accusing him of shortchanging workers, taking kickbacks, and inflating the price of wharf logs. Deblois replied that Marbury trumped up the charges so he could replace Deblois with one of his relatives.[4]

Not a few were eager to lambaste the commissioners, but Stoddert kept disputes out of the newspaper. On September 29 he heard from Wolcott that Law had been told by the paving contractor Lovell that the commissioners had decided not to carry the Pennsylvania Avenue footpath all the way to the Capitol. After dinner Thornton, Stoddert, and Scott rode to the avenue toward the Capitol, found Lovell, who was building the bridge over the Tiber, and had him sign a "certificate" attesting that he had told Law exactly the opposite, that he was about to ask the board exactly where they wanted the footpath from the Tiber to the Capitol. Scott and Thornton sent that to Wolcott "as a proof how little dependence is to be placed in city reports, particularly when they respect the commissioners."

Unfortunately for the board, Stoddert was no longer president of the Bank of Columbia. With money running out, the bank was the only available resource. Its new president, John Mason, squire of the large island just below Georgetown, never liked giving the board a blank check. On September 23 Scott and Thornton asked the bank for at least $15,000 until Congress arrived. A weary Scott wrote the plea. "We have in vain tried sales. They produce nothing but bad paper and perplexity." They had no security to offer but their own, which they gave "in full confidence" that Congress would reimburse the bank. On October 1 the bank turned them down. Scott tried again, offering property as security: lots advertised for sale in November on which $18,000 was due, "so well situated that no doubt ought to exist that it *will* raise the money solicited" from the bank. Moreover, they still held 800 lots on which $64,000 was due. Scott reiterated that the commissioners had "the fullest reliance on the honor of our government." Congress would reimburse them.

The bank did not reply. On October 8 Scott and Thornton sent over a note for $5,000 to be cashed, suggesting that just $10,000 might "keep the several works now on hand in progression until the meeting of Congress." They warned that without the money, the president's house and the Capitol would not be completed. The bank cashed the $5,000 check and drew the line at that.[5]

The work of the carpenters, plasterers, and glaziers at the president's house continued. George Andrews ornamented the walls with stucco animals. The board signed a contract for a 20-by-13-by-8-foot wooden "necessary" on Capitol Hill to be ready by November 1 at a cost of $234. Stoddert asked Thomas Claxton, not the commissioners, to furnish the president's house. Six of his upholsterers got sick at the beginning of October, and Claxton could find no replacements. Work had to be done at the Capitol too, so when the sick men recovered he had them work at the president's house during the day and shifted them to the Capitol at night.

Despite his resolve, Thornton had done little to improve the president's yard. Stoddert pressed the board to at least remove the temporary buildings surrounding the house. The board promptly ordered the workers residing in the houses in the squares at both the president's house and the Capitol, exempting Claxton and his assistant, to vacate. The board even notified Hoban that his salary would end at that date.

The resulting petition from the carpenters did not mince matters: "You cannot be ignorant of the utter impossibility of procuring houses for the married, or lodging for the unmarried carpenters employed at the President's house." With winter coming, men who had the money to build had to work for themselves, and their friends would help out. The carpenters in the houses offered to pay rent until March 1 or buy the houses. "But if you persevere in taking them down, we shall every man leave the employ." They expected an answer by return of the boy who delivered their petition.

The board did not return an answer, and some, but not all, of the carpenters quit. The board took the matter to Stoddert, who went to see the carpenters. He exorted the workers but also promised an immediate raise of one shilling, six pence, a day and continued occupancy of the houses on the square if they paid rent. Impressed with what had to be done before the president arrived, Stoddert told the board to hire six more carpenters as soon as possible, which the board did, offering $2 a day to lure some men off private jobs during the waning days of the building season.

No one seemed more surprised at the idea that work would be finished by November 1 than the men doing it. When he got notice, Hoban complained that with so much left to be done, he had turned down two private jobs. He also objected to such perfunctory treatment because he had not taken his pay since March. While the board mulled that over, it ordered Hoban back to the Capitol to supervise the completion of the painting.

Though much was unfinished, the community was not about to hang its head in shame. A general meeting was called to determine the proper way to officially greet the government. The citizens decided to form a procession at the Little Hotel and accompany the president to the Capitol on the day he opened Congress.

Many citizens were proudly showing the city off. In the Treasury there was a full-length portrait of George Washington by Stuart, which was to hang in the president's house. There was such a crowd at the president's house that Claxton demanded that the board ban visitors. "The crowds of people . . . ," he informed them on October 28, "interrupt the upholsterers and c. who are exerting every nerve to prepare for the reception of the President."[6]

*   *   *

Margaret Smith began her days by studying the Bible if the stories from boarders at Stelle's breakfast did not last all morning. Then she visited tradesmen, walking, since hacks cost 25 cents for every 100 yards. She found a cabinetmaker from Trenton who knew her father. The poverty in the city was disconcering, though when she went to the hut of her washerwoman, her five children and sick husband all seemed happy.

When her husband was free, they took long walks. He proved the poet in a letter to his sister describing their situation: on "a commanding hill bounded by one of the handsomest streams in our country, now descending into a cool valley covered with wood and watered by gently flowing rills." She liked the sweetbriers in their yard, he "the noble oaks." The first issue of his *National Intelligencer* came out at the end of October. Their household articles arrived by ship, and she got curtains ready for their house. They still found time to ramble. After one walk over a high plain with a view of the river she exclaimed, "I seldom enjoyed a walk more than this, and had scarcely resolution to return, altho' the sun had set." The next day they collected herbs in the woods.

They did not like the luxurious president's house. "The impression of its folly was stronger than that of its greatness." She preferred the "honest industry" at the Navy Yard, where, walking along an uneven, broken shore, she found "an hundred men were employed in digging away a hill and piling up a wharf." They also admired the sugarhouse.[7]

83. Fair Promises—But

On Saturday, November 1, Mrs. Thornton was at the silversmith. She looked out and saw "the President, with his secretary Mr. Shaw, pass bye in his chariot and four, no retinue only one servant on horseback." He went right to his house, moving in without ceremony. In a letter to his wife he reported that "the building is in a state to be habitable," which was a nice way of saying that every room in it was in some respect unfinished. He also offered a prayer: "May none but honest and wise men ever rule under this roof!" Stoddert and Marshall called, as did Thornton. What Adams thought of the improvements made since June is not known, but he did not like the stucco ornaments. The board promptly ordered Andrews to "take down figures at the President's house intended to represent man or beast" and replace them with plaster urns.

Claxton sent a note to the president apologizing for the unreadiness of the house. He had been assigned the job of furnishing it only seven weeks before and had difficulty furnishing what was unfinished. Furthermore, it was a bad time of year to buy household goods because the new imports from England had not arrived and the old "were nearly exhausted." "The great distance the most trifling articles in all instances were to be brought from added to these difficulties." Then he explained the sickness of his hands.[1]

Claxton was the only one to make a written apology even though much was undone, including half of the interior of the president's house. The back stairs, a 10-by-4-foot "necessary" with three holes, and "a hall" for the servants with two doors to the oval room were needed immediately. At the Capitol there was no convenient toilet for congressmen. They would have to go all the way to the cellar. There were no windows in the building for the State and War departments. The biggest headaches were on the grounds. There was still rubbish around the president's house and clay pits around the Capitol, the drains dug on Pennsylvania Avenue were proving too small, and neither the bridge over Rock Creek nor the path to it were finished.

The board did not act as if there were any crisis. It met once in the first week of November and instructed the paving contractor Lovell not to carry the footpath up to the north wing of the Capitol. Stoddert wanted Pennsylvania Avenue prepared, and it stopped at the foot of Capitol Hill. That the street running from the avenue up the hill remained unopened was Carroll's fault. He had kept it in crops too long. Carriages could use the old path through his field. Carroll responded by threatening to fence the square, closing the old road. Stoddert saw that a suitable road was graveled and footpath laid from the avenue to the building.

The board had so little money that it had to ask Stoddert for the $150 it would take to repair the bridges over James and Tiber creeks connecting the point to the rest of the city. Mindful of the snide comments about the point, the commissioners ordered the removal of the wooden buildings still in the streets. That roused citizens of the point to defend the poor carpenters and their families who would be displaced. But the dispute had to simmer because the board broke up for a week. Thornton went to the horse races in Alexandria, White went home for a respite before returning for the opening of Congress, and Scott suffered his old bodily complaint.

The auction of lots brought them back together again. Scott hoped it would raise $18,000, but the city's being the seat of government did not magically bring lots up to their supposed true value. There were no bidders on the 10th, nor were there any bidders for the rest of the week. At the end of the week the board gamely placed an ad explaining that the sale would be continued "to give gentlemen from remote parts of the country a chance."[2]

* * *

No one made much of the War Department building not being completed on time. Whether that bothered Jonathan Jackson, Harbaugh's head carpenter, when he died on November 8 is not known. No one recorded the deathbed confessions of a carpenter struggling to get rich in real estate. His offer to sell a lot at Connecticut and K with a lovely spring had been in the newspaper for some time. His family kept a roaring fire in the room where the corpse lay, even though it was a warm day. Around seven o'clock the building next door, which housed the War Department, caught fire. Men rushed to the scene, too late to bring up water. The nearest fire engine was at the Treasury building, five long blocks away down Pennsylvania Avenue.

On investigation it was found that Jackson's chimney wall backed up against the War Department library. On the second floor the thickness of the party wall was no greater than a brick, and interspersed among real bricks were wooden blocks. At first, blame centered on the lack of firefighting equipment. Then the commissioners took the heat for not having the war office ready in time and not policing the party walls. But soon editors in places where men were still voting could not help hinting that burned in the fire were some yet unrevealed scandals of the administration.[3]

* * *

After a harrowing ride in which they got lost between Baltimore and the city, Mrs. Adams, her son Thomas, her niece, and her servant arrived on the 16th. "As I expected to find it [the city] a new country, with houses scattered over a space of ten miles, and trees and stumps in plenty with a castle of a house, so I found it," she wrote to her sister Mary Cranch. "The President's house is in a beautiful situation in front of which is the Potomac with a view of Alexandria. The country around is romantic but a wild, a wilderness at present." After pledging not to complain, she admitted that she preferred the house in Philadelphia: "not one room or chamber is finished of the whole. It is habitable [only] by fires in every part, thirteen of which we are obliged to keep daily, or sleep in wet and damp places."

To her daughter she voiced more complaints: bells to ring the servants "are wholly wanting"; a contract to deliver firewood was not being fulfilled, and the few cords delivered had to be used to dry the rooms before the family arrived; their servant got some coal, "but we cannot get grates made and set"; "not a single apartment finished", not a "twentieth part lamps enough to light it"; "the great audience room I make a drying room of, to hang up the clothes in"; "not the least fence, yard, or other convenience" outside; and of the belongings she shipped down, "many things were stolen, many more broken, . . . my tea china is more than half missing."

She did admit that "six chambers are made comfortable. . . . Upstairs there is the oval room, which is designed for the drawing-room, and has the crimson furniture in it. It is a very handsome room now; but, when completed, it will be beautiful." That furniture was Claxton's touch. He had been able to get hold of a large amount of red Morocco leather.

Thomas Adams was somewhat impressed at the progress in the city since he had last seen it in 1799. It had "increased rapidly," he told his brother John Quincy, "and begins to assume somewhat the appearance of an inhabited region, much wood, stubble and stumps however still standing." He stayed only a week, tramping about the city to party. A gentleman who joined him one night recalled it years later. After dinner at the president's house, he, Thomas Adams, and three others, guided by Shaw, went to the Johnsons' house and then to a party at General Wilkinson's, who lived in one of the six buildings. "Upon opening the door we saw by the light of the entry lamp how muddy our shoes were; they were altogether unfit to walk upon a carpet or to be seen in a lady's drawing room." Since only Shaw had been invited, the others wanted to withdraw, but Shaw assured them that everybody's boots were muddy.

Abigail Adams did not find the dirt and disorder romantic. As she looked from her window she saw twelve slaves carting dirt and rubbish from the front of the house using four carts. While four went to dump the carts a half mile away, the other eight leaned on their shovels. She thought "two of our hardy N. England men would do as much work in a day as the whole twelve."[4]

*   *   *

On the 17th Congress was supposed to convene, but the House could muster only forty-two members and the Senate fifteen, both short of a quorum. The week was given over to socializing, beginning with the president's usual Tuesday levee. There was much to talk about since there was so much to dislike. Robert Liston, the retiring British minister, thought the president "extremely well lodged in about one-half of the palace" and Congress "sufficiently well accommodated" in the Capitol. But the members "complain with some reason of the narrow size of their private lodgings in the scattered houses of the new city, and of the extravagant price of the necessaries and conveniences of life." Liston blamed the congressmen themselves, since the uncertainty of removal had slowed development. He expected that with Congress on hand, "great and rapid exertions will be made by the proprietors of the valuable soil to remove every cause of just complaint."

Prices in the city were high. At Stelle's, boarders paid $15 a week, plus $5 for a servant, $3 for wood and candles. Congressmen were paid $6 for every day Congress met, which meant their maximum weekly pay was only $36. No congressman was going to make money. At Conrad's and McMunn's, boarders paid $15 a week, but that included candles, wood, and liquors. One had to share a room with another, however, and a dinner table with twenty-four to thirty people. Of course the proprietors advertised the rooms as "spacious." Cranch decided to take in a few boarders too and charge $15 a week for a room alone and $10 if one shared it, but he did not include wood, candles, and liquor. If Cranch filled all his spare rooms he would make $65 a week, but since Congress would adjourn on March 3, Cranch thought the boarders "will not more than pay for our extra expenses in preparing for them."

Most members came expecting to suffer. Young Harrison Gray Otis, who thrived on parties as much as on flights of oratory, brought his wife. "The place . . . is more pleasant than I had anticipated," he confessed to his brother-in-law, but he had to admit that they were better lodged than most. The arrival of such a wealthy young couple relieved Margaret Smith from some walking. On Sunday Mrs. Otis sent her carriage to pick up the Smiths and bring them to church, where they heard "a good sermon . . . preached to a small but respectable congregation."[5]

Then, of all things, it snowed three inches. Petrified that leaks would drip down the walls of the House Chamber, the board hired Lovering to take some men onto the roof to see what could be done. The universal grumbling about the lack of firewood increased. The Treasury Department had advertised for wood early in the season, and the response was so dissatisfactory that Wolcott sent to Philadelphia for wood. Northerners blamed slavery for such seemingly easily overcome inconveniences. As Abigail Adams explained to a correspondent, the area was "abounding with wood," but no one would cut it. "The effects of slavery are visible everywhere." The overseers had become lazier than the slaves. "The lower order of whites," she continued, "are a grade below the negroes in point of intelligence and ten below them in point of civility. They look like the refuse of human nature; the universal character of the inhabitants is want of punctuality, fair promises—but he who expects performance will rapidly be disappointed."

Northerners arriving in earlier years had scarcely mentioned slavery, but in 1800 slavery was much on the mind of the friends of Adams. Since each slave counted as 60 percent of a person, the electoral power of Virginia was greater than that of Massachusetts. North Carolina carried more weight than New York. From the slave's perspective, the city was still a place of refuge but not necessarily a congenial one. A mulatto boy named Tom ran away from a Frederick County, Virginia, master to, it was expected, the federal city, where his mother, "a black woman," was a slave. Then there was Robert, who had been sold by a parson to an Alexandria merchant and by him to a barkeeper and by him to an Orange

County, Virginia, planter who had heard he "has been seen in the employ of Mr. James R. Dermott and supposed to be concealed by said Dermott." Dermott, who, to maximize profits from his city houses, had moved across the Eastern Branch to a farm called St. Elizabeth's, was no joy for an Afro-American to be with. He offered a reward for jailing or flogging Fidelio, "well known about the city," who he suspected was lurking about "Mrs. Young's where he has a wife."

To blame what was lacking in the city on slavery was to miss what had been going on. Few promises to the city had been fulfilled. L'Enfant's housemate, Richard Soderstrom, came to the city as Swedish consul and also presented L'Enfant's petition to Congress, not with much hope. As he explained to L'Enfant, most congress-men considered the 500 guineas he had refused in 1792 to be adequate compensation for all his labors. Soderstrom warned him that if he did not send a short, pointed petition, instead of the dozen or so pages he had filled, accompanied by an account of daily expenses, he had no hope of getting more than 500 guineas, if that. Collen Williamson was off to Annapolis, still pressing his case to wrest back pay from the commissioners. Blodget finally got loose from his New York creditors, and after a brief visit to his old hometown Boston, he came to Washington to try once and for all to dispose of the hotel built by the lottery. Hadfield was quite aware of the latest mission to stop the leaks in the Capital roof, but having got nothing from the Adams administration, he was biding his time before demanding vindication for his design for the roof. One of Morris's sons came to the city, but like everyone else, he was mute while another week of the auction passed without a bidder.

And Abigail Adams lived on the wrong side of town, in a virtual suburb of Georgetown. The only show of enterprise on the west side was made by Samuel M'Intire, next to O'Neale's boardinghouse, who began selling "jelly glasses, sugar basons, gilt and lettered 'Prosperity to the City of Washington.'" The east side of town was coming into its own. In late November Mrs. Thornton paid a rare compliment to a store there. The new hardware store was "better . . . than any in Georgetown."

Newcomers, however, could not appreciate the improvements. One congressman painted a rather grim picture of enterprise around the Capitol. "Our local situation is far from being pleasant or even convenient," he wrote to his wife. "Around the Capitol are seven or eight boarding houses, one tailor, one shoemaker, one printer, a washing-woman, a grocery shop, a pamphlets and stationery shop, a small dry-goods shop, and an oyster house."

Indeed, when congressmen arrived Law published an explanation, writing as "Justice." Yes, "Justice." explained, there was a lack of development around the Capitol, but "it can be solely attributed to the little encouragement given." Georgetown even got another bridge, quite "unnecessary," as were the footpaths to it. "Justice" recalled the efforts to move Congress into the president's house and closed with a warning. "It would have been wise in the first instance, to have placed the public buildings in the vicinity of each other, but as that cannot be now remedied, Congress will of course adopt every precaution to prevent any possible counteraction or impediment to the growth of buildings near the Capitol."

Law was ready to guide them. Congressmen soon became acquainted with that human dynamo. In a November 16 letter to her sister, Margaret Smith tried to portray him, beginning with the disclaimer that "it is impossible to describe this man." "He is one of the strangest men I ever met with; all good nature and benevolence; his ruling passion is to serve every one, which keeps him perpetually busy, about others. Scarcely a day passes without his calling, and at all hours; the other morning he was almost in the room before we were up."[6]

84. Many Salutary Regulations May Be Enacted

The procession organized by the citizens of Washington fizzled. There was a fight over who would be master of ceremonies. The president managed to get to the Capitol by noon on November 22 anyway, along with a considerable crowd of citizens. The galleries filled up and ladies joined the members on the floor of the Senate chamber. Congress had never convened in a room so elegant. The half-elliptic shape, galleries supported by arches and columns, and red Morocco leather chairs delighted everyone, or almost everyone. A writer in the *Baltimore American* objected to "expending 20 dollar to build a gaudy, sumptuous chair for the seat of members of Congress." The red Morocco leather on the Senators' chairs, the goatskins on the House chairs, and the mahogany used throughout the building, the critic noted, all came from England or its colonies. The placing of the portraits of Louis XVI and Marie Antoinette on each side of the vice president's chair was ignored by Republican commentators. Federalist wags took comfort in knowing that if Jefferson looked to the left or right he would see royalty. For the moment, however, Jefferson was not in the city.

Adams congratulated Congress "on the prospect of a residence not to be changed." He noted "that accomodations are not now so complete as might be wished" but found "great reason to believe that this inconvenience will cease with the present session.' He then looked to heaven and implored that "in this city may that piety and virtue, that wisdom and magnanimity, that constancy and self-government, which adorned the great character whose name it bears be forever held in venerations!" He reminded them of the need to pass laws for the federal territory, then went on to relations with France and England, and the need for a building a strong navy and reforming the federal judiciary. Of course, no mention was made of what was on everyone's mind, the election.

Mrs. Thornton thought "the whole appearance was solemn and conducted with order." Afterward, despite the clouds and cold, visiting was the order of the day for ladies with carriages. Mrs.

Adams and her niece repaid a visit by Mrs. Thornton and took a look at the plans for the Capitol.[1]

By tradition, a delegation from each house returned the president's favor and went to his house to offer replies to his message. The Senate's reply on the 25th rued the death of Washington, for "great indeed would have been our gratification if his sum of earthly happiness had been completed by seeing the Government thus peaceably convened at this place." They reminded the president of the need for a mausoleum for the hero. The House reply was traditionally more businesslike and more important. It promised to consider a government for the District of Columbia. In Philadelphia it had been easy for the House to go in procession to deliver its reply to the president. Despite the distance to the president's house, the House managed to keep the tradition alive.[2]

The city of Washington was finally doing the business it was intended to do. It was founded. But historically, little business of importance transpired in Congress between the opening of the session and the holidays. It was a time for balls. The rival dancing assemblies opened their seasons. The Washington Assembly at Stelle's opened on November 26 to all who would pay the $15 subscription. The *Intelligencer* described the crowd as "above 100 ladies and gentlemen" enjoying the "good humor and gaiety," which was not a phrase idly thrown out. Tension over the election was increasing. Federalist victories in New Jersey and Delaware meant that South Carolina, whose legislature met in early December, would determine the winner. Speaker Sedgwick expected that South Carolina would manage the vote so that its favorite son, General Pinckney, would be president.

The Georgetown Assembly opened December 9. It was not an entirely happy occasion. News had just arrived of the death, not unexpected, of the Adams's son Charles in New York. He had been a heavy drinker and well unwell. As his mother put it, "food has not been his sustenance." Those attending the usual Tuesday levee at the president's house wore crepe bands. But the ball in Georgetown that night went famously. There were thirty-nine ladies, which was about the usual complement, "and a great many gentlemen." Needless to say, the president and his wife did not attend. Abigail was getting more set against the damp house she was in. But two weeks there, her niece Susan woke up laboring with a "dreadful hoarse cough." The physician nearest came quickly and "gave her calomil, soaked her feet in warm water, and steamed her with warm vinegar. She puked and that seemed to relieve her." Then Abigail herself was "afflicted with a loss of voice & a bad cough."[3]

*　　　*　　　*

The beginning of Congress and commencement of the social season did not make the ongoing auction of lots any more lively. There was a bid on November 25. Thomas Sims Lee bought a lot near the new bridge over Pennsylvania Avenue for $194. The next day, George Andrews, whose stucco animals had been banished from the president's house, bought two lots near Blodget's hotel for three cents a square foot. The lots offered were not off the beaten track: on the next day, lots bounded by New York Avenue and 14th, 13th, and K Streets attracted no bids.

Such dismal results did not deter George Walker, who announced an auction of one hundred lots at Tunnicliff's. Walker wanted half in cash and half in notes of sixty days. In private sales, the commissioners tried to keep lot prices up, offering lots just north and northeast of the Capitol for 12 cents a square foot and lots south of Pennsylvania Avenue at 11th Street Northwest for 8 cents. In December, they made one sale, some lots on the north side of Pennsylvania Avenue between 12th and 13th Streets, for 7 cents a square foot. This sluggish business was in spite of their sending maps to the boardinghouses and a special map to the House and Senate with the publicly owned lots colored in red and lots sold for default in yellow. (On December 5, the day after they sent the maps over, John Nicholson died after four months in Prune Street prison, leaving a wife and eight children.)[4]

*　　　*　　　*

The commissioners were bankrupt, and more than merely financially. The proprietors looked to Congress to save the city. If

Congress assumed jurisdiction, not only would the commissioners be out of business, but the state of Maryland could no longer tax property. And as "Justice" argued in the *Intelligencer,* "many salutary regulations may be enacted to promote the prosperity and the happiness of the inhabitants of Columbia."

The House and Senate promptly appointed a committee to draw up laws for the district, but on the floor the mausoleum took center stage. That summer Benjamin West, the American who had become a great artist in England, submitted a design to the U.S. minister in London for a pyramid-shaped mausoleum 150 feet square that would cost $170,000. Henry Lee, who had always been the driving force behind the monument, liked the idea. This alarmed the friends of Capitol Hill because there was talk of putting the large pyramid in another part of the city. The rival sides of the city began fighting over Washington's bones.

Law had his friends in Congress argue that, rather than an expensive monument, "a plain but neat apartment should be speedily prepared" in the Capitol. In a newspaper essay he ridiculed the pyramid and the bill leaving the selection of a site to the four secretaries, "who may have it in contemplation to place a Mausoleum on some sublime rugged Eminence near Georgetown, and with that view have already made a footway toward it, and a bridge otherwise superfluous over Rock Creek." Thornton had the *Intelligencer* print portions of the letter he had written to John Marshall last winter about how the monument could spur the completion of the Capitol. (About the same time, a news item from France reported the arrest of the sculptor Ceracchi for conspiring to assassinate Napoleon. The ill-fated sculptor soon met the guillotine.)

Congress frankly did not care about the competing sides of the city. Plain Republicans like lanky Nathaniel Macon objected to wasting money on a pile for a man everyone already venerated. Then Randolph of Virginia and Harper of South Carolina squared off on whether the proposal served, as Randolph put it, "most cruelly, (however pure in intention,) to violate the feelings of a lady, so much troubled already."[5]

*　　*　　*

The commissioners did not hurry to lay their affairs before Congress. They managed to pay off their $5,000 note at the Bank of Columbia with a $5,000 note from Uriah Forrest payable in ninety days. He paid his note with an apology: "I know that I have disappointed you, and regret it." Forrest persuaded the bank to accept the arrangement. The money men of the community decided it was not the time to call attention to the rather tenuous financial situation of the Bank of Columbia.

The commissioners could with difficulty go to Congress for money when the footpaths and carriageways remained unfinished. Not until December 19 did men get to work on grading Pennsylvania Avenue to the new bridge over Rock Creek, including filling up a six-foot-deep hollow. On the 18th Alexander White toured the other end of the avenue and found ditches not opened so water could drain and other ditches already filled in. If all the ditches were not opened and kept open, the whole project would soon become useless. Furthermore, he could see why no one used the new bridge over the Tiber. The turn to it from the hill was too sharp, and carriages still had to go over "a considerable space of low ground." After writing his report, White went home for the holidays, promising to be back January 10. That left the city without a board, since Scott was sick again. On Christmas Eve he was "insensible," and on Christmas Day he died, leaving a wife and seven children.

Although the commissioners withheld their bills, Congress was soon pressed to make good on others. On December 11, Senator Langdon of New Hampshire presented L'Enfant's memorial, not shortened, as Soderstrom had advised, and with nothing so picayune as daily expenses itemized. He still wanted almost $100,000. The Committee on Claims asked the commissioners for their file on L'Enfant. The committee also fielded a more pressing claim. James Clark asked Congress to pay him for the blinds he had made for the Treasury building. His beef was really with Wolcott. As Clark told the story, he was in Wolcott's office hanging sashes when the secretary came in and said the window needed blinds. Clark suggested other windows in the building needed them too, and Wolcott told him to make them. After he completed the work, Clark went to Wolcott for payment. Wolcott sent Clark to the comissioners, and they said they had never ordered blinds. Clark asked whether, when

Wolcott had told him to make them, he should have "insult[ed] him by asking, sir, who is to pay me?"[6]

*   *   *

General Pinckney refused to be a part of any scheme to have electors vote for him while not voting for Adams, and as a result, South Carolina went for Jefferson and Burr. The news reached Washington on December 12, where it was "snowing, hailing, blowing, raining," so badly that a sale of slaves by Mrs. Burnes had to be postponed. No one recorded the reaction of Jefferson or Adams. Dr. Thornton called on the president elect, inviting him to see the plans of the Capitol and also samples of Andrews's ornaments, hoping the future resident of the president's house would vindicate his judgment in having them done.

Residents of the city naively assumed that with the election over, the statesmen of the nation would devise a government for them. As one essayist put it, "In the collision and agitation which have attended the Presidential election, there has not been found in the public councils a mind sufficiently calm to elevate itself above the storm; and to devote some attention to the interests of the respectable body of people, comprehended in the Territory of Columbia, and in the City of Washington in particular."

Augustus Woodward, a young man from New York City who, with money given to him by his father, had bought as many as sixty-six lots in the city, published a five-part essay in the *Intelligencer* telling Congress what to do. First, the Constitution should be amended to give the city representation in the House and one senator. Then, since "it would impair the dignity" of the federal government "to be occupied with all the local concerns of the Territory of Columbia," there should be a governor appointed by the president and an elected house and senate for the district. At the same time, Congress should bear some responsibility for completing the city. The federal government should build and keep in repair the public buildings, the public docks, the naval hospital, "the great canal," the monuments, and the national university. For everything else the citizens themselves should pay. He cautioned that "every inhabitant ought to pride himself in this pecuniary independence; and to discourage a constant application to Congress for donations and charities, which cannot fail in the end to make every state in the union our enemy."[7]

*   *   *

Then it dawned on politicians that the election was not over at all. No knowledgeable Republican could guarantee that one Republican elector had not voted for Burr. There was a very good chance that Jefferson and Burr would have an equal number of votes for president, which meant that the House would have to determine the winner, with each state delegation having one vote. The Federalists controlled only six delegations so could not elect a president. But the Republicans controlled only eight delegations, one shy of a majority. Two state delegations, Maryland and Vermont, were split between the parties. The Federalists could prevent the election of Jefferson. In its Christmas Eve issue the *Intelligencer* hoped that the suggestion was "merely the playful ebullition of a sportive fancy, and not the effect of deliberate design."

With doubt cast on the certainty of his election, Jefferson stopped offering appointments in his new administration. He did not go to Thornton's lest that be construed as an attempt to prematurely impose his ideas on the commissioners. He did not trust the Federalists, was uncertain of Burr, and so confronted the constitutional crisis by adhering strictly to his constitutional duties, making his way along the footpath from Conrad and McMunn's to the Senate chamber and back again, avoiding the growing swamp of intrigue all around him. One afternoon he dined at the president's house. He sat next to Abigail Adams and asked her about the other guests at the president's table. He confessed, "I do not know 1 in 20" Republican congressmen; "they complain, and say that I will not take my hat off to theirs when I pass them, but I cannot help it, I have no means of knowing them."[8]

1801

85. Turkey Carpets to Lie upon Would Not Be Amiss

"The Jacobins in the House . . . [are] more civil in their attentions than I have ever known them," Speaker Sedgwick chortled. The Federalists were in no hurry to let the opposition off the hook. The ballots would be officially counted on February 11. Until then, much good could be done for the country: the Sedition law could be extended for another two years and the federal judiciary reformed so that Adams could appoint almost two dozen new judges.

Most Federalists made no mistake about whom they favored in the election. Many sincerely thought Burr would make the better president. They believed their own propaganda. Jefferson was an atheist and impractical philosopher, whereas Burr was just a convenient tool. They hoped to make him their tool. They even ignored long letters that Hamilton sent, painting Burr as an unprincipled and dangerous man.

The Republicans were unable to end the crisis themselves. Not having an official reason to be in Washington, Burr did not come. On December 30 he did write to Samuel Smith, Republican of Maryland, to say that he would not stand in Jefferson's way. Those words struck many as equivocal. Republicans had hoped he would say that he would not serve as president. Federalists read the letter as merely an invitation for them to do the dirty work. As Senator Uriah Tracy, Federalist of Connecticut, put it, "If he [Burr] cannot outwit all the Jeffersonians, I do not know the man."

So Smith went to see Burr and asked what he would do if the House remained deadlocked. Burr replied that the Republicans could make him president. To demand he renounce the presidency impugned his honor. "I was made a candidate against my will," he fumed, "God knows, never contemplating or wishing the result which has appeared. And now I am insulted by those who use my name for having suffered it to be used. . . ." Republicans in Washington suspected every newcomer from New York of being an agent for Burr.[1]

                                *   *   *

James Madison did not serve in the Sixth Congress, so the Republican leader in the House was Albert Gallatin. He crossed the snow-covered Appalachians and reached the federal city on January 10. He disliked everything about the city. Gallatin was no rude frontiersman. Born and educated in Geneva, Switzerland, he came to America to make his fortune and thought the transshipment point between the Potomac and Ohio valleys was the place to do it. Politics saved him from penury on the frontier. If Jefferson did not become president, he would go to New York City to make his fortune.

The new capital was not enough city for him. He not only bemoaned the lack of accommodations; he denigrated the site, which most observers extolled. On the 15th he described it to his wife. Dividing Greenleaf's Point from the Capitol was "a large swamp." The same swamp separated the Capitol from the president's house, and any house built on the "causeway" between the two buildings would condemn "its wretched tenant to perpetual fevers."

Gallatin took some comfort, however, in the wasteland around him. The salvation of Jefferson's candidacy lay in the general loathing of the federal city. Maryland's Federalist congressmen would vote for Jefferson, thus making him president, because they were "afraid about the fate of the federal city, which is hated by every member of Congress without exception of persons or parties." They could not afford to divide the union.

A week passed, and none of the four Maryland Federalists signaled support for Jefferson. Gallatin rethought his analysis. The inconvenience of the city would not solve the crisis; it fed it. Members stayed in boardinghouses. "A few, indeed, drink, and some gamble, but the majority drink naught but politics, and by not mixing with men of different or more moderate sentiments, they inflame each other. . . . On that account, principally," he explained to his wife, "I see some danger in the fate of the election which I had not before contemplated."

Gallatin thought through the worst case. If the House remained deadlocked, the Federalists could have the presidency devolve on a caretaker—Secretary of State Marshall was talked of—and ask the states to hold new elections. Then they could use their control of the state senates of Pennsylvania, New York, Maryland, and South Carolina to prevent any new election in those states, which they had just done in Pennsylvania, thus forcing each of those states to divide its votes. The Federalists' control of New England would give them a five-vote majority. There would be nothing unconstitutional about the scenario.

In Virginia and Pennsylvania, Republicans talked of raising the militia to prevent a usurper, some self-styled Napoleon, from gaining power.[2]

*   *   *

A place that so quickly became an Armageddon was not about to impress many as destined to be an emporium. When most Americans finally directed their attention to the city, it was to calculate the forces of good and evil, not the value of lots. Those still wrapped up in the parochial, albeit grandiose, dreams of the would-be emporium were isolated in the very city that they thought only they understood. It was a cruel twist for residents who trusted that once the election was over, Congress would spend much time on their affairs. Citing that "precarious vortex from that political chaos from which it is impossible to tell the result," Samuel Davidson complained, "our city property is rarely thought worthy of being made the topic of common conversation."

The fact that Adams had lost the election, however, was of some service. He did not hem and haw when it came to making appointments. Replacing Scott was made easy when some proprietors advised him that Cranch was just the man. Washington had taken months to appoint new commissioners. Adams appointed Cranch on January 11. Cranch accepted the appointment, well knowing the office might soon be abolished. Of course he did not give up his law practice. The day his uncle appointed him commissioner, he tried to get Virginia authorities to arrest James Piercy for his client Law. The sugar baker had fled the federal city with equipment from his factory, running out on $30,000 in debts.

Thornton, who expected to be Jefferson's governor of the territory of Washington, still had enough enthusiasm for his job to come up with such ideas as having Clephan the housepainter paint panels in the Senate chamber "in imitation of Prophyry." Cranch, a realist, spent his first ten days in office trying to fanthom the financial plight of the board. By keeping up the value of the remaining 5,000 public lots, the board could claim that it was over $670,000 in the black, which left plenty to spare to pay back $360,000 in loans. But it had no cash on hand, and interest had to be paid to Maryland before it could consider going ahead with work on the buildings. The only possible source of revenue was a sale of Morris's and Nicholson's lots, since the board's lots were pledged to repay the loans. The solution the board thought of was for Congress to pass a law guaranteeing the validity of titles to city lots, disband the commissioners, and let the federal government complete the public buildings and sell the remaining public lots.[3]

*   *   *

When Federalists caucused on January 19 they decided to put the House in secret session the 11th and stay in session, always voting to a man for Burr, and wait for the Republicans to break.

The evening after the caucus the Treasury building caught fire. William O'Neale spotted the fire as he was on his way to Dr. Coningham's. He cried "Fire!" and Coningham was sure it was just wood shavings. Eventually the president himself joined the bucket brigades. O'Neale directed the effort, which allowed him to first inspect the auditor's office, where the fire had started. He found a "hickory chunk about 12 or 15 inches long, and about 3 inches in diameter; it appeared to be burnt at one end to a coal; there was bark on one end." He announced that the fire had been set "by some evil disposed person.'' Then the fire, which had seemed to be extinguished, spread upstairs. When several men rushed up to fight it, they stumbled on a group of men packing papers. Wolcott was also up there. O'Neale begged for orders. Wolcott refused to give them since he had just resigned and was busy saving his private papers, with which he could vindicate his conduct as Treasury secretary. He spied his replacement, Samuel Dexter, and introduced him to O'Neale, and Dexter told O'Neale what public papers to save first.

Such were the political tensions that no one calculated how great a loss the fire was to the commissioners' depleted reserves of cash. The charge that Wolcott himself had set the fire became so insistent that Robert G. Harper, a Federalist from South Carolina, insisted Congress investigate the fires at the Treasury and War departments to allay all suspicion. The investigation did not redound to the credit of the commissioners. Once again, wooden bricks were found in profusion, as well as wooden sticks pushed in the cracks of uneven brickwork.

To prevent another catastrophe, the board directed Hoban to take down parts of the walls near the extra stoves in the House chamber and to remove flammable wood. Hoban also put a scaffold up under the grand staircase, where decorations were threatening to fall down. Clephan was asked no longer to imitate porphyry, but to check the putty used on the skylights instead. The roof was still leaking.

At least no one slept at the Capitol. After a January thaw there was such dripping in her chamber that Abigail Adams had to get out of bed and summon servants ''to sit tubs to catch the water.'' A week after that disaster, her room was still not dry. Being in the damp house was annoying, but so was getting out of it. Between her and Mrs. Johnson, she complained, lay ''such a quagmire that our intercourse is much injured.'' Mrs. Adams managed to get to the Capitol for church services and visited Mount Vernon, but she hoped to get out of the city before the end of January.[4]

*   *   *

The city proprietors tried to entertain congressmen. Thomas Johnson's party was, Otis thought, "made brilliant by the presence of several really fine and fashionable Annapolitans." But the food was "shabby beyond all former precedent," cold beef and ham "which the dear ladies were obliged to eat on their blessed knees." Commandant Burrows had good music and an elegant supper and "Ben Huger [a Federalist from South Carolina] danced on his toes as usual with every flirt in the room, while his sedate and venerable lady bedizzened and bejeweled kept a steadfast and deploring eye upon his eccentric follies." But as February 11 approach parties became strained. Otis thought a ball at Lingan's ruined by the presence of five Republican congressmen. He was outnumbered, since only four Federalist members attended.

So few attended because Lingan's was on the heights of Georgetown. Members learned the hazards of venturing out too late in the wilderness surrounding them. One visitor found walking in the city at night easy, "as for the whole length of Pennsylvania Avenue our path was illuminated by brick kilns." But Otis's horse threw him into a clay pit, and he joked to his wife that getting into difficulties at night was "not uncommon with members of our honorable house." James Bayard, Federalist of Delaware, was thrown from a carriage into a ditch as he and his friends tried to climb New Jersey Avenue to their boardinghouses after a dinner party at Law's. If Bayard had died, the joke went, Delaware would have been unrepresented, giving Jefferson a majority in the House. Members could stay close to home for entertainment. "The Learned Pig" performed nightly at Conrad and McMunn's tavern.[5]

* * *

The city's newest permanent residents, the government clerks, petitioned for a raise, blaming the city for their financial woes. They cited the "extravagant price of most of the necessaries of life; the inconvenience and expense in attending to the public business from remote situation; the exorbitant demands for house rent"; and the fact that there were no jobs in town with which they could supplement their income. Unfortunately for them, their petition, which

Congress denied, seemed but a drop in the sea of discontent swelling in the district. Some petitioners asked for a government. Some merely wanted Congress to claim jurisdiction, so the citizens of the district could avoid Maryland taxes.

A House committee reported a bill for a territorial government that divided the district into its Virginia and Maryland parts and gave each equal representation in an elected house with two-year terms, an appointed senate modeled on the U.S. Senate, and a governor appointed by the president to serve for three years. It limited the franchise to men of property, and to answer the worries of Alexandrians that they would be taxed to pave the city of Washington, the bill forbade the territorial legislature from taxing to open or improve streets. The citizens of Washington were nonplused. "Washington" worried in the pages of the *Intelligencer* that "the inevitable result will be the entire prostration of Washington."

In early February the House debated the bill at length but not the issues of taxation and relative representation that worried their landlords. Republicans called for more republican provisions, such as annual elections and no senate, and, not eager for Adams to appoint the officers of the new government, they were in no hurry to pass it. The citizens of Alexandria protested the measure, and while the speculators of Georgetown and landlords of Washington wanted a government, they did not want the one proposed. Federalist did not have the stomach to push the bill through. With members of both parties numbed by the controversy, a conviction to do as little as possible for the federal district began to grow.

But the public buildings had to be finished. In late January a House committee reported a bill carrying on the public buildings without commissioners. Congress would ante up $100,000 annually, a loan secured by lots, and the four secretaries would supervise "suitable architects, agents and workmen." The House tabled that bill while the Ways and Means Committee investigated to see if there were hopes of any loan being repaid.[6]

*   *   *

Sometime in early February the president and vice president met by chance on Pennsylvania Avenue. Jefferson brought the conversation around to the crisis. He told Adams that if the Senate named someone to lead the country during "an interregnum," "such a measure would probably produce resistance by force." He suggested that Adams announce that he would veto such a bill. Adams replied that he thought such a bill justified. While Adams had no part in formulating Federalist strategy nor wanted any, he was aware that the party's House leaders had come up with terms of surrender. He told Jefferson that he, Jefferson, could "fix the election by a word in an instant by declaring [he] would not turn out the federal officers, not put down the navy, nor sponge the national debt." Jefferson broke off the discussion. A senator had already presented the same deal, and he had explained that he would not enter office under any obligation to anyone.

On the eve of the House vote, Adams let off steam in a letter to his old friend Elbridge Gerry. "I know no more danger of a political convulsion, if a President pro-temp of the Senate or a Secretary of State or Speaker of the House should be made President by Congress than if Mr. Jefferson or Mr. Burr is declared such. The President would be as legal in one as in either of the others in my opinion, & the people as well satisfied. This however must be followed by another election & Mr. J. would be chosen. I should in that case decline the election. We shall be at any rate in the tempestuous sea of liberty for years to come & where the bark can land but in political convulsion I cannot see."

The Republicans, however, incorrectly assessed the animus of the Federalists. They were less interested in perpetuating their power than in defeating Jefferson. They expected Burr to persuade his friends in the New York and New Jersey delegations to vote for him, thus adding two states to the six the Federalists could deliver. Then they had to get a vote in Maryland or Vermont. Bayard, Federalist of Delaware, approached General Smith, once a Federalist, and mentioned future appointment to whatever he wanted as a reward for switching. Chauncey Goodrich, Federalist of Connecticut, approached the man Federalists had already branded a coward, Matthew Lyon, and mentioned money. The Republicans hoped that the Maryland Federalists would at last relent. The proprietors pressed Craik to end the crisis.

At noon on the 11th, Vice President Jefferson opened the ballots cast by the states' electors. He certified the tie between himself and Burr. At one o'clock the House convened, operating under a rule not to adjourn until there had been an election. Otis, only half in jest, had suggested that the House "committee rooms must be garnished with beefsteaks, and a few Turkey carpets to lie upon would not be amiss." However, members were left to make their own provisions. Otis told his wife that he did not think "the obstinacy of parties will endure beyond the second day." Muhlenberg and Lieb, both Republicans from Pennsylvania, assured friends that they would lay in "a store of ham, turkey and wine for the election." Dana, Federalist of Connecticut, decided to starve himself in hopes of curing a nagging fever.

The House convened in surprising good cheer, each member cast secret ballots, and both parties were more gratified than alarmed that party discipline was absolute, which meant that eight states voted for Jefferson, six for Burr, and two, Maryland and Vermont, were divided. The Maryland vote was something of a surprise because few expected that the Republican Joseph Nicholson would attend. Sick though he was, he voted from a bed made for him in a room beside the chamber. Between 1:00 P.M. and 8:00 A.M. the House voted twenty-seven times, with the same results. There were no reports then or remembrances afterward of any ill feeling expressed in the chamber during the nineteen-hour ordeal. A year later in a congressional debate, when someone who had not been there tried to describe the scene as acrimonious and a prelude to civil war, Archibald Henderson, Federalist of North Carolina, who had been there, objected that in fact relations between members had never been more cordial.

As members had no offices and were accustomed to do other work at their seats in the chamber while the House was in session, it was not all time lost. The most popular pastime was writing letters to the president recommending men to be judges. Twenty-three new ones had to be appointed thanks to passage of the bill reforming the judiciary.

Roger Griswold, Federalist of Connecticut, had a more diverting task: picking over the accounts of the commissioners as he prepared a report on the financing of the public buildings. Two months earlier he had told his sister that he found the place "both melancholy and ludicrous . . . a city in ruins.'' To his amazement given the results, the board had spent over $1 million. As for the nearly $1 million the board claimed it could raise with the sale of lots, Griswold looked over the record of sales and saw that the government could not rely on the sale of lots to complete the buildings and properly accommodate the government. Most amazing of all, Griswold found that the proprietors who had been buzzing in his ear about there being no true plan of the city were right. The original trustees had still not conveyed land to the government, and the commissioners' actions had not necessarily conformed to what plans there were.

At 8:00 A.M. the members agreed to suspend balloting until noon. When members left the Capitol to go to their boardinghouses, they were not greeted by a throng of curious onlookers. The talk of raising militias was in Richmond and Philadelphia, and from the latter city six of the "stoutest butchers and bloodiest bullies" were on their way to the federal city. But in the city born when the Pennsylvania line carried its mutiny to Congress accompanied by the cheers of Philadelphians, no mob assembled. As weary members trod the footpaths to their boardinghouses, they found that snow had fallen during the night.[7]

Epilogue

"Nearly blood warm." So the waters of the Potomac felt to Secretary of State John Quincy Adams just before dawn, August 20, 1820, as he took his customary swim off the rocks just southwest of the White House grounds. Adams liked to float on his back, slip off his green goggles, and watch the sun rise over the Capitol. He became the first of America's great men to really get the city in his blood.

When he returned to America in the summer of 1801, his mother's bad report did not keep him away from the city. She had not stayed around to witness Jefferson's triumph after thirty-six ballots—worried about the fate of his small state if the union came asunder and thinking he had Jefferson's promise, through the agency of Samuel Smith, that he would not undo what the Federalists had done, Bayard of Delaware ended the stalemate. Cranch described to her the mob of "40 or 50 . . . strangers' who forced him to illuminate his windows in celebration of Jefferson's victory.

When John Quincy landed in Philadelphia he sent his wife on to her family in Washington, while he went to Quincy to see his. His mother told him not to go to Washington before October, the end of the sickly season, advice he did not obey. His wife, Louisa, was sending him glowing reports of the city: "I'm quite delighted with the situation of this place, and I think should it ever be finished it will be one of the most beautiful spots in the world. The President's house and the Capitol are the two most superb buildings and very well worth coming to see. The publick offices are likewise very handsome."

Applying lessons they had learned in Virginia and reinforced by their experiences along the Delaware, Jefferson and Madison religiously left the city by August and did not return until the end of September. They would not stay on tidewater during those months. When duty called, John Quincy always stayed the summer.

Like all mortals, he marveled at how unrelieving an August in Washington could be. At one in the morning, on August 15th, the night after his blood-warm swim, the clouds burst. Lightning struck near his house off Judiciary Square, and when he came out the next morning to assess the damage, he could not believe how hot and muggy it had already become. The great storm afforded no relief.[1]

* * *

There was enough damage in the area that the newspapers talked about it. The torrents coming down the hills wrecked newly laid sewers and drowned a slave in Georgetown. Within the week a newspaper editorial pondered this: if a downpour caused such damage in a city with so much vacant space, "What, then, must we expect, when closely built streets occupy these spaces and shut up these outlets?"

Twenty-nine years after its founding, the city still did not have a drainage system. In 1815, Benjamin Latrobe and Robert King, Jr., the city surveyors, sensed that maybe the time had come. Congress was financing the reconstruction of the Capitol and the president's house, which had been burned by the British on a sweltering August day in 1814 (a mighty storm came up in the night, humbled the barbaric troops, and put out the fires.) Latrobe and King pointed out that the expansive city had good natural drainage, but that "in forming the plan . . . no attention" had been paid to it. So after a bad rain the valley running from 14th and K down to 9th and Pennsylvania usually became "covered with water some feet deep." King's father had made the same point in 1798. The 1815 report elicited no response.[2]

* * *

On either August 22, 1820, a week after the storm Adams described, civic-minded residents gathered under a "scorching" sun to lay the cornerstone of the new City Hall on Judiciary Square. While the population of the city, in a day when both Philadelphia and New York housed more than 100,000 souls, barely topped 13,000, George Hadfield designed a City Hall with a classical look and ample insides worthy of a metropolis. His original design had a price tag of $375,000. The city divided into parties over the design, cost, and site. As a compromise, it was decided to build it piecemeal, although the friends of Hadfield argued that the whole building could be finished for under $100,000. Despite the acrimony generated, the building was a triumph for Hadfield and a belated victory over Thornton, who was embittered by Jefferson's not appointing him to run the city and then letting Latrobe redesign the south wing of the Capitol. Thornton had given up any pretense to being an architect, devoting himself, as commissioner of patents, to invention.

Thomas Law's son John gave the major address at the ground breaking. The son of a Bengali mother, a member of the Harvard class of 1805, he was the rising young man in the city (he died during a fever epidemic in 1822). He began his career by defending his father in a case brought by the trustees of the aggregate fund, which the Supreme Court finally laid to rest in 1815. The case became the most massive in early court history, with 900 folios, and Law won $62,644.45 for land never conveyed to his father by Greenleaf, Morris, Nicholson, and the trustees. Young Law developed into an adept in real estate law. His oration began with personal remembrances but soon speculated on land values.

"He remembers the surprise he felt," Law began, speaking of himself in the third person, "when he understood that the woods and fields around him were dignified with the name of a city; and over this very spot, now surrounded with numerous buildings, he used to walk in solitude to school." Gesturing to Pennsylvania Avenue on the plain below, he continued, ". . . The largest part of the beautiful avenue which connects the principal public edifices together was an impassable wilderness; and the streets were not distinguished by any visible lines: how great is the contrast between its present desolate condition at that period and the prospect of its present prosperity!"

Law reviewed the economic indicators, which in those days spelled good times: $6 million worth of assessed property, city revenues of $40,000, and 30 miles of streets "open and improved."

The city was ready to boom. Echoing the enthusiastic descriptions of the 1790s, he exalted at the city's "salubrious and delightful climate, equally removed from the extremes of heat and cold, and a circle of elevated hills around, form which the eye may range over an amphitheater presenting all the beauties of nature. . . ."

Having delivered the old salute to nature, he did not notice how little Congress had done. Despite popular belief that the federal government paid for building the city, it had actually contributed no more than $110,000 in loans, which had been repaid with interest.

Young Law knew he had a pleasing theme when he blamed Congress for the state of the city. "From the slight exertion made at its establishment to forward its growth," he quipped, "we might infer that it was believed there was a magic power in the term Metropolis, which, when applied by the Congress of the United States, to a houseless heath, would immediately convert it into a splendid city, as Amphion of yore is said to have built the walls of Thebes by the miraculous magic of his lyre." He then contrasted the stingy Congress with the "power and resources of the Autocrat of Russia," who, within nine years, built St. Petersburg on "an uninviting morass on the banks of the Neva."[3]

It being August, no congressmen were in the audience. Of the early members, only Van Ness of New York remained in the city, quite an exception since he had married David Burnes's daughter and managed the old man's estate well enough to afford the mansion on 17th Street that Burnes had first planned with L'Enfant back in 1791. But some in the crowd with long memories must have had some sympathy for the sufferings of those early congressmen. At least when part of the roof of the Senate chamber fell in 1803, it hit no members. Latrobe was so appalled at the bad workmanship at the Capitol that he suggested in one of his reports that those who built it had left such evidence of "gross ignorance, or of fraud" (Blagden excepted) as to invite criminal proceedings. Jefferson crossed that accusation out before the report was published.[4]

Law did not have to look far to cite an example of congressional negligence. The Mall that his father wanted improved back in 1796 lay neglected; "not a tree has been planted, not even a common fence encloses it." He could even shift blame for the lack of private development from the city's residents. "The unsettled parts of the city may be attributed to the injudicious subdivisions of squares into small lots of one-eighth of an acre." Many were sold to faraway speculators. "Hence it became impossible for an individual to purchase a sufficient space for shrubbery or a garden." Until parcels of land owned by farflung speculators could be consolidated, "nearly 2,000 acres which might contribute to the support and ornament of this place, are thus destined to remain a desert."

That made the proprietors of city property seem defenseless before marauding speculators. Law conveniently forgot the desperation of Benjamin Stoddert. Before the spring of 1801 ended, his old partner Forrest had become an object of charity. Cranch repaid an old debt and appointed Forrest as clerk of the District of Columbia court, to which his uncle had appointed him judge in the waning hours of his administration. Desperate to avoid a similar fate, Stoddert packaged all his holdings as a tontine and sent salesmen from Charleston to Boston literally begging his Federalist friends to buy a share for $40, not for themselves, but for their children. "If gentlemen at Charleston, who can spare money and have children, can believe the truth, that this plan . . . affords fair, and as I think certain means of disposing of money to be returned to the children many fold, I should think it likely to succeed," Stoddert pleaded in 1804. It did not and Stoddert died in 1813, a poor man.

In 1806 Benjamin Latrobe pitied most of all the master workmen who had come to the city with such hopes, saving their wages to buy lots and build houses "which in any other spot would have given to them ease, and to their children education." In the federal city it afforded them "distress." ". . . Want of employ has made many of them sots; few have saved their characters, most of them hate, envy, and calumniate each other, for they are all fighting for the scanty means of support, which the city affords." Latrobe did not forget the speculators, "who brought large fortunes to this grand vortex, that swallowed every thing irrecoverably that was thrown into it. Law, Duncanson, Stoddert, and many others from affluent circumstances, are involved by their sanguine hopes in embarrassments from which nothing but the grave will set them free." When Latrobe wrote, Blodget was in prison, still collecting "$5 subscriptions for the establishment of the University." He died in 1814.

Greenleaf outlived them all, periodically visiting the city "for the purpose of testing titles," and selling lots for the aggregate fund. He had begun his agency in 1803. Managing the trustees' suits, battling Stoddert for control of lots still unpaid for, and fortified by the resources of his wife Ann Allen, he tried in 1807 to buy all the property of the aggregate fund for $50,000, but on terms that were too easy for Pratt to bear.

Between 1801 and 1820, Washington lots did have their moments. In 1808, Thomas Munroe, whom Jefferson appointed supervisor of the city, replacing the three commissioners, complained that bidders colluded at forced sales, bought lots for a pittance, and then turned around and sold them for 1,000 percent markup. In 1817 Harrison Gray Otis returned to the city from a long absence and reported that lots along Pennsylvania Avenue, which had become the major street of the city, were selling for 75 cents a square foot. Elsewhere, the story was different. Between January 1818 and February 1819 Greenleaf sold $1,774.70 worth of lots, earning a commission of $177.47. The siting of City Hall helped him sell lots at the northwest corner of Judiciary Square for four cents a square foot. When Greenleaf died in 1843 in Washington, where he had been living since 1826, the heirs of the trustees of the aggregate fund trusted that "the great obstacle in the closing the concern is removed." Greenleaf could no longer test titles in court. Most of the trust's lots sold for less than the assessed value of one cent a square foot, some sold for a thirtieth of that. The lawyer managing the liquidation warned claimants on the trust to expect nothing.

"The former trustees," he explained in an 1848 letter, had long ago ". . . looked upon the concern as perfectly desperate in so far as the certificate holders were concerned, and as quite doubtful even in regard to the payment of their advances. The event has shown the correctness of their anticipation, and that all their troubles and anxiety about this business, great and long continued as it was—only resulted in throwing good money after bad."[5]

*   *   *

Law set up his peroration by taking a last swipe at Congress for depressing property values by its frequent debates on moving the government out of the city. Not until 1814, when Congress resolved to rebuild the Capitol and the president's house could residents feel comfortable about Congress's commitment to the city. Law credited President James Madison with having forced Congress to do it. Indeed, it was to the presidents that the city owed so much. With thumping cadence, Law lauded Washington, Adams, Jefferson, Madison, and Monroe for aiding a city so obviously about to come into its own and prove worthy of the great City Hall it was about to build.

In 1802, before going off to England in a vain attempt to raise money for the Washington canal, Thomas Law had rued Jefferson's budget cutting as one of the major drags on the city's development. Finally, in 1803, Jefferson got Congress to begin making annual appropriations to finish the buildings and appointed Latrobe to do it. But work on the buildings and improving that stretch of Pennsylvania Avenue between them is all that he wanted done.

To the regret of such speculators as Law, Jefferson had no trouble reconciling the construction of grand buildings in a rural setting. Jefferson found the city's rural character its major charm and seemed to cultivate more botanists than investors in the city. As long as it remained unfinished, the city served as butt for the anti-Americanism, or antirepublicanism, of many visitors and foreign ministers. But anyone with sensitivity for nature truly delighted in the place. The British minister in 1804, Anthony Merry, compared it to a wasteland. The minister in 1809, Francis Jackson, likened it to the finest resort area of England, Tunbridge Wells.

An American, David Baile Warden, penned the greatest tribute to the city's natural charms. While serving as U.S. consul in Paris, he tried to correct misimpressions "Washington will, for a long time, have a moral advantage over other great cities, as the sublime scenery of a majestic river, beautified by the luxuriant hangings of woods, rocks, and meadows, keep alive in the breasts of the beholders the native feelings of truth and nature, and prevent their minds from being corrupted by the artificial lures of emasculated softness and gregarious vices."

In the face of such Romantic assertiveness, the Enlightenment plan of L'Enfant had no chance. The central element of it, however, the canal, was finally completed. (Law had failed in his effort to raise money for the canal in 1802. The notable result of his trip to England was his wife's infatuation with marine officers. The Laws separated. He said she was "insane," and of course everyone in the city had a file of stories demonstrating his insanity.)

Construction of the canal began in 1810, and it was completed in 1815, but when the ceremonies ended in 1820, at the cornerstone of City Hall, none walked down to the canal to summon their private gondola.

L'Enfant had originally placed City Hall along the canal south of the Capitol, where it divided into two branches. In 1818 there had been talk of putting the building there to bring life to the canal and to the point below where the trustees had long ago sold the brick houses for $1,000 each. The area was very much a backwater, with no constituency to attract improvements.

L'Enfant was still in the vicinity. He lived on his grand avenue for a while at Rhodes Tavern on 15th Street, and then on an estate in Prince Georges County, but he took no part in debates about the city's development. By 1803 one old friend in the city decided that the charming, inventive, impossible man he had known in 1791 was no longer worthy of respect. Samuel Davidson forgave L'Enfant his old debts totaling £15, writing in his ledger, "knowing you now to be a pitiful dirty fellow and very poor, I give up the debt." L'Enfant accused Davidson of being part of the cabal that had stolen his trunk back in 1792.

L'Enfant ceaselessly pursued his cause in Congress. In 1803 Congress offered him the 500 guineas he had rejected in 1792. He rejected it again, and creditors attached the sum anyway. In 1804 he turned on Soderstrom, accusing him of stealing all he had. In 1806 Benjamin Latrobe described him: "daily thro' the city stalk the picture of famine, L'Enfant and his dog. . . . He is too proud to receive any assistance, and it is very doubtful in what manner he subsists." In 1808 Rhodes threatened to throw him out of his room unless he paid. L'Enfant finally humbled himself to ask the superintendent of the city for a portion of the money Congress had given him—just $300 for Rhodes and $100 "for the most pressing of other little demands.'' He insisted, however, that his taking any money in no way signified that he relinquished his claim for $95,000.

His latter years were eased by a powerful friend, Thomas Digges, who was close to James Monroe. While Monroe was secretary of war, L'Enfant was hired by the army as an engineer to rebuild a fort south of the city next to the Digges estate which became L'Enfant's home. As in most of his projects his work at Fort Washington was problematical and unsatisfying. Shortly afterward, in 1816, Digges described the "old Major," as he called the 62-year-old L'Enfant, in a letter to Monroe. He was still "an inmate with me, quiet, harmless and unoffending as usual. I fear from symptoms of broken shoes, rent pantaloons, out at elbows & c. & c., that he is not well off—manifestly disturbed at his getting the go by, never facing toward the Fort, tho' frequently dipping into the eastern ravines and hills on the plantation—picking . . . periwinkles. Early to bed and rising—working hard with his instruments on paper 8 or ten hours every day as if to . . . complete surveys of his works, but I neither ever see or know what his plans are." Digges admired him as "always incorruptibly honest and with the cleanest hands as to public money."

In 1823 he was still pressing his claim explaining to a Washington lawyer that he had evidence that the commissioners had made at least 21,000 sterling, or almost $100,000 from sales of his plan in Holland alone. The lawyer promised "I will do all in my feeble power that I can to further your wishes." L'Enfant died in 1825.

He may not have felt as unfulfilled during those years as posterity romantically believes. In one way of thinking, every failure in the city confirmed the brilliance of his original conceptions. If only they had been followed. City Hall was no exception. The prosperity that young Law boasted was sure to come did not come soon enough. The city tried to finance construction of City Hall through a lottery. But the New York manager of the adventure walked off with some money, and the city fathers took comfort in blaming a spate of legislation banning interstate lotteries as crippling their worthy effort. They decided to ask Congress to specifically exempt their lottery from state regulation so that they could sell tickets for it everywhere.

It behooved someone to come up with a rationale for why the

628 *Epilogue*

federal city had taken thirty years to build a City Hall in the first place and why the city itself could not finance it. In 1820 John Law had lauded the city's natural advantages. In 1821 city leaders decided it was expedient to finally agree with its critics, and, to justify indulgences thirty years later, they invented the swamp that daunted and almost defeated the first settlers. The mayor (Samuel Smallwood, the former slave driver at the Capitol), the aldermen, and the common council for the city sent a memorial to Congress asking for a special law for their lottery, explaining: "When it is considered that little more than twenty years ago the grounds on which this city is laid out was for the most part covered only with woods and impassable marsh, . . . the labor which has devolved on its first settlers may be conceived, but can hardly be realized. . . ."[6]

Notes

I have tried to show readers what a good story the history of Washington is, rather than tell them what to think about it. In these notes I want to show scholars what a wealth of information there is about the city in hopes that they will tap the same lode. Since I feared that too many footnotes in the text would get in the way of the story, I decided not to hand scholars each citation on a silver platter. Several citations are bunched under one note, but a close reader should be able to figure out what is referred to. The collection of material most quoted is the correspondence of the commissioners. Unless otherwise noted, letters to and from the commissioners are in that National Archives collection that has been microfilmed.

In those documentary editions of papers where letters follow in chronological order, I've not given volume and page number. The dates of the letter will invariably lead you to the right volume and page. The Nicholson microfilm reels, called JN reels in my notes, are arranged chronologically under the name of Nicholson's correspondent. Not a few of the collections I've used are quite a jumble, namely the Van Ness–Phillip papers which has Burnes material, the North American Land Company papers, and the Thornton papers. To find what one is looking for, one just has to be a little bit patient, enjoy, and in the case of the North American Land Company papers, try not to get dirty hands.

In quoting materials I have changed punctuation in cases where it will make the text read more smoothly. In general I have corrected spelling in those cases where I suspect it was simply proper to spell the word that way back then; for example, I made George Washington's "accomodating" read "accommodating." The letters of L'Enfant present a special problem. Elizabeth Kite cleaned up his language far too much, and the originals are often too confusing. I've left most of his misspellings when I felt they gave an impression of a man whose mind was racing toward ideas. Where a reader might smile at his rendition, for example "pound" instead of "pond," I transcribed it "pond." In cases where correspondents genuinely don't know how to spell, I've kept most of the mistakes to show the gap in education between slave drivers and commissioners, for example. Anyone who is so taken with a quote that he or she is going to chisel it in granite is advised to go back to the original first.

Key

GW: George Washington
JG: James Greenleaf
JN: John Nicholson
RM: Robert Morris
TJ: Thomas Jefferson

AFP: Adams family papers, MHS
CHS: *Columbia Historical Society Records*
Commrs.: Commissioners of the Public Buildings
CR LC: Commissioners of the District of Columbia records, LC
FO: Foreign Office Copying Project, LC
GW LC: George Washington papers, LC
HLC: Holland Land Company papers
HSP: Historical Society of Pennsylvania
HSW: Historical Society of Washington, D.C.
JN LB: John Nicholson letterbooks, HSP
JN reels: Microfilmed edition of Nicholson correspondence, Historical Museum of Pennsylvania
LB: Letterbook(s)
LC: Library of Congress
MHS: Massachusetts Historical Society
NA RG: National Archives Record Group
NALC papers: North American Land Company papers, HSP
NYPL: New York Public Library
Proceedings: Commrs.' proceedings, National Archives
RM LB: Robert Morris letterbook, LC

Chapter 1

1. Freeman, *Washington,* vol. 7, for a full account of Washington's death.

2. GW to Thornton, to White, both Dec. 8, 1799, Fitzpatrick, *Writings*. Almost all of Washington's letters pertaining to the city of Washington were compiled by the Columbia Historical Society in 1914. These two last letters were not included.

3. CHS, vol. 17, pp. 208–32. On GW's inability to get a loan in 1789, see GW to Carey, May 22, 1789, Abbot, *Papers*, Presidential Series, vol. 2.

4. Brighton, *Lear*. Latrobe to Mazzel, May 29, 1806, Latrobe, *Correspondence*, vol. 2, pp. 227–28. All of these themes will be developed later.

5. Latrobe, *Virginia Journals*, on the dilapidated state of Williamsburg.

Chapter 2

1. Burnett, *Continental Congress*, pp. 576–79. Rush to Montgomery, July 12, 1783, Burnett, *Letters*. Bingham papers, Thomson to wife, Aug. 21, 1783, Burnett, *Letters*.

2. Madison to GW, August 24, 1788, Rutland. *Papers*, Madison to Randolph, Sept. 14, 1788, Rutland, *Papers*.

3. On L'Enfant in New York, see Kite, *L'Enfant*, and Caemmerer, *L'Enfant*.

4. Primary sources for the debate and intrigues over the residence of Congress include *Annals* and Bowling and Veit, *Diary*. Good secondary sources are Bowling, *Federal City*; Renzullia, *Maryland*, pp. 132ff.

Chapter 3

1. GW, Sept. 25, 1784, Fitzpatrick *Diaries*, Bowling in *Federal City*, attributes the article in the January 23,1789, *Maryland Journal* to Walker.

2. Memorial in Bowling & Veit, *Documentary History*, vol. 6, p. 1785. Stephen, "Expostulations." O'Connor, "Political Opinions." Bowling in *Federal City* attributes "Expostulations" and "Political Opinions" to Stephen and O'Connor. List of Young's slaves in CHS, vols. 35–36.

3. *Annals*. Maclay gives the most detailed accounts of the discomfiture of the friends of assumption; see Bowling and Veit, *Diary*. Ford, *Jefferson*, vol. 1, p. 226. Smith, "Politicks." Cazenove to the Six Houses, June 23, 1790, Cazenove LB, HLCLC. Gerry description in *Journals of Continental Congress*, May 27, 1784. Boyd, in his essay on this topic in *Papers*, makes the case that contemporaries thought Morris had scored a victory over the friends of the Potomac.

Chapter 4

1. Boyd, *Papers*, vol. 17, pp. 460–61. Boyd's two essays on fixing the seat of government are in vols. 17 and 20. Early editors of TJ's papers gave

a later date, Nov. 29, 1790, to his memorandum on what should be done to effect the Residence Act. Boyd moved that to Aug. 29, 1790. I accept Boyd's dating. Throughout his early association with the city, TJ was always rushing ahead with his ideas on town planning and architecture. The copy of Madison's notes on the meeting is in Rutland, *Papers.*

2. Letter from Thomas Shippen to William Shippen, Boyd, *Papers,* Sept. 15, 1790, Boyd, *Papers,* vol. 17, p. 464. Most modern treatments of GW's trip up the river—Bowling, *Federal City; Boyd Papers;* Flexner, *Geo. Washington,* Green, *Washington*—characterize it as a ruse to keep land speculators off balance, arguing that GW never seriously considered an upriver site. It is a rather safe guess, but the seriousness and thoroughness with which GW quizzed upriver leaders argues against a ruse, and no one has identified any land speculators kept off balance.

3. Oct. 13, 1790, offer, CHS, vols. 35–36, p. 23. *Maryland Journal,* Oct. 26, 1790, CHS, vols. 35–36, p. 26. Davidson to Burton, Nov. 6, 1790, Davidson letterbook. CR LC has several maps of competing areas at the end of the reel. Otho Williams to GW, Nov. 1, 1790, GW LC. Deakins to GW, Nov. 12, 1790, GW LC. Chapland and Goods to GW, Dec. 4, 1790, GW LC. Darnall to Deakins, Nov. 7, 1790, GW LC.

4. Burnes folder, Van Ness-Phillip papers. Burnes alludes to such an offer, but the offer itself has not been found. Davidson to Dunlop, Nov. 28, 1790, Davidson letterbook. Deakins and Stoddert to GW, Dec. 9, 1790, GW LC. Richardson, *Messages,* vol. 1, p. 86.

Chapter 5

1. Bowling and Veit, *Diary,* p. 368. White to Simms, Feb. 20, 1791, Simms papers. Delaplaine, *Johnson.* Geiger, *Carroll.* Cazenove to Johnson, Feb. 14, 1971, Cazenove LBHLC.

2. GW to Deakins and Stoddert, Feb. 3, 1791, CHS, vol. 17. There is no direct documentary evidence of Carroll undertaking such an agency, but it is obvious someone was getting offers from the so-called Carrollsburg interests, and it was not Stoddert. The name of the holdout is obliterated in GW papers. If it was Burnes, certainly no one would have scratched out the name, since it remains in other letters not flattering to Burnes. Peter's son married Martha Washington's granddaughter, and so a member of the Peter family would have had motive and opportunity to obliterate Peter's name. GW to Deakins and Stoddert, Feb. 17, 1791, CHS, vol. 17. Record of Deakins's and Stoddert's purchase of Hamburg lots in National Archives. Much material on Burnes's early land dealings is in the Burnes folder of the Van Ness-Phillip papers, Mar. 1783 inventory, e.g., *Carroll lessee v.*

Burnes, May 10, 1785. GW to Deakins and Stoddert, Mar. 2, 1791, CHS, vol. 17.

3. L'Enfant's letter to GW is in Kite, *L'Enfant,* and Caemmerer, *L'Enfant,* as is information of his early career. TJ to L'Enfant, Padover, *Jefferson,* p. 42. Remembrances of the Peter houses are in Dermott to commrs., Nov. 15, 1799. A list of other early houses, although some in it were built after 1791, is in Busey, *Pictures,* p. 136. L'Enfant to TJ, Mar. 10 and 11, 1791, Padover, *Jefferson* and Boyd *Papers.*

4. *Ledger,* Mar. 12, 1791. The remarks about Banneker and L'Enfant are in the same article, and the black astronomer got top billing. Bedini, *Banneker.* GW to TJ, Mar. 16, 1791, Padover, *Jefferson.* TJ to L'Enfant, Mar. 17, 1791, Padover, *Jefferson.* Burnes to GW, Feb. 26, 1791, and Stoddert to Burnes, Mar. 11, 1791, Burnes papers.

5. Carroll to Madison, Apr. 6, 1791, Rutland *Papers.* L'Enfant to TJ, Caemmerer, *L'Enfant,* p. 136.

Chapter 6

1. L'Enfant to Hamilton, Apr. 8, 1791, Syrett, *Papers.* Ellicott to his wife, Mar. 21, 1791, Mathews, *Ellicott,* p. 86.

2. GW's diary, excerpted in CHS, vol. 17. L'Enfant claimed credit for persuading GW to take all the land under consideration. The ease with which GW and TJ adjusted to the idea argues that they had been hoping for it all along and that they had resigned themselves to one side of the area or the other from fear of landowners holding out for too high a price. No one thought of recording exactly what went on at the meeting. GW recalled his argument about the size of the city in his May 7, 1791, letter to the commrs., CHS, vol. 17. Agreement with the proprietors, CHS, vols. 35–36, p. 44. Prout to his brother, Apr. 1791, and May 7, 1791, Prout papers. GW diaries, CHS, vol. 17.

3. *Maryland Journal,* Apr. 8, 1791, CHS, vols. 35–36, p. 49. L'Enfant to Hamilton, Apr. 8, 1791. GW to Stoddert and Deakins, Apr. 1, 1791. GW to commrs., Apr. 3, 1791. GW to L'Enfant, Apr. 4, 1791, CHS, vol. 17. TJ to L'Enfant, Apr. 10, 1791, Padover, *Jefferson.*

4. Walker's deal, CHS, vols. 35–36, p. 95. Prout to his brother, May 7, 1791, Prout papers, HSW. Davidson to Walker, Apr. 8, 1791, and to Shore, Apr. 12, 1791, Davidson letterbook. Apr. 21, 1791, clipping from unidentified newspaper in HLC D.C. file.

5. Peter et al. to commrs., Apr. 14, 1791, and Walker et al. to commrs., Apr. 14, 1791, CHS, vols. 35–36, pp. 54ff. GW to commrs., May 7, 1791, CHS, vol. 17.

Chapter 7

1. Smith, "Journal".
2. Carroll to Madison, Apr. 23, 1791, Rutland, *Papers.*
3. Caemmerer, *L'Enfant,* and Kite, *L'Enfant.*
4. Carroll to Stuart, June 9, 1791, Haverford College. Fitzpatrick, *Diaries.* Stoddert to Monroe, Jan. 18, 1805, commrs.' letters received. Young to commrs., Jan. 7, 1792. *Maryland Journal,* July 5, 1791, quoted in CHS, vols. 35–36, p. 61.
5. Proceedings, June 30, 1791, Aug. 2, 1791, and Jan. 9, 1792, for expenses. Ellicott to his wife, June 26, 1791, Mathews, *Ellicott,* p. 89. Davidson account with L'Enfant in ledger, Davidson papers. Walker's move to Eastern Branch, *Ledger* ad dated June 10, 1791.
6. Commrs. to French, Aug. 2, 1791. Carroll to Madison, July 24, 1791, Rutland, *Papers.* Commrs. to GW, Aug. 2, 1791, Jan. 8, 1972.
7. L'Enfant to GW, Aug. 19, 1791, L'Enfant papers LC. Kite and Caemmerer gave a cleaned up version of the letter.

Chapter 8

1. TJ to GW, Sept. 8, 1791, Boyd, *Papers,* vol. 22, p. 136. Queries for D.C. commrs., Aug. 28, 1791, Boyd, *Papers,* vol. 22, p. 89. TJ's notes on commrs., Sept. 8, 1791, Padover, *Jefferson.*
2. Ellicott to commrs., Sept. 9, 1791. Ellicott to L'Enfant, Kite, *L'Enfant.*
3. Commrs. to Maryland legislature, Sept. 8, 1791, Proceedings.
4. Commrs. to L'Enfant, Sept. 9, 1791. Ellicott to L'Enfant, Kite, *L'Enfant. Ledger,* Sept. 17, 1791.
5. Journal of Victor Dupont, 1791, Hagley Museum and Library, Wilmington, Del. Hallet biography in Butler, *Competition.* Hallet to Dermott, Jan. 25, 1794, commrs.' letters received.
6. Ellicott to wife, Nov. 11, 1791, Ellicott papers. GW to Stuart, Nov. 20, 1791, CHS, vol. 17. GW to L'Enfant, Feb. 28, 1792, CHS, vol. 17. TJ notes on design competition, "Idea of the public buildings to be erected at the Federal seat," TJ papers, LC, at end of 1791 correspondence.
7. Commrs. to L'Enfant and Ellicott, Sept. 24, 1791. Davidson ledger. Huston to parents, Oct. 23, 1791, Prout papers.
8. *Maryland Journal,* Sept. 30, 1791.

Chapter 9

1. Carroll to L'Enfant, Oct. 2, 1791, L'Enfant papers.
2. Lear to GW, Oct. 6, 9, and 11, 1791, GW LC. GW to Lear, Oct. 2

and 14, 1791, Fitzpatrick, *Writings*.

   3.. Proceedings, Oct. 16, 1791. Map NCP-0-51, NA RG42.

   4. Shippen papers. Stuart to GW, Oct. 21, 1791, GW LC.

   5. Proceedings, Oct. 17–20, 1791. Shippen papers. Commrs. to GW, Oct. 21, 1791. Davidson to Barker, Nov. 12, 1791, Davidson papers. Forde to Reed, Oct. 28, 1791, Reed and Forde papers. Lingan to Coxe, Nov. 11, 1791, Coxe papers. Prout to brother, Oct. 23, 1791, Prout papers. *Gazette of the United States*, Nov. 5, 1791. Ternant letter, Oct. 24, 1791, *American Historical Association Report*, 1903.

   6. GW to Stuart, Oct. 18, 1791, Fitzpatrick, *Writings*. TJ to Ellicott, Nov. 21, 1791, Boyd, *Papers*, Commrs. to GW, Oct. 21, 1791. *New York, an American City*, p. 234.

Chapter 10

   1. L'Enfant to Lear, Oct. 19, 1791, Caemmerer, *L'Enfant*, p. 173.

   2. GW to Stuart, Nov. 20, 1791, CHS, vol. 17.

   3. The demolition of Carroll's house generated a considerable file; see CHS, vol. 17, pp. 34–45; Padover, *Jefferson*, pp. 78–86; commrs.' report on matter to GW in their letters sent, Dec. 21, 1791, Jan. 7, 1792; Carroll to commrs., Jan. 2, 1792; Kite, *L'Enfant;* Caemmerer, *L'Enfant;* Carroll to Madison, Dec. 13, 1791, Rutland, *Papers*.

   4. Commrs. to Cabot, Nov. 26, 1791. Cabot to commrs., Dec. 11, 1791, Feb. 11, 1792.

   5. For L'Enfant's last days in the city, see Kite, *L'Enfant,* and Caemmerer, *L'Enfant*. For Ellicott's activities and concern about his expenses, Ellicott to TJ, Nov. 30, 1791, and to commrs., Dec. 10, 1791; commrs. to GW, Jan. 7, 1791.

Chapter 11

   1. Roberdeau to L'Enfant, Kite, *L'Enfant*. Roberdeau to commrs., Jan. 9, 1792, Jan. 10, 1792 (two letters), Jan. 21, 1792. Young to commrs., Jan. 7, 1792. Commrs. to Roberdeau, Jan. 7, 9, and 10, 1792. Commrs. to Boraff, Jan. 8, 1792. Commrs. to Williams, Jan. 10, 1792. Commrs. to GW Jan. 9 and 21, 1792.

   2. Commrs. to Walker, Jan. 20, 1792. Walker to commrs., Jan. 21, 1792. Faw to Johnson, Jan. 24, 1792. Faw to commrs., Jan. 28, 1792 (indexed under Law). Commrs. to King, Jan. 21, 1792. Carroll to Madison, Jan. 18 and 26, 1792, Rutland, *Papers*.

   3. Davidson, Ledger.

Chapter 12

1. Jan. 5, 1792, *Gazette of the United States*. Ellicott to commrs., Feb. 23, 1792. Cazenove to Lee, Feb. 15, 1792, Cazenove LB, HLC papers, also on Cazenove trip to Potomac see Cazenove to Willink, June 16,1791. On the interest of Dutch banks in loans, see Short letters to Hamilton, Syrett, *Papers*.

2. Caemmerer, *L'Enfant*.

3. TJ to L'Enfant, Jan. 7, 1792, Boyd, *Papers*. GW to TJ, Jan. 15, 1792, Padover, *Jefferson*. GW to commrs., Jan. 17, 1792, Fitzpatrick, *Writings*. Commrs. to GW, Jan 9, 1792. GW to TJ, Jan 18, 1792, Padover, *Jefferson*. TJ to GW, Feb. 1, 1792, Boyd, *Papers*.

4. GW to TJ, Feb. 7, 9, 11, and 15, 1792, Fitzpatrick, *Writings*. L'Enfant to GW, Feb. 6, 1792, L'Enfant papers. L'Enfant to Lear, Feb. 17, 1792, Kite, *L'Enfant*. Ellicott to commrs., Feb. 23, 1792. On difference in plans to see National Capitol Planning Comm., *Downtown Urban Renewal*.

5. GW to TJ, Feb. 15, 1792, Padover, *Jefferson*. TJ to L'Enfant, Feb. 22, 1792, Padover, *Jefferson*. L'Enfant to TJ, Feb. 22, 1792, Boyd, *Papers*. GW to Madison and Randolph, Feb. 25, 1792, Fitzpatrick, *Writings*. GW to TJ, Mar. 14, 1792, Padover, *Jefferson*. TJ to Walker, Mar. 1, 1792, Padover, *Jefferson*. TJ to L'Enfant, Feb. 28, 1792. L'Enfant to GW, Feb. 28, 1792, Kite, *L'Enfant*. GW to L'Enfant, Feb. 28, 1792, CHS, vol. 17.

Chapter 13

1. TJ to Walker, Mar. 1, 1792. TJ to Carroll, Mar. 1, 1792, Boyd, *Jefferson*. Walker to TJ and proprietors to Walker, Mar. 9, 1792, Padover, *Jefferson*. Proprietors to L'Enfant, Kite, *L'Enfant*.

2. L'Enfant to proprietors, Kite, *L'Enfant*. She leaves out the portion threatening a public attack on the changes in the plan. The original is the L'Enfant papers. GW to Stuart, Mar. 8, 1792, Fitzpatrick, *Writings*. Two long letters from Stuart to GW, Feb. 26, 1792, and Johnson to TJ, Feb. 29, 1792, both in GW LC, give their side of the struggle with L'Enfant.

3. Stuart to GW, Feb. 26, 1792, GW LC. Johnson to TJ, Mar. 8, 1792, Padover, *Jefferson*. GW to commrs., Mar. 6, 1792. GW to Stuart, Mar. 8, 1792.

4. GW to TJ, Mar. 4, 1792, Fitzpatrick, *Writings*. James, *Biography*, pp. 11ff. TJ to commrs. Mar. 6, 1792, Padover, *Jefferson*. TJ to Johnson, Mar. 8, 1792, Padover, *Jefferson*.

5. GW to TJ, Mar. 14, 1792, TJ to Walker, Mar. 14, 1792, Padover, *Jefferson*.

Chapter 14

1. Commrs. to TJ, Mar. 14, 1792, Padover *Jefferson*. Commrs. to GW, Mar. 14, 1792. Carroll to Madison, Mar. 8, 1792, Rutland, *Papers*.

2. L'Enfant to commrs., Mar. 18, 1792, Kite, *L'Enfant*, p. 174. Roberdeau to L'Enfant, Mar. 21 and 23, 1792, L'Enfant papers. Proprietors to Walker, Mar. 21, 1792, Walker to TJ, Mar. 21, 1792, Padover, *Jefferson*.

3. Roberdeau to L'Enfant, Mar. 28, 1792, L'Enfant papers. L'Enfant to Walker, Apr. 1, 1792, L'Enfant papers.

4. On the financial panic and L'Enfant's association with Paterson, N.J., see Syrett, *Papers*, GW to TJ, Mar. 21, 1792, Padover, *Jefferson*.

Chapter 15

1. Roberdeau to L'Enfant, Mar. 26 and 28, 1792, L'Enfant papers.

2. Proceedings, Mar. meetings. On commrs.' house see Apr. proceedings. Commrs. to TJ, Mar. 30, 1792, Padover, *Jefferson*.

3. A drawing of Harbaugh's bridge and a map of the mouth of Rock Creek are in CR LC. A sketchy biography of Harbaugh is in Butler, *Competition*. TJ to commrs., Apr. 5, 1792, Padover, *Jefferson*.

4. Ellicott to TJ, Apr. 3, 1792, Padover, *Jefferson*. Ellicott to commrs., Apr. 11, 1792.

5. Ceracchi to Randolph, May 11, 1795, misc. letters, State Department, recalls his efforts in 1792. TJ to commrs., Apr. 9, 1792, Padover, *Jefferson*. Commrs. to TJ, Apr. 11 and 14, 1792, Padover, *Jefferson*. Commrs. to TJ, Apr. 14, 1792. On keeping labor cool, commrs. to TJ, Jan. 5, 1793, Padover, *Jefferson*. Proceedings, Apr. 13, 1792.

Chapter 16

1. TJ to Commrs., Apr. 20, 1792, Padover, *Jefferson*. On TJ's designs and patronage of Hallet, Butler, *Competition*. Prout to brother, Nov. 11, 1792, Prout papers. Proceedings, Apr. 12, 1792.

2. Forrest to L'Enfant, Apr. 27, 1792, L'Enfant papers. Burnes to commrs., Apr. 13, 1792. Commrs. to Burnes, Apr. 13, 1792. Davidson to Commrs., Mar 27, 1792, Davidson papers. Commrs. to Davidson, Apr. 12, 1792. Davidson to GW, May 28, 1792, Davidson papers. Davidson to commrs., June 1, 1792. Walker to L'Enfant, June 6, 1792, L'Enfant papers. Ad in *Ledger*, July 26, 1792. Davidson ledger. Roberdeau to L'Enfant, July 2, 1792, L'Enfant papers.

3. Proceedings, Apr. meetings. Ellicott to TJ, May 13, 1792, Padover,

Jefferson. Brighton, *Lear*, p. 104. Commrs. to TJ, June 2, 1792, Padover, *Jefferson.* Proceedings, May 1792. Commrs. to Ellicott, May 4, 1792, June 6, 1792. Harbaugh to commrs., July 3, 1792. Dermott's meeting with Stuart, commrs. to GW, Mar. 23, 1794.

Chapter 17

1. GW to Lear, July 30, 1792, Fitzpatrick, *Writings*. French to commrs., July 19, 1792. An article on the importance of the bridge is in the *Ledger*, Mar 31, 1792.

2. Biographical information on Hoban is in Seale, *President's House*. GW to Stuart, July 9, 1792, CHS, vol. 17. Commrs. to GW, July 19, 1792. Butler, *Competition*. GW to commrs., July 23, 1792, CHS, vol. 17.

3. Blodget to commrs., July 11, 1792. Blodget to TJ, June 25, 1792, July 5, 1792, Padover *Jefferson*. TJ to commrs., July 11, 1792, Padover, *Jefferson*. TJ to Blodget, July 12, 1792, Padover, *Jefferson*. Governor of Virginia to commrs., June 29, 1792.

4. Hamilton to directors of the Society for the Promotion of Useful Manufactures, Aug. 16, 1792, Syrett, *Papers*, vol. 12, p. 216. Stuart and Carroll to Johnson, Aug. 3, 1792, commrs.' letters received. Carroll to GW, Aug. 15, 1795, GW LC. Proceedings, Aug. 3, 1792, Sept. 1, 1792.

Chapter 18

1. Williamson to Adams, Apr. 26, 1797, AFP. Burnes Folder, Van Ness-Phelps papers. Currie, *Historical Account*, p. 235. Ellicott to wife, Sept. 3, 1792, Ellicott papers. GW to Lear, Aug. 31, 1792, Fitzpatrick, *Writings*.

2. Commrs. to Blodget, Aug. 29, 1792. L'Enfant to Hamilton, Sept. 17, 1792, Syrett, *Papers*. Wells Bennett, "Hallet," *AIA Journal*, June 1916.

3. Ellicott to wife, Oct. 10, 1792, Ellicott papers. Hammond to Grenville, Oct. 3, 1792, FO 4, vol. 16. Sales book, NA RG 42. Blodget to commrs., Sept. 8, 1792. Walker to GW, Oct. 8, 1792, GW LC. Stuart and Carroll to commrs., Nov. 21, 1794. Davidson to Adams, Nov. 27, 1797, commrs.' letters received. Commrs. to TJ, Nov. 5, 1792, Padover, *Jefferson*. Stuart to GW, Oct. 13, 1792, GW LC. Blodget to Burnes, Oct. 23, 1792, Van Ness-Phelps papers.

Chapter 19

1. Stoddert to GW, Oct. 24, 1792, GW LC. GW to Stuart, Nov. 30, 1792, CHS, vol. 17. Biographical information on Blodget is in James, *Biography*, pp. 11ff.

2. Butler, *Competition*. Wright to commrs., Dec. 3, 1792. Proceedings, Jan. 1, 1793, Dec. 4, 1792. The names of Hoban's slaves come from carpenters' time rolls at the president's house, NA RG 39.

3. Ellicott to commrs., Nov. 5, 1792. Burnes to commrs., Nov. 4, 1792. Walker to commrs., Nov. 1, 1792. Carroll to commrs., Dec. 1, 1792. Briggs to commrs., Jan. 1, 1793. Stuart to GW, Dec. 10, 1792, GW LC. Ellicott to wife, Dec. 14, 1792, Ellicott papers.

4. Hoban to commrs., Dec. 1, 1792. W. A. Washington to commrs., Dec. 11, 1792. Commrs. to W. A. Washington, Jan. 2, 1793.

5. On indentured servants in Maryland and Virginia, see Bailyn, *Voyagers*, p. 209. Laird to commrs., Nov. 15, 1792. Van Staphorst to commrs., Sept. 9, 1792. GW to commrs., Dec. 18, 1792. TJ to commrs., Dec. 17 and 23, 1792, Padover, *Jefferson*, p. 163. Commrs. to Traquair, Jan. 2, 1793. Commrs. to Fenwick, Jan. 5, 1793.

Chapter 20

1. Bingham to Walker, Nov. 28, 1792, Bingham letterbook. Walker to JN, Jan. 14, 1793, JN reels.

2. Ellicott letter, *Maryland Journal*, Feb. 4, 1793. Ellicott to commrs., Jan. 4 and 8, 1793. Commrs. to Ellicott, Jan. 8, 1793. GW to Forrest, Jan. 20, 1793, CHS, Vol. 17.

3. Commrs. to Blodget, Jan. 5, 1793. Ad for lottery in many newspapers of the period. Undated letter from Blodget to Randolph, CR LC.

4. TJ to Ellicott, Jan. 15, 1793, Padover, *Jefferson*. GW to Forrest, Jan. 20, 1793. Dermott to Ellicott, Feb. 6, 1793, GW LC. *Ledger*, Feb. 16, 1793. Stuart to GW, Feb. 10 and 18, 1793. I am unable to locate Chronicle's attack on Judas, so I reconstruct it based on Judas's Feb. 16 reply. Ellicott to his wife, Jan. 15, 1793, Ellicott papers. Commrs. to GW, Mar. 23, 1794.

5. Blodget to commrs., Jan 26 and Feb. 1, 1793. Commrs. to Blodget, Feb. 2, 1793. GW to Commrs., Jan 31, 1793, CHS, vol. 17. Butler, *Competition*. Commrs. to TJ, Jan 5, 1793, Padover, *Jefferson*. "Memorandum Relative to Commissioners," Mar. 11, 1793, Padover, *Jefferson*.

Chapter 21

1. *Maryland Journal*, Mar. 1, 1793.

2. Commrs. to GW, Mar. 11, 1793. Thornton to commrs., undated, Thornton papers.

3. Commrs. to Ellicott, Mar. 11, 12, and 13, 1793. Ellicott to commrs.,

Mar. 12, 1793. Forrest to commrs., Mar. 14, 1793. Commrs. to Forrest, Mar. 14, 1793.

4. Walker pamphlet in Phillips, *Beginnings*, p. 18. Davidson to JN, Mar. 20, 1793, Davidson papers.

5. Burnes to commrs., Mar. 11, 1793, Apr. 6, 1793. Commrs. to Burnes, Apr. 8, 1793. Williamson to commrs., Mar. 25, 1793.

6. Ellicott to TJ, Mar. 26, 1793, Padover, *Jefferson*. GW to commrs., Apr. 3, 1793, CHS, vol. 17. Commrs. to Ellicott, Apr. 5, 1793. Proceedings, Apr. 4, 5, and 9, 1793.

Chapter 22

1. Williamson to Adams, Apr. 26, 1797, AFP. Roberdeau to L'Enfant, L'Enfant papers. Traquair to commrs., Apr. 4, 1793.

2. Commrs. to GW, Apr. 9, 1793. Thornton to commrs., undated, Thornton papers. Blodget ad, *Maryland Journal*, May 20, 1793. Blodget undated letter, CR LC. Proceedings, Apr. 10, 1793. Davidson to Cabot, May 23, 1793, Davidson papers. Fenwick to commrs., Apr. 4, 1793. J. Johnson to commrs., Apr. 4, 1793.

3. Roberdeau to L'Enfant, June 18, 1793, L'Enfant papers. Lear to GW, June 17, 1793, GW LC. Commrs. to GW, June 23, 1793. Ellicott to commrs., June 7, 1793, July 19, 1793. Briggs and Ellicott to Commrs., July 27, 1793.

4. GW to TJ, June 30, 1793, Padover, *Jefferson*. Undated draft in Thornton papers, reels 1329–32. TJ to GW, July 17, 1793, Padover, *Jefferson*. Sept. 23, 1793, ad by Joseph Mitchell, *Maryland Journal*.

5. Commrs. to Carroll, June 26, 1793. Article on hotel cornerstone, *Philadelphia General Advertiser*, July 16, 1793, printed in CHS, vols. 35–36. Blodget to commrs., July 7 and 17, 1793.

6. Proceedings, Aug. 1, 1793. Article on census, CHS, vols. 35–36, p. 78. Johnson to Stuart, Aug. 5, 1793, commrs.' letters received.

Chapter 23

1. Murray to Coxe, Sept. 1, 1793, Coxe papers. Powell, *Bring Out Your Dead*.

2. Proceedings, Sept. 2, 1793. *Maryland Journal,* Sept. 17, 1793. Deakins report of sale of tickets, Commrs.' letters received, Sept. 9, 1793. Notices of Bank of Columbia, *Maryland Journal,* Jan. 13, 1794. Newspaper notice of Washington tontine, HLC D.C. file.

3. Clark, *Greenleaf and Law,* pp. 81ff., 145ff. Agreement with Lear,

NALC papers. Blodget's undated letter, CR LC. GW to commrs., Aug. 13, 1793, CHS, vol. 17. GW to commrs., Aug. 20, 1793, GW LC. Ford, *Webster*.

    4. Sales book, NA RG 42. GW to commrs., Apr. 11, 1794, CHS,vol. 17.

    5. Stuart to Carroll. Aug. 18, 1793, commrs.' letters received. *Columbian Centinel* (Boston), Oct. 5, 1793, quoted in Hazleton, *National Capitol,* p. 22. *Intelligencer,* Aug. 29, 1847. *Columbian Centinel,* Oct. 9, 1793. Blodget to commrs., Sept. 24, 1793.

Chapter 24

    1. JG's agreement with Johnson, Sept. 25, 1793, NALC papers. Johnson to JG, Sept. 25, 1793, HSW. Sept. 23, 1793, agreement between commrs. and JG, NALC papers. Clark, *Greenleaf and Law,* pp. 67ff. Carroll to JG, Sept. 24, 1793, JG papers, NYPL.

    2. Proceedings, Sept. 22, 1793. JG to Webster, Sept. 26, 1793, Ford, *Webster,* p. 365. GW to Lear, Sept. 25, 1793, CHS, vol. 17.

    3. Burnes's bill of chancery against commrs., Sept. 14, 1793, Van Ness-Phillip papers.

    4. GW to Pearce, Aug. 2, 1793, Fitzpatrick, *Writings,* Madison to TJ, Sept. 16, 1793, Rutland, *Papers.* TJ to GW, Oct. 17, 1793, Padover, *Jefferson.*

    5. Briggs and Ellicott to commrs., Sept. 13, 1793, Oct. 15, 17, and 18. 1793. Briggs to A. Ellicott, Jan. 6, 1794, Ellicott papers. Commrs. to Briggs and Ellicott, Oct. 17, 1793.

    6. Proceedings, Oct. 15, 1793.

    7. Report of auditors, Proceedings, Oct. 31, 1793. Commrs. to GW, Oct. 26, 1793, Nov. 3, 1793. Commrs. to Lee, Sept. 23, 1793, Dec. 22, 1793. Proceedings, Dec. 16, 1793.

Chapter 25

    1. JG to Webster, Ford, *Webster,* p. 365. Journal, Kent papers. On Morris, see Clark, *Greenleaf and Law.* On the particularly cash poor condition of RM and JN in the summer of 1793, see JN to RM, July 12, 1793, JN reel 1.

    2. RM to JG, Aug. 3 and 9, 1793, Oct. 11 and 23, 1793, Nov. 9, 1793, JG papers, NYPL.

    3. Commrs. to JG, Oct. 18, 1793, Nov. 20, 1793.

    4. Cazenove to the Six Houses, Dec. 15, 1793, Cazenove LB HLC. Agreement with Kinsley for brick machine, Nov. 16, 1793, is mentioned in their Jan. 6, 1794, agreement, NALC papers. Nov. 30, 1793, agreement

with Simmons, NALC papers. Appleton to Webster, Nov. 23, 1793, Ford, *Webster*, p. 376.

5. TJ to Madison, Nov. 2, 1793, Rutland, *Papers*.

6. Lingan to Forde and Reed, Jan. 16, 1794, Reed and Forde papers. Commrs. to Casanave, Nov. 22,1793. Johnson to GW, Dec. 23, 1793, Delaplaine, *Johnson*. Johnson ad in *Maryland Journal* dated Nov. 26, 1793. Johnson to JG, Nov. 20, 1793, Haverford College. On the value of Difficult Run land, see GW to Lewis, Aug. 26, 1793, Fitzpatrick, *Writings*.

7. Forst to GW, Oct. 16, 1793, GW LC. Manley to commrs., Dec. 9, 1793. Blodget to commrs., Nov. 28, 1793, Dec. 5 and 13, 1793. Carroll to Blodget, Dec. 10, 1793.

Chapter 26

1. Dec. 10 and 12, 1793, agreements between RM, JN, and JG in NALC papers. I attribute the Columbian Society to RM because of his facility in making such plans, and none of the houses JG contracted for were like the houses the society promised to build. Prospectus of the society is in the Holland Land Co. D.C. file. GW to Carroll, Dec. 16, 1793, CHS, vol. 17.

2. Lear's *Observations*, CHS, vol. 51, also in Kent papers. Kent to his brother, Jan. 2, 1794, Kent papers.

3. Ellicott's parting letter is dated Dec. 21, 1793. Commrs. to Ellicott, Dec. 17, 1793.

4. Clark, *Greenleaf and Law*, p. 68. Blodget to commrs., Dec. 13, 1793. Commrs. to RM, Dec. 23, 1793. Commrs. to GW, Dec. 23, 1793.

5. Hoban to commrs., Nov. 19, 1793. Commrs. to JG, Dec. 23, 1793. Templeman to commrs., Dec. 22, 1793. Proceedings, Jan. 24, 1794.

6. Commrs. to GW, Dec. 24, 1793. Proceedings Dec. 23–25, 1793. Johnson to GW, Dec. 23, 1793, in Delaplaine, *Johnson*. Journal, Kent papers.

Chapter 27

1. Blodget to commrs., misdated Jan. 4, 1793, and filed in 1793 letters received. RM to Cazenove, Jan. 27, 1794, HLC D.C. file. Cazenove to the Four Houses, Feb. 8, 1794, Cazenove LB HLC.

2. Randolph to GW, Jan. 3, 1794, domestic letters, State Department. JG to Randolph, Jan. 7, 1794, CR LC. Randolph to commrs., Jan. 19, 1794.

3. JG agreement with Kinsley, Jan. 6, 1794, NALC papers. JG to Carroll, Feb. 20, 1794, Carroll papers.

4. Johnson to GW, Dec. 23, 1793, GW LC. GW to Johnson, Jan. 23,

1794, CHS, vol. 17. Blodget to commrs., misdated Jan. 12, 1793. Undated letter of Blodget to Randolph, CR LC. Commrs. to Randolph, Jan. 28, 1794. Commrs. to Blodget, July 11, 1794. Ad for second lottery, CR LC. Stuart to GW, Feb. 6, 1794, GW LC.

5. Commrs. to GW, Jan. 28, 1794. Briggs to Ellicott, Jan. 7, 1794, Ellicott papers. Ads are in Dermott to GW, Mar. 22, 1794, GW LC. Commrs. to B. Ellicott, Jan. 25, 1794.

Chapter 28

1. Information on slaves in the city is rather sketchy. The names and owners of slaves can be found in NA RG 39. Short was listed in the time rolls, which were first kept in 1795. The time rolls also include white laborers, Ambrose Moriarty was a laborer and a literate one, as his letter of Apr. 20, 1795, to the commissioners attests. The number of slaves is in Proceedings, contract with Crocker, Apr. 24, 1794.

2. Roe to commrs., Jan. 30, 1794, in Proceedings, Apr. 24, 1794. Walsh to Carroll, Feb. 28, 1794. Johnson to GW, Feb. 6, 1794. GW LC. Stuart to GW, Feb. 6, 1794, GW LC.

3. Ellicott to GW, Feb. 28, 1794, June 27, 1793, GW LC. Ellicott, Briggs, and Ellicott to GW, June 29, 1793. GW to commrs., Mar. 14, 1794, CHS, vol. 17. Proceedings, Mar. 25, 1794. Commrs. to GW, Mar. 23, 1794.

4. JG to Templeman, Jan. 1794, JG papers, LC. Commrs. to JG, Mar. 25, 1794. Commrs. to Randolph, Mar. 23, 1794. RM ledger, HSP. GW to commrs., Mar. 14, 1794. Commrs. to GW, Mar. 23, 1794.

5. Lingan to Forde, Feb. 7, 1794, HSP. *Centinel,* Feb. 19, 1794.

Chapter 29

1. Commrs. to Fenwick, Apr. 19, 1794. Purcell to commrs., Sept. 13, 1798. Proceedings, Apr. 24, 1794. Deblois to JN, Apr.–June 1794, JN reels. Walker to commrs., Dec. 12, 1793. Dalton to JG, May 20, 1794, HSP.

2. Stoddert to commrs., April 23, 1794. Proceedings, Apr. 24, 1794, May 1794. Commrs. to GW, Apr. 23, 1794. L'Enfant to Hamilton, Sept. 15, 1794, Syrett, *Papers. American State Papers,* Military Affairs, vol. 1, pp. 71–107. Deakins to commrs., Apr. 22, 1794.

3. JG to Randolph, Apr. 9, 1794, GW LC. GW to RM, May 26, 1794, Fitzpatrick, *Writings.* Proceedings, Apr. 14, 1794. Stoddert to JG, Apr. 24, 1794, May 12, 1794, NALC papers. JG's agreements with Lovering, May 8, 1794, O'Neale, May 9, 1794, Clarke, May 11, 1794, NALC papers.

4. Commrs. to Deakins, Apr. 21, 1794. Commrs. to Harrison and Taylor, Apr. 23, 1794.

5. Proceedings, Jan–May 1794. Caffry to commrs., Apr. 14, 1794. Commrs. to Crocker et al., Apr. 17, 1794. Worthington, Coningham, and Crocker to commrs. (three letters), Apr. 18, 1794.

Chapter 30

1. Harrison to commrs., May 2, 5, and 29, 1794. Commrs. to Randolph, May 17, 1794. Randolph to commrs., May 17, 1794, CR LC.

2. Carroll to Williamson, May 7, 1794. Commrs. to Williamson, May 17 and 19, 1794, June 7, 1794. Commrs. to Hicks, Maitland, Ore, and Hakesly, May 19, 1974. Stoddert to Carroll, May 26, 1794. Williamson to commrs., June 5, 1794. Brown, Maitland, and Delahunty to commrs., June 23, 1794. Hoban to commrs., May 16, 1794, June 20, 1794.

3. Commrs.' letters to Hallet are also in *Documentary History of the Capitol.* Hoban's June 28 letter is in Proceedings, as are commrs.' actions against Hallet. Commrs. to Key, June 28, 1794.

4. Hodgson to commrs., June 5, 1794. Dalton to JG, May 20, 1794. Hoban to commrs., June 20, 1794.

5. Blodget's June 7, 1794, letter published in *Philadelphia Gazette,* June 25, 1794. The newspaper war follows in July issues.

6. On GW's fall from his horse, GW to secretary of war, June 25, 1794, Fitzpatrick, *Writings.* GW to commrs, June 1, 1794, CHS, vol. 17. GW to Johnson, June 27, 1794, CHS, vol. 17. For the considerable correspondence on the causeway deal, commrs. to Dorsey, June 28, 1794. Johnson to GW, in Delaplaine, *Johnson.* June 28, 1794.

Chapter 31

1. Notice for Columbian Society in HLC D.C. file. RM ledgers. Cazenove letters, May 5, 1794, June 5, 1794, Cazenove LB, pp. 128, 148, HLC. JG to Bourne, June 25, 1794, Bourne papers.

2. Appleton to JG, June 23, 1794, JG papers, NYPL. JG agreement with Macomb, June 16, 1794, NALC papers. Lovering description of buildings on Greenleaf's Point, undated, NALC papers, book 68. Appleton to Cranch, Feb. 2, 1795, Cranch papers, NYPL. Deblois to JN, June 18, 1794, JN reels.

3. Commrs. to Vermonnet, June 27, 1794. Vermonnet to commrs., July 5, 1794. Commrs. to JG, July 10, 1794. Commrs. to GW, July 10, 1794.

4. Proceedings, July 11, 1794. Commrs. to JG, July 11, 1794. JG to

Johnson, July 11, 1794, NALC papers. Lingan to Forde, July 7, 1794, Reed and Forde papers.

5. *Centinel,* summer 1794. Burnes papers. Davidson to Stoddert, July 25, 1794, Davidson papers.

6. The newspaper war between Blodget and the commrs. in July *Philadelphia Gazette.* JG to commrs., quoted in Commrs. to GW, July 31, 1794.

7. Randolph to commrs., July 18 and 30, 1794, domestic letters, State Department. Johnson to commrs., July 29, 1794. GW to commrs., July 23, 1974, CHS, vol. 17.

Chapter 32

1. Proceedings, July 30, 1794. NA RG 39. O'Neale to commrs., Sept. 19, 1794. Williamson to Adams, Apr. 17, 1797, AFP.

2. Brighton, *Lear.* Accounts of Appleton purchases, NALC papers. Agreement with Coningham, Aug. 1, 1794, NALC papers.

3. Bourne agreement with Mylius, May 6, 1794, NALC papers. A copy of the loan agreement with Crommelin is in HLC, in Dutch; a translation is in JN reels under Bourne. For the difficulty of raising loans in Holland, see Syrett papers, e.g., Willink et al. to Hamilton, Oct. 15, 1794. Bourne to JG, May 9, 1794, JN reels. Dalton to JG, Aug. 17, 1794. HSP.

4. JG to commrs. (extract), July 26, 1794, CR LC. Dalton to JG, July 27, 1794, HSP. JG et al. to Bourne, July 28, 1794, Clark, *Greenleaf and Law,* p. 89. RM to Bourne, Aug. 1, 1794 (extracts), HSP. JG to JN, Aug. 16 and 21, 1794, JN reels. Commrs. to JG, July 31, 1794. Commrs. to Randolph, July 31, 1794.

5. Appleton to Webster, July 26, 1794, Ford, *Webster,* p. 384.

6. GW to Lee, July 25, 1794, to Lear, Aug. 28, 1794, CHS, vol. 17. Randolph to Potts, July 24, 1794, domestic letters, State Department. Lear to GW, Sept. 5, 1794, GW LC.

Chapter 33

1. *Centinel,* Aug. issues. GW to Pearce, Aug. 3, 1794, Fitzpatrick. *Times* (London) Nov. 25, 1794, Dec. 2, 1974. D'Invernois to J. Adams, Aug. 30, 1794, AFP. GW to Adams, Nov. 15, 1794, CHS, vol. 17. Trumbull papers, Conn. Hist Soc. Trumbull to Lear, Sept. 15, 1794, commrs.' letters received.

2. Hopkins to commrs., Sept. 9, 1794. JG to commrs., Sept. 18, 1794. Commrs. to Randolph, Sept. 19, 1794. Stoddert to commrs., Sept. 19, 1794. Commrs. to governor of Virginia, Sept. 16, 1794. Randolph to commrs.,

Oct. 2, 1794.

3. Davidson to Willcocks, Nov. 6, 1794, Davidson papers. O'Neale to commrs., Sept. 19, 1794. Crocker to commrs., Oct. 25, 1794. Leclair is listed in NA RG 39. Carroll to JG, Sept. 30, 1794, Oct. 25, 1794, JG papers, NYPL.

4. Agreement with Hallet, Oct. 1, 1794, NALC papers. RM ledger, Sept. 30, 1794, "Washington Lots."

5. Adams to wife, Nov. 9, 1794, AFP. Cranch to Adams, June 14, 1798, AFP. Cranch to mother, Oct. 26, 1794, MHS.

Chapter 34

1. Proceedings, Oct. 15, 1794. Casanave, Deakins, and Lee to commrs., Dec. 12, 1794. Deakins to commrs., Nov. 14, 1794. Carroll to commrs., Oct. 13, 1794. Walker to commrs., Oct. 24, 1794.

2. Harrison and Taylor to Carroll, Nov. 11, 1794. Blodget to commrs., Oct. 9, 1794, Nov. 26, 1794. Commrs. to JG, Oct. 18, 20, 27, 29, 30, and 31, 1794, Nov. 3, 1794. Commrs. to Randolph, Oct. 18, 1794, CR LC. Deakins to commrs., Nov. 16, 1794.

3. Deblois to JN, Nov. 5, 12, 17, and 20, 1794, Dec. 8, 1794, Jan. 19, 1795, JN reels.

4. Stewart to commrs., Nov. 6 and 20, 1794, Dec. 4, 1794. Commrs. to Stewart, Nov. 7 and 11, 1794. Parkyns to commrs., Nov. 7, 1794. Commrs. to Parkyns, Nov. 7, 1794. *Virginia Gazette,* Nov. 10, 1794.

Chapter 35

1. JG to JN, Nov. 26, 1794, JN reels.

2. Law to JG, Mar. 21, 1795, Apr. 10, 1808, JG papers, NYPL. Clark, *Greenleaf and Law,* pp. 94–102. La Tour du Pin, *Memoirs.* Cranch to father, Dec. 8, 1794. *Pratt v. Law,* Supreme Court Appelate file, pp. 245ff., for several letters from Law to JG.

3. JG to commrs., Dec. 1, 1794, CR LC. Commrs. to JG, Dec. 5, 1794, CR LC. Cazenove to Stadnitski, Dec. 8, 1794, Cazenove LB HLC papers. Blodget to commrs., Dec. 3, 1794. Commrs. to Blodget, Dec. 2 and 9, 1794.

4. Commrs. to Virginia Assembly, Nov. 25, 1794. Dobson to commrs., Dec. 7, 1794. Contract between Dobson and commrs. in Proceedings, Dec. 31, 1794. Freeman to commrs., Jan. 7, 1795, NA RG 39. Commrs. to Williamson, Dec. 2, 1794. Thornton to Trumbull, Jan. 6, 1795, Thornton papers. Peter to commrs., Dec. 1, 1794. Roll of masons, carpenters, and laborers, Dec. 1794, NA RG 39. Proceedings, Nov. 6, 1794 through Decem-

ber. Ledger, Davidson papers.

5. JG to JN, Dec. 22, 26, and 29, 1794, JN reels.

6. Lear to GW, Dec. 17, 1794, GW LC. GW to Lear, Dec. 21, 1794, CHS, vol. 17.

Chapter 36

1. GW to Carroll, Jan. 7, 1795, CHS, vol. 17. Carroll to GW, Jan. 13, 1795, GW LC.

2. Hopkins to commrs. regarding Virginia's donation, Jan. 21, 1795, CR LC. Reports on expenses, CR LC. Report to GW, Jan. 30, 1795. Hallet to commrs., Jan. 21, 1795. Proceedings, Dec. 24 and 31, 1794.

3. *Georgetown Chronicle,* Jan. 12, 15, and 19, 1795. Masons' rolls, NA RG 39. Stonecutters' petition, Jan. 21, 1795, commrs.' letters received. Johnson to GW, Feb. 12, 1795. JG agreement with Johnson, Jan. 8, 1795, NALC papers.

Chapter 37

1. Henry to commrs., Feb. 16, 1795. Cranch's several letters to Henry, Cranch papers, NYPL. Mitchell to commrs., Feb. 11, 1795.

2. Deblois to JN, Jan. 2 and 19, 1795, JN reels.

3. RM to JG, Dec. 23, 1794, RM LB. Adams to wife, Jan. 29, 1795, AFP. RM to Swanwick, Jan. 12, 1795, to Hall, Feb. 23, 1795, to Carth, Jan. 6, 1795, RM LB. Ward to Constable, Nov. 20, 1794, Constable papers.

4. GW to commrs., Jan. 28, 1795, CHS, vol. 17. Parkyns Prospectus, Jan. 18, 1795, JN reels. Feb. 14, 1795, articles on subscription to and description of Ceracchi's monument, JN reels. Parkyns to GW, Feb. 21, 1795, misc. letters, State Department. Blodget to Thornton, Jan. 5, 1795. Thornton papers. Ralph to commrs., Jan. 21, 1795.

Chapter 38

1. The controversy with Johnson generated a sizable file, much in Johnson's barely legible hand, redeemed somewhat by his biting sarcasm. Johnson to commrs., Feb. 11, 13, and 15, 1795. Stuart to GW, Feb. 22, 1795, GW LC. Commrs. to Johnson, Feb. 15 and 18, 1795. Commrs. to Randolph, Feb. 21, 1795, CR LC. Proceedings, Feb. 18, 1795.

2. Dermott to Stewart, Feb. 20, 1795, Mar. 24, 1795, HSP. Thornton to commrs., Mar. 13 and 25, 1795. Scott to Thornton, Mar. 4 and 13, 1795, Thornton papers. Commrs. to Thornton, Mar. 20, 1795. Commrs. to Randolph, Mar. 20, 1795.

3. Commrs. to Cranch, Mar. 5, 1795. Account of work on bridge, Feb. 17, 1795, NA RG 39. Law to Rose, Oct. 20, 1794, in catalogue description in HSW Law file. Law to JG, Mar. 21, 1795, JG papers, NYPL. Law to RM, JN, and JG, Mar. 9, 1795, JG papers, NYPL. JN to JG, Mar. 20, 1795, JN LB. RM to JG, Mar. 12 and 16, 1795, RM LB. Clark, *Greenleaf and Law*, pp. 101–5.

4. RM to Willink, Mar. 16, 1795, to Constable, Mar. 14, 1795, Apr. 3, 1795, to Bourne, Mar. 30, 1795, RM LB.

5. Deblois to JN, Mar. 9 and 20, 1795, Mrs. Deblois to JN, Mar. 25, 1795, JN reels. JN to Deblois, Mar. 23, 1795, JN LB.

Chapter 39

1. Thornton to GW (draft), Mar. 12, 1795, Thornton papers. Commrs. to Randolph, Mar. 20, 1795.

2. Lear to GW, Feb. 23, 1795, Mar. 8 and 18, 1795, GW LC. GW to commrs., Mar. 24, 1795, CHS, vol. 17.

3. Ceracchi to GW, Mar. 28, 1795, GW LC. Runaway ads dated Jan. 19, 1795, Mar. 3, 1795, Apr. 19, 1795, *Chronicle. Look Before You Leap.*

4. Scott to Thornton, Mar. 4, 1795, Thornton papers. Proceedings, Feb. 18 and 25, 1795, Mar. 4, 5, and 11, 1795, Apr. 2, 1795. Commrs. to Lee, Mar. 12, 1795. Deblois to JN, Apr. 8, 1795, JN reels. O'Neale to commrs., Mar. 5 and 12, 1795. Hoban to commrs., Mar. 12 and 28, 1795. Deakins to commrs., Mar. 21, 1795. Mason to commrs., Apr. 1, 1795. Carters' accounts, NA RG 39.

5. Johnson to commrs., Mar. 4, 5, 6, 15, and 18, 1795. Johnson to GW, Feb. 28, 1795, Mar. 21, 1795, GW LC. Commrs. to GW, Apr. 20, 1795.

Chapter 40

1. Commrs. to Pryor, Apr. 9, 1795. Hoban to commrs., Apr. 10, 1795. Pryor et al. to commrs., May 14, 1795. RM to Law, Apr. 20, 1795, RM LB. Law to JG, undated, CR LC (canal material).

2. RM to JG, Mar. 26, 1795, Apr. 3 and 24, 1795, RM LB. JN to JG, Mar. 26, 1795, Apr. 4 and 13, 1795, JN LB. JN to RM, Apr. 13 and 24, 1795, JN LB. Agreement with Polock, Mar. 3, 1795, NALC papers. Polock to JN, July 15, 1795, JN reels.

3. Proceedings, Apr. 27, 1795. GW to Carroll and White, both May 17, 1795, CHS, vol. 17. Carroll to GW, May 10 and 25, 1795, GW LC.

4. Roe to commrs., Apr. 22, 1795. Williamson to Adams, June 9, 1797, AFP. Commrs. to Williamson, May 15, 1795. Commrs. to Clark, Lovering,

and Henderson, June 10, 1795. Information on Roe's work force is in NA RG 42 (estimates). Proceedings, May 28, 1795. Commrs. to Cooke and Brent, May 15 and 26, 1795. Brent to commrs., May 24, 1795. Dunbar to commrs., May 18, 1795. Commrs. to Dunbar, May 26, 1795. Commrs. to Hallet, Apr. 27, 1795. Mrs. Hallet to GW, May 1, 1795 in commrs. letters received. GW to Hallet and commrs., May 5, 1795, CHS, vol. 17. Mitchell to commrs., May 2, 1795. GW to White, May 17, 1795, CHS, vol. 17. Commrs. to JG, May 18, 1795.

5. Ceracchi generated a flurry of letters before he left the country; see GW LC and misc. letters, State Department. GW to Ceracchi, May 3, 1795 (misdated in book), Fitzpatrick, *Writings.* Ceracchi to Randolph, May 11, 1795. Ceracchi to GW, Apr. 23, 1795, May 7, 9, and 10, 1795.

Chapter 41

1. Lear to GW, May 26, 1795, GW LC.

2. Deblois to JN, Apr. 29, 1795, May 25, 1795, JN reels. JN to Deblois, May 30, 1795, to JG, May 22, 1795, to Cazenove and Nephew, May 27, 1795. RM to Watson, Apr. 22, 1795, May 1, 1795, to Carey, Apr. 17, 1795, to W. Morris, June 1, 1795, RM LB. Dundas to JN, Apr. 15, 1795, JN reels. RM to JG, Apr. 25, 1795, May 27, 1795, June 1, 1795, RM LB.

3. Law to JG, Apr. 10, 1808, JG papers, NYPL. Lear to GW, June 3 and 4, 1795, GW LC. JG to Carroll, June 8, 1795, Carroll papers.

4. Commrs. to Randolph, May 26, 1795. Randolph to commrs., June 23, 1795, domestic letters, State Department. Blodget to commrs., June 6, 1795. *Observer,* June 12, 19, and 25, 1795, July 1, 1795.

5. Commrs. to Martin, May 7, 1795. Martin to commrs., May 22, 1795. Johnson to GW, June 15, 1795, with enclosures. Law to commrs., June 7, 1795. Commrs. to Randolph, May 26, 1795, June 10, 1795. RM to JG, June 1, 1795, RM LB.

Chapter 42

1. Customs records on *Two Sisters,* NA RG 36. Barry ledger, HSW. *Look Before You Leap.*

2. White to GW, June 8, 1795, GW LC. Proceedings, June 1795.

3. Estimates of damage in NA RG 42 (estimates and proposals). Randolph to commrs., July 6, 1795, domestic letters, State Department. Commrs. to Randolph, July 6 and 13, 1795. Thornton to commrs., July 18, 1795. Proceedings, July 22, 1795. Harbaugh to commrs., Oct. 27, 1795.

4. Wells to Randolph, July 6, 1795, commrs.' letters received. Commrs. to Stoddert, July 13, 1795.

5. RM to JG, June 22 and 30, 1795, to Franklin, July 18, 1795, to Constable, July 27, 1795, RM LB. JG to JN, July 17, 1795. JN reels. JN to JG, July 20, 1795, JN LB. RM to Cranch and JG to Law in Clark, *Greenleaf and Law,* pp. 109, 112. JN to King, July 24, 1795, JN LB.

Chapter 43

1. Commrs. to Randolph, July 20, 1795. Commrs. to Law, July 20, 1795. Clark, *Greenleaf and Law,* pp. 108 & 156.

2. RM to Cranch, July 26, 1795, RM LB. JG agreement with Lovering, July 6, 1795, with Frost, June 27, 1795, with Henderson June 19, 1795. The last includes a description of work to be done. NALC papers. Deblois to JN, June 19, 1795, July 22, 1795, JN reels. Stansborrough to JN, July 10 and 16, 1795, JN reels.

3. Commrs. to Cranch, July 17, 1795. GW to Randolph, July 22, 1795, Fitzpatrick, *Writings.*

4. Freeman to commrs., July 4, 1795. *Centinel,* July 17, 1795, Aug. 4, 1795. White to commrs., Aug. 17, 1795. Commrs.' secretary to Dumoko, July 17, 1795. Commrs. to GW, July 24, 1795. Proceedings, July 20, 1795. Commrs. to Carroll, July 30, 1795.

5. *Centinel,* June 19, 1795. Thornton deed, *U.S. v. Morris et al.,* p. 2462. GW to Randolph, Aug. 3, 1795, Fitzpatrick, *Writings.* Maitland et al. to commrs., July 31, 1795.

Chapter 44

1. Blagden to commrs., Aug. 6, 1795. Mitchell to commrs., Aug. 4 and 18, 1795. Brent to commrs., Sept. 17, 1795. Dunbar to commrs., Sept. 21, 1795. Commrs. to Mitchell, Aug. 21, 1795. Commrs. to Lee, Aug. 10, 1795.

2. RM to Cranch, July 26, 1795, Aug. 19, 1795, RM LB. Commrs. to Randolph, Aug. 17, 1795.

3. RM to Lovering, Aug. 17, 1795, RM LB. JG's clerk to Cranch, Aug. 26, 1795, Cranch papers, NYPL. JN to Cazenove and Nephew, July 28, 1795, to JG, July 28 and 31, 1795, to Joseph Ball, Aug. 6, 1795, to Allison, Sept. 28, 1795, to Ashley, Sept. 19, 1795, JN LB.

4. Cazenove report, HLC D.C. file.

5. Carroll to GW, Aug. 7, 1795, GW LC. Mitchell to commrs., Oct. 8, 1795. GW to RM, Sept. 14, 1795, CHS, vol. 17. RM to GW, Sept. 21, 1795, RM LB.

Chapter 45

1. Wolcott to Hamilton, Sept. 26, 1795, Syrett, *Papers,* vol. 29, RM to Marshall, Oct. 16, 1795, to Cranch, Aug. 14, 1795, Sept. 21, 1795, Oct. 1, 1795, to Law, Oct. 1, 1795, to Constable, Aug. 10, 1795, to Bourdieu, Oct. 7, 1795, to Law and Duncanson, Sept. 11, 1795, RM LB.

2. Deblois to JN, Aug. 29, 1795, Sept. 25 and 30, 1795, Oct. 16, 1795, JN reels. JN to Deblois. Aug. 31, 1795, Sept. 21, 1795, Oct. 2 and 5, 1795. JN LB.

3. Commrs. to RM, Sept. 28, 1795, to JN, Sept. 28, 1795. Commrs. to Casanave, Oct. 10 and 20, 1795. Commrs. to GW, Sept. 27, 1795, Oct. 5, 1795. Blagden to commrs., Oct. 19, 1795. Commrs. to Key, Oct. 22, 1795. Commrs. to Reintzel, Oct. 27, 1795. GW to commrs., Sept. 18, 1795, CHS, vol. 17. Forrest to Commrs., Oct. 24, 1795.

4. Commrs. to Law, Oct. 1, 1795. Commrs. to Barry, Oct. 5, 1795. Burr to Theodesia, Sept. 23 and 26, 1795, Davis, *Memoirs*. Hallet to Cazenove, Nov. 9, 1795, HLC D.C. file.

5. Draft of Thornton memo on Hadfield's changes, Thornton papers. White to GW, Sept. 17, 1795. Trumbull to Hadfield, Mar. 9, 1795, Trumbull papers. Hadfield to commrs., Oct. 28, 1795.

Chapter 46

1. Forrest to Commrs., Oct. 24, 1795. Commrs. to GW, Oct. 26, 1795. Scott to GW, Nov. 13, 1795, GW LC. White to GW, Oct. 31, 1795, GW LC. GW to commrs., Oct. 30, 1795, Nov. 4, 1795, to White, Nov. 9, 1795, CHS, vol. 17.

2. Commrs. to GW, Oct. 31, 1795. Thornton to GW (draft), Nov. 2, 1795, Thornton papers. GW to Thornton, Nov. 9, to commrs., Nov. 9, 1795, CHS, vol. 17. Commrs. to Hadfield, Nov. 30, 1795. Hadfield to commrs., Nov. 17, 1795. Thornton to commrs., Nov. 17, 1795.

3. RM to commrs., Nov. 2, 1795, to Cranch, Nov. 2 and 13, 1795, RM LB. Deblois to JN, Nov. 9 and 25, 1795, Dec. 11, 1795, JN reels. JN to Deblois, Oct. 30, 1795, Nov. 17, 18, and 25, 1795, Dec. 3, 14, and 18, 1795, JN LB.

4. Clark to JN, Nov. 3, 1795, JN reels. Isabella Clark to RM and JN, Nov. 28, 1795, JN reels. RM to Fox, Dec. 3, 1795, RM LB. JN to Isabella Clark, Dec. 4, 1795. JN LB.

Chapter 47

1. White to commrs., Dec. 6, 10, 14, and 21, 1795. White to Thornton, Dec. 21, 1795, Thornton papers.

2. Scott to GW, Nov. 18, 1795, Dec. 14, 21, and 23, 1795, GW LC. Commrs. to GW, Nov. 30, 1795, Mar. 17, 1796. Commrs. to White, Dec. 10, 15, 22, and 31, 1795.

3. White to commrs., Dec. 25 and 27, 1795. Commrs. to White, Dec. 31, 1795.

4. CHS. vols. 35–36, p. 91. Commrs. to White, Dec. 31, 1795.

Chapter 48

1. RM to Field, Dec. 12, 1795, RM LB. Prentiss to JN, Dec. 28, 1795, Jan. 4 and 6, 1796, Oct. 27, 1797. Cranch to mother, Jan. 13, 1796, Cranch papers, MHS. RM to Cranch, Feb. 10, 1796, RM LB. Richmond's account of slave hire, NA RG 42 (ledgers). Ralph to commrs., Dec. 22, 1795. *Centinel,* Jan. 8, 1796.

2. JN to White, Dec. 25, 1795, JN LB.

3. White to Thornton, Jan. 14 and 18, 1796, Thornton papers. White to commrs., Jan. 8, 13, 18, and 20, 1796. Memorial to Congress, committee report, and debates on loan bill, *Documentary History of the Capitol,* pp. 38 ff. Commrs. to White, Jan. 6 and 18, 1796. RM to White, Jan. 9, 1796, RM LB.

Chapter 49

1. White to commrs., Jan. 23, 1795. Commrs. to White, Feb. letters.

2. RM to Cranch, Feb. 10, 12, and 22, 1796, to Marshall, Jan. 16, 1796, RM LB. Young et al. to commrs., Feb. 6, 1796, CR LC. Duncanson to commrs., Feb. 17, 1796. Stuart to GW, Feb. 25, 1796, GW LC. *Pratt v. Law,* Supreme Court Appelate file, interrogatory of Cranch, and Carroll to Cranch, Feb. 29, 1796. JN to JG, Feb. 13, 1796, JN LB. Commrs. to Law, Dec. 15, 1795.

3. Burns to Commrs., Feb. 8, 1796. Deakins account, 1796, ledger, NA RG 42. Commrs. to Stoddert, Feb. 3, 1796. Commrs. to Lee, Deakins, and Casanave, Jan. 22, 1796. Commrs. to Constable, Jan. 12, 1796. Mitchell to Commrs., Jan. 30,. 1796, Feb. 20, 1796.

4. White to commrs., Jan 31, 1796. Commrs. to White, Feb. letters.

Chapter 50

1. White to commrs., Feb. letters. Debate is in *Annals* and *Documentary History of the Capitol,* pp. 47ff. White to Thornton, Feb. 26, 1796, Thornton

papers. Goodrich to Wolcott, Feb. 21, 1796, Gibbs, *Memoir,* p. 302. Sedgwick to Smith, Mar. 24, 1800, W. L. Smith papers.

2. RM to Cranch, Feb. 29, 1796, Mar. 6, 1796, to Marshall, Mar. 4, 1796, RM LB.

3. Law to Commrs., Mar. 20, 1796. Deblois to JN, Mar. 21, 1796, JN reels. Prentiss to JN, Feb. 29, 1796, Apr. 8, 1796, JN reels. JN to Deblois, Mar. 29, 1796, JN LB. Williamson to commrs., Mar. 11, 1796. Walker ad, *Centinel,* Mar. 4, 1796. Carters' receipts and work rolls, NA RG 39.

4. Commrs. to White, Jan. 27, 1796, Feb. 20, 1796, Mar. 1 and 7, 1796. Thornton to White, Mar. 4, 1796, Thornton papers.

5. White to commrs., Mar. letters.

Chapter 51

1. White to commrs., Mar. letters. Stewart to commrs., Mar. 28, 1796. Commrs. to White, Jan. 22. 1796, Mar. 29, 1796. Commrs. to GW, Mar. 17, 1796, which White was to read first. Attorney general's opinion, Mar. 20, 1796, CR LC. Commrs. to White, Mar. 29, 1796.

2. White's Mar. letters. *Annals.* Coit letters, New England Genealogical Society. Smith letters, Plumer papers, LC. *Pennsylvania Magazine of History,* vol. 97, pp. 131–82. Weld, *Travels.*

3. RM to Cranch, Apr. 15, 1796, RM LB. Lee to commrs., Apr. 9, 1796. Dermott to Stewart, Apr. 15, 1796, HSP. White's Mar. and Apr. letters. Commrs. to White, Mar. & Apr.

4. Weld, *Travels.* Cranch to mother, Apr. 25, 1796, Cranch papers, MHS.

Chapter 52

1. White's Apr. letters to commrs.

2. RM to Barry, Apr. 2, 1796, to Cranch, Apr. 12, 1796, RM LB. Commrs. to White, Apr. 19, 1796.

3. White's Apr. and May letters to commrs. White to Thornton, Apr. 20, 1796, Thornton papers. Combs, *Jay Treaty,* p. 184. *Annals.*

4. Twining, *Travels,* pp. 96ff.

Chapter 53

1. White to commrs., May 9, 1796.

2. Forrest to Clifford, Mar. 4, 1796, Clifford-Pemburton papers, HSP. Carpenters to commrs. June 6, 1796. Deakins to GW, May 27, 1796, GW

LC. White to GW, May 25, 1796, GW LC. GW to commrs., May 22 and 30, 1796, to Scott, May 25, 1796, to White, June 5, 1796, to Deakins, June 6, 1796, CHS, vol. 17.

3. Law to commrs., June 1, 10, and 14, 1796. Barry to commrs., June 17, 1796. Ralph to commrs., June 16, 1796. Law to JN, May 11, 1796, JN reels. Barry account book.

4. Blagden to commrs., May 17, 1796. Accounts, June 8, 1796, NA RG 39. Commrs. to Lee, Apr. 13, 1796, May 12, 1796. Commrs. to Parrot and Blake, May 3, 1796. Hoban report, May 18, 1796, HLC D.C. file. Account for shoes, July 7, 1796, NA RG 39. Commrs. to GW, June 20, 1796. Cooke and Brent to commrs., June 9, 1796, NA RG 42 (estimates). Commrs. to Anderson, May 23, 1796.

5. Scott to Gilmore, May 4, 1796, HSP. Commrs. to Gilmore and Willink, May 13, 1796. Commrs. to Wolcott, June 20, 1796. Commrs. to GW, May 13, 1796. Commrs. to GW, June 3 and 20, 1796. GW to commrs., June 10 and 26, 1796, CHS, vol. 17.

Chapter 54

1. Cazenove to the Four Houses, July 13, 1796, to Ten Cates, May 25, 1795, June 22, 1795, Cazenove LB, HLC papers. *Gazette,* Aug. 10, 1796. Stewart, *Opposition Press,* p. 77.

2. Commrs. to Hadfield, June 27, 1796. Commrs. to GW, June 22 and 29, 1796. Ad for leveling in *Gazette,* June 29, 1796. Thornton on Hadfield, undated, Thornton papers. Johnson to commrs., June 20, 1796. GW to commrs., June 26, 1796, July 1, 1796, CHS, vol. 17. GW to Scott, July 4, 1796, CHS, vol. 17.

3. *Look Before You Leap.* RM to Marshall, May 24, 1796, to Cranch, May 22 and 30, 1796, June 27, 1796, July 10, 1796, to Law, June 12, 1796, RM LB. JN to Barrell and Servante, June 2, 1796, JN LB.

4. Deblois to JN, May 2 and 27, 1796, JN reels. JN to Deblois, May 6, 1796, to commrs., May 19, 1796, to Morris, July 12, 1796, to Carroll, July 1, 1796, JN LB. Harrison, *Philadelphia Merchant,* p. 51.

5. Cranch to father, Sept. 4, 1796, Cranch papers, MHS. Prentiss to JN, June, July, and Aug., 1796, JN reels. Lovering to JN, June, July, and Aug. 1796, JN reels. RM to Cranch, July 12, 1796, RM LB. *Pratt v. Law,* Supreme Court Appelate file, Cranch accounts, p. 595. Cranch to JG, Feb. 1797, NALC papers.

6. Commrs. to RM, July 15, 1796. RM to commrs., July 25, 1796, RM LB. Commrs. to Tilghman, Aug. 3, 1796. Commrs. to RM, Aug. 9, 1796. JN to Jarvis, Aug. 2, 1796, to Fitzsimmons, July 22, 1796, JN LB.

Chapter 55

1. Mrs. Liston to her uncle, Sept. 9, 1796, National Library of Scotland, FO5. Latrobe, *Journals,* July 19, 1796, p. 170.

2. Barry to Law, Aug. 4, 1796, Law papers, LC. Law to Lagarenne, Aug. 22, 1796, Law papers, NYPL. Law to GW, Aug. 1796 (enclosed in Oct. 6, 1796), GW LC. Law to commrs., Aug. 15, 1796. Commrs. to Forrest, Aug. 17, 1796.

3. An impressive display of dry goods from the three stores is in the *Gazette,* Nov. 23, 1796. *Gazette,* July 9, 16, and 27, 1796, Aug. 31, 1796, Sept. 17, 1796. Commrs. to Stoddert, June 30, 1796. Stoddert to commrs., Sept. 9, 1796. Weems to Carey, July 28, 1796, Weems, *Letters,* p. 23. Davidson to Covachiche, Aug. 3, 1796, Davidson papers. Blodget to commrs., Aug. 13, 1796.

4. JN to RM, Aug. 5 and 22, 1796, Sept. ?, 1796, JN LB. RM to JN, Aug. 29, 1796, RM LB. Prentiss to JN, Sept. 3, 1796, JN reels.

Chapter 56

1. RM to Marshall, Sept. 7 and 16, 1796, to Lee, Sept. 30, 1796, RM LB. RM ledgers. Lingan to Reed and Forde, Aug. 26, 1796, Reed and Forde papers. Smith to Reed and Forde, Sept. 14 and 23, 1796, Reed and Forde papers.

2. Prentiss to JN, Sept. 19 and 21, 1796, JN reels. *Gazette* quote in Clark, *Greenleaf and Law,* p. 129. Prentiss and Carroll testimony in *Pratt v. Carroll,* Supreme Court Appelate file.

3. Murray to McHenry, Sept. 9, 1796, Steiner, *McHenry,* p. 197. Thornton to GW, Oct. 1, 1796 (draft), Thornton papers. Commrs. to GW, Oct. 1, 1796. JN to commrs., Sept. 28 and 30, 1796. Commrs. to JN, Oct. 1, 1796. Walker to commrs., Oct. 4, 1796. JN, Prout, et al. to commrs., Sept. 27, 1796.

4. Hoban to commrs., Sept. 28, 1796. Blagden to commrs., Aug. 22, 1796. Wiley to commrs., Aug. 29, 1796. Hadfield to commrs., Sept. 8, 1796.

5. Prentiss to JN, Aug. letters. Agreement with Langley, Sept. 26, 1796, NALC papers.

6. Correspondence between Hamilton and JG in Syrett. Sept. 29, 1796, *Claypool*'s *Gazette* has JN's attack on auction; newspaper war follows throughout Oct. Reed and Forde to Smith, Sept. 30, 1796, Oct. 3, 1796, Reed and Forde papers. JN to Gibson, Oct. 5, 1796, JNLB.

Chapter 57

1. *Gazette,* Aug. 20, 1796, Oct. 26 and 29, 1796. Law to GW, Oct. 6, 1796, GW LC. Commrs. to Millard, Oct. 4, 1796. GW to commrs., Oct. 21,

1796, CHS, vol. 17. Davidson to GW, Oct. 25, 1796.

2. JN to RM, Nov. 14, 1796, JN LB. JN diary, Oct. 10 and 11, 1796. RM to Mrs. Stewart, Oct. 21, 1796, to Fitzsimmons, Oct. 16, 1796, to Thompson, Oct. 28, 1796, to Field, Oct. 28, 1796, to Marshall, Nov. 1, 1796, to Rees, Oct. 30, 1796, to Sansom, Oct. 31, 1796, RM LB. Prentiss to JN, Oct. 3, 5, 17, and 27, 1796, Nov. 1, 1796, JN reels. Barry to Law, Nov. 6, 1796, Law papers, Law to commrs., Nov. 8, 1796. Smith to Reed and Forde, Oct. 24, 1796, Nov. 7, 1796, Reed and Forde papers. Copy of agreement for loan from Deakins, Duncanson, and Forrest, Oct. 26, 1796, NALC papers.

3. Willink to commrs., Sept. 10, 1796. Commrs. to Willink, Oct. 31, 1796. Commrs. to GW, Oct. 31, 1796. Commrs. to Wolcott, Oct. 31, 1796. Commrs. to Bowie, Nov. 31, 1796. Wolcott to commrs., Nov. 8, 1796.

4. Forrest to Clifford, Nov. 15, 1796, Clifford-Pemburton papers. Law to RM and JN, Nov. 3, 1796, JN reels. Barry to Law, Sept. 4, 1796, Law papers, LC. Wescott to JN, Dec. 26, 1796, JN reels. RM to Duncanson, Dec. 4, 1796, RM LB. Walker to GW, Jan. 25, 1797, GW LC. Newspaper war between Walker and commrs., *Gazette,* Nov. 26 and 30, 1796. JN to RM, Nov. 14 and 23, 1796, JN LB.

5. Bank of U.S. to Wolcott, Nov. 18, 1796, commrs.' letters received. Commrs. to GW, Nov. 21, 1796.

Chapter 58

1. *Gazette,* Nov. 19, 23, and 26, 1796, Dec. 7, 1796.

2. Harrison and Sterret to JN, Nov. 3, 1796, JN reels. JN to Dunlop and Carleton, Nov. 16, 1796, JN reels. RM to JN, Nov. 14 and 20, 1796, JN LB. JN diary, Nov. 14, 1796, JN papers, LC.

3. JN to RM, Nov. 18, 1796, JN LB.

4. Cranch to JG, Dec. 5, 1796, Cranch papers (Cranch's account of how JN tried to thwart him from recording JG's claim on lots). JN to RM, Nov. 23, 1796, to Barrell and Servante, Nov. 25, 1796, JN LB.

5. March to Reed and Forde, Dec. 12, 1796, Reed and Forde papers. Steiner, *McHenry,* pp. 206–7. Payroll of cutters, Feb. 27, 1797, NA RG 39.

6. *Annals,* Fourth Congress.

7. RM to JN, Nov. 29, 1796, Dec. 1, 8, 11, 13, 22, and 28, 1796, to Cranch, Dec. 23, 1796, to Marshall, Dec. 3, 1796, RM LB. Fox to trustees of aggregate fund, Feb. 14, 1799, NALC papers. Morris agreement with Ball et al., Dec. 14, 1796, NALC papers.

Chapter 59

1. White to GW, Dec. 15, 1796, GW LC. Tunnicliff to JN, May 19, 1797, Oct. 5, 1797, Nov. 18, 1797, JN reels. *Gazette,* Dec. and Jan. issues. GW to White, Dec. 26, 1796, to Scott, Dec. 26, 1796, to Thornton, Dec. 26, 1796, to commrs., Dec. 26, 1796, CHS, vol. 17.

2. JN to RM, Dec. 28, 1796, Jan. 9, 11, 16, and 27, 1797, JN LB. On the refusal to provide bail, Dorsey to JN, Jan. 8, 1797, Levy to JN, Jan. 7, 1797, JN reels. Lovering to JN, Jan. 17, 1797, JN reels. Prentiss to JN, Dec. 26, 1796, JN reels.

3. Law to JN, Jan. 10, 1797, JN reels. Law to commrs., Jan. 24, 1797, Feb. 2, 1797. JN to RM, Jan. 17 and 23, 1797, JN LB.

4. Clark, *Greenleaf and Law,* pp. 245ff. Piercy to JN, Jan.–Mar. 1797, JN reels. Commrs. to GW, Jan. 31, 1797. Walker to GW, Jan. 31, 1797, commrs.' letters received. Walker to JN, Mar. 2, 1797, JN reels. Carroll to GW, Feb. 6, 1797, GW LC. Law to GW, Feb. 4, 1797, GW LC; the poem is not Law's best: "You'd suppose that at first they made streets for the many / And next that the Congress's house were begun / Ah no! for the public they care not a penny / And only attend to the flattering of One. . . ."—that is, by building the president's house.

5. RM to Scott, Jan. 29, 1797, RM LB. RM to JN, Jan. 10. 1797, Feb. 5, 1797, Roberts collection, Haverford College. RM to JN, Dec. 29, 1796, Jan. 1, 4, 12, 18, and 24, 1797, RM LB. JN to RM, Jan. 17 and 23, 1797, Feb. 8, 1797, JN LB. Commrs. to RM, Jan. 23, 1797. Commrs. to JN, Feb. 3, 4, and 7, 1797, Mar. 9, 1797. Clark to JN, Feb. 7, 1797, JN reels.

Chapter 60

1. Dawes to D. Greenleaf, Dec. 29, 1796, Greenleaf papers, HSW. Webster to D. Greenleaf, Jan. 5, 1797, Greenleaf papers, HSW. Law to GW, Feb. 8, 1797, GW LC. Commrs. to GW, Feb. 6, 1797. GW to Walker, Jan. 26, 1797, to commrs., Jan. 29, 1797, Feb. 15, 17, 20, and 27, 1797, Mar. 3, 1797, CHS, vol. 17. King diary, Jan. 20, 1797, King papers. Davidson memorial, Jan. 31, 1797, commrs.' letters received. Thornton to GW, Feb. 14, 1797, Thornton papers.

2. RM to JN, Feb. 9, 1797, to Marshall, Feb. 14, 1797, to Cranch, Feb. 17, 1797, RM LB.

3. Attorney general's opinion, Feb. 19, 1797, *Pratt v. Law,* Supreme Court Appelate file, p. 779. Law to JN, Mar. 9, 11, 14, and 19, 1797, JN reels. RM to JN, Mar. 6, 1797, RM LB. Law to commrs., Feb. 6, 1797. RM to Law, Mar. 19, 1797, RM LB. Cottineau to JN, Mar. 18, 1797, JN reels.

Law to JG, Feb. 21, 1797, JG papers, NYPL. Commrs. to RM and JN, Mar. 9, 1797.

4. Tunnicliff diaries for Feb. & Mar., JN reels. Deblois's runaway ad, *Gazette,* dated Feb. 27, 1797.

5. TJ to White, Sept. 17, 1797, Padover, *Jefferson.* Commrs. to GW, Feb. 20, 1797. *Gazette,* Feb. 8 and 22, 1797. Cranch to Adams, Mar. 5, 1797, AFP. Ruth Dalton to A. Adams, Jan. 14, 1797, AFP. Law to Adams, Feb. 26, 1797, Mar. 19, 1797, AFP.

Chapter 61

1. Adams to wife, Jan. 28 and 31, 1797, Apr. 7, 1797, AFP. Adams to commrs., Mar. 28, 1797, Apr. 17, 1797, commrs.' letters from presidents, LC. Correspondence between Adams and the governor of Pennsylvania about Philadelphia's president's house, *Gazette,* Mar. 18, 1797; also in Adams, *Works.* Commrs. to Adams, Mar. 22, 1797, Apr. 3 and 11, 1797. Law to commrs., Mar. 15, 1797. Adams to Cranch, Mar. 23, 1797, AFP.

2. Hadfield to commrs., Mar. 25, 1797. Carpenters to commrs., Apr. 12, 1797. Smallwood to commrs., Mar. 7, 1797. Monroe to commrs., Mar. 30, 1797. Carvers to commrs., Mar. 17, 1797. Proceedings, Mar. 22, 1797, Apr. 3, 1797, May 3, 1797.

3. Commrs. to Cooke and Brent, Apr. 21, 1797, to Lee, Apr. 7, 1797, to Parrot and Blake, Apr. 7, 1797, to Mitchell, May 2, 1797. Mitchell to commrs., May 3, 1797. Blake to commrs., Apr. 23, 1797.

4. Cranch to Adams, Apr. 18, 1797, AFP. Tunnicliff diary, Apr. 15, 1797, JN reels. Lovering's valuation of the property, NALC papers.

5. Tunnicliff's diary, Apr. 18, 1797, JN reels. *Gazette,* Apr. 18, 1797. Louis-Philippe, *Diary,* pp. 21ff. La Rochefoucauld-Liancourt, *Travels.*

6. JG's caution, dated Mar. 16, 1797, appeared frequently in the *Gazette;* the ensuing newspaper war lasted into May. JG to commrs., Mar. 10, 1797. RM to Marshall, Apr. 3, 1797, RM LB. Tunnicliff to JN, Apr. 23, 1797, Prentiss to JN, Apr. 14, 1797, Lovering to JN, Apr. 19 and 28, 1797, JN reels. RM to Scott, May 1, 5, and 8, 1797, RM LB.

Chapter 62

1. Cranch to Adams, Apr. 18, 1797, AFP. RM to Scott, May 5, 8, 10, and 25, 1797, June 7, 1797, RM LB. Scott to RM, May 10, 1797, to JN, May 3, 1797, HSP. RM to Cranch, May 14, 1797, RM LB.

2. Carroll to RM, May 14, 1797, *Pratt v. Carroll,* Supreme Court Appelate file. McNantz to JN, May 5, 1797, JN reels. Prentiss to JN, May 3

and 19, 1797, June 14, 1797, JN reels. Tunnicliff diary, June 11, 1797, Tunnicliff to JN, Apr. 26, 1797, June 12, 1797, JN reels. RM to Lovering, May 3, to McNantz, May 4, 1797, RM LB.

3. Nesmith to commrs., May 8, 1797. Farrell to commrs., May 26, 1797. Proceedings, May 26 and 30, 1797. Work rolls, NA RG 39. Report on expenditures, May 18, 1797, HLC D.C. file. Thornton to commrs., June 20, 1797.

4. Proceedings, May 2, 1797. GW to Lee, Apr. 2, 1797, to Scott, Apr. 22, 1797, Fitzpatrick, *Writings*. GW to Humphreys, June 26, 1797, CHS, vol. 17. Martha Washington to Powel, May 20, 1797, Washington family papers.

5. Commrs. to Willink, May 10, 1797. *Gazette,* June 7, 1797. Commrs. to RM and JN, May 4, 1797. RM and JN agreement with JG and trustees, June 26, 1797, NALC papers.

Chapter 63

1. Williamson to Adams, June 9, 1797, AFP. Dalton to Adams, June 28, 1797, AFP. Forrest to Adams, June 23, 1797, AFP. Adams to Dalton, July 1, 1797, AFP.

2. RM to Scott, July 7, 29, and 30, 1797, to Dunlop July 8, 1797, to Forrest July 12 and 29, 1797, RM LB.

3. RM to trustees, Aug. 11, 1797, RM LB. RM and JN to commrs., July 30, 1797, to Martin, July 11, 1797, RM LB. Commrs. to RM and JN, July 19, 1797. Commrs. to trustees, July 26, 1797, Aug. 4 and 8, 1797, Sept. 13, 1797. Pratt to commrs., July 30, 1797. Trustees to RM and JN, July 30, commrs.' letters received. Dorsey to commrs., Aug. 7, 1797. Trustees' certificate, Chalmers Allen papers, HSP.

4. HLC D.C. file. Gilbert to commrs., July 19, 1797, Aug. 14, 1797. Law to commrs., Aug. 12, 1797. Law to GW, Dec. 22, 1797, GW LC. *Gazette,* June 21, 1797. Gridley to commrs., Aug. 11, 1797. Prentiss to JN, Aug. 6, 1797, JN reels. Tunnicliff to JN, July 28, 1797, JN reels. RM to Cranch, Aug. 30, 1797, RM LB. Prout to brother, Oct. 17, 1797, Prout papers. Lovering to JN, Sept. 5, 1797, JN reels. Ralph to commrs., Aug. 25, 1797.

5. Proceedings, Aug. 28 and 29, 1797. Commrs. to Stoddert, Aug. 30, 1797. Commrs. to Dorsey, Sept. 28, 1797. Commrs. to Hadfield and Hoban, Oct. 3, 1797. Stoddert to commrs., Sept. 7, 1797.

6. Cranch to mother, June 30, 1797, Cranch papers. Frost to commrs., Oct. 17, 1797. *Gazette,* Sept. 16 and 30, 1797.

Chapter 64

1. RM to JN, Sept. 16, 22, and 24, 1797, Oct. 15 (two letters), 19, and 24, 1797, to trustees, Sept. 23 and 28, 1797, Oct. 6 and 27, 1797, RM LB. Lewis & Burd to Trustees, Mar. 6, 1798, NALC papers. Trustees to RM and JN, Oct. 29, 1797, NALC papers. Report of trustees, Apr. 22, 1799, NALC papers. RM to Scott, Oct. 2, 16, and 26, 1797, to Boone, Oct. 24, 1797, to Forrest, Aug. 11, 1797, Oct. 5, 1797, to Law, Sept. 16, 1797, RM LB.

2. *Gazette,* Oct. 28, 1797. Proceedings, Oct. 18, 19, and 20, 1797. Commrs. to trustees, Oct. 15, 1797.

3. Trustees to commrs., Nov. 2, 1797. RM to JN, Nov. 1, 1797, RM LB. JG to brother, Nov. 26, 1797, Greenleaf papers, HSW. RM to JG, Oct. 20, 1797, RM LB.

4. Adams to Wolcott, Oct. 27, 1797, Gibbs, *Memoir,* p. 572. Commrs. to Hadfield, Nov. 16, 1797. Report on Public Buildings, Nov. 18, 1797, HLC, D.C. file. Hoban estimate, Nov. 2, 1797, Hadfield estimate, Nov. 18, 1797, NA RG 42 (estimates). Proceedings, Nov. 14 and 15, 1797. Williamson to Adams, Nov. 27, 1797, CR LC.

5. Commrs. to trustees, Oct. 20, 1797, Nov. 9 and 23, 1797. Commrs. to Adams, Oct. 10, 1797, Nov. 3, 25, and 26, 1797. Davidson to Adams, Nov. 27, 1797, commrs.' letters received. Cranch to A. Adams, Nov. 21, 1797, AFP. Adams to commrs., Oct. 31, 1797, Dec. 5, 1797, to Pickering, Oct. 31, 1797, AFP.

6. Lee to commrs., Dec. 16, 1797. Scott to GW, Dec. 21, 1798, GW LC. Commrs. to Adams, Dec. 13, 1797. Scott to commrs., Dec. 23, 1797. Forrest to commrs., Nov. 27, 1797.

Chapter 65

1. Thornton to GW, Oct. 6, 1797, GW LC. GW to Law, Oct. 2, 1797, CHS, vol. 17. White to GW, Jan. 8, 1798, GW LC. Commrs. to Adams, Jan. 3, 1798. GW to White, Jan. 11, 1798, CHS, vol. 17.

2. Thornton to Fell, Oct. 5, 1797, to commrs., Jan. 9, 1798, Thornton papers. Thornton memorandum, June 1798, Thornton papers. Hadfield to commrs., Nov. 2, 1797. Commrs. to Hadfield, Jan. 1, 1798. Proceedings, Jan. 6, and 10, 1798.

3. *Gazette,* Oct. 21, 1797, Dec. 9 and 16, 1797, Jan. 20, 1798, Feb. 10, 1798.

4. Proceedings, Jan. 22, 1798. *Gazette,* Nov. 11 and 25, 1797. Mrs. Prentiss to JN, Nov. 13, 1797, JN reels. Lovering to JN, Jan. 14, 1798, JN

reels. Cranch to D. Greenleaf, Jan. 28, 1798, Greenleaf papers, HSW. Cranch to J. Q. Adams, Mar. 8, 1798, AFP. RM to Cranch, Feb. 26, 1798, RM LB.

    5. RM to JN, Dec. 30, 1797, Feb. 26 and 28, 1798, RM LB.

Chapter 66

    1. White to GW, Feb. 20, 1798, GW LC.

    2. White to commrs., Feb. 11 and 18, 1798. Dalton to Adams, Feb. 12, 1798, AFP. Commrs. to Forrest, Jan. 30, 1798.

    3. Farrell to commrs., Jan. 29, 1798. Purcell to commrs., Feb. 20, 1798, Mar. 7, 12, and 20, 1798. Hadfield to commrs., Feb. 26, 1798, Mar. 10 and 16, 1798. *Gazette,* Mar. 3, 1798. Proceedings, Mar. 13 and 28, 1798.

    4. Scott to Dennis, Feb. 21, 1798. Proceedings, Mar. 22, 1798, Lee contract. Dennis to commrs., Feb. 18, 1798. Dunbar to commrs., Feb. 12, 1798. Blagden to commrs., Mar. 5, 1798. Proceedings, Feb. 27, 1798. Time rolls, NA RG 39.

    5. Lovering to JN, Mar. 30, 1798, JN reels. *Boston Gazette,* Feb. 5, 1798, in Phillips, *Beginnings,* p. 10. *Gazette,* Feb. 24, 1798. Forrest to Clifford, May 22, 1797, Clifford papers.

    6. King diary, Apr. 4, 1797, King papers. King to commrs., Mar. 7, 1798. Proceedings, Feb. 13, 1798. King to unidentified, June 5, 1802, Jefferson Papers. Cranch to A. Adams, Mar. 12, 1798, AFP.

Chapter 67

    1. White to GW, Mar. 10, 1798, GW LC. White to commrs., Mar. 8, 11, 18, 22, and 27, 1798, Apr. 5 and 8, 1798. White to Thornton, Feb. 25, 1798, Mar. 17, 1798, Thornton papers. Commrs. to White, Mar. 13 and 16, 1798, Apr. 12, 1798. TJ to Madison, Mar. 29, 1798, Ford, *Jefferson,* vol. 8. GW to White, Mar. 25, 1798, CHS, vol. 17. *Annals* and *Documentary History of the Capitol,* pp. 80–83. Law diary, Mar. 22, 1798, Law papers. Madison to TJ, Apr. 15, 1798, Hunt, *Writings,* vol. 6.

    2. Thornton never explicitly said he was loath to begin the south wing until Hadfield was gone, but it seems a reasonable explanation for the behavior of a rather jealous man. Commrs. to Adams, Apr. 18, 1798, May 7, 1798.

    3. Proceedings, Apr. 23, 1798. Commrs. to stonecutters, Apr. 16, 1798. White to Miller, Apr. 18, 1798. Blagden to commrs., Apr. 21, 1798. Miller to White, May 1, 1798, commrs.' letters received. Hadfield to commrs., Apr. 24 and 30, 1798.

4. Niemcewicz, *Under Their Vine,* pp. 78ff. Hadfield to commrs., May 14 and 16, 1798. Commrs. to Hoban, May 12, 1798. Smallwood to commrs., June 5, 1798. Purcell to commrs., May 1 and 25, 1798. Commrs. to Hadfield, May 10, 15, 18, and 23, 1798. Commrs. to Hoban and Hadfield, May 4, 1798.

Chapter 68

1. RM to JN, Apr. 13, 1798, Morris letters, Haverford College. Attorney general's opinion, May 1, 1798, commrs.' letters received. Commrs. to Adams, June 8, 1798. Memo in Burnes papers. Mason to Simms, Nov. 30, 1798, Simms papers. Proceedings, May 7, 1798, June 20, 1798. Harbaugh to commrs., Mar. 19, 1802.

2. Polock to commrs., Apr. 12, 1798. Proceedings, June 20, 1798. Commrs. to Thornton, June 22, 1798, Thornton papers. Commrs. to Freire, May 23, 1798. Stoddert to unidentified, July 22, 1798, Stoddert letters HSW.

3. Law diary, Jan. 1798 entries, Law papers, Law to GW, Apr. 1798, GW LC. GW to Law, May 7, 1798, CHS, vol. 17. Piercy to GW, May 23, 1798, GW LC. Niemcewicz, *Under Their Vine.*

4. GW to Adams, June 17, 1798, CHS, vol. 17. Pickering to commrs., June 22, 1798, domestic letters, State Department. Commrs. to Pickering, June 21 and 25, 1798. Thornton memorandum, Thornton papers. Monroe to proprietors, May 8, 1798. Commrs. to Carroll, May 7 and 18, 1798. Cranch to Adams, June 14, 1798, AFP. Duncanson letter in *Alexandria Times,* Oct. 12, 1798. A. Adams to Cranch, July 12, 1798, and to Mrs. Johnson, July 14, 1798, AFP.

Chapter 69

1. Proceedings, Aug. 21, 1798. Commrs. to Hoban, Aug. 21, 1798. Work rolls, NA RG 39. Harbaugh to commrs., Sept. 16, 1798. Blagden to commrs., Sept. 17, 1798. Thornton's plans are in the Thornton papers. Ruth Dalton to A. Adams on absence of commissioners, July 28, 1798, AFP.

2. King to commrs., June 30, 1798. Commrs. to King, Aug. 7, 1798. King memorandum, *U.S. v. Morris,* p. 2253. Pickering to commrs., July 25, 1798. Davidson to Stoddert, Sept. 7, 1798, Davidson papers.

3. Wescott to Law, Sept. 3, 1797 (she did her boasting in 1797 and died during the 1798 epidemic). All newspapers of the period give much coverage to the yellow fever epidemics. *Medical Repository,* 1798, p. 407. Thornton to unidentified, Oct. 10, 1798, Thornton papers. *Gazette* quoted in Phillips,

Beginnings, p. 9. Thornton to GW regarding Francis, Sept. 15, 1798, GW LC.

4. Announcement of sale, Sept. 11, 1798, signed by Monroe, commrs.' letters received. Proceedings, Sept. 11 and 12, 1798. JG to commrs., Sept. 22, 1798. Commrs. to JG, Sept. 24, 1798. Commrs. to Maryland legislature, Dec. 4, 1798.

5. Newspaper clippings, JG papers, LC. A. Adams to Cranch, undated, filed under 1798, AFP.

6. Proceedings, Oct. 2, 1798. Commrs. to Maryland legislature, Oct. 30, 1798. GW to Lee, Sept. 29, 1798, CHS, vol. 17. Lee to commrs., Oct. 9, 1798.

Chapter 70

1. GW to commrs., Sept. 28, 1798, Oct. 4, 17, 22, and 27, 1798, CHS, vol. 17. Commrs. to GW, Oct. 3 and 4, 1798. GW to Thornton, Oct. 18 and 28, 1798, CHS, vol. 17. Law to GW, Sept. 22, 1798, GW LC. Stoddert to GW, Sept. 16, 1798, GW LC. GW to Stoddert, Sept. 26, 1798, Fitzpatrick, *Writings,* vol. 37.

2. Report on Capitol, Nov. 18, 1798, *Documentary History of the Capitol.* Commrs. to Solomon Cotton Co., Oct. 30, 1798.

3. Commrs. to Lee, Apr. 4, 1799. Lee to commrs., Mar. 29, 1799, Apr. 5, 1799. Polock to commrs., Nov. 5 and 20, 1798. Commrs. to Polock, Nov. 5 and 20, 1798. Tax records for 1798, Maryland Archives.

4. Commrs. to Coningham, Nov. 22, 1798. Coningham to commrs., Nov. 24, 1798. Dr. May's accounts, NA RG 39, allowed Apr. 14, 1800. Commrs. to managers of canal lottery, Oct. 22 and 30, 1798.

5. Carroll to commrs., Nov. 12, 1798. Commrs. to Adams, Nov. 29, 1798. Proprietors' memorial, Nov. 10, 1798, *Annals,* Seventh Congress, p. 1306.

Chapter 71

1. Stoddert to Wolcott, Oct. 15, 1798, Wolcott papers. Stoddert to Adams, Nov. 24, 1798, Wolcott papers. Stoddert on recruits, Syrett, *Papers,* vol. 22 p. 298. Adams to his wife, Nov. letters, AFP.

2. Latrobe report, Dec. 29, 1798, Latrobe, *Correspondence,* vol. 1, p. 111. *Centinel,* Feb. 5, 1799.

3. Craik to Lingan et al., Mar. 15, 1799, American Philosophical Society.

4. GW to Thornton, Dec. 20 and 30, 1798, Jan. 30, 1799, Feb. 15, 1799, to Lewis, Jan. 23, 1799, to Lear, Mar. 31, 1799, CHS, vol. 17.

5. Commrs. to Blagden, Jan. 23, 1799. Proceedings, Jan. 15 and 23, 1799. Hoban to commrs., Apr. 18, 1799. Middleton to commrs., Feb. 19, 1799.

6. Harbaugh to commrs., Sept. 29, 1799. Commrs. to Carroll, Jan. 21, 1799. Carroll to commrs., Jan 15, 1799. Attorney general's opinion, Jan. 7, 1799, commrs.' letters received. Commrs. to Pickering, Jan. 31, 1799. Dermott to commrs., Feb. 28, 1799.

7. Clippings, JG papers, LC. *Centinel,* Jan. 18, 25, and 29, 1799. Cranch to mother, Jan. 16, 1799, Cranch papers, MHS.

Chapter 72

1. *Centinel,* Jan. 4, 1799. Reed and Forde papers.

2. Fox to Wallace and Muir, June 3, 1798, NALC papers. Fox to Miller, Feb. 15 and 16, 1799, NALC papers. Lovering to JN, Nov. 5, 1798, JN reels. Commrs. to trustees, Mar. 22, 1799. Agreement with commrs. in Fox's hand, Mar. 22, commrs.' letters received. Trustees to commrs., Mar. 14, 1799.

3. King ad, Apr. 12, 1799, Carroll ad, Mar. 19, 1799, Burnes ad, Feb. 8, 1799, Prout ad, Apr. 12, 1799, Fitzhugh ad, Apr. 19, 1799, Dermott ad, Apr. 2, 1799, all in *Centinel.* Gridley ad, dated Dec. 31, 1798, *Centinel.* Lovering to JN, Mar. 9, 1799, JN reels. Nicklin and Griffith to commrs., Jan. 22, 1799. Brighton, *Lear,* p. 158.

4. Hoban to commrs., Mar. 12 and 28, 1799, Apr. 15, 16, and 18, 1799. Proceedings, Mar. 18, 1799, Apr. 3, 1799. Commrs. to Hoban, Mar. 28, 1799, Apr. 11, 1799. Middleton to commrs., Apr. 1, 1799. Tompkins to commrs., Apr. 9, 1799. *Centinel,* Apr. 9, 12, and 16, 1799. Commrs. to Thornton, Apr. 17, 1799. Thornton to commrs., Apr. 17, 1799, Thornton papers. Purcell to commrs., Apr. 3, 1799. White to commrs., June 4, 1799. Hadfield to commrs., Apr. 23, 1799. White to TJ, July 13, 1802, Padover, *Jefferson,* p. 276.

Chapter 73

1. Law to GW, Apr. 5, 1799, GW LC. Cranch to mother, May 22, 1799, Cranch papers, MHS. Proceedings, Apr. 30, 1799, May 1, 1799. Commrs. to Williams, Mar. 26, 1799.

2. Trustees' report, Apr. 22, 1799, NALC papers. Trustees to commrs., Apr. 27, 1799. Proceedings, Mar. and Apr. 1799, esp. Mar. 21, for sales at

auction. Commrs. to Trustees, May 2, 1799. Turner to JN, Apr. 5, 1799, JN reels.

3. Beall and Gantt to commrs., May 8, 1799. Commrs. to Beall and Gantt, May 9, 1799. Commrs. to Pickering, June 5 and 6, 1799. Thornton to commrs., May 22, 1799. Thornton to GW, May 31, 1799, *Annals,* Seventh Congress, p. 1318. Walker to commrs., May 15, 1799. Walker to GW, Aug. 5, 1799, commrs.' letters received.

4. T. Adams to mother, June 9, 1799, to J. Q. Adams, June 3, 1799, AFP. Tunnicliff to JN, Apr. 9, 1799, JN reels. *Centinel,* Mar. and Apr. 1799. Slipper ad, *Centinel,* June 19, 1799. Wheat to commrs., May 15, 1799. Lovering to JN, Mar. 26, 1799, JN reels. Thornton to GW, Apr. 19 and 24, 1799, June 5, 1799, GW LC. Lincoln to GW, June 4, 1799, GW LC. A. Adams to T. Adams, June 15, 1799, AFP.

5. Commrs. to Dennis, May 22, 1799, June 11, 1799. Dennis to commrs., June 1, 1799. Commrs. to Pierce, May 6, 1799. Proceedings, June 12, 1799.

Chapter 74

1. RM to JN, Jan. 2, 1799, Morris papers HSP. RM and JN deed to trustees, June 1799, Morris papers HSP. Boone to JN, summer 1799; the former sheriff kept up a running commentary on threats to jail JN and himself, JN reels. Cranch to Adams, July 16, 1799, AFP. Trustees to commrs., May 25, 1799. Commrs. to trustees, July 12, 1799. Circular of *Potomac Company,* July 2, 1799, GW LC.

2. Thornton to GW, July 3, 1799, GW LC. Proceedings, July 3, 1799. Hoban to commrs., June 6, 1799, July 20, 1799. King to commrs., Aug. 1, 1799. Commrs. to Hodgson, July 22, 1799. Templeman to commrs., Sept. 3 and 21, 1799. Ad about Dick, *Centinel,* May 24, 1799.

3. Harbaugh to Commrs., July 8, 1799. Commrs. to bidders, July 23, 1799. Proceedings, Aug. 6 and 14, 1799. Marbury ad, *Centinel,* June 18, 1799. Article on Treasury building, Aug. 9, 1799. Law to GW, Aug. 10, 1799, GW LC. Polock to commrs., Aug. 8, 1799.

4. Cranch to parents, Sept. 15, 1799, Cranch papers, MHS. Hanley, *Carroll Papers,* several letters refer to the hospitality of the Youngs. Law to GW, Aug. 10, 1799, GW LC. Blodget to commrs., Sept. 19, 1799. Proceedings, Aug. 27–Sept. 4, 1799. White to Wolcott, Sept. 5 and 19, 1799, Wolcott papers. Thornton to GW, Sept. 1, 1799, GW LC. Ads for lot sales, *Centinel,* Aug. 20, 1799, Sept. 3 and 6, 1799. Forrest attack on trustees, *Centinel,* Sept. 10, 1799.

Chapter 75

1. Commrs. to Adams, Sept. 25, 1799. Proceedings, May 15, 1799. National Capital Planning Commission, *Downtown Urban Renewal,* p. 57. Ridout, *Building the Octagon,* p. 86.

2. Commrs. to Adams, Sept. 25, 1799. Pickering to GW, Aug. 22, 1799, commrs.' letters received.

3. GW to commrs., Aug. 28, 1799, to Francis, Aug. 14, 1799, CHS, vol. 17. Francis to GW, Aug. 17, 1799, GW LC. Thornton to GW, July 19, 1799, GW LC.

4. Proceedings, Sept. 17, 1799, Oct. 1, 1799. Stoddert to Humphreys, Aug. 31, 1799, Humphreys papers. Carroll to commrs., Aug. 20, 27, and 30, 1799. Commrs. to Carroll, Aug. 21, 1799. Marbury to commrs., Nov. 1, 1799. Commrs. to Stoddert, Oct. 30, 1799, Nov. 12, 1799.

5. Commrs. to Kearney, Oct. 16, 1799. Commrs. to Harvey, Sept. 19, 1799. Keepser to Harvey, Oct. 5, 1799, commrs.' letters received. Pickering to commrs., Oct. 30, 1799. Commrs. to Pickering, Nov. 5, 1799.

Chapter 76

1. GW to Thornton, Sept. 29, 1799, Oct. 1 and 6, 1799, CHS, vol. 17. Thornton to GW, July 3, 1799, GW LC.

2. Davidson to Jones, Oct. 30, 1799, Davidson papers. Prout to brother, Oct. 30, 1799, Prout papers. Sheriff's sale ad, Sept. 23, 1799, Langley sale, Oct. 22, 1799, Dalton insolvency, Oct. 24, 1799, O'Neale ad, Nov. 25, 1799, Fenwick runaway, Nov. 26, 1799, all in *Centinel.* Cranch to mother, Nov. 23, 1799, Cranch papers, MHS. JG to Pratt, Nov. 7, 1799, NALC papers. Proceedings, Nov. 12, 1799.

3. Commrs. to Maryland legislature, Dec. 9, 1799. Proceedings, Dec. 9, 1799. Commrs. to Adams, Nov. 21, 1799. Hoban's report on buildings, Nov. 18, 1799, CR LC. Stoddert to commrs., Nov. 29, 1799. Stoddert to trustees, Dec. 5, 1799, Knox, *Quasi War,* vol. 4.

4. Liston papers and Mrs. Liston's journal, FO5, LC. GW to Thornton, Dec. 8, 1799, to White, Dec. 8, 1799, Fitzpatrick, *Writings,* vol. 37. Thornton to GW, Nov. 13, 1799. GW to Thornton, Nov. 18, 1799, CHS, vol. 17. *Annals,* Sixth Congress, p. 208.

5. Monroe to commrs., Dec. 16 and 22, 1799. Scott to commrs., Dec. 23, 1799.

6. Description of Washington, misc. MS., LC. White to Adams, Dec. 13, 1799, AFP.

Chapter 77

1. Mrs. Washington to Adams, *Annals.* Thornton to Marshall, Jan. 2, 1800, Thornton papers. White to Adams, Dec. 13, 1799, AFP. Stoddert to commrs., Jan 2, 1800, Knox, *Quasi War,* vol. 5, p. 28. Commrs. to Dennis, Jan. 6, 1800. Proceedings, Jan. 1800. Commrs. to Stoddert, Jan. 7, 1800. White to Adams, Jan. 15 and 28, 1800, AFP.

2. Forrest to commrs., Jan 7, 1800. Commrs. to Key, Feb. 18, 1800. Key to commrs., Feb 5, 1800. Thornton to unidentified, Feb. 21, 1800, Thornton papers. Commrs. to J. Davidson, Jan. 6, 1800. J. Davidson to commrs., Jan. 12, 1800. Commrs. to Lingan, Feb. 24, 1800, to governor of Maryland, Feb. 15 and 28, 1800. Forrest and Lingan to commrs., Feb. 28, 1800.

3. Thornton to Stoddert, Jan. 30, 1800, Thornton papers. Stoddert to Thornton, Jan. 20, 1800, Thornton papers. CHS, vol. 10, p. 91. Cranch to A. Adams, Jan. 28, 1800, AFP. A. Adams to Cranch, Feb. 3, 1800, AFP. Thornton to unidentified, Feb. 21, 1800, Thornton papers.

4. Lovering ad, *Centinel,* May 1, 1800. Thornton's ownership of northeast corner of square 171, in CHS, vol. 18. Most sources describing Thornton's design of the Octagon cite no specific contemporary references, nor is there any reference to Lovering having designed it, but he was a far less prominent man, and no mention is made of other houses he designed. CHS, vol. 10, pp. 92, 102, 215.

Chapter 78

1. Stoddert to Tingey, Jan. 22, 1800, Knox, *Quasi War,* vol. 5, p. 113. Tingey to Stoddert, Knox, *Quasi War,* vol. 5, p. 212. Tingey to wife, Jan. 25, 1800, Tingey papers HSW. Tingey to commrs., Feb. 25, 1800. Johnson ad, *Centinel,* dated Apr. 19, 1800.

2. Forrest to Pickering, Feb. 26, 1800, Pickering papers. Commrs. to Caldwell, Apr. 21, 1800. Forrest to commrs., Apr. 22, 1800. Agreement for Dalton house, Aug. 18, 1800, War Department, letters received, National Archives.

3. CHS, vol. 10, pp. 112, 116. Cranch to mother, Jan. 29, 1800, Cranch papers, MHS. Law to JG, Apr. 9, 1800, AFP.

4. Johnson to Adams, Apr. 8, 1800, AFP. Thornton to TJ, May 7, 1800, Thornton papers. On letter to White, CHS, vol. 10, p. 107. *Annals,* Sixth Congress, Apr. 4, 1800. Lee to Carroll, Apr. 26, 1800, Carroll papers. Liston to Grenville, May 28, 1800, FO 5.

5. Highflyer ad, Mar. 28, 1799, Punch ad, Mar. 24, 1799, Holt ad, Mar.

7, 1799, all in *Centinel*. CHS, vol. 10, p. 100. Cranch to mother, May 18, 1800. Commrs. to Smallwood, Mar. 12, 1800. Proceedings, Apr. 15 and 21, 1800. Dove to commrs., Mar. 31, 1800. Commrs. to Stoddert, Apr. 19, 1800. Rogers to commrs., Apr. 23, 1800.

Chapter 79

1. A. Adams to Mrs. W. Cranch, Apr. 17, 1800, Cranch papers, LC. Carroll to Cranch, Apr. 19, 1800, AFP. Cranch to A. Adams, Apr. 24, 1800, AFP. Liston to Grenville, May 28, 1800, FO 5.

2. L'Enfant to commrs., May 30, 1800, Caemmerer, *L'Enfant*, p. 397.

3. Commrs. to Stoddert, Apr. 14 and 19, 1800, May 21, 1800. Stoddert to commrs., May 15, 1800, Knox, *Quasi War*, vol. 5, p. 518. Stoddert to secretaries of war, state, and the Treasury, May 15, 1800, Knox, *Quasi War*, vol. 5, p. 519. Proceedings, May 28, 1800.

4. Steiner, *McHenry*. On removal, Busey, *Pictures*, pp. 64ff. Stoddert to clerks, June 7, 1800, Knox, *Quasi War*, vol. 6, p. 26. Steele to commrs., May 24, 1800.

5. Harrison and Maynadier Co. to commrs., May 27, 1800. Commrs. to Keepser, May 29, 1800. Dennis to commrs., May 17, 1800. Commrs. to Harbaugh, May 9, 1800. Work rolls, NA RG 39. CHS, vol. 10, pp. 151–52. Shaw to A. Adams, June 8, 1800, AFP. *Centinel*, June 6 and 13, 1800. Adams to wife, June 13, 1800, to Gerry, June 13, 1800, AFP.

Chapter 80

1. Cranch to mother, June 14, 1800, Cranch papers, MHS. List of balances due, CR LC, also in commrs. to President Bank of Columbia, Oct. 10, 1799. Tingey ad on not disputing sales, *Centinel*, June 27, 1800. Bourne to Lear, Mar. 29, 1799, Perkins to Lear, Mar. 6, 1800, Lear papers.

2. Stoddert to Truxton, June 24, 1800, to Burrows, June 23, 1800, Knox, *Quasi War*, vol. 6, pp. 74, 77. Proceedings, June 4, 1800. Commrs. to cabinet, June 18, 1800. Commrs. to Stoddert, June 23, 1800.

3. King to commrs., May 8, 1800, July 9, 1800. Commrs. to cabinet, July 10, 1800. Proceedings, June 24, 1800.

4. Wolcott to wife, July 4, 1800, Gibbs, *Memoir*, p. 376. Wagner to Pickering, Pickering papers. General accounts, NA RG 217. Claxton to commrs., July 18, 1800.

5. Wilkinson to Hamilton, July 28, 1800, Syrett, *Papers*, vol. 25. CHS, vol. 10, p. 179. *Centinel*, July 11, 1800. Commrs. to Huddlestone, July 9,

1800, to O'Hara and Craig, July 10, 1800, to Grundy, July 30, 1800. Harrison and Maynadier Co. to commrs., July 28, 1800.

6. Commrs. to Stoddert, July 31, 1800. Commrs. to Mason, July 25 and 28, 1800. Proceedings, Sept. 12, 1800, regarding Johnson. Commrs. to Forrest, July 30, 1800.

Chapter 81

1. S. H. Smith to Bayard, Aug. 5, 12, and 22, 1800, Smith papers. Bayard to Smith, Aug. 14, 1800, Smith papers. Dermott to commrs., May 13, 1800. House census in Padover, *Jefferson*, p. 252. Claxton to commrs., July 18, 1800. Sweeny ad, June 10, 1800, Carroll ad, Sept. 30, 1800, *Centinel*. Hunt, *Forty Years*, p. 9.

2. CHS, vol. 10, pp. 163, 221. Wignall to commrs., July 8, 1800. Blodget to commrs., May 8, 1800, Aug. 25, 1800.

3. *Dunlop, Carleton, and Scott v. Morris, Nicholson, and Trustees*, Feb. term, 1800, Chancery Court cases. Tingey to commrs., Aug. 1, 1800. Proceedings, Aug. and Sept. 1800. CHS, vol. 10, p. 177. Commrs. to Forrest, Aug. 28, 1800. Commrs. to Marshall, Aug. 27, 1800.

4. Commrs. to Prater, Aug. 13, 1800. Proceedings, Aug. 19 and 21, 1800. Sale of material, Proceedings, Sept. 16, 1800. Rush to commrs., Aug. 20, 1800. Stoddert to Law, Sept. 9, 1800, to commrs., Sept. 9, 1800, Knox, *Quasi War*, vol. 6, p. 336. Contract with Harbaugh, Proceedings, Sept. 11, 1800. Commrs. to Stoddert, Sept. 3 and 16, 1800.

5. Barry to commrs., Aug. 4, 1800. Commrs. to Mrs. Fenwick, Aug. 8 and 21, 1800. Carroll to commrs., Aug. 2 and 25, 1800. King to commrs., July 30, 1800.

6. "Pastoral on the Epidemic," Aug. 26, 1800, Hanley, *Carroll Papers*. CHS, vol. 10, p. 193.

Chapter 82

1. Margaret Smith to sister, Oct. 5, 1800, S. H. Smith papers, with letters to her father.

2. Wagner to Pickering, Sept. 23, 1800, Pickering papers. *Norwich Courier*, Sept. 3, 1800, Oct. 8, 1800.

3. Cranch to mother, Oct. 11, 1800, Cranch papers, MHS. A. Adams to Mrs. Johnson, Oct. 10, 1800, AFP.

4. Knox, *Quasi War*, vol. 6, p. 105. On Bridge St, *Centinel*, Aug. 12, 1800. Polock ads, *Centinel*, Aug. 15 and Sept. 15, 1800. Deblois v. Marbury, *Centinel*, Sept. 24, 1800.

5. CHS, vol. 10, p. 196. Commrs. to Wolcott, Sept. 30, 1800. Commrs. to Mason, Sept. 23, 1800, Oct. 2 and 8, 1800.

6. Proceedings, Oct. 3, 20, 22, 24, and 27, 1800. Claxton to Adams, Nov. 3, 1800, AFP. Carpenters to commrs., Oct. 1800. Commrs. to Stoddert, Oct. 24, 1800. Commrs. to Hoban, Oct. 24, 1800. Hoban to commrs., Oct. 29, 1800. Claxton to commrs., Oct. 28, 1800. CHS. vol. 10, p. 191.

7. Margaret Smith journal, Oct. entries, Smith papers. Smith to his sister, Oct. 10, 1800, Smith papers.

Chapter 83

1. CHS, vol. 10, p. 208. Adams to wife, Nov. 2, 1800, AFP. Proceedings, Nov. 15, 1800. Claxton to Adams, Nov. 3, 1800, AFP.

2. Margaret Smith journal, Nov. 4, 1800, S. H. Smith papers. Proceedings, Nov. 3, 1800. Claxton to commrs., Nov. 8, 1800. Carroll to commrs., Nov. 12, 1800. Commrs. to cabinet, Oct. 31, 1800. Hogan to commrs., Nov. 10, 1800. Proceedings, Nov. 14, 1800.

3. Jackson's ad for lot, *Intelligencer*, Nov. 12, 1800. *Annals*, seventh Congress, p. 1363. Many newspapers had reports on the fire; one is in Steiner, *McHenry*, p. 476.

4. A. Adams to sister, Nov. 21, 1800, Adams, *New Letters*. A. Adams to Smith, Nov. 22, 1800, Adams, *Letters*. A. Adams to Tufts, Nov. 28, 1800, AFP. T. Adams. to J. Q. Adams, Dec. 6, 1800, AFP. *National Democratic Quarterly*, Nov. 1859, L'Enfant papers.

5. Liston to Grenville, Nov. 28, 1800, FO 5. Bayard to Rodney, Jan. 5, 1801, Donnan, *American Historical Association Report*, p. 117. Cranch to mother, Jan. 11, 1801, Cranch papers, MHS. Gallatin to wife, Jan. 15, 1801, Adams, *Gallatin*. Otis to Foster, Nov. 25, 1800, Otis papers.

6. A. Adams to Tufts, Nov. 28, 1800, Otis papers. Ad for Tom, *Intelligencer*, Dec. 26, 1800. Ad for Robert, *Centinel*, Dec. Ad for Fidelio, *Intelligencer*, Dec. 19, 1800. McIntyre ad, *Centinel*, Nov. 4, 1800. Justice article, *Intelligencer*, Dec. 3, 1800. Soderstrom to L'Enfant, Dec. 27, 1800, L'Enfant papers. Hadfield to TJ, Mar. 27, 1801, Padover, *Jefferson*, p. 200. CHS, vol. 10, p. 215. Gallatin to wife, Jan. 15, 1801, Adams, *Gallatin*. Hunt, *Forty Years*, p. 4.

Chapter 84

1. Wolcott to wife, Dec. 4, 1800, Gibbs, *Memoir*, p. 456. CHS, vol. 10, p. 214. *Baltimore American*, Nov. 22, 1800.

2. Richardson, *Messages*, vol. 1, pp. 298ff. Perhaps the most frequently

quoted description of the city in 1800 is by Representative John Cotton Smith, Federalist of Connecticut, who described Pennsylvania Avenue as a morass covered with alder bushes. Smith wrote it sometime in the 1840s, however, and by that time descriptions of Washington (as well as those of New York, Baltimore, and other cities) emphasized the rude conditions of earlier times, the better to highlight the advances made. For a similar reason, I do not make much use of the descriptions of Christian Hines, who recalled what the city was like seventy years after his boyhood experiences in it. On the price of the Washington Assembly, CHS, vol. 10, p. 215.

3. *Intelligencer*, Nov. 28, 1800. A. Adams to sister, Dec. 1, 1800, Adams, *New Letters*. CHS, vol. 10, p. 219.

4. Proceedings, Nov. 1800. Commrs. to Lee, Dec. 10, 1800. Walker ad, *Intelligencer*, Nov. 26, 1800. *Annals*, sixth Congress, p. 730. Proceedings, Dec. 3 and 6, 1800. Arbuckle, *Nicholson*.

5. *Annals*, pp. 816ff. *Intelligencer*, Dec. 3 and 17, 1800.

6. Forrest to commrs., Nov. 21, 1800. Proceedings, Dec. 19, 1800. White to commrs., Dec. 20, 1800. CHS, vol. 10, p. 224. L'Enfant to Congress, Dec. 10, 1800, Kite, *L'Enfant*, and Caemmerer, *L'Enfant*. Clark to commrs., Jan. 12, 1801. Clark to Wolcott, Jan. 10, 1801, Wolcott papers.

7. CHS, vol. 10, p. 220. *Intelligencer*, Dec. 24, 26, 29, and 31, 1800; Woodward essays also formed a pamphlet.

8. *Intelligencer*, Dec. 24, 1800. A. Adams undated memo, Jan. 1801, AFP.

Chapter 85

1. Biographies of all the major characters in the historical drama cover the election crisis. Steiner, *McHenry*, has the most primary documents generated by Federalists.

2. Gallatin to wife, Jan. letters, Adams, *Gallatin*.

3. Davidson to Swan, Feb. 20, 1801, Davidson letterbook. Blodget and others to Adams, Jan. 5, 1801, AFP. Cranch to Simms, Jan. 11, 1801, Simms papers. Commrs. to Adams, Jan. 29, 1801. Proceedings, Jan. 19, 1801. Mrs. Thornton's biography of her husband in Thornton papers.

4. *Annals*, p. 1371. Proceedings, Jan. 31, 18012. A. Adams to T. Adams, Jan. 15, 1801, AFP.

5. *National Democratic Quarterly*, Nov. 1859, L'Enfant papers. Otis to wife, Morison, *Otis*, p. 8. Hunt, *Forty Years*, p. 10. *Intelligencer*, Feb. 1801.

6. Clerk's memorial, Jan. 29, 1801, NA RG 233 (petitions to Congress). *Annals*. Alexandria petition, NA RG 233. Report on meeting of citizens, *Intelligencer*, Jan. 16, 1801. Essays on city government, *Intelligencer*, Jan. 30, 1801, Feb. 2, 1801.

7. TJ's *Anas*, Washington, *Works*, vol. 9, p. 210. Adams to Gerry, Feb. 10, 1801. Morison, *Otis*, p. 10. Smith to Coxe, Feb. 13, 1801. Griswold report, *Annals* and *American State Papers*, class 10. Griswold letter, Green, *Washington*, p. 23. Tyler to Monroe, Feb. 11, 1801, Monroe papers. Tazewell to Monroe, Feb. 12, 1801, Monroe papers. Cranch to A. Adams, Feb. 20, 1801, AFP.

Epilogue

1. J. Q. Adams diary, Aug. 14 and 15, 1820, AFP. Cranch to A. Adams, Feb. 20, 1801, A. Adams to J. Q. Adams, Sept. 13, 1801, Louisa to J. Q. Adams, Sept. 16 and 22, 1801, all in AFP. Bemis, *Adams and the Foundations*, p. 276.

2. *Intelligencer*, Aug. 20, 1820. King and Latrobe to superintendent, Oct. 18, 1815.

3. *Intelligencer*, Aug. 23, 1820. National Capital Planning Commission, *Downtown Urban Renewal*, pp. 21ff.

4. Latrobe report, footnote to Dec. 1, 1804, Report on Public Buildings, Latrobe, *Correspondence*, vol. 1, p. 583.

5. Stoddert to Rutledge, Apr. 21, 1804, Rutledge papers. Latrobe, *Journal*, Aug. 12, 1806. Tilghman to Dulany, Apr. 19, 1848, NALC papers. Otis to S. H. Otis, Feb. 2, 1817, Otis papers. Munroe to TJ, Nov. 15, 1808, Padover, *Jefferson*.

6. Law to Eustis, Aug. 4, 1802, Eustis papers. Willson, *Friendly Relations*, p. 66. Warder, *Chorographical and Statistical Description*. Louisa to J. Q. Adams, 1804 letters, AFP. Davidson ledger, Dec. 31, 1803. L'Enfant on Soderstrom, 1804; L'Enfant to Commrs., Apr. 28, 1808; Digges to Monroe, Oct. 26, 1816; L'Enfant to Bailey, Nov. 18, 1823; Bailey to L'Enfant, Feb. 4, 1824, L'Enfant papers. *Intelligencer*, Dec. 12, 1821.

Bibliography

Manuscript Sources

Entries marked with an asterisk are the more important sources.

Library of Congress

William Bingham papers
Sylvanus Bourne papers
Daniel Carroll of Duddington papers*
Commissioners of the District of Columbia records*
William Cranch papers
Samuel Davidson letterbook and ledger*
Andrew Ellicott papers
William Eustis papers
Foreign Office Copying Project (Great Britain, Foreign office) vols. 4 and 5
James Greenleaf papers
Holland Land Company papers (which include the Theophile Cazenove letterbook)*
Thomas Jefferson papers*
James Kent papers
Nicholas King papers
Thomas Law papers
Tobias Lear papers
Pierre L'Enfant papers in Digges-L'Enfant-Morgan papers*
Mr. and Mrs. Robert Liston journals and letters
James Monroe papers
Robert Morris letterbook*
John Nicholson papers
Shippen papers
Charles Simms papers
Samuel Harrison Smith papers*
William L. Smith papers
Walter Stewart papers

Benjamin Stoddert papers
Rebecca Lowndes Stoddert papers
William Thornton papers*
Thomas Tingey papers
Washington family papers
George Washington papers*

Historical Society of Pennsylvania

Chalmers Allen papers
Clement Biddle letterbook
William Bingham letterbook
Clifford-Pemburton papers
Tench Coxe papers
James Greenleaf papers*
Joshua Humphreys papers
Robert Morris ledgers and papers*
John Nicholson letterbooks*
North American Land Company papers*
Reed and Forde papers
Walter Stewart papers

Historical Museum of Pennsylvania

John Nicholson correspondence* (no copy of this crucial collection, which
    is microfilmed, is in Washington, D.C.)

Massachusetts Historical Society

Adams family papers*
William Cranch papers*
Harrison Gray Otis papers
Timothy Pickering papers

Connecticut Historical Society

John Trumbull papers
Oliver Wolcott papers

Haverford College Quaker Collection

Robert Morris letters

American Philosophical Society

A few very interesting letters

New York Historical Society

Van Ness-Phillip papers for Burnes material*

New York Public Library

William Constable papers
William Cranch papers*
James Greenleaf papers[1]
Thomas Law papers

Duke University

Rutledge papers

Historical Society of Washington, D.C.

James Barry account book
James Greenleaf papers*
William Prout papers*
A few letters from Benjamin Stoddert

Maryland Archives

Chancery Court cases
Tax records of 1798

National Archives

Commissioners' proceedings, letters sent, and letters received (on microfilm)*
Record Group 42: ledgers; division sheets; contracts; estimates and proposals; schedule of sales of public lots; platbook of Carrollsburg and Hamburg; records relating to selections by Greenleaf, Morris, and Nicholson; records relating to accounts of Greenleaf, Morris, Nicholson, Forrest, and Stoddert; and papers relating to accounts of various persons and

firms exclusive of the accounts of Greenleaf, Morris, Nicholson, Forrest, and Stoddert

Record Group 39: vouchers and time rolls of the commissioners, arranged by date of payment

Record Group 233: petitions to Congress

Domestic letters and miscellaneous letters of the State Department (on microfilm)*

War Department letters received (on microfilm)

Record Group 217: general accounts (on microfilm)

Supreme Court Appelate file (on microfilm), containing the voluminous record of Pratt et al. v. Law, v. Duncanson, and v. Carroll*

Newspapers

There are considerable gaps in the newspaper record.

Georgetown Weekly Ledger
Georgetown Centinel of Liberty
Washington Impartial Observer
Washington Gazette
National Intelligencer
Washington Federalist
Maryland Journal
Virginia Gazette

Boston and Philadelphia papers had periodic reports on the federal city, including the *Gazette of the United States, Claypool's Gazette, Philadelphia Gazette,* in Philadelphia; *Columbian Centinel* and *Boston Gazette* in Boston. Also consulted were the *Norwich Current* and *Medical Repository*, a magazine, published in New York City.

Primary Sources

Abbot, W. W., *The Papers of George Washington*. Charlottesville: University Press of Virginia, 1987.

Adams, Abigail, *New Letters of Abigail Adams*. Stewart Mitchell, ed. Boston: Houghton Mifflin, 1947.

Adams, Charles Francis, *Letters of Mrs. Adams*. Boston: Little, Brown, 1841.

———, *The Works of John Adams*. Boston: Little, Brown, 1854.

Adams, Henry, *Life of Albert Gallatin*. Philadelphia: Lippincott & Co., 1879.

American Historical Association Report, 1903. "Letters of French Ministers to the United States." Washington, D.C.: Government Printing Office, 1945.

American State Papers: 1789–1809. Class 10, Vol. 1. Washington, D.C.: Gales and Seaton, 1834–61.

Annals of Congress, 1789–1802. Washington, D.C.: Gales and Seaton, 1835–56.

Blodget, Samuel, *Economica: A Statistical Manual for the United States of America.* New York: A. M. Kelley, 1964.

Bowling, Kenneth R. and Helen E. Veit, eds., *The Diary of William Maclay.* Baltimore: Johns Hopkins University Press, 1988.

———, *Documentary History of the First Federal Congress.* Baltimore: Johns Hopkins University Press.

Boyd, Julian, ed. *The Papers of Thomas Jefferson.* Princeton: N.J.: Princeton University Press, 1950–89.

Burnett, Edmund C., *Letters of Members of the Continental Congress.* Washington, D.C.: Government Printing Office, 1941.

Currie, William, *An Historical Account of the Climates and Diseases of the United States of America.* Philadelphia: 1792.

Documentary History of the Constitution and Development of the United States Capitol Building and Grounds. House Report 646, 58th Congress, 2nd session. Washington, D.C.: Government Printing Office, 1904.

Donnan, Elizabeth, *American Historical Association Report 1913: Papers of James A. Bayard.* Washington, D.C.: Government Printing Office, 1915.

"Expostulations of Potowmac," Broadside collection, LC, Evans microfilm 22076.

Fitzpatrick, John C., ed. *Diaries of George Washington.* New York: Houghton Mifflin, 1925.

———, *The Writings of George Washington. Vols. 30–37.* Washington, D.C.: Government Printing Office, 1931–40.

Ford, Emily, *Notes on the Life of Noah Webster.* New York: privately printed, 1912.

Ford, Paul L., *The Writings of Thomas Jefferson.* New York: G. P. Putnam, 1892–99.

Gibbs, George, *Memoir of the Administration of Washington and John Adams.* New York: W. Van Norden, 1846. For Wolcott's letters.

Hanley, Thomas O'Brien, S.J., ed., *The John Carroll Papers*. Notre Dame, Ind.: University of Notre Dame Press, 1976.

Harrison, Eliza Cope, *Philadelphia Merchant*: the Diary of Thomas P. Cope 1800–1851. South Bend Ind.: Gateway Editions, 1978.

Hunt, Galliard, ed., *The First Forty Years of Washington Society in the Family Letters of Margaret Bayard Smith*. New York: F. Ungar Publishing Co., 1965.

————ed., *The Writings of James Madison*. New York: G. P. Putnam, 1900–1910.

Journals of the Continental Congress. Washington, D.C.: Government Printing Office, 1904–37.

Knox, Dudley, ed., *The Quasi War*. Washington, D.C.: Naval Historical Foundation, 1937.

La Rochefoucauld-Liancourt, François Alexandre Frederic, Duc de, *Travels through the United States of North America in the Years 1795, 1796, 1797*. London: R. Phillips, 1799.

La Tour du Pin, Gouvernet, Henriette Lucie (Dillon) Marquise de, *Memoirs of Madame La Tour du Pin*. New York: McCall Publishing, 1971.

Latrobe, Benjamin, *Correspondence and Miscellaneous Papers of Benjamin Henry Latrobe*. John Van Horne, ed. New Haven: Conn.: Yale University Press, 1984.

————, *The Virginia Journals of Benjamin Henry Latrobe*. Edward Carter, ed. New Haven, Conn.: Yale University Press, 1977.

————, *The Journals of Benjamin Henry Latrobe*. Edward Carter, ed. New Haven, Conn.: Yale University Press, 1980.

Look Before You Leap, or a Few Hints to such artisans, mechanics, labourers, farmers and husbandmen, as are desirous of emigrating to America, being a genuine collection of letters from persons who have emigrated, . . . particularly to the Federal City of Washington. London: 1796.

Louis-Philippe, *Diary of My Travels in America*. New York: Delacorte Press, 1977.

Niemcewicz, Julian, *Under Their Vine and Fig Tree: Travels Through America 1797–1799, 1805*. Metche Budka, ed. Elizabeth, N.J.: Grassman Publishing Co., 1965.

O'Connor, John, "Political Opinions." Rare book collection, LC. Evans microfilm, 22072.

Padover, Saul K., ed., *Thomas Jefferson and the National Capital*. Washington, D.C.: Government Printing Office, 1946.

Pugh, Wilma J., *Talleyrand in America as a Financial Promoter*. Washington, D.C.: Government Printing Office, 1942.

Richardson, J. D., *A Compilation of the Messages and Papers of the President. Vol. 1*. Washington, D.C.: Government Printing Office, 1896.

Rutland, Robert, et al., eds., *Papers of James Madison*. Charlottesville: University of Virginia Press, 1977.

Smith, William L., "Journal of William Loughton Smith 1790–91." Massachusetts Historical Society Proceedings, vol. 51. Boston: 1958.

Smith, William L. (attributed to), "Political Opinions Particularly Respecting the Seat of the Federal Empire," Rare book collection, LC, Evans microfilm 22072.

Stephen, Adam, "The Expostulations of Potowmac." Broadside collection, LC, Evans microfilm 22076.

Syrett, Harold, et al., eds. *Papers of Alexander Hamilton*. New York: Columbia University Press, 1961–79.

Twining, Thomas, *Travels in America 100 Years Ago*. New York: Harper and Brothers, 1894.

United States v. Martin F. Morris et al. Record in the Supreme Court of the District of Columbia (The Potomac Flats Case). Washington: 1898.

Warden, David B., *A Chorographical and Statistical Description of the District of Columbia*. Paris: 1816.

Washington, H. A., *The Writings of Thomas Jefferson*. Washington, D.C.: Taylor & Maury, 1854.

Weems, Mason Locke, *Mason Locke Weems, his Works and Ways*. Emily Ford Skeel, ed. New York: Plimpton Press, 1929.

Weld, Isaac, Jr., *Travels through the States of North America and Provinces of Upper and Lower Canada during the years 1795, 1796, 1797*. London: John Stockdale, 1799.

Secondary Sources Pertaining to Washington, D.C.

Bemis, Samuel F., *John Quincy Adams and the Foundations of American Foreign Policy*. New York: Knopf, 1956.

———*John Quincy Adams and the Union*. New York: Knopf, 1956.

Bowling, Kenneth, *Creating the Federal City 1774–1800*. Washington, D.C.: American Institute of Architects Press, 1988.

Brown, Glenn, *History of the United States Capitol*. U.S. Senate Document 60, 56th Congress, 1st session. Washington, D.C.: Government Printing Office, 1902.

Bryan, Wilhelmus B., *A History of the National Capital*. New York: Macmillan, 1914.

Busey, Samuel, *Pictures of the City of Washington in the Past*. Washington, D.C.: William Ballantyne and Sons, 1898.

Butler, Jeanne F., *Competition 1792: Designing a Nation's Capitol*. Washington, D.C.: U.S. Capitol Historical Society, 1976.

Caemmemer, H. Paul, *The Life of Pierre Charles L'Enfant, Planner of the City Beautiful, The City of Washington*. Washington, D.C.: National Republic Publishing Co., 1950.

Clark, Allen C., *Greenleaf and Law in the Federal City*. Washington, D.C.: W. F. Roberts, 1901.

Columbia Historical Society Records. Vol. 10, "Mrs. Thornton's Diary." Vol. 17, "Writings of Washington Relating to the National Capital. Vol. 18, "Dr. and Mrs. William Thornton." Vols. 35–36, "Origins of the Federal City." Washington, D.C.: Historical Society of Washington, D.C.

Eberlein, Harold, and Cortlandt Hubbard, *Historic Houses of Georgetown & Washington City*. Richmond, Va.: Dietz Press, 1958.

Green, Constance M., *Washington: Village and Capital 1800–1878*. Princeton, N.J.: Princeton University Press, 1962.

Hazleton, George, Jr., *The National Capitol: Its Architecture Art and History*. New York: J. J. Little, 1897.

Hines, Christian, *Early Recollections of Washington City*. Washington, D.C.: Junior League, 1981.

Kite, Elizabeth, *L'Enfant and Washington, 1791–1792*. Baltimore: Johns Hopkins University Press, 1929.

National Capital Planning Commission, *Downtown Urban Renewal Landmarks*. Washington, D.C.: Government Printing Office, 1970.

Phillips, P. Lee. *The Beginnings of Washington as Described in Books, Maps, and Views*. Washington, D.C.: privately printed, 1917.

Ridout, Orlando V., *Building the Octagon*. Washington, D.C.: American Institute of Architects Press, 1989.

Seale, William, *The President's House*. Washington, D.C.: White House Historical Association, 1986.

Thatcher, Erastus, *Founding of Washington City*. Washington, D.C.: Law Reporter Co., 1891.

Tindall, William, *Standard History of the City of Washington*. Knoxville, Tenn.: H. W. Crew and Co., 1914.

Other Secondary Sources

Alberts, Robert C., *The Golden Voyage: Life and Times of William Bingham*. Boston: Houghton Mifflin, 1969.

Arbuckle, Robert, *Pennsylvania Speculator and Patriot: John Nicholson*. University Park: Pennsylvania State University, 1975.

Bacon-Foster, Cora, *Early Chapters in the Development of the Potomac Route to the West*. Washington, D.C.: Historical Society of Washington, D.C., 1912.

Bailyn, Bernard, *Voyagers to the West*. New York: Knopf, 1986.

Bedini, Silvio, *The Life of Benjamin Banneker*. New York: Scribner, 1972.

Brant, Irving, *James Madison: Father of the Constitution*. Indianapolis: Ind.: Bobbs-Merrill, 1948.

Brighton, Ray, *The Checkered Career of Tobias Lear*. Portsmouth, N.H.:Portsmouth Marine Society, 1985.

Burnett, Edmund C., *The Continental Congress*. New York: Macmillan, 1941.

Combs, Jerald A., *The Jay Treaty*. Berkeley: University of California Press, 1970.

Craven, Avery, *Soil Exhaustion as a Factor in the Agricultural History of Virginia and Maryland*. Urbana: University of Illinois Press, 1926.

Davis, Joseph S., *Essays in the Earlier History of American Corporations*. Cambridge, Mass.: Harvard University Press, 1917, For information on the Society for the Promotion of Useful Manufactures.

Davis, Matthew L., *Memoirs of Aaron Burr*. New York: Harper & Row, 1837.

Delaplaine, Edward S., *Life of Thomas Johnson*. New York: Hitchcock, 1927.

Doerflinger, Thomas M., *A Vigorous Spirit of Enterprise: Merchants and*

Economic Development in Revolutionary Philadelphia. Chapel Hill: University of North Carolina Press, 1986.

Flexner, James, *George Washington and the New Nation*. Boston: Little, Brown and Company, 1969.

Freeman, Douglas S., *George Washington: A Biography*. New York: Scribner, 1948–57.

Geiger, Mary Virginia, *Daniel Carroll*. Washington, D.C.: Catholic University of America Press, 1943.

Goebel, Julian, Jr., and Joseph H. Smith, *The Law Practice of Alexander Hamilton*. New York: Columbia University Press, 1964. Primarily of interest for essays on Morris's land speculations in New York.

James, Marquis, *Biography of a Business: Insurance Company of North America*. Indianapolis, Ind.: Bobbs-Merrill, 1942.

Matthews, Catherine V., *Andrew Ellicott: His Life and Letters*. New York: Grafton Press, 1908.

Morison, Samuel E., *Life and Letters of Harrison Gray Otis*. Boston: Houghton Mifflin, 1913.

Palmer, Michael, *Stoddert's War*. Columbia: University of South Carolina Press, 1987.

Pomerantz, Sidney I. *New York: an American City*. New York: Ira J. Friedman, 1965.

Powell, John H., *Bring Out Your Dead*. Philadelphia: University of Pennsylvania Press, 1949.

Renzullia, L. Marx, *Maryland: The Federalist Years*. Rutherford, N.J.: Fairleigh Dickinson University Press, 1973.

Reps, John W., *The Making of Urban America: A History of City Planning in the United States*. Princeton, N.J.: Princeton University Press, 1965.

Riley, James C., *The Eighteenth Century Campaign to Avoid Disease*. New York: St. Martin's Press, 1987.

Schama, Simon, *The Breaking of the Dykes: Revolution and Government in the Netherlands*. New York: Knopf, 1977.

Scharf, J. Thomas, *History of Western Maryland*. Baltimore, Md.: Regional Publishing Co., 1968.

Steiner, Bernard C., *Life and Correspondence of James McHenry*. Cleveland, Ohio: Burrows Brothers Co., 1907.

Stewart, Donald H., *The Opposition Press of the Federalist Period*. Albany: State University of New York Press, 1969.

Willson, Beckles, *Friendly Relations: A Narrative of Britain's Ministers and Ambassadors to America*. Boston: Little, Brown, 1934.

The Massachusetts Historical Society gave permission to quote from the Adams family papers, the Cranch family papers, the Otis papers, and the Pickering papers. The New York Historical Society gave permission to quote from the Van Ness–Phillip papers.

Index

Adams, Abigail: in president's house, 594–96, 598, 601, 602, 606, 613; opinion of city, 487–88, 554, 563; *see also* William Cranch

Adams, John: argues with White, 478–80; lack of interest in city, 463, 464, 525, 534; and president's house, 549, 550, 553, 592ff; and residence debate, 15, 16; supports commissioners, 429ff, 445; visits city, 568–70; *see also* elections of 1796 and 1800

Adams, John Q., 587, 595, 619, 620

Adams, Thomas, 502, 523–25, 594, 595

African Americans, 25, 39, 121, 153, 187, 408, 412, 457, 512, 574; *see also* slaves

Alexandria, Va., 15, 18, 23, 33, 34, 300, 615

amusements, 387, 434, 485, 584, 614

Andrews, George, 562, 590, 592, 602, 605

anti-Irish sentiment, 290, 355, 444, 456, 457

anti-Semitism, 256, 433

Appleton, Nathaniel, 184, 185, 224ff, 233, 237, 239, 242

Architects and Carpenters Society, 225

art and artists, 105, 107, 113, 115, 116, 156, 249, 272, 292, 293, 354, 406, 424, 523, 544, 555, 579, 580, 591, 603

auctions of city lots, 44, 53ff, 66–73, 122, 123, 132ff, 159, 171ff, 443, 444, 450, 454, 492, 494, 513, 514, 522, 527, 529ff, 577, 580, 581, 589, 593, 594, 598, 602, 612, 618, 624

axe-men, 57, 81, 149, 410

bakers, 113, 226, 354, 380, 415, 427, 432

Baltimore, 13, 21, 23; yellow fever in, 239, 243, 584

Bank of Columbia: loans to commissioners, 212, 241, 303, 317, 332, 340, 357, 376, 377, 387, 450, 499, 589; loans to Morris and Nicholson, 313, 389ff, 401, 437, 439, 444, 445; organized, 171, 199, 209; overextended, 246, 247, 285, 604

Bank of United States, 34; refuses loan to commissioners, 377, 387, 403, 405

Banneker, Benjamin, 39

barracks for workers, 85, 87, 97, 160, 167, 205, 206, 285, 322, 500

Barry, James, 322, 353, 386, 401, 403ff, 409, 571; buys lots, 262, 285, 287, 374, 513, 540; dispute

685